# Legal Canons

# Legal Canons

EDITED BY

*J. M. Balkin and Sanford Levinson*

*New York University Press*

NEW YORK AND LONDON

NEW YORK UNIVERSITY PRESS
New York and London

© 2000 by New York University

Library of Congress Cataloging-in-Publication Data
Legal canons / edited by J. M. Balkin and Sanford Levinson.
        p.   cm.
    ISBN 0-8147-9857-8 (cloth : acid-free paper)
1. Law—Study and teaching—Unites States.  2. Law—United
                States—Sources.
    I. Balkin, J. M.  II. Levinson, Sanford, 1941–
            KF272.L426  2000
        340—dc21            00-009019

New York University Press books are printed on acid-free paper,
and their binding materials are chosen for strength and durability.

Manufactured in the United States of America

10  9  8  7  6  5  4  3  2  1

*To Bruce Ackerman,*
*who taught us how to challenge canons*

# Contents

# Preface

Every discipline, because it is a discipline, has a canon, a set of standard texts, approaches, problems, examples, or stories that its members repeatedly employ or invoke, and which help define the discipline as a discipline. If the study of law is a discipline, it too must have its canons and its own sense of the canonical. Discovering those features is the task of the present volume. In order to understand how the twin ideas of canons and canonicity operate in law, we commissioned a series of essays from some of the most respected scholars in the American legal academy. We assigned each of them a topic and then asked them to write about what, in their opinion, is or should be canonical in law. As the reader will discover, the answers are complicated and wide-ranging, not only in terms of substance but also in terms of methodological and political commitments.

We have structured this book into four parts—a general theoretical introduction to canons in law followed by three groups of essays. The first set of essays concern the canon in the curriculum: the canon of materials and approaches in standard law school courses. In fact, the curricular canon is a dual canon: Not only does each course have its own canon, but the collection of courses in the law school curriculum itself constitutes a kind of canon. The essays in this section move gradually from private law to public law (itself a canonical distinction). The section concludes with an essay about what has been (in our opinion) the most successful interdisciplinary innovation in the traditional law school curriculum, Law and Economics.

Most of the subjects covered in this section of the book have traditionally been taught in the first year of law school, but this is no longer the case. Both property and criminal law have become second year or even elective courses at some institutions. Of course, the question of what properly belongs in the first year, and what can be relegated to the status of "elective," is one of the most familar ways in which canons get debated by law school faculties.

The next section of essays, on the canon and groups, takes on directly issues that people most often associate with debates about the canon in liberal arts: the representation of particular groups (or the lack thereof) in canonical texts. The groups most often mentioned in this context are racial and ethnic groups, women, and, in recent years, gays and lesbians. To this end, this section of the book includes two different essays on race. One is written by a white feminist scholar sympathetic to the aims and goals of critical race theory. The other is written by an African American man who has often been critical of the same movement. We have also commissioned essays on feminism and on sexual orientation.

We by no means think this exhausts the possible group affiliations that might fruitfully be discussed, but we do think that these have been the most central bones of contention in debates over canons both in law and in the liberal arts. There are important ideological issues in these debates, including which groups will be counted as needing to be brought into the canon. Ironically, these questions tend to turn on which of these heretofore marginalized groups are themselves considered canonical, in the sense that they are seen as most representative of marginalized groups or most in need of representation.

The final section of the book concerns the canon in constitutional law. This is a special interest of ours, and for that reason, we have included three different essays on the constitutional canon, each taking very different approaches. We should note, moreover, that our introductory theoretical essay also offers many examples drawn from constitutional law, and the essays on race, gender, and sexual orientation inevitably trench on constitutional questions. This bounty is not accidental. We expect that more readers will want to read about the canon in constitutional law than any other subject—especially those readers who are interested in comparisons between law and literary studies. As we mention in our introductory essay, for better or worse, constitutional law has become the canonical subject for talking about many issues in legal thought generally. We hope that this book will be the beginning of a conversation about canons and canonicity, not the end of the discussion. And so we invite our audience to consider the choices we have made and the ways they would choose differently. That, after all, is what canon construction is all about.

All canons are limited by considerations of time and space, and our book—which forms a canon of its own—is no exception. There is much more to be said about the canons of curricular subjects, and about the representation of particular social groups, and about the marginalization of particular approaches to the study of law. Nevertheless, we think that the diverse essays in this book will allow readers to see why we think that the question of canonicity is an endlessly fascinating subject. We hope our readers will be as excited by the question as we have been, and that a long and fruitful conversation about legal canons can now begin.

*Part I*

# Introduction

# Chapter 1

# Legal Canons
## *An Introduction*

# *J. M. Balkin and Sanford Levinson*

## *I. Introduction*

To some readers, a discussion of "legal canons" might suggest a treatise on church law, or perhaps, for creative spellers, a discussion of gun control. Our subject is somewhat different. It concerns what is and what ought to be canonical in the study of law. In our view, there is no better way to understand a discipline—its underlying assumptions, its current concerns and anxieties—than to study what its members think is canonical to that discipline. The study of canons and canonicity is the key to the secrets of a culture and its characteristic modes of thought.[1]

In the liberal arts, debates about "the Western canon" have been going on for some time, often through controversies about what texts should be assigned in basic humanities courses.[2] Analogous debates about canonicity have occurred in the legal academy too, but by other names and using different vocabularies. They have been debates about interdisciplinarity, about narrative scholarship, about identity politics, about the structure of the law school curriculum, and about the preservation of the liberal precedents of the Warren Court and early Burger Court eras as normative icons. Legal academics have their own ways of discussing what is canonical, even if they never use that particular word.

Questions about legal canonicity have arisen during a time of great excitement and ferment in the American legal academy. In the past twenty-five years, legal scholars have witnessed the entry (some would say invasion) of interdisciplinary approaches, the ascendance of law and economics, the development of feminism, critical race theory, and gaylegal studies, and the increasing influence of both rational-actor methodology and postmodernism. The demographics of the law school have also changed dramatically: More and more women and minorities have attended law schools, and slowly but surely they have gained entry to the ranks of the legal professoriat. Simultaneously, the comparatively insular American law school is "going global." After many years of smug self-assurance, American legal education is finally showing interest in the legal systems and constitutional problems of other countries. To be sure, this newfound concern is partly a means of exporting American legal culture to other lands, but it also reflects an increasing curiosity about how things might be done otherwise here in the United States.

It is precisely at such times of ferment, growth, change, and innovation that anxieties about canons arise in any discipline. The discipline seeks either to reconstitute itself or to close ranks by considering what, if anything, can be said to be canonical about its practices, its methods, or its materials of study. In discussions about the legal canon, analogies to debates that have taken place in the liberal arts at Stanford and other universities have proved too tempting to resist.[3] After all, such debates have drawn considerable controversy and press coverage, with some of the participants suggesting at times that nothing less than the future of Western civilization depends on accepting their particular position in the debate.

Nevertheless, such comparisons conceal as much as they reveal. In this essay, we want to consider both the similarities and the differences in debates over literary and legal canons. More importantly, we want to consider what is really at stake in asking whether any field of law is constituted by a canon. The question of what is canonical must be approached sociologically as well as prescriptively. We cannot debate the content of "the canon" until we understand the purposes for which the question is being asked and the reasons why the question is being asked at a particular moment in the development of legal culture. Moreover, we must understand debates about canons with reference to their particular institutional contexts, for these debates are part of more general forms of ideological and cultural development and struggle. Because we are both teachers of constitutional law, we draw many of our examples from that field, but we hope that the reader will see these as exemplary of more general features of legal canons.

In this chapter, we discuss the different ways of constituting or defining a canon. We argue that what is regarded as canonical in law depends very much on the audience for whom and the purposes for which the canon is constructed. For example, legal materials can be canonical because they are important for educating law students, because they ensure a necessary cultural literacy for citizens in a democracy, or because they serve as benchmarks for testing academic theories about the law. Because legal materials have multiple audiences and functions, there is no reason to think that law, or any field of law, has a single canon. By contrast, different forms of canonicity are more closely linked with one another in the liberal arts than they are in law, and this linkage gives the appearance of a unified canon over which participants fight. Finally, we argue that some of the most important forms of canonicity have less to do with the choice of materials than with the tools of understanding that people use to think about the law—the background structures of "law-talk" that shape conversations within and concerning the law.[4] These elements of "deep canonicity" include characteristic forms of legal argument, characteristic approaches to problems, underlying narrative structures, unconscious forms of categorization, and the use of canonical examples.

## II. Pedagogy, Cultural Literacy, and Academic Theory

When we think about debates over the canon in the liberal arts, we normally focus on the question of what books or authors should be assigned and read in university courses. But in fact, many of the books actually assigned in liberal arts courses are collections of preselected materials in the form of anthologies. Consider a sampling of the books offered by the Norton Publishing Company: *The Norton Anthology of American Literature*,[5] *The Norton Anthology of Short Fiction*,[6] *The Norton Anthology of English Literature*,[7] *The Norton Anthology of World Masterpieces*,[8] *The Norton Anthology of Modern Poetry*,[9] *The Norton Anthology of Literature by Women: The Tradition in English*,[10] and *The Norton Anthology of African American Literature*.[11] These anthologies save the harried liberal arts professor time and energy both by choosing what books and poems to assign and by editing the chosen works, and that is one reason why they are so popular. Nor is this economy accidental. Offering people ready-made categories to think with and providing texts to think about are some of the most important functions of canon construction. This labor saving is due to the work of anthology editors, who carefully screen and select the relevant materials, providing updates as required. In fact, there have been multiple editions of several of these anthologies, suggesting either that the category of "world masterpieces" is not altogether stable,[12] or, more happily, that new "world masterpieces" are being published every year.[13]

In any case, the editors' decisions as to which among many potential candidates will be canonized in these anthologies may call for exquisite judgment.[14] As Sandra Gilbert and Susan Gubar discovered when they published a Norton anthology of literature by women that purported to offer "*The* Tradition in English,"[15] anthology editors are often subjected to severe criticism, both for their choices and for those choices' pretensions to hegemonic status.[16]

Law professors also rely on anthologies, though we call them "casebooks." Indeed, it is safe to say that no part of the academy relies more on anthologies than do American law schools. Energetic law professors sometimes add supplemental materials of their own devising and may even recommend a hornbook or two, but for the most part American law students are fed a steady diet of increasingly thick (and increasingly expensive) casebooks.[17]

Just as literature professors decide what poems and novels to teach, editors of casebooks decide what "cases and materials" students ought to be exposed to on their intellectual journey from uninitiated laypersons to well-educated, "disciplined" lawyers. We have no doubt that the purposes and agendas of the people who create these collections often differ; we are equally certain that the academy would benefit from a far more explicit (and contentious) debate than the present muffled discussion about what visions of law underlie any given casebook. Thus, one purpose of this commentary is to provoke a long overdue discussion among would-be constructors of the legal canon about the reasons for their particular decisions—a discussion not simply about what texts they include and exclude, but also about *why* these texts are included or excluded.[18]

We begin, however, with a legal document that generates no contention at all: John Marshall's opinion in *McCulloch v. Maryland*,[19] which established an expansive view of national power under the U.S. Constitution. At least within the field of constitutional law, almost everyone seems to agree that *McCulloch* is canonical. Indeed, in a recent study of eleven major constitutional law casebooks entitled "Is There a Canon of Constitutional Law?" *McCulloch* was one of only ten cases included in all of the casebooks.[20] This unanimity only confirms the intuition that every law student should be exposed to *McCulloch* and should be able to offer some informed commentary about its holding and arguments.[21] Yet articles about *McCulloch* rarely appear in American law reviews.[22] If one attempted to determine what is canonical by examining the work product of legal academics as revealed in American law reviews, *McCulloch* would leave almost no traces at all.

In short, we may find a wide divergence between what professors of law teach and what they write about. Liberal arts professors are in a somewhat different position. Contrast the law professor's treatment of *McCulloch* with the literature professor's treatment of Shakespeare's plays. These plays are not only taught to the young, but also continue to be written about with great zeal by many important members of the literary academy, even—and perhaps especially—when these scholars apply trendy contemporary methods of interpretation like deconstruction, the new historicism, and Lacanian psychoanalytic theory.[23] Methodologies wax and wane, but each one gets applied to Shakespeare in turn.

What is "canonical" in law varies according to how the canon is defined, and how the canon is defined depends on the purpose of the canon. For example, consider three different ways that the question of the canon might be articulated in the field of constitutional law. First, we might ask what key cases and materials should be taught in constitutional law courses and reprinted in constitutional law casebooks. We call this the "pedagogical canon." Second, we might ask what key cases and materials any educated person should be aware of in order to participate in serious discussions about American constitutional development. We call this the "cultural literacy canon." Third, we might ask what key cases and materials any serious legal academic—as distinguished from the ordinary lawyer or the well-educated generalist—should know and any serious theory of constitutional law must take into account. We call this the "academic theory canon."

The example of *McCulloch* suggests that these canons can and do diverge. In designing a casebook, an editor concerned with preparing lawyers to litigate contemporary issues might choose to focus on current issues in constitutional law at the expense of those cases and materials that contribute to cultural literacy. For example, we assume that, as a matter of cultural literacy, students of the Constitution (and of the Supreme Court) should know something about *Dred Scott v. Sandford*—a case that has often been viewed as precipitating the conflagration of civil war. This is so even though *Dred Scott* is almost completely irrelevant to contemporary constitutional litigation. Similarly, many cases and materials that are valuable for the purpose of cultural literacy are not necessarily crucial for any serious academic theory to explain. Few constitutional scholars believe that the principles or the holding of *Dred Scott* is important for modern constitutional theory (except perhaps as a symbol continually to be vilified).[24]

## III. Audience and Function

Each of our formulations of a canon of constitutional law implicitly assumes an "audience" for the canon. The audience is the group of persons who are supposed to be edified or instructed by the canon or (in the case of the academic theory canon) who are supposed to utilize the canon as a set of standard problems or materials that need to be explained and justified. Our earlier description of the pedagogical canon, for example, presumed that the appropriate audience was law students; our definition of the theoretical canon assumed that the relevant audience was legal academics. But these are not the only possible choices, and as we vary the intended audience for a given canon, the canon's contents may also vary. The key cases and materials of constitutional law that every political scientist should know, for example, are not necessarily the same ones that we should expect ordinary citizens to be familiar with.

Moreover, the contents of a canon may vary depending on the appropriate function of that canon for a particular audience. Consider the pedagogical canon, for example. What precisely are we law professors preparing our students to do? If we are concerned only with preparing students for everyday law practice, should we care whether they know about *Prigg v. Pennsylvania*,[25] in which Pennsylvania tried to create due process protections for blacks accused by slave catchers of being fugitive slaves?[26] After all, as many students who are assigned *Prigg* are quick to point out, slavery has long been outlawed in this country. Spending time on an 1842 case obviously means less time to spend on the latest pronouncements from the Supreme Court, which are far more likely to interest the judges before whom our students may someday practice. Indeed, if preparation for the practical realities of legal practice is the central aim of pedagogy, then why should law students spend so much time on constitutional issues at all, given that most students will rarely be confronted with such issues?

If law professors think it important to introduce their students to non-business-related topics of constitutional law—or, to put it another way, if these topics properly form part of the pedagogical canon for law students—then it must be at least in part because legal educators believe that lawyers perform (or ought to perform) a special "citizenship" function in a democracy. Presumably this citizenship function requires that lawyers know something about the basic foundations of the American legal system, including the U.S. Constitution. Hence, legal educators, as the teachers of lawyers, should structure their courses with this role in mind. Of course, when the functions of the pedagogical canon are fixed in this way, it overlaps predictably with the canon of cultural literacy.

Next, consider the possible functions served by the cultural literacy canon—the materials that any educated person should know about in order to participate in and contribute to serious general discussions about American law. It is important to recognize that these discussions are usually normative rather than merely descriptive, especially when conducted among Americans themselves; they often concern whether the United States is in fact well served by particular aspects of its law and whether certain radical changes might not be desirable.

In addition, people may think that cultural literacy in constitutional matters is important because it fosters pride in and attachment to the American political community. At least some cases may form part of the canon because they seem to promote an appealing portrait of "America-the-good." Moreover, the desire to engender pride may lead to the omission of certain cases and legal events from the cultural literacy canon because they present a less attractive picture of the rule of law in the United States.

On the other hand, if the function of cultural literacy is to help us learn from past misdeeds and mistakes and to understand how these have irrevocably shaped the world in which we live today, we might include a different selection of cases and materials: for example, cases and materials about slavery, Jim Crow, controls on the immigration and liberties of Chinese laborers, and the mistreatment of Native Americans. Such a cultural literacy canon might supplement presumably affirmative icons like *Brown v. Board of Education*[27] and *New York Times Co. v. Sullivan*[28] with less inspiring cases like *Dred Scott*, United States v. Debs,[29] *Korematsu v. United States*,[30] and *The Chinese Exclusion Case*.[31]

The theoretical canon may have still other functions. It prescribes the materials that constitute the central foci of professional constitutional theorists. That is, it concerns the materials that a young assistant professor ought to study if he or she wants recognition as an active participant in the field.[32] Because this function of the academic theory canon is so closely linked to the quest for disciplinary solidarity, status, and respect within the profession of legal academics, we should not be surprised that it differs greatly from the pedagogical canon directed at fledgling lawyers. The legal academy has become increasingly interdisciplinary, even as law schools still perform their traditional professional function of training future members of the bar. As a result, the audience for legal scholarship has increasingly become other legal academics rather than students (the audience for the pedagogical canon) or fellow citizens (the presumed audience for the cultural literacy canon).

The academic theory canon today certainly includes "materials" as well as "cases"; more importantly, it increasingly includes the work of nonlegal academics. Some familiar examples include the works of the philosopher John Rawls and the economist Ronald Coase.[33] Even though neither of these scholars is a lawyer, ignorance of their work would be a sign of incompetence in a law professor who taught in certain fields. Indeed, we suspect that the work of Rawls and Coase is more canonical—at least within the world of legal academics striving for professional success—than many clearly legal materials, such as the Supreme Court's opinion in *Prigg v. Pennsylvania*.

This is, of course, an empirical claim, and one might try to prove it by laboriously counting citations in articles published in "leading" law journals (like the *Harvard Law Review*). Indeed, Fred Shapiro has done precisely this, and he determined that the most frequently cited article of all time in articles published in legal journals (and presumably directed at legal academics) is Coase's *The Problem of Social Cost*.[34] Because Shapiro did not count citations to books, we do not know the actual frequency of citations to Rawls's *A Theory of Justice*, but we would place a substantial bet that it shows up very frequently indeed.

Yet a simple thought experiment should prove equally convincing. Canonicity is not simply a matter of what one thinks important; it is also a matter of what one thinks *others* think important. In his classic academic novel *Changing Places*, David Lodge describes the academic's game of "Humiliation," in which a player names a work that he or she has *not* read and wins a point for every other person who *has*.[35] The winner of the game is the person best able to demonstrate how ignorant he or she is, as judged by the collective reading habits of his or her colleagues. Hence, winning requires a knowledge of what others are likely to think important enough to read. Lodge describes an especially competitive young member of the Euphoric State University English Department who could not resist one-upping everyone by admitting that he had never read *Hamlet*.[36] He won the game, though he was later denied tenure as a consequence.[37]

One way to construct a theoretical canon for academics, then, is by playing an imaginary game of "Humiliation." The "winner" would be the person who has failed to read works in the operative canon. Thus, to understand the current role of interdisciplinary scholarship in the academic theory canon, ask yourself which would be the greater academic embarrassment to a law professor: to confess, at a professional gathering, that you had not read *A Theory of Justice* or *The Problem of Social Cost*, on the one hand, or *Prigg v. Pennsylvania*, on the other?[38]

As this example suggests, the canon of interest to academics may be quite different from the canon that is important to the practicing lawyer.[39] One reason for significant differences in canon formation among various sociolegal groups is that each group constitutes a different community with different interpretive assumptions, purposes, and practices. Thus, an increasing divergence in canon construction among these groups may be a symptom of an increasing division among interpretive communities and an increasing differentiation in purposes among academics, lawyers, and judges (in addition to the professional differentiation that has always existed between lawyers and citizens). Each interpretive community may have its own canon (or set of canons), and although these canons surely overlap, they may also diverge in particular respects.

This divergence suggests a point that we shall return to later in this essay. One reason for renewed interest in canons and in questions of canonicity may be a desire to reestablish commonality within an imagined interpretive community of judges, lawyers, and academics that many fear is falling apart.[40] Enforcement of canons is invariably a sort of policing action, no matter how benign its motivations,[41] and police often step up their vigilance when they fear that social order is breaking down.

## IV. Canons Legal and Literary

We have argued that there are multiple canons in law that vary by audience and function. There are multiple ways of defining the canon, and there are multiple interpretive communities that might each have a canon, each of which is increasingly separated from the others. Recognizing these features of legal culture helps us understand why comparisons to debates about the canon in English literature and in the liberal arts generally are especially likely to be misleading.

First, in the liberal arts, the pedagogical canon *is* very often closely linked to the cultural literacy canon and the academic theory canon. The question of what one should teach in English departments is very much connected to the questions of what educated people should know, what the "best" literature is (including what literature has the best effects on its readers), what literary works every theory of artistic greatness must take into account, and what sorts of things (including works of literature) literary critics should write about. Many (but certainly not all) liberal arts educators see the function of cultural literacy—the notion that every educated person should know something about Dante or (from a different perspective) should be exposed to literature describing racial oppression—as directly connected to the pedagogical goal of producing edified, if not virtuous, people. Just as William Bennett thinks that exposing youngsters to classic literature will produce better citizens,[42] so too his critics on the left seek to introduce novels and poems about race and gender to edify and enlighten their educational charges.

In short, we strongly suspect that the pedagogical, cultural literacy, and academic theory canons are more closely linked in debates about the canon in liberal arts curricula than they are in academic law. Transferring these debates root and branch into the legal milieu is likely to confuse the issue. As scholars who have explored analogies between artistic and legal modes of thought,[43] we think it important to emphasize that one cannot usefully explore these analogies without noting significant differences where they arise. Analogies to debates about the literary canon can be helpful only if we separate out issues that literary debates may tend (for institutional reasons) to collapse.

A second difference follows from the first. English professors, unlike law professors, do not usually offer badly written or badly reasoned literature in their courses to provoke discussion.[44] Law professors, however, regularly include such literature in their pedagogical canon. Legal casebooks in the United States often contain cases that the casebook authors think are wrongly decided or, even if the correct result is reached, offer styles of reasoning that the authors wish to question or criticize. First-year textbooks, especially in the common law subjects, often feature seemingly contradictory sets of cases and materials selected to introduce competing policy considerations or otherwise stimulate discussion and provoke thought. It follows that, for sound educational reasons, the pedagogical canon of cases to which law students should be exposed may contain something more than the academic theory canon of materials that any sound legal theory must discuss and explain.[45]

In fact, law professors routinely include cases and materials that are not only badly reasoned, but also unjust, because they are insensitive to the poor and oppressed, because they justify violations of civil liberties, or because they are racist or sexist. *Plessy v. Ferguson*,[46] which gave constitutional blessing to Jim Crow,[47] is probably the canonical example of such a case. English professors sometimes do offer texts that they regard as racist and sexist, but usually not in order to enshrine them in the canon. Rather, the point is to reveal the racism and sexism of what is currently regarded as canonical. Indeed, one senses an urge in some quarters to boot out of the canon (or at least deemphasize) famous works now viewed as irredeemably racist or misogynist.

Perhaps the most striking difference between the legal and literary academies is institutional. An important part of the canons of law consists of the authoritative materials produced by courts and legislatures. These institutions strongly influence the content of what law professors teach and law students learn. For example, it would be rather extraordinary if a casebook on welfare rights law omitted the euphemistically titled Personal Responsibility and Work Opportunity Reconciliation Act of 1996 simply because the authors found it normatively dreadful or stylistically objectionable. Indeed, a law teacher who completely neglected the pronouncements of legislatures and courts would not simply be idiosyncratic; she would be committing professional malpractice.

By contrast, the literary academy has no single institution or set of institutions that successfully proclaims its right to produce new texts that *must* become the object of close study by literary academics or its right to offer singularly authoritative interpretations of "classic" texts. The denizens of certain literature departments may well think of themselves as "supreme" and of members of other literature departments as "inferior."[48] They may regard their own work as authoritative and insist that it be accepted by those they consider lesser lights. But even the most megalomaniacal of these professors will concede that, for better or worse, no official designation of authoritative interpretations exists. No scholar or group of scholars can plausibly claim a right "ultimately" to decide whether Hamlet was feigning madness or what William Blake really meant in his famous poem on the tiger.[49]

Nor can any "literary legislature" publish poems or novels that automatically become the central focus of the academy.

Law, on the other hand, is blessed—or afflicted, depending on one's point of view—by institutions that proclaim the privileged status of their own pronouncements. This is the most obvious reason why judicial opinions (and especially U.S. Supreme Court opinions) dominate American legal casebooks. Few legal academics now believe that the individuals who compose the Supreme Court are so wise that their views deserve pride of place over the views of academics. (In any case, the opinions of judges are increasingly written by their clerks, who are barely a year out of law school.) Some law professors even insist that the Supreme Court's pronouncements are not authoritative as to the true meaning of the Constitution.[50] But all of these scholars spend valuable time in their classes and use up valuable space in their teaching materials studying the pronouncements of that Court. It is almost impossible, as a practical matter, to overcome the view that the Constitution is what the Supreme Court says it is and that the law is what courts, legislatures, and administrative agencies say it is.

It would be easy and wrong, we think, to explain this difference solely on the ground that the study of law is the study of power and the study of literature is not.[51] There is plenty of power at stake in any academic institution. Careers are made and destroyed, reputations are elevated and besmirched, funds are raised and distributed, and the minds of students are refined or coarsened. The substantial power that can be exercised through the seemingly harmless "pursuit of knowledge" is a major reason why contemporary critics of the academy are so alarmed by what occurs within its ivory towers. The question is not the presence or absence of power, but the form of that power and the ways in which that power is organized. The study of the legal system in the United States is organized around institutions that are separate from the academy and can claim canonical status without the help of the professors who study them. We doubt that any set of political or cultural institutions has the same relationship to the work of liberal arts professors.

## V. Deep Canonicity

We can approach the question of canonicity in yet another way. Our three examples of canons in constitutional law presume that what makes a legal canon canonical are "cases and materials," in the same way that the Western canon is a collection of particular books, plays, and poetry. Yet educators who defend the Western canon are not interested in these manuscripts merely for their own sake; they want students to read them because they will introduce students to basic approaches and questions that have been central to Western culture from the Greeks onward. This suggests a very different notion of canonicity: the canonicity of certain ways of thinking, talking, and arguing that are characteristic of a culture. We call these forms of thinking, talking, and arguing "deep canonicity."[52] They are an important part of what makes canons constitutive of a particular culture or a particular discipline. For convenience, we note four different forms of deep canonicity.

*1. Canonical Arguments.* The first form of deep canonicity consists of the kinds of arguments that members of a particular culture or a particular discipline characteristically employ. Philip Bobbitt, for example, argues that American constitutional culture is distinguished and legitimated by its characteristic forms of argument.[53] Bobbitt claims that six modalities—textual, structural, historical, prudential, doctrinal, and ethical—underlie all constitutional interpretation; that each mode of argument is of equal constitutional status; and that following these modalities—and no others—gives constitutional argument its legitimacy.[54] We are somewhat skeptical of Bobbitt's claims about exclusivity and legitimacy; yet we think that his general approach to legal rhetoric is both sound and important.[55] The "lawtalk" that lawyers, judges, politicians, and citizens employ in discussing the Constitution is structured in a set of repeatable rhetorical *topoi* (topics for argument), such as text, structure, intentions, consequences, fundamental values, and so on.[56] These topoi provide the common basis through which Americans talk and reason about the Constitution. A large part of learning the law is acquiring the ability to memorize, recognize, and master these topoi, and making their use in argument and discussion second nature. The canon of permissible constitutional topoi—a canon that alters over time—is one of the central determinants of our constitutional culture.

*2. Canonical Problems and Approaches.* A second variety of deep canonicity consists of the approaches and questions that a culture or a discipline employs or asks itself. These approaches and questions include the kinds of issues that the culture or discipline finds interesting, as opposed to those that it views as tedious or irrelevant. They also include those ideas so basic that they do not even appear on the "radar screen" of the imagination. This canon includes both what is overtly problematized and what is thought so obviously important that its articulation is not even necessary to the members of the culture. We call this the "canon of problems and approaches." Just as Thomas Kuhn pointed out that certain generations of scientists share common "paradigms" of research,[57] so too members of a culture or discipline may have their own distinctive problematics and methods of framing and solving problems.

The canon of problems and approaches is as characteristic of any academic discipline as its purported subject matter. Different groups of academics—for example, rational choice political scientists and cultural anthropologists—often have very different ways of approaching a question and often find very different things important in a particular situation. Indeed, they may tend to characterize the situation in quite disparate and even contradictory ways. To the extent that law is an academic discipline, it too has its characteristic ways of formulating and approaching questions. Pierre Schlag has repeatedly tried to show, for example, that legal academics routinely frame matters in terms of what Schlag calls "normative legal thought."[58] In other words, for legal academics, the point of analysis is to develop norms that might be followed by some court or some legislature, or to offer methods for deciding cases correctly. Even when legal academics eschew specific policy reforms, Schlag insists, they still speak in terms of advancing particular normative political positions, a rhetorical style that is very similar to and indeed is ultimately derived from their legal habits of debating rules and policies.[59]

Thus, Schlag points out, American legal academics routinely attempt to turn the teaching of other disciplines into knowledge that can be used in a doctrinal test or offered as authority for a legal argument before a judge or legislature.[60] Because other disciplines do not research questions or produce information with these goals in mind, normative legal thought inevitably reshapes and (in Schlag's view) domesticates their work.[61] Yet as long as legal academics are shaped by their canonical approaches—indeed, as long as the academic practice of law is constituted by these approaches—legal academics will continue to imagine, pose, and answer questions in precisely this way. The assumptions of normative legal thought are so central to the work of legal academics that they are usually not even discussed; they literally go without saying.

3. *Canonical Narratives.* An equally important and pervasive part of the rhetorical canon are "canonical narratives." Every society has a set of

stock stories about itself, which are constantly retold and eventually take on a mythic status.[62] These stories explain to the members of that society who they are and what values they hold most dear. These stock stories are both descriptive and prescriptive: they not only frame our sense of what has happened and how events will unfold in the future, but also explain how those events should unfold.[63]

Constitutional interpretation is full of such stock stories. There are stock stories about Americans as courageous pioneers who won the West, stories about the United States as a nation of immigrants who came to these shores in search of liberty and equal opportunity, and stories about the United States as a distinctive country that has always existed free from those forms of feudalism and social hierarchy characteristic of the Old World or has self-consciously thrown them off.[64] These stories, and others like them, are as central to constitutional interpretation as the opinions of any jurist. Indeed, they are so familiar that we often do not recognize the many ways they are invoked to frame and justify legal arguments.

Take, for example, that most canonical of constitutional cases, *McCulloch v. Maryland*. In *McCulloch* we find Chief Justice John Marshall justifying an expansive conception of federal power not merely through textual and structural interpretation, but also by telling a story about what the United States was and what it would become. "Throughout this vast republic, from the St. Croix to the Gulph of Mexico, from the Atlantic to the Pacific," Marshall argued, "revenue is to be collected and expended, armies are to be marched and supported. . . . Is that construction of the constitution to be preferred which would render these operations difficult, hazardous, and expensive?"[65] It is particularly telling that Marshall chose to ascribe borders to the United States much larger than those actually existing in 1819, when *McCulloch* was written. In Marshall's narrative—one that would be retold countless times under the more familiar name of "Manifest Destiny"—the United States was to become a great country, not only in spirit but also in resources and size; and great countries need constitutions that give them the flexibility to grow and attain their promised greatness.

As Lewis Henry LaRue has pointed out, it is this familiar narrative of American destiny, as much as anything else, that underpins and justifies the expansive constitutional interpretation of national power in *McCulloch*.[66] The narrative is not everything, but it is surely something. If we told a different story—a Jeffersonian story of a tranquil land of agrarian farmers who hoped to avoid the corruptions of ambition and avarice characteristic of

European monarchies, who sought merely to live their lives in peace and harmony in small, close-knit communities—we might well imagine that it should be "difficult, hazardous, and expensive" for the national government to gather revenues, raise armies, sweep across the continent, and conquer all in its path. If we told a story that opposed the depravity and overreaching of grasping monarchs and their prime ministers to the simple virtues of a self-reliant republican citizenry, we might well want to nip in the bud any potential mechanisms of national aggrandizement.

In like fashion, a stock story about Protestant dissenters fleeing religious persecution in Great Britain seems to undergird much of the law of religious freedom in this country. This stock story portrays religion as a dangerous and potentially oppressive element in civil society that fosters intolerance and social strife and therefore must be kept strictly separated from the organs of state power. According to this stock story, the more fervent a religious belief, and the more determinedly a religious movement asserts authority over its followers, the more threatening it is: fanatical or exotic forms of religious enthusiasm, on the one hand, and the hierarchy of the Catholic Church on the other, become representative examples of religion's most divisive and oppressive features. Conversely, religious expression is most welcome when it most resembles watered-down or domesticated versions of mainline Protestantism. In the past, this stock story has been used to justify oppression of Mormons and Catholics in the name of protecting American governments (even though, ironically, the persecutions that originally led to the exodus from Great Britain were conducted by fellow Protestants). In the present, the myth is invoked against evangelical Protestants, Christian conservatives, Orthodox (and especially Hasidic) Jews, and all manner of contemporary religions and cults.[67]

The stock story of the flight of the first European Americans from religious persecution is now being contested by a new myth of pluralism and multiculturalism. Not surprisingly, this new myth helps generate very different doctrinal conclusions: because Americans are a deeply religious people with many different forms of spirituality, the state should accommodate religion and should recognize and even help foster our spiritual values. The difference between this new myth and the previous one is symbolized by the difference between the hostility expressed by Justices Black, Douglas, and Brennan toward state support of parochial schools and the relaxation of those strictures in the opinions of the contemporary Supreme Court.[68]

Perhaps the most basic stories used in American constitutional interpretation are stories about the progress of the American nation and its
laws. Robert Gordon has observed that "American legal argument from
the Founding onward consistently relied upon a core narrative of liberal
progress, the story of liberal modernization, by which law both followed
and facilitated the evolution of society away from feudalism, tyranny and
superstition and towards increasing freedom."[69]

Because the narrative of progress is so deeply ingrained in American
culture, it is not surprising that both liberals and conservatives have employed it. The story of inevitable progress has allowed progressives to
harmonize the injustices of the past with their aspirations for the future.
In the progressive imagination, principles immanent at the time of the
Revolution (or the founding or Reconstruction) unfold and are realized
through historical struggle, emerging and working themselves pure from
the parochialism and injustices of the past.[70]

Gordon offers Abraham Lincoln's theory of the Declaration of Independence as an example of this progressive narrative.[71] Through a narrative account of the inevitable progress of American liberty, Lincoln resolved the tension inherent in a document that "declared all men to be
equal even as it established a polity that legalized slavery."[72] The authors
of the Declaration, Lincoln explained,

> did not mean to assert the obvious untruth that all were then actually en-
> joying that equality, nor yet that they were about to confer it immediately
> upon them. In fact they had no power to confer such a boon. They meant
> simply to declare the *right*, so that the *enforcement* of it might follow as fast
> as circumstances should permit. They meant to set up a standard maxim
> for free society, which should be familiar to all, and revered by all; con-
> stantly looked to, constantly labored for, and even though never perfectly
> attained, constantly approximated, and thereby constantly spreading and
> deepening its influence, and augmenting the happiness and value of life to
> all people of all colors everywhere.[73]

Yet the narrative of progress (whether inevitable or hard fought) can
also work in a conservative direction. People can invoke comparisons between the present and the injustices of the past as proof that the country
has left behind white supremacy or the denial of civil liberties, and that
further reforms are unnecessary or are deviations from the path of
progress. Precisely because we no longer live in the McCarthy era, precisely because of the past successes of the civil rights movement and the
women's movement, contemporary claims of deeply ingrained racism,

sexism, and other remaining injustices can be discounted or dismissed as hyperbolic or, at the very least, viewed with a skeptical eye. In this way, the progressive narrative can be turned against progressive causes. As Reva Siegel has pointed out, hierarchical regimes of injustice do not vanish in the face of legal reforms but often reconfigure themselves to thrive in new legal environments.[74] The happy story of progressive legal reform can mask the elements of unjust status hierarchies that still remain, aided and abetted by the very rules that purported to disestablish them.[75]

Perhaps because of the success of conservative uses of the progressive narrative, many progressive and radical critics of American law have offered a counternarrative of permanence, stasis, or inevitable return. This narrative is usually pessimistic: it argues that American society has been, and will always continue to be, racist or sexist, or otherwise deeply unfair. From the vantage point of the narrative of stasis, successive decisions, statutes, and reforms appear as ever new ways by which status hierarchies are preserved, the interests of the powerful confirmed, good intentions blunted, and injustices perpetuated.[76] Often scholars on the left attempt to complicate matters by yoking the narrative of permanence with the narrative of progress. Although racism and sexism are persistent and pervasive, they have been weakened over time; nevertheless, we must be ever vigilant to their continuing presence in our lives and to their potential resurgence. Reva Siegel's argument that unjust status hierarchies achieve "preservation-through-transformation" modifies the narrative of permanence by emphasizing the dynamic features of social hierarchies and by admitting significant elements of progress, but this story nevertheless retains deep ambivalence about the prospects for reform.[77]

Narratives of permanence can also be effective tools of conservative rhetoric. People can justify the status quo by arguing that human nature remains constant, that our traditions remain essentially unchanged from their earliest days, or that, as the Supreme Court asserted in *Plessy v. Ferguson*, law "is powerless to eradicate racial instincts or to abolish distinctions based upon physical differences."[78] In our own day, the word "cultural" can be substituted for the word "physical" with similar effect.

A third and very familiar kind of canonical narrative assumes change rather than stasis, but argues that the change is for the worse. Examples include narratives of a Golden Age, against which the present must seem debased and debauched, and stories about a moment when the Constitution was properly understood, a benchmark from which later courts and politicians have repeatedly strayed. These narratives urge us to recognize our failings, to confess our sins, and to return to the old ways. At first glance, these narrative constructions seem exclusively conservative in tone. Robert Bork's vivid comparisons of contemporary American culture (and contemporary constitutional jurisprudence) to Sodom and Gomorrah are only the most recent examples.[79] Yet progressives have also appealed to golden ages and called for a return to a more just and sensible past. Even revolutionaries find it useful to call for restoration of an invented tradition. A good example is the story of the commerce clause as told by supporters of the New Deal. According to this story, the Supreme Court's narrow, formalist theory of federal regulatory power during the pre–New Deal era was an abandonment of the sensible, pragmatic approach of John Marshall and the founding generation.[80] Hence, the New Deal conception of a broad-ranging, flexible commerce power was not a judicial deformation of the Constitution, but rather a return to a correct understanding of the relation between federal and state power.[81]

*4. Canonical Examples.* The final form of deep canonicity works on a somewhat different level from the others. It concerns the kinds of examples that legal academics, lawyers, judges, and students of the law take as characteristic of a particular category or problem. We call this phenomenon the selection of "canonical examples."

Cognitive psychologists from Eleanor Rosch onward have noted that human beings tend to focus on certain members of categories that they regard as most representative or salient. Rosch called these examples "prototypes."[82] Prototypes are synecdoches for categories, synecdoche being the classical trope in which the part is taken to represent the whole. They are the canonical examples by which and through which individuals reason about categories, and hence they are the examples through which a great deal of human reasoning occurs. Rosch found that individuals tend to remember prototypes more easily than nonprototypical examples and that they are more likely to use them in drawing inferences about other members of a category.[83] Rosch collectively called these various psychological habits of mind "prototype effects."[84]

One of the most important ways to understand legal culture is to study the canonical examples that members of the culture routinely call upon to formulate problems and discuss issues. Situations, categories, factual hypotheticals, and even problems themselves can be the canonical examples around which legal academics and other legal thinkers naturally tend to focus and organize their thought.[85]

Accordingly, we offer two examples of what we mean by canonical examples in legal thought (although we express no opinon whether they are canonical examples of canonical examples). First, we believe that certain subjects are canonical in discussions of legal theory. When jurisprudence scholars talk about how legal reasoning works, they often draw their canonical examples from common law subjects, and even more often from constitutional law. These subjects are probably canonical because of their centrality to the culture of the first year of legal education and because many American academics who teach legal theory also teach some form of constitutional law. Indeed, the fact that we draw on constitutional law for so many of our examples in this essay is simply further evidence of constitutional law's hold on many people interested in legal theory. Common law subjects and constitutional law have become, for good or ill, the canonical examples of law for American legal theorists. Elsewhere we have noted that a majority of the most frequently cited articles of all time are about constitutional law subjects, even though there are many subjects of equal or greater importance to government policymakers and to the practicing bar.[86] Every year the *Harvard Law Review* begins its initial issue with a foreword by a noted scholar on the previous year's Supreme Court term. These much-heralded essays are almost never about antitrust, Social Security, or the regulatory problems of the Federal Deposit and Insurance Corporation. They are almost always about constitutional law, even in years when a significant majority of the Supreme Court's work involves nonconstitutional cases. These forewords symbolize the hegemony of constitutional law in the imagination of both the academics who read and write them and the students who edit them.

Nevertheless, when making arguments about how lawyers reason, or how pervasive legal indeterminacy is, or even about the nature of legal obligation, using examples based on constitutional law may be very misleading. The problems of law are not always the problems of constitutional law. The Uniform Commercial Code, the Federal Communications Act, or the Texas Rules of Civil Procedure might prove to be much better examples. Obviously, before other audiences, and for other purposes, any or all of these statutes might provide canonical examples. But that is simply further evidence of the role that prototypical examples play in structuring thought. When we say that constitutional law tends to provide canonical examples for legal theorists, we are not claiming that this tendency is a good thing. We are simply adverting to what many professors of commercial and corporate law have recognized for years: legal theorists seem to be overly concerned with constitutional law even though the vast majority of the sources of the law—and the problems that need addressing in the law—lie elsewhere.

This same canonical field provides us, not surprisingly, with our second example. Because of America's sorry history of slavery and racism, African Americans have become the canonical example of a disadvantaged or oppressed minority, the canonical example of a social group deserving of legal protection, and, indeed, the canonical example of a racial group. The Reconstruction Amendments were written largely with blacks in mind, and African Americans were surely Justice Stone's canonical example of a "discrete and insular minority."[87] As social movements gradually have sought to obtain equality for other disadvantaged groups—including women, Hispanic Americans, Asian Americans, the disabled, and most recently, homosexuals—analogies have routinely been drawn to the problem of discrimination against African Americans. African Americans, in short, are the canonical example for thinking about issues of equality in the United States. Yet racial and gender discrimination differ in important ways. The histories of unequal treatment of women and African Americans differ. The stereotypical judgments leveled against each group, the institutions and social practices through which inequality has traditionally been enforced, and the traditional justifications offered for those inequalities often differ considerably for racial and sexual inequality, to say nothing of the special problems faced by women of color.[88] One can make a similar point about discrimination against gays and the disabled. Even within the class of ethnic minorities, Hispanic Americans and Asian Americans face different problems than do African Americans.[89]

The use of African Americans as the canonical example of a racial group in legal thought has many other interesting and important effects. It tends to make discussions about race relations bipolar, even as the multicultural and multiracial status of the United States is becoming increasingly obvious. Equally important, viewing African Americans as the canonical example of a racial group tends to make white racial identity invisible. Seeing blacks as the most representative example of a race tends to make whites seem like a much less good example, and it reinforces the idea that to have a race is to be more like a black person and less like a white person.

Once we recognize this form of canonicity, we discover that American legal culture is full of canonical examples. Consider the use of disputes between farmers and ranchers to explain the workings of the Coase theorem, the use of automobile accidents to discuss the operation of tort law, and the use of the requirement that the president be thirty-five years old to illustrate an "easy case" that symbolizes the determinacy of legal texts. Each era also has its canonical examples of judicial activism that affect its views about the role of the judiciary: *Lochner v. New York*[90] in one era, *Brown v. Board of Education* in another, *Roe v. Wade*[91] in still another.

Examples of canonical examples could be multiplied, but two points are important for our purposes. First, the selection of canonical examples often operates in the background rather than as a conscious choice; that is precisely why these examples are forms of deep canonicity. Second, the use of canonical examples often has important ideological effects—effects that may be just as powerful and just as important as the choice of which cases and materials to study in the canonical first-year course.

## VI. Prescriptive and Sociological Approaches

The idea of deep canonicity suggests that much of canon formation occurs beyond the conscious apprehension of the members of a culture or discipline. Much of what is canonical is the result not of conscious planning but of the serendipitous development of the ever-shifting contours of a culture, a discipline, or an interpretive community. To be sure, individuals and groups may fight vigorously over what is canonical, but what emerges may be very different from what they desire. To paraphrase Marx, individuals and groups construct canons, but not as they intend. Moreover, the contending sides may already agree on things that are so taken for granted, and thus already so canonical to their thought, that the idea of contesting them does not even arise. Ultimately, canons and the canonical are collective enterprises involving both the conscious and unconscious elements of a culture. They are historical creations in which rational design and precision engineering are wishful thinking.

Initially we described the question of canonicity in prescriptive terms: we asked what cases and materials *should* be included in a particular version of the canon, whether pedagogical, cultural literacy, or theoretical. Of course, the notion of what ought to be canonical presupposes the possibility of shaping the canon nearer to our hearts' desire. However, we can also approach the question of canonicity sociologically. We can ask how a particular interpretive community actually forms its canon and why. In the latter case, we are especially interested in why people converge or diverge in their sense of what is canonical and in how and why their judgments change over time.

The sociological study of the canon (what social forces explain the creation of a given set of canonical materials) and the prescriptive study of the canon (what materials one ought to read or assign to others) can intersect. Once we understand how a canon gets constructed, we may be able to offer an ideological critique of its substance and the processes by which it is formed. For example, we may discover that a particular construction of a canon gives short shrift to certain types of questions (for example, how chattel slavery was integrated into every aspect of American law)[92] and that, as a result, this construction gives a particular normative slant to what people consider the important questions facing anyone in the business of thinking about law.[93] If one believes that setting agendas and framing questions significantly affect how these questions are answered, then a sociological approach to canon formation may have considerable normative importance for the study of law.

Indeed, a sociological approach leads us to a more fundamental question about canonicity than the particular contents of various canons: Why should debates about the canons of law arise at this particular time in the history of the legal academy? Debates about the canon arise when what is canonical is no longer taken for granted, no longer "goes without saying," but becomes controversial in some significant way. As noted above, debates may also occur when an imagined unity of thought and practice seems to be breaking down. They may occur when the forces of cultural reproduction that ensure the replication of interpretive assumptions in successive generations of a discipline's membership no longer operate as smoothly as they once seemed. When a previous generation cannot reproduce a relative uniformity of interpretive assumptions in a new generation—whether due to changes in demographics, to recalcitrant experience, or to economic factors—a crisis of confidence emerges that manifests itself in debates about the purposes of the common enterprise. One way in which this crisis surfaces is in controversies about what is canonical. These controversies occur repeatedly throughout the history of any discipline. Now it is the turn of the legal academy to be seasoned by its own discontents.

One clue to the source of concern about the canon, therefore, is demographic changes in the composition of the legal academy and corresponding changes in the makeup and practices of the organized bar. An increasingly "diverse" academy will almost certainly generate diverse notions about what is most worth teaching, studying, and discussing. Indeed, the same phenomenon has occurred in American liberal arts colleges, as a more varied group of people has gained entry into the academy in the past generation, producing predictable struggles over the canon in humanities departments. In like fashion, because of changes in demographics, economics, and politics, members of the legal academy may begin to ask themselves whether casebooks should include materials from "new" or "different" perspectives—for example, citations to the feminist and critical race theory literature, excerpts from novels and plays, increased coverage of slavery, and so forth.

A second possible source of concern over the legal canon is the emergence of interdisciplinary scholarship. The entry of other disciplines into the study of law threatens to change the pedagogical canon, the cultural literacy canon, and the academic theory canon at a single stroke. At some point hermeneutics, public choice theory, and feminist theory threaten to become as important to the legal academy as the dormant commerce clause or the doctrinal refinements of promissory estoppel. (Perhaps this point has already been reached.) Of course, the rise of interdisciplinary study may not be so much the cause of present-day concern with the canon as a symptom of more general social and institutional changes that, in turn, have given rise to questions about canonicity. In any case, when a distinguished jurist and former academic writes a volume on jurisprudence entitled *Overcoming Law*,[94] one might guess that traditional views of what is canonical to legal study are in for stormy weather.

A third reason for increasing interest in the composition of the constitutional canon in particular has to do with the perceived threat to the beloved precedents of the Warren Court, which seem daily under assault by current members of the U.S. Supreme Court. Posed in this light, the question of the constitutional canon appears to concern whether cases like *Miranda v. Arizona*[95] and *Brown v. Board of Education* are sacred cows that cannot be touched or whether they are revisable like everything else. A constitutional canon becomes a means of ensuring their continued vitality. For example, Cass Sunstein, a well-known liberal constitutional theorist, has insisted that "an approach to constitutional interpretation is unacceptable if it entails the incorrectness of *Brown v. Board of Education*."[96] This is more than a claim that *Brown* must be taught to law students; after all, that is also the case with *Lochner v. New York*. Rather, Sunstein is arguing that *Brown* is normatively canonical.

One can no more criticize it than one can suggest that Mozart is a wildly overrated composer of music for eighteenth-century dinner parties. One establishes oneself as a cultured person by affirming Mozart's genius; one establishes oneself as a properly acculturated lawyer by affirming *Brown*'s correctness.

Note that in this debate about canonicity it is liberals who defend the academic theory canon against the "barbarians" on the right. There is a certain irony here. Clinging to these Warren Court and early Burger Court cases as canonical is "foundationalist" in a sense that left-liberals in the current academy might loudly disdain if the issue were posed in epistemological terms. In studying the constitutional canon sociologically, therefore, we might consider the curious relationship between the antifoundationalist pragmatist who asserts that all knowledge is revisable if good enough reasons can be provided and the constitutional theorist who demands that any theory of constitutional law must explain and justify *Roe v. Wade*, while showing why *Bowers v. Hardwick*[97] is wrongly decided. There is just something unavoidably foundationalist about canons and the canonical, which we take to include all claims of the form: "An approach to constitutional interpretation is unacceptable if it entails the incorrectness of *X*." The idea of a *truly* antifoundationalist canon, if not an oxymoron, must at least create a perpetual state of intellectual tension.[98]

## VII. Institutional Contexts and Strange Bedfellows

Liberal attempts to canonize liberal precedents remind us that we must understand debates about the canon in their institutional context. Indeed, institutional factors help produce some of the most significant differences between literary and legal debates over the canon. Both debates involve a struggle for authority, but the terms of the struggle are different in each case because the institutional context differs. Differences in the political meaning of the attack on the canon stem in large part from differences in how authority is created in law and liberal arts and in who has control over the respective canons.

In liberal arts departments, traditional canons are being attacked primarily from the left side of the political spectrum. However, the pedagogical and academic theory canons in constitutional law are contested from both the left and the right. It is hardly surprising that critical race theory and feminism might wish to challenge parts of the pedagogical canon in ways reminiscent of the debates waged in liberal arts departments. Less analogous is the attack on the theoretical canon—the set of correctly decided cases that any serious theory of constitutional law must explain— from the political right. Here we find left-liberals defending a normative canon that includes cases like *Roe v. Wade* against assaults by the political right, led and symbolized by the right wing of the Supreme Court and the Reagan-Bush judiciary.

This two-front war in law can produce some interesting role reversals. When the liberal constitutional scholar Cass Sunstein declared the lasting correctness of *Brown v. Board of Education*, he was playing a role not unlike that of cultural conservatives Donald Kagan and E. D. Hirsch, who have tried to preserve the Western canon of great books from the onslaughts of multiculturalism and deconstruction.[99] In similar fashion one could imagine liberal scholars defending *Roe* or *Regents of the University of California v. Bakke*[100] against the likes of Antonin Scalia or William Rehnquist. Yet Sunstein's defense of the canon was directed not at some conservative jurisprude hoping to wreak havoc with liberal precedents; it was aimed at a still more left-wing scholar—Stanley Fish.[101] Politics makes strange bedfellows, but the ones canons make may be stranger still.

This curious state of affairs is due in large part to the institutional differences between legal and liberal arts education, and in particular, differences in the ways in which authority is created and defended in the legal and liberal arts academies. We noted previously that the attack on the liberal arts canon has come primarily from "the left." However, this expression conflates many different strands of thought. Let us separate out two of them. The first tendency, which might be termed the "political left," promotes radical egalitarianism on issues of race, class, gender, and sexual orientation. The second tendency, which we might call the "methodological left," is an epistemological and methodological attack on all received forms of canonicity and objectivity; it can take the form of antifoundationalism, poststructuralism, postmodernism, the study of culture as a form of power/knowledge, and so on.[102] Whether this stance is truly culturally relativist, it is often so portrayed by its opponents. Now one can be methodologically "on the left" without being politically on the left, and vice versa, but in today's liberal arts academy the two tendencies seem to travel together. Conversely, attacks on the methodological left and commitment to the canon seem to be identified with, if not political conservatism, at least the forces of political moderation. (Nevertheless, in the hothouse of the contemporary liberal arts academy, one can be quite liberal and still find oneself on the starboard side of these debates.)

As a result, contemporary attacks on the liberal arts canon from "the left" often serve *both* a particular political agenda and a methodological agenda, which, in the present context, seems to serve that political agenda.[103] Nevertheless, one of the most important features of alliances—including intellectual alliances—is that they are never permanent and acontextual, but take their strength from the institutional and political contexts in which they occur. If one changes that context ever so slightly, one sometimes finds stunning shifts, and hence, strange bedfellows.

So it is with the legal academy, at least when viewed from the standpoint of the liberal arts academy. The left-liberal who wishes to defend the canonical status of the Warren Court's liberal precedents must fend off attacks from the political right and the *methodological* left, but not necessarily from the *political* left. Critical race scholars—who are presumably even further to the political left than Professors Sunstein or Fish—would also regard the defense of *Brown v. Board of Education* as a sine qua non of any serious constitutional theory. They might claim that *Brown* stands for something quite different from what Antonin Scalia believes it stands for, but that goes to its meaning and not to its canonical status.

Professor Fish, by contrast, has been playing an altogether different game. In suggesting that all canons can be historicized,[104] Fish has simply adverted to the inherent tension between currently fashionable methodologies and Warren Court fundamentalism. Scratch a liberal pragmatist, Fish seems to say, and you will find a Warren Court fundamentalist. Even though many of the younger generation of scholars recognize (and loudly pronounce) that the Warren Court is dead and gone, they still want to preserve large parts of the Warren Court canon.

But is the preservation of this canon really in the hands of law faculties? This brings us to our second point about the importance of institutional context. Differences in the debates over the canon in legal and liberal arts faculties stem from differences in the mechanism of authority in law and the liberal arts. Liberal arts scholars have more control over the academic theory canon of their discipline than do legal academics. They teach the courses, assign the books, and become the arbiters of quality and taste in intellectual production and in significant parts of "high culture." Thus, for example, what gets studied in history departments and

what is considered good or bad history are, not surprisingly, largely defined by what historians want to teach, what they think is worth studying,
and what history they think is well done and well written. Of course, because liberal arts scholars do not have control over popular culture, they
do not fully control what is canonical in their disciplines; yet they have
considerable authority nevertheless.

In contrast, constitutional law professors have much less control over
the content of the academic theory canon of their discipline. This canon
is largely shaped and controlled by forces beyond their direct control—
the courts and the political branches. Law professors exercise their control primarily through influence over their students and their fellow academics and through their work as legal advisors and advocates. This
influence is not insignificant: much of our essay on the canon in constitutional law is devoted to showing that the way in which constitutional
law is taught may affect the development of constitutional doctrine. Nevertheless, the power of law professors over the academic theory canon of
constitutional law pales in comparison to the control that historians have
over the question of what is considered good history or a proper subject
of historical study.

Thus, left-liberal constitutional theorists are defenders of an academic
theory canon over which they have comparatively little control. When the
political forces that surround them demand a reassessment of liberal
precedents, they are forced into a jurisprudential posture that celebrates
stare decisis and the rule of law—in short, one that celebrates the canonical nature of these precedents. Not so for the left-wing liberal arts professor: the power to change the pedagogical, cultural literacy, and academic
theory canons of her discipline is largely hers. She may take the offensive,
knowing that to carry the day is simultaneously to win control of the
canon-making apparatus. Liberal legal academics in a conservative age,
on the other hand, must continually fight a rearguard action until like-
minded judges ascend to the bench. Even at that point, they do not gain
control of the academic theory canon, but once again find themselves
largely as cheerleaders for what has now become the winning team. In
any case, during the most urgent moments of their struggle to preserve
the work of the Warren Court and its timeless precedents, probably the
last thing they feel they need is some joker from the English department
pointing out that the whole thing is socially constructed. Thus, in comparing the institutional differences between law and the liberal arts, we

might note that canons are most likely to make the strangest bedfellows when one has the least choice about where one spends the night.

## VIII. Postscript: The Canons of This Book

Many of the issues that our remarks raise about canon construction also apply, with suitable modification, to the construction of this book. When we originally planned this volume, we attempted to offer a wide sampling of authors discussing various features of legal theory and legal education that might be canonical or raise issues about inclusion or exclusion in a canon. We chose to commission essays on the canon in subjects studied in the first-year curriculum (contracts, property, constitutional law), canonical approaches to legal theory (law and economics), and the canon as viewed from the perspective of particular group identities (race, gender, sexual orientation). The authors were given a general instruction to write about what was canonical or should be canonical in their particular subject area. The resulting essays take very different approaches to the subject and yet also often overlap in their concerns, producing a complicated conversation that we could not have completely predicted in advance.

Constructing a group of essays and commissioning a group of authors are themselves the formation of a certain kind of canon, and one that no doubt can and will be a fruitful subject for discussion by others. We wish that there had been more space to include more essays by more scholars on more subjects. What we discovered, however, in the formation of this particular canon, is that real canons are never wholly the result of conscious planning and deliberate choice. Rather, they always also involve haphazard events and unexpected turns that confound any attempt to produce a perfectly rational plan of organization. As we solicited the essays, we had our own ideas of what subjects and what authors should be included in the mix. We wanted, quite frankly, to achieve diversity not only of subject matter, but of ideology, institutional affiliation, and demographics. But as we began the process of soliciting manuscripts, the lineup and the canon we were constructing began to change and mutate as some authors accepted readily, others turned us down flat, and still others suggested different subjects and treatments. The resulting very distinguished lineup of authors, and the diversity of their treatments, are partly the result of conscious planning, but also partly the result of serendipity and forces beyond our control.

We think that this is very much the way canons and the canonical get created and formed in many different institutional settings. If we are more candid about the way this book was constructed than the authors of many other collections of essays, it is because the very process of putting together the volume has been a lesson in the nature of its subject matter. We hope that the essays in this book will stimulate useful discussions about the state of legal theory and legal education at the beginning of a new century. We have learned much from the study of the canon, and we hope that our readers will too.

NOTES

We are grateful to Akhil Amar, Bruce Ackerman, John Langbein, Carol Rose, and Reva Siegel for their helpful comments on an earlier draft of this essay.

1. The word "canon" comes from the Greek *kanon*, meaning "rod" or "rule," and originally meant a "rule, law, or decree of the Church." THE OXFORD ENGLISH DICTIONARY 838 (2d ed. 1989). Later it came to mean a "standard of judgement or authority [or] a test, criterion, [or] means of discrimination." *Id.* Hence one speaks of the "canons" of polite society. Historically, one of the most important forms of discrimination was the decision whether to count a particular text as Holy Scripture and include it in the Bible. Thus, the word "canon" came to mean a collection that is selected and organized according to a rule or set of rules, like the books of the Bible or the canon of saints in the Catholic Church. Musical canons, for example, are compositions organized according to a strict rule of imitation. *See* THE AMERICAN HERITAGE DICTIONARY OF THE ENGLISH LANGUAGE 281 (3d ed. 1992). From these various usages, the word *canon* has acquired the additional connotations of authenticity and sacredness.

2. *See* DAVID DENBY, GREAT BOOKS: MY ADVENTURES WITH HOMER, ROUSSEAU, WOOLF, AND OTHER INDESTRUCTIBLE WRITERS OF THE WESTERN WORLD (1996); HENRY LOUIS GATES, JR., LOOSE CANONS: NOTES ON THE CULTURE WARS (1992); LAWRENCE W. LEVINE, THE OPENING OF THE AMERICAN MIND: CANONS, CULTURE, AND HISTORY (1996). A particularly notable (and for some, notorious) debate took place at Stanford University about, among other things, required readings in its basic Western civilization course. *See* Mary Louise Pratt, *Humanities for the Future: Reflections on the Western Culture Debate at Stanford, in* THE POLITICS OF LIBERAL EDUCATION 13 (Darryl J. Gless & Barbara Herrnstein Smith eds. 1992).

3. *See, e.g.,* Frances Lee Ansley, *Race and the Core Curriculum in Legal Educa-*

*tion*, 79 CAL. L. REV. 1512, 1513 & n.3 (1991); Francis J. Mootz III, *Legal Classics: After Deconstructing the Legal Canon*, 72 N.C. L. REV. 977, 978–80 (1994); Judith Resnik, *Constructing the Canon*, 2 YALE J.L. & HUMAN. 221, 221 (1990). The constitutional canon was the subject of a 1993 panel at an Association of American Law Schools (AALS) Conference on Constitutional Law at the University of Michigan. *See* AALS Conference Program, *Conference on Constitutional Law* (Ann Arbor, Mich., June 12–16, 1993). The more general question "Do We Have a Legal Canon?" was the subject of the plenary session of the 1993 AALS Convention. For a collection of the papers presented at this meeting, see Symposium, *Do We Have a Legal Canon?*, 43 J. LEGAL EDUC. 1, 1–26 (1993).

4. For a discussion of the concept of "law-talk," see J. M. Balkin & Sanford Levinson, *Constitutional Grammar*, 72 TEX. L. REV. 1771, 1774–78 (1994).

5. THE NORTON ANTHOLOGY OF AMERICAN LITERATURE (Nina Baym, Wayne Franklin, Ronald Gottesman, Laurence B. Holland, David Kalstone, Arnold Krupat, Francis Murphy, Hershel Parker, William H. Pritchard & Patricia B. Wallace eds., 4th ed. 1994).

6. THE NORTON ANTHOLOGY OF SHORT FICTION (R. V. Cassill ed., 3d ed. 1986).

7. THE NORTON ANTHOLOGY OF ENGLISH LITERATURE (M. H. Abrams ed., 5th ed. 1986).

8. THE NORTON ANTHOLOGY OF WORLD MASTERPIECES (Maynard Mack ed., 5th ed. 1985) [hereinafter WORLD MASTERPIECES, Fifth Edition].

9. THE NORTON ANTHOLOGY OF MODERN POETRY (Richard Ellmann & Robert O'Clair eds., 1973).

10. THE NORTON ANTHOLOGY OF LITERATURE BY WOMEN: THE TRADITION IN ENGLISH (Sandra M. Gilbert & Susan Gubar eds., 1st ed. 1985).

11. THE NORTON ANTHOLOGY OF AFRICAN AMERICAN LITERATURE (Henry Louis Gates, Jr. & Nellie Y. McKay eds., 1997).

12. It is interesting to compare the tables of contents for the fourth and fifth editions of volume 2 of the *Norton Anthology of World Masterpieces*, which includes literature from the seventeenth century to the present. Among the authors present in the fourth edition who are omitted from the fifth are François, Duc de la Rochefoucauld, whose maxims are included, *see* 2 THE NORTON ANTHOLOGY OF WORLD MASTERPIECES 128–31 (Maynard Mack ed., 4th ed. 1979) [hereinafter WORLD MASTERPIECES, Fourth Edition]; Jean de la Fontaine, *see id.* at 132–36, Lord Byron, whose *Don Juan–Canto II* is included, *see id.* at 504–52; François René de Chateaubriand, *see id.* at 567–88; André Gide, whose *The Return of the Prodigal Son* is included, *see id.* at 1371–84; Anna Akhmatova, whose *Requiem* is included, *see id.* at 1599–1605; Vladimir Nabokov, whose *Cloud, Castle, Lake* is included, *see id.* at 1785–92; Jean-Paul Sartre, whose *No Exit* is included, *see id.* at 1793–1825; and Richard Wright, whose *Big Boy Leaves Home* is included, *see id.* at 1826–56. Moreover, some of the authors who are included in both editions are

now adjudged to have written different "masterpieces." Thus William Faulkner is represented in the fourth edition by *Old Man, see id.* at 1648–1720, whereas the fifth edition offers *Barn Burning, see* 2 WORLD MASTERPIECES, Fifth Edition, *supra* note 8, at 1781–95, and *Spotted Horses, see id.* at 1796–1815. Camus's *The Renegade, see* WORLD MASTERPIECES, Fourth Edition, *supra*, at 1857–70, is now apparently thought inferior to *The Guest, see* 2 WORLD MASTERPIECES, Fifth Edition, *supra* note 8, at 1895–1906. The fifth edition, moreover, welcomes a host of new authors into the canon, including Jorge Luis Borges, Samuel Beckett, R. K. Narayan, Ralph Ellison, Alexander Solzhenitsyn, Doris Lessing, Alain Robbe-Grillet, Yukio Mishima, Gabriel García Márquez, and Wole Soyinka. *See id.* at xvi–xvii. All of these authors had published significant work prior to the fourth edition, which was published in 1979, so whatever explains their inclusion, it cannot be the existence of brand-new work available to the editors of the 1985 edition.

13. There is also the possibility that textbook publishers like Norton expect their editors to produce new editions every few years or so to undercut the market for used copies of previous editions. This possibility gives new meaning to the expression "marketplace of ideas."

14. *See, e.g.*, Henry Louis Gates, Jr., *The Master's Pieces: On Canon Formation and the African-American Tradition, in* THE POLITICS OF LIBERAL EDUCATION, *supra* note 2, at 95, 107–08.

15. THE NORTON ANTHOLOGY OF LITERATURE BY WOMEN: THE TRADITION IN ENGLISH, *supra* note 10 (emphasis added). Perhaps in response to criticism, the title of the second edition has been slightly altered. *See* THE NORTON ANTHOLOGY OF LITERATURE BY WOMEN: THE TRADITIONS IN ENGLISH (Sandra M. Gilbert & Susan Gubar eds., 2d ed. 1996).

16. For example, Gail Godwin complained that Gilbert and Gubar gave too much space to "little-known works of significant feminist content" while neglecting women writers "whose prose or poems do not always deal with female experience or lend themselves to feminist explication." Gail Godwin, *One Woman Leads to Another*, N.Y. TIMES, Apr. 28, 1985, § 7, at 13. Thus, according to Godwin, the anthology should have been subtitled "The Feminist Tradition" rather than "The Tradition" of women writers in English. *Id.* Joyce Carol Oates noted that the anthology "had the perhaps unanticipated effect of polarizing women into two contending camps: those who denied the claims of gender and those who acknowledged them." JOYCE CAROL OATES, (WOMAN) WRITER: OCCASIONS AND OPPORTUNITIES 30 (1988). Criticisms of the anthology, Oates suggested, sometimes came from "women writers whose sense of themselves is 'genderless,' though their writing has been aimed toward a specifically female audience and their literary reputations nourished, in large part, by feminist support." *Id.*

17. We emphasize American practice here, for in Great Britain and continental Europe (as elsewhere), American-style casebooks have not caught on so read-

ily. Often, professors in these countries assign their students treatises or simply give them lists of cases and statutes to find in the library and send them on their merry way.

18. Although this debate is long overdue, it is not unprecedented. *See* Christopher D. Stone, *Towards a Theory of Constitutional Law Casebooks*, 41 S. CAL. L. REV. 1 (1968). More recently, there have been occasional discussions about the role of race in the legal curriculum, *see, e.g.*, Ansley, *supra* note 3, at 1515 & n.8; about the gendered selection of materials in contracts casebooks, *see, e.g.*, Mary Joe Frug, *Re-reading Contracts: A Feminist Analysis of a Contracts Casebook*, 34 AM. U.L. REV. 1065, 1076–1113 (1985); and about the presuppositions underlying the structure of civil procedure casebooks, *see, e.g.*, Linda S. Mullenix, *God, Metaprocedure, and Metarealism at Yale*, 87 MICH. L. REV. 1139, 1556–65 (1989). There is even a literature discussing the famous Hart and Wechsler approach to federal jurisdiction. *See* Akhil Reed Amar, *Law Story*, 102 HARV. L. REV. 688 (1989) (reviewing PAUL BATOR, DANIEL J. MELTZER, PAUL J. MISHKIN & DAVID L. SHAPIRO, HART AND WECHSLER'S THE FEDERAL COURTS AND THE FEDERAL SYSTEM (1988)); Richard H. Fallon, Jr., *Comparing Federal Courts "Paradigms,"* 12 CONST. COMMENTARY 3 (1995); Michael Wells, *Who's Afraid of Henry Hart?*, 14 CONST. COMMENTARY 175 (1997).

19. 17 U.S. (4 Wheat.) 316 (1819).

20. See Jerry Goldman, *Is There a Canon of Constitutional Law?*, AM. POL. SCI. ASS'N NEWSL. (Law and Courts Section) Spring 1993, at 2–4. Goldman's list of truly canonical cases, *see id.* at 3, is as follows (in alphabetical order):

1. Brown v. Board of Educ., 347 U.S. 483, 495 (1954) (holding segregation of public schools unconstitutional)
2. Garcia v. San Antonio Metro. Transit Auth., 469 U.S. 528, 555–57 (1985) (upholding federal regulation of state employees under the commerce clause)
3. Gibbons v. Ogden, 22 U.S. (9 Wheat.) 1, 221–22 (1824) (construing the commerce clause and defining the concept of interstate commerce)
4. Griswold v. Connecticut, 381 U.S. 479, 485–86 (1965) (recognizing the constitutional right to privacy and striking down a law banning the sale of contraceptives to married persons)
5. Lochner v. New York, 198 U.S. 45, 64–65 (1905) (striking down a maximum hour law for bakery employees)
6. Marbury v. Madison, 5 U.S. (1 Cranch) 137, 177–80 (1803) (invoking the power of judicial review over congressional legislation)
7. McCulloch v. Maryland, 17 U.S. (4 Wheat.) 316, 425 (1819) (upholding the constitutionality of the Second Bank of the United States)
8. New York Times Co. v. United States (The Pentagon Papers Case), 403 U.S. 713, 714 (1971) (per curiam) (rejecting a request for an injunction against

the publication of materials claimed to compromise national security interests)

9. Roe v. Wade, 410 U.S. 113, 164–67 (1973) (extending the right of privacy to a woman's right to abortion)

10. Youngstown Sheet & Tube Co. v. Sawyer, 343 U.S. 579, 582, 588–89 (1952) (striking down President Truman's seizure of steel mills as violating the separation of powers)

Goldman notes, incidentally, that if he had omitted the casebook with the fewest cases (PAUL BREST & SANFORD LEVINSON, PROCESSES OF CONSTITUTIONAL DECISIONMAKING (3d. ed. 1992), at least five additional cases would have been added to the list of ten cases common to all eleven of the surveyed books, *see id.* at 4:

11. Dennis v. United States, 341 U.S. 494, 516–17 (1951) (upholding the convictions of leaders of the Communist Party for conspiring to attempt to teach the necessity of the violent overthrow of the U.S. government)

12. Heart of Atlanta Motel, Inc. v. United States, 379 U.S. 241, 261–62 (1964) (upholding the Civil Rights Act of 1964 under Congress's power to regulate interstate commerce)

13. Miller v. California, 413 U.S. 15, 24 (1973) (offering a three-part test for the definition of obscenity)

14. New York Times Co. v. Sullivan, 376 U.S. 254, 288–92 (1964) (establishing a constitutional standard for state defamation law)

15. NLRB v. Jones & Laughlin Steel Corp., 301 U.S. 1, 30–32, 49 (1937) (upholding the National Labor Relations Act as a proper exercise of Congress's power to regulate interstate commerce)

Finally, as Goldman notes, there are three other likely candidates included in BREST & LEVINSON but omitted by one of the other books surveyed, *see id.* at 3–4:

16. Plessy v. Ferguson, 163 U.S. 537, 551–52 (1896) (upholding the "separate but equal" doctrine as applied to the segregation of railway carriages traveling intrastate)

17. Home Bldg. & Loan Ass'n v. Blaisdell, 290 U.S. 398, 447–48 (1934) (upholding a Minnesota mortgage moratorium law as consistent with the contracts clause).

18. The Slaughterhouse Cases, 83 U.S. (16 Wall.) 36 (1873) (construing the privileges or immunities clause of the Fourteenth Amendment narrowly to apply only to rights of national citizenship)

21. It is worth noting that Daniel A. Farber, William N. Eskridge, Jr., and Philip P. Frickey, in their self-consciously presentist *Cases and Materials on Constitutional Law: Themes for the Constitution's Third Century* (which was not included in Goldman's survey), devote a dozen pages to *McCulloch*, even given their

successful attempt to create a casebook that is far shorter than any of their competitors. *See* DANIEL A. FARBER, WILLIAM N. ESKRIDGE, JR. & PHILIP P. FRICKEY, CASES AND MATERIALS ON CONSTITUTIONAL LAW: THEMES FOR THE CONSTITUTION'S THIRD CENTURY 774–86 (1993). The book is 1,206 pages long, including the preface, the tables of contents and cases, end materials, and index. More typical is the most recent edition of what is said to be the most widely adopted casebook in the field, GEOFFREY R. STONE, LOUIS M. SEIDMAN, CASS R. SUNSTEIN & MARK V. TUSHNET, CONSTITUTIONAL LAW (3d ed. 1996), which totals 1,917 pages and devotes only two more pages to *McCulloch* than does the Farber casebook, *see id.* at 57–71. Both the Farber and the Stone casebooks edit *McCulloch*. Paul Brest and Sanford Levinson are unique in reprinting an unedited version of the case. *See* BREST & LEVINSON, *supra* note 20, at 19–31, 42–47.

22. Moreover, contemporary legal scholars rarely find it necessary to explain or justify *McCulloch*. However, the powerful surges of political conservatism we are currently witnessing in the United States soon may change all that. The changing political currents of our age have opened a space for increasingly radical positions on the rights and powers of states and have emboldened both judges and academics to make federalism arguments that would have been roundly dismissed as extreme only a few decades ago, even by many conservatives. *See* Printz v. United States, 117 S. Ct. 2365, 2383–84 (1997); U.S. Term Limits, Inc. v. Thornton, 514 U.S. 779, 845–926 (1995) (Thomas, J., dissenting); United States v. Lopez, 514 U.S. 549, 584–602 (1995) (Thomas, J., concurring); Randy E. Barnett, *Necessary and Proper*, 44 UCLA L. REV. 745, 758–59, 788–93 (1997); Gary Lawson & Patricia B. Granger, *The "Proper" Scope of Federal Power: A Jurisdictional Interpretation of the Sweeping Clause*, 43 DUKE L.J. 267, 271–74 (1993).

23. *See, e.g.*, STEPHEN J. GREENBLATT, LEARNING TO CURSE: ESSAYS IN EARLY MODERN CULTURE 80–98 (1990); STEPHEN GREENBLATT, SHAKESPEAREAN NEGOTIATIONS: THE CIRCULATION OF SOCIAL ENERGY IN RENAISSANCE ENGLAND *passim* (1988).

24. This vilification comes especially from contemporary "originalists" who are naturally eager to disassociate themselves from the self-consciously originalist methodology adopted by Taney. *See, e.g.*, ROBERT H. BORK, THE TEMPTING OF AMERICA: THE POLITICAL SEDUCTION OF THE LAW 28–34 (1990) (finding in *Dred Scott* the origins of an illegitimate and undesirable substantive due process).

25. 41 U.S. (16 Pet.) 536 (1842).

26. *See id.* at 550–55 (discussing the text of the 1826 Pennsylvania "Act to give effect to the provisions of the Constitution of the United States relative to fugitives from labour, for the protection of free persons of color, and to prevent kidnapping").

27. 347 U.S. 483 (1954).

28. 376 U.S. 254 (1964).

29. 249 U.S. 211 (1919). *Debs* upheld a conviction on the ground that Debs's

remarks implied that he approved of conscientious objection to the draft in violation of the Espionage Act of 1917. *See id.* at 216–17. Because of the fortuity that Oliver Wendell Holmes coined the clear and present danger test in the companion case of *Schenck v. United States*, 249 U.S. 47, 52 (1919), *Schenck* almost always has pride of place in casebooks, with *Debs* sometimes relegated to a footnote. *See, e.g.*, WILLIAM COHEN & JONATHAN D. VARAT, CASES AND MATERIALS ON CONSTITUTIONAL LAW 1200–01 & n.2 (10th ed. 1997) (describing Debs simply as "a prominent socialist").

Thus, we wonder how many students never learn that the United States imprisoned Eugene V. Debs, undoubtedly the most important socialist leader of his time, who amassed almost 6 percent of the vote (over 900,000 votes) for the presidency in the 1912 election (and who received roughly the same number of votes in 1920 while he was serving a ten-year sentence that had been unanimously upheld by the Supreme Court). *See* BREST & LEVINSON, *supra* note 20, at 330–32; THE READER'S COMPANION TO AMERICAN HISTORY 270 (Eric Foner & John A. Garrity eds., 1991); STONE, SEIDMAN, SUNSTEIN & TUSHNET, *supra* note 21, at 1096–97. Instead, the emphasis on *Schenck* and on *Abrams v. United States*, 250 U.S. 616 (1919), leads many students to assume that the governmental oppression of dissidents was indeed restricted to what Holmes memorably called "puny anonymities," *id.* at 629 (Holmes, J., dissenting). We therefore think that there are good reasons to reverse the treatment accorded to *Schenck* and *Debs*, even in those casebooks that currently recognize *Debs*'s significance, *see* GERALD GUNTHER & KATHLEEN M. SULLIVAN, CONSTITUTIONAL LAW 1038–40 (13th ed. 1997); WILLIAM B. LOCKHART, YALE KAMISAR, JESSE H. CHOPER, STEVEN H. SHIFFRIN & RICHARD H. FALLON, JR., CONSTITUTIONAL LAW 617–18 (8th ed. 1996); STONE, SEIDMAN, SUNSTEIN & TUSHNET, *supra* note 21, at 1096–97. The Lockhart casebook appropriately quotes Harry Kalven's statement that, "[t]o put the case in modern context, it is somewhat as though George McGovern had been sent to prison for his criticism of the [Vietnam] War." LOCKHART, KAMISAR, CHOPER, SHIFFRIN & FALLON, *supra*, at 617 n.a (second alteration in original) (quoting Harry Kalven, *Ernst Freund and the First Amendment Tradition*, 40 U. CHI. L. REV. 235, 237 (1973)) (internal quotation marks omitted). Of course, their very need to identify the war in brackets also suggests that soon most of our students will need to be told who George McGovern was.

30. 323 U.S. 214 (1944). *Korematsu* upheld the constitutionality of wartime internment of Japanese American citizens. *See id.* at 223–24.

31. Chae Chan Ping v. United States (The Chinese Exclusion Case), 130 U.S. 581 (1889). *The Chinese Exclusion Case* upheld the plenary power of the federal government to expel Chinese aliens working as laborers in the United States. *See id.* at 610–11.

32. We have previously considered one aspect of this subject in our commentary on Fred Shapiro's list of the hundred most-cited law review articles of all

time. *See* J. M. Balkin & Sanford Levinson, *How to Win Cites and Influence People*, 71 CHI.-KENT L. REV. 843, 854–56, 860–66 (1996) (discussing Fred R. Shapiro, *The Most Cited Articles Revisited*, 71 CHI.-KENT L. REV. 751 (1996)). We have suggested, for example, that someone wishing to become a "player" in the legal academy is well advised to become adept in the jurisprudence of the First and Fourteenth Amendments, rather than to study and write about the power of the president to engage in foreign adventures without prior approval of Congress. *See id.* at 854–56. Whether this allocation of energies is socially useful is quite another question. But there is no reason to think that canons are always socially useful, at least outside the confines of their respective disciplines.

33. *See, e.g.,* JOHN RAWLS, POLITICAL LIBERALISM (1993); JOHN RAWLS, A THEORY OF JUSTICE (1971); R. H. Coase, *The Problem of Social Cost*, 3 J.L. & ECON. 1 (1960).

34. *See* Shapiro, *supra* note 32, at 759, 767.

35. *See* DAVID LODGE, CHANGING PLACES: A TALE OF TWO CAMPUSES 135 (Penguin Books 1992) (1975).

36. *See id.* at 136.

37. *See id.*

38. Other readers might imagine which admission of ignorance would be less harmful to give to a law school appointments committee, or which would be less damaging if placed in one's tenure file. With suitable amendment, the game can be employed to discern the canon of cases and materials that any practicing lawyer should know. For example, imagine the following exchange at an oral argument:

> *Federal judge:* Well, that's a very interesting argument, counselor, but doesn't it conflict with *Marbury v. Madison*?
> *Lawyer:* I confess I'm unfamiliar with that case.

39. The canon of interest to academics may also differ from the canon that is important to a judge seeking competent law clerks. *See* Harry T. Edwards, *The Growing Disjunction Between Legal Education and the Legal Profession*, 91 MICH. L. REV. 34, 34–42 (1992) (arguing that the gap between legal academics and judges should be bridged by means of "practical" scholarship that combines theory with doctrine); Sanford Levinson, *Judge Edwards' Indictment of "Impractical" Scholars: The Need for a Bill of Particulars*, 91 MICH. L. REV. 2010, 2012–18 (1993) (agreeing with Judge Edwards that a gap between academics and the legal profession exists, but disagreeing with Judge Edwards's conclusions).

40. This certainly seems to be the basis of Judge Edwards's heartfelt attack on the contemporary legal academy. *See* MARY ANN GLENDON, A NATION UNDER LAWYERS: HOW THE CRISIS IN THE LEGAL PROFESSION IS TRANSFORMING AMERICAN SOCIETY 199–229, 288 (1994); Edwards, *supra* note 39, at 61–63.

41. There is a reason, after all, that one refers to "disciplines." See the discussion

in J. M. Balkin, *Interdisciplinarity as Colonization*, 53 WASH. & LEE L. REV. 949, 952–57 (1996). We have made a similar point in evaluating Philip Bobbitt's claim that constitutional lawyering is constituted by the use of a given legal grammar. *See* Balkin & Levinson, *supra* note 4, at 1775 (positing that Bobbitt is a "grammarian of our constitutional culture, determined to identify—and to police—the boundaries of what counts as the particular . . . language of constitutional 'law talk'").

42. *See* WILLIAM J. BENNETT, THE BOOK OF VIRTUES: A TREASURY OF GREAT MORAL STORIES 11 (1993) ("This book . . . is a 'how to' book for moral literacy.").

43. *See, e.g.,* Sanford Levinson & J. M. Balkin, *Law, Music, and Other Performing Arts*, 139 U. PA. L. REV. 1597 (1991).

44. An advanced course may offer what we today believe to be badly written material, but the purpose would be to reveal the vast differences in taste and sensibility between the earlier age and our own.

45. Conversely, the pedagogical canon may contain far fewer of the materials that legal academics debate in their own work, because pedagogical considerations (plus the sheer scarcity of time) often prevent a law teacher from assigning the entire theoretical canon in a course.

46. 163 U.S. 537 (1896).

47. *See id.* at 550–51.

48. *Cf.* U.S. CONST. art. III, § 1 (distinguishing the Supreme Court from "such inferior Courts as the Congress may from time to time ordain and establish").

49. *Cf.* Cooper v. Aaron, 358 U.S. 1, 18 (1958) (asserting the supremacy of the judiciary and of the Supreme Court in matters of constitutional interpretation). For a recent defense of such hierarchical superiority in the law, see Larry Alexander & Frederick Schauer, *On Extrajudicial Constitutional Interpretation*, 110 HARV. L. REV. 1359, 1372–86 (1997).

50. *See, e.g.,* SANFORD LEVINSON, CONSTITUTIONAL FAITH 9–53 (1988); Michael Stokes Paulsen, *The Most Dangerous Branch: Executive Power to Say What the Law Is*, 83 GEO. L.J. 217, 220–22 (1994).

51. This distinction is, of course, a familiar trope in the study of law and literature. *See, e.g.,* Robin L. West, *Adjudication Is Not Interpretation: Some Reservations About the Law-as-Literature Movement*, 54 TENN. L. REV. 203, 205, 207 (1987); *cf.* Robert M. Cover, *Violence and the Word*, 95 YALE L.J. 1601, 1609–10 (1986) (asserting that adjudication involves a violence that is "utterly real," as opposed to the violence found in literature). For a critique of this distinction in the context of musical performance, see Levinson & Balkin, *supra* note 43, at 1612–14.

52. We are indebted to Stanley Fish for this term.

53. *See* PHILIP BOBBITT, CONSTITUTIONAL INTERPRETATION 8–10 (1991).

54. *See* PHILIP BOBBITT, CONSTITUTIONAL FATE: THEORY OF THE CONSTITUTION 5–8 (1982); BOBBITT, *supra* note 53, at 11–22.

55. *See* Balkin & Levinson, *supra* note 4, at 1774–78.

56. On the topical approach to legal interpretation generally, see THEODORE VIEHWEG, TOPICS AND LAW: A CONTRIBUTION TO BASIC RESEARCH IN LAW (W. Cole Durham, Jr., trans., 1993), and J. M. Balkin, *A Night in the Topics: The Reason of Legal Rhetoric and the Rhetoric of Legal Reason, in* LAW's STORIES: NARRATIVE AND RHETORIC IN THE LAW 211–24 (Peter Brooks & Paul Gewirtz eds., 1996).

57. *See* THOMAS S. KUHN, THE STRUCTURE OF SCIENTIFIC REVOLUTIONS 43 (2d ed. 1970).

58. Pierre Schlag, *Normativity and the Politics of Form*, 139 U. PA. L. REV. 801, 808 (1991).

59. *See* Pierre Schlag, *Normative and Nowhere to Go*, 43 STAN. L. REV. 167, 177–80, 184–85 (1990); Schlag, *supra* note 58, at 808–10. The canonical approach is evident in the typical "job-talk" in which aspirants seeking positions in the legal academy routinely feel it necessary to offer proposals for legal reform that correct some deficiency identified in the main body of the talk. Few candidates dare to eliminate such a normative prescription, much less assert the irrelevance of normativity to successful legal scholarship. (Perhaps for the same reason, even fewer are willing to acknowledge the more modest position that they do not yet have sufficient education or experience to presume to offer solutions to significant problems of law or society.)

60. *See* Pierre Schlag, *Clerks in the Maze*, 91 MICH. L. REV. 2053, 2059–60 (1993).

61. *See id.* at 2060.

62. For a discussion of "stock stories" in law, see Gerald P. López, *Lay Lawyering*, 32 UCLA L. REV. 1, 5–9 (1984).

63. On the role of narrative constructions in shaping belief, see J. M. BALKIN, CULTURAL SOFTWARE: A THEORY OF IDEOLOGY (1998); JEROME BRUNER, ACTS OF MEANING 35–36 (1990); L. H. LARUE, CONSTITUTIONAL LAW AS FICTION: NARRATIVE IN THE RHETORIC OF AUTHORITY (1995); and RICHARD SLOTKIN, GUNFIGHTER NATION: THE MYTH OF THE FRONTIER IN TWENTIETH-CENTURY AMERICA 10–21 (1992).

64. The canonical argument for the distinctiveness of America is LOUIS HARTZ, THE LIBERAL TRADITION IN AMERICA: AN INTERPRETATION OF AMERICAN POLITICAL THOUGHT SINCE THE REVOLUTION (1st ed. 1955). The locus classicus for the myth of the frontier—although expressed not as myth but as fact—is FREDERICK JACKSON TURNER, THE FRONTIER IN AMERICAN HISTORY (1920). Richard Slotkin has reinterpreted Turner's frontier thesis as part of a grand series of interlocking American myths deeply embedded in American culture, including myths of "The Savage War," the "Bonanza," and "Regeneration through Violence." RICHARD SLOTKIN, THE FATAL ENVIRONMENT: THE MYTH OF THE FRONTIER IN THE AGE OF INDUSTRIALIZATION, 1800–1890, at 51–63 (1985); SLOTKIN, *supra* note 63, at 1–21; *cf.* RICHARD SLOTKIN, REGENERATION THROUGH VIOLENCE: THE MYTHOLOGY OF

THE AMERICAN FRONTIER, 1600–1860, at 563–65 (1973) (describing the myth of re-generation through violence in American history, culture, and rhetoric).

65. McCulloch v. Maryland, 17 U.S. (4 Wheat.) 316, 408 (1819).

66. See LaRUE, *supra* note 63, at 88–90. LaRue calls this the "story of change and growth." *Id.* at 90.

67. *See id.* at 16–31.

68. *See* Agostini v. Felton, 117 S. Ct. 1997, 2016–17 (1997) (overruling Aguilar v. Felton, 473 U.S. 402 (1985)); Rosenberger v. Rector of the Univ. of Va., 515 U.S. 819, 845–46 (1995).

69. Robert W. Gordon, *The Struggle over the Past*, 44 CLEV. ST. L. REV. 123, 129–30 (1996).

70. *See id.* at 128–29.

71. *See id.* at 130.

72. *Id.*

73. Abraham Lincoln, The Dred Scott Decision: Speech at Springfield, Illinois (June 26, 1857), *in* ABRAHAM LINCOLN: A DOCUMENTARY PORTRAIT THROUGH HIS SPEECHES AND WRITINGS 88, 91 (Don E. Fehrenbacher ed. 1964).

74. *See* Reva Siegel, *Why Equal Protection No Longer Protects: The Evolving Forms of Status-Enforcing State Action*, 49 STAN. L. REV. 1111, 1113, 1119, 1129–31 (1997).

75. *See* Reva B. Siegel, *"The Rule of Love": Wife Beating as Prerogative and Privacy*, 105 YALE L.J. 2117, 2179–81 (1996); Siegel, *supra* note 74, at 1147–48.

76. Perhaps the most eloquent representative of this narrative form is Derrick Bell, whose heartfelt reflections on the permanence of American racism are collected in various works. *See* DERRICK BELL, AND WE ARE NOT SAVED: THE ELUSIVE QUEST FOR RACIAL JUSTICE (1987); DERRICK BELL, FACES AT THE BOTTOM OF THE WELL: THE PERMANENCE OF RACISM (1992); DERRICK BELL, RACE, RACISM AND AMERICAN LAW (1970).

77. Siegel, *supra* note 75, at 2180; Siegel, *supra* note 74, at 1113.

78. Plessy v. Ferguson, 163 U.S. 537, 551 (1896).

79. *See* ROBERT H. BORK, SLOUCHING TOWARDS GOMORRAH: MODERN LIBERALISM AND AMERICAN DECLINE (1996).

80. The canonical example of this story is Robert L. Stern, *The Commerce Clause and the National Economy, 1933–1946*, 59 HARV. L. REV. 645 (1946).

81. Bruce Ackerman's theory of constitutional moments is a story of punctuated moments of popular self-definition and self-discovery (if not progress); it views the New Deal narrative of return as one of dissimulation. *See* 1 BRUCE ACKERMAN, WE THE PEOPLE: FOUNDATIONS 159–62 (1991) [hereinafter ACKERMAN, FOUNDATIONS]; 2 BRUCE ACKERMAN, WE THE PEOPLE: TRANSFORMATIONS (1998) [hereinafter ACKERMAN, TRANSFORMATIONS]. For Ackerman, the *Lochner*-era Court was more likely the true heir of the original understanding. *See* ACKERMAN, FOUNDATIONS, *supra*, at 153–56. However, it is important to recognize that

Ackerman's generous interpretation of the *Lochner* era is crucial to his own narrative: it helps establish the necessary break with the past (and the tinges of illegality) that Ackerman believes are characteristic of constitutional moments.

82. *See* Eleanor Rosch, *Cognitive Reference Points*, 7 COGNITIVE PSYCHOL. 532, 544–46 (1975); Eleanor Rosch, *Cognitive Representations of Semantic Categories*, 104 J. EXPERIMENTAL PSYCHOL. GEN. 192, 193–94 (1975); Eleanor Rosch, *Principles of Categorization, in* COGNITION AND CATEGORIZATION 36 (Eleanor Rosch & Barbara B. Lloyd eds. 1978) [hereinafter Rosch, *Principles of Categorization*]; Eleanor Rosch & Carolyn B. Mervis, *Family Resemblances: Studies in the Internal Structure of Categories*, 7 COGNITIVE PSYCHOL. 573, 574 (1975).

83. *See* GEORGE LAKOFF, WOMEN, FIRE, AND DANGEROUS THINGS: WHAT CATEGORIES REVEAL ABOUT THE MIND 40–43 (1987) (summarizing the phases of Rosch's experimental work).

84. Rosch, *Principles of Categorization, supra* note 81, at 37; *see also* LAKOFF, *supra* note 83, at 40–45 (describing Rosch's contributions to cognitive theory).

85. *Cf.* Jed Rubenfeld, *Reading the Constitution as Spoken*, 104 YALE L.J. 1119, 1122 (1995) (offering a normative theory of constitutional interpretation based on the application of "paradigm cases"); Steven L. Winter, *Transcendental Nonsense, Metaphoric Reasoning, and the Cognitive Stakes for Law*, 137 U. PA. L. REV. 1105, 1107 (1989) (emphasizing the importance of cognitive modeling to legal thought).

86. *See* Balkin & Levinson, *supra* note 32, at 854.

87. United States v. Carolene Prods. Co., 304 U.S. 144, 153 n.4 (1938).

88. The canonical discussion of the differences between racial and gender discrimination is Richard A. Wasserstrom, *Racism, Sexism, and Preferential Treatment: An Approach to the Topics*, 24 UCLA L. REV. 581 (1977). *Cf.* Sylvia A. Law, *Rethinking Sex and the Constitution*, 132 U. PA. L. REV. 955, 965 (1984) (noting that arguments about categorical physical differences can be more plausibly invoked in gender cases than in race cases because of women's reproductive capacity). Obviously, women do not fit the canonical definition of a "discrete and insular minority" because they constitute a majority. *See* JOHN HART ELY, DEMOCRACY AND DISTRUST 164–70 (1980). Finally, special complications affect women of color. *See* Kimberle Crenshaw, *Demarginalizing the Intersection of Race and Sex: A Black Feminist Critique of Antidiscrimination Doctrine, Feminist Theory and Antiracist Politics*, 1989 U. CHI. LEGAL F. 139–40; Angela P. Harris, *Race and Essentialism in Feminist Legal Theory*, 42 STAN. L. REV. 581, 586–90 (1990).

89. *See* RONALD TAKAKI, STRANGERS FROM A DIFFERENT SHORE: A HISTORY OF ASIAN AMERICANS 474–84 (1989); Richard Delgado, *Rodrigo's Fifteenth Chronicle: Racial Mixture, Latino-Critical Scholarship, and the Black-White Binary*, 75 TEX. L. REV. 1181, 1197 (1997); Jerry Kang, *Negative Action Against Asian Americans: The Internal Instability of Dworkin's Defense of Affirmative Action*, 31 HARV. C.R.-C.L. L. REV. 1, 20 (1996); Deborah Ramirez, *Multicultural Empowerment: It's Not Just Black*

and White Anymore, 47 STAN. L. REV. 957, 959–60 (1995); Frank H. Wu, *Changing America: Three Arguments About Asian Americans and the Law*, 45 AM. U. L. REV. 811, 812 (1996); Frank H. Wu, *Neither Black nor White: Asian Americans and Affirmative Action*, 15 B.C. THIRD WORLD L.J. 225, 281–84 (1995); Note, *Racial Violence Against Asian Americans*, 106 HARV. L. REV. 1926, 1930–33 (1993).

90. 198 U.S. 45 (1905).

91. 410 U.S. 113 (1973).

92. The general answer is all too easily. See the magisterial analysis in THOMAS D. MORRIS, SOUTHERN SLAVERY AND THE LAW, 1619–1860, at 61–65 (1996).

93. For a discussion of this point, see Sanford Levinson, *Slavery in the Canon of Constitutional Law*, 68 CHI.-KENT L. REV. 1087, 1087 (1993).

94. RICHARD A. POSNER, OVERCOMING LAW (1995).

95. 384 U.S. 436 (1966).

96. Cass R. Sunstein, *In Defense of Liberal Education*, 43 J. LEGAL EDUC. 22, 26 (1993).

97. 478 U.S. 186 (1986).

98. Obviously, these prescriptive debates about the academic theory canon may have consequences for the construction of the pedagogical canon as well. For example, depending upon our bedrock commitments, we might focus on either *Miranda* or the writings of the Anti-Federalists. This is one of many ways in which the construction of the academic theory canon affects the content of the pedagogical canon and the cultural literacy canon.

99. *See* Sunstein, *supra* note 96, at 26.

100. 438 U.S. 265 (1978).

101. *See* Sunstein, *supra* note 96, at 22.

102. For a critical perspective on these trends in legal scholarship, see Suzanna Sherry's contribution to this volume, "The Canon in Constitutional Law."

103. *But see* J. M. Balkin, *Transcendental Deconstruction, Transcendent Justice*, 92 MICH. L. REV. 1131, 1138, 1149–57, 1159–62, 1174–76 (1994) (arguing that this connection is overstated because progressive political uses of deconstruction can be flipped to serve a very different politics).

104. See Stanley Fish, *Not of an Age, But for All Time: Canons and Postmodernism*, 43 J. LEGAL EDUC. 11, 20 (1993) (noting that "the insight that canons are socially constructed, rather than undermining their claims, merely directs us to the history in the course of which those claims have been established").

# Part II

# The Canon in the Curriculum

# Chapter 2

# Empire or Residue

## *Competing Visions of the Contractual Canon*

## *Ian Ayres*

Is the domain of contract waxing or waning? Lawrence Friedman's path-breaking 1965 book *Contract Law in America* characterized contract law as covering a residual category of relatively unimportant transactions. He argued that whenever particular types of transactions became sufficiently salient—such as those concerning employment or insurance—specialized regulation was promulgated that "robbed contract [law] of its subject-matter."[1] Nine years later, Grant Gilmore expressed this idea similarly in *The Death of Contract*: "[T]he general law of contract is merely a residual category—what is left over after all the specialized bodies of law have been added up."[2]

In stark contrast to this residual conception, many scholars have trumpeted a much more imperialist conception of contract's domain. John Langbein, for example, has recently opined:

> Contract has become the dominant doctrinal current in modern American law. In fields ranging from corporations and partnership to landlord and tenant to servitudes to the law of marriage, scholars have come to understand our legal rules as resting mainly on imputed bargains that are susceptible to alteration by actual bargains.[3]

Under this view, the bedrock principles of contract inform (or should inform) an ever-increasing range of legal relationships.[4]

What gives? The easiest way to reconcile these radically different claims about the domain of contract is to recognize that authors employ varying definitions about what makes a particular area of law "contractual." A residualist might only consider an area contractual if disputes are decided by common law courts using common law principles such as the consideration requirement.[5] Imperialists on the other hand might consider any field to be contractual if the parties have substantial freedom to privately reorder their legal relationship.

Arthur Corbin long ago cautioned against scholars' being diverted by such definitional misunderstandings:

> Definitions [of contract] have been constructed by almost all writers on law and in many thousands of judicial opinions. . . . It is a very common error to suppose that legal terms, such as contract, have one absolute and eternally correct definition. The fact is that all such terms have many usages, among which every one is free to select. One usage is to be preferred over another only in so far as it serves our necessity and convenience.[6]

Corbin wisely warned that we should not particularly care whether a field is characterized as contractual—unless something turns on the characterization. Our first response to someone's impassioned suggestion that a particular area is or is not contractual should be "Who cares?" or perhaps more precisely "*Why* should we care?"[7]

We should be quite skeptical of any canon definitions that are divorced from consequentialist considerations. Essentialist debates about what is contract not only are semantic in the most pejorative sense of the word, but may divert attention from what is really at stake. Common law decision making is prone toward error when judges divorce the meaning of words from their legal consequences.[8] For example, in struggling to determine whether a rent-to-own transaction—whereby a consumer rents, say, a television with an option to buy—is appropriately characterized as a "credit sale," courts often lose sight of the fact that what turns on this designation is whether the seller needs to disclose an implicit interest rate.[9] Even nonactivist judges who want only to be faithful to the legislature's intent should ask whether the legislature in using this term intended to force rent-to-own businesses to disclose this type of information. But in the most egregious examples of this type of reifying interpretation, the standards for characterizing behavior are wholly divorced from the legal consequences of the characterization.[10]

Given my extreme skepticism about the utility of defining a contractual canon, I will now cautiously argue for the following definition: An area of law should be considered contractual if parties can privately reorder a substantial proportion of their legal relations.[11] While I have no stake in maintaining that this is the only valid definition, I hope to show

that the definition might, in Corbin's terms, prove to be convenient because it might lead policymakers (and scholars) when speaking of contract to focus on a central aspect of contract: whether and how parties
contract around default rules.

This definition puts me squarely within the imperialist camp, but in
three senses I claim only to be a "wimpy imperialist." First, the focus on
rules that are susceptible to private reordering does not necessarily include areas of law where the rules conform to the "hypothetical contract"
that parties would enter into if they could costlessly contract.[12] Thomas
Jackson, for example, has claimed that bankruptcy rules conform to the
hypothetical bargain that creditors would strike amongst themselves.[13]
But as Jules Coleman has acutely observed, these theories are really arguments that a particular set of rules is efficient, supplemented by the su-
perfluous assumption that the parties would have contracted for the efficient rule.[14] The hypothetical bargain approach is routinely used to describe areas of law that are not contractual in the sense that the rules are
largely mandatory—that is, not susceptible to private reordering—such
as bankruptcy or professional ethics. Describing such areas as contractual
is not useful. Because hypothetical bargaining theories routinely assume
monolithic preferences (i.e., every contracting pair is assumed to want
the same contract), these theories divert policymakers from making the
difficult but important assessments about whether particular rules
should be susceptible to private reordering or not.

Second, my definition of contract is wimpy because it does not incor-
porate a presumption that contractual rules should be defaults (susceptible to private reordering), or a presumption that hypothetical or majoritarian defaults should be chosen.[15] In contrast, Fred McChesney represents what I would call a strong-form imperialist. To his credit, he clearly
states what turns on calling corporate law contractual:

> Since the firm is best explained in the contractarian paradigm as a set of
> contractual rules that reduce transaction costs, mandatory law overriding
> contracts is the exception. Those advocating legal coercion must bear the
> burden of showing why coercion should trump contracts.[16]

But the fact that a substantial number or even a majority of rules *are* susceptible to private reordering does not create a presumption that other
rules in the area *should* be. McChesney here is leaping from "is" to
"ought" without sufficient justification. My wimpy brand of contractarianism more modestly hopes to focus policymakers and scholars on the

consequences of making particular rules mandatory. A conclusion that particular rules should be susceptible to private reordering also does not lead me to presume that these defaults should be set at what the majority of contractual parties favor. Indeed, Rob Gertner and I have shown that "penalty" or "information-forcing" defaults might produce more efficient contractual equilibria than so-called majoritarian defaults.[17] My wimpier conception of contract intends to induce a more explicit consideration of how parties would bargain in the shadow of a variety of possible defaults.

Finally, by demanding that a substantial number of rules be susceptible to private reordering, the definition does not include areas where parties make all-or-nothing decisions to consent to a whole set of legal rules. The definition thereby excludes vast areas of tort and regulatory law that individuals opt into by consenting to undertake particular activities— such as driving cars. While there are interesting positive and normative issues about how particular sets of mandatory rules affect individuals' decision to participate in particular activities, characterizing such areas as contractual might divert attention from the core issues that should be in the foreground of policymakers' and scholars' minds.

In particular, my thesis is that my "default-centric" definition of the contractual canon can help illuminate three normative issues:

1. Should particular rules be mandatory or merely defaults (which may be privately changed)? And if defaults,
2. Which default should be chosen? and
3. What should be the necessary and sufficient conditions for contracting around the default?

The impulse of too much scholarship is to analyze legal rules as though— like much of tort law—they were not or could not be susceptible to private reordering. But a host of related normative questions arises in contexts where parties have or should have the freedom to reorder substantial parts of their legal relationship.

Before discussing each of these three normative issues, it is useful to step back and place this definition of canonicity in the larger context of this book. Balkin and Levinson have suggested three major categories of canons: the pedagogical canon, consisting of what law students/lawyers should know; the academic theory canon, consisting of what every "serious legal academic" should know and what theoretical approaches should be central to the field; and the cultural literacy canon, consisting of what every "well-educated generalist" should know.[18] I intend for my default-centric contractual canon to apply to all three audiences. My most basic claim is that a default-centric definition of the contractual cannon makes visible important normative questions that are currently (or especially in the past were) invisible. Making law students more sensitive to issues of private reordering will ultimately produce better advocates–ones who are sensitive to whether and how particular rules can be privately displaced. Making legal academics more sensitive to default rules can lead to a more informed debate about what our laws should be. In what follows, for example, I hope to show that some of the analysis of Ronald Dworkin and Richard Epstein could have been improved if they more reflexively asked the three aforementioned, primordial default questions when advocating particular legal rules. Finally, to the extent that lawmakers and other well-educated generalists want to engage in ought talk, it would be useful to have default sensitivity become part of the cultural literacy canon. The current discussions of libertarianism are often only about whether there should be contractual freedom and not about how the law can shape the ways that contractual freedom is exercised. However, this cultural literacy claim is my weakest. There would be some value in including all kinds of information in the canon of what it means to be culturally literate–but not all this information can be maintained within the limited human RAM. So ultimately, I make no claim that it is more important for the well-educated generalist to learn the wisdom of defaults than, say, the wisdom of Sojourner Truth.[19] But with this discussion of canonicity as background, let me now turn to the three core normative issues themselves.

*1. Immutability Considerations.* In deciding whether particular rules should be mandatory, policymakers should consider whether restrictions on the parties' freedom of contract is justified either by "externalities" or "paternalism"—in that lawmakers might make rules mandatory to protect people not in privity with the contract (e.g., as in the mandatory prohibition of criminal conspiracies) or to protect people inside the contract (e.g., as in the mandatory prohibition against contracting with infants).[20] Consequentialists will also want to carefully consider the interaction between mandatory and default terms of contracts and the effect of mandatory rules on the ability of people to contract at all. For example, the mandatory prohibition against usurious interest rates might limit the ability of high-risk consumers to borrow money, or induce sellers with bargaining power to extract their profits in a less efficient manner.

Many prophylactic rules which are initially characterized as mandatory can often in reality be modified to give even more protection to one of the contracting parties. For example, the mandatory duty of good faith can be contracted around to enhance a promisor's fiduciary duties. Policymakers should consider whether a mandatory restriction should prohibit all private reorderings or whether it should merely establish mandatory ceilings or floors to the contractual duties.

Finally, when establishing mandatory restrictions on freedom of contract, the law perforce needs to establish how it will react to parties' attempts to contract around these restrictions. The law of contracts has displayed two generic responses to such attempts at violating immutability. One response—which is captured by the equitable doctrine of *cy pres*—reforms the offending provision to the "closest" nonoffending term. For example, if an employer contracts for an unreasonably long covenant not to compete, the law might respond by enforcing only a reasonable covenant not to compete. The second broad legal response is structured to deter such attempts by punishing the responsible party. The law can deter immutability violations not only by criminally sanctioning the attempts (as with conspiracies to violate mandatory criminal rules), but also by reducing the contractual rights of one contracting party. The "blue pencil" interpretive method of striking out offensive contractual provisions may have such a penalizing effect. For example, if an employer extracts a covenant not to compete for an unreasonable time, the blue pencil method may result in the employer's having no protection against competition (instead of reducing the duration of the covenant to a reasonable period).[21] A subtler way that the law might deter attempts to contract around mandatory restrictions is to promote contractual opportunism by the parties within such invalid contracts. If courts countenance contractual opportunism by one or more of the parties, they might no longer find it in their interest to contract initially. While controlling contractual opportunism is usually one of the primary purposes of contract law, courts might want to foster contractual opportunism when parties contract for prohibited provisions in order to deter parties from entering into such contracts in the first place. For example, if the courts void all contractual and restitutionary duties with regard to such "illegal" contracts, parties will be unwilling to rely in advance on the other side's performance for fear that the other side will walk away from its unenforceable duty to perform.[22] A classic example of the law struggling to choose between the *cy pres* and *deterrence* responses to contracting around mandatory rules can be found in the trial court and appellate decisions in *Fros-*

*tifresh v. Reynoso.*[23] The trial court responded to a seller's unconscionably high markup on a freezer by deciding that the buyer was not required to pay any profit;[24] the appellate court affirmed the unconscionability decision but instead reformulated the contract to require the buyer to pay a "reasonable profit."[25]

*2. Choosing the Default.* Even if the law allows freedom of contract to reign, it still must decide how to fill obligational gaps in agreements— where parties fail to fully specify their respective contractual duties.[26] There are several competing theories on how to choose defaults.[27] The most widely accepted standard is to choose the default that most parties would choose if they could costlessly contract. This "majoritarian" standard has the intuitive appeal that choosing the default that most parties want promotes efficiency by minimizing the transaction costs expended to contract around a particular rule.

While the "majoritarian" standard has acquired the status of presumptive correctness, as a wimpy imperialist I am intrigued with both empirical and theoretical counterexamples. Empirically, it may be difficult to identify a majoritarian rule for the simple reason that there may be several rules that a majority of parties fail to contract around. In other contexts, there may be three or more popular provisions—so that policymakers could do no better than identify a "plurality" rule.

Theoretically, it is has been shown that nonmajoritarian default rules can be more efficient for a variety of reasons. First, it might be more efficient to select a default that only a minority of contractors prefer if this minority would bear particularly high costs of contracting around or failing to contract around.[28] Second, inducing parties to contract around a nonpreferred default might induce contractors to disclose private information to each other or to third parties (including courts).[29]

Regardless of whether policymakers embrace majoritarianism, they often must also decide two other dimensions: whether the default should be "tailored" or "one-size-fits-all," and whether the default should be a "rule" or a "standard."[30] The majoritarian default approach commands lawmakers to provide the gap fillers that most people want, but does not define the population over which to calculate the majority. As the population size is reduced, the default choice becomes "tailored" to more particularized characteristics of the contracting party. At the extreme, a tailored default seeks to provide the hypothetical contractual provision that each particular contracting pair would have contracted for ex ante. A related, but separate, issue concerns whether the chosen default should be rule-like or standard-like. Legal standards are muddier provisions whose contours are often determinable only after the fact—unlike the more crystalline provisions of legal rules which are more readily knowable ex ante.[31] Lawmakers choose the degree of tailoring and muddiness in noncontractual areas as well. For example, in deciding the due care standard for torts, the law inevitably must establish whether this generally mandatory duty is tailored to particular characteristics of the tort feasor or victim, as well as the degree of muddiness ("reasonable man" v. *res ipsa loquitur*). However, it is extremely dangerous to import tort (read: mandatory) theories about tailoring or muddiness to the contractual area. The consequences of choosing an untailored standard are likely to be very different when parties can obliterate the law literally with a few strokes of a pen.

*3. Prerequisites for Private Reordering.* Even after deciding that a particular legal relationship will be subject to private reordering and after choosing what default provision will govern when the parties have been silent, the law must still establish what constitutes nonsilence—that is, the law must identify the necessary and sufficient conditions for supplanting or contracting around defaults. A number of cases turn on the question of sufficiency. The parties to a contract attempt to contract around a default, and the court must decide whether the attempt was sufficient to create an alternative contractual obligation. For example, in *Jacob and Youngs v. Kent*[32] and in *Peeveyhouse v. Garland Coal Co.*,[33] the courts, while upholding the private parties' freedom to contract for contrary results, found that the contractual language was not sufficient to give rise to "cost of performance" damages. These cases establish that certain manifestations are not sufficient to contract around a "diminution in value" damage measure, but do not establish what would be sufficient. Judicial holdings and statutes that find particular wording to be sufficient have the effect of creating safe harbors for parties who want to establish an alternative program. At other times, contract law establishes necessary conditions for contracting around a particular default—as in the U.C.C. provision requiring waivers of the implied warranty of merchantability to use the word "merchantability" and to be conspicuous.[34]

The legal choice of these necessary and sufficient conditions can provide valuable information to a variety of people. Most importantly, the words used to supplant default provisions are the most direct manifestations of the parties' consent. Rules regarding the verbal as well as the non-verbal conditions (e.g., conspicuousness, separate initialing) can insure that the nondrafting party is aware of the particular term and thus help police the quality of the parties' consent. But manipulating the conditions for contracting around defaults can also provide information to third parties. Most importantly, requiring explicit manifestations of intent can give courts information about the scope of the contract. And at times policymakers might want to provide information to ancillary members of society. Especially when a penalty default is chosen because of its information-forcing quality, policymakers will want to make sure that the method that parties use to contract around the default reveals the intended type of information. For example, the default damages for lost profit on consumer sales might usefully be set to zero dollars as a penalty default in order to encourage sellers to contract for liquidated damages and thereby to provide consumers with better information about the seller's expected profit.[35] Providing profit information might both allow consumers to take more efficient precautions against breach (such as searching for financing) and give consumers more bargaining power. The first goal (of facilitating efficient consumer precaution) can be accomplished by simply requiring that the liquidated damages clause make clear to consumers that the consequence of not purchasing will be a certain amount of money. But to further the second goal, the law might want to enforce damages for lost profit only if the damages clause explicitly designates the liquidated amount as being compensation for lost profit. A consumer negotiating to buy a compact car—upon learning that she was about to sign a contract in which the seller claims $4,000 in lost profits—might be put on notice that she should continue negotiating or search elsewhere.

An important, unexplored puzzle concerns the seemingly intentional fuzziness of legal standards for contracting around particular default rules. Many areas of law—even after decades of decision—resist clear statements of the necessary and sufficient conditions for contracting to a particular result.[36] In classic "sufficiency" cases such as *Peeveyhouse* and *Jacob and Youngs* it still is unclear what ex ante contractual language would have reversed the result. Cynics might view this as the backdoor creation of mandatory rules,[37] but an interesting issue for further research is whether there might be other reasons why the law would intentionally make it difficult or unclear how to contract around. A different way of characterizing these cases is that they are attempting to make particular provisions mandatory for some contractual parties but not for others (who are willing to undertake the difficult and uncertain process of attempting to contract around).[38]

My thesis is that defining the contractual canon to focus on *private reorderings* focuses attention on whether and how default rules might be reordered. In confronting each of these issues, the most persuasive normative analysis will explicitly compare the predicted equilibrium of alternative rules. Too many articles argue for the efficiency of a particular rule without adequately describing what the contractual equilibrium would look like under that rule and comparing it with the contractual equilibria under alternative rules. Better still are the very few articles that try to bring real world contracting evidence to bear in developing their consequentialist claims.[39]

To illustrate the normative payoff of thinking "contractually"—in the sense of focusing on these three core gap-filling issues—I intentionally choose to discuss an area of law where the leading scholars are apt to ignore contract. My illustration concerns Ronald Dworkin's recent suggestion that the First Amendment should ban most actions for libel.[40] What would it mean to think about this proposal through the lens of contract? I will argue that thinking contractually raises interesting questions about each of the three core default issues and that consideration of these three issues ultimately undermines (or at least substantially modifies) the proposal itself.

First, one should consider whether the rule (banning all actions except for malicious libel) should be mandatory or merely a default rule. Dworkin, like most constitutional theorists, is so used to thinking only about mandatory rules that he does not consider this most basic issue. Currently many contractual parties warrant the truthfulness of their representations—and thereby contract for liability if one of their representations is false (even if the misrepresentation was not made maliciously). I doubt that Dworkin believes that such affirmative contracts violate his conception of the First Amendment. The Constitution similarly should not prohibit laws that allow individuals to affirmatively opt into potential libel liability for (nonmalicious) misrepresentations. Just as the makers of Carbolic Smoke balls offered warranties to its users to make its claims of effectiveness more credible,[41] I see no reason why the Constitution should prohibit newspapers from guaranteeing that all of their news is accurate and offering to pay damages to anyone who would be injured as a way of convincing readers that their product (the news) is truthful. It would be a strange result indeed if the First Amendment were read to prohibit giving people the option to "stand behind" the truthfulness of their statements. This analysis suggests that Dworkin's proposed ban is merely a default rule and not (as it seems) mandatory.

But the conclusion that a particular legal rule is a default ineluctably leads contract thinkers to ask the second ur–default question: Which default is most appropriate? If the First Amendment does not prohibit firms from opting into such a regime, why should it prohibit a legislature from creating an opt-out regime? In particular, why couldn't the legislature require that speakers in particular public fora open themselves up to pay libel damages for falsehoods unless the speakers explicitly opted out by expressly disclaiming such potential liability? Dworkin needs to provide a reason why a "no liability" default is to be constitutionally preferred to a "potential liability" default. Dworkin might argue that forcing speakers to disclaim potential liability is too burdensome, so that as a categorical matter opt-out regimes are unconstitutional.

But this defense of Dworkin's proposal itself necessitates an investigation of the third default issue: the necessary and sufficient conditions for contracting around particular defaults. As a theoretical matter, it is unclear whether an opt-in or opt-out regime would be more burdensome to freedom of speech. If the majority of speakers wants to credibly signal the truthfulness of its statements, then forcing these speakers to opt into potential liability may be more burdensome than forcing other speakers to opt-out. Instead of banning all opt out regimes, the First Amendment might only restrict the words of disclaimer required in order to opt out. For example, requiring a speaker to say that her statement may include malicious falsehoods as a precondition for avoiding libel damages may overly burden the free speech right. But putting listeners on notice that the speaker is not willing to be legally accountable for her misstatements is not, as an a priori matter, inimical to the underlying goals of the First Amendment.

At the minimum, this contractual reconception has refocused the terms of the debate. Instead of arguing whether libel laws are immutably unconstitutional, we ask whether the default rule should be "potential libel damages" or "no potential libel damages" and what should be sufficient to opt in or opt out of such liability.[42] Once one accepts that private parties should be able to opt into libel liability, it is a short step to seeing that the state might constitutionally force parties to opt out of such liability by forcing speakers to indicate (in not overly burdensome ways) that they do not wish to be legally accountable for their misrepresentations. Recast this way, Dworkin's bold proposal loses much of its oomph. The point here is not that an "opt out" regime is necessarily constitutional, but that it is a serious enough contender to deserve more thorough and explicit consideration.

This First Amendment analysis is by no means unique. The contractual impulse can be applied—like the name game—to virtually any rule of law. And while free market proposals often are thought to have a conservative political valence, thinking contractually can defang conservative as well as liberal proposals. For example (and in contrast to Dworkin's liberalism), contractual analysis can undermine Richard Epstein's proposal to repeal Title VII and its prohibition of racial or sexual discrimination in the workplace.[43] Recast in contractual terms, Epstein makes several (questionable) arguments against Title VII as a mandatory rule and suggests that these arguments are sufficient for repeal. But as long as Epstein would allow decision makers to covenant that they will not discriminate (and as a hard-core believer in freedom of contract, Epstein would), his proposal is really that Title VII become an opt-in regime—with "no potential liability" being merely a default. But just as Dworkin needs to provide some reason why a "no liability" default is to be preferred to a "potential liability" default, Epstein needs to explain why repealing Title VII is preferred to merely making Title VII a default rule. While I am not in favor of either change, I think that changing Title VII to a default that an employer could disclaim only with sufficiently public disclosures would not lead to any significant change in the current equilibrium: most employers would be ashamed to contract for the right to discriminate on the basis of race.[44] Again, the point here is that legal analysts can profit by thinking about the contractual dimensions of problems even in areas that seem far removed from the traditional canon of contract.

In studying for the Illinois bar, I was forced to learn dozens of corporation rules that were dutifully squibbed in my review materials. But I remember being frustrated that the materials invariably failed to indicate whether particular rules could be contracted around, and if so, how. This method of teaching law was an unfortunate part of many curriculums. Increasingly, however, professors in their scholarship and in their teaching are emphasizing whether and how private parties can reorder particular legal rules. While I remain highly dubious about the project of canon building, I confess that I hope to instill a certain contractual impulse or reflex, if you will, in my students: whenever they learn a new legal rule in any field, I hope they will ask whether and how it should be contracted around.

The debate over what it means to be "contractual" has been probably most intense in the area of corporate law. Dozens of articles have been written with the contractarian/noncontractarian divide fracturing much of the literature.[45] I propose no magic resolution to this conflict. Give me your definition of contract and I will try to tell you whether, as a descriptive matter, corporate law conforms. If like Victor Brudney[46] you believe that contract requires a certain amount of bargaining or market competition to ensure that contractual provisions are properly "priced," then you might reasonably conclude that a corporation is not usefully described as a nexus of contracts. On the other hand, corporate law seems to meet my wimpy imperialist definition, because a substantial number of rules are susceptible to private reordering. What I have characterized as the three core contractual questions are of great importance in determining the scope of corporate law. But as a wimpy imperialist, my contractual view of the corporation does not close my mind to using mandatory rules or information-forcing defaults or manipulating the requirements for contracting around defaults to improve social welfare. The quintessentially "relational" nature of management's contract with the firm raises distinct issues of corporate governance: The quality of consent at a corporation's inception is often high, but the inception is so temporally removed from future contingencies that complete contracting is impossible, and inducing diversified investors to seriously consider amendments (the so-called "midstream" problem) significantly reduces the quality of consent for subsequent attempts to reorder the terms of the governance contract.[47] To me, however, the midstream problem and similar difficulties underscore the importance of thinking about the consequences of properly regulating the scope and method of private reordering.

Unlike other theories, my vision of the contractual canon has not made "promise," "consent," or "bargain" the defining theme.[48] Indeed, my definition does not even strictly require two contracting parties, hence, wills and estates are "contractual" for me because the laws of intestacy are merely defaults that individuals have the option to contract around.[49] Placing "gap filling" at the core focuses our attention on consequences of granting individuals the option to mutate their legal obligations—the consequences of contractual freedom.[50]

NOTES

Jennifer Brown provided helpful comments.

1. Lawrence Friedman, Contract Law in America: A Social and Economic Case Study 24 (1965).

2. GRANT GILMORE, THE DEATH OF CONTRACT 7 (1974).

3. John H. Langbein, *The Contractarian Basis of the Law of Trusts*, 105 YALE L.J. 625, 630 (1995).

4. *See also* Richard Painter, *Game Theoretic and Contractarian Paradigms in the Uneasy Relationship Between Regulators and Regulatory Lawyers*, 65 FORDHAM L. REV 149 (1996).

5. *See* for example Austin Scott's arguments that trust law is not contractual because of its roots in the law of equity. Austin W. Scott, *The Nature of the Rights of the Cestui Que Trust*, 17 COLUM. L. REV. 269, 270 (1917). Langbein uses a more modern definition of contract in criticizing Scott. Langbein, *supra* note 3, at 645–50.

6. A. CORBIN, CORBIN ON CONTRACTS § 3 (1952) (footnote omitted). *See also* Robert Clark, Agency Costs Versus Fiduciary Duties in *Principals and Agents: The Structure of Business* 55, 60 (John Pratt & Richard Zeckhauser eds. 1985) ("The term *contract* is more frequently used, even by lawyers in varying senses than is the term *agency*, so it would be neither right nor prudent for me to claim that one particular specification of the term is the definitive legal notion of contract").

7. I admit, however, to having irrational commitment to some arbitrary word meanings—where little turns on the meaning. For example, like Jack Balkin, I was born and raised in Kansas City and have found myself in heated debates on whether or not I am a "Midwesterner." I am.

8. *See* RICHARD POSNER, OVERCOMING LAW 178 (1996) (arguing that analogic reasoning "is not reasoning but is at best preparatory to reasoning").

9. *See* Palacios v. ABC TV & Stereo Rental of Milwaukee, 365 N.W.2d 882 (Wis. App. 1985).

10. *See* Delta Life & Annuity Co. v. Freeman Fin. Servs. Corp., 1995 U.S. App. LEXIS 14897; 1995-2 Trade Cas. (CCH) ¶ 71, 141 (9th Cir. 1995). This case (which I unsuccessfully argued in the appellate court) forced the court to decide whether the remarketing of annuities constituted the "business of insurance" under the three-part standard announced in Hartford Fire Ins. Co. v. California, 509 U.S. 764 (1993). But neither the Supreme Court's standard nor the Ninth Circuit court's application was tied to the legal consequence: exemption from antitrust liability under section 2(b) of the McCarran-Ferguson Act, 15 U.S.C. § 1012(b).

11. This definition is close to many others in the field. *See*, e.g., Langbein, *supra* note 3, at 629 ("The bedrock elements of contract are consensual formation and consensual terms").

12. See Henry N. Butler & Larry E. Ribstein, *Opting Out of Fiduciary Duties: A Response to the Contractarians*, 65 Wash. L. Rev. 1, 17 (1990) (It is "a mistake to identify the hypothetical bargain approach with the contract theory of the corporation. Yet several commentators have done that, and have then proceeded to criticize the contract theory because the hypothetical bargain approach is inconsistent with it, or otherwise defective. If anything, the defects of the hypothetical bargain approach provide another argument in favor of the contract theory: To the extent that courts and legislators follow this approach in adopting default provisions, it is important to permit the parties to opt out of it in order to escape its defects.")

13. Thomas H. Jackson & Robert E. Scott, *On the Nature of Bankruptcy: An Essay on Bankruptcy Sharing and the Creditor's Bargain*, 75 Va. L. Rev. 155, 156 (1989); Thomas H. Jackson, *Bankruptcy, Non Bankruptcy Entitlements, and the Creditor's Bargain*, 91 Yale L.J. 857, 860 (1982); Thomas H. Jackson, the Logic and Limits of Bankruptcy Law 228–48 (1986). Ron Gilson has similarly argued that many mandatory rules of professional responsibility are consistent with the hypothetical bargain that clients would collectively strike. Ronald J. Gilson, *The Devolution of the Legal Profession: A Demand Side Perspective*, 49 Md. L. Rev. 869 (1990).

14. Jules L. Coleman, Douglas D. Heckathorn & Steven M. Maser, *A Bargaining Theory Approach to Default Provisions and Disclosure Rules in Contract Law*, 12 Harv. J.L. & Pub. Pol'y 639 (1989).

15. For a discussion of the difference between hypothetical and majoritarian defaults, *see* Ian Ayres & Robert Gertner, *Majoritarian v. Minoritarian Defaults*, 51 Stan. L. Rev. (1999).

16. Fred S. McChesney, *Contractarianism Without Contracts? Yet Another Critique of Eisenberg*, 90 Colum. L. Rev. 1332, 1335 (1990).

17. Ian Ayres & Robert Gertner, *Filling Gaps in Incomplete Contracts: An Economic Theory of Default Rules*, 99 Yale L.J. 87 (1989) (with Robert Gertner) [hereinafter Ayres & Gertner I].

18. Applying the alternative definitions to constitutional law, Balkin and Levinson have argued:

First, we might ask what key cases and materials should be taught in constitutional law courses and reprinted in constitutional law casebooks. We call this the "pedagogical canon." Second, we might ask what key cases and materials any educated person should be aware of in order to participate in serious discussions about American constitutional development. We call this the "cultural literacy canon." Third, we might ask what key cases and materials any serious legal academic—as distinguished from the ordinary lawyer or the well-educated generalist—should know and any serious theory of constitutional law must take into account. We call this the "academic theory canon."

*See* J. M. Balkin & Sanford Levinson, *The Canons of Constitutional Law,* 111 HAR. L. REV. 964, 975–76 (1998).

19. However, as discussed below, sensitivity to defaults can have important implications for qualifying Richard Epstein's argument that Title VII should be repealed.

20. Ayres & Gertner I, *supra* note 17, at 88; Anthony T. Kronman, *Paternalism and the Law of Contracts,* 92 YALE L.J. 763 (1983).

21. *See* G. Richard Shell, *Contracts in the Modern Supreme Court,* 81 CALIF. L. REV. 431, 442 (1993).

22. Countenancing ex post opportunism by one side of the contract will deter ex ante contracting only if the potential victim has sufficient knowledge to know that it should not enter into this type of contract. Buyer opportunism should increase the buyer's willingness to contract and decrease the seller's willingness to contract. The latter effect will dominate (to deter contracting) only if sellers know at the time of potential contracting about the legal system's likely reaction. Thus, deciding that employers do not need to pay undocumented workers will reduce illegal immigration only if the potential workers in question know that they may be subject to such ex post exploitation. *See* Gates v. Rivers Constr. Co., 515 P.2d 1020 (Alaska 1973).

23. Frostifresh Corp. v. Reynoso, 54 Misc. 2d 119, 281 N.Y.S. 2d 964 (1967).

24. 52 Misc.2d 26, 274 N.Y.S.2d 757 (1966).

25. 54 Misc. 2d 119, 281 N.Y.S. 2d 964 (1967).

26. Lawyers refer to obligational gaps as rendering contracts "incomplete," while economists use the same term to refer to contracts that are not sufficiently state contingent. Ian Ayres & Robert Gertner, *Strategic Contractual Inefficiency and the Optimal Choice of Legal Rules,* 101 YALE L.J. 729 (1992) (hereinafter Ayres & Gertner II); Gillian K. Hadfield, *Judicial Competence and the Interpretation of Incomplete Contracts,* 23 J. LEGAL STUD. 159 (1994).

27. *See e.g. Symposium on Default Rules and Contractual Consent,* 3 S. CAL. INTERDIS. L.J. 1 (1993); Randy E. Barnett, *The Sound of Silence: Default Rules and Contractual Consent,* 78 *Va. L. Rev.* 821 (1992); Jason Scott Johnston, *Strategic Bargaining and the Economic Theory of Contract Default Rules,* 100 YALE L.J. 615 (1990); David Charny, *Hypothetical Bargains: The Normative Structure of Contract Interpretation,* 89 MICH. L. REV. 1815 (1991); Ayres & Gertner I, supra note 17.

28. Ayres & Gertner I, supra note 16, at 108–18 (providing algebraic example).

29. *Id.*

30. *See* Ian Ayres, *Making a Difference: The Contractual Contributions of Easterbrook and Fischel,* 59 U. CHI. L. REV. 1391 (1992) (discussing whether fiduciary duty defaults should be rules or standards); Ian Ayres, *Preliminary Thoughts on Optimal Tailoring of Contractual Rules,* 3 S. CAL. INTERDIS. L.J. 1 (1993) (discussing whether default rules should be "tailored" or "off-the-rack").

31.  *See* Louis Kaplow, *Rules Versus Standards: An Economic Analysis*, 42 Duke L.J. 557 (1992); Carol M. Rose, *Crystals and Mud in Property Law*, 40 Stan. L. Rev. 577 (1988).

32.  230 N.Y. 239, 129 N.E. 889 (1921).

33.  382 P.2d 109 (Okla 1962), *cert. denied*, 375 U.S. 906 (1963).

34.  U.C.C. § 2–316(2).

35.  Ayres & Gertner I, *supra* note 17, at 104; Victor Goldberg, *An Economic Analysis of the Lost-Volume Retail Seller*, 57 S. Cal. L. Rev. 283 (1984).

36.  There are also mandatory provisions within contract law where courts almost intentionally seem to resist precise characterization. For example, in most jurisdictions it would be difficult to describe the exact maximum enforceable length of covenants not to compete.

37.  Alan Schwartz, *The Default Rule Paradigm and the Limits of Contract Law*, 3 S. Cal. Interdis. L.J. 390 (1993); Charles J. Goetz & Robert E. Scott, *The Limits of Expanded Choice: An Analysis of the Interactions Between Express and Implied Contract Terms*, 73 Calif. L. Rev. 261 (1985).

38.  Ayres & Gertner I, *supra* note 17, at 125 (discussing possible channeling function of such sticky default).

39.  *See, e.g.*, J. Hoult Verkerke, *An Empirical Perspective on Indefinite Term Employment Contracts: Resolving the Just Cause Debate*, 4 Wis. L. Rev. 838 (1995).

40.  Ronald Dworkin, Freedom's Law: The Moral Reading of the American Constitution (1996) (arguing that all plaintiffs must prove actual malice). *See* Cass R. Sunstein, Book Review, New Republic 35 (May 13, 1996).

41.  Carlill v. Carbolic Smoke Ball Co., [1893] 1 Q.B. 256.

42.  For a similar analysis of liability under security law for false statements by corporate directors, see Ian Ayres, *Back to Basics: Regulating How Corporations Speak to the Market*, 77 Va. L. Rev. 945 (1991).

43.  Richard Epstein, Forbidden Ground: The Case Against Employment Discrimination Laws (1992). For my fuller thoughts on this book, *see* Ian Ayres, *Price and Prejudice*, New Republic 30 (July 6, 1992), and Ian Ayres, *Alternative Grounds: Epstein's Discrimination Analysis in Other Market Settings*, 31 U. San Diego L. Rev. 67 (1994).

44.  There might, however, be a significant number of employers who contract out of disparate impact and/or reasonable accommodation duties.

45.  *See, e.g.*, Frank H. Easterbrook & Daniel R. Fischel, the Economic Structure of Corporate Law (1991); William W. Bratton, Jr., *The New Economic Theory of the Firm: Critical Perspectives from History*, 41 Stan. L. Rev. 1471 (1989); Henry N. Butler, *The Contractual Theory of the Corporation*, 11 Geo. Mason U. L. Rev. 99 (1989); William W. Bratton, Jr., *The "Nexus of Contracts" Corporation: A Critical Appraisal*, 74 Cornell L. Rev. 407, 416 (1989); McChesney, *supra* note 16, at 1333–34; Henry N. Butler & Larry E. Ribstein, *Opting out of Fiduciary Duties: A Response to the Contractarians*, 65 Wash. L. Rev. 1, 23 (1990);

Barry D. Basinger and Henry N. Butler, *Antitakeover Amendments, Managerial Entrenchment, and the Contractual Theory of the Corporation*, 71 VA. L. REV. 1257 (1985); Victor Brudney, *Corporate Governance, Agency Costs, and the Rhetoric of Contract*, 85 COLUM. L. REV. 1403 (1985); Clark, *supra* note 6; John Coffee, *No Exit?: Opting Out, the Contractual Theory of the Corporation and the Special Case of Remedies*, 53 BROOKLYN L. REV. 919 (1988); John Coffee, *The Mandatory/Enabling Balance in Corporate Law: An Essay on the Judicial Role*, 89 COLUM. L. REV. 1618 (1989); Deborah Demott, *Beyond Metaphor: An Analysis of Fiduciary Obligation*, 1988 DUKE L.J. 879; Michael C. Jensen & William H. Meckling, *Theory of the Firm: Managerial Behavior, Agency Costs and Ownership Structure*, 3 J. FIN. ECON. 305 (1976); Armen A. Alchian & Harold Demsetz, *Production, Information Costs, and Economic Organization*, 62 AM. ECON. REV. 777 (1972).

46.  Brudney, *supra* note 42.

47.  *See, e.g.*, Lucian A. Bebchuk, *Limiting Contractual Freedom in Corporate Law: The Desirable Constraints on Charter Amendments*, 102 HARV. L. REV. 1820 (1989).

48.  *See, e.g.*, CHARLES FRIED, *Contract as Promise: A Theory of Contractual Obligation* 1 (1981); Randy E. Barnett, *A Consent Theory of Contract*, 86 COLUM. L. REV. 269, 269 (1986); Melvin Eisenberg, *The Bargain Principle and Its Limits*, 95 HARV. L. REV. 741 (1982).

49.  Similarly, Akhil Amar's interpretation of the Fourth, Fifth and Sixth Amendments focuses on the ability of criminal defendants to waive or contract around a variety of rights. AKHIL AMAR, THE CONSTITUTION AND CRIMINAL PROCEDURE: FIRST PRINCIPLES (1996).

50.  Richard Craswell has usefully distinguished between two different types of default rules: "background rules" and "agreement rules." As discussed earlier, background rules define the exact substance of a party's obligation, by specifying (among other things) the conditions under which her nonperformance will be excused, and the sanctions which will be applied to any unexcused nonperformance. By contrast, agreement rules specify the conditions and procedures the parties must satisfy in order to change an otherwise applicable background rule. Agreement rules thus include most of the rules governing offer and acceptance, as well as such doctrines as fraud or undue influence, which define the conditions necessary for a party's apparent consent to be counted as truly valid. To be sure, these two categories are not mutually exclusive, for some rules serve both functions simultaneously. Richard Craswell, *Contract Law, Default Rules, and the Philosophy of Promising*, 88 MICH. L. REV. 489, 503 (1989). The term "agreement rules" then captures not only the necessary and sufficient conditions for contracting around a rule ("the conditions and procedures the parties must satisfy in order to change an otherwise applicable background rule"); this term also seems to include rules about what behavior is necessary and sufficient to form a contract. These latter formation rules are themselves often defaults that parties can

contract out of, for example by specifying a particular offer can be accepted only in writing. For excellent analysis of agreement rules, *see* Richard Craswell, *Offer, Acceptance, and Efficient Reliance*, 48 STAN. L. REV. 481 (1996), and Avery Katz, *The Strategic Structure of Offer and Acceptance: Game Theory and the Law of Contract Formation*, 89 MICH. L. REV. 215 (1990).

# Chapter 3

# Canons of Property Talk, or,
# Blackstone's Anxiety

## *Carol M. Rose*

How do legal scholars talk about property? Here is one set of lines they are quite likely to quote:

> There is nothing which so generally strikes the imagination, and engages the affections of mankind, as the right of property; or that sole and despotic dominion which one man claims and exercises over the external things of the world, in total exclusion of the right of any other individual in the universe.[1]

The author of this statement, of course, was William Blackstone, who made it early in the second volume of his weighty and influential *Commentaries on the Laws of England*, at the point where he turned his attention to the subject "Of the Rights of Things"—that is to say, property.[2]

Since Blackstone's time, his definition of property as exclusive dominion has been cited again and again and again, by practicing lawyers, scholars, and everyone else interested in the law of property. Even James Madison used a slightly garbled version of the famous definition (without attribution) in a short essay on property.[3] For their part, modern legal scholars refer to it often, whether they do so with approbation or disapproval.[4]

But perhaps it is the fate of canonical texts to be cited rather than read, because it seems that if property lawyers and scholars have read Blackstone, they have not read *much* Blackstone. If those who quote Blackstone's definition read further, they might come to think that Blackstone posed his definition more as a metaphor than as a literal description—and as a slightly anxiety-provoking metaphor at that. They might well notice too that the famous definition was only a point of departure, an occasion for a set of discussions that have become "canonical" in a much broader sense. That is to say, beyond the well-known opening lines, Blackstone set out a range of argumentative moves that can be recognized even today as the standard strategies for talk about property—particularly talk among legal scholars.

Instead of discussing particular cases, treatises, or texts as the canon of property law, in this chapter I propose to take up as "canonical" the strategies for property talk that Blackstone so interestingly prefigured. By calling them canonical, I mean that despite some ebbs and flows, each of these strategies has enjoyed a certain constancy over time. They are canonical too in the sense that the adherents to each seem confident of the foundations of their own respective perspectives, regarding them as the more or less unproblematically proper stance for discussing property. But whereas modern scholars take sides in choosing one or another strategy, the capacious Blackstone managed to give each its due.

Hence this essay begins with Blackstone and his treatment of property in the *Commentaries*, describing how he took up the various argumentative modes that now reappear in modern property scholarship. His discussion proceeded through three stages. First—a point that is very seldom noticed—immediately after those famous remarks on exclusivity, Blackstone cast into doubt the patterns of existing ownership. Next, he answered his own doubts with a utilitarian story to show the social usefulness of property. Finally, he ducked the whole messy business, diving instead into a mass of descriptive doctrine.

In our own age, Blackstone's moves have ripened into three classic strategies for modern property scholarship: the posing of doubts, the utilitarian justification, and the doctrinalist deflection, with the latter two moves answering the doubts raised by the first, just as they did for Blackstone. In discussing the more recent incarnation of these strategies in legal scholarship, I will reverse Blackstone's order to match the actual chronological pattern of modern property scholarship—doctrinalism first, followed by utilitarianism, followed by still newer doubts.

Of course, the modern echoes of Blackstone's strategies raise another question: Have modern scholars taken their strategies from Blackstone? It would be hard to say they have in any direct sense, since so few actually appear to read Blackstone on property in modern times, at least beyond the first few pages, or indeed beyond the first few lines. No doubt there remains some lingering inheritance from Blackstone's work across the generations. Perhaps the greatest part of that inheritance is simply the ringing words defining property as exclusive dominion. It may be that this very definition somehow constantly elicits similar argumentative strategies—raising worrisome doubts about existing entitlements or eliciting soothing appeals to usefulness on the one hand or to tradition on the other. Be that as it may, I will conclude by arguing that within this tripartite division of canonical strategies in legal property talk, none has sufficiently explored the *metaphoric* quality of Blackstone's opening definition of property as exclusive dominion, because it is as metaphor, as trope, that this idea still molds our thinking about property.

## I. Blackstone Sets the Stage

### A. Axiom and Anxiety

When Blackstone described property as exclusive dominion, he may have had little idea of the resonance his words would have for later writers on property. Indeed, the notion of property as exclusive dominion—a notion to which I will refer as the Exclusivity Axiom—is far from self-evident, and it was even less self-evident when Blackstone wrote these lines. The axiom put aside the earlier medieval traditions in which property ownership had been hemmed in by intricate webs of military and other obligations; it ignored the family ties encapsulated in such devices as the entailed fee; and it ignored as well the general neighborly responsibilities of riparian and nuisance law. Blackstone himself was thoroughly aware of these pervasive and serious qualifications on exclusive dominion. Indeed, he discussed them at great length, particularly with respect to the feudal system and its later permutations.[5] Moreover, as at least one modern commentator has observed,[6] Blackstone asserted that the law properly recognizes claims by the destitute to some minimal assistance from those who are more prosperous.[7] This position links Blackstone to a traditional view tying property to social and political obligation—a view that clearly creates some tension with the idea of property as absolute or exclusive dominion.[8] Hence it might be best to conclude that for Blackstone, the Exclusivity Axiom was in a sense a trope, a rhetorical figure describing an extreme or ideal type rather than reality.[9]

Taken as a trope, however, the Exclusivity Axiom is powerfully suggestive.[10] A right to exclude would not necessarily mean that property owners *do* exclude others; it would mean only that they can *decide* whether to exclude or not. This decision-making authority is what makes property a central libertarian value: The property owner has a small domain of complete mastery, complete self-direction, and complete protection from the whims of others. This authority is also what makes property so important in utilitarian thinking. The right to exclude means that an owner is solely responsible for the fate of her assets. Thus, whether she chooses to hold, share, or trade those assets, she has good reason to make her decisions prudently. In identifying property with the right to exclude, then, Blackstone struck a central nerve in modern discussions of property, and meditations, transmutations, and fulminations on the theme of exclusivity continue to run through modern cases and commentaries.[11]

Perhaps the power of the trope explains the pattern in which modern scholars quote only those first few confident lines of Blackstone's observations on property.[12] But what they fail to notice are the extremely nervous sentences that follow immediately thereafter:

> And yet there are very few, that will give themselves the trouble to consider the original and foundation of this right. Pleased as we are with the possession, we seem afraid to look back to the means by which it was acquired, as if fearful of some defect in our title.[13]

We do not really want to learn too much about such matters, Blackstone continues, because we do not

> car[e] to reflect that (accurately and strictly speaking) there is no foundation in nature or in natural law, why a set of words upon parchment should convey the dominion of land . . . or why the occupier of a particular field or of a jewel, when lying on his death-bed and no longer able to maintain possession, should be entitled to tell the rest of the world which of them should enjoy it after him.[14]

The hidden skeleton in property's closet is what I shall call the Ownership Anxiety—that is, anxiety over the foundations for existing distributions. Notice that this anxiety does not directly target the Exclusivity Axiom. Exclusive dominion, of course, is indeed related to distribution in a general way, because the right to exclude in itself implies that there will be *some* distribution of property rights. If Ann can exclude Bart (and all the world) from *X*, then Ann has *X* and Bart (and the rest of the world) does not; this is clearly a distribution of rights. Yet the principle of exclusive dominion on its face is indifferent as between Ann and Bart; Bart might have owned X instead, and Ann might have owned Y, or Z, or nothing at all. Thus, even though the Exclusivity Axiom entails *some* distribution, no particular distribution can be gleaned from the Exclusivity Axiom itself.

As I shall argue later, there is more to be said on the relationship of axiom to anxiety,[15] but on the face of things, it is the axiom's very indifference toward specific distributions that triggers the Ownership Anxiety. Granting that property in general entails some set of exclusive dominions, why does Ann have exclusive dominion over X? Why does Bart not have X instead? That is the focus of the anxiety—not so much that the world of property is divided into exclusive rights, as that rights come to be distributed in one way rather than another. What justifies any particular distribution of rights? And, most importantly, do current claimants really have any solid foundation for the things they claim?

That was the question that Blackstone raised, but it seemed to make the gentlemanly author very uncomfortable indeed. Such close questioning of entitlements, he remarked, would only be "useless and even troublesome in common life." Better, he said, that "the mass of mankind . . . obey the laws when made, without scrutinizing too nicely into the reasons of making them."[16]

No wonder, then, that Blackstone no sooner had created this enormous ripple than he followed with two efforts to smooth the waters and steer the great ship of the common law back on course. One of these efforts was short in the telling but rather long on theory: He told a story that provided both a pseudohistory of the origins of property and a theoretical justification for the existence of the institution. The second effort, on the other hand, was very long in the telling but vanishingly small in theory: He deflected the reader from all such concerns, drowning doubts in an ocean of doctrine. And in making all three moves, Blackstone prefigured the directions of modern legal scholarship across the entire domain of property. One direction casts doubts on the natural justice of property; a second direction justifies property on utilitarian grounds; and a third direction deflects the entire issue by moving to a seemingly neutral, positive description of property's legal structures. Given these modern echoes, Blackstone's versions deserve closer attention.

### B. Righting the Ship Theoretically: The Utilitarian Just-So Story

The Ownership Anxiety arises because property rights come to rest permanently in some hands rather than others. But why should this be so? As soon as he raised this question, Blackstone set out to answer it through "rational science."[17] To that end, Blackstone turned to a kind of concocted history of property, very like the one that John Locke had told almost a century earlier. It is a story that begins by placing human beings in a primitive state that Blackstone (like Locke) likened to that of pre-Columbian America, where, he said, the bounties of nature were a great commons given to all by their creator.[18] In that condition, human beings created property through "occupancy": First they took temporary use of natural products like plants for foodstuffs and fibers; then later, as they "increased in number, craft, and ambition" and as resources became correspondingly scarce, they began to claim more permanent rights in chattels and ultimately in land. Permanent claims allowed the "occupiers" to avoid conflicts with one another and encouraged them to labor on the things to which they now claimed a durable right.[19] That, of course, is the great utilitarian claim for the exclusive character of property: Exclusive dominion is useful because it reduces conflicts and induces productive incentives. As Blackstone observed, no one would bother working and cultivating if someone else could "seise upon and enjoy the product of his industry, art, and labour."[20] But given exclusive rights, presumably people would avoid conflicts, work hard, trade, and grow collectively wealthier. Thus, he concluded, "[n]ecessity begat property," and to preserve property "recourse was had to civil society" and to government.[21]

This justificatory story leaves rather ambiguous the status of property as a natural right, at least insofar as property means anything beyond that early temporary "occupancy."[22] Nevertheless, more enduring rights are clearly essential to the creation and protection of wealth; and if lasting property is not based directly on nature, then perhaps it is seminatural in the indirect or social sense that David Hume had discussed a few years earlier. That is, it is a part of human nature to invent useful things. In that sense, a common institution as useful as property is at least indirectly "natural."[23]

But notice how little this just-so story actually does to placate the Ownership Anxiety. First, the story is not a very convincing tale on its own terms about the emergence of the institution of property. Even if it is true that exclusive property does induce people to work and to treat resources conscientiously (and in fact, there is very considerable evidence that it does),[24] that happy possibility in itself scarcely means that people will introduce this useful institution. In general, the fact that some institution would be *nice* does not mean that people will invent it and enforce its precepts.[25] After all, the person who introduces the idea of permanent entitlements is rather like the cultivator who lacks property in his crop: He may do all the organizing to get people to stop brawling and accept the institution of property, but then the fruits of his labors are effectively appropriated by everyone else, with no special reward for himself. Later on, there is the problem of policing. This too is a thankless chore, and why should anyone undertake it? Perhaps the neighbors would pay a night watchman to keep an eye on things, but who will get them organized to hire an appropriate person? Who will monitor them later to make sure that none is shirking on the dues? Who will watch the watchman, to be sure that he is not stealing from his charges? Inventing property to solve the problems of conflict and free riding, in short, only introduces the need to invent other institutions to solve still other problems of conflict and free riding.[26] At the end of Blackstone's short story, the institution of property is as mysterious as it was at the beginning.

Quite aside from all that, the story really has precious little to do with the anxiety that ownership provokes. However useful property may be as an institution, that anxiety focuses on another question: Why do *I* have what I am fond of saying is *mine*? The problem is this: Suppose you were to accept as true the proposition that durable exclusive dominion gives people incentives to invest their labor in the things they own; suppose that this labor does indeed enhance the value of things; suppose that those enhanced values aggregate into vastly greater total social wealth; and suppose that this greater social total makes everyone better off, so that both rich and poor are wealthier with a property regime than they would be without one.[27] Suppose all those general points about property regimes to be true, and you still have the question: What justifies any *specific* claims to portions of that wealth? Why is the *specific* distribution of "exclusive dominions" a just one?

Blackstone did glance at this question in his just-so story, but he left it rather hurriedly. Title to resources does come to vest permanently in individuals, he observed, but whether this was justified simply by occupancy or by the universal consent of mankind was a question, he said, "that savours too much of nice and scholastic refinement"![28] Occupancy was the simple original fact of the matter, according to all the schools, and that, in a sense, is that.

But with a moment's thought, that is not that after all. Quite aside from begging the normative question of how occupancy turns into particular permanent entitlements (by the consent of all?), there is a practical problem with occupancy itself. The problem is that a first-occupancy principle invites everyone to grab at everything, and everyone winds up fighting with everyone else. At some point, to become a set of permanent claims in which people can fruitfully invest, property needs not more grabbing via occupancy but rather more mutual forbearance.[29]

Hence the claim to exclusive title is not really entirely exclusive after all. Each such claim depends on everyone else's going along with the program in the form of mutual respect and forbearance. While Blackstone's account shows how useful it would be if everyone behaved in this way, the account does not say why people do, or why they *should* forbear with respect to any specific distribution of property.

### C. Sailing out of Anxiety: The Doctrinal Deflection

The utilitarian story did not take Blackstone long to tell, and he quickly moved on to the actual details of property law, which constitute the bulk of his text. With these details, he swamped the Ownership Anxiety in a veritable flood of doctrine. His opening doctrinal gambit itself is revealing: Did he begin with some relatively simple device like conveyancing or wills? Not at all. He opened with the crushingly arcane subject of "hereditaments,"[30] and indeed with "incorporeal hereditaments," themselves subdivided into the "ten sorts" of "advowsons, tithes, commons, ways, offices, dignities, franchises, corodies or pensions, annuities, and rents."[31] Thereafter, Blackstone navigated a maze of detail, describing a very formidable array of rights within rights, including those of the feudal system and its later permutations.

Even Blackstone seemed embarrassed about the wealth of detail of his subject, observing that it may well have "afforded the student less amusement and pleasure" than his discussions of other areas of the law, owing to the complications that had "been heaped one upon another for a course of seven centuries, without any order or method, [making] the study of this branch of our national jurisprudence a little perplexed and intricate."[32]

Still, at least two features of Blackstone's doctrinalism indirectly give comfort to the anxious property holder. The first is simply forgetfulness. One can quickly lose one's fears and gain confidence in this massive layering of rights wrinkled within rights. One can quickly forget those embarrassing questions that one might have about *one's own* entitlements and snuggle up in this luxurious doctrinal blanket. As David Lieberman has observed, Blackstone was aware of his own gargantuan detail, and in another discussion he even explained it in an only slightly apologetic paragraph that itself suggests the comforts of a well-known abode.[33] The British law, Blackstone said, resembles

> an old Gothic castle, erected in the days of chivalry, but fitted up for a modern inhabitant. The moated ramparts, the embattled towers, and the trophied halls, are magnificent and venerable, but useless. The inferior apartments, now converted into rooms of convenience, are cheerful and commodious, though their approaches are winding and difficult.[34]

Ultimately, the doctrinal deflection rests on an unspoken but underlying justification of convention or prescription—the supposedly universal, though tacit, acquiescence to whatever has come to be known for long enough that "the memory of man runneth not to the contrary,"[35] a usage that was papered over with the pretense of a "lost grant."[36] In that prescriptive sense, Blackstone's doctrinalism once again brings to mind David Hume's defense of convention and custom.[37] On such an account, particular entitlements may originate in some indifferent manner, but, once begun, custom and expectancy render their continuation nonarbitrary and indeed just (at least in the eighteenth-century sense of the word).[38] The nooks and crannies of comfortable doctrine supplement the sheer passage of time, reinforcing people's tendency to settle in and think that their "rights" must have always been there.

Aside from the comforts of custom, there is a second subtly soothing feature in Blackstone's doctrinal description of property. This feature derives from his choice of subjects. In his whole discussion "Of the Rights of Things," *land* clearly takes the predominant role. There were undoubtedly good reasons for this: Land had been and continued to be a major source of wealth in Blackstone's time. He did devote a few chapters to personal property, where he described some commercial instruments such as bills of exchange and even the arcana of "bottomry" (a mortgage on a ship).[39] But on the whole, nonlanded sources of wealth took a distinctly secondary role to traditional landed property in the *Commentaries*.[40] He may have understood the growing use of water power for new industrial mills, for example, but he had only a few scattered and somewhat misleading remarks on this rather unsettling form of property, so full of portent for the future.[41]

Whether intended or not, Blackstone's concentration on land strikes a particularly calming note about property. Land is fixed, enduring, stable.

It stands still when you put a fence around it to solidify your claims. And whatever the importance of "occupancy" for his *theory* of property, Blackstone's massive doctrinal sections disclosed very little to remind readers of the self-seeking, possibly violent, and certainly problematic initial grabs of initial occupancy. Once past his opening utilitarian just-so story, Blackstone's examples of first possession are not drawn at all from land, which is largely stable and well owned in his discussions; his examples come instead from the acquisition of wild animals and moving resources like air, water, and—more figuratively—literary products.[42]

Notice, however, how the doctrinal elaboration of rights within rights undermines the idea of property as exclusive possession. Exclusivity of dominion is rescued only by the casuistic division of larger properties into vanishingly small miniclaims, each supposedly "exclusive." This classic doctrinal maneuver continues in the modern notion of property as a "bundle of sticks," but the maneuver also suggests how artificial is the description of property as exclusive dominion.[43]

I have gone on at length about Blackstone's discussion of property law, because his account is a wonderful capsule version of the three canonical topoi that define the plane on which so much of the discussion of property takes place. The anxious doubts, the confident utilitarian riposte, the seemingly neutral but covertly comforting detail of doctrine—those features continue to define the basic strategies for talking about property. The next part will describe the ways in which these three poles have turned into the modern canonical strategies for discussing property. In keeping with the chronology of the late twentieth century's trends in property scholarship, the next part reverses the order of the strategies, taking Blackstone's progression through the looking glass to a modern arena where neutral doctrine leads off, utilitarian theory gives a rationale, and critical questioning revives anxious doubts.

## II. The Modern Mirror of Blackstone's Strategies: Doctrinalist, Utilitarian, Problematizing

How do aspiring lawyers learn to talk about property now, at the end of the twentieth century? By looking at the three best-selling property casebooks of the mid-1990s, one can see the very strategies that Blackstone's discussion introduced. The oldest entry, and now the second most popular, is John E. Cribbet's *Property*,[44] a standby that has certainly changed with the times (and with new editions and co-authors) but whose basic intellectual energy is devoted to laying out the black letter about Black-acre. A newer entry, and now by far the leader of the pack, is Jesse Dukeminier and James Krier's *Property*.[45] This book also includes a good deal of doctrine, but it is a favorite of those who favor economic approaches, and indeed its popularity suggests the degree to which a utilitarian strategy has become the predominant way to discuss property law. A still newer entry, however, is gaining ground on both its rivals. This is Joseph W. Singer's *Property Law*,[46] and it too has a goodly dose of doctrine. But it also stirs up the old Ownership Anxiety at every plausible turn, undermining the comfortable notion that existing distributions of property are *justified* simply because they are intricately detailed and interrelated, or because the general institution of property may happen to be a useful one. Despite the considerable overlap in these textbooks, their central tendencies suggest not only the dominant ways of talking about property today, but also the relative academic satisfactions over each of these three discursive modes.[47]

## A. The Modern Conventional Strategy: Doctrinalism

The doctrinal strategy dominated academic property discussions through the nineteenth century and up to the blossoming of law and economics scholarship a generation ago. One need only look at the nineteenth-century treatises on property—Angell on Tidelands,[48] Wood on Nuisance[49]—to get a sense of the overwhelming importance that those property scholars placed on the elaboration of doctrinal nuance.[50]

Treatises of this sort have fallen out of fashion in modern property scholarship, as indeed they have in most other areas of the law. Still, doctrinalist elements maintain a robust existence in modern property law. One continuing doctrinalist pattern is the treatment of land as the central subject of property. There are, of course, many other forms of property—securities, for example, or intellectual property, or even what is called "human capital," notably education—and these forms of property now constitute a very substantial proportion of the modern representations of wealth. Moreover, land itself certainly need not be discussed in purely doctrinalist modes, as is amply illustrated in Robert Ellickson's wide-ranging utilitarian and sociological presentations.[51]

Nevertheless, "property unmodified" still means land, and land has a peculiar affinity to doctrinalism. By virtue of its durability, land invites an intricate layering of rights over time. Lawyers have never bothered to create an elaborate doctrine of, say "estates in automobiles" or "covenants running with automobiles"; nor have they done so with any other non-landed property. That is because after only a limited number of years, any given automobile will end in the junk heap. This finite life span keeps encumbrances on automobiles relatively simple and few in number.[52]

Land, on the other hand, sticks around indefinitely, while claims against land can go on and on, in layer after layer, to be lost, found, banished, restored, relished, then lost again to long-standing practice and prescription. This enduring quality is one reason why claim-clearing doctrines like "adverse possession" and prescription are essential with respect to land. But land's durability is also the reason why land is so central to doctrinalism: Land offers a gold mine of doctrinal variation, a subject on which taxonomic exactitude—rather like Blackstone's—is the central effort.

The very fact that "property unmodified" still means land is a strong hint that doctrinalism is alive and well as a canonical strategy. Aspiring lawyers still face queries on bar exams about many arcane interests in land, no doubt because bar examiners are sure that law schools teach them, and of course law schools continue to teach these doctrines because they are on the bar exam. Putting to one side that exasperatingly circular pattern, there are some other payoffs to doctrinalism for lawyers: the confidence that comes with mastery of a set of complex conceptions, the aesthetic enjoyment of identifying the rooms of the old house, and the pleasure of finding the corridors that run between them with a kind of hidden logic. There is also, of course, the satisfaction of deflecting the Ownership Anxiety and instead treating property as a subject that requires detailed positive explication rather than normative justification.

All these doctrinalist satisfactions entail and in a way illuminate one of the chief functions of the Exclusivity Axiom, which continues to serve as an unspoken heuristic for doctrinalism. Here the trope of exclusivity serves (as it did for Blackstone) an essentially linguistic function: The conceit of exclusivity allows the lawyer to divide and subdivide interests into separate and exclusive "things," each analyzable on its own terms. Indeed, in modern cases even the right to exclude itself is treated as one of several separately identifiable interests.[53]

At the same time, modern doctrinalism also illustrates some of the more problematic aspects of the linguistic trope of exclusivity. For one thing, doctrinalist separations of mutually "exclusive" property interests may obfuscate commonsense notions of property.[54] More seriously, they may place subtle intellectual barriers in the way of understanding normal practices like sharing and neighborly give-and-take, where exclusivity melts into the more fluid pattern of keeping reciprocal favors on a roughly even basis.[55]

Politically, a certain conservatism inheres in doctrinalism. Conceptual explication itself can easily shade into a defense of existing property categories, if for no other reason than for protection of one's own intellectual capital.[56] A more subtly conservative aspect of doctrinalism is the way in which its underlying presumption—that rights can be fully identified, specified, and labeled—implicitly nourishes a libertarian justification for existing property rights, a justification that is at once historical and oddly ahistorical. As Robert Nozick put it, the libertarian justification of existing holdings is "historical" insofar as any given entitlement derives from a series of just transfers, linking all the way back to its original just acquisition.[57] But the justification is ahistorical too, in its supposition that property rights never really change over time in meaning or content. It is no accident that Richard Epstein, whose work has strong though not exclusively libertarian currents,[58] frequently refers to the categories of the common law and even Roman law. Implicit in his work is the view that these venerable legal systems generate categories of rights that are unchanging over time and fully specifiable—and, of course, just the ticket as a basis for modern property rights.[59]

This is a way of thinking that can create some practical problems: Doctrinal "rights talk" can run wild. An unfortunate example is given by the radical right-wing groups who hearken back to a home-cooked and half-baked version of the "common law" in order to justify what is basically a revolutionary disregard of ordinary legal duties and neighborly behavior.[60] Even at considerably higher theoretical levels, the doctrinal presumption that rights can be justly acquired and then justly transferred usually lies either insufficiently examined[61] or is left to rest on pragmatic considerations.[62] As Blackstone was well aware, too close an inquiry into such matters can be troublesome and awkward.

Doctrinalism is by no means all conservative. At war with the view of doctrine as a set of philosophical "natural kinds" is a whole set of evolutionary views and reformist impulses that also abide in American doctrinal explication. Indeed, the playing out of doctrine in the past absorbed the energies of very capable reformist commentators, while within the last thirty years, perhaps one of the most noticeable changes in modern property law has derived primarily from the analysis of doctrine. Indeed, this legal sea change technically revolves around the doctrine of estates in land. This is the so-called revolution in landlord-tenant law, whose subject is the estate for years, known to normal people as a lease.[63] Since the 1960s, courts led by the District of Columbia Circuit (and egged on by scholarly commentators) have largely split the doctrine of residential leases away from commercial leases, and in the former they have substituted large elements of contract for the prior property approaches. Residential leases are now generally regarded as in large part contracts for residential services, and they include remedies like warranties of quality and rules requiring mitigation of damages—rules that have been drawn from contract law.[64] Despite a nod or two to economic analysis,[65] this important legal change has been largely driven by a modernizing analysis of doctrine.[66]

Such developments suggest a rather pragmatic version of doctrinalism, a version that would cast in a different light the luxuriantly complex elaboration of doctrinal distinctions. As in Blackstone, that pragmatic drift would bring doctrinalism back to Humean convention, which itself supposes a human psychology that gets attached to things as they are— or, perhaps, as they have become over time, after their provenance is largely forgotten.[67] Understood in this way, as an explicator of gradual legal change, doctrinalism is linked to modern property scholars' interest in cognitive psychology, especially to the exploration of what is now called the "endowment effect"—that is, roughly speaking, people's widespread tendency to place a higher value on the things that they actually have (their current "endowments") than on things they do not possess.[68] Doctrinalism would explore the legal causes and consequences of changing endowment effects.

The passage of time and the lapses of human memory, however, cannot fully paper over the Ownership Anxiety about current distributions. Fancy psychological talk about endowment effects does not help any more than the earlier doctrinal talk about prescription, with its ridiculous conceit of a "lost grant."[69] Quite the contrary, the Ownership Anxiety fixes on the possibility that some essential flaw occurred in times *beyond* current memory—that is, the fear is that current endowments ultimately have no firm foundation. A shifting conception of entitlements only allows the uncomfortable Ownership Anxiety to come back to the surface, in full view.

Moreover, an evolving and pragmatic version of endowments challenges the doctrinalist deployment of the trope of exclusivity itself, in which each entitlement is an exclusive and lasting nugget. Like Zeno's Arrow, this intellectual technique is hard put to explicate dynamic change. Yet if there is current life in doctrinalism, it is in doctrinalism as process and change, which entails some loosening of the Exclusivity Axiom and some recognition of the porosity of property categories.[70]

If doctrinalist deflection still leaves the Ownership Anxiety in view and even begins to shake the Exclusivity Axiom, what about the modern updating of Blackstone's chief normative answer to that anxiety, namely, the utilitarian strategy? Does it do a better job at soothing anxieties directly than doctrinalism does indirectly? The answer, briefly, is "no," although as in modern doctrinalism, there are plenty of new angles.

### B. The Utilitarian Just-So Story Updated: Law and Economics

Blackstone's utilitarian maneuver finds its modern counterpart in the law and economics approach, an intellectual movement that must count as one of the most important success stories in the history of American legal scholarship, legal education, and even to some degree in practice as well, since judges and lawyers now at least occasionally talk the talk of "transaction costs" and "externalities."[71] If the movement is now graying at the temples, it is still a vital and changing theoretical force—in property as in other legal areas. Indeed, so vital is it that I can illustrate its modern canonical stature through only a few central examples.

The original theorist of utilitarianism, Jeremy Bentham, was a great disparager of Blackstone's doctrinalism.[72] Like Bentham, the modern law and economics scholars often barely hide their disdain for doctrinal hairsplitting. But if Bentham generally blasted Blackstone's *Commentaries*, Bentham's modern successors found just the right brief section of Blackstone to cite: the utilitarian just-so story.[73] This is the very text that Richard Posner's law and economics text cites for the proposition that it has been known "for hundreds of years" that property rights encourage labor and investment.[74] Indeed, the economist Harold Demsetz retells Blackstone's just-so story in a modern version, a version that incidentally appears early in the most popular American property law textbook.[75] Like Blackstone's story, this version describes the invention of property as a response to scarcity. Demsetz illustrates his version through an account of Native American hunters in the Hudson Bay area during the early colonial period, when the Europeans' ardent demand for furs created unprecedented pressures to capture fur-bearing animals. Under those new circumstances, the native hunters began to overhunt the common grounds, each hunter imposing "external" costs on all the others, as all needed to expend more hunting effort to catch the increasingly scarce animals. But according to Demsetz, these indigenous hunters realized they could prevent overhunting by turning their formerly common hunting grounds into private property. Once they had done so, the story goes, the individual owners husbanded wildlife resources on their respective territories, and the now-private hunting grounds became productive again. In Demsetz's more technical economic terms, property rights enabled people to "internalize externalities."[76] As in Blackstone's story, property is justified by its utility and particularly by the way in which it promotes peaceable and productive labor, investment, planning, and resource management.

The trouble with this story is that it can be told without the happy ending. Indeed, it *has* been told without the happy ending, most notably by the biologist Garrett Hardin, and earlier, if less flamboyantly, by the economist Scott Gordon.[77] Their story too, or at least Hardin's version, is now a staple item in law and economics property law teaching materials. In the story as told by Gordon and Hardin—the former using the example of fishing, the latter of grazing—nobody organizes a property regime when a common resource comes under pressure. Instead, the resource is simply used to exhaustion (or something near exhaustion), at which point all economic rents are dissipated. This is the well-known phenomenon of the "tragedy of the commons"—the very catchy title of Hardin's article—and it is actually a variant on another modern economic story, the so-called prisoner's dilemma. In the prisoner's dilemma, the parties would be better off collectively if they could come to agreement, but they have individual motivations to cheat instead.[78]

The tragedy of the commons, of course, directly confronts Blackstone's optimistic utilitarian just-so story as retold by Demsetz and others.[79] Indeed, the tragic version shows what was the matter with that optimism: However wealthy and happy the institution of property might make us, there is nothing in the logic of the story that means we actually *will* invent it.

So will we or won't we? Which story about the institution of property is correct? Do we get happy property or the gloomy tragedy of the commons? Law and economics writers may occasionally be faulted for telling both stories without much attention to the contradiction between them, but those scholars do have ways to answer the question. They focus on "transactions costs," an idea derived from Ronald Coase's pivotal article "The Problem of Social Cost"[80] and worked out in enormous detail by law and economics scholars thereafter. In brief, on this analysis, a system of property rights depends on implicit or explicit agreement—as it did in Blackstone's story and in Demsetz's too, though neither made much of the point. If agreement is easy and the costs of definition are low, property rights are likely to be sharply defined; if not, they will be mushier or nonexistent.[81]

Transactions costs analysis is a central enterprise in the law and economics movement, in property law as elsewhere. As Guido Calabresi and Douglas Melamed famously pointed out, transactions costs analysis can help to explain both why property normally is transferred only with the consent of the owner and why, when consent is difficult to organize, it may be transferred by forced sales.[82] Transactions costs analysis also yields a way to make sense of some old doctrinal distinctions, for example, between trespass and nuisance.[83] It suggests reasons to decide some property arrangements by majority votes rather than unanimous decisions, as in condominium associations or indeed governments, and it suggests reasons for some public intervention in property use, as in the case of environmental damage, where the large numbers of affected parties cannot easily cut a deal.

In general, the very concept of transactions costs *means* an absence of clearly defined property rights,[84] and hence the concept subtly suggests that all other things being equal, it is better that property rights be defined firmly rather than mushily. That is because firmly defined rights reduce externalities and transactions costs, allowing the free flow of goods and services among producers and consumers.[85]

In this way, of course, transactions costs analysis adopts the Blackstonian axiom of exclusivity as a normative goal. Exclusive control over entitlements concentrates appropriate incentives entirely on the individual owner, encouraging this owner to plan and deal carefully. At the same time, exclusivity enables trades to proceed smoothly, relieving the parties from worrying about vague objections from other unknown stakeholders.

Notice, however, that in taking this positive stance toward exclusivity, law and economics scholarship in effect reveals another tropelike characteristic of the Exclusivity Axiom: Exclusivity is a metaphor for the incentive power of self-interest, the self-interest that drives individual investment and social wealth.

The embarrassing fact, of course, is that property rights are not thoroughly exclusive in any commonsense way, and the even more embarrassing fact is that an insistence on the Exclusivity Axiom would only obscure matters that are of great interest to the production of social wealth. Law and economics scholarship borrows from the doctrinalists the move to divide and subdivide rights into conceptually separable and exclusive "sticks" in a bundle, but a person's use of any of those sticks depends powerfully on what other people do. Landlords and tenants have widely shared but sometimes conflicting interests. So do neighbors, co-op owners, and shareholders.

To deal with such interdependencies, some modern institutional economists, instead of subdividing individual rights into smaller and smaller shards, take the opposite and interesting tack of *enlarging the rights holder*. That is, they describe whole communities as joint owners of common property regimes, which are the exclusive property of the community vis-à-vis other communities.[86]

An interest in groups is creeping into law and economics approaches from another angle as well. As Robert Cooter has shown, even low transactions costs scenarios give opportunities for strategic bargaining, suspicion, and betrayal.[87] Potentially beneficial deals may go begging because the parties fritter them away in endless jockeying for position, each wanting to take the lion's share of the gains from trade. In effect, each trade potentially presents a new version of the prisoners' dilemma. In short, it is not enough that trading partners have low transactions costs. They must also have some reason to trust each other, and in Robert Ellickson's terms, it helps if they are in a "close-knit" community.[88]

Game theory identifies and analyzes such issues, and it is no surprise that game theory is moving very rapidly into a prominent position in the economic analysis of property law (and other areas of law as well).[89] But that is not all. Game-theoretic analysis opens the door to a much broader study of psychology and culture, and of the social contexts and patterns that make property and commerce possible.[90] In effect, there is a kind of mystery of "niceness"[91] and trust at the center of economic transactions, and understanding the conditions for such niceness and trust involves moving out into many other disciplines—anthropology, social psychology, the study of different kinds of communities. That is why, for example, in reworking a 1976 essay collection, my co-authors and I changed the title from *The Economic Foundations of Property Law* to the more general *Perspectives on Property Law* and included already-canonical insights from other disciplines.[92] That is also why the modern utilitarian strategy may yet extend a hand back to the basic impulses behind doctrinalism— to the sociology of custom and convention, to the psychological comfort of things well-known.

The graying of law and economics, then, may mean a certain mellowing and a growing consciousness of the importance of social context. But what is interesting is that these very mellowing trends implicitly cast doubt on the Exclusivity Axiom. As it turns out, a fixation on exclusive dominion could obscure the social interactions that are now emerging as an important new interest in law and economic thinking.

Finally, all the economic offshoots still never completely answer the Ownership Anxiety. The fundamental utilitarian move is to argue that human beings are better off with the institution of property than without it. But the benevolence of the institution of property, taken as a whole, is not much of an excuse for *existing distributions* of property. Indeed, the celebrated Coase Theorem itself is well-known for its once-scandalous position that, from the perspective of society as a whole, it really does not matter which of two competing claimants has a property right as long as transactions costs are low and the parties can trade.[93] Indeed, law and economics approaches are quite explicit in pointing out that different starting points can lead to quite different distributions, and that any one of those distributions can be efficient.[94]

This clearly is no answer to the Ownership Anxiety, and it is that very anxiety that is stirred up by the third modern canonical strategy.

### C. The Problematizing Strategy: Angst and Critical Prodding

The third canonical strategy in property law I will call critical, largely because problematizing is such an awkward word. In this critical strategy, I certainly include the adherents of the modern critical legal studies movement (CLS), but I will include some other writers as well.

Like the doctrinal and utilitarian strategies, the critical strategy also echoes a part of Blackstone—but a different part. By critical, I refer to the scholars whose work recalls Blackstone's opening nervousness about entitlements. Rather than salve that anxiety, however, the critical strategy pokes at it, stirs it up, stokes it, all in an attempt to show that existing distributions of property have no special claim on justice.

All this troublemaking has a venerable ancestral line. The list of antecedents includes such well-known tracts as Proudhon's *What Is Property?*[95] in which the author responds that property is theft. It also includes Marx's chapter in *Capital* on "The So-Called Primitive Accumulation," where he fulminates about the force and fraud that he claims lie at the basis of feudal and bourgeois property.[96]

The modern CLS scholars are heirs not only to this destabilizing tradition, but also to some degree to the historic left's egalitarian and utopian aspirations. These aspirations can act as a platform from which to criticize current legal structures, a point seen in its most visionary form in the work of Roberto Unger. Putting it very briefly, Unger argues that individual human liberation and flourishing occur only in self-creating communities of affection and mutual assistance, whereas the fetishization of rights generally—and property rights in particular—divides people from community and entrenches patterns of domination and subordination that further poison communal life.[97] Hence our current thinking about property, like our other legal discourse, must be disrupted and dramatically reconceived so that claims can be based on social sharing and responsibility.[98]

In any such project of disruption and reconception, the obvious targets in existing property law discourse are doctrinalism on the one hand and utilitarianism on the other—the one because it deflects anxieties about distribution, the other because it purports to answer those anxieties. Indeed, for critical destabilizers, the doctrinalist and utilitarian strategies are linked by a profound conservatism, by their replication of an intellectual technology of hierarchy, and by their ideological service to an inegalitarian, anomic, and unjust status quo.

First, the critical attack on doctrinalism. The doctrinal maneuver tries to bury ownership anxieties in the cake of custom and implicitly justifies property by convention. But a chief claim of CLS scholars is that doctrine itself is indeterminate, since in virtually any case mutually contradictory doctrines could lead any given legal decision in quite different directions.[99] Hence a doctrinal mode of analysis is likely to mask choices made for conscious or subconscious reasons that are quite independent of doctrine itself.[100]

Indeed, CLS scholars have become famous for peeling away the temporal layers of received doctrine, refuting earlier accounts of natural progress, and instead suggesting darker influences in the directions in which dominant legal doctrine has drifted over time.[101] On such accounts, far from stabilizing expectations, property doctrine may actually add up to a shifting set of apologia that has subtly furthered the cause of hegemonic interests at the expense of the less powerful. A now-classic exposition is Morton Horwitz's description of water rights doctrine in the nineteenth century. According to Horwitz, fixed rights in riparian property were modified to accommodate industrial development and then rehardened around the rights that industrialists came to claim for themselves.[102] Joseph Singer recounts a similar thesis with respect to the solemn legal refutations of Native American claims.[103] In these as in other instances, say such critics, doctrine may appear to be neutral, but this appearance itself allows doctrine to disarm the less fortunate and render complacent the more fortunate, all the while reinforcing a culture of hierarchy and persuading everyone that all is for the best in this best of all possible worlds.[104]

Even sharper is the critique of the utilitarian strategy in its modern incarnation as law and economics. Particularly interesting in this critique is the implicit link that the critics draw between Blackstone's Exclusivity Axiom and his Ownership Anxiety. While the principle of exclusive dominion may imply no particular distribution of entitlements, after a given distribution is in place any unconsented alteration runs contrary to the principle of exclusive dominion. In this way, the Exclusivity Axiom becomes a bulwark to protect existing distributions. Thus, to cast doubt on the justice of existing distributions—to stir up the old Ownership Anxiety—is to confront the Exclusivity Axiom as well. A comment by Jeremy Bentham, the original utilitarian, illustrates the point strikingly. Bentham exhorted his readers that even blatantly unequal distributions of property, including serfdom, should not excuse disturbance of property rights, lest society's aggregate welfare suffer.[105]

On the other hand, one might look at this picture differently. That is to say, normatively, if existing distributions are unjust, then the principle of exclusive dominion must yield in order to rectify them; and positively, if the wealth-producing function of exclusive dominion is itself weak, then the case for redistribution is much greater. As a part of a general program of dismantling hierarchy, the modern CLS scholars have mounted both types of attack on the Exclusivity Axiom.

On the normative side, Duncan Kennedy has made what is now a classic distinction between "rules" and "standards" in approaches to law. In so doing, he attacked a central idea in the utilitarian idea of property—bright-line rules. In property law, the most central incarnation of such rules is the axiomatic and awesome Blackstonian power to exclude: What is inside the line is all mine, what is outside I must trade to get. Under the utilitarian argument, bright-line rules create the security that allows autonomous individuals to plan, invest, and trade; the presence of such rules is the essential reason why property works to produce wealth. But Kennedy strongly suggested that bright-line rules are morally inferior to looser "standards."[106] Clearly demarcated and propertylike rules, he said, may protect the autonomous individual, but they also permit the clever and unscrupulous to dupe the rest of us. The Holmesian "bad man" will closely study the limits of bright-line rules, and he will use his knowledge to skate as closely as possible to the line, to the detriment of more trusting folk. On the other hand, flexible and porous "standards" (such as principles of fairness and reasonableness, which assess actions and outcomes after the fact) protect the good person because they rectify injustice ex post, vindicating those who acted with trust and goodwill rather than those who took advantage of their fellows.[107] Thus, while law and economics scholars eschew mushy standards in favor of the bright-line rules that, they say, encourage foresight and chastise sloppiness, critical scholars see the general legal preference for bright-line rules—such as the Exclusivity Axiom—as a bias subtly causing entitlements to gravitate toward the canny, the endowed, and the grasping.[108]

Quite aside from this normative attack, Frank Michelman, individually and together with Duncan Kennedy, mounted a controversial challenge on the positive logic of the utilitarian defense of property—that is, on the argument that private property and freedom of contract promote social wealth and well-being. Not so, said these destabilizers; compared with a rule of force on the one hand or with obligatory sharing of wealth on the other hand, private property does not necessarily induce more labor or its consequence, greater social wealth.[109] Whether a property regime does or does not induce labor is simply a matter of empirical fact, they said.[110] The implication is that the utilitarian privileging of private property, like the doctrinal pretense of parsing cases, represents not a logical conclusion but rather a political choice, an ideology that favors the status quo even when clothed as liberalism.[111]

Needless to say, utilitarians do not take this attack argument lying down. Richard Posner has argued somewhat cryptically that the Kennedy-Michelman argument simply misunderstands the character of economic incentives.[112] Undeterred by such counterattacks, critical strategists are inventive in developing new versions of property—versions that effectively call for some level of redistribution from the rich to the poor, implicitly undermining the idea of ownership's exclusive claims. A generation ago, Charles Reich argued that no one can really take part in politics without some minimum level of assets—and hence democracy necessitates redistribution.[113] Frank Michelman and Greg Alexander have developed Reich's idea, building on J. G. A. Pocock's rediscovery of the historical "civic republican" tradition in early American political thought[114]—a tradition, they say, that supports a modern redistributionist state.[115] Margaret Radin has argued that property is an essential vehicle for the development of the personality—and hence that the property that is especially close to people's self-definition (e.g., their homes) deserves special protections from the law and precedence over other property rights.[116]

Numerous other scholars have cast doubt on existing distributions while attacking the Exclusivity Axiom as an impediment to justice. A particularly well-known way to do so is to pose the question that John Rawls asked: What distribution of property would sensible people choose if they could make their choices without knowing where they would wind up on the social pecking order? Behind that "veil of ignorance," according to Rawls, they would choose a modicum of free enterprise along with a social safety net—that is, some private holdings along with a lot of sharing of resources, including the sharing of "natural talents."[117] So long, exclusion! Hello, redistribution!

Notice how sharply all this stirs up Blackstone's anxiety. The Blackstonian anxiety stemmed from the fear that when one traced back one's title, it would be found to rest on nothing at all; hence, one's current property might be the fruits of larceny. Larceny from whom? In older times, the answer was from all mankind, to whom God gave the earth in the first place, and who may or may not have "consented" to particular "occupancies" by particular individuals.

The critical strategists pursue this anxious logic. They point out that the doctrinalist and utilitarian strategies fail to solve the question of entitlement and instead simply drag red herrings across the trail.[118] Hence, any particular property right has no firm foundation and is still subject to the claims of all humankind. In turn, all humankind may have something to say about the way you use your property—an idea that has a practical embodiment, for example, in the developing world's calls for technology transfers from more developed nations.[119] When all is said and done, on the critical view, property is a social construction and a product of law, a way to get at some larger social goals, of which, of course, redistribution may be one[120]—a position, incidentally, that is not entirely foreign to Blackstone's own.[121]

Critical arguments about the socially constructed and socially malleable nature of property have met some vociferous and very serious rejoinders, both from the doctrinalist camp's defense of justly acquired rights[122] and even more extensively from the utilitarian position that overly enthusiastic redistribution may discourage productive work, leaving less wealth to redistribute.[123] But perhaps less predictably, the pure-social-construction approach has also raised some internal problems, as well as warning flags from the left. Insofar as critical strategists claim that existing property distributions are unjust, they themselves often seem to imply that some exclusive property was once justly held and only later unjustly removed—as in the case of Native American peoples.[124] In a closely related development, feminist and critical race theory scholars have argued that the talk of rights (possibly including property rights) is not to be so lightly eschewed, because rights-talk holds considerable attraction for the powerless.[125] Indeed, the rhetoric of rights may be all the more revealing and all the more powerful when applied to unexpected persons and areas—the rights of children, the rights of mentally disabled persons, the distribution of rights within intimate settings like the family.[126] In this vein, the exclusivity axiom is a particularly potent metaphor for dignity and personal efficacy, which may explain why ordinary working people are loath to give up a Blackstonian notion of property as their own exclusive dominion.[127] Simply as rhetoric, something like the Exclusivity Axiom—e.g., in the exclusive right to one's own body—rings powerful chords for the very once-disdained groups whose interests the CLS writers wish to vindicate.[128]

Hence, there may be some muting of the critical prodding of the Ownership Anxiety insofar as it entails an attack on the Exclusivity Axiom. The axiom is a very forceful species of rights-talk,[129] and the critics' own critics suggest why that kind of talk, for all its frailties, carries important symbolic freight in the very kind of distributional and liberationist projects that so engage the critics.

## III. Conclusion

Immediately after he made his sweeping and highly quotable assertion equating property with exclusive dominion, Blackstone professed anxiety about the distributional foundations of existing property rights. There are indeed many important questions about the distributional aspects of property, but as this essay has suggested, Blackstone might have done well to expend some of his anxiety on his first assertion, the purported Exclusivity Axiom. The delicate nature of the axiom appears in Blackstone's own discussion of property, and it unfolds even more dramatically in the modern permutations on Blackstone's three canonical strategies. Each one of these permutations suggests in its own way that while there is something to be gained from the Exclusivity Axiom, property may be much more porous and changeable than is suggested by the assertion of simple exclusive dominion.

The axiom itself exercises a powerful hold on all three canonical strategies, although for different reasons. For doctrinalists, the Exclusivity Axiom is a necessary linguistic device, permitting ever more refined statements of just who has what. For utilitarians, the axiom is a normative background principle, a goal to be attained in order to drive down the dreaded costs of transactions. For critical strategists (or at least many of them), the axiom is a target to be attacked because it constitutes an obstacle to a more just and less hierarchical distribution of property.

At the same time, however, the Exclusivity Axiom poses problems for all three canonical strategies. For doctrinalists, the division of ever more nuanced "exclusive" rights is an artifice that disguises the interactions among entitlements and that ill describes transformations of entitlements over time. For utilitarians, the drive to create exclusive rights may mask more sociable, non-rights-based ways that people overcome transactions costs and prisoners' dilemmas. The problem for critics is different: They may eschew the principle of exclusive dominion, yet the principle still retains a sub-rosa attraction—not only for securing entitlements when they come into the hands of the previously powerless, but also for the dignitary metaphoric force that the Exclusivity Axiom shares with rights-talk generally.

Indeed, metaphor is the heart of the matter. The very notion of property as exclusive dominion is at most a cartoon or trope, as Blackstone himself must have known—a trope to make complex systems of rights intelligible by the Cartesian practice of division and separate analysis; a trope to suggest the unique motivating power of self-interest (and correspondingly, as the critics have acerbically insisted, a trope to insinuate the pretended pitfalls of sharing or redistribution); and finally, as the critiques of the critics have suggested, a trope that can extend personal dignity and efficacy even to the powerless.

But as a practical matter, property rights have always overlapped social claims with individual ones, just as they have always mixed stability with change over time. Property regimes always consist of some individual rights, mixed with some rights shared with nearby associates or neighbors, mixed with still more rights shared with a larger community, all held in relatively stable but nevertheless changing and subtly renegotiated relationships.[130]

There are profound reasons why property rights have never been held in an exclusive vacuum. People need property only because there are other people who might contest their control of scarce resources. The institution of property mediates among property owners and would-be interlopers. But property regimes quickly fall apart when people do not understand, respect, and tolerate the property claims of others.[131] In its own way, the trope of exclusive dominion can encourage respect for the claims of others. But at the same time, if the trope of exclusivity does any major disservice, it is to overstate the case, concealing the interactive character of property and giving an inappropriately individualistic patina to this most profoundly sociable of human institutions. That is one reason why, when scholars read Blackstone's ringing words about property as exclusion, they should read the rest of the paragraph too—to appreciate Blackstone's anxiety and to consider how much of that anxiety redounds back to the seemingly mighty axiom of exclusive dominion.

NOTES

This chapter originally appeared as "Canons of Property-Talk, or, Blackstone's Anxiety," in 108 Yale Law Journal 601 (1998), and is reproduced with the permission of the *Yale Law Journal*. Thanks go to Ian Ayres, Jack Balkin, and Laura Underkuffler for their helpful comments on earlier drafts; to Shelley White for her very able research assistance; and to Alison LaCroix for her thoughtful and thorough edit.

1. 2 WILLIAM BLACKSTONE, COMMENTARIES ON THE LAWS OF ENGLAND 2 (facsimile ed. 1979) (1765–69). Subsequent citations will cite to the star edition, the pages of which are the same as those in the facsimile edition. For discussion of some of the citation issues on the *Commentaries*, including confusion over the star edition, see Albert W. Alschuler, *Rediscovering Blackstone*, 145 U. PA. L. REV. 1, 3 n.4 (1996).

2. 2 WILLIAM BLACKSTONE, COMMENTARIES *1.

3. *See* James Madison, *Property*, NATL GAZETTE, Mar. 27, 1792, *reprinted in* 14 THE PAPERS OF JAMES MADISON 266 (Robert A. Rutland et al. eds. 1983). On Blackstone's influence in the United States, see Alschuler, *supra* note 1, at 5–8, which stresses Blackstone's influence in America through the nineteenth century; and Dennis R. Nolan, *Sir William Blackstone and the New American Republic: A Study of Intellectual Impact*, 51 N.Y.U. L. REV. 731, 767 (1976), which concludes that Blackstone's influence was diffuse but very significant. Alschuler claims that Blackstone is now largely treated as a historical figure, generally somewhat negatively. *See* Alschuler, *supra* note 1, at 16–17. On the other hand, negative treatment implies a continuing influence, in the sense that it signals a necessity to refute Blackstone or to distance oneself from his views.

4. For modern scholars' citation of this passage as illustrative of Blackstonian property, see, for example, GREGORY S. ALEXANDER, COMMODITY AND PROPRIETY: COMPETING VISIONS OF PROPERTY IN AMERICAN LEGAL THOUGHT, 1776–1970, at 87 (1997); MARGARET JANE RADIN, REINTERPRETING PROPERTY 131 (1993); and Robert C. Ellickson, *Property in Land*, 102 YALE L.J. 1315, 1317 (1993).

5. *See* 2 BLACKSTONE, *supra* note 2, at *44–119; *see also* Joseph William Singer, *No Right to Exclude: Public Accommodations and Private Property*, 90 NW. U. L. REV. 1283, 1308–10 (1996) (discussing Blackstone's treatment of merchants' duty to serve the public).

6. *See* Alschuler, *supra* note 1, at 34.

7. *See* 1 BLACKSTONE, *supra* note 2, at *127.

8. *See* CAROL M. ROSE, PROPERTY AND PERSUASION 58, 62 (1994) (describing the medieval and early modern view of property as "propriety," a tradition in which property ownership was expected to carry a number of responsibilities, including caring for the impoverished).

9. Early American commentators evidently so understood Blackstone. *See* ALEXANDER, *supra* note 4, at 87 (noting that Daniel Webster and American lawyers regarded the "Blackstonian conception" as a "myth" with respect to its English context).

10. For some of the symbolic freight of the exclusivity trope, see Louise A. Halper, *Tropes of Anxiety and Desire: Metaphor and Metonymy in the Law of Takings*, 8 YALE J.L. & HUMAN. 31, 57–58 (1996).

11. *See, e.g.*, Nollan v. California Coastal Comm'n, 483 U.S. 825, 831 (1987) (concerning the right to exclude); Loretto v. Teleprompter Manhattan CATV Corp., 458 U.S. 419, 435–36 (1982) (same); Halper, *supra* note 10, at 57–58 (describing the "anxiety of boundaries"); *see also infra* notes 53–55, 85–86, 104–17 and accompanying text.

12. *See supra* note 4; *see also* Alschuler, *supra* note 1, at 30 n.175 (complaining that the passage is generally cited out of context).

13. 2 BLACKSTONE, *supra* note 2, at *2.

14. *Id.* One of the few analyses to go on to quote the nervous later lines is Robert P. Burns, *Blackstone's Theory of the "Absolute" Rights of Property*, 54 U. CIN. L. REV. 67, 75 (1985). Without quoting these lines, however, some other scholars have observed that Blackstone did not think property was strictly founded on natural law. *See* Alschuler, *supra* note 1, at 28–36; Duncan Kennedy, *The Structure of Blackstone's Commentaries*, 28 BUFF. L. REV. 209, 311–16 (1979).

15. *See infra* text accompanying notes 117–21.

16. 2 BLACKSTONE, *supra* note 2, at *2; *see also* Herbert J. Storing, *William Blackstone*, in HISTORY OF POLITICAL PHILOSOPHY 622, 624–31 (Leo Strauss & Joseph Cropsey eds., 3d ed. 1987) (stressing that Blackstone wrote for an audience of practical gentlemen rather than philosophers and that he therefore emphasized stability and practice over first principles and theoretical extremes).

17. 2 BLACKSTONE, *supra* note 2, at *2.

18. *See id.* at *2–3.

19. *Id.* at *2–5.

20. *Id.* at *7.

21. *Id.* at *8.

22. In Blackstone's presentation, property has a place as a natural right, but it is at best incomplete, applying to current occupancy but evidently not to more permanent claims, and especially not to claims based on inheritance. *See id.* at *11; Kennedy, *supra* note 14, at 313–15 (arguing that only occupancy or use rights were natural for Blackstone in primitive society); *see also* Alschuler, *supra* note 1, at 28–36 (discussing Blackstone's distinction between "absolute" rights, which were derived from nature, and "relative" rights, which were derived from society); Burns, *supra* note 14, at 71–72 (same); *cf.* Storing, *supra* note 16, at 631 (noting Blackstone's interest in blurring conventional systems with nature, especially with respect to property). David Hume had also argued that lasting property was not a direct product of human nature because it was based on convention and the "artificial" or learned respect for the rights of others. *See* DAVID HUME, A TREATISE OF HUMAN NATURE 488–91 (L.A. Selby-Bigge ed., Oxford Univ. Press, 2d ed. 1978) (1739–40).

23. As Hume argued,

Mankind is an inventive species; and where an invention is obvious and absolutely necessary, it may as properly be said to be natural as any thing that proceeds immediately from original principles, without the intervention of thought or reflexion. . . . Nor is the expression improper to call them *Laws of Nature* [principles of justice]; if by natural we understand what is common to any species, or even if we confine it to mean what is inseparable from the species.

HUME, *supra* note 22, at 484; *see also* Burns, *supra* note 14, at 85 (arguing that civil institutions as well as property are in a sense "providential").

24. See, for example, reports on the greater productivity of private farming over collective farming in socialist or formerly socialist states, such as Richard Critchfield, *Why Soviet Breadbasket Is Never Full*, CHRISTIAN SCI. MONITOR, Apr. 22, 1980, at 12, which describes the disastrous Chinese collectivization of agriculture and the greater productivity caused by the reintroduction of private farming; and Gail DeGeorge & Gail Reed, *Private Farming: Ten Acres and a Loan*, BUS. WK. (Int'l Editions), Mar. 17, 1997, at 37, which describes the greater agricultural productivity caused by the introduction of private farms in Cuba.

25. *See, e.g.*, GARY D. LIBECAP, CONTRACTING FOR PROPERTY RIGHTS 19–26 (1989) (describing impediments to productive changes in property institutions); *cf.* MANCUR OLSON, THE RISE AND DECLINE OF NATIONS: ECONOMIC GROWTH, STAGFLATION, AND SOCIAL RIGIDITIES 77–79 (1982) (describing the decline of growth-producing governmental policies in stable democracies such as Great Britain due to the increasing power of rent-seeking special interest groups).

26. *See* ROSE, *supra* note 8, at 37–38; James E. Krier, *The Tragedy of the Commons, Part Two*, 15 HARV. J.L. & PUB. POL'Y 325, 335–39 (1992).

27. *See, e.g.*, Geoffrey P. Miller, *Comment: Economic Efficiency and the Lockean Proviso*, 10 HARV. J.L. & PUB. POL'Y 401 (1987) (arguing that the Lockean proviso—that first possessors leave "enough, and as good" for later claimants—may be satisfied by the greater wealth that first possessors produce simply by introducing a wealth-enhancing property regime).

28. 2 BLACKSTONE, *supra* note 2, at *8.

29. *See* Carol M. Rose, *"Enough, and as Good" of What?*, 81 NW. U. L. REV. 417, 438–39 (1987) (describing a private property regime as a large-scale agreement not to succumb to the "prisoners' dilemma"); *see also* Carol M. Rose, *Trust in the Mirror of Betrayal*, 75 B.U. L. Rev. 531, 531–33 (1995) and sources cited therein (discussing similar difficulties of mutual forbearance in various contexts).

30. 2 BLACKSTONE, *supra* note 2, at *16–17.

31. *Id.* at *21.

32. *Id.* at *382–83.

33. *See* David Lieberman, *Property, Commerce, and the Common Law: Attitudes to Legal Change in the Eighteenth Century*, *in* EARLY MODERN CONCEPTIONS OF PROPERTY 144, 148 (John Brewer & Susan Staves eds. 1995).

34. 3 BLACKSTONE, *supra* note 2, at *268; *see also* Storing, *supra* note 16, at 630 (analogizing this passage to Blackstone's larger effort to reform while preserving the old). This passage is one of the many singled out for attack in Jeremy Bentham's venomous critique of the *Commentaries*. Bentham criticized Blackstone for failing to recognize the darker forces that might live in old structures. *See* JEREMY BENTHAM, *A Fragment on Government*, *in* A FRAGMENT ON GOVERNMENT AND AN INTRODUCTION TO THE PRINCIPLES OF MORALS AND LEGISLATION 1, 19 & n.1 (Wilfrid Harrison ed., Basil Blackwell 1948) (1776).

35. 1 BLACKSTONE, *supra* note 2, at *76; *see also* Storing, *supra* note 16, at 628–29 (arguing that Blackstone consistently rested law on custom).

36. *See* 2 BLACKSTONE, *supra* note 2, at *265.

37. *See* HUME, *supra* note 22, at 489–91 (arguing that property and justice arise not from human nature but from convention).

38. *See id.* at 490–91 (associating justice with stability of possession); *see also* ADAM SMITH, LECTURES ON JURISPRUDENCE 5 (R.L. Meek et al. eds. 1978) (1762) (asserting that the chief aim of government is to "maintain justice; to prevent the members of a society from incroaching on one another's property.... The design here is to give each one the secure and peacable possession of his own property. {The end proposed by justice is the maintaining [of] men in what are called their perfect rights.}").

39. *See* 2 BLACKSTONE, *supra* note 2, at *458–59, *466.

40. *See* Lieberman, *supra* note 33, at 147–49 (arguing that, while Blackstone may have had more interest in commerce than is apparent from his text, he ultimately had less familiarity with a commercial society).

41. *See* ROSE, *supra* note 8, at 172–73 (arguing that Blackstone's brief remarks on water use ignored the existing doctrine, although they may have encouraged the development of mills).

42. *See* 2 BLACKSTONE, *supra* note 2, at *402–06.

43. *See* Frank I. Michelman, *Ethics, Economics, and the Law of Property, in* NOMOS XXIV: ETHICS, ECONOMICS, AND THE LAW 3, 8–21 (1982) (arguing that property requires a principle of "composition"). Thomas Grey argues that the modern "bundle of sticks" metaphor undermines the commonsense and moral understanding of property. *See* Thomas C. Grey, *The Disintegration of Property, in* NOMOS XXII: PROPERTY 69, 76–77 (1980). But the complexities of eighteenth-century property that Blackstone described suggest an even less integrated view of property in that era.

44. JOHN E. CRIBBET ET AL., PROPERTY: CASES AND MATERIALS (7th ed. 1996). This text was adopted by 57 law schools in 1994–95, according to an informal survey by Foundation Press. *See* Foundation Press, Subject Area: Property (1995) (unpublished informal survey of textbook adoptions distributed to the Board of Editors of Foundation Press, on file with author and cited with permission of Foundation Press).

45. JESSE DUKEMINIER & JAMES E. KRIER, PROPERTY (4th ed. 1998). The third edition was adopted by 110 law schools, according to the Foundation Press survey. *See* Foundation Press, *supra* note 44.

46. JOSEPH W. SINGER, PROPERTY LAW: RULES, POLICIES, AND PRACTICES (1993). There were 27 law school adoptions in 1994–95, an increase from 18 in 1993–94. *See* Foundation Press, *supra* note 44.

47. It is instructive to compare these casebooks' treatment of one of the chestnuts of property law, *Pierson v. Post*, 3 Cai. R. 175 (N.Y. Sup. Ct. 1805), an

early nineteenth-century New York case concerning the conditions for reducing a wild animal to possession. Cribbet treats it as a footnote in the doctrine of the law of "finds." CRIBBET, *supra* note 44, at 105. Dukeminier and Krier use it as the opening case in a sequence that ends with a discussion of the economic concept of "externality." DUKEMINIER & KRIER, *supra* note 45, at 19. Singer sandwiches the case between materials illustrating the indeterminate and political character of legal definitions of property. *See* SINGER, *supra* note 46, at 56.

48.  JOSEPH K. ANGELL, A TREATISE ON THE RIGHT OF PROPERTY IN TIDE WATERS AND IN THE SOIL AND SHORES THEREOF (1847).

49.  H.G. WOOD, A PRACTICAL TREATISE ON THE LAW OF NUISANCES IN THEIR VARIOUS FORMS; INCLUDING REMEDIES THEREFOR AT LAW AND IN EQUITY (3d ed. 1893). The title page notes that the author is also "Author of 'The Law of Master and Servant,' 'Fire Insurance,' 'Landlord and Tenant,' 'The Limitation of Actions,' etc., etc., etc."

50.  Duncan Kennedy suggests that property was a particularly retrograde academic area after the later nineteenth century, one left behind by the Langdellian revolution in "scientific" legal thinking. *See* Kennedy, *supra* note 14, at 349.

51.  *See, e.g.*, ROBERT C. ELLICKSON, ORDER WITHOUT LAW: HOW NEIGHBORS SETTLE DISPUTES (1991) (deriving a theory of norms from the behavior of a community of landowners); Ellickson, *supra* note 4 (using social theory to analyze a broad spectrum of landownership practices).

52.  Similarly, it is relatively easy to establish a simple registration system for automobiles, since any secured claims die with the vehicle. Landed claims, because they can last so long, can more easily get lost in the records, or refer to non-record events, fouling up simple systems—including the Torrens system, which was borrowed from the registration of vessels. *See* ROSE, *supra* note 8, at 205–08.

53.  *See, e.g.*, Nollan v. California Coastal Comm'n, 483 U.S. 825, 831 (1987); Loretto v. Teleprompter Manhattan CATV Corp., 458 U.S. 419, 435–36 (1982).

54.  For example, the scholarly division of a right of "use" from a right of "income" may obscure the fact that these are in a sense *alternatives*, rather than rights simultaneously held. A person's decision whether to use property herself is influenced by the amount another might pay her for it. *See* ROSE, *supra* note 8, at 281.

55.  For a description of the preference for informality in neighborly give-and-take, see ELLICKSON, *supra* note 51, at 76–81.

56.  Tocqueville's famous commentary on the conservatism of American lawyers argues that this conservatism derives in part from the lawyers' knowledge of an arcane system of precedents. *See* ALEXIS DE TOCQUEVILLE, 1 DEMOCRACY IN AMERICA 276 (Phillips Bradley ed., Alfred A. Knopf 1945) (1834).

57.  *See* ROBERT NOZICK, ANARCHY, STATE AND UTOPIA 150–53 (1974).

58.  *See* RICHARD A. EPSTEIN, TAKINGS: PRIVATE PROPERTY AND THE POWER OF EMINENT DOMAIN 334–38 (1985) (admiring but criticizing Nozick).

59. *See, e.g.*, Richard A. Epstein, *Possession as the Root of Title*, 13 GA. L. REV. 1221, 1222–23, 1226 n.6, 1241 (1979) (arguing for the advantages of common law sources, describing Roman law sources, and arguing that the first possession doctrine persists through all time). For somewhat similar identifications of fundamental rights with common law practices, see Douglas W. Kmiec, *The Coherence of the Natural Law of Property*, 26 VAL. U.L. REV. 367, 383–84 (1991), which argues that the natural rights tradition foresees the prevention of harms, as in the common law doctrine of nuisance; and *Johnson v. M'Intosh*, 21 U.S. (8 Wheat.) 543, 567–68 (1823), in which the defendants argued that Indians had no property under American positive law because they had none either in the law of nature or in the common law of former British colonies. For a critique of Epstein's "conceptualism" and presupposition of a single unchanging concept of property, *see* Margaret Jane Radin, *The Consequences of Conceptualism*, 41 U. MIAMI L. REV. 239 (1986).

60. *See* Michael Janofsky, *Home-Grown Courts Spring Up as Judicial Arm of the Far Right*, N.Y. TIMES, Apr. 17, 1996, at A1.

61. See the rather inconclusive discussion in NOZICK, *supra* note 57, at 150–82.

62. *See* Epstein, *supra* note 59, at 1241–43 (defending the first possession principle on the basis of long-standing practice and social need, not philosophy).

63. *See, e.g.*, Mary Ann Glendon, *The Transformation of American Landlord-Tenant Law*, 23 B.C. L. REV. 503 (1982) (assessing the transformation of American landlord-tenant law); Edward H. Rabin, *The Revolution in Residential Landlord-Tenant Law: Causes and Consequences*, 69 CORNELL L. REV. 517 (1984) (describing the causes, history, and effects of the "revolution" in landlord-tenant law).

64. *See* Glendon, *supra* note 63, at 521–28.

65. *See, e.g.*, Robinson v. Diamond Hous. Corp., 463 F.2d 853, 860 (D.C. Cir. 1972) (citing Bruce Ackerman, *Regulating Slum Housing Markets on Behalf of the Poor: Of Housing Codes, Housing Subsidies and Income Redistribution Policy*, 80 YALE L.J. 1093 (1971) (arguing that market forces prevent landlords from passing on the increased costs of code enforcement to tenants through rent increases)).

66. In fact, this doctrinal change has been treated with great skepticism by economic theorists. *See, e.g.*, Charles Meyers, *The Covenant of Habitability and the American Law Institute*, 27 STAN. L. REV. 879 (1975) (criticizing the *Restatement* draft position supporting the landlord's duty of habitability); *see also* Chicago Bd. of Realtors v. City of Chicago, 819 F.2d 732, 741–42 (7th Cir. 1987) (Posner & Easterbrook, JJ., concurring) (criticizing a variety of landlord-tenant "reforms").

67. *Cf.* Oliver Wendell Holmes, *The Path of the Law*, 10 HARV. L. REV. 457, 476–77 (1897) (referring to the law of prescription and remarking on the way that something one has "enjoyed and used" for a long time "takes root in [one's] being").

68. *See, e.g.*, Jack L. Knetsch, *The Endowment Effect and Evidence of Nonreversible Indifference Curves*, 79 AM. ECON. REV. 1277–83 (1989) (describing the endowment effect and the original literature giving rise to the idea). Interestingly enough, Hume also noticed the endowment effect. *See* HUME, *supra* note 22, at 482 ("Men generally fix their affections more on what they are possess'd of, than on what they never enjoy'd: For this reason, it wou'd be greater cruelty to dispossess a man of any thing, than not to give it him").

69. *See* 2 BLACKSTONE, *supra* note 2, at *265.

70. This reality is not lost on modern doctrinalists. *See, e.g.*, John Edward Cribbet, *Concepts in Transition: The Search for a New Definition of Property*, 1986 U. ILL. L. REV. 1 (describing burgeoning special cases, and exceptions to rules that collectively show a "social side" of property).

71. *See, e.g.*, Westfarm Assocs. v. Washington Suburban Sanitary Comm'n, 66 F.3d 669, 679 (4th Cir. 1995) (discussing "externalities"); Gail v. United States, 58 F.3d 580, 585 n.7 (10th Cir. 1995) (discussing "transaction costs").

72. *See* BENTHAM, *supra* note 34, at 3–4, 8–9, 15–22 (accusing Blackstone of impeding criticism and reform and describing passages of particular complacency).

73. *See supra* section I.B.

74. RICHARD A. POSNER, ECONOMIC ANALYSIS OF LAW § 3.1, at 30 n.1 (3d ed. 1986).

75. *See* Harold Demsetz, *Toward a Theory of Property Rights*, 57 AM. ECON. REV. 347–59 (1967), *reprinted in part in* DUKEMINIER & KRIER, *supra* note 45, at 40. Demsetz gives no indication that he read Blackstone's story.

76. Demsetz, *supra* note 75, at 350.

77. *See* H. Scott Gordon, *The Economic Theory of a Common-Property Resource: The Fishery*, 62 J. POL. ECON. 124 (1954); Garrett Hardin, *The Tragedy of the Commons*, 162 SCIENCE 1243 (1968).

78. For an explanation of this classic game theory problem in the context of similar problems, see Jack Hirshleifer, *Evolutionary Models in Economics and Law: Cooperation Versus Conflict Strategies*, 4 RES. IN LAW & ECON. 1, 17 (1982).

79. For some other variations on the optimistic creation-of-property stories, see ROSE, *supra* note 8, at 287, and the authorities cited therein.

80. R. H. Coase, *The Problem of Social Cost*, 3 J.L. & ECON. 1 (1960).

81. *See, e.g.*, LIBECAP, *supra* note 25, at 12–26 (describing factors that impel and impede "contracting for property rights").

82. *See* Guido Calabresi & A. Douglas Melamed, *Property Rules, Liability Rules, and Inalienability: One View of the Cathedral*, 85 HARV. L. REV. 1089, 1106–07 (1972) (describing the use of liability rules instead of property rules where transactions costs would defeat value-enhancing transfers). For a modern reconsideration, see Louis Kaplow & Steven Shavell, *Property Rules Versus Liability Rules: An Economic Analysis*, 109 HARV. L. REV. 713 (1996).

83. *See* Thomas W. Merrill, *Trespass, Nuisance, and the Costs of Determining Property Rights*, 14 J. LEGAL STUD. 13 (1985).

84. *See* Steven N. S. Cheung, *The Structure of a Contract and the Theory of a Non-Exclusive Resource*, 13 J.L. & ECON. 49 (1970).

85. *See* Clifford G. Holderness, *A Legal Foundation for Exchange*, 14 J. LEGAL STUD. 321 (1985); *see also* Frank H. Easterbrook, *The Supreme Court 1983 Term—Foreword: The Court and the Economic System*, 98 HARV. L. REV. 4, 10–12 (1984) (arguing that the Supreme Court is increasingly likely to consider cases from an "ex ante" perspective of defined rights, in order to ease transactions, rather than from the blurred "ex post" perspective of fairness).

86. *See, e.g.*, BONNIE MCCAY & JAMES ACHESON, THE QUESTION OF THE COMMONS: THE CULTURE AND ECOLOGY OF COMMUNAL RESOURCES (1987); ELINOR OSTROM, GOVERNING THE COMMONS: THE EVOLUTION OF INSTITUTIONS FOR COLLECTIVE ACTION (1990).

87. *See* Robert Cooter, *The Cost of Coase*, 11 J. LEGAL STUD. 1, 17–18 (1982).

88. ELLICKSON, *supra* note 51, at 177–82.

89. *See, e.g.*, Randal C. Picker, *Simple Games in a Complex World: A Generative Approach to the Adoption of Norms*, 64 U. CHI. L. REV. 1225 (1997) (giving a game-theoretic account of norm change through social learning that has implications for a wide variety of legal issues).

90. *See, e.g.*, ROBERT H. FRANK, PASSIONS WITHIN REASON: THE STRATEGIC ROLE OF THE EMOTIONS (1988); Avner Greif, *Reputation and Coalitions in Medieval Trade: Evidence on the Maghribi Traders*, 49 J. ECON. HIST. 857 (1989). For a popular presentation of the social organizations of commerce, see FRANCIS FUKUYAMA, TRUST: THE SOCIAL VIRTUES AND THE CREATION OF PROSPERITY (1995).

91. In Robert Axelrod's much-cited study of the "tit for tat" strategy that he regards as a prototype of successful cooperation, the players must begin with a "nice" move or the relationship will not get off the ground. ROBERT AXELROD, THE EVOLUTION OF COOPERATION (1984).

92. ROBERT C. ELLICKSON ET AL., PERSPECTIVES ON PROPERTY LAW at xii (1995) (revising BRUCE A. ACKERMAN, ECONOMIC FOUNDATIONS OF PROPERTY LAW (1975)).

93. *See generally* Coase, *supra* note 80. *But see, e.g.*, Mark Kelman, *Consumption Theory, Production Theory, and Ideology in the Coase Theorem*, 52 S. CAL. L. REV. 669, 672–73, 678–79, 681–82, 688–91 (1979) (giving examples of the ways in which individuals value existing endowments more highly than opportunities and criticizing the Coase Theorem for neglecting these differences' effects on trading outcomes).

94. *See, e.g.*, Herbert Hovenkamp, *Arrow's Theorem: Ordinalism and Republican Government*, 75 IOWA L. REV. 949, 968 (1990) (describing a multiplicity of Pareto optimal distributions that depend on initial entitlements).

95. PIERRE JOSEPH PROUDHON, WHAT IS PROPERTY? (Benjamin R. Tucker trans., Howard Fertig 1966) (1840).

96. 1 KARL MARX, CAPITAL: A CRITIQUE OF POLITICAL ECONOMY 713–74 (Frederick Engels ed., Int'l Publishers 1967) (1887).

97. *See* ROBERTO MANGABEIRA UNGER, THE CRITICAL LEGAL STUDIES MOVEMENT 36–38 (1986) [hereinafter UNGER, CLS]; ROBERTO MANGABEIRA UNGER, WHAT SHOULD LEGAL ANALYSIS BECOME? 163–64 (1996) [hereinafter UNGER, LEGAL ANALYSIS]; *see also* Thomas F. McInerney III, *Common Ground: Reconciling Rights and Communal Concerns in Real Property Law*, 25 B.C. ENVTL. AFF. L. REV. 831, 846–50 (1998) (discussing Unger's views of property).

98. *See* UNGER, CLS, *supra* note 97, at 38–40; UNGER, LEGAL ANALYSIS, *supra* note 97, at 157–60.

99. *See* MARK KELMAN, A GUIDE TO CRITICAL LEGAL STUDIES 258 (1987) (observing that while ordinary outcomes may be predictable, contrary doctrines are always available).

100. *See id.* at 294–95 (giving examples of instances where the supposed principle of neutrality can misdescribe legal outcomes and mask bias).

101. For various strands of critical historiography, *see* Robert W. Gordon, *Critical Legal Histories*, 36 STAN. L. REV. 57, 71–100 (1984).

102. *See* MORTON J. HORWITZ, THE TRANSFORMATION OF AMERICAN LAW, 1780–1860 at 32–42, 101–02 (1977). *But see* ROSE, *supra* note 8, at 165–88 (offering a different account); Stephen F. Williams, *Transforming American Law: Doubtful Economics Makes Doubtful History*, 25 UCLA L. REV. 1187 (1978) (book review) (criticizing Horwitz's thesis).

103. *See* Joseph William Singer, *Sovereignty and Property*, 86 Nw. U. L. REV. 1, 5–6 (1991).

104. *See* Gordon, *supra* note 101, at 98–100, 109–12; *see also* KELMAN, *supra* note 99, at 270–71 (noting that critical thinkers believe property law categories block the reimagination of existing distributions); James L. Kainen, *Nineteenth Century Interpretations of the Federal Contract Clause: The Transformation from Vested to Substantive Rights Against the State*, 31 BUFF. L. REV. 381, 399–401, 451, 476–77 (1982) (describing the process by which nineteenth-century legal elites shifted the concept of rights from "vested" to "substantive," leading to the reification of the laissez-faire principle of "freedom of contract"); Mark Tushnet, *An Essay on Rights*, 62 TEX. L. REV. 1363, 1382–84 (1984) (criticizing the "reification" of rights). Kelman appears to think that legal doctrine's flaw is less its bias (though it may indeed be biased) than its tendency to deny contradictions and promote complacency. *See* KELMAN, *supra* note 99, at 286.

105. *See* JEREMY BENTHAM, *Principles of the Civil Code, in* THE THEORY OF LEGISLATION 88, 119–20 (C. K. Ogden ed. & Richard Hildreth trans., Kegan Paul, Trench, Trubner & Co. 1931) (1802).

106. Duncan Kennedy, *Form and Substance in Private Law Adjudication*, 89 HARV. L. REV. 1685, 1710 (1976).

107.*See id.* at 1742–45, 1773–74.

108. A reprise of this argument appeared in Laurence Tribe's critique of an influential article by Frank Easterbrook. *See* Laurence H. Tribe, *Constitutional Calculus: Equal Justice or Economic Efficiency?*, 98 HARV. L. REV. 592, 600–01 (1985) (critiquing Easterbrook, *supra* note 85). *But see* Frank H. Easterbrook, *Method, Result, and Authority: A Reply*, 98 HARV. L. REV. 622, 624–26 (1985) (acknowledging that ex ante approaches are not always dispositive but reasserting that they are informative, productive of social wealth, and more appropriate for judges than Tribe's constitutive approach).

109. *See* Duncan Kennedy & Frank Michelman, *Are Property and Contract Efficient?*, 8 HOFSTRA L. REV. 711 (1980); Frank I. Michelman, *supra* note 43, at 25.

110. Cf. KELMAN, *supra* note 99, at 159 (noting instances where forced sharing overcomes inefficiencies).

111. *See* Duncan Kennedy, *Law-and-Economics from the Perspective of Critical Legal Studies*, *in* 2 THE NEW PALGRAVE DICTIONARY OF LAW AND ECONOMICS 465, 471–73 (1998).

112. *See, e.g.*, POSNER, *supra* note 74, § 3.1, at 30–31 n.1 (responding to Michelman). *But see* KELMAN, *supra* note 99, at 329 n.4 (criticizing Posner's response).

113. *See* Charles A. Reich, *The New Property*, 73 YALE L.J. 733, 785–86 (1964); *see also* STEPHEN R. MUNZER, A THEORY OF PROPERTY 241–47 (1990) (discussing the minimum entitlements necessary for "a decent human life in society").

114. J. G. A. POCOCK, THE MACHIAVELLIAN MOMENT: FLORENTINE POLITICAL THOUGHT AND THE ATLANTIC REPUBLICAN TRADITION 506–52 (1975).

115. *See* Gregory S. Alexander, *Takings and the Post-Modern Dialectic of Property*, 9 CONST. COMMENTARY 259, 275 (1992); Frank I. Michelman, *Possession vs. Distribution in the Constitutional Idea of Property*, 72 IOWA L. REV. 1319, 1329–30 (1987).

116. *See* Margaret Jane Radin, *Property and Personhood*, 34 STAN. L. REV. 957 (1982).

117. JOHN RAWLS, A THEORY OF JUSTICE 101 (1971).

118. *See, e.g.*, KELMAN, *supra* note 99, at 142–44, 165 (arguing that efficiency concerns cannot justify property rules because supposedly efficient outcomes vary depending on the distribution of initial entitlements).

119. For an exploration of some of the conflicting demands, *see* Klaus Bosselmann, *Plants and Politics: The International Legal Regime Concerning Biotechnology and Biodiversity*, 7 COLO. J. INT'L ENVTL. L. & POL'Y 111 (1996).

120. *See, e.g.*, KELMAN, *supra* note 99, at 260; *see also* Singer, *supra* note 5, at 1450–51 (concluding, after an extensive discussion of public accommodations

law, that property incorporates "built-in distributive principles" reflecting wider social organization and changing social values).

121. *See* Alschuler, *supra* note 1, at 34.

122. *See, e.g.*, EPSTEIN, *supra* note 58, at 334–36; NOZICK, *supra* note 57, at 155–64.

123. *See, e.g.*, Thomas W. Merrill, *Wealth and Property*, 38 UCLA L. REV. 489, 495 (1990) (book review). Richard Epstein, wearing his utilitarian hat, makes this point as well. *See* EPSTEIN, *supra* note 58, at 336–37.

124. *See, e.g.*, SINGER, *supra* note 46, at 23–24; Robert A. Williams, Jr., *Encounters on the Frontiers of International Human Rights Law: Redefining the Terms of Indigenous Peoples' Survival in the World*, 1990 DUKE L.J. 660, 687–89; *see also* Michael J. Perry, *Taking Neither Rights-Talk nor the "Critique of Rights" Too Seriously*, 62 TEX. L. REV. 1405, 1415 (1984) (arguing that the critique of "rights-talk" gives no better alternative to those in need).

125. *See* Kimberlé Williams Crenshaw, *Race, Reform, and Retrenchment: Transformation and Legitimation in Antidiscrimination Law*, 101 HARV. L. REV. 1331, 1364–65 (1988). For a review of the differences that emerged between critical race theorists and the critical legal studies movement, *see* KIMBERLÉ WILLIAMS CRENSHAW ET AL., *Introduction* to CRITICAL RACE THEORY: THE KEY WRITINGS THAT FORMED THE MOVEMENT at xiii, xxii–xxvii (1995). Among the critics themselves, Duncan Kennedy has been interested in the ways that legal forms interplay with autonomy. Interestingly enough, Kennedy's most explicit discussion is in *The Structure of Blackstone's Commentaries*, in which he describes the "fundamental contradiction" in the belief that the protection of individual freedom entails legal coercion. Kennedy, *supra* note 14, at 211–13.

126. *See* Martha Minow, *Interpreting Rights: An Essay for Robert Cover*, 96 YALE L.J. 1860, 1866–67, 1892–93, 1907–08, 1910–11 (1987) (arguing that the language of rights can invite serious consideration of unconventional claims); Reva B. Siegel, *Home as Work: The First Women's Rights Claims Concerning Wives' Household Labor, 1850–1880*, 103 YALE L.J. 1073, 1111 (1994) (arguing that feminists' early property claims in marriage opened up at least a partial challenge to the then-current "gendered aspects of the market ideology").

127. On the importance that working-class people place on property, *see* SALLY ENGLE MERRY, GETTING JUSTICE AND GETTING EVEN: LEGAL CONSCIOUSNESS AMONG WORKING-CLASS AMERICANS 44–47 (1990). *See also* Maria Newman, *Housing Plan: From Projects into Co-ops*, N.Y. TIMES, Sept. 27, 1992, at 33 (describing public housing tenants' "almost obsessive" wish to be included in conversions to privately owned units because owners can control their environment and exclude persons they do not want as neighbors). An especially interesting example of property's relation to personal efficacy is seen in ERVING GOFFMAN, ASYLUMS: ESSAYS ON THE SOCIAL SITUATION OF MENTAL PATIENTS AND OTHER INMATES 18–21 (1961), which describes inmates' tremendous efforts to

reestablish property-like claims in personal spaces, personal effects, and "stashes" following institutional divestment of their property.

128. *See* Alschuler, *supra* note 1, at 49 n.266, 51 n.269 (criticizing critical scholars for failing to pay attention to their own wishes to maintain a zone of autonomy from the community).

129. *See* Carol M. Rose, *Property as the Keystone Right?*, 71 NOTRE DAME L. REV. 329, 348–49 (1996) (describing both the argument that property symbolizes other rights and critiques of that position).

130. *See* Ellickson, *supra* note 4, at 1322–26 (classifying land regimes according to the number who may enter and use the land and discussing the ramifications thereof); Laura S. Underkuffler, *The Perfidy of Property*, 70 TEX. L. REV. 293, 311 (1991) (book review) (arguing that the concept of property contains both individual and collective elements).

131. *See* Rose, supra note 129.

# Chapter 4

# Vanished from the First Year
## *Lost Torts and Deep Structures in Tort Law*

## *Martha Chamallas*

Changes to the mandatory first-year curriculum of law schools are rare and tend to be of the small-order variety, rather than fundamental. In the past few years, one such minitrend has been to cut down on the number of hours devoted to torts, as part of a more general streamlining of the first-year package of courses. The once-standard two-course, six-hour sequence is now being replaced by a single torts course of four hours. Forced to slash topics from their torts syllabi, torts professors have become more self-conscious about what they regard as crucial to their students' appreciation of tort law as a field and what they consider to be essential cases for instructing students in the arts of legal reasoning and argument. One by-product of this curricular revision has been to make the pedagogical canon in torts more visible (and perhaps less contested) and to underscore the many important issues and questions that never see the light of day.

The core of the pared-down torts course is the negligence claim, which sometimes even pushes intentional torts from its position as the first topic discussed in the course. Many professors explain that negligence liability takes center stage because most suits are brought under this theory of liability and tell their students that an exploration of "fault" is central to understanding the rationale for state intervention in private disputes. The need to compensate accident victims for unexpected tragedy in their lives is still discussed, but often tends to be addressed as a special-interest concern for plaintiffs and their lawyers, rather than as a general societal problem.

In this configuration of the subject, the major "problem" addressed by tort law becomes how to allocate losses from unintentional injury and how society should handle the costs of accidents.[1] For many students, torts is the first class in which they have an opportunity to discuss the cost-benefit analysis that lies beneath the law's determination of "reasonableness," a construct that crops up at almost every corner. Thus, a must-read case in torts is Learned Hand's opinion in *United States v. Carroll Towing*[2] in which he devised an algebraic formula to decide whether human conduct was negligent. Professors with a "law and economics" bent often use the case to introduce students to an economics analysis of negligence and to provoke discussion about whether tort rules of liability are efficient and whether they create optimal levels of deterrence.

This turn to efficiency in torts courses, however, is a relatively recent development, dating mostly from the mid-1980s. Prior to that time, high courts in some states—most prominently California—had liberalized tort law to allow plaintiffs a greater chance at recovery in a wide variety of contexts. This liberalization of tort law reflected events in the larger society in the late 1960s and early 1970s, particularly the push for equality of the black civil rights and women's rights social movements. Looking back, this period probably also represented the high-water mark for strict liability for defective products[3] and for recognition of new torts such as wrongful birth[4] and mental distress claims for witnessing the negligent killing and injury of family members.[5] Often the plaintiffs in these cases were ordinary consumers, patients, and mothers and other caretakers of children whose lives had been disrupted because of a catastrophic injury. The defendants were typically corporate entities and other institutional "deep pockets" who were said to be more capable of absorbing and spreading the loss through raising the price of their products or services. Commentators of the day discussed the "redistributive potential" of tort law, seeing the private liability system as one way to shift resources from the hands of wealthy defendants to less affluent plaintiffs. "Tort reform" at this time was most often linked to innovations, such as comparative negligence, that softened the effect of restrictive doctrines (like contributory negligence and assumption of risk) and permitted at least partial recovery for some groups of seriously injured tort victims.

A shift occurred in the 1980s when conservative forces emerged on the political scene and began to have an impact on tort law and how it was taught in the legal academy. Many believed that the liberalization of tort law of the preceding two decades had produced a "litigation explosion" that drove up the costs of insurance and had a depressing effect on business growth. At the state legislative level especially, there were two waves of "tort reform," the first spurred by the medical malpractice "crisis" which aimed to make it more difficult for patients to recover in negligence suits against their physicians, followed by a more general assault on tort recoveries, particularly with respect to award of noneconomic types of damages, such as sums for pain and suffering, mental distress, and punitive damages.[6] By the end of the century, "tort reform" became a code word for initiatives to limit tort liability and to curb what business representatives and their supporters decried as frivolous lawsuits and excessive jury awards. Practitioners sometimes reported that even juries, the institution with a reputation for sympathizing with the plight of ordinary citizens, had begun to worry about the effect of damage awards on insurance premiums and had become more skeptical about the legitimacy of claims brought before them.

These developments did not always have a direct or immediate effect in the classroom, particularly given that most torts professors professed that they did not have the time to devote to nontraditional topics, such as tort reform. Rather, I suspect that the ideological shifts that occurred in practice and in cultural debates about the value of litigation were felt in the glosses and interpretations that academics gave to canonical cases (such as Cardozo's classic opinions in *Palgraf v. Long Island Railroad Co.*[7] and *Martin v. Herzog*[8]) and in their selections of new cases, generally placed under "old" topical headings in casebook revisions and unpublished supplementary materials. What is thought to be important about a case—the social meaning of a text—can change over time and subtly change the pedagogical canon in tort law, even when there appears to be considerable continuity in the core syllabus.

In addition to reflecting on how texts are understood and approached, it is also critical to take note of those topics, issues, and questions in torts that seem to have vanished from the first year. In the contemporary curriculum, for example, there is rarely room for discussion of relational interests—those torts such as wrongful death, loss of consortium, and alienation of affections which compensate for interference with or loss or impairment of important family or intimate relationships. In the "lost tort" category, we might also place many claims for invasion of nonphysical interests, from the old cases dealing with the mishandling of corpses to newer claims for negligent infliction of mental distress. As a general matter, there is also likely to be less extensive classroom exploration of dignitary harms, including the ancient causes of action for battery, assault, and false imprisonment, even as these claims are being revised to redress such contemporary harms as date rape, sexual harassment, and domestic violence. Moreover, now more than ever, remedial issues, including the type and amount of damages awarded and the adequacy of awards, are likely to be relegated to the margins of the course or "saved" for upper-class, small-enrollment electives such as advanced torts or remedies. It is not that these topics are never covered, or at least mentioned, in the required torts course. I suspect, however, that they are the first to go when time is short and instructors are forced to focus on the basics. Contrasting and comparing the doctrinal frameworks of negligence and strict liability can easily occupy the bulk of the semester.

At the same time this winnowing of torts has occurred, however, a new genre of scholarship has emerged which applies the insights of legal feminism, critical race theory, and other critical discourses to torts.[9] One project of this group of writers has been to uncover hidden biases based on race, gender, and other important dimensions of personal identity and to question the basic equity of tort rules created within a predominantly white, male-dominated legal system. This growing body of literature suggests that no dimension of law tort has escaped the influence of gender or race. The literature discusses how the four elements of the basic negligence claim—duty, breach, causation, and damages—derive their meaning within specific cultural contexts in which understandings about gender and race play a prominent role. For example, the "reasonable person" standard, a staple in tort law, is now recognized as a problematic construct that needs to be unpacked to expose its nonneutrality and propensity to reproduce the status quo.[10]

What is most striking about the new critical scholarship, however, is that it finds its most persuasive evidence of gender and race bias precisely in those areas of tort law that are gradually being taken out of the canon or have already lost their place in the core curriculum. It is through examination of "lost torts" and marginal topics that we can see most clearly that tort law is not evenhanded, that systemic biases persist even though explicit gender and race classifications no longer form part of the formal legal doctrine.[11] As in so many other areas of contemporary law, moreover, the bias that pervades tort law is subtle in nature. It is best described as cognitive or structural bias (rather than the more familiar disparate treatment) and operates within a system that is facially neutral with respect to gender and race. Most often, bias finds its way into tort law through hidden mechanisms, notably implicit hierarchies of values and habits of dichotomous thinking. Only by looking at the whole of tort law beyond the first-year canon is it possible to divide the subject into its privileged and nonprivileged parts. Through this process we can tease out the judgments of value—the deep structures of tort law—that reproduce gender and race disparities in what purports to be a color-blind and gender-neutral regime.

The following are some examples from my research[12] of neglected areas in tort law that are saturated with implicit gender and race bias. The first example, from the law of damages, shows how the lives and potential of women and racial minorities have been devalued in personal injury and death cases and consequently are judged to be worth less than the lives and potential of white men. The remaining examples mine the various subfields of tort law to discover implicit hierarchies. They reveal the inner structures of the law that provide a ranking of types of injuries and types of damages, most often to the detriment of marginalized social groups. These examples demonstrate that the tort hierarchies disproportionately harm women of all races and minority men and produce a legal regime that provides inadequate protection for the recurring injuries in their lives.

## Gender and Race in the Law of Damages: Reproducing Bias in Predicting the Future

Even before the recent contraction of the torts curriculum, the subject of damages rarely received attention either in the classroom or in the academic literature. Perhaps because professors do not possess the detailed knowledge of practicing attorneys and the topic appears to lack the theoretical importance of more general principles of liability, there has been surprisingly little debate about how injuries of different social groups are valued under the law.

The empirical studies of damage awards in personal injury and wrongful death suits, however, indicate that women of all races and minority men receive significantly lower awards than white men. Some of these data have been generated by the movement to study gender and race bias in the courts,[13] in which task forces created in the 1980s and 1990s investigated aspects of the civil justice system to determine whether gender and ethnic groups were being treated fairly. For example, a study of wrongful death cases between 1984 and 1988 conducted by the bias task force in Washington state found that the mean damage award for a male decedent was $332,166, compared to a mean award of $214,923 for a woman.[14] Similar disparities were documented in a nationwide study of jury awards in personal injury cases, showing that in virtually all age groups, women received significantly lower mean and median compensatory damage awards than men.[15] My own calculations from tort judgments and settlements reported in a 1996 guide for personal injury lawyers also indicate that, in the aggregate, male plaintiffs received awards that were 27 percent higher than those of female plaintiffs.[16] Although there are fewer data analyzing tort awards along racial lines, a Washington state study of asbestos cases in the 1980s did find substantial disparities between settlement amounts of minority and nonminority plaintiffs.[17]

These data confirm that in the realm of torts a higher value is placed upon the lives of white men and that injuries suffered by this group are worth more than injuries suffered by less privileged groups in society. Although the empirical studies are not refined enough to pinpoint the source of the disparity, it is likely that some portion of the gap is traceable to the way the law measures the potential of female and minority plaintiffs, specifically, the calculation of their loss of future earning capacity. Particularly in cases in which plaintiffs are injured or killed when they are young, little reliable information may be available to predict how much they would have earned during their lifetime. This speculation about potential earning power is critically important on both a practical and a symbolic level. Loss of future earning capacity is a "big ticket" item of damages, which can make the difference between a modest and a sizable award. Because it is a measure of human potential, moreover, the price the law attaches to lost earning capacity tells us something about societal judgments concerning worth, specifically the worth of the individual plaintiff and the groups to which the individual belongs.

Judges and practitioners serving on bias task forces report that it is commonplace in tort litigation to use gender-based and sometimes also race-based tables to determine lost earning capacity.[18] Briefly stated, two important components go into calculating this element of damages—the work-life expectancy of the plaintiff and the average wage the plaintiff likely would have earned in the future. Loss of future earning capacity is typically measured by estimating the number of years the plaintiff would have worked had she not been injured (work-life expectancy) and the amount the plaintiff would have earned each year, reduced to present value.

Estimates of each of these two significant components are often infected with race and gender bias—bias that is hidden from view by statistics. In calculating the work-life expectancy of plaintiffs, economists frequently rely upon race-specific and gender-specific work-life tables, which predict that women and racial minorities will spend fewer years in the labor force. This is because work-life expectancy is distinct from life expectancy. Work-life expectancy is a statistical measure derived from the past working experience of all people in a plaintiff's gender or racial group. It incorporates rates of unemployment, both voluntary and involuntary, as well as expected retirement age. Because women in the past stayed out of the workplace to raise children, women have a lower work-life expectancy than men, despite the fact that women live longer than men. Because of higher rates of unemployment and of incarceration, minority men also have a lower work-life expectancy than white men. Thus, based on data from the U.S. Bureau of Labor Statistics, the work-life expectancy for a white man injured at the age of thirty was estimated to be 4.7 years more than that of a minority man, 8.7 years more than that of a white woman, and 9.2 years more than that of a minority woman.[19] Embedded within the seemingly neutral concept of "work-life expectancy" is thus the history of unequal treatment of female and minority workers, including the exclusion and discouragement of married women and mothers from employment and the relegation of minority men to sporadic employment with little job security.

Gender and race also affect the calculation of average wages. When a plaintiff has no individualized track record of earnings, economists acting as expert witnesses frequently resort to gender-based and race-based tables of earnings to estimate future earnings. Because of wage discrimination and occupational segregation, predictions of future earnings for women and minorities are considerably lower than for white men, even when controlled for such factors as educational attainment. One technique for calculating future earning capacity in these cases is to predict the level of education that the plaintiff would have achieved. This can be done by considering a number of factors, such as the plaintiff's scores on aptitude tests, the socioeconomic status of the plaintiff's family, and the parents' and siblings' education levels. Gender and race explicitly enter the calculation when economists refer to tables of average earnings to estimate a plaintiff's lifetime earnings, broken down by sex, race, and education levels. Using such gender-specific and race-specific economic data can have enormous consequences for a plaintiff's total award. Thus, the projected lifetime earnings, discounted to 1990 present value, of a female college graduate have been estimated to be only 65 percent of those of a similarly situated male college graduate.[20] This means that if two twins—a boy and a girl—were simultaneously severely injured in a car accident, the boy would be entitled to a considerably higher amount for loss of future earning capacity than his sister, a disparity solely attributable to gender.

The size of the male/female disparity in projected earning capacity is not surprising given the persistence of the wage gap between men and women of all races. In 1991 the median income of white women employed full time was 69 percent of the median income for white men; African American women, 62 percent of the median income for white men; Hispanic women, 54 percent; African American men, 74 percent; and Hispanic men, 65 percent.[21] Relying on past earnings to make predictions about the future ties these predictions to current race and gender disparities. Use of these data also means that discrimination in one area—the setting of pay rates—will influence valuation in another area: calculating personal injury and wrongful death awards.

The widespread acceptance[22] of the use of race-based and gender-based economic data in tort litigation stands in sharp contrast to judicial hostility against the use of such explicit race and sex classifications in other contexts. In constitutional challenges involving explicit gender and race classifications, the Supreme Court has embraced an individualistic perspective, insisting that race and gender not be used as a proxy for economic dependency and that group-based generalizations and stereotypes are not proper substitutes for the "thoughtful scrutiny of individuals."[23] Even when the pattern that emerges from statistics is accurate to some degree, equal protection requires that individuals not be saddled with race- and gender-based presumptions about their group. Thus, in a series of cases starting in the 1970s,[24] the Court showed its distaste for the very domestic and maternal assumptions underlying the calculation of women's future earning capacity—that women will become stay-at-home mothers and that when they do work, they will have less demanding and lower-paying jobs. Because racial classifications are inherently suspect and reviewed with the strictest scrutiny,[25] a black torts plaintiff would seem to have a strong case if he argued that it was unfair to calculate his individual award on race-based work-expectancy tables reflecting the fact that a disproportionately high number of African American men lose working years while in jail or have their working life shortened because of a higher exposure to violence. Particularly given the willingness in recent years to find sufficient "state action" in civil trials to trigger constitutional protection,[26] it is a bit surprising that the bias in tort damages has not yet spawned a constitutional challenge.

It may be that the highly contestable cultural assumptions underlying use of gender-based and race-based tables have largely escaped notice precisely because they are camouflaged under a maze of statistics and because the law of damages is not part of the torts canon. The economists who testify as expert witnesses and the lawyers who try personal injury cases are unlikely to be primed to identify race and gender inequities in a context totally removed from a civil rights case.

Experts also tend not to question the fairness of using gender-based and race-based tables, particularly because such use is standard practice outside the litigation context. What economists regard as an accurate measure of loss of future earning capacity has dominated the legal determination. When the inquiry is so pared down, there is little room for discussion of the equity of the process and little awareness that predictions about the future involve social as well as economic judgments.

Deep-seated judgments about the importance of gender and race differences do, however, lie beneath the use of the statistical disparities and result in the devaluation of the potential of women and minorities. In projecting future earning capacity, only a few characteristics of the plaintiff are routinely used as guides to predict the future—notably, age, sex, and race. To some extent, it seems reasonable to rely on these factors to calculate future earnings. A person's age does affect how long he or she will likely be able to earn money and remain in the workforce. In our society, moreover, race and gender do matter: Being a woman or being an African American does dampen one's earnings prospects. However, what is not often noticed is that many other variables, such as religion, ethnicity, and marital status, also have predictive power. Yet they are not used to predict earning potential. The use of race- and sex-based data is thus highly selective. And it is this selectivity through which the process of devaluation takes place. The judgment to focus on race and gender—but not other personal traits—amounts to a judgment that race and gender tell us more about what a person will become, more about what a person will achieve, than other traits that have been correlated in the past with the acquisition of wealth. When race-specific and gender-specific data are used, it signals that white men are worth more, and reinforces beliefs that they will achieve more in their lives than white women or minority men and women.

Importantly, the selective use of statistics makes the process appear neutral and rational. The past is uncritically accepted as a guide to the future, even though most people acknowledge that the past was hardly free of race and gender bias. Hidden from view is the process by which we actively select the factors we will use to predict the future. Devaluing the potential of women and minorities is thus accomplished in an updated, subtle form that looks more like economic expertise than race or gender bias.

## The Ranking of Injuries and Damages

Aside from the computation of damage awards, gender and race bias finds its way into torts through the construction of legal categories that purport to describe types of injuries and types of damages. In contemporary tort law, these types of injuries and damages are ranked in importance, with the higher-ranked injuries receiving more extensive legal protection than lower-ranked injuries. Although these hierarchies of value purport to rank injuries and damages neutrally, they often end up having a disparate negative effect on women plaintiffs as a class, and to some degree also disproportionately harm minority male plaintiffs as well. Most significantly, injuries of low value are more often associated with women, while injuries of high value are more often linked to men.

Although the standard texts generally do not explicitly state so, there is little question that a higher value is placed on physical injury and property loss than on emotional or relational harm. This implicit hierarchy of value was even more apparent in an earlier era when the scope of recovery in tort was more restricted and there were fewer possibilities for recovering for marginal harms. Despite the liberalization of tort law, the basic hierarchy has remained intact.

The hierarchy of types of injuries is evident in the typical law school curriculum, particularly if we focus on what is left out as well as what is covered in the classroom. As mentioned above, most first-year torts courses focus almost exclusively on the "privileged" types of injury, omitting extensive discussion of topics such as wrongful death, loss of consortium, and negligent infliction of mental distress. The message is that "real" injuries involve physical harm and loss of property and that we should be more skeptical about the legitimacy or worth of claims of emotional loss or relational injury. Recently, moreover, an implicit hierarchy of types of damages has been constructed that complements the hierarchy of types of injury. The trend is toward favoring or privileging pecuniary or economic losses, such as lost wages and medical expenses, as opposed to nonpecuniary or noneconomic damages, such as pain and suffering, mental distress, lost companionship and society, loss of enjoyment of life, and punitive damages.

In the abstract, the implicit hierarchies of value look neutral in the sense that they are not tied to any gender or other social group. Because all persons have a body, emotions, and personal relationships, it is often assumed that people possess "privileged" and "nonprivileged" interests in equal proportions. As they operate in social context, however, the hierarchies of value tend to place women at a disadvantage. The important and recurring injuries in women's lives tend more often to be classified as lower-ranked emotional or relational harm, or noneconomic loss. The ranking thus assigned to "women's injuries"[27] makes it more likely that relief will be denied or that recoveries will be devalued.

## The Devaluation of Emotional Harm

One type of injury that has received only marginal protection is emotional harm, whether caused by intentional wrongdoing or negligence. Until well into the twentieth century, the law purported to draw a sharp line between physical injury and property loss on the one hand, and mental distress and relational harm on the other. An 1861 English case, *Lynch v. Knight*,[28] was often cited for the proposition that mental disturbance alone did not qualify as a legally cognizable harm. When plaintiffs recovered for pain and suffering or other mental distress associated with physical injuries, the courts were careful to explain that these damages were "parasitic" and that the cause of action was fundamentally based on physical injury. The ancient intentional torts of assault, false imprisonment, and offensive battery, which often compensated plaintiffs for nonphysical injury, were dismissed as exceptional cases. They provided protection against only the narrowest range of harms (e.g., loss of liberty, fear of imminent physical injury) and only to the extent necessary to assure that the injured party or his relatives would not seek revenge through violent retaliation.

The recognition of tort causes of action based principally on mental distress has been a slow and uneven process. The independent tort of intentional infliction of mental distress, free from any requirement of proof of physical injury, was first incorporated into the Restatement of Torts in 1948. This "new tort," however, is not yet recognized in every state and is still approached cautiously by courts. The threshold requirements that the defendant's action must be "extreme and outrageous" and that the plaintiff's distress must be "severe" serve as significant limitations on recovery. In theory at least, the intentional infliction of the most trivial physical harm is a legal wrong. With respect to emotional harm, however, the law responds only to severe injuries and only if the wrongdoer is of the worst order and deliberately oversteps the bounds of common decency.

One consequence of the nonprivileged status of emotional harm is that tort law has never provided a solid basis for recovering for sexual harassment. Although some harassment takes the form of physical contact amounting to battery or assault, the far more common type of harassment consists of claims of hostile working environments, and involves verbal conduct and patterns of abuse that do not fall neatly into the traditional intentional tort categories. It is telling that no legal category captures the full dimensions of sexual harassment as an injury. Tort law treats it primarily as a dignitary harm under the rubric of emotional distress.

The numerous empirical studies of sexual harassment in the workplace indicate that the vast majority of harassment victims are women,[29] although there is growing recognition of the phenomenon of same-sex harassment of men by male supervisors and co-workers.[30] The law's treatment of sexual harassment is thus of special importance to women, and any lack of protection tends to have a profound disparate impact on women.

When making claims for intentional infliction of mental distress, victims of sexual harassment face an initial hurdle of proving that the defendant's behavior was "outrageous." Although some plaintiffs have overcome this obstacle, most courts still do not regard sexual harassment as per se outrageous conduct, with the result that the scope of liability under tort law is more restrictive than that provided under Title VII, the major civil rights statute prohibiting sex discrimination and sexual harassment in employment.

This disparity in coverage has substantive as well as procedural disadvantages, because the newly expanded civil rights remedies under Title VII impose a cap on compensatory and punitive damages for harassment victims.[31] This means that, unless the plaintiff can meet the more onerous requirements of proof for intentional infliction of mental distress, she may not receive full compensation for her injury. Moreover, outside the employment and educational contexts, there is generally no special statutory protection for women who are harassed on the street or who suffer from intentional sexual exploitation by professionals such as divorce lawyers and physicians.

Beyond the precedents limiting liability for intentional infliction of mental distress, the law is even more restrictive when it comes to recovery for negligent infliction of emotional distress. Most jurisdictions have retained what is known as the "physical injury" or "physical manifestations" rule, which limits recovery to plaintiffs who can prove that their emotional trauma had physical consequences. The courts regard the physical injury requirement as a validation of the genuineness of the emotional harm, and allow the presence of the higher-ranked type of harm to lessen anxieties about expanding the boundaries of tort recovery. Another limiting doctrine that has substantially curbed tort recovery is the "bystander rule"—the doctrine which once prohibited all recovery by persons who suffered trauma through witnessing the injury or death of their children, family members, or other persons. The courts still tend to impose substantial restrictions in "bystander" cases, beyond the general negligence requirement that some injury to the plaintiff be foreseeable. The majority of courts continue to deny recovery, unless the plaintiff who witnesses the injury is located in the zone of physical danger, regardless of the plaintiff's trauma or close relationship to the accident victim. Thus, at present, recovery for a mother who witnesses her child's injury or death depends on the jurisdiction in which the accident occurs and the number of feet she happens to be from the site of the accident.

The precarious status of the claim for negligent infliction of mental distress has had a disproportionately negative impact on women, the classic plaintiffs in such suits. Although emotional harm is not gender-specific, women in our society have traditionally been assigned the emotional work of maintaining human relationships, particularly within the family. Historically, women have tended to bring claims for emotional distress more often than men, and these claims have been cognitively associated with women and their interests.[32] Recently, the Texas Supreme Court abolished the claim for negligent infliction of mental distress. The only woman on the Texas Supreme Court, Justice Spector, dissented from the ruling, arguing that it would deny protection to a predominantly female class of plaintiffs "in exactly those instances where it is most needed."[33] The debate in the Texas Supreme Court was unusual because the connection between emotional harm and gender has not generally been visible. Most commentators debate only the efficiency of allowing recovery for nonphysical injuries, and even the once-famous "bystander" cases are likely to be squeezed out of the first-year course. In this respect, the law's devaluation of emotional harm mirrors the marginalization of the subject in the pedagogical canon.

## *Placing Relationships at the Margins of Tort Law*

Like emotional harms, relational injuries continue to rank at the bottom of the legal hierarchy for injuries. At different historical periods, certain relational claims have gained visibility, but there has never been widespread legal protection for this type of injury. Many of the old intentional torts which sought to protect intimate and family relationships, such as criminal conversation (i.e., the husband's suit against his wife's lover for adultery), seduction, breach of a promise to marry, and alienation of affections either have been abolished or have little impact in the law. Notably, there has been no development comparable to the emergence of the tort of intentional infliction of mental distress that provides general protection against intentional interference with important relationships.

There has been some modest growth in the recognition of negligent infliction of relational injury, but the law is still characterized by discrete, narrowly bounded causes of action. The two most important contemporary legal bases for compensation for negligent interference with relationships—wrongful death and loss of consortium—did not exist in their current form at common law. Relatives had no common law right to recover for wrongful death of a family member, which was afforded only much later by statute. Loss of consortium claims arising from nonfatal injuries were originally limited to a husband's claim for loss of his wife's services, sex, and society, and a father's claim for loss of his child's services. Both consortium claims were likened to a master's claim for deprivation of his servant's services and characterized as a material loss to the "owner." Both claims were given only to the dominant party: A wife or child suffered no legally cognizable injury when the husband or father was harmed. In fact, the one-sided nature of these claims made it difficult to characterize them as relational injuries at all, at least insofar as relational harms rest on a recognition of interdependency among persons, distinct from both individual property rights and emotional harm.

Under current negligence law, courts do routinely allow claims for wrongful death and spousal consortium on a gender-neutral basis. Nonetheless, it is still fair to say that recovery for relational injuries remains at the outer margins of the law. In most states, there is no cause of action for the loss of companionship and society of family members other than spouses, and recovery virtually never extends beyond traditional relationships. Even legal commentators rarely debate the merits of affording compensation for relational injuries to partners of same-sex or other nonmarital relationships, or for damage to lifelong friendships. In life, the existence and quality of these intimate relationships may well be essential to a person's happiness or well-being. Tort law, however, generally treats relational injuries merely as supplemental to "primary" claims for physical harm, serving principally to increase the total recovery for the family unit.

The gender impact of the low status of relational harms is most evident in the legal treatment of injuries sustained by persons who care for children. When a child suffers injury or death, people who have a special responsibility for caring for the child typically also suffer a grievous injury. Particularly after a serious nonfatal accident, the caretaker must learn to deal with the child's resulting physical disability and the enormous change in daily routine that this often causes. Such an injury is likely to change the relationship significantly, and the caretaker will often feel grief, guilt, and anxiety. For both the caretaker and the child, such an accident can be a life-altering event.

However, tort law most often treats the caretaker's losses as derivative or secondary, failing to recognize the full extent of the caretaker's relational and emotional loss. The law has been reluctant to recognize a cause of action for what is known as "filial consortium"—the loss of a child's society and companionship which the parent suffers as a result of the reverberating effects of a child's serious injury. Denying this kind of relational claim largely affects women in their roles as primary caretakers of children. In our culture, the care of children has been disproportionately assigned to women, so much so that mothers, grandmothers, other female relatives, and hired female nannies and babysitters tend to spend more time with children than their male counterparts. As their primary caretakers, women have a greater responsibility for the safety and happiness of children on a daily basis and are likely to place a very high value on the emotional and relational ties to the children under their charge.

Under current law, the child has a "primary" tort claim for the injury suffered, including an amount for medical or other rehabilitative expenses associated with her physical, mental, and relational injury. The devastating impact of the accident on the daily life of the caretaker, however, is eclipsed because there is generally no separate claim allowed for the caretaker's loss of consortium. Even in those few states that permit claims for loss of filial consortium, moreover, there may well be a further negative racial impact. This impact occurs because the law restricts such filial consortium claims to biological or adoptive parents and gives no recognition to the injury of others who take on primary caretaking roles. This limitation likely has a disproportionate impact on African Americans and other ethnic groups in which extended family members—most often grandparents—may have the primary responsibility for raising children. Even in the most liberal states, courts generally have refused to extend consortium claims beyond the nuclear family, perhaps not fully appreciating that families may be defined differently in different communities.

There is a wide gulf between the importance placed by society on maintaining and preserving human relationships and the legal valuation of relational interests. Popular culture valorizes the role of the "soccer mom" and makes much of middle-class women staying home to raise children. However, the hierarchy of torts claims does not place so high a value on the contributions of parents and other caretakers. The most painful event in a caretaker's life may not be actionable in tort.

### Privileging Economic over Noneconomic Loss

The implicit hierarchy of types of damages, which ranks pecuniary over nonpecuniary damages, is of more recent origin than the hierarchy of injuries. At first blush, this hierarchy may appear to duplicate the hierarchy of types of injuries in that both privilege tangible over nontangible harms. However, many types of injuries give rise to both pecuniary and nonpecuniary damages. Thus, for example, plaintiffs who suffer physical injury seek recovery not only for pecuniary damages consisting of medical expenses, wage loss, and loss of future earning capacity, but for nonpecuniary damages of pain and suffering and loss of enjoyment of life. A plaintiff suing for negligent infliction of mental distress is likely to have medical expenses and loss of income; a wrongful death beneficiary may recover for loss of pecuniary support and maintenance as part of the relational injury. The hierarchy of damages thus operates within categories of types of harm to give higher priority to the pecuniary or economic aspects of the damage claim.

The implicit hierarchy of damages is most evident in statutory proposals for tort reform and judicial pronouncements rejecting challenges to such measures. Beginning with the movement for workers' compensation, tort reform has most often targeted nonpecuniary damages, suggesting that these damages are somehow less essential to a fair system of compensation than damages for economic loss. To be sure, workers' compensation and automobile no-fault schemes were not designed to disfavor plaintiffs: the quid pro quo for giving up noneconomic loss was a quicker recovery for plaintiffs who were no longer saddled with the difficult task of proving negligence. Nevertheless, these insurance systems reflected a choice to curtail recovery for nonpecuniary loss, and thus implicitly set a higher priority on recovery for pecuniary loss.

The more recent waves of tort reform clearly follow the damages hierarchy. They have provided the political impetus for a variety of statutory caps on noneconomic damages, particularly in actions against health care providers. By the 1990s, some kind of cap had been extended in well over half the states, some extending to all personal injury suits.[34] Most recently, there has been support for federal legislation that would force all states to cap noneconomic losses in health care liability actions.[35]

This sharp curtailment on noneconomic damages, particularly without the quid pro quo found in earlier reforms, has prompted constitutional challenges, so far with mixed results and no clear determination of the legality of the caps. However, some important courts, including the highest courts in California[36] and New York,[37] have expressed a clear preference for economic damages over noneconomic damages. The opinions cast noneconomic damages as suspect and express the view that such recoveries rest on a "legal fiction" that money can compensate for such harms as pain and suffering and loss of enjoyment of life.

The judicial mistrust of noneconomic damages has been echoed by the torts establishment, particularly those who approach torts from a law and economics perspective. Their influence has been felt by the American Law Institute, as evidenced by a 1991 report addressing awards for pain and suffering.[38] The authors' commitment to the hierarchy of damages is most apparent in the structure they selected to examine the issue. The report deals at length with the question of whether there should be any award for pain and suffering, discussing the possible abolition of noneconomic damages quite seriously. Although the authors fall short of recommending total abolition, they include no comparable discussion of the wisdom of expanding recovery for noneconomic damages. The report contains no treatment, for example, of whether the law fails to compensate for important noneconomic losses suffered by victims of negligence or other fault. What is presented as a balanced discussion of the issues is actually quite skewed. The wisdom of the hierarchy of damages is largely presumed, with the focus on the more limited question of how far the law should cut back on its traditional rules governing noneconomic loss.

Critics of these cutbacks are now beginning to assess the negative gender impact of tort reform. An empirical study by Thomas Koenig and Michael Rustad[39] demonstrates that women stand to lose more when "nonprivileged" types of damages are curtailed, particularly noneconomic damages in actions involving health care. Their study reveals that two out of three plaintiffs receiving punitive damages in medical malpractice litigation are women, often in gender-linked cases involving mismanaged childbirth, cosmetic surgery, sexual abuse, and neglect in nursing homes. Because so much mass tort litigation has centered on women's reproductive health and other gender-linked injuries—from Dalkon Shield and Norplant birth-control methods to superabsorbent tampons and breast implants—reforms that would curb noneconomic awards for health care liability also threaten to curtail this new focus on gender-specific injuries.

The Koenig and Rustad study further shows that capping noneconomic damages for pain and suffering and loss of enjoyment of life would disproportionately affect women. This is because the noneconomic portion of the tort award is crucial to women plaintiffs. Since women tend to earn lower wages and bear greater unpaid responsibility for child care and housekeeping, as a group women plaintiffs tend to have smaller economic losses than men of the same age. Even physical injuries to women may not translate into large awards for medical expenses, particularly if there is no current treatment for the condition. Thus, when a homemaker suffers reproductive injury from being forced to undergo a hysterectomy caused by damage from an intrauterine device (IUD), the primary measure of her injuries will be noneconomic. Caps on noneconomic damages in health care actions thus would double the disadvantage for women, by restricting an important element of damages in those very cases women tend to bring.

In general, noneconomic damages are particularly significant to women because they serve to offset the disproportionately low value placed on women's claims when the measures of value are solely economic. They also serve as the only means of expressing the value of certain gender-linked injuries, such as the loss of fertility. The recent legislative and judicial trend to solidify the implicit hierarchy of damages and to privilege economic over noneconomic damages thus has the potential to further slant the torts system against women's interests.

## Perceptual Bias: The Image of the Prototypical Plaintiff

The foregoing examples relating to emotional harm, relational interests, and noneconomic loss indicate that the hierarchies of value disadvantage women. In tort law, as in many other areas of contemporary law, the mechanisms that maintain the hierarchies of value are cognitive processes that influence the thinking of even people who believe they are unbiased. The hierarchies of value not only set up a ranking of different types of injuries and types of damages; they also establish pairs of opposites or dualisms. Embedded within the hierarchies are three contrasting categories: physical/emotional, property/relational, and economic/noneconomic. These categories are themselves "gendered," meaning that if we were asked to link each type of damage or harm with the adjective "male" or "female," there would be widespread agreement that the left side of the pair (physical, property, economic) should be labeled "male," while the right side of the pair (emotional, relational, noneconomic) should be labeled "female."

At work here is a perceptual process which categorizes injury sustained by women as emotional, relational, or noneconomic, even when the same injury could, as a matter of logic, be characterized as physical, property-like, or economic. The basic point is that in deciding how to categorize a loss, we consider not only the nature of the injury, but also *who* we believe suffers the loss. The gender of the prototypical plaintiff affects the way we categorize the nature of the harm.

This perceptual process is akin to the process that occurs when people interpret ambiguous behavior. Social psychologists have conducted experiments measuring human perception, asking their subjects, for example, to describe an interaction between two people involving a poke or a shove.[40] The action is ambiguous, in the sense that it could possibly be classified as benign (dramatizes, gives information, plays around) or threatening (aggressive, violent, mean). The studies indicate that the race of the actor is important in determining how the action will be interpreted or categorized. Thus, whites tend to interpret the ambiguous behavior of black actors as being more threatening and more hostile than the same behavior undertaken by white actors. The identity of the actor affects how we perceive the nature of the action.

If the gender of the prototypical plaintiff likewise affects legal categorization, it makes sense to view legal categorization as an active process that involves human choice. By this account, the basic legal categories in tort law are not objective entities, but socially constructed. The deep structures of tort law are "man-made," allowing cognitive bias to find its way into tort law through the legal categorization process itself.

I first understood the process behind the social construction of basic tort categories, such as "emotional harm" and "pecuniary loss," when I read the opinions in *Lynch v. Knight,*[41] the old English case that established the proposition that mental disturbance alone does not qualify as a legally cognizable harm. I found Lord Campbell's opinion the most revealing. He discusses the question why men, but not women, were given the right to sue for "criminal conversation," the adultery-type claim brought by a husband against a man who had intercourse with the plaintiff's wife. Lord Campbell sincerely believed that when a wife was unfaithful to her husband, the husband suffered a loss akin to a permanent loss of property. To him, the husband's loss of exclusive sexual access to his wife was a material harm, propertylike in nature. However, when Lord Campbell analyzed the losses the wife suffered from her husband's sexual betrayal, he saw only hurt feelings and emotional harm. Harm to the wife in such a comparable situation was described as subjective, intangible, and transitory. What we would now describe as the same harm—the harm stemming from adultery—was then conceptualized in gender-specific terms, with the man's loss treated as the property loss, while the woman's loss was cast as emotional and relational.

This perceptual process is still at work in the social construction of tort categories, affecting where the line is drawn between physical and mental injuries and economic and noneconomic loss. For example, in a study of fright-based injuries, historian Linda K. Kerber and I analyzed the classic "mental distress" cases involving female plaintiffs who suffered miscarriages and stillbirths as a result of emotional trauma.[42] In a very real sense, these plaintiffs suffered physical injuries, and as many early commentators pointed out, their cases could easily have been determined by the same principles and doctrines applied to ordinary negligence litigation. Instead, their claims were categorized as "emotional harm" cases. In this one class of litigation, the law fixed on fright, the mechanism of the injury, rather than on the ultimate physical consequences of the defendant's actions. Once classified as emotional harm, moreover, the various restrictive doctrines came into play to reduce the chances of recovery. To some extent, the classification of fright-based physical harms as "mental distress" persists to this day, as the organization of basic torts casebooks and treatises attest. When faced with a choice—a choice that is always present when we construct categories—the law matched the type of injury (emotional) to the prototypical plaintiff (pregnant woman).

Lucinda Finley has also observed this perceptual process in the law's treatment of women's reproductive and sexualized injuries.[43] Finley asserts that tort law follows the medical profession's tendency to treat an injury to a woman's reproductive system or to a sexualized part of her body (e.g., breasts) as an emotional, rather than a physical, injury. As an example, she cites a case in which the court refused to allow women who were injured by the "anti-miscarriage" drug DES to recover for "purely emotional harm."[44] The court characterized the women's harm as emotional, even though many DES daughters had malformations of their cervixes and uteruses, as well as cellular changes to the vaginal and cervical lining which necessitated extensive medical monitoring. A similar dynamic takes place when the effects of physical deformities arising from breast reduction or enlargement surgeries are treated by the courts primarily as emotional injuries. Finley's research on women's reproductive and sexualized injuries reinforces a basic feature of the perceptual process, showing that the characterization of the nature of the injury is capable of being influenced by the gender of the person suffering the harm.

With respect to the line between economic and noneconomic harm, the most clear-cut example of the operation of this perceptual bias is the law's valuation of household services, a kind of work performed dispro-

portionately by women.[45] Until quite recently, the law placed no economic value on a homemaker's domestic services, a category which encompasses not only cleaning the house, but also caring for children and
other dependents. This dramatic undervaluation of "women's" work not
only has had consequences for distribution of assets upon divorce, when
homemakers tried to demonstrate their contributions to the marriage,
but also has played a significant role in tort cases for wrongful death and
personal injury.

Several of the final reports of gender bias task forces have discussed
the continued devaluation of homemaker services and the effects of such
devaluation on stay-at-home mothers, employed women, and men.
Plaintiffs' attorneys believe that juries harbor negative stereotypes about
the value of housework and impose artificial ceilings on the value of a
homemaker's life. There is even some evidence that, for comparable injuries, employed women receive higher damage awards for pain and suffering than homemakers, suggesting that negative attitudes toward this
kind of work carry over and affect other elements of damages. The devalued status of household services reduces awards for employed women
and men as well: working mothers are often awarded paltry sums for
their duties in the home, and the household tasks that men perform are
sometimes invisible. What is classified as "economic" is tied closely to the
market, disproportionately leaving women undervalued in the domestic
sphere of the home and family. In this respect, the hierarchy of damages
placing highest priority on "economic" losses is a subtle way of using
men's activities as the sole benchmark of value.

The most noteworthy feature of the many examples of structural bias in
the law of torts discussed above is that few have attained the status of
major issues or problems in the commentary or case law. The pedagogical
canon in torts in particular misses the gender and race effects of important doctrines because those doctrines themselves are located at the margins of the course of study. The lost torts governing relational interests,
like the claim of filial consortium, are rarely discussed, even though they
may be the only legal vehicles for protecting important relationships in a
person's life. The devaluation of the lives and potential of racial minorities is hidden within the law of damages and may not surface in the classroom, even as we debate the same phenomenon in the implementation of
the death penalty and other controversies in the criminal justice system.
The cognitive connection between the construction of the canons of tort

law and the investigation of gender and race bias in the body of tort law is close and mutually reinforcing. Teasing out the bias in the deep structures of tort law entails retrieving marginal torts and going beyond analysis of negligence and strict liability. Maybe it even requires a few more changes to the first-year curriculum.

### NOTES

1. Guido Calabresi's influential book is aptly titled *The Costs of Accidents* (1970).

2. 159 F.2d 169 (2d Cir. 1947).

3. *See* Cronin v. J.B.E. Olson Corp., 501 P.2d 1153 (Cal.1972).

4. *See* Custodio v. Bauer, 59 Cal. Rptr. 463 (Cal. App. 1967); Berman v. Allan, 404 A.2d 8 (N.J. 1979).

5. *See* Dillon v. Legg, 441 P.2d 912 (Cal. 1968).

6. *See* Dan B. Dobbs, Torts and Compensation 792–93 (2d ed. 1993).

7. 248 N.Y. 339 (1928).

8. 228 N.Y.164 (1920).

9. *See, e.g.,* Regina Austin, *Employer Abuse, Worker Resistance, and the Tort of Intentional Infliction of Emotional Distress*, 41 Stan. L. Rev. 1 (1988); Leslie Bender, *An Overview of Feminist Torts Scholarship*, 78 Cornell L. Rev. 575 (1993); Leslie Bender, *Teaching Torts As If Gender Matters: Intentional Torts*, 2 Va. J. Soc. Pol'y & L. 115 (1994); Thomas Koenig & Michael Rustad, *His and Her Tort Reform: Gender Injustice in Disguise*, 70 Wash .L. Rev. 1 (1995); Lucinda M. Finley, *Female Trouble: The Implications of Tort Reform for Women*, 64 Tenn. L. Rev. 847 (1997).

10. *See, e.g.,* Nancy S. Ehrenreich, *Pluralist Myths and Powerless Men: The Ideology of Reasonableness in Sexual Harassment Law*, 99 Yale L. J. 1177 (1990); Lucinda A. Finley, *A Break in the Silence: Including Women's Issues in a Torts Course*, 1 Yale J. L. & Feminism 41 (1989).

11. The old doctrines that explicitly limited recovery to one gender have either been abolished or extended on a gender-neutral basis. Thus, women as well as men may now recover for such claims as loss of spousal consortium and loss of a child's services. The disabilities that once prevented slaves, free persons of color, and married women from filing suit on their own behalf and giving testimony in court have been lifted by legislation guaranteeing access to the courts. Juries are now integrated, and even peremptory challenges may no longer be exercised on the basis of race or gender.

12. A fuller examination of these issues is contained in Martha Chamallas, *The Architecture of Bias: Deep Structures in Tort Law*, 146 U. Pa. L. Rev. 463

(1998); *Questioning the Use of Race-Specific and Gender-Specific Economic Data in Tort Litigation: A Constitutional Argument,* 63 FORDHAM L. REV. 73 (1994); *Women, Mothers and the Law of Fright: A History,* 88 MICH. L. REV. 814 (1990) (with Linda K. Kerber).

13. *See, e.g.,* Ninth Circuit Gender Bias Task Force, *The Effects of Gender in the Federal Courts* (1993), *reprinted in* 67 CAL. L. REV. 745 (1994); Judith Resnik, *Asking About Gender in Courts,* 21 SIGNS: J. WOMEN IN CULTURE & SOC'Y 952 (1996).

14. WASHINGTON STATE TASK FORCE ON GENDER AND JUSTICE IN THE COURTS, GENDER AND JUSTICE IN THE COURTS 89–90 (1989).

15. 5 JURY VERDICT RESEARCH, INC., PERSONAL INJURY VALUATION HANDBOOKS: THE AGED AS PLAINTIFFS, pts. I & II (1987), *cited in* ILLINOIS TASK FORCE ON GENDER BIAS IN THE COURTS, THE 1990 REPORT 181 n.3 (1990).

16. The 27 percent figure was calculated by totaling the 1995–96 awards and settlements recorded across twenty-eight categories of specific types of injuries (from abdominal to wrist injuries, including wrongful death).

17. WASHINGTON STATE MINORITY AND JUSTICE TASK FORCE, FINAL REPORT 123–25 (1990).

18. *See* EQUALITY IN THE COURTS TASK FORCE, STATE OF IOWA, FINAL REPORT 113–22 (1993).

19. *See* 9 PAUL M. DEUTSCH & FREDERICK A. RAFFA., DAMAGES IN TORT ACTIONS § 110.13 tbls.7b.2 & 7b.5 (1997).

20. Professor Richard Stevenson of the University of Iowa's College of Business projected lifetime earnings for a female college graduate at $1,174,772, compared with a male college graduate's projected income of $1,815,850. Interview in Iowa City, Iowa, on August 25, 1993.

21. United States Department of Labor, *Money Income of Households, Families, and Persons in the United States: 1991* in P-60 Series of the Current Population Reports (1991).

22. Only two cases in the United States have questioned the use of such data. *See* Reilly v. United States, 665 F.Supp. 976 (D.R.I. 1987), *aff'd,* 863 F.2d 149 (1st Cir. 1988) (rejecting use of gender-based tables to calculate work-life expectancy); Wheeler v. Tarpeh-Doe, 771 F.Supp. 427 (D.D.C. 1991) (rejecting use of race-based and gender-based tables to determine average income).

23. Manhart v. United States, 435 U.S. 702, 709 (1978).

24. *See, e.g.,* Califano v. Goldfarb, 430 U.S. 199 (1977); Weinberger v. Weisenfeld, 420 U.S. 636 (1975); Frontiero v. Richardson, 411 U.S. 677 (1973).

25. *See, e.g.,* Palmore v. Sidoti, 466 U.S. 702 (1978).

26. The argument for finding state action in these cases is that by allowing the admission of explicit race-based or gender-based data, the courts endorse a common law rule of damages that turns on the race or gender of the plaintiff. *Cf.* Edmonson v. Leesville Concrete Co., 500 U.S. 614 (1991) (state action found in

exercising peremptory challenge based on race); J.E.B. v. Alabama ex rel. T.B., 511 U.S. 127 (1994) (accord, gender-based peremptory challenge).

27. I put "women's injuries" in quotation marks to signal that I do not regard these injuries as somehow naturally or biologically linked to women. Instead, the disparate impact of these injuries on women stems from the particular social roles assigned to women and societal obliviousness to the gender dimensions of legal injury.

28. 11 Eng. Rep. 854 (H.L. 1861).

29. Two studies of the federal workplace found that 42 percent of women experienced some form of harassment during a two-year period. See DEBORAH L. SIEGEL, NATIONAL COUNCIL FOR RESEARCH ON WOMEN, SEXUAL HARASSMENT: RESEARCH AND RESOURCES 9 (Susan A. Hallgarth & Mary Ellen S. Capek, eds. 1991). In comparison, from 1992 to 1996, approximately 10 percent of the sexual harassment claims filed with the EEOC were filed by men. Telephone interview with EEOC headquarters (Mar. 3, 1998).

30. See amicus brief authored by Catharine MacKinnon in Oncale v. Sundowner Offshore Services, Inc., 118 S. Ct. 998 (1998) published in 8 U.C.L.A. WOMEN'S L. J. 9 (1997).

31. The Civil Rights Act of 1991 amended Title VII to permit plaintiffs alleging intentional discrimination to try their cases before a jury and to receive compensatory and punitive damages. Damages are capped, however, at $50,000 to $300,000, depending on the size of the employer. See 41 U.S.C. § 1981a (a) (1), (b), (c)(1) (1994). Prior to the 1991 act, there was no right to a jury trial and no recovery of compensatory and punitive damages.

32. See Martha Chamallas with Linda K. Kerber, Women, Mothers and the Law of Fright: A History, 88 MICH. L. REV. 814 (1990).

33. Twyman v. Twyman, 855 S.W.2d 619, 644 (Tex.1993) (Spector, J., dissenting).

34. DOBBS, supra note 6 at 792–93.

35. These cases include claims of medical malpractice as well as products liability cases involving a medical product.

36. See Fein v. Permanente Med. Group, 695 P.2d 665 (Cal.1985).

37. See McDougald v. Garber, 536 N.E.2d 372 (N.Y. 1989).

38. See 2 AMERICAN LAW INST., REPORTER'S STUDY, ENTERPRISE RESPONSIBILITY FOR PERSONAL INJURY 201–03 (1991).

39. Thomas Koenig & Michael Rustad, His and Her Tort Reform: Gender Injustice in Disguise, 70 WASH. L. REV. 64–77 (1995).

40. These experiments are discussed in Jody Armour, Stereotypes and Prejudice: Helping Decisionmakers Break the Prejudice Habit, 83 CAL. L. REV. 733, 752–54 & n.90 (1995).

41. IX H.L. Cas.576, 11 Eng. Rep. 854 (1861).

42. See Chamallas with Kerber, supra note 32.

43. *See* Lucinda M. Finley, *Female Trouble: The Implications of Tort Reform for Women*, 64 TENN. L. REV. 847, 858–67 (1997).

44. *See* Payton v. Abbott Labs, 437 N.E.2d 171 (Mass. 1982).

45. *See* Katharine Silbaugh, *Turning Labor into Love: Housework and the Law*, 91 Nw. U. L. REV. 1 (1996).

# Chapter 5

# Criminal Law

## Robert Weisberg

I write in the imperative (more modestly, in the exhortative) in answer to the question, What must one read to understand our criminal law? And since this essay will address the relationship between desert and utility, let "canon" here mean a combination of those works most deserving to be read for their merit and those most *useful* to read, even as only data (though crucial data).

Few associate Blackstone with the criminal law, but read the section of his *Commentaries* on " Public Wrongs."[1] You will be chastened: However much we believe in elemental principles, we are all probably anti-Langdellian enough to be embarrassed by the near sufficiency of Blackstone in laying out, over two centuries ago, the fundamentals of criminal jurisprudence and the elements of major crimes. Perhaps most strikingly, Blackstone quickly recognizes the main problem in generating prescriptive principles of criminal liability. He posits the various potential purposes of criminal punishment, and he recognizes that any combination of two or more of them will thwart any very systematic formula for correlating crime to punishment. And he makes no effort to finesse the problem by suggesting any easy pluralism.

> For though the end of punishment is to deter men from offending, it never can follow from thence that it is lawful to deter them at any rate and by any means; since there may be unlawful methods of enforcing obedience even to the justest laws. . . . Where the evil to be prevented is not adequate to the violence of the preventive, a sovereign that thinks seriously can never justify such a law to the dictates of conscience and humanity.[2]

Blackstone worries over punishments for inchoate crimes, where culpability exceeds harm. He rejects the *lex talionis* for most crimes, because sometimes it fails to explain the punishment—i.e., the "execution of a needy decrepit assassin" is hardly recompense for the murder of a worthy youth, and, contrarily, because sometimes the punishment should *exceed* the injury, "especially as the suffering of the innocent is past and irrevocable, [while] that of the guilty is future, contingent, and liable to be escaped or evaded."[3] Thus recognizing that rational punishment cannot escape contradiction, Blackstone proceeds to catalog elements of crimes and issues of interpretation that leave little for successors to amend.

He recognizes that no abstract notion of a "reasonable person" can capture the variety of impassioning circumstances:

> The age, education, and character of the offender: the repetition (or otherwise) of the offense; the time, the place, the company, wherein it was committed; all these, and a thousand other incidents, may aggravate or extenuate the crime.[4]

He heroically assays the problem of defining murder in abstract terms, recognizing that "malice" is both an originary concept and yet also merely a name for a collection of types of moral and mental conditions which, by common intuition, seem to merit a similar degree of punishment.[5] He recognizes that in laying out the terms of mental and moral culpability, one can establish ends of the culpability continuum at careless accidents and premeditated harm.[6] But Blackstone knows we still have to face the convergence of the key concerns about severity of punishment on a collection of acts that exhibit what we now call recklessness—that subtle midpoint on the continuum, that elusive condition of *willingness* to bear the risk of antisocial harm for antisocial purposes.[7]

You will find Blackstone asking all the key questions: How do we generate consistent rules on the basis of inconsistent premises? What manifestations of character merit moral condemnation? How do we avoid degrading character into a mere sum of acts? Why should it matter whether a criminal causes harm? Because if he has caused harm he deserves punishment, or because if he caused harm then punishing him will prevent future harm? If we do require harm, how can one volitional person cause another to exercise his volition to commit crime? And so most generally, Blackstone recognizes that criminal law cannot help but worry over a fundamental agony of liberalism: How do we reconcile the deserved with the useful?

Blackstone's questions underlie the effort to sustain the legal authority of the liberal state, a state in which the government may engage in force and violence against individuals who break or threaten a social contract so severely as to merit that higher form of sanction called punishment. In so doing, the criminal law must respect the volitional capacity of individuals. Arguably, it *can* punish only where in some sense the antisocial action is volitional. It *may* punish in that circumstance, and from the Kantian perspective, it *must* punish in that circumstance, because not to do so is to disrespect the power of individuals to break a contract, and thus to devalue our civilization- and soul-saving capacity to make and fulfill a contract. But what has that do do with more mundane social utility? And what happens when mundane social utility becomes the dominant, indeed, exalted end of punishment?

Read Bentham's *Theory of Legislation*, which is concerned that punishment may be unfair, that it may be "inefficacious," when it acts on those who cannot or will not fear criminal sanctions, and also that it is potentially "too expensive" in light of its social costs, i.e.:

> —1st. Evil of coercion. It imposes a privation more or less painful according to the degree of pleasure which the thing forbidden has the power of conferring. 2nd. The sufferings caused by the punishment, whenever it is actually carried into execution. 3rd. Evil of apprehension suffered by those who have violated the law or who fear a prosecution in consequence. 4th. Evil of false prosecutions. This inconvenience appertains to all penal laws, but particularly to laws which are obscure and to imaginary offences. . . . 5th. Derivative evil suffered by the parents or friends of those who are exposed to the rigour of the law. . . .[8]

Note that this is Blackstone retold in what is really only slightly different form—with an express analytical vocabulary of cost-benefit analysis.

But to commit to instrumental behavioral control and economic efficiency as the purposes of punishment is not necessarily to adopt a simplified view of the human nature of the criminal. Effective and efficient behavioral control requires understanding and manipulating the whole person, including the inner psyche. And so the ambitious utilitarian, even if ultimately concerned only with outward behavior, must enter the soul, and, to a critic of theory, this means that the theorist of utilitarianism must "invent" its human object.

Thus, now turn to Foucault's *Discipline and Punish*, and do not fear being ostentatiously chic, because this is one Foucault book that undeniably speaks substance and common historical sense. Foucault shows us how the Benthamite approach to crime ultimately overcame the earlier jurisprudence of violent punishment.[9] Between 1760 and 1840, says Foucault, Europe and the United States saw a "redistribution" of "the entire economy of punishment." As modern codes were drawn up across Europe, one decisive change in penal justice occurred: the end of torture as a public spectacle. Foucault reluctantly acknowledges that this change could be merely viewed as part of the process of "humanization," that it may be a mere footnote to such great reforms as

> the formulation of explicit, general codes and unified rules of procedure, with the almost universal adoption of the jury system, the definition of the essentially corrective character of the penalty and the tendency . . . to adapt punishment to the individual offender.[10]

But he finds something subtler and more important in the end of torture: "The body as the major target of penal repression disappeared," and the new object of penal policy became the soul, "the heart, the thoughts, the will, the inclinations."[11] So read Foucault's famous description of the new utilitarian prison, with its goals of incarceration and rehabilitation, and its design of a new individual:

> Bentham's Panopticon is the architectural figure of this composition.
> . . . Each individual, in his place, is securely confined to a cell from which he is seen from the front by the supervisor; but the side walls prevent him from coming into contact with his companions. He is seen, but he does not see; he is the object of information, never a subject in communication. . . . The crowd, a compact mass, a locus of multiple exchanges, individualities merging together, a collective effect, is abolished and replaced by a collection of separated individualities. From the point of view of the guardian, it is replaced by a multiplicity that can be numbered and supervised; from the point of view of the inmates, by a sequestered and observed solitude. . . .
>
> Hence the major effect of the Panopticon: to induce in the inmate a state of conscious and permanent visibility that assures the automatic functioning of power. . . .[12]

Foucault views this "panoptic modality of power" as the " other, dark side of the bourgeoisie's establishment of an explicit, coded and formally egalitarian juridical framework, made possible by the organization of a parliamentary, representative regime."[13]

> Certainly the 'crimes' and 'offences' on which judgement is passed are juridical objects defined by the code, but judgement is also passed on the

passions, instincts, anomalies, infirmities, maladjustments, effects of environment and heredity; acts of aggression are punished, so also through them, aggressivity; rape, but at the same time perversions; murders, but also drives and desires . . . the knowledge of the criminal, one's estimation of him, what is known about the relations between him, his past and his crime, and what might be expected of him in the future.[14]

With this new psychology of punishment in mind, we can return to the conventions of legal doctrine to see how the psychological subject of economical punishment emerges in a legal typology of the mental and the punitive. Examine George Fletcher's work on the history of theft offenses, as it traces the gradual shift toward greater emphasis on mental and moral culpability than on manifest act or harm.[15] As theft law developed at the turn of the nineteenth century, the actor's wrong came to have less to do with the manner of acquiring physical control over the object than with the intent of the actor as evidenced by his unauthorized exercise of control over the property. You can then link larceny law to the very changes Foucault describes: the nineteenth century's legislative codification of criminal law, the development of professional police forces, and the shift from corporal and capital punishment of crime to reliance on incarceration in penitentiaries. And look below the vocabulary to see what is after all a rather minor elision from the postmodernist notion of "the subject" to the more comfortable and merely modern notion of "the subjective."

> Under [the subjective] conception, the intent to violate a legally protected interest constitutes the core of the crime. . . . The critical implication of subjective criminality is that an act "quite innocent on its face" may qualify as a criminal act. It does not matter whether mounting the horse [picking up the cravats or receiving the bails] incriminates the actor. We trust the police to elicit other forms of evidence to establish the required intent. Confessions are good evidence, as are admissions to friends of the suspect. Prior convictions will do, as will secretive conduct after the incident. [By contrast, the older] principle of manifest criminality rejects the possibility of convicting someone of larceny. . . on the basis of an act not incriminating on its face.[16]

Most modern statutes have incorporated these developments under a unified definition of theft, focusing on the thief's intent and his exercise of dominion and control over the property. Where Foucault might speak of the pragmatic creation of a proper type of moral mentality for punitive discipline, Fletcher speaks more modestly of the versatility of new doctrines of mens rea in defining and then sanctioning culpability.

> In addition to its intuitive plausibility, the standard of intent has important political significance in generating a widely acceptable theory of criminal sanctions. Unlike the issues of harm and objective criminality, the concept of intent appeals both to protectionists, whose central concern is identifying dangerous persons, and retributivists, whose focus is punishing the blameworthy. . . . More significantly, neither retributivists nor traditionalists have seen a reason to criticize the ascendancy of intent, precisely because it seems so closely related to moral blameworthiness. As the common denominator of contemporary theory, the concept of criminal intent provides a foundation for the ideologically fragile system of criminal justice to enjoy wide support.[17]

But however versatile the new rules of mental and moral culpability, they left courts with heavy burdens of interpretation and rhetoric. To appreciate the early modern efforts to refine these culpability standards, scan the seriatim opinions in such classic and quaint British cases as *Faulkner* and *Prince*, as they descant upon the nuances of subjective criminality:

> —[I]n order to establish the charge . . . the intention of the accused forms an element in the crime to the extent that it should appear that the defendant intended to do the very act with which he is charged, or that it was the necessary consequence of some other felonious or criminal act in which he was engaged, or that having a probable result which the defendant foresaw, or ought to have foreseen, he, nevertheless, persevered in such other felonious or criminal act.[18]

> —[A]ll questions of intention and malice are closed by the finding of the jury, that the prisoner committed the act with which he was charged whilst engaged in the commission of a substantive felony. . . irrespective of all refinements as to "recklessness" and "wilfulness. . . ."[19]

> —The act forbidden is wrong in itself, if without lawful cause; I do not say illegal, but wrong. I have not lost sight of this, that though the statute probably principally aims at seduction for carnal purposes, the taking may be by a female with a good motive. Nevertheless, although there may be such cases, which are not immoral in one sense, I say that the act forbidden is wrong.[20]

> —[Mens rea] exists where the prisoner knowingly does acts which would constitute a crime if the result were as he anticipated, but in which the

result may not improbably end by bringing the offence within a more serious class of crime. . . .[21]

In their legalistic fussing over criteria of culpability, the English judges
are stuggling to define the relevant features of the modern individual.
How much ethical frailty do we allow this individual? Does she owe her
allegiance to positive law or common morals? Must she take care to heed
the signals she receives from the world of experience? To obey the legislature? Do her legal duties set the minimum or the maximum of her social
duties? It takes not a subversive rereading, but a change in vocabulary, to
view these cases as " inventing" the subjects of their jurisprudence.

Now return to Blackstone for a moment to note that the dilemma between desert and utility creates one other great mysterious problem for
the substantive criminal law—the problem of *cause*:

> And yet, generally, a design to transgress is not so flagrant an enormity as
> the actual completion of that design. For evil, the nearer we approach it, is
> the more disagreeable and shocking; so that it requires more obstinacy in
> wickedness to perpetrate an unlawful action, than barely to entertain the
> thought of it: and it is an encouragement to repentance and remorse even
> till the last stage of any crime, that it is never too late to retract; and that if
> a man stops even here, it is better for him than if he proceeds. . . .[22]

The key to that mystery, however, does not lie in the question of what it
means to cause a result. On that score, the familar vagaries of actual and
proximate cause plague the criminal law as they do tort law. Rather, the
mystery more peculiar to the matter of criminal punishment is that of
*why* cause matters at all. Hence we face the problem of distinguishing attempts from both completed crimes and from actions or mental phenomena that fall short of crime. And then we face the even subtler difficulties of determining the reach of complicity and conspiracy law.

No one text easily comprehends the problem, but no student or
scholar can fully appreciate the criminal law without spending an hour
with one of the great common law cases, *State v. Tally*,[23] which explores
the mystery with literary elegance and philosophical candor beyond anything we will find in modern jurisprudence. Here is the raw plot of this
late Victorian novel-in-an-appellate-opinion: Ross, the seducer of Tally's
sister in law, flees Scottsboro for Stevenson, with Tally's kinsmen in pursuit. Ross's kinsman sends a telegram of warning to Ross at Stevenson.
Tally sends a telegram to the telegraph operator at Stevenson, urging him
to prevent Ross from escaping. The Stevenson telegraph operator ends up

not delivering the warning to Ross, who is killed. There is really one key problem in *Tally*: As exquisitely analyzed by the court, it is impossible to determine for sure whether Tally's actions played any causal role in Ross's death.

> It is quite enough if the aid merely rendered it easier for the principal actor to accomplish the end intended by him and the aider and abettor, though in all human probability the end would have been attained without it. *If the aid in homicide can be shown to have put the deceased at a disadvantage, to have deprived him of a single chance of life which but for it he would have had,* he who furnishes such aid is guilty, though it cannot be known or shown that the dead man, in the absence thereof, would have availed himself of that chance; as, where one counsels murder, he is guilty as an accessory before the fact, though it appears probable that murder would have been done without his counsel; and as, where one being present by concert to aid if necessary is guilty as a principal in the second degree, though, had he been absent murder would have been committed, so where he who facilitates murder *even by so much as destroying a single chance of life the assailed might otherwise have had,* he thereby supplements the efforts of the perpetrator, and he is guilty as [a] principal in the second degree at common law, and is [a] principal in the first degree under our statute, notwithstanding it may be found that in all human probability the chance would not have been availed of, and death would have resulted anyway. . . .[24]

We do not know how or whether one person can cause another volitional actor to choose to act. Equally important, we do not know for sure why we care, since a system based solely on manifest culpability would indeed not care. Modern legal doctrine is then riddled with generic rationalizations, such as that of Justice Frankfurter in explaining why conspiracy to commit a crime can be a crime independent of the target crime:

> [C]ollective criminal agreement—partnership in crime—presents a greater potential threat to the public than individual delicts. Concerted action both increases the likelihood that the criminal object will be successfully attained and decreases the probability that the individuals involved will depart from their path of criminality. Group association for criminal purposes often, if not normally, makes possible the attainment of ends more complex than those which one criminal could accomplish. Nor is the danger of a conspiratorial group limited to the particular end toward which it has embarked. Combination in crime makes more likely the commission of crimes unrelated to the original purpose for which the group was formed. In sum, the danger which a conspiracy generates is

not confined to the substantive offense which is the immediate aim of the enterprise.[25]

But one might prefer the less pretentious statement in *Tally*, which quietly assumes, without bothering to argue, that the "why" question has been settled as well as human wisdom allows, and then shows exquisite moral realism in finding a workable rule for merely human judges and lawyers to follow.

In sum, the plagues of liberal criminal jurisprudence have been the difficulties that Blackstone himself delineated. The best of modern criminal scholarship implicitly demonstrates the stubborn endurance of these difficulties but recasts them in light of our new self-understanding of the economics of law: not through simplistically inapt mathematical models, but through a self-critical *social* economics that sees social meaning as part of the capital at play in legal and poltical markets. Thus, read Louis Michael Seidman's "Soldiers, Martyrs, and Criminals: Utilitarian Theory and the Problem of Crime Control."[26] Seidman shows how utilitarianism ultimately turns on itself if it serves as an instrument of the liberal state's criminal jurisprudence. Although, as Bentham would say, harsh punishments may overdeter crime by creating too much social cost, Seidman notes that the cost of *inflicting* punishment is greater than the cost of *threatening* it. And so if there is no decline in the marginal productivity of punishment, then at some point the threat of hideous punishment is costless, because it deters all crime. So long as the cost of catching is higher than the cost of punishing, a risk-preferring system makes sense— and hence a system of extreme legal harshness.[27]

Put differently, notes Seidman, if particularized cost-benefit analysis is the legal norm, the law will not deter much at all, since every individual will perform the same cost-benefit analysis as the legislature. Thus, a defendant who is aware that special circumstances are exculpatory may not weigh the cost of punishment in deciding whether to commit a crime. If so, then the only way to ensure that a criminal has weighed the value of the crime to him against social cost is to threaten to punish him regardless of any of the particular circumstances of his condition or situation. Hence we may need an acoustic separation of conduct rules and decision rules.

This is a version of the "sorting paradox"—the paradox that everyone who violates the law thereby proves he was not deterrable at that level. As laid out succinctly in a gemlike essay by H. L. A. Hart,[28] the paradox of general deterrence is that for every person who commits a crime we can identify some characteristic or factor that made him undeterrable.[29] But as Seidman notes where the cost of identifying relevant characteristics is high, and the risk of missorting is great, the only practical solution is to take the Holmesian path and acknowledge that we are necessarily sacrificing some of the undeserving along with the deserving to better serve the common good. Hence the very effort to put in a no-fault utilitarian punishment system weakens the deterrent effect of punishment; it is the "premium" of moral condemnation that makes efficiency analysis more effective, because without it efficiency analysis would be self-defeating.

Read any modern liberal treatise on substantive criminal law, and find yet another restatement of this agony of liberalism—the reconciliation of the deserved and the useful. Inevitably, read of Packer's "due process" and "crime control" models in *The Limits of the Criminal Sanction*,[30] but for a more elegantly concise version of this classic liberal agony, and for an almost Panglossian solution to it, read Henry Hart's "The Aims of the Criminal Law."[31] Hart recognizes that there can be no unifying principle of criminal punishment, but he insists that it would in fact be bad if there were a single principle. Glibly assuming that all competing values are important, he offers the pragmatic institutionalism of the legal process school, arguing that the matter of priority of principles is always a matter of solving a particular problem through a particular agency. The criminal law, for Hart, simply tells people what to do or not do. It is agnostic in defining crime, except to involve the notion of condemnation independent of severity of sanction; it is mainly—or merely—a taxonomy of rules of recognition. Hart knows that his era aspires toward rehabilitation as punishment's goal, but

> even if it were possible to gauge in advance the types of conduct to be forbidden by the expected need for reformation of those who will thereafter engage in them, would it be sensible to try to do so? Can the content of the law's commands be rationally determined with an eye singly or chiefly to the expected deficiencies of character of those who will violate them? Obviously not. The interests of society in having certain things not done or done are also involved. . . .

> Is the correlation between describable types of conduct (acts or omissions), on the one hand, and the need for cure and rehabilitation of those who engage in them, on the other hand, so close that the need can be taken as a reliable index of the types of conduct to be forbidden and the differentiation among offenses to be made? . . . The danger to the individual is that

he will be punished or treated, for what he is or is believed to be, rather than for what he has done. . . . The danger to society is that the effectiveness of the general commands of the criminal law as instruments for influencing behavior so as to avoid the necessity for enforcement proceedings will be weakened.[32]

If Packer wrote with grave solemnity and Henry Hart with sunny finessing optimism, the 1959 Tentative Draft of the ALI Commentary to the Proposed Model Penal Code[33] sets the not-quite-happy mean of serious intellectual conflict resolved in soberly clear-eyed, businesslike legal doctrine. Written on the verge of the explosion of political sentiment and intellectual ambition of 1960s political liberalism, the MPC, with its concern for highly precise specifications of acts and mental states, and its disdain for strict liability and upgrading forms of vicarious liability, is not only an effort to codify the common law of crimes and to clean up the excrescences of common-law-based criminal statutes. It is also a kind of constitutional moment, in Bruce Ackerman's sense,[34] a set of model statutes establishing certain quasi-constitutional principles that guide and restrain legislatures themselves.

As background, ponder Justice Harlan's famous dictum about the death penalty in *McGautha v. California*:

To identify before the fact those characteristics of criminal homicides and their perpetrators which call for the death penalty, and to express these characteristics in language which can be fairly understood and applied by the sentencing authority, appear to be tasks which are beyond present human ability.[35]

Also examine what is the virtual founding document of the ALI's exemplary liberal jurisprudence in homicide law—Michael's and Wechsler's famous "A Rationale of the Law of Homicide."[36] Michael and Wechsler exhibit a subtle blend of respect for, acquiescence in, or condescension toward public preferences about crime, while also tinkering with schemes of social engineering. They assume the possibility of drawing coherent moral distinctions among killers, and draw from those distinctions a sentencing plan that accommodates the competing goals of punishment—or more specifically the competing ways of preventing crime. Finally, they unembarrassedly see rehabilitation as a possible form of punishment. After laying out a fundamental taxonomy of aspects of killings and killers, they acknowledge that "it is impossible in the present state of knowledge to determine with any precision what weight should be given the various aggravating and extenuating circumstances, either absolutely or relatively."[37] And of the death penalty specifically, they pose the question thus:

> If the death penalty is commonly regarded with greater dread than even life imprisonment, as we think it usually is; if criminal homicides are disturbingly frequent; if the attempt to apply the death penalty will not lead to nullification; and if it can be applied without exciting too much public hysteria, without brutalizing the population and without destroying too many lives, then there is a strong case for employing it in the most aggravated cases for deterrent purposes, although from other points of view its use may be objectionable. . . . To the extent that imprisonment is employed for terms less than life, it is obviously desirable that severity be attained by protracting the period of imprisonment rather than by cruel or exceptionally arduous conditions of incarceration; to release men unfit for a non-criminal life, embittered and determined to exact their revenge, may produce as much crime as such harshness prevents. A prison program must be reformative in purpose even if the requirements of deterrence demand that men be detained after they could safely be released and that less be done to reform them than could be done.[38]

This confident, even self-congratulatory language reflects the reform spirit of the legal process era, yet it also sounds so absurdly anachronistic in its moral delicacy and its cautious confidence in social science that it could come from the era of Beccaria or Bentham. Again, recur to Foucault, in this case his analogous survey of the utilitarian reform movement:

> The true objective of the reform movement . . . was not so much to establish a new right to punish based on more equitable principles, as to set up a new "economy" of the power to punish, to assure its better distribution, so that it should be neither too concentrated at certain privileged points, nor too divided between opposing authorities; so that it should be distributed in homogenous circuits capable of operating everywhere, in a continuous way, down to the finest grain of the social body.[39]

So the post-MPC history of American death penalty law, through the temporary judicial nullification of capital punishment[40] and then its reinstatement,[41] test our efforts at working out this "economy of justice." Where did this experiment in the economizing of justice end? Compare the MPC plans and hopes with the reflections of Justice Powell for the Court in *McCleskey v. Kemp*,[42] an opinion of almost perversely candid intellectual honesty. Rejecting the claim that de facto discrimination in death sentencing based on the race of the victim was unconstitutional, Powell said:

> McCleskey's claim, taken to its logical conclusion, throws into serious question the principles that underlie our entire criminal justice system. The Eighth Amendment is not limited in application to capital punishment, but applies to all penalties. Thus, if we accepted McCleskey's claim that racial bias has impermissibly tainted the capital sentencing decision, we could soon be faced with similar claims as to other types of penalty. . . . Similarly, since McCleskey's claim relates to the race of his victim, other claims could apply with equally logical force to statistical disparities that correlate with the race . . . of other actors in the criminal justice system, such as defense attorneys, or judges.[43]

Justice Powell implicitly warns us that we cannot accept the logical conclusions of our own principles, for to coherently cure capital punishment of the taint of racist attitudes would be to undo the whole criminal justice system.

And so for moral and political clarification, read the candid response to *McCleskey* of Randall Kennedy, whose searing article on the case admonishes us to see how desert and utility bear a hopelessly vexing relation.[44] Kennedy shows that the victim-race discrimination issue presents an impossible conflict for blacks: To give black victims "equal protection" from heinous murder with whites, the state must execute the killers of blacks as often as it executes the killers of whites—and thereby must execute more blacks. Kennedy then tests the limits of social engineering aimed at reconciling desert and utility by hypothesizing any solution to victim-race discrimination as a form of affirmative action. He notes that in employment discrimination cases, the courts have permitted the advantaging of minorities in hiring but have drawn the line at layoffs, on the premise that in the latter case the "social tax" of affirmative action is too high and too focused on disadvantaging particular whites. Kennedy then wryly recasts the capital punishment issue in parallel terms.[45] He recognizes that "levelling downwards"—essentially abolition of capital punishment—would usefully signal the principle that the death penalty cannot be administered at all unless administered equally. But he also unsentimentally recognizes the death penalty as a "highly valued public good," so that abolition would be viewed as an across-the-board "reduction in services."[46] He offers no simple remedy, but rather a challenge to the Court to find some solution better than the worst one, the one they chose: i.e., to act as if no constitutional problem even exists.

Now consider what social science and social theory tell us about these efforts to design a fair and efficient criminal jurisprudence. Indeed, consider the even larger criminological questions of the sort traditionally asked by Marxists. Marx and Engels themselves had little to say about penal policy, and many of their progeny have shown more than the average tendency toward reductionism. Marxists generally regard criminology itself as a "problematic" discipline; they cannot in good faith collude in searching for the cures of crime according to the tenets of modern positivism. But there are several basic premises of Marxist criminology which, though all arguable and susceptible to reductionism, enable students of criminal law to at least open, if not answer, the more global questions that American liberalism and positivism rarely ask. To the Marxist punishments are historically specific phenomena which appear in concrete social forms; punishment forms are reflections of the means of production, reflect class interests, are intricately related to other social institutions, but also take on some "relative autonomy" as cultural forces; the operations of these forces both reflect and are disguised and distorted by ideology.[47]

But simply read Franklin Zimring and Gordon Hawkins's magisterial *The Scale of Imprisonment*[48] to realize that one need not take on orthodox Marxism to think dialectically about criminal justice. The elegantly simple and profound premise of their book is that a society's rate of imprisonment may depend on factors having little to do with its rate of crime. Indeed, they show, empirical studies cannot convincingly correlate rates of imprisonment to the rate of crime (in part because crime is still so rarely punished by imprisonment, in part because so much crime is committed by juveniles); to public opinion or political pressure (which make largely symbolic demands, and whose calls for punishment get dissipated in the complex bureaucracies of financial and prosecutorial power); to the percentage of young males in the population (which varies far less than rates of imprisonment); to economic conditions (the deadest horse in criminology if viewed in terms of general indicators like national unemployment); or to the rate of drug use (which cannot really be measured, but in any event largely affects short-terms stays in local jails).[49]

If the criminal law is an engine designed to send the appropriate people to prison, there is a bewildering variety of forces that control its throttle. Questions of prosecutorial and judicial discretion and financial resources may, of course, help determine the size of our incarceration product, but Zimring and Hawkins's survey of historical theories and current empirical research leaves one amazed at how little we know of the breadth and complexity of these forces. In the 1930, the Marxists Rusche and Kirchheimer[50] postulated that the rate of imprisonment depends on a society's stage of industrial development and surplus or deficit of labor. Though their studies now seem theoretically quaint and empirically questionable, they were clearly right that penal systems are not isolated phenomena subject to their own special laws but are embedded in wider social forces. Modern empiricists[51] have challenged the old Marxists with a Durkheimian theory that the rate of imprisonment in a society is in fact relatively constant, since societies essentially find the level of imprisonment they need to ensure social solidarity. That theory, too, has been subject to vigorous empirical challenge, but its implicit theoretical premise is as remarkable as that of Rusche and Kirchheimer. Yet again, to study crime is to study our own paradoxes. Zimring and Hawkins's work illustrates how the criminal justice system is the textbook example of externalities, where virtually the only agents in government or society who have no effect on the imprisonment rate are the people who pay for or the people who run the prisons.

Now turn more in the direction of the modern humanities for another perspective on how we attempt to control—and therefore how we attempt to define—"crime." Postmodern observers of this agony of liberalism will suggest that we "construct" the crime we seek to punish. Clichés of social constructionism aside, moral philosophy and related art help us understand how we shape the objects of our fears. Who is the criminal we fear? As noted earlier, even in the quaint legal technology of turn-of-the-century English mens rea cases, liberalism has made a "homo juridicus"—an amalgam of partial or assumed free will and partial or assumed determined behavioral responses—that can be captured by our culpability codes. But we suffer a disconnection between the social phenomena of crime and their representation in philosophies of punishment. Kant's ideal of rational individualism clashes with a shadowy world full of incentives to criminality, yet the Kantian model survived in legal codes whose formal boundaries of character, act, and will are regularly violated by the motley crew of killers and thieves who plague our system.

Our Willie Hortons, black or white, homicidal or merely thieving, are characters who manifest a pathological indifference to the fears and desires of normal people. What they are pathologically indifferent to may vary, at least if we worry about formal doctrinal categories. Sometimes they are pathologically indifferent to facts, such as the likely physical consequences of their pleasure-seeking actions; sometimes these facts are the "facts" of another person's volition, as in some rape cases; sometimes they are pathologically indifferent to legal rules, such as those determining the boundaries of property; and sometimes their indifference is harder to capture in doctrine, because it is neither about facts nor law per se, but about whether social norms, legal or otherwise, or the needs of other human beings, are worth attending to at all. In the abstract, the Model Penal Code stresses the key mens rea of recklessness, an intriguing formulation of a state of mind of pathological indifference to norms that in older state laws carries with it the more colorfully connotative vocabularies of "extreme indifference" and "malice." Nothing in the history or construction of the code has recognized the teasing but unexamined fit between this key doctrinal component of its mental-state structure and the social psychology of pathology. Yet when courts have had to confront some of the more socially and politically charged issues of mental culpability in new criminal contexts, it has been precisely the amorphousness of the concept of reckless indifference, as lying between purpose and negligence, that has tested their ability to create sound doctrine.

For two powerfully imaginative renderings of this problem, read the work of Peter Arenella and Jack Katz. To rethink the problem of pathology, we must recognize our ambivalence over holding a person responsible for his apparent inability—or is it his unwillingness?—to exhibit appropriate moral empathy. Can one be held responsible for his moral values, unless we locate the point at which he formed those moral values or had the chance to reform them? This is exactly what the criminal law (somewhat unconsciously) does; we rely on what Arenella calls a theory of "fair attribution," which is essentially a rhetorical rationalization for avoiding the very question he poses.[52] What Arenella calls our "thin" theory of rationality permits liberalism to adopt a "soft" determinist view of behavior that protects the issue of moral agency from scrutiny.

Shift from Arenella and reflective moral philosophy to Jack Katz and dramatic demonstration in an empirical and yet literary form. In his great work *Seductions of Crime*, the "text" for Katz is the inner and outer behavior of the criminal, as recorded in Katz's interviews and observations, and as captured, and misrecognized and reconstructed, by legal categories.[53] Katz reviews a wide variety of criminal artists-in-the-self-making: the "righteous slaughterer" who kills out of moral justification even where no law recognizes the defense; the petty shoplifter who acts out a sensual fantasy of "sneaky thrills"; the "senseless killer"; the "badass" young man who is "tough, not easily influenced, highly impressionable, or anxious about the opinions that others hold of him . . . not morally malleable." Katz's criminals are perverse moral artists, and perverse utilitarians. They perpetually compose alien aspects of their selves and script conduct hostile to civilization. It would be superficial to view their violence as gratuitous. Rather, it backs up their meaning without any utilitarian analysis, since their public selves are not to be adjusted to contingent social expectations. They alone understand—and overtly manipulate—the difference between rationality and irrationality, and let the world know that they are not obligated to make this meaning intelligible to others by clarifying the distinction.

In Katz's chapter "Doing Stick-Up," the most "professional" robbers create elaborate symbols that attest to rational utilitarian justifications for their professionalism, yet the overall shape of their lives is self-destructively irrational. Katz's robbers fulfill some existential need by creating situations that limit their utilitarian control, and within those artificial boundaries they appear to meet high standards of rationality. In short, they script dramas full of exogenous limits on their action in order to demonstrate or test their ability to sustain personal integrity in the face of an (artificially) recalcitrant universe.[54] Robbery for them is therefore often really aesthetic recreational violence; indeed this process entails dissipation of the proceeds of the crime. And in this aesthetic sense, the causes of crime are composed by the offenders themselves—as lures and pressures they experience as exogenous. Chaos is produced so it can be transcendentally controlled. Being "bad" is fundamentally not a matter of acting criminally or immorally, or even acting with physical aggression, but something that is more precisely defined with a morally charged, spatial metaphor: charting out a big space in public interactions and claiming to be able to fill it.

What of Katz's killers? They often act with the fatalistic sense that their actions are demanded and foretold and destined, and the fact that they do ultimately kill only proves that the killings are ordered by law. Thus, if one sees the infamous subway vigilante Bernhard Goetz[55] as wounding senselessly because he shot the last boy as the latter lay utterly helpless and harmless, then Goetz's defense is that this was only an "apparently senseless" shooting—not that it was practically necessary to save his own life, but that it was in defense of a higher moral order he wanted to restore to the subways. Many spousal killings, Katz shows, occur over disputes concerning the proper handling of domestic business, such as a dispute over the proper priority (by legal or moral standards) among a couple's financial obligations—that is, over the principle of how one affirms to the world that one is a debtor of integrity. Many killings occur over slight insults, such as disputes over parking places or proper respect or civility in a bar or over a pool table,[56] but it is important, Katz argues, to see that such trivial matters are viewed psychologically not only as assertions of legitimate property rights, but as affirmations of the general principle of property ownership and civil order. Ironically, though this form of killing is greater among the poorer classes, it might be seen as a defense of bourgeois values—marital order, property rights, responsible debt.[57]

Finally, turn from the substantive law of crime to criminal procedure. This is a legal world of social "interest-balancing"—with the "desert" side of the desert-utility pair focused on deontological rights deemed of constitutional stature. Start, for inspiration, with one of the great old cases, cited now as ancient historical background but almost never read anymore, to realize that constitutional law brought moral grandeur to criminal justice when the system was honestly brutal, not hypocritically liberal. Recur to the era when the Supreme Court had to declare that police could not beat and whip a poor defendant into confessing a crime when there was little or no other evidence that he had committed it. Thus, from *Brown v. Mississippi*:[58]

> The State may abolish trial by jury. It may dispense with indictment by a grand jury and substitute complaint or information. . . . But the freedom of the State in establishing its policy is the freedom of constitutional government and is limited by the requirement of due process of law. Because a state may dispense with a jury trial, it does not follow that it may substitute trial by ordeal. The rack and the torture chamber may not be substituted for the witness stand. The State may not permit an accused to be hurried to conviction under mob domination—where the whole proceeding is nothing but a mask—without supplying corrective process. . . .

Decades later criminal procedure became a duller matter of the fine-tuning of utilitarian rules of restraints on police, backgrounded by a vague sense of deontological rights encoded in the Bill of Rights. We speak of the "Warren Court revolution" and the "Burger-Rehnquist Court counterrevolution." Certainly, the student must read *Mapp v. Ohio*,[59] *Miranda v. Arizona,*[60] *Gideon v. Wainwright.*[61] But do not read this brief historical episode too melodramatically: Perhaps the most important Warren Court decision is the murky, politically and intellectually ambivalent one in *Terry v. Ohio.* There, Chief Justice Warren himself sided with the police in declaring the "stop-and-frisk" permissible under the Fourth Amendment, even in the absence of true probable cause to believe a crime had occurred. Remarkably, Warren worried over the futility of utility, over whether a system built around enforcing rights through rules of exclusion could carry out its own norms.

> Street encounters between citizens and police officers are incredibly rich in diversity. They range from wholly friendly exchanges of pleasantries or mutually useful information to hostile confrontations of armed men involving arrests, or injuries, or loss of life. . . . Some of them begin in a friendly enough manner, only to take a different turn upon the injection of some unexpected element into the conversation. Encounters are initiated by the police for a wide variety of purposes, some of which are wholly unrelated to a desire to prosecute crime. . . . Doubtless some police "field interrogation" conduct violates the Fourth Amendment. But a stern refusal by this Court to condone such activity does not necessarily render it responsive to the exclusionary rule. . . . Proper adjudication of cases in which the exclusionary rule is invoked demands a constant awareness of these limitations. The wholesale harassment by certain elements of the police community, of which minority groups . . . complain, will not be stopped by the exclusion of any evidence from any criminal trial. Yet a rigid and unthinking application of the exclusionary rule, in futile protest against police practices which it can never be used to control, may exact a high toll in human injury and frustration of efforts to prevent crime. No judicial opinion can comprehend the protean variety of the street encounter.[62]

The drama of criminal procedure is now subtler, but it remains the perennial cultural macrodrama captured by Thurman Arnold in his aptly titled book *The Symbols of Government.* His dramaturgic image of law finds more than a resolution of guilt or innocence of the conventional sort. The criminal trial is as much a social ritual as a legal instrument, valuable in part because it can affirm our many values at once.

> For most persons, the criminal trial overshadows all other ceremonies as a dramatization of our spiritual government, representing the dignity of the State as an enforcer of law, and at the same time the dignity of the individual when he is an avowed opponent of the State, a dissenter, a radical, or even a criminal. So important is the criminal trial to the whole ideological

structure of government that its disappearance in favor of an efficient and speedy way of accomplishing the incarceration of persons supposed to be dangerous to the social order, is always a sign of psychological instability of a people.[63]

If viewed functionally, Arnold argues, the criminal trial is inherently a failure. The rules of evidence are a woefully inefficient tool of investigation; the definitions of criminal responsibility rarely accord with sensible psychology; the criminal sentence often fails to serve any social purpose, and so on. But all this may be irrelevant since

> the only function which the criminal trial can perform is to express currently held ideals about crime and about trials. It can act as a brake against a popular hysteria, which insists upon following any one of the ideals to its logical conclusion. . . . Obviously, therefore, the public administration of criminal justice is not a method of controlling crime. It is rather one of the problems which must be faced by those who desire to control crime. Without the drama of the criminal trial, it is difficult to imagine on just what institution we would hang our conflicting ideals about public morality.[64]

A word about *Miranda* law itself. Despite right-wing symbolic protestations, it has been pretty fully absorbed into police "culture." The empirical studies suggest it may not have unduly restricted law enforcement.[65] Despite occasional conservative attacks and the lingering concern about "judge-made" rules, it faces little threat of overruling, and the case law has largely involved tinkering and even some mild expansion. The fruitful line of inquiry, both descriptive and normative, is to examine how *Miranda* addresses the problem of human autonomy in relation the state. That, after all, is what is supposed to make criminal law more important than any other kind of law if we remain, as we seem to be remaining, within a liberal culture.

How can one rationally choose a self-harming act?[66] Criminal law generally assumes free volition, but "intersubjectivity" renders compulsion meaningless because no will is truly free of other wills. Little of the criminal procedure scholarship has appreciated the odd practical result of the inherent paradoxes of self-incrimination, and certainly no academic writing has captured it as well as the journalistic account in David Simon's book *Homicide*, a Damon Runyonesque slice of the life of Baltimore detectives and their prey.[67] A detective gives a murder suspect the warnings, and then:

The detective assures you that he has informed you of these rights because he wants you to be protected, because there is nothing that concerns him more than giving you every possible assistance in life. If you don't want to talk, he tells you, that's fine. And if you want a lawyer, that's fine too, because first of all, he's no relation to the guy you cut up, and second, he's gonna get six hours overtime no matter what you do. But he wants you to know—and he's been doing this a lot longer than you, so take his word for it—that your rights to remain silent and obtain qualified counsel aren't all they're cracked up to be.

. . . Once you up and call for that lawyer, son, we can't do a damn thing for you. No sir, your friends in the city homicide unit are going to have to leave you locked in this room all alone and the next authority figure to scan your case will be a tie-wearing, three-piece bloodsucker—a no-nonsense prosecutor from the Violent Crime unit with the official title of assistant state's attorney for the city of Baltimore. And God help you then, son. . . .

What the hell is wrong with you, son? . . . I got three witnesses in three other rooms who say you're my man. I got a knife from the scene that's going down to the lab for prints. I got blood spatter on the Air Jordans we took off you ten minutes ago. . . .

. . . Look, punk, I'm giving you a chance. He came at you, right? You were scared. It was self-defense.

Your mouth opens to speak.

He came at you, didn't he?

"Yeah," you venture cautiously, "he came at me."

Whoa, says the detective, holding up his hands. Wait a minute, If we're gonna do this, I gotta find your rights form. Where's the fuckin form? Damn things like cops, never around when you need 'em.[68]

Simon's cops suggest that the state cannot afford to give defendants the rights it purports to guarantee them, a view which is confirmed by express statement in John Langbein's pitiless rendering of our rights-based criminal procedure reforms. Why, asks Langbein, has the rights revolution become largely a background or shadow world of legal rules behind the daily grind of plea bargaining? With wry nostalgia for the old medieval systems of proof, Langbein argues that most modern reforms are futile efforts to mitigate the consequences of having handed the adjudication of guilt to juries and then having come to worry over how to constrain what the jury hears and does.

The Anglo-American trial system has been caught up over the last two centuries in an effort to protect the accused against the dangers of the jury system, in which laymen ignorant of the law return a one- or two-word verdict that they did not explain or justify. Each system found itself unable to recant directly the unrealistic level of safeguard to which it had committed itself, and each then concentrated on inducing the accused to tender a confession that would waive his rights to the safeguards.

The European law of torture preserved the medieval law of proof undisturbed for those cases in which there were two eyewitnesses or voluntary confession. But in the more difficult cases (where, I might add, safeguard was more important), the law of torture worked an absolutely fundamental change within the system of proof; it largely eliminated the adjudicative function. Once probable cause had been determined, the accused was made to concede his guilt rather than his accusers to prove it.

In twentieth-century America we have duplicated the central experience of medieval European criminal procedure; we have moved from an adjudicatory to a concessionary system. We coerce the accused against whom we find probable cause to confess his guilt. To be sure, our means are much politer; we use no rack, no thumbscrew, no Spanish boots to mash legs. But like the Europeans of distant centuries who did employ these machines, we make it terribly costly for an accused to claim his right to the constitutional safeguard of trial. . . . The sentencing differential is what makes plea bargaining coercive. Like the Medieval Europeans, the Americans are now operating a procedural system that engages in condemnation without adjudication.[69]

An ironic complement to Langbein comes in one final canonical work, perhaps the most lauded modern essay on the history of criminal law: Douglas Hay's "Property, Authority and the Criminal Law."[70] How is it, Hay asks, that in Renaissance England capital statutes multiplied, yet few were executed and many were pardoned? Hay's piece is about criminal law demonstrating the state in a condition of conspiracy and dramaturgy. Its goal, he says, was not to *maximize* punishment, but to *epitomize* it. Thus the Crown and Parliament were concerned not just with financial cost-effectiveness but with moral cost-effectiveness, fearing that too brutal a law would lose its moral force. So the government, or the rich people whose property the brutal criminal law was designed to protect, would episodically and mysteriously pardon or acquit the guilty, to create miracle, mystery, and authority. "The criminal law was critically important in maintaining bonds of obedience and deterrence, in legitimizing the status quo, in constantly recreating the structure of authority which arose from property and in turn protected its interests."[71] And, argues Hay, the advent of strict procedural rules was the key step in reform and legitimation. Code-pleading technicalities were invoked selectively to defeat prosecutions, and rich forgers were chosen selectively to be hanged.

> Here was the peculiar genius if the law. It allowed the rulers of England to make the courts a selective instrument of class justice, yet simultaneously to proclaim the law's incorruptible impartiality, and absolute determinacy. ... Its majesty, justice and mercy helped to create the spirit of consent and submission, the "mindforged manacles," which Blake saw binding the English poor.[72]

Langbein sees the liberal jurisprudence of rights lapsing helplessly into irrelevance because of its impossible costs in thwarting necessary punishment. Hay sees this jurisprudence as a brilliant conspiracy to both disguise and render more efficient the raw dictatorial utility that underlies punishment. All they agree on is the most important theme in the canon of criminal law—that a jurisprudence aimed at enhancing both desert and utility can make certain adjustments but can hardly achieve resolution.

### NOTES

1. WILLIAM BLACKSTONE, 4 COMMENTARIES ON THE LAWS OF ENGLAND (George Sharswood ed. 1908).

2. *Id.* at 8.

3. *Id.* at 12.

4. *Id.* at 14.

5. *Id.* at 193–95. 198.

6. *Id.* at 26.

7. *Id.* at 198.

8. JEREMY BENTHAM, THE THEORY OF LEGISLATION 322–24, 338 (1950).

9. MICHEL FOUCAULT, DISCIPLINE AND PUNISH: THE BIRTH OF THE PRISON (1977).

10. *Id.,* at 7–8.

11. *Id.* at 8.

12. *Id.* at 8, 16; see id at 3, 6–8, 16, 29–30, 200–06, 217, 221.

13. *Id.* at 200–01.

14. *Id.* at 221–22.

15. *Id.* at 17–18.

16. George Fletcher, *The Metamorphosis of Larceny*, 89 HARV. L. REV. 469 (1976).

17. George Fletcher, *Manifest Criminality, Criminal Intent, and the Metamorphosis of Lloyd Weinreb*, 90 YALE L.J. 119, 338 (1976).

18. Regina v. Faulkner, 13 Cox's Cases Res. 550 (1877) (Fitzgerald, J.).

19. *Id.* (Keogh, J.)

20. Regina v. Prince, L.R. 2, Crown Cases. Res. 154 (1875) (Bramwell, B.).

21. *Id.* (Brett, J.).

22. BLACKSTONE, *supra* note 1, at 12.

23. 102 Ala. 25, 15 So. 722 (1894).

24. *Id.* at 102 Ala. 69–70, 15 So. 738–39 (emphasis added).

25. United States v. Callanan, 364 U.S. 587 (1939).

26. 94 YALE L. J. 315 (1984).

27. *Id.* at 323.

28. H. L. A. HART, PUNISHMENT AND RESPONSIBILITY 18–20 (1968).

29. *Id.* at 329–30.

30. HERBERT PACKER, THE LIMITS OF THE CRIMINAL SANCTION 149–73 (1968).

31. Henry Hart, *The Aims of the Criminal Law*, 23 LAW & CONTEMP. PROB. 401 (1958).

32. *Id.* at 407 & n.17.

33. American Law Institute, Model Penal Code and Commentaries (Tentative Draft No. 9, 1959).

34. BRUCE ACKERMAN, RECONSTRUCTING AMERICAN LAW (1984).

35. 402 U.S. 183, 204 (1971).

36. Jerome Michael & Herbert Wechsler, *A Rationale of the Law of Homicide*, 37 COLUM. L. REV. 701 (Part I), 1281 (Part II) (1937).

37. *Id.*

38. *Id.* at 1306–07

39. FOUCAULT, *supra* note 9, at 80–81.

40. Furman v. Georgia, 408 U.S. 238 (1972).

41. Gregg v. Georgia, 428 U.S. 153 (1976).

42. 481 U.S. 279 (1987).

43. *Id.* at 314–17.

44. Randall Kennedy, *McCleskey v. Kemp: Race, Capital Punishment, and the Supreme Court*, 101 HARV. L. REV. 1388 (1988).

45. *Id.* at 1437–39.

46. *Id.* at 1439–40.

47. DAVID GARLAND, PUNISHMENT AND MODERN SOCIETY 90–92 (1990) (discussing GEORG RUSCHE, PUNISHMENT AND SOCIAL STRUCTURE (1939).

48. FRANK ZIMRING & GORDON HAWKINS, THE SCALE OF IMPRISONMENT (1991).

49. *Id.* at 167–75. One difficulty is that the measures are so imprecise that even, for example, the most sophisticated efforts at cost-benefit analysis produce hilarious results like mathematical conclusions than an extra expenditure of $6

billion per year will eliminate crime in America. *Id.* at 92–94, citing E. Zedlewski, *Making Confinement Decisions, in* NATIONAL INSTITUTE OF JUSTICE, RESEARCH IN BRIEF (1987).

50. G. RUSCHE & O. KIRCHHEIMER, PUNISHMENT AND SOCIAL STRUCTURE (1939).

51. *E.g.,* Alfred Blumstein & Jacqueline Cohen, *A Theory of the Stability of Punishment,* 64 J. CRIM. L. & CRIMINOLOGY 198 (1973); see FRANKLIN ZIMRING & GORDON HAWKINS, *supra* note 48, at 14–29.

52. Peter Arenella, *Character, Choice and Moral Agency: The Relevance of Character to our Moral Culpability Judgments,* 7 SOC. PHILOSOPHY & POL'Y 59 (1990).

53. JACK KATZ, SEDUCTIONS OF CRIME (1989).

54. *Id.* at 164–93.

55. *See* People v. Goetz, 68 N.Y.2d 96, 497 N.E.2d 41 (1986).

56. Significantly, the modal time for these killings is during the casual hours of Saturday night or Sunday morning, when the expected release from the workaday humiliations of job and schedule produce a sense of entitlement to peace and respect, an entitlement so viscerally assumed that its violation produces violent rage. KATZ, *supra* note 53, at 21–22, 46.

57. *Id.* at 17–18, 45.

58. 297 U.S. 278 (1936).

59. 367 U.S. 643 (1961).

60. 384 U.S. 436 (1966).

61. 372 U.S. 335 (1963).

62. 392 U.S. 1, 13–14 (1967).

63. THURMAN ARNOLD, THE SYMBOLS OF GOVERNMENT 130 (1935).

64. *Id.* at 147–48.

65. *See* YALE KAMISAR, WAYNE LAFAVE & JERROLD ISRAEL, MODERN CRIMINAL PROCEDURE 542–43 (1990) (summarizing sources); *but see* Paul Cassell, *Miranda's Social Costs: An Empirical Reassessment,* 90 Nw. U.L. REV. 387 (1996).

66. George Thomas & Thomas Bilder, *Aristotle's Paradox and the Self-Incrimination Puzzle,* 82 J. CRIM. L. & CRIMINOLOGY 243 (1991).

67. DAVID SIMON, HOMICIDE: A YEAR ON THE KILLING STREETS (1991).

68. *Id.* at 194–96.

69. John Langbein, *Torture and Plea Bargaining,* 46 U. CHI. L. REV. 3, 12–13 (1978).

70. Douglas Hay, *Property, Authority, and the Criminal Law,* in ALBION'S FATAL TREE (Douglas Hay, Peter Linebaugh, John G. Rule, E. P. Thompson & Cal Winslow eds., 1975). The irony is that Langbein has written a vitriolic critique of Hay, claiming that Hay's notion of legitimation is completely circular. *See* Langbein, *Albion's Fatal Flaw,* 98 PAST AND PRESENT 96 (1983).

71. Hay, *supra* note 70, at 25.

72. *Id.* at 48–49.

# Chapter 6

# Teaching American Civil Procedure since 1779

## Paul D. Carrington

### The Demand for Civil Procedure: Competence

If there is a traditional law school curriculum, it has no author. In its structure, it expresses no coherent premise. In its details, it is the result of myriad responses of teachers to their students. While students are seldom aware of the power they exercise, they hold their teachers in the same thralldom that other audiences impose on artists performing before them. Moral cowardice tends to be the standard of such industries. For this reason if no other, the curriculum, like other legal institutions, is the product of experience, not logic.

This is not to say that individual teachers have no power to decide what to teach. We teachers have power over our classroom agendas and are to some degree free to choose what sort of contracts or civil procedure course to present to our students. But we have considerably less freedom than teachers of literature, for the reason that there is but one law applicable to the deeds and misdeeds of our fellow citizens, and it is not made, selected, or necessarily approved by us, and our students know that.[1] Our students come to see Shakespeare, and it won't do to perform Ibsen however much better Ibsen may or may not be. In this important respect, there is no canon in the law curriculum comparable to the high fashion in literature courses that has been the object of recent concern and debate.

To the extent that there is an American legal canon, Civil Procedure has not always been a part of it. The subject was irregularly taught in university law departments before the twentieth century. Perhaps the reason was the one in the mind of Albert Venn Dicey when he affirmed that "English law must be learned and cannot be taught, and that the only places where it can be learned are the law courts and chambers."[2] English civil procedure was not amenable to intellectual discourse. In any case, it seems that nineteenth-century students studying law in universities did not necessarily expect instruction in civil procedure.

But then it was not until the latter part of that century that Americans in number began to enroll in university law schools for the purpose of acquiring salable competence. Students now expect to acquire competence, i.e., professional status associated with information that can be sold in exchange for a suitable income. If this were not otherwise the case, the high price of today's legal education requires that it be so. We teachers deny students satisfaction of that appetite at the peril of rejection, potentially acute rejection, which no performing artist will withstand for long. It is that demand that dictates the teaching of civil procedure as a basic course, and no teacher of the subject will long resist it. The demand is, however, easily satisfied by teachers of civil procedure because students uninformed about the mechanisms of civil justice are unlikely to be able to employ usefully any information they might assimilate about other legal texts and traditions of private law or public.

Yet few who devote their careers to law teaching are pleased to think of themselves as mere fillers of passive vessels or as trainers of Hessians. In the first place, we know (if we are realistic) that teachers are largely dispensable in the acquisition of the information our students seek. For that purpose, for the most part, students could as well go straight to Gilbert's Outline or any of its competitors and bypass their teachers. CALI and others now provide excellent means of autoinstruction. Moreover, if legal education were purely human capitalism, most of us who provide it would as soon do something else, such as maximize our own wealth rather than that of our students.

## The Suppliers: Civil Procedure and Truth

As members of the academic profession, we are prone to align ourselves with a different pursuit than the pursuit of Competence. The academic profession's preference is the search for Truth. Fortunately, Truth is at least sometimes useful. Our students generally bring to law study a profound misconception of the nature of law. It is their original sin to suppose that one who assimilates a sufficient number of legal rules or principles is thereby made a lawyer. They start with the ignorant assumption that rules of court bind judges to a ceremony that leads to the correct application of law to discerned reality. While a knowledge of court rules and statutes such as a commercial outline can provide is not as useless as some sophisticates might have it, it is chiefly wisdom and judgment, or prudence as Anthony Kronman would have it,[3] not often information, that makes a lawyer competent to render service valuable to paying clients. Effectively to endow students with that insight and to elevate their professional judgment are, in a sense, to lead them on a pursuit of Truth.

Even this joint service to Truth and Competence is not always welcomed by those to whom it is provided. We now live and work in an age of consumerism, driven in part by high tuitions. Unfortunately, because law students seldom bring to their enterprise a sound opinion about what it is they need to learn, teachers are at risk of disserving their students by giving them what they think they want. This problem may be especially acute for teachers of civil procedure because of the high level of indeterminacy in much adjective law. Teaching civil procedure therefore sometimes requires us to gauge just how much truth our students are willing to stand.

On the other hand, there is also a finite limit to the amount of Truth there is available to share with law students. Most of the great truths about law were fully revealed by the time of Justinian. Moreover, the system of civil procedure we teach rests on the assumptions of the Enlightenment. Our premises are that it is possible to discern reality about past events and to apply legal texts to resolve disputes arising out of those events. It is not useful to students to re-examine those premises, or seriously to contemplate a different system resting on different premises.

For these reasons, if there were a Nobel Prize in law, it would be a great challenge to identify a credible nominee. In that respect, much law resembles gross anatomy, a subject that must be mastered by novice medical doctors, but must be taught by teachers with no greater chance of discovering a new truth in their field than a modern explorer would have of discovering a new continent on the planet Earth. While Holmes called upon us to employ "the lightning of our genius,"[4] Thomas Cooley, a man with his feet more firmly on the ground, cautioned those of Holmesian genius that law is a commonplace and of little value or effect if it does not express "the common thoughts of men."[5] At least with respect to civil procedure, Cooley was plainly right and Holmes wrong.

Ours is a humdrum discipline not easily adapted to the role of genius engaged in a soaring search for Truth.

And even those striving to discern and reveal smaller truths about civil justice are imprisoned by the reality that the only law we have is made by persons holding appropriate commissions, persons who must themselves negotiate and compromise their utterances. What matters in reality (as our students know at the outset) is what those persons do and say, and a curriculum taking leave of the texts to which they pay homage is disseminating neither Competence nor Truth. There being only one body of adjective law applicable to the resolution of civil disputes, it is unsurprising that all law teachers from one school to another tend to teach more or less the same stuff.

Nevertheless, the desire to escape the doom of being an academic pedestrian at least partly explains the impulse of many law teachers to seek the intellectual excitement and status of more abstract and hence more honorific disciplines. Such teachers might, if their own preferences were the only consideration, prescribe a first-year law curriculum of, say, public choice, game theory, hermeneutics, distributive justice, and ascriptive metaphysics (a subject I think I just invented as a candidate for next season's intellectual fad). While there may indeed be unrevealed truth at the bottom of these several wells, we cannot convince first-year students of civil procedure that they need to drink from them as a precondition to becoming lawyers. If good law teaching cannot be a search for previously unrevealed truth, nevertheless, even ascriptive metaphysics (whatever that might be) probably has some illumination that it can shed on the ceremonies of civil justice. The teacher can therefore indulge herself in occasional forays into such marginalia without betraying her students' ambition to understand what courts actually do.

## Civil Procedure and the Public Good

Competence and Truth are not the only available themes or purposes of instruction in civil procedure. *University* law departments, unlike the proprietary sort, were created not by teachers, or by students, or by those chiefly concerned with the welfare or amusement of either of those groups, nor even with the social status associated with academic or professional credentials, but by those who imagined that law teaching would serve the public interest. The hope was that those favored with such education would find themselves under a duty to serve the public.

The need for such a profession abides. Even if students pay tuition equal to or greater than the operating cost of today's professional school, there are real social costs associated with our operations to be kept in mind by those who benefit. We ought not to forget that we take three years of our students' lives, causing them to forgo income and incur debt; that this time-serving requirement restricts the delivery of legal service to persons willing and able to invest in human capitalism, a willingness not evenly distributed across the population; that professional incomes are heightened by our exclusivity, but so are the costs of legal services paid by those who need them; and that we nurture intellectual arrogance and class bias by being who we are. The public should not be asked to suffer our continued existence if all we do is to indulge the student demand for Hessian training in the form of costly information transmission valued for its effect in separating them from the lumpenproletariat, or indulge our own desire for academic status.

The founding purpose of American legal education was not to impart Competence nor to reveal Truth, but to nurture Virtue in the institutions of democratic government. Tocqueville found American lawyers to be like European aristocrats not because of their pretensions of social status, but because of the stabilizing role they played in democratic government.[6] It was to promote that role that law teaching emerged in America in the eighteenth century.[7] While this founding purpose has been confounded by students seeking Competence and academics pursuing Truth, public Virtue remains needful, and law teachers are the group having the best opportunity to foster it.

Teachers who perform their duty to nurture Virtue can enhance their students' understanding of the moral duties of officers exercising power over fellow citizens in a democracy. A polity served by a profession understanding those moral duties has a good chance of remaining a republic; a polity lacking such a profession, our ancients believed, is unlikely to be self-governing for long. Civil procedure is the premier opportunity for teachers to conduct such moral education.

Curricular choices are made with a mix of these purposes in mind; Competence, Truth, and Virtue compete for place in civil procedure as in other courses of instruction. Within the parameters of a single course conducted by a single teacher, we are free to respond to the uninformed student demand for Competence as little as we may think we can get away with; we can pursue Truth for a few orbits around the planet; and we can try in different ways to initiate students to the demanding moral discipline of public Virtue. The mix of these aims is, hour by hour, the freedom and responsibility of the law teacher. No subject is better suited to the simultaneous pursuit of Competence, Truth, and Virtue than civil procedure.

## A Short History of the Civil Procedure Course

Nevertheless, the two of our forebears in American law teaching who had the best opportunities to shape a curriculum in law omitted to teach civil procedure. They came to this common failure from opposing positions.

The first of the two was George Wythe, who had an open choice at the time of his appointment as professor of law and politics at William and Mary in 1779. Wythe understood his mission to be the nurturing of public virtue. Although a scholar of repute, he was not an academic person in the contemporary sense; he was, indeed, a sitting judge while also a teacher. And it was not his purpose, nor did he seek to attract students, to prepare them to appear in court. He was preparing his students for public life in the Commonwealth of Virginia. He had his students for a single academic year, and he was their only law teacher.[8]

Wythe was constricted in his choices of content by the availability of reading materials. His lectures were in part a guide to Blackstone, the one generally available and readable law book. His students read not only those parts of Blackstone depicting the English law of contracts and property and the common law of crimes, but also the account of the English constitution, which Wythe apparently employed as an occasion to extol the greater virtues of the Virginia constitution he had helped write.[9] He also lectured on Roman law, a subject on which he was acknowledged to be the most learned American.[10] In addition, he introduced his students to the literature of political economy, notably the then-recent works of Adam Smith and Baron Charles Montesquieu. He also conducted moot courts and fortnightly meetings of his students organized as a legislative body.[11]

Wythe's successor, St. George Tucker, followed a similar pattern and at the conclusion of his teaching career, in 1803, published an Americanized edition of Blackstone,[12] eliding Blackstone's royalisms and adding an extended treatment of American constitutional law based on Tucker's own lectures. The Transylvania University Law Department, perhaps the most important in antebellum times because of the large number of its graduates who participated in our national public life, followed Wythe's leadership in emphasizing public law, comparative law, and political economy, while also affording access to Kent's *Commentaries on American Law,*[13] a work, like Blackstone's, giving short shrift to adjective law.[14]

By the 1830s, there seems to have been a general understanding that an academic law program would occupy about five months of the year, and that students completing the program would be expected to be in residence two such years. Topics were often studied in alternating years. Transylvania may have been the first American university to conduct a final examination in law; it was given at the end of the program; only those who passed received a degree; and most failed the exam, which was OK, because the credential meant very little, anyhow. Antebellum Harvard under Story and Greenleaf gave a degree to all who were present for the prescribed period.[15] Thomas Cooley's Michigan[16] and Theodore Dwight's Columbia[17] did almost the same.

To hear systematic lectures on common law pleading in the time of Wythe or Tucker, one would have had to enroll at the proprietary school in Litchfield, where James Gould taught the subject with elan.[18] Indeed, shortly before he retired, he published his lectures on pleading;[19] they were an extended encomium to the intricacies of the forms of action. But Litchfield was not a university law school; its profit-seeking aim was to market Competence, not Virtue of the sort that Wythe, Tucker, and Cooley sought to nurture.

A reason that eighteenth-century pleading may have commended itself to Litchfield as a subject to teach was its arcane character. Only a lawyer could master the difference between trespass and trespass on the case, and to know that distinction marked one as anointed because common law pleading was a task for which common sense was useless. A proprietary institution selling resalable information could hardly afford to pass up the opportunity to celebrate such a subject. On the other hand, it was a subject having little interest to most university law teachers, for much the same reason.[20] The system was only marginally more rational than trial by ordeal, or the Japanese alternative of Sumo, both of which were religious ceremonies invoking the will of God to resolve disputes. It had no more political content, and far less intellectual content, than other complex games such as chess.

Gould's teaching of the subject was, however, poor teaching, whatever his aim. Common law pleading was already in eclipse in England as well as America. Jeremy Bentham had likened aspects of common law pleading to a syphilis of government.[21] This view was widely shared, and there was in the early nineteenth century a movement afoot on both sides of the Atlantic to discard this barbaric sport. The forms of action he extolled in 1832 were abolished in England in 1836.[22] Among those sharing Bentham's scorn of common law procedure were Jacksonians who regarded English procedure as just another burden the aristocracy imposed on honest folk as a means of preserving the wealth and status of lawyers.[23]

New York University was founded by Benthamite utilitarians who admired the pragmatism of the new German universities and of the University of London.[24] One of its first achievements was to open in 1838 a law school under the leadership of Benjamin Butler, President Jackson's attorney general.[25] Butler proposed that the first year of his three-year, part-time curriculum be devoted to the "science" of pleading, with supplementary work on jurisprudence and constitutional law; the attention to pleading was given not without apology:

> Nor will the task of instructing in these branches be unworthy the efforts of an able and learned jurist. Our forms of proceedings, though generally prolix, and often encumbered with needless technicalities, are yet intimately connected with the principles of Law. And as a general rule, he who best understands the nature and design of the instruments which the Law employs, will not only be most qualified to look above the mere form, and to lay hold of, and appropriate to their true uses, the higher parts of the profession.[26]

One of Butler's first steps was to employ Professor David Graham, the author of an 1832 book on New York practice. Graham was an associate of David Dudley Field in the effort to abolish common law procedure in New York, an effort that achieved success in 1848.[27] It was Graham who lectured on civil procedure that founding year. Alas, for reasons that are not fully known, the school closed after one year, to be reopened two decades later.[28]

Max Weber explained the movement uniting Bentham, Field, and Graham as a response to the Enlightenment.[29] What they sought to do was to persuade those with the power to do so to delete dysfunctional formalities to assure, insofar as it is possible, that the judgments of law courts would be based on the law and the facts, and not the result of a misstep of counsel. One evident purpose in teaching pleading at New York University was to enlist support in the profession for the reforms that would be forthcoming a decade later. Timothy Walker, the founder of the Cincinnati Law School, was not a Jacksonian, but he shared their interests in law reform, and he did some teaching of pleading in the 1840s to the same reformist end.[30] John Norton Pomeroy, also a reformer,[31] in the 1870s also gave attention to the subject in his curriculum at the Hastings College of Law of the University of California.[32]

Joseph Story may have been the first American law professor to teach the topics of jurisdiction and judgments. These lectures, presented in the 1830s, were part of a longer treatment of conflict of laws, a subject on which Story was the first American author.[33] There was little national law on those topics until the Fourteenth Amendment was ratified in 1868.[34] Story's colleague, Simon Greenleaf, lectured on evidence and published the first work on that subject in 1852.[35] The law of evidence was largely the product of American judicial decisions accommodating the institution of the jury trial to the conditions of nineteenth-century America. Greenleaf's book would go through many editions before his subject was reworked by his former student, James Bradley Thayer,[36] and then by Thayer's student, John Henry Wigmore.[37]

All of the works mentioned, and the teaching they expressed, were instruments of law reform. They were written in the spirit of the Jacksonian reforms of pleading, and were a part of the tradition marked by Weber. The moral premise underlying the teaching of Graham, Walker, Story, Greenleaf, Thayer, and Pomeroy was that courts ought to seek in their procedures and administrative arrangements the means of providing judgments disinterestedly by applying law made by a government of the people to facts, and thus to impose a resolution on disputes. Implicit in their teaching was the duty of the legal profession to support courts engaged in that enterprise. These teachers were, unlike Gould, children of the Enlightenment. They were also missionaries for a secular faith that law can be an effective instrument of popular self-government.

There is an additional reason for the stunted development of civil procedure teaching in university law schools in the nineteenth century. This was the local character of much of the applicable law. Butler's New York University was among the few schools deigning to teach the law of a state;

most were desperate to attract students from more than one state. This was especially true of Story at Harvard, who had been summoned by the benefactor Nathan Dane to celebrate the national law, not the localisms that were dividing the republic.

Civil procedure does not appear to have had a significant place in the curriculum of Simeon Eban Baldwin's Yale Law School[38] or Theodore Dwight's Columbia.[39] Cooley's Michigan curriculum, however, included lectures on equity, evidence, and code pleading, and it even offered instruction in trial practice through a moot court.[40]

The second important moment for the law curriculum was, of course, Langdell's.[41] There was much that was fresh about his approach.[42] He appears to have known nothing about Wythe or those who followed him, or about any events or institutions west of the Hudson River. He did not, so far as we know, consider the possibility of teaching law to nurture public virtue. He had no interest in social or political reform of any kind; a royalist at heart, he placed no value on the traditions of self-government. His charge, given him by President Eliot, was to elevate the status of the Harvard Law School by making it exclusive, apolitical, and academic.[43] Like many New Englanders more English than the English, he did not regard the Constitution of the United States, or even the legislative enactments of Congress, as law.[44] Law, in his view, is what life-tenure judges make while unencumbered by any texts drafted by the amateurs in legislative committees and constitutional conventions. Hence, he preferred to consign constitutional law to the undergraduate curriculum so that professional law students might never have their minds sullied by the vulgarities of politics.

As a part of the scheme to make a Harvard legal education more valuable in the marketplace, Langdell proposed to extend the period of study from the usual two terms of about five months to three academic years of nine months each. This decision was in no way driven by a demand of Harvard students for more instruction, or by Harvard teachers for more time in which to cover material they deemed important. The purpose, and the only purpose, was to make Harvard Law more rigorous and hence more exclusive, as President Eliot had directed him to do. Thus, he needed to provide twenty-seven months' worth of curriculum in lieu of the traditional ten, while if possible diminishing the place in the curriculum of public law or other matters soiled by politics. This created a huge vacuum for private law courses, and thus a fresh canvas to which he was free to apply his crayon. His acolyte, James Barr Ames, was thus the author of no fewer than nine casebooks used to fill the time created by Langdell.[45] It can be no surprise that in Langdell's lifetime, the Harvard Law dropout rate was very high—a minority of those not excluded by the novel examinations bothered to stay three years to imbibe much repetition, and many entered the profession with but a piece of a Harvard Law education.[46]

Prominent among the new courses was torts, a subject never before taught to law students anywhere. Indeed, the first book ever written about torts[47] had been published as recently as 1861. Also added to the Harvard curriculum was formal instruction in civil procedure. But not American procedure fashioned by such low-minded Jacksonians as David Dudley Field, but English civil procedure, the only kind worthy of study by good Anglophiles such as Langdell and Ames.

Ames, if it can be believed, taught his students at Harvard in 1880 the rigors of pleading under the Hilary Rules.[48] The Hilary Rules were the first English manifestation of Bentham's influence on procedural law reform. They were adopted by Parliament in 1836 as the result of the strenuous efforts of Henry Brougham, who challenged his legislative brethren:

> It was the boast of Augustus, that he found Rome of brick and left it of marble. . . . But how much nobler will be the sovereign's boast when he shall have it to say that he found law dear, and left it cheap; found it a sealed book, left it a living letter; found it a patrimony of the rich, left it the inheritance of the poor; found it the two-edged sword of craft and oppression, left it the staff of honesty and the shield of innocence.[49]

Alas for Brougham, and even more for Ames, the Hilary Rules proved to be a disaster in practice and were repealed in 1848,[50] a quarter century before Ames began to teach them at Harvard. Their fault lay in the unrealistic demands they imposed on counsel, a fault to which Ames, who never in his life appeared in court, proved to be quite blind. For that reason, it is as well that the pleading course was given only a minor place in the Langdell curriculum.

Because Langdell's Harvard was promoting university legal education as the route to Competence rather than Virtue, it sought to overcome the disadvantage of being a national institution and to solve the problem of filling out three full years of instruction by offering specialized third-year courses on local practice in the states to which the largest numbers of its students went. Generally these were taught by practitioners from the several states involved.[51]

## Civil Procedure and Judicial Law Reform

The teaching of civil procedure received a powerful impulse from the Progressive era. Roscoe Pound, then the dean at Nebraska, made a celebrated address to the American Bar Association in 1905[52] signaling the beginning of a new era of reform. Pound was joined in leading this endeavor by his sometime colleague at Northwestern, Wigmore.[53] By the time of Pound's address, the 1848 Field Code had been transmogrified by the New York legislature into the Throop Code, one of the most elaborate and least workable schemes ever devised for the resolution of disputes.[54] Disenchanted by the propensity of American legislatures to ornament procedural systems with dissonant provisions favorable to the interests of whatever faction or interest group might for a moment hold their attention, the Progressive reformers favored court rule making as the mechanism for reform.[55] This was an English innovation of 1873 expressed for the first time in America in the Wyoming constitution of 1890.[56] They also promoted enactment of the early precursors of long-arm legislation,[57] "merit selection" of judges,[58] more thorough merger of law and equity, and liberal joinder of parties and claims.[59] Among the most passionate advocates for procedural reform was William Howard Taft,[60] a man not otherwise given to radical ideas.

This Progressive reform movement was taking shape at the same time that the academic legal profession was emerging as a group somewhat apart from the practicing bar. A whole generation of the newly minted career law teachers were imbued with an interest in civil procedure and a keen sense of the promise of reform to make civil law enforcement more effective. Among those who were active in reform efforts and who influenced the teaching of civil procedure in the era after World War I were Charles Clark at Yale,[61] Edson Sunderland at Michigan,[62] and Arthur Vanderbilt at New York University.[63] Also influential as teachers were Austin Scott of Harvard[64] and Jerome Michael at Columbia.[65] Casebooks prepared in that era integrated for the first time the teaching of pleading with the teaching of jurisdiction and the basic features of the civil jury trial.[66] Their presentations were uniformly historical in orientation; their students were taught to appreciate the difference between the forms of action and code pleading, and to prepare themselves for further reforms along the lines of those appearing in the Federal Rules promulgated in 1938. Much of the teaching of procedure in those decades was done in the upper-class years, although an introductory first-year one-semester course was not uncommon.

Many teachers of procedure became active reformers of legal institutions. The most important success was achieved by Clark and his associates, including Sunderland, who were responsible for the promulgation of the Federal Rules of Civil Procedure in 1938. Clark was the principal proponent of summary judgment and notice pleading; Sunderland can be said to have invented the pretrial conference. Vanderbilt also enjoyed dramatic success in leading radical reform of the legal institutions of New Jersey. But there were numerous others. Harold Medina of Columbia took up the cause of reforming the municipal courts of New York City.[67] Single-handedly, he took on Mayor LaGuardia in legislative chambers at Albany. Thurman Arnold at the University of West Virginia began to gather empirical data to inform efforts to improve the administration of civil justice.[68]

The 1938 rules were a hit.[69] Examined in a cold light today, they were no triumph of professional draftsmanship. In fairness, they were not presented at the time as a permanent solution to the problem posed by rule 1 of achieving speedy, just, and efficient disposition of every civil case. Even the reformers of 1938 were aware of the iron law of unintended consequences, and they were mindful that vigorous advocates would exploit any weakness they might find in the structure created. But the new rules lent unaccustomed strength to the traditional purpose of discerning the truth with respect to disputed facts; more than a few malefactors made generous settlement offers rather than face the horrors of a "deposition upon oral examination." The new rules also obliterated some arcane distinctions, such as the false dichotomy made in English law between law and equity, and thus made it harder for unjust litigants to take refuge in technicality. By liberalizing joinder, they fostered comprehensive resolution of disputes. And the rules were drafted with studied looseness of text to free judges from the duties to observe procedural niceties impeding their efforts faithfully to apply the substantive law. Procedure became more a servant, albeit not a slave, to substance.

The broad acceptance with which the Federal Rules were received led to a further round of reform at mid-century. Many states adopted variations on the national rules, and some even adopted them *in haec verba*.[70] Among the major state reforms was a renovation of the New York Civil Practice Act in which Jack Weinstein, then of Columbia, was instrumental.[71] Characteristic of these reforms of state practice was the merger of law and equity, i.e., the abolition of the ancient traditions of the English Court of Chancery as a distinct feature of American law. The learning of equity scholars such as John Norton Pomeroy[72] became substantially obsolete, and teachers such as Zechariah Chafee[73] retired, not to be replaced. Much of the reform of state procedures was effected through the participation of teachers of civil procedure.

Discourse over the possible improvement of the Federal Rules was maintained by the Advisory Committee whose work was conducted out of the offices of James William Moore at Yale,[74] and then of Benjamin Kaplan[75] and Albert Sacks[76] at Harvard. Interest in empirical testing of procedural institutions was manifested in the career of Maurice Rosenberg at Columbia[77] and in the establishment in 1966 of the Federal Judicial Center.[78]

Through the 1960s, much of the most respected scholarship in the field of civil procedure illuminated and criticized rules of court; premier work was done by Moore[79] and by Charles Alan Wright at Texas,[80] but also significant were narrower and sometimes more penetrating treatments such as the thorough job done on requests for admissions by Ted Finman of the University of Wisconsin,[81] on directed verdicts by Edward Cooper,[82] then at Minnesota, on judicial notice of foreign law by Arthur Miller,[83] then at Michigan, and on summary judgment by Martin Louis of the University of North Carolina.[84]

No sooner were the new rules promulgated in 1938 than the Court decided *Erie R. R. v. Tompkins.*[85] For generations of teachers and students, this would prove to be a great moment in the life of the law. If given the full range of application favored by Justice Frankfurter,[86] *Erie* would have killed the new rules and remanded the federal courts back to the ancient practice of conforming their procedure to that of local state courts. The line between substance and procedure, between what is properly a matter of state law and what is a matter of federal practice, or between what is properly a subject of a rule enacted by the Supreme Court rather than Congress, evoked a rich literature,[87] and a formidable line of Supreme Court decisions culminating in *Hanna v. Plumer* in 1965.[88] The United States was aboil in national procedural issues.

Also a continuing issue with high visibility was the federal constitutional limits on state court jurisdiction over persons and property. By the mid-sixties, most states had adopted extended long-arm legislation, often extending the reaches of their courts to the outer limit allowed by the

Fourteenth Amendment.[89] Much scholarly writing was devoted to this subject, and many teachers introduced their course with an extended treatment of the due process limits of state court jurisdiction, beginning with *Pennoyer v. Neff*,[90] extending through *International Shoe v. Washington*,[91] to *Hanson v. Denckla*.[92]

Another enlarged element of instruction centered on the text of the Seventh Amendment. The interface of the new rules of court merging law and equity and allowing liberal joinder of parties and claims with the ancient distinction embedded in the 1791 text proved to be an intractable problem that still troubles the Supreme Court of the United States.[93] This has proved to be one area in which legal history has continuing and direct pertinence to the disposition of contemporary litigation.[94] State courts have struggled with similar issues arising under the texts of state constitutions,[95] but the decisions of the Supreme Court have dominated discourse.

Numerous other procedural issues arising in state court litigation have been found in recent years to be subject to parameters established by the Fourteenth Amendment. Among these are adequacy of notice of proceedings,[96] the right to notice before provisional remedies are granted,[97] applicability of statutes of limitations,[98] res judicata,[99] the right to be represented by counsel,[100] the right to proceed in forma pauperis in some proceedings,[101] allocation of the burden of proof,[102] peremptory strikes of jurors,[103] and, most recently, the settlement of class actions.[104] Although all of these topics have been constitutionalized by the Supreme Court, they have been left to the instruction of civil procedure teachers.

The literature and teaching of civil procedure in the decades following World War II reflected the maturation of the legal process as a means not merely of resolving disputes, but of enforcing rights and duties. Disenchantment with the administrative process of law enforcement[105] led legislative bodies increasingly to rely upon private law enforcement by individual plaintiffs employing modern civil procedure to bring malefactors to account. In this important respect, American civil litigation became unique in the world.

Localism as an impediment to teaching the national law diminished in its importance. The ascendant nationalization of the academic profession meant that law teachers absorbed in issues of local law would lose status within the academic discipline, so that professional considerations were incentives to teachers to direct their attention to federal practice. And the increasing mobility of lawyers gave additional weight to the attractions to students of a study of the national law on the subject.

## The Modern Course Emerges

These developments all stimulated the teaching of civil procedure as a course integrating pleading with jurisdiction and other facets of the process, and now also as a course centered on the new body of national adjective law, much of which was rooted in the Constitution. The first casebook to present such a course was edited by Richard Field and Benjamin Kaplan; their first edition appeared in 1953.[106] They soon had several competitors,[107] but to them must go the palm for designating the canon, if such it be. Accordingly, there was in the mid-1960s virtual unanimity that the first year of law school should include a yearlong six-semester-hour course in civil procedure devoted primarily to federal practice and constitutional limitations on the practices of state courts. If there is a canon in civil procedure, it is not forty years old.

Except with respect to a few matters such as the Seventh Amendment, the history of civil procedure began to fade from view. Even though many casebooks included historical material, it got short shrift from teachers because of the student reaction it engendered. By 1975, few students wanted to know of the evolution commencing in the early nineteenth century, and marked by the adoption of the Field Code in 1848 and the Rules Enabling Act of 1934. In part, this transformation was effected by a reduction in the number of first-year class hours devoted to the subject. To the extent that the purpose of reducing the number of hours in the yearlong first-year courses was intended to accommodate courses presenting a broader perspective on law, the change may in this respect have been counterproductive.

While the historical perspective has been lost, few teachers have otherwise encountered difficulty in persuading first-year law students that civil procedure is an important subject worthy of their attention as novitiates to the profession. The course has what it takes to be taken seriously by preprofessional students: the understanding it imparts enlarges the possibility that students will achieve Competence. The Truth they learn along the way is that mere information about the legal texts governing the process by which civil disputes are resolved will not go far in enabling the novitiate to earn a living as a trial advocate, even though a rough familiarity with those texts is essential. Competence, students soon perceive, cannot be achieved by those who resist the truth about the indeterminacy of many legal texts, because procedure rules are written to enable the courts applying them to reach substantively appropriate results; the law of procedure is, in truth, handmaiden to substance.

Civil procedure also retains appeal for teachers indulging a broad spectrum of intellectual interests. A teacher combining an interest in history, politics, economics, behavioral science, philosophy, anthropology, classics, or literature can find outlets for the expression of such interests within the reasonable ambit of a course on civil procedure. A growing and increasingly useful body of scientific data is now available to evaluate procedural arrangements; while the student appetite for such information is limited, the field is one in which students can be challenged to subject the premises of discourse to empirical testing. Even the craft of literary criticism can be brought to bear, although it is somewhat deflected by the tendency of modern procedural rules to anticipate some of its insights; by acknowledging the wisdom of the precept that "tight will tear, wide will wear,"[108] the tailors of court rules have often preempted the possibilities for "dynamic" interpretation. Thus, while there is meager opportunity to discern important and previously unrevealed truth, the academic enterprise can be pursued by one teaching civil procedure.

More important is the opportunity civil procedure affords for law teaching that aims to serve the traditional, public purpose pursued by Wythe and Story, the Transylvanians and the Jacksonians. Underlying the legislation, rules of court, and court decisions marking the field are the moral premises that make democratic government an imaginable possibility. Some of those moral premises were synthesized by Lon Fuller in his lectures on the morality of law.[109] Some are expressed in the text of the Fourteenth Amendment due process and equal protection clauses. Some are expressed in rule 1 of the Federal Rules of Civil Procedure exhorting the courts to make decisions that are just, speedy, and economic. Together, these moral premises express the hope if not always the expectation that courts in a democratic government can and will apply the lash of the law faithfully and evenhandedly.

No sensible teacher would exhort his or her students to believe that their system works reliably. After all, what people bring to court is the refuse of our national and community life. Mendacity, greed, brutality, sloth, and neglect are the materials with which we work, and there will never be enough justice in the world to supply the demand. It is not uncommon in 2000 to find those who despair, who hold that it is not worth the effort and cost to achieve such results as we are able to achieve. Thus, in some of its aspects, the alternative dispute resolution (ADR) movement is a protest against law's enforcement, and a throwback to pre-Enlightenment ceremony.[110] Often, however, those who are heard first to grieve about the failures of modern civil procedure in its effort to enforce duties and protect rights are those who have been brought to book in civil court and suffered for their misdeeds.

## Postmodern Reactions

The yearlong course is now seldom found in the curricula of the most elite law schools. Semesterization seems to have been driven less by any dissatisfaction with the content or form of yearlong courses than by the convenience of faculty members coming and going on leave and by the desire of anxious students for more frequent examinations. Whatever its cause, the trend has forced teachers to be more selective. Because diverse selections seem equally reasonable, there is now, I believe, considerable difference in the content of the first-year course. Most of the published course books present material that is an updated but fundamentally unchanged version of the 1953 Field and Kaplan course, but fewer students are led through the whole of the subject thus viewed.

A more creative response devised by Robert Cover and Owen Fiss[111] has been to conduct the inquiry at a more abstract level embracing problems and issues of administrative procedure as well as judicial procedure in a single intellectual undertaking. "Metaprocedure" tends to short the importance of the statutes and rules of court that are the plumbing and electric wiring of the great edifice the editors strive to erect. An exercise in the search for Truth, it risks disparagement of Competence. Linda Mullenix finds the approach pedantic and hopelessly snobbish,[112] but it appeals to teachers and those few students who are given to philosophy. Metaprocedure does not, however, address the problem of the abbreviation of the course; the editors insist that their 1,877-page work requires a full year of study.[113]

At the same time that their course has been abbreviated, postmodern civil procedure teachers have also been exhorted to find a place for ADR.[114] There is a problem in doing so that some champions of ADR do not fully appreciate. It is that the issues with which proceduralists deal, such as territorial jurisdiction, notice, access to proof, right to be heard, qualifications and disinterest of the decision maker, fidelity to legal texts, and finality of decisions, are equally present when disputants are directed to ADR.[115] They cannot be avoided, but must be resolved, if crudely; crude resolutions tend to be less respectful of rights. There is, in short, no completely satisfactory way around the law's cost and delay. Indeed, contractual jurisdiction may be a prime method for avoiding the lash of the law and favoring those who prey on the rights of others.[116]

Postmodern teachers of civil procedure may be less interested than their immediate predecessors in the possibilities of judicial law reform. It remains the case that there are many opportunities to participate in reform activities of genuine value to the public. These seem to be somewhat neglected, particularly opportunities to work with state courts and state legislatures. It is often said that the states are useful laboratories, and certainly this could be true with respect to civil procedure. The Arizona courts are presently experimenting with sweeping disclosure requirements[117] and with jury instructions;[118] if more law teachers took a greater interest in promoting and evaluating such experiments, significant benefits might be achieved. It is at least imaginable that the next generation of procedure teachers will have an opportunity to promote and bear witness to extraordinary reforms exploiting the potential of the computer chip. That technology may obsolesce large chunks of what my generation of civil procedure teachers knew and taught.[119] The opportunities for useful experiments are certain to be better in the future than they have ever been in the past. To exploit those opportunities, teachers of civil procedure would need both to participate in state government and to master and deploy tbe methodologies of social science. While no prudent reformer will ever forget or repeal the law of unintended consequences,[120] there is much useful knowledge to be gained.[121]

Unfortunately in my view, the reward system in place in the academic profession tends to direct attention away from such work. Academic recognition tends to come to those engaged in more theoretical work; while there is excellent work done in the field, possibilities for reform are less frequently addressed than they might be. Thus, for a time, a decade or so ago, it was fashionable to write of the possibility of "non-transubstantive procedural law" as a promising direction for reform.[122] This form of discourse seemed to derive in part from the observation that procedure rules tend to be notably indeterminate. It was apparently the hope that special systems might be devised that would be less determinate in order to favor particular classes of civil litigants, such as plaintiffs in employment discrimination cases, by constricting the discretion of judges in such matters.

A flaw in this "movement," if a few articles can be so described, is that it proceeded at so theoretical, or architectural, a level that it missed an elementary point about the plumbing: If special rules are written for such a class of cases, they will not be written by the class of litigants who it was the apparent aim of the proponent to advance. At least in the federal structure, any such systems would have to be enacted by Congress, for they would be too substantive to be an appropriate subject for judicial rulemaking under the Rules Enabling Act.[123] If one wishes to advance the cause of a particular group of civil litigants, there is no way to avoid direct contact with the soil of legislative politics.[124]

Moreover, although the federal courts decide a very small and diminishing percentage of the civil cases litigated in the United States, they receive almost all the attention of those law teachers who do serious scholarship on the subject. For example, in 1998, I had occasion to study the literature on the law governing judicial elections. No issue arising in the conduct of civil litigation is more important than this, but the issues pertain entirely to the conduct and organization of state courts. I did find some useful work on the subject, but I think it slights no one to say that the literature is thin. Much of what one finds is written by political scientists; while there is nothing wrong with their interest in the field, it is remarkable that there are, for example, much richer literatures in the law reviews on long-arm jurisdiction, class actions, and the role of state law in federal diversity litigation, just to pick a few topics at random.

One of the attractions of these topics of greatest interest to most civil procedure teachers is that they can be studied from an armchair. A contribution to more promising empirical literature requires training and an investment of time that law teachers, for diverse reasons, are reluctant to make. For the most part, the field has been left to social psychologists and institutions such as the Civil Justice Institute, the Federal Judicial Center, or perhaps the American Bar Foundation. One may hope that the proceduralists of the future will be more given to empirical work than the present writer.[125]

The Civil Justice Reform Act of 1990 may be taken as an adverse comment by Congress on the state of civil procedure teaching and research. That enactment expanded in some measure the procedural lawmaking authority of district courts, encouraged the use of mandatory ADR, and called for empirical study of the results. Most academic observers scorned the legislation as impulsive and illconceived, an assessment that I continue to share.[126] One reason for this reaction may, however, be that those who proposed the act disregarded the available academic literature, apparently assessing it to be useless. Another may be that decentralization of procedural lawmaking threatens to deprive the current generation of law teachers of the livelihood they have acquired through a knowledge and understanding of national law. A third may be that the evaluation phase of the experiment envisioned a resort not to the human resources of law schools, but to the institutions engaged in empirical work.

## Prospect

It is surely possible, indeed maybe it is certain, that the achievements of modern civil procedure were oversold in the 1960s and 1970s. Just as teachers of torts may have caused a national sorrow by elevating to greater prominence our Calvinist preoccupation with blame, teachers of civil procedure may have contributed to what some see as a similar national disorder sometimes denoted as hyperlexis,[127] that is, our alleged excessive preoccupation with the use of law to enforce individual rights to the detriment of our social duties and community relations. I leave that speculation to the reader unobstructed by the self-justifications of an aged proceduralist. I will, however, venture the forecast that the premises derived from the Enlightenment will abide, that whatever utility may be derived from the ADR movement and postmodern disdain for legal textualism, there will long be a need for a system that, as best we can, decides cases on the law and the facts. And it will be the privilege and the duty of those who teach civil procedure to share in the satisfaction of that public need.

### NOTES

1. Accord, J. M. Balkin & Sanford Levinson, *The Canons of Constitutional Law*, 111 Harv. L. Rev. 964, 983 (1998): "[I]t would be rather extraordinary if a casebook on welfare rights law omitted the Welfare Reform Act of 1996 simply because the authors found it normatively dreadful or stylistically objectionable."

2. Albert Venn, Dicey, Can English Law Be Taught in the Universities? 1 (1883).

3. ANTHONY T. KRONMAN, THE LOST LAWYER: FAILING IDEALS OF THE LEGAL PROFESSION (1993).

4. Address of Chief Justice Holmes at the Dedication of the Northwestern University Law School Building, Chicago, Oct. 20, 1962, in COLLECTED LEGAL PAPERS 272, 276–77 (1920).

5. Harvard University, A Record of Commemoration, November Fifth to Eighth, 1886, On the Two Hundred and Fiftieth Anniversary of the Founding of Harvard College 95 (Cambridge, John Wilson & Son, 1886).

6. ALEXIS DE TOCQUEVILLE, DEMOCRACY IN AMERICA 106–50, 264–65, 268–70 (J. P. Mayer, George Lawrence trans. 1969) (1835).

7. Paul D. Carrington, *The Revolutionary Idea of University Legal Education*, 31 W&M L. REV. 527 (1990); Paul D. Carrington, *Teaching Law and Virtue at Transylvania University: The George Wythe Tradition in the Antebellum Years*, 41 MERCER L. REV. 673 (1990); Paul D. Carrington, *Teaching Law in the Antebellum Northwest*, 23 U. TOL. L. REV. 3 (1992).

8. *See* Carrington, *Revolutionary Idea, supra* note 7, at 533–38.

9. ALONZO THOMAS DILL, GEORGE WYTHE, TEACHER OF LIBERTY 43 (1979).

10. *William Wirt, Sketches of the Life and Character of Patrick Henry* 65–66 (1859).

11. Carrington, *Revolutionary Idea, supra* note 7 at 535–36.

12. ST. GEORGE TUCKER, BLACKSTONE'S COMMENTARIES ON THE LAWS OF ENGLAND WITH NOTES OF REFERENCE TO THE CONSTITUTION AND THE LAWS OF THE FEDERAL GOVERNMENT OF THE UNITED STATES (Philadelphia 1803).

13. JAMES KENT, COMMENTARIES ON AMERICAN LAW (Boston 1826–30).

14. *See generally* Carrington, *Teaching Law and Virtue, supra* note 7.

15. 2 CHARLES WARREN, HISTORY OF THE HARVARD LAW SCHOOL AND OF EARLY LEGAL CONDITIONS IN AMERICA 88–92 (2d ed. 1970); ARTHUR E. SUTHERLAND, THE LAW AT HARVARD: A HISTORY OF IDEAS AND MEN, 1817–1967 at 123–24 (1967). 16. ELIZABETH GASPAR BROWN, LEGAL EDUCATION AT MICHIGAN 1859–1959 at 740 (1959).

17. Dwight was required to administer an examination before awarding a degree to his students. JULIUS GOEBEL, A HISTORY OF THE SCHOOL OF LAW, COLUMBIA UNIVERSITY 50 (1955).

18. MARIAN C. MCKENNA, TAPPING REEVE AND THE LITCHFIELD LAW SCHOOL 81–106 (1986); *and see* Simeon Eben Baldwin, *James Gould in* TWO GREAT AMERICAN LAWYERS 455 (William Draper Lewis ed. 1907).

19. JAMES GOULD, A TREATISE ON THE PRINCIPLES OF PLEADING IN CIVIL ACTIONS (New York 1936).

20. Asahel Stearns, the professor of law at Harvard from 1817 to 1829, may have been an exception. *See* ARTHUR E. SUTHERLAND, THE LAW AT HARVARD: A HISTORY OF IDEAS AND MEN, 1817–1967 at 72 (1967). Nathaniel Beverley Tucker,

who was the professor of law and police at William and Mary from 1834 to 1851, may have been another. *See* Professor Beverley Tucker's Valedictory Address to His Class, 1 SOUTHERN LITERARY MESSENGER 597, 599 (1835), *reprinted in* ESSAYS ON LEGAL EDUCATION IN NINETEENTH CENTURY VIRGINIA 103, 107 (W. Hamilton Bryson ed. 1998).

21. JEREMY BENTHAM, A FRAGMENT ON GOVERNMENT; OR A COMMENT ON THE COMMENTARIES BEING AN EXAMINATION OF SIR WILLIAM BLACKSTONE'S COMMENTARIES (Wilson, London 1823).

22. William S. Holdsworth, *The New Rules of Pleading of the Hilary Term, 1834*, 1 CAMBRIDGE L. J. 261, 270–78 (1923).

23. Steven N. Subrin, *David Dudley Field and the Field Code: A Historical Analysis of an Earlier Procedural Vision*, 6 LAW & HIST. REV. 311 (1988).

24. THEODORE F. JONES, NEW YORK UNIVERSITY 1832–1932, at 6 (1933); on the University of London, *see* HUGH HALE BELLOT, THE UNIVERSITY COLLEGE, LONDON 1826–1926 (1929).

25. RONALD L. BROWN, THE SCHOOL PAPERS OF BENJAMIN F. BUTLER 5–9 (1987).

26. Quoted *id.* at 124.

27. ROBERT W. MILLAR, CIVIL PROCEDURE OF THE TRIAL COURT IN HISTORICAL PERSPECTIVE 43–51 (1952); *supra* note 23.

28. Brown, *supra* note 25, at 9–11.

29. MAX WEBER, ECONOMICS AND SOCIETY 657 (G. Roth & C. Wittich eds. 1968); FROM MAX WEBER: ESSAYS IN SOCIOLOGY 214 (H. H. Gerth & C. Wright Mills eds. 1946).

30. WALTER T. HITCHCOCK, TIMOTHY WALKER: ANTEBELLUM LAWYER 56, 79–81, 153–88 (1990).

31. *See, e.g.*, JOHN NORTON POMEROY, THE CODE OF REMEDIAL JUSTICE REVIEWED AND CRITICIZED (Van Bethuysen, New York 1877).

32. THOMAS BARNES, HASTINGS COLLEGE OF LAW: THE FIRST CENTURY 88–114 (1978).

33. 1 Warren, *supra* note 15, at 492–93; Sutherland, *supra* note 15, at 113–15; R. KENT NEWMYER, SUPREME COURT JUSTICE JOSEPH STORY: A STATESMAN OF THE OLD REPUBLIC 296–300 (1985).

34. Pennoyer v. Neff, 95 U.S. 714 (1878); Harris v. Balk, 198 U.S. 215 (1905); on the background of Pennoyer, *see* Wendy Collins Perdue, *Sin, Scandal and Substantive Due Process: Personal Jurisdiction and Pennoyer Reconsidered*, 62 WASH. L. REV. 479 (1987).

35. SIMON GREENLEAF, A TREATISE ON THE LAW OF EVIDENCE (Boston 1842).

36. JAMES BRADLEY THAYER, A PRELIMINARY TREATISE ON EVIDENCE AT COMMON LAW (Boston 1898). On the relationships of these works, *see* WILLIAM TWINING, THEORIES OF EVIDENCE 5–9 (1985).

37. JOHN HENRY WIGMORE, A TREATISE ON THE SYSTEM OF EVIDENCE IN TRIALS AT COMMON LAW INCLUDING THE STATUTES AND JUDICIAL DECISIONS OF ALL JURISDICTIONS IN THE UNITED STATES (4 vols., 1904–08).

38. FREDERICK C. HICKS, YALE LAW SCHOOL: 1869–94 INCLUDING THE COUNTY COURT HOUSE PERIOD (1937).

39. GOEBEL, *supra* note 17, at 44–68.

40. BROWN, *supra* note 16, at 226 et seq.

41. 2 WARREN, *supra* note 15, at 359–78; SUTHERLAND, *supra* note 15, at 166–84.

42. *See* Paul D. Carrington, *Hail! Langdell!*, 20 LAW & SOC. INQUIRY 691, 707–16 (1995).

43. 2 WARREN, *supra* note 15, at 397; 2 HENRY JAMES, CHARLES W. ELIOT, PRESIDENT OF HARVARD UNIVERSITY 1869–1900 at 87 (1930); Charles W. Eliot, *Langdell and the Law School*, 33 HARV. L. REV. 518 (1920).

44. *See* Christopher Columbus Langdell, *Dominant Opinion in England During the Nineteenth Century in Relation to Legislation as Illustrated by English Legislation, or The Absence of It During That Period*, 19 HARV. L. REV. 151 (1906). *Compare* ALBERT VENN DICEY, LAW AND OPINION IN ENGLAND (1905).

45. THE CENTENNIAL HISTORY OF THE HARVARD LAW SCHOOL 1817–1917, at 190–292 (1917).

46. SUTHERLAND, *supra* note 15, at 180–81; WARREN, *supra* note 15, at 521.

47. FRANCIS HILLIARD, THE LAW OF TORTS OR PRIVATE WRONGS (Boston 1861).

48. MILLAR, *supra* note 27, at 45–46.

49. 2 SPEECHES OF HENRY BROUGHAM 485 (London 1838).

50. 15 WILLIAM HOLDSWORTH, A HISTORY OF ENGLISH LAW 108–11 (Goodhart & Hanbury eds. 1965).

51. 2 WARREN, *supra* note 15, at 446–48.

52. Roscoe Pound, *The Causes for Popular Dissatisfaction with the Administration of Justice*, 40 AM. L. REV. 729 (1906).

53. WILLIAM R. ROALFE, JOHN HENRY WIGMORE: SCHOLAR AND REFORMER 111–13, 207 (1977); Paul D. Carrington, *The Missionary Diocese of Chicago*, 44 J. LEGAL. ED. 467, 502, 507–10 (1994).

54. HERBERT PETERFREUND & JOSEPH M. MCLAUGHLIN, NEW YORK PRACTICE 2 (1968); HAROLD R. MEDINA, IMPORTANT FEATURES OF PLEADING AND PRACTICE UNDER THE NEW YORK CIVIL PRACTICE ACT 2–3 (1922); MILLAR, *supra* note 27, at 55–56.

55. Steven B. Burbank, *The Rules Enabling Act of 1934*, 130 U. PA. L. REV. 1015, 1035–98 (1982).

56. WYO. CONST. art. 5, § 2

57. *E.g.*, "doing business" legislation, upheld in Commercial Mut. Acc. Co. v.

Davis, 213 U.S. 245 (1909), and nonresident motorist legislation, upheld in Kane v. New Jersey, 242 U.S. 160 (1916) and Hess v. Pawloski, 274 U.S. 352 (1927).

58. The concept was proposed by Albert Kales, of Northwestern University, and was promptly adopted as the chief cause of the newly organized American Judicature Society. MICHAEL R. BELKNAP, TO IMPROVE THE ADMINISTRATION OF JUSTICE: A HISTORY OF THE AMERICAN JUDICATURE SOCIETY (1990).

59. MILLAR, *supra* note 27, at 98–142.

60. *E.g.*, William Howard Taft, *The Selection and Tenure of Judges*, 38 ABA REP. 418 (1913).

61. *See* PROCEDURE: THE HANDMAID OF JUSTICE: ESSAYS OF CHARLES E. CLARK (Charles A. Wright & Harry M. Reasoner eds. 1966); JUDGE CHARLES EDWARD CLARK (Peninah Petruck ed., 1991).

62. *See* Edson Sunderland, *The English Struggle for Procedural Reform*, 39 HARV. L. REV. 725 (1926); *A Reply to Senator Walsh*, 6 OR. L. REV. 73 (1926); *The Regulation of Legal Procedure*, 35 W. VA. L. Q. 131 (1927); *The Grant of Rulemaking Power to the Supreme Court of the United States*, 32 MICH. L. REV. 1118 (1934).

63. EUGENE C. GERHART, ARTHUR T. VANDERBILT: THE COMPLEAT COUNSELLOR 77–89, 140–83, 205–52 (1980).

64. Scott joined the Harvard faculty in 1909 and is best known for his work in trusts. But he was a magnetic teacher, and his casebook published in 1919, *A Selection of Cases and Other Authorities on Civil Procedure in Actions at Law*, was a creative work. *See also* AUSTIN W. SCOTT, FUNDAMENTALS OF PROCEDURE IN ACTIONS AT LAW (1922).

65. Michael's work was primarily devoted to evidence, which led him, like Wigmore, to a study of psychology and to a long association with Mortimer Adler. His tightly crafted casebook for a first-year introductory course was very widely adopted and is worthy of examination today. THE ELEMENTS OF LEGAL CONTROVERSY: AN INTRODUCTION TO THE STUDY OF ADJECTIVE LAW (1948).

66. *See, e.g.*, THURMAN W. ARNOLD & FLEMING JAMES, JR., CASES AND MATERIALS ON TRIALS, JUDGMENTS, AND APPEALS (1936); EDSON R. SUNDERLAND, CASES AND MATERIALS ON JUDICIAL ADMINISTRATION (1937); ARTHUR T. VANDERBILT, CASES AND OTHER MATERIALS ON MODERN PROCEDURE AND JUDICIAL ADMINISTRATION (1952).

67. A brief account of Medina's career is in GOEBEL, *supra* note 17, at 287–88.

68. LAURA KALMAN, LEGAL REALISM AT YALE, 1927–1960, at 31–32 (1986); VOLTAIRE AND THE COWBOY: THE LETTERS OF THURMAN ARNOLD 162–174 (Gene M. Gressley ed. 1977).

69. CHARLES ALAN WRIGHT, THE LAW OF FEDERAL COURTS 429–30 (5th ed. 1994). "The Federal Rules may be Bleak House, but everyone seems to want to live there." Geoffrey C. Hazard, Jr., UNDEMOCRATIC LEGISLATION, 87 *Yale L. J.* 1284, 1287 (1978).

70.  John B. Oakley & Arthur F. Coon, THE FEDERAL RULES IN STATE COURTS: A SURVEY OF STATE COURT SYSTEMS OF CIVIL PROCEDURE, 61 WASH. L. REV. 1367 (1986).

71.  On the history of the act, see 1 JACK B. WEINSTEIN, HAROLD L. KORN & ARTHUR R. MILLER, THE NEW YORK CIVIL PRACTICE ACT (1967).

72.  JOHN NORTON POMEROY, A TREATISE ON EQUITY JURISPRUDENCE: AS ADMINISTERED IN THE UNITED STATES OF AMERICA, ADAPTED FOR ALL THE STATES AND FOR THE UNITED STATES (3 vols., 1881–83).

73.  ZECHARIAH CHAFEE, CASES ON EQUITY, JURISDICTION AND SPECIFIC PERFORMANCE (1934); SOME PROBLEMS OF EQUITY (1950).

74.  Robert Cover, *For James Wm. Moore: Some Reflections on A Reading of the Rules*, 84 YALE L. J. 718 (1975).

75.  Benjamin Kaplan, *Continuing Work of the Civil Committee: 1966 Amendments to the Federal Rules of Civil Procedure*, 81 HARV. L. REV. 356 (1967).

76.  Mary Kay Kane, *The Golden Wedding Years: Erie R. R. v. Tompkins and the Federal Rules*, 63 NOTRE DAME L. REV. 671 (1988).

77.  *See* Paul D. Carrington, *Maurice Rosenberg*, 95 COLUM. L. REV. 1901 (1995).

78.  JOSEPH L. EBERSOLE, THE FEDERAL JUDICIAL CENTER: A NONTRADITIONAL ORGANIZATION IN THE FEDERAL JUDICIARY OF THE UNITED STATES (1979).

79.  JAMES WILLIAM MOORE, FEDERAL PRACTICE: A TREATISE ON THE FEDERAL RULES OF CIVIL PROCEDURE (1938). This work evolved into a twenty-volume set.

80.  In 1959, Wright became editor of William W. Barron & Alexander Holtzoff, *Federal Practice and Procedure* (7 vols., 1950).

81.  Ted Finman, *The Request for Admission in Federal Civil Procedure*, 71 YALE L.J. 371 (1962).

82.  Edward Cooper, *Directions for Directed Verdicts: A Compass for Federal Courts*, 55 MINN. L. REV. 903 (1971).

83.  Arthur Miller, *Federal Rule 44.1 and the "Fact" Approach to Determining Foreign Law: Death Knell for a Die-Hard Doctrine*, 65 MICH. L. REV. 613 (1967).

84.  Martin Lewis, *Federal Summary Judgment Doctrine: A Critical Analysis*, 83 YALE L.J. 745 (1974).

85.  304 U. S. 64 (1938).

86.  Guaranty Trust v. York, 326 U. S. 99 (1945).

87.  Paul D. Carrington, *"Substance" and "Procedure" in the Rules Enabling Act*, 1989 DUKE L.J. 281, reviews the literature.

88.  380 U.S. 460 (1965).

89.  1 ROBERT C. CASAD, JURISDICTION IN CIVIL ACTIONS 4-3 to 4-10 (2d ed. 1991).

90. 95 U.S. 714 (1877).

91. 326 U.S. 310 (1945).

92. 357 U.S. 235 (1958).

93. Beacon Theatres, Inc. v. Westover, 359 U.S. 500 (1959); Dairy Queen, Inc. v. Wood, 369 U.S. 469 (1962).

94. Charles Wolfram, *The Constitutional History of the Seventh Amendment*, 57 MINN. L. REV. 639 (1973).

95. *See generally* Randy J. Holland, *State Constitutions: Purpose and Functions*, 69 TEMPLE L. REV. 989 (1996); Randall T. Shepard, *The Maturing Nature of State Constitutional Jurisprudence*, 30 VAL. U.L. REV. 421 (1996).

96. *E.g.*, Greene v. Lindsey, 456 U.S. 44 (1982).

97. *E.g.*, North Georgia Finishing, Inc. v. Di-Chem, Inc., 419 U.S. 601 (1975); Mitchell v. W. T. Grant Co., 416 U.S. 600 (1974).

98. *E.g.* Tulsa Professional Collection Services v. Pope, 485 U.S. 478 (1988).

99. *E.g.*, Martin v. Wilks, 490 U.S. 755 (1989).

100. *E.g.*, Walters v. National Association of Radiation Survivors, 473 U.S. 305 (1985).

101. Boddie v. Connecticut, 401 U.S. 371 (1971).

102. Hicks Acting on Behalf of Feiock v. Feiock, 485 U.S. 624 (1988); Santosky v. Kramer, 455 U.S. 745 (1982).

103. *E.g.*, Edmonson v. Leesville Concrete Co., Inc., 500 U.S. 614 (1991); J. E. B. v. Alabama ex rel. T. B., 511 U.S. 127 (1994).

104. Amchem Products, Inc. v. Windsor, 117 S. Ct. 2331 (1997).

105. MORTON HORWITZ, THE TRANSFORMATION OF AMERICAN LAW 1870–1960, at 213–46 (New York 1993).

106. RICHARD FIELD & BENJAMIN KAPLAN, MATERIALS FOR A BASIC COURSE IN CIVIL PROCEDURE (1953).

107. MAURICE ROSENBERG & JACK B. WEINSTEIN, ELEMENTS OF CIVIL PROCEDURE (1962); JAMES H. CHADBOURN & A. LEO LEVIN, CASES AND MATERIALS ON CIVIL PROCEDURE (1962); DAVID W. LOUISELL & GEOFFREY C. HAZARD, JR., CASES AND MATERIALS ON PLEADING AND PROCEDURE (1962).

108. FRANCIS LIEBER, LEGAL AND POLITICAL HERMENEUTICS OR PRINCIPLES OF INTERPRETATION AND CONSTRUCTION IN LAW AND POLITICS WITH REMARKS ON PRECEDENTS AND AUTHORITIES 125 (William G. Hammond ed., St. Louis 1880).

109. LON FULLER,THE MORALITY OF LAW (1964).

110. *See* JOHN S. MURRAY, ALAN SCOTT RAU & EDWARD F. SHERMAN, PROCESSES OF DISPUTE RESOLUTION: THE ROLE OF LAWYERS 436–99 (2d ed. 1996); EMERGING ADR ISSUES IN STATE AND FEDERAL COURTS (Frank E. D. Sander ed. 1991); *but see* Harry Edwards, *Alternative Dispute Resolution: Panacea or Anathema?*, 99 HARV. L. REV. 668 (1986).

111. ROBERT M. COVER, OWEN M. FISS & JUDITH F. RESNIK, PROCEDURE (1988).

112. Linda S. Mullenix, *God, Metaprocedure and Metarealism at Yale*, 87 MICH. L. REV. 1139, 1170 (1989).

113. COVER, FISS & RESNIK, *supra* note 111, at vii.

114. It should be noted that I have been engaged in ADR work as a founder in 1983 of the Private Adjudication Center, Inc., an organization I presently serve as Chairman of the Board. Also, I do teach in the basic course a few hours on the law governing ADR proceedings.

115. Paul D. Carrington, *Civil Procedure and Alternative Dispute Resolution*, 34 J. LEGAL. EDUC. 298 (1984); *ADR and Future Adjudication: A Primer on Dispute Resolution*, 15 REV. OF LITIGATION 1 (1996).

116. Paul D. Carrington & Paul Haagen, *Contract and Jurisdiction*, 1996 SUP. CT. REV. 331 (1997).

117. Lawrence M. Frankel, *Disclosure in the Federal Courts: A Cure for Discovery Ills?*, 23 ARIZ. ST. L.J. 219 (1993).

118. B. Michael Dunn & George Logan III, *Jury Reform: The Arizona Experience*, 79 JUDICATURE 280 (1996).

119. Paul D. Carrington, *Virtual Civil Litigation: A Visit to John Bunyan's Celestial City*, 98 COLUM. L. REV. 501 (1998).

120. Thomas D. Rowe, *Repealing the Law of Unintended Consequences: A Comment on Walker*, 23 J. LEG. STUD. 615 (1994).

121. Laurens Walker, *Avoiding Surprise from Federal Civil Rule Making: The Role of Economic Analysis*, 23 J. LEG. STUD. 569 (1994); *and see* Laurens Walker, *A Comprehensive Reform for Federal Rulemaking*, 61 GEO. WASH. L. REV. 455 (1993).

122. *E.g.*, Cover, *supra* note 74; *and see* Stephen N. Subrin, *Federal Rules, Local Rules, and State Rules: Uniformity, Divergence, and Emerging Procedural Patterns*, 137 U. PA. L. REV. 1999 (1989); Judith Resnik, *The Domain of Courts*, 137 U. PA. L. REV. 2219 (1989).

123. *See* Paul D. Carrington, *Exorcising the Bogy of Non-Transsubstantive Rules and Making Rules to Dispose of Manifestly Unfounded Assertions*, 137 U. PA. L. REV. 2067 (1989); David L. Shapiro, *Federal Rule 16: A Look at the Theory and Practice of Rulemaking*, 137 U. PA. L. REV. 1969 (1989); Geoffrey C. Hazard, Jr., *Discovery Vices and Trans-Substantive Virtue in the Federal Rules of Civil Procedure*, 137 U. PA. L. REV. 2237 (1989).

124. Stephen N. Subrin, *Uniformity in Procedure Rules and the Atrributes of a Sound Procedural System: The Case for Presumptive Limits*, 49 ALA. L. REV. 79, 91 (1997).

125. I am not completely innocent. *See* Paul D. Carrington, *United States Appeals: A Field and Statistical Analysis*, 11 HOUSTON L. REV. 1104 (1974).

126. For an expression of my views and a review of the literature, *see* Paul D.

Carrington, *A New Confederacy? Disunionism in the Federal Courts*, 45 Duke L.J. 929 (1996).

127. *E.g.*, Walter K. Olson, The Litigation Explosion: What Happened When America Unleashed the Lawsuit (1991); *but see* Marc Galanter, *The Debased Debate on Civil Justice*, 71 Denver U.L. Rev. 77 (1993); Lauren K. Robel, *The Politics of Crisis in the Federal Courts*, 7 Ohio St. J. Disp. Resol. 115 (1991).

# Chapter 7

# Of Coase and the Canon
## *Reflections on Law and Economics*

## *Daniel A. Farber*

One highlight of my environmental law class is the day I teach the Coase Theorem.[1] I introduce Coase right after I cover a classic nuisance case, *Atlantic Cement Co. v. Boomer*.[2] The issue in *Boomer* was whether a court should close a pollution source when the company's economic value is much greater than the measurable harm to the plaintiffs. The students usually disagree strongly with the court's ruling in favor of the company. After allowing the spirited discussion to run its course, I pull my surprise. "Does it really matter," I ask, "how the court rules?" Then, simplifying a bit for dramatic effect, I add that Ronald Coase won the Nobel Prize for proving that the court's ruling is irrelevant. I spend the rest of the class on the Coase Theorem, usually provoking vehement arguments from the students against applying the theorem to the *Boomer* case.

I spend class time on the Coase Theorem for several reasons. Probably the strongest personal motivation is that it's incredibly fun to teach. Coase's conclusion is not merely counterintuitive but an outrage to lawyerly common sense, yet the argument is simple and powerful. Thus, teaching Coase is like pulling a rabbit out of a hat before a disbelieving audience. Another reason is that economic analysis is important in a variety of contexts in environmental law. In most environmental situations, the Coase Theorem doesn't actually apply, but it is important for the students to understand why it does not. And Coase's argument does turn out to be useful later when I reach the subject of marketable pollution permits, which operationalize Coase's conception of bargaining over pollution. Finally—and probably the best justification, if not the strongest motivation—is that I consider the Coase Theorem to be part of a modern lawyer's basic liberal education. Many of my students do not encounter it in their other classes, and they should not leave law school without it.

The Coase Theorem is a central result in legal scholarship. From the beginning, the theorem was perceived as momentous. It originated in a seminar that Coase presented to the University of Chicago economics department in 1960. Future Nobel Prize winner George Stigler later called that seminar "one of the most exciting intellectual events of my life."[3] At the beginning of the seminar, the participants took a vote. Like my students, the audience was initially skeptical. Coase received only a single vote (apparently his own). The conventional view originated by Arthur Pigou received twenty. Milton Friedman took the lead and pummeled Coase with penetrating questions. At some point in the evening, however, Friedman changed sides and began attacking Pigou's position. By the end of the evening, the vote was Coase 21, Pigou 0.[4]

After this auspicious beginning, Coase's article quickly attained a central position in law and economics. Richard Posner has observed that the article "as everyone knows—it's silly to dwell on it—is basic to the whole economic analysis of law."[5] Posner has also noted that "The Problem of Social Cost" is "widely believed to be the most frequently cited article in all of economics."[6] By 1989, the article had received 1,109 citations in the Social Science Index, about half of them in law journals.[7] It is also probably one of the most frequently cited articles in the history of legal scholarship.[8] Indeed, according to one study of the period 1981–88, it was the single work mostly frequently cited in law review articles.[9]

Besides the sheer volume of citations, the article is also notable for the close attention it has received from major legal scholars, including key figures in law and economics such as Richard Posner and Bob Cooter, liberals like Bruce Ackerman and Owen Fiss, and critical legal scholars such as Mark Kelman. As Stewart Schwab says, "For both supporters and opponents, Coase has helped set the terms of debate about the legal system."[10] Little wonder that Robert Ellickson views the Coase Theorem as "undoubtedly . . . the most fruitful, and the most controversial, proposition to arise out of the law-and-economics movement."[11]

In other words, if anyone has ever established a new paradigm in legal scholarship, that person was Ronald Coase.[12] And if there is anything that can be described as the canon of "law and economics," the Coase Theorem is at the heart of that canon.[13] As Balkin and Levinson have said, it is clearly part of the "academic theory" canon.[14] Indeed, it is so basic to understanding major portions of legal theory that only the most vocational version of law school could omit it. It is for this reason that I believe it is a necessary part of the intellectual toolkit of any well-educated lawyer. For the same reason, the Coase Theorem serves as an ideal focal point for an exploration of the entire canon of law and economics.

A canonical work exercises its influence not only through scholarship but through teaching, as part of what Balkin and Levinson call the pedagogical canon. In any event, we often think most seriously about the content of the canon in the classroom context. Consequently, in discussing the canon, I will draw upon my own experience in using economic analysis in the classroom.

## I. The World of the Coase Theorem

In my environmental law class, I explain the Coase Theorem with a simplified version of *Boomer v. Atlantic Cement Co.*[15] I begin by showing the effect of liability rules. Suppose that Mr. Boomer suffers $2,000 harm from the pollution. If Atlantic is liable for Boomer's damages, it won't pollute unless it profits from the pollution by $2,000 or more. If its profits are any lower, it will actually lose money by polluting, after it pays damages to Boomer. But if the profits are higher than $2,000, Atlantic will choose to pollute, pay damages, and still come out ahead. In effect, tort liability forces Atlantic to perform a cost-benefit analysis that includes both benefits to itself and costs to others. Hence, tort liability will lead to an economically efficient outcome.[16] This was essentially Pigou's point.[17]

Where Pigou may have gone astray, however, was in assuming that unless the company had to pay for the harm it caused, an inefficient level of pollution would result. It seems intuitively obvious that, without some form of cost internalization, the polluter would simply ignore its neighbors. Coase observed, however, that another mechanism exists for the victims to influence the polluter's activities.

Coase's insight was that bargaining can sometimes produce an economically efficient outcome even without tort liability. Suppose there is no tort liability, and that Atlantic's profits are less than Boomer's $2,000 in damages. At first blush it seems Atlantic will choose to pollute and make its profit, even though a societal cost-benefit analysis would come out negative. After all, what does Atlantic care about Boomer's harm if it doesn't have to pay damages? But there's another way to eliminate the pollution: Boomer can pay Atlantic not to pollute. For example, if Atlantic's profits are $1,000 and Boomer's harm is $2,000, Boomer could offer Atlantic $1,500 not to pollute. This is a winning deal for both sides—each is $500 better off than in the situation where Atlantic pollutes.[18]

This hypothetical exemplifies a more general truth. According to the Coase Theorem, unless transactions costs prevent contracting around legal rules, the legal rules don't matter—or more precisely, the parties will always bargain their way to an economically efficient outcome, regardless of the legal rule. In short, bargaining washes out legal rules.

In the real world, as Coase himself stressed, judicial decisions do affect total social wealth because bargaining may not occur. Coase observed that transactions are "often extremely costly, sufficiently costly at any rate to prevent many transactions that would be carried out in a world in which the pricing system worked without cost" (16).

Where transactions costs are high, Coase suggested, courts should make the initial assignment of rights in a way that maximizes total social wealth. (p. 19) "In a world in which there are costs of rearranging the rights established by the legal system, the courts, in cases relating to nuisance, are, in effect, making a decision on the economic problem and determining how resources are to be employed" (28). Indeed, Coase says, "courts are conscious of this" and often compare, at least implicitly, "what would be gained and what lost by preventing actions which have harmful effects" (id).

Thus, Coase's analysis would suggest, we should proceed upon the following lines in analyzing a legal rule. We should begin by determining how rights would be allocated after bargaining in the absence of transactions costs. This allocation is, according to the Coase Theorem, economically efficient, and thus provides a normative baseline. Then, we identify the relevant transactions costs and determine whether they are sufficiently large to interfere with bargaining. If so, we allocate the legal entitlement to the party who would have ended up with it in the absence of transactions costs, using law to mimic the results of the market. Often, we will discover that the courts have already arrived at this result without the benefit of a formal economic analysis. Here is the blueprint for a new method of legal analysis.[19]

## II. The Economic Analysis of Law

What insights has economics added to legal analysis? The literature of law and economics is extensive. Posner's treatise on the subject is almost seven hundred pages in length in its most recent edition. The author index runs to about six hundred names, though not all of them would identify themselves as belonging to the law and economics movement. Much of this work carries forward Coase's project of evaluating whether legal rules are economically efficient. Law and economics scholarship is not only plentiful but diverse. Virtually the entire field of law is covered; the level of sophistication ranges from Econ. 101 to graduate level; and the viewpoints of the authors span the political spectrum. Although most scholarship is based on standard microeconomic market analysis, much of the most interesting recent work uses game theory to analyze nonmarket phenomena. (For instance, the work on public choice theory discussed later tends to fall in the game theory tradition.) It would require a book longer than Posner's to evaluate the degree to which economics has enriched—or instead, merely confused—the analysis of law. Even to deal adequately with the contribution of economics to a single field of law would require a lengthy article in its own right.[20]

Rather than attempting an evaluation of how economics has contributed to legal scholarship, I will focus on the more manageable question of its role in legal pedagogy. One key indication of the extent to which economics belongs in the legal canon is its role in the classroom. As a law teacher, this is a question I have had to face in a number of courses. Indeed, the fact that I have "*had* to face" this issue would itself be an indication of the increasingly canonical status of economics, even if I had ultimately decided against discussing economics in class. But in fact, I do not believe that teachers in a number of areas of law can properly avoid considering economic arguments.

I probably use economics more extensively in environmental law than in any other course I have taught. Given the central role of economics in environmental regulation, minimal competence as an environmental lawyer requires familiarity with economic concepts. In addition, the course provides a nice opportunity to acquaint students with some basic ideas which they can use in a variety of other contexts.

For example, my environmental law class always includes a brief presentation of the standard economic analysis of pollution. As with the Coase Theorem, I use a simple example to make the basic idea clear. Suppose that catalytic converters are cost-justified, so that their benefits in pollution control outweigh their costs. But any particular car owner receives only a tiny return (in the form of improved air quality) from her individual investment in pollution control. Performing this cost-benefit analysis, the owner decides not to pay for a catalytic converter, although she would of course be happy to enjoy the cleaner air resulting from the purchases of converters by other car owners. Since every car owner goes through the same calculation, none of them buys a converter, though all would be better off if they had each made the contrary decision. The government can improve everyone's welfare by mandating converters. This is the classical economic argument for government regulation of pollution.

As the Coase Theorem indicates, this argument overlooks the possible role of bargaining. It is theoretically possible to avoid this dilemma of underinvestment if the individuals involved can feasibly bargain with each other. But in the pollution example, this is impossible, as my students invariably point out to me in our discussions of the Coase Theorem. There are thousands or millions of car owners, so that even contacting each of them would be expensive, let alone persuading them to make a deal. The situation would be quite different if there were only a handful of polluters, each with a large potential stake in the issue of pollution control. Such a small group would be far easier to organize effectively because transactions costs would be much lower. While it would be hard for consumers to bargain with each other, it would be much easier for the major car companies to make an agreement with each other over pollution control, as the Big Three allegedly once did.

This simple example allows me to introduce some crucial economic concepts: public goods, negative externalities, and the prisoner's dilemma. These concepts are crucial to environmental policy analysis, and a lawyer who lacked an understanding of these concepts would be badly handicapped in policy debates. Economics is a foreign language, and a regulatory lawyer needs, at the very least, a tourist-level knowledge of that language.

It's more difficult to know how much economics to include in common law courses like torts and contracts. As it happens, I taught torts for the first time two years ago, and had to give considerable thought to how much economics to include. Explicit economic reasoning is still infrequent in judicial opinions in torts and contracts, although influential judges like Posner are making significant inroads.[21] Still, I would guess that most highly successful torts lawyers are entirely ignorant of economics, except to the extent that economists or accountants provide expert testimony relating to the amount of damages. Moreover, my own tentative sense of the case law is that economic efficiency has done less to shape the law than other notions relating to group norms, moral responsibility, and social insurance. Nevertheless, I decided to include a significant amount of economics in the course, for three reasons.

One reason is cultural literacy. Our students should have at least a glancing encounter with the major ideas that are circulating in the legal academy, and Minnesota's law and economics contingent is small enough that students might well get through law schools without running into much economics. They may never need to use the Coase Theorem in practice, but then, they will also probably never need to cite *Brown v. Board of Education* in a brief. We would be remiss in graduating students who are ignorant about either one.

Another reason for teaching economics is that economic analysis is one way to get students to think seriously about policy. Tort reform has been a simmering public issue for the past fifteen years or so, and may well continue to be controversial when my current students have attained responsible positions in government. Policy arguments are not also uncommon in legal arguments before courts, and I suspect that lawyers will be increasingly likely to run into judges who want to discuss the economics of the tort rules. In some ways, torts is likely to become a particularly fertile field for economics because some of the traditional legal concepts, such as Judge Learned Hand's famous definition of negligence, do lend themselves to economic analysis. Lawyers are apt to view references to public policy as conversation stoppers; I want them to learn that it's possible to think hard about policy issues rather than just staking out a political position.

Finally, economic analysis is useful as a source of cognitive dissonance. Law students are too inclined to take the pronouncements of the courts as gospel. Economic analysis is a useful way of shaking them up from time to time, so they do not unthinkingly internalize current law. For example, after several weeks discussing the nuances of the negligence concept, I spent some time explaining a basic economic result, which is that strict liability and negligence law induce individuals to take exactly the same level of care.[22] This result throws open the question of why we have a negligence standard at all, just when the students have been taking the existence of that standard completely for granted and focusing entirely on how to define its parameters.

Perhaps it's worth mentioning that my original plan for this particular class period ended with a discussion of the Coase Theorem. I was planning to use one of my hypotheticals to show that if the parties could bargain freely, they would end up at exactly the same level of care even if there was no tort liability rule at all. This is a significant point, because substantial portions of tort law involve parties who can engage in some degree of bargaining, yet courts often seem to apply the same tort rules as they do to interactions between complete strangers. Unfortunately, it took so long to work through the more basic parts of the argument that I never had a chance to get to Coase. I had to wait until I got to products liability before putting forward the Coasean argument.

## III. Public Choice Theory

In its simplest terms, Coase's argument is that it is unfair to compare the flawed operations of the real market with the idealized perfection of a hypothetical government regulation. If the market operated perfectly, it could cure all of society's problems; so could a perfect government. Hence, we must compare the market's imperfections with the government's. Government regulations may or may not be effective in advancing the public interest. Indeed, they may or may not be *designed* to advance the public interest. Coase's work suggests grounds for skepticism about government regulation, but does not discuss the question in detail.

It remained for other economists to probe the flaws of government regulation. Their work is the heart of the field of public choice, a discipline which now spans law, economics, and political science. Essentially, public choice is an effort to apply economic methodology to political institutions.

The central insight of the economic theory of legislation is that political participation is much like pollution control. It is costly (if only in terms of time and effort), and the benefits overwhelmingly flow to the public at large rather than to the individual citizen. Hence, every individual citizen will underinvest in political participation, just as she will underinvest in catalytic converters. Because of transaction costs, it is difficult for this diffuse group to act collectively. In contrast, when a political issue involves a small group with high individual stakes, Coase's analysis suggests that they may do better at bargaining their way to an "efficient" outcome—efficient for them, that is, not necessarily for the rest of society. The result is a built-in skew in group dynamics: small, concentrated groups tend to dominate politically over large, diffuse groups, all other things being equal, because of their inherent organizational advantages. In short, small groups tend to be more "Coasean" than large groups, and this gives them an edge in terms of pursuing the welfare of their members.

The credit for applying this analysis to politics goes to Mancur Olson.[23] The implication, as he observed, is that political activity should be dominated by small groups of individuals seeking to benefit themselves, usually at the public expense.[24] These groups are able to mobilize a disproportionate share of political resources in order to influence the government. These groups may be able to capture administrative agencies through control over the selection of agency staff or over the flow of information to the agency. Their views may influence not only the substance of legislation, but also the procedural mechanisms used for enforcement, which may be designed to favor those groups. To gain this influence, as Dan Rodriguez points out, they may use several tools: "They may deliver votes, campaign contributions, or outright bribes. They may extract rents from legislators who would receive value from having information which the groups exclusively possess. Additionally, they may threaten to support a legislator's opponent in the next election."[25]

A classic example of interest group influence is provided by tariffs. On balance, according to economic theory, free trade is generally more beneficial to a nation than a trade barrier even if other countries follow protectionist policies. (This may seem counterintuitive, but trade barriers are really not unlike blockading your own harbors: a bad idea, even if your trading partners do it to themselves first.) Thus, nations do not face a prisoner's dilemma; on the contrary, free trade is normally the dominant strategy in terms of national interest. The political balance of power within each individual nation, however, may not reflect the overall national interest. The beneficiaries of free trade are consumers, a diffuse group with small individual stakes. The beneficiaries of tariffs are concentrated industries and their (often unionized) employees, who are much easier to organize politically and therefore wield considerable political clout. The result is a political tendency toward protectionism, despite its economic flaws.

As Einer Elhauge explains, interest group theory holds that these "fundamental distortions in the political process" cause systematic divergences from the public interest."[26] The political process, in short, is inherently rigged in favor of special interests. Hence, legislation can enjoy no presumption of alignment with the public interest. As Elhauge summarized in his survey, this model of politics has led a wide range of scholars to propose substantial revisions in legal doctrine:

Erwin Chermerinsky argues that the susceptibility of the politically accountable branches to interest group pressure undermines the case for deferential constitutional review. Richard Epstein advocates far-reaching substantive judicial review under the Takings and Contract Clauses to curb rent seeking. Jerry Mashaw uses interest group theory to support his argument that the Supreme Court should invalidate some "private-regarding" legislation. Martin Shaprio argues that, at least in the First Amendment area, the Court should not defer to a political process driven by interest group politics but rather should advance the cause of the groups the political process underrepresents. Bernard Siegan believes that interest group theory helps justify a return to *Lochner*-era substantive due process review of economic regulation. Finally, Cass Sunstein argues that more rigorous constitutional scrutiny is needed to invalidate the legislation that rewards the raw political power of interest groups.[27]

As Elhauge goes on to point out, proposals for legal change are not limited to constitutional law. For example, John Wiley, Frank Easterbrook, and others argue for revisions in the "state action" defense in antitrust law. Easterbrook, Macey, Sunstein, and Eskridge have all argued for changes in judicial techniques of statutory interpretation on the same basis.[28]

A related theory casts additional doubts on the legitimacy of democratic governments. Some prominent scholars have argued that inherent logical flaws in voting procedures, first identified by Kenneth Arrow, leave the legitimacy of democratic decision making in doubt. In *Liberalism against Populism*,[29] William Riker argues that voting is so susceptible to cycling and strategic behavior that outcomes cannot be meaningfully connected with the voters' values. Hence, "the meaning of social choices is quite obscure" because those choices may reflect either the voters' true values, the results of manipulation, or the accidental result of both factors.[30]

The basic conclusion of the public choice literature, Jerry Mashaw concludes in a thoughtful survey, is that no stable relationship between individual preferences and collective choice can exist except in special circumstances.[31] At its most extreme, he continues, positive political theory predicts that political outcomes are completely fortuitous. According to Mashaw, this prediction can be given a cynical "spin," by stressing the ability of legislative players to manipulate the process. Alternatively, he adds, it can be given a more agnostic interpretation, which simply says that collective decisions are "probably meaningless because it is impossible to be certain that they are not simply an artifact of the decision process that has been used."[32] The natural implication is that courts should be less deferential toward legislative decisions, which do not have any strong claim to reflect either any coherent public opinion or any meaningful public interest.

This body of work does not stem in any direct way from Coase, but it is a perfect fit with his call for an investigation of the relative defects of the market and government. It also reinforces his suggestion that the government's defects are more glaring than the market's, suggesting that we should be skeptical of government intervention even when there is a plausible claim of market failure.

So far, public choice has not yet attained the same position in the legal canon as law and economics generally. On the other hand, it was later in reaching the legal academy than microeconomics, so perhaps its impact will grow.[33] In the previous section, I said that it would take a long book to evaluate the contribution of law and economics to scholarship. As it happens, I have co-authored a book attempting such an evaluation of public choice, along with Phil Frickey.[34] Our conclusion, in a nutshell, was that public choice is a useful tool in thinking about some kinds of problems in public law, provided that it is used carefully and its limits are respected. On the other hand, there seem to be large and important areas of public law, such as discrimination law, where it has no apparent relevance.

What role should public choice play in the classroom? In constitutional law, I have found it most relevant to two issues. First, it arguably supports giving a lower degree of deference to economic regulations, and hence suggests a more aggressive judicial role in protecting economic rights. Because these arguments have some political resonance, it seems worthwhile to spend some class time evaluating them, even though I do not myself find them persuasive. Second, public choice might have something useful to say about issues concerning the structure of government, such as the legislative veto. Although there is an expanding body of interesting scholarship on the subject, the theories are complex and in considerable disagreement; I have never found a way to deal with them intelligibly given the time constraints of the basic constitutional law class. If anything, I have tended to spend less time on them over the years.

Public choice looms larger in the course on legislation. Here, it seems to me that a substantial discussion of public choice is unavoidable simply because much of the leading judicial discussion of the statutory interpretation is by former academics such as Frank Easterbrook, Richard Posner, and Antonin Scalia. Their views cannot be comprehended, let alone intelligently evaluated, without some background on public choice. Public choice is highly controversial in the field of legislation, much like the law and economics movement twenty years ago. It is unclear whether it will ever achieve the level of acceptance of economic analysis in private law. Nevertheless, its advocates have succeeded in setting much of the agenda for debate, so even their strongest opponents need to know something about public choice, if only for purposes of self-defense. In the legislation course, part of my motive for teaching public choice is to inoculate the students, who might otherwise come down with a virulent case of legal formalism if they are later exposed to the views of the Scalia school for the first time.

No doubt other teachers make contrary decisions about course coverage. It is probably more important to consider the assumptions underlying my pedagogical decisions than to debate whether I've worked out the implications correctly. There are basically three reasons for covering law and economics or public choice in class. The first is the "legal practice" rationale. Economic reasoning is by no means canonical on the part of judges, outside of some special areas like antitrust, but it has growing importance, and I believe that a well-trained lawyer should have at least some superficial acquaintance with it. Second is the "citizen lawyer" rationale. Many of my students will someday be judges, legislators, and bureaucrats, with some influence over the making of public policy, particularly at the state level. I believe that familiarity with the economic analysis of legal issues will be helpful to them later. Finally, there is the "liberal education" rationale. Although I believe that the main purpose of law school is to prepare professionals, it also seems to me that our students should be exposed to the main currents of thought regarding the nature of law. Perhaps this will make them more effective as lawyers, but even if it doesn't, it may make them more reflective about their work.

For some of these purposes, the actual validity of economic analysis is quite irrelevant. If judges are going to be using it, students need to know about it even if it is nonsense. And if students need exposure to the academic legal canon, what matters is the actual content of the canon at any given time, not the desirability of that content. But it is also important to consider the normative question of whether economic analysis deserves a home in the legal canon. In the final two sections of the chapter, I will reflect upon the question of whether economic analysis has anything useful to contribute to law.

## IV. The Empirical Question

Does economics actually provide a useful way of evaluating legal policies? One issue is whether the world of economic theory matches up with the reality. Economics isn't going to be much help in formulating policy if it's empirically worthless. Obviously, it's not easy to evaluate the empirical validity of an entire discipline. My own view is that economics is fairly robust empirically—for a social science. But some might consider that a matter of damning with faint praise.

The Coase Theorem is a nice illustration of both the strengths and weaknesses of economic theory. The theorem can be tested empirically in two ways. First, an experiment may be used to study bargaining under controlled conditions. Second, real-world behavior may be investigated to see whether it follows Coase's predictions.

Elizabeth Hoffman and Matthew Spitzer set up some careful experiments to test the Coase Theorem. Their experiments, which involved artificial bargaining situations, did confirm Coase's predictions. Indeed, they found that individuals reached efficient bargains even when the number of bargainers was fairly high, despite the fact that transaction costs might be expected to be higher.[35] Other experiments, which were designed to study game theory rather than the Coase Theorem, raise some questions about the Coase Theorem. Some games have "cores"— agreements which are optimal in the sense that neither any individual nor any combination of individuals can better themselves by defecting from the agreement. Game theory predicts that outcomes should always be in the core if one exists, since otherwise some individuals could better their situations by defecting. This prediction, which is very similar to Coase's prediction of optimal bargains, has had only modest empirical success.[36]

Nonexperimental empirical results are not very supportive of Coase. Drawing on Coase's example of damage by cattle, Robert Ellickson studied how ranchers responded to different rules regarding liability for damage by stray cattle. He investigated an area where some regions were covered by a rule of strict liability for strays ("closed range") and others by a rule of nonliability with narrow exceptions ("open range"). He found that actual conduct regarding cattle was unaffected by the legal rule— which seems to confirm the Coase Theorem—but also that the legal rule failed to provide even a starting point for bargaining, contrary to Coase's model. Rather, individuals simply ignored the legal rule, followed precepts of neighborliness in their interactions with others, and viewed litigation as a form of deviant misconduct.[37]

A particularly interesting study by John Donohue straddles the line between experiment and field investigation, making use of a "natural experiment" by a state government. In order to study the effects of incentives on the length of periods of unemployment, the state established a program of bonuses for selected workers who found jobs. One program provided for payment of the bonus to the new employer, the other to the employee. Under these circumstances, the Coasean prediction would be that outcomes in the two programs would be identical: it should make no difference whether the employer or the employee receives the check. Instead, Donohue reports, the programs operated substantially differently, with very different participation rates and different effects on unemployment.[38]

The Donohue and Ellickson studies are both somewhat inconsistent with Coase. Ellickson's findings suggest that high transaction costs actually may prevent legal rules from being relevant but may not be a barrier to efficient understandings between landowners. Donohue's suggest that low transaction costs may not produce efficient bargains, and that even very low transaction costs may not make legal rules irrelevant. In response, Coase might point to Hoffman and Spitzer's experimental results and to Ellickson's evidence that people are sometimes remarkably good at working out economically efficient, consensual arrangements. The Coase Theorem points to a theoretical possibility which seems to be erratically realized in practice. Given the spotty empirical record, it would be foolish to base public policy solely on Coase's predictions. Instead, we would do better to take the Coase Theorem as a hypothesis in need of careful testing in any concrete setting.

It's hard to generalize about the empirical validation for law and economics across various fields. In torts, the subject that I mentioned earlier, probably the most comprehensive survey of the empirical literature was published in 1994 by Gary Schwartz.[39] After examining a multitude of studies, he concluded that tort law probably does have a significant deterrent effect, but that the linkage between tort rules and conduct may be looser than assumed by economic analysts. He found some indications that the costs of the tort system were justified by the increased safety produced by the threat of tort liability, particularly for medical malpractice. His overall conclusion is that economic analysts may be investing too much effort in fine-tuning tort rules in a search for theoretical perfection, though he admitted that "over time some fraction of these exercises will probably yield findings with actual social payoffs."[40]

A similar conclusion can be drawn regarding public choice theory. The logic of interest group theory is compelling, but its empirical validity is less clear-cut. As the protectionism example shows, the interest group story is at least incomplete. Despite the political pressures toward protectionism, which have indeed triumphed at times, the current tendency is strongly in the other direction. The success of the Uruguay Round in liberalizing trade and creating the World Trade Organization is a striking illustration. On the other hand, it's hard to gainsay the idea that special interests play a significant role in the political process.

The empirical literature confirms that constituent interest, special interest groups, and ideology all help determine legislative conduct.[41] Interest group theory accounts poorly for many aspects of politics, most notably individual voting behavior.[42] Nevertheless, it is difficult to believe that interest group theory is completely fallacious. All other things being equal, organizing a group would clearly seem to become more difficult the larger the group and the smaller the individual stakes relative to the marginal cost of group participation. Thus, although other factors undoubtedly play a role in politics, the special interest theory seems likely to have some validity.

In short, economic theory seems to have significant but limited empirical validity as applied to the legal system. The best the economist can probably claim is to identify general tendencies which are often subject to considerable unexplained deviations. But, so long as we keep in mind the fallibility of the theories, it would be foolish not to obtain whatever empirical insights we can gain from economics. It is not, after all, as if we had some other, markedly more reliable basis for predicting the impacts of legal rules. The economist may well claim to be the one-eyed person in the kingdom of the blind—perhaps even a myopic one-eyed person—but still, a useful source of guidance, at least when the light is good and the target is near.

## V. The Normative Limits of Economic Efficiency

Economic analysis may sometimes tell us about how the world works, but can it also give normative direction? The answer depends on whether we find any substance in the underlying norm of economic efficiency used in law and economics. As we saw earlier, Coase recommended establishing legal rules in order to maximize social wealth. Or, in more familiar terms, the standard is one of cost-benefit analysis. But does this standard have any legitimacy?

The norm of economic efficiency was most hotly debated in the early 1980s, though portions of the dispute linger on today. The most vocal defender of efficiency was Richard Posner, who came close to arguing that efficiency is the only norm which judges should use. His fullest discussion of the subject is found in a 1980 article, written after he had already exchanged initial shots with some of his critics. The crux of the argument was as follows. Because there is no way of determining whether individuals actually consent to legal rules, the best we can do is to look for implied consent. One way of doing this is to ask whether the parties would have agreed to the legal rule in advance, if transaction costs were zero. This procedure, he said, "resembles a judge's imputing the intent of parties to a contract that fails to provide expressly for some contingency." Thus, he said, "an institution predicated on wealth maximization may be justifiable by reference to the consent of those affected by it even though the institution authorizes certain takings, such as the taking of life, health, or property of an individual injured in an accident in which neither party is negligent, without requiring compensation ex post."[43]

Because of his reliance on a form of implicit consent as the basis for determining fairness, Posner's argument has some resemblance to John Rawls's use of the "original position" in his theory of justice. Posner distinguished his approach from that taken by Rawls in that it does not assume that the parties are ignorant about their positions in society. His objection to Rawls is that in the original position, no one knows whether he has "productive capabilities," so the choices of the unproductive receive equal weight.[44] Thus, he explained, his rejection of Rawls is based on the premise that "those who have no productive assets have no ethical claim on the assets of others."[45]

In retrospect, it is easy to see why Posner's argument sparked such a hostile response. There was first of all his unblinking assertion that those who cannot work—the very young, the very old, and the handicapped— have no moral claim on society, even for the minimum needed to survive. This is not an easy assertion to stomach. Given the timing of the debate, just at the start of the Reagan administration, liberals may also have been alarmed by Posner's seeming rationale for the conservative agenda of un-regulated markets and government cost-benefit analysis. Whatever the reasons, Posner attracted a vigorous and distinguished array of critics.[46]

Ronald Dworkin led the charge against Posner. He argued that wealth is not a value at all, let alone one which should be the primary guide for judicial decisions.[47] His argument went like this: Suppose Derek has a book Amartya wants; Derek would be willing to sell the book for two dol-lars, and Amartya would be willing to pay three. Then a forced transfer from Amartya to Derek is economically efficient because Amartya would have been willing to pay Derek enough to compensate him for his loss. In Coasean terms, we could defend the forced transfer on the grounds that the entitlement to the book would end up with Derek in a zero transac-tion cost world; if transaction costs prevent bargaining, the court should assign the right to Derek. But, Dworkin says, make the example more spe-cific: "Derek is poor and sick and miserable, and the book is one of his few comforts. He is willing to sell it for $2 only because he needs medi-cine. Amartya is rich and content. He is willing to spend $3 for the book, which is a very small part of his wealth, on the odd chance that he might someday read it, although he knows that he probably will not." In this case, Dworkin concludes, "that goods are in the hands of those who would be pay more to have them is as morally irrelevant as the book's being in the hands of the alphabetically prior party."[48] Dworkin minces no words about his conclusion:

> I did not argue that maximizing social wealth is only one among a number of plausible social goals, or is a mean, unattractive, or unpopular social goal. I argued that it makes no sense as a social goal, even as one among others. It is preposterous to suppose that social wealth is a component of social value, and implausible that social wealth is strongly instrumental to-wards a social goal. . . .[49]

The Amartya/Derek hypothetical fails to justify this sweeping conclu-sion.[50] If we want to know whether something is a morally relevant fea-ture of the world, we need to know whether two otherwise identical situ-ations differ morally because of a difference in this quality. We cannot show that social wealth is irrelevant by taking two states of the world, and triumphantly pointing out that one of them has greater social wealth but is morally inferior, when it also differs in other morally relevant respects, such as the distribution of wealth and the use of coercion.

In addition, Dworkin ignores the heart of the argument for economic efficiency. The strongest argument for efficiency is that it will "increase the size of the pie" rather than just reallocating existing wealth. So we should really compare a world in which Amartya has $2 but the book does not exist, with a world in which Amartya does not have the money but Derek has the book, which he values at $5. Unless we have some reason to be partial toward Amartya over Derek, we might very well be inclined to favor the latter state of affairs. There are, of course, economic systems that make a point of ignoring efficiency in allocating resources, but these systems have not on the whole been appealing. Indeed, millions of people in Eastern Europe made their rejection of that approach unmistakably clear a few years ago.

It seems hard to argue that economic efficiency is morally irrelevant. Yet it would be even harder to argue for efficiency as the sole controlling norm. Even Posner himself says that economic efficiency is not the sole principle of justice. According to Posner, this has always been his position; it is clear at any rate that it is his current position. For example, he now believes that the moral case against slavery is based on liberty rather than efficiency.[51] The standard view among economists is that distributional norms are needed along with the efficiency norm in order to evaluate government policies.

Even taken together, the three norms of efficiency, liberty, and equality may not fully encompass our moral vision. Early in the semester, I ask my environmental law class to consider why we should be concerned about the survival of the whales. They typically respond with a volley of utilitarian arguments, which may well have some validity. These arguments, however, do not exhaust the students' reasons for wanting to save the whales; indeed, under probing, they generally admit that they would be willing to save the whales despite a contrary cost-benefit analysis. This seems to me a legitimate (and widely shared) moral position. So there are clearly some policies that we wish to further in areas like environmental law, and they may not be reducible to any single metric or measure of analysis. In many circumstances, economic efficiency cannot be considered to the exclusion of other moral values.

That conclusion would not have been a surprise to Coase. Economists are often criticized for reducing all values to questions of economic efficiency. Pragmatists tend to believe that human beings should pursue multiple goals, which cannot necessarily be quantified or reduced in a foundationalist way to a single value. Coase did not address the matter extensively, but he seemed to be in the pragmatist camp:

> In this article, the analysis has been confined, as is usual in this part of economics, to comparisons of the value of production, as measured by the market. But it is, of course, desirable that the choice between different social arrangements for the solution of economic problems should be carried out in broader terms than this and that the total effect of these arrangements in all spheres of life should be taken into account. As Frank H. Knight has so often emphasized, problems of welfare economics must ultimately dissolve into a study of aesthetics and morals. (p. 43)

With respect to the economics canon, Coase's view may or may not be typical, but it is clearly the better attitude for lawyers to take toward economic analysis.[52]

At the heart of much of the opposition to law and economics is a sense that economics may undermine valuable social norms by making us insensitive to these other moral dimensions. As two writers recently put it, "choices among alternative approaches to law and policy making—especially the choice between cost-benefit and other approaches—are significant apart from the results they produce." Such choices "reflect *how* we think about various social 'goods'—and how we think is a matter of independent ethical significance because it helps define the kind of community we will have."[53] According to critics, economics celebrates the marketplace but markets are "isolating, competitive, mean-spirited arenas."[54] Or, as Ron Cass phrases the objection in a thoughtful essay on law and economics, the analogy is to the doctor who refers to patients by disease rather than by name ("the ruptured disc in Room 102"), and no longer thinks of his patients as real people: "For him, the problem no longer is how George Johnson feels and functions but what mechanical treatment seems necessary to a particular organ or muscle or other sub-part. Such language may be appropriate to the efficient discussion of a technical problem, but it has a long-term, subtle, corrosive effect."[55]

This is a worrisome objection, and like Cass, I find myself in some doubt about how to respond.[56] A society in which people thought about themselves and others purely in the language of economic theory would be a disturbing spectacle, and it would be terrible if we somehow lost the capacity to use any other language than that of economics to describe our social world. To that extent, the critics are surely right. But this argument falls short of making the case for exiling economics from legal discourse.

First, the real question is not whether economics should be our sole means of discourse, but whether it should be included in the mix. Admittedly, it would be a grim world in which we could speak only the language of economics. But it would also be a grim world in which we could speak only the language of law (or even only the language of literary criticism). Our instinctive revulsion against a world of unitary economic discourse may be as much against the whole idea of unitary discourse as against economics as such.

Second, to use a cliché of First Amendment law, the remedy for speech may be more speech. If we find economic analysis useful but fear that it will distort our discourse, perhaps the best response is to open the door to other discourses as well, which may help counter the distortion. For instance, we might find it useful to make room for increased use of narrative techniques as a counter to the excessive abstraction of economic analysis.[57]

Finally, while we should not forget the expressive function of law, we should not allow that function to blind us to its instrumental significance. It would be morally bankrupt to focus solely on beautifying the language of the law while being heedless of the direct impact on the subjects of legal decisions. Cass's essay was prompted by the debate over Posner's famous (or infamous) proposal to use market mechanisms to deal with a shortage of adoptable babies. In essence, Posner wanted to implement a system of Coasian bargains to deal with the baby shortage. Posner's use of market language in this context is indeed troubling, and Cass thoughtfully canvasses the objections to this use of the depersonalized language of economics. He closes, however, with an observation about how the debate over depersonalization may sacrifice the individuals most affected:

> [T]here should be at least a pang of regret that it is so difficult to look at a proposal like Judge Posner's apart from the general combat over methodology. For people whose lives are vitally affected by legal and institutional constraints on the adoption process, a straightforward evaluation of what truly is gained or lost by *this* proposal is of immense importance.[58]

One point of economic analysis is that we should never lose track, in considering any legal rule, of the need for a "straightforward evaluation of what truly is gained or lost by *this* proposal." Of course, broader issues may also be involved in a legal question, but it is important not to ignore the direct impact of a rule on human welfare. At its best, that is what law and economics seeks to investigate. Despite all its shortcomings—which are not insignificant—it has thereby made a contribution to legal thought.

An apt example is provided by the constructive role which the Coasean perspective has indirectly played in environmental law. From Coase's point of view, the problem with pollution is that transaction costs prevent individuals from bargaining their way to an optimal level of pollution, taking into account the harm done by pollution and the costs of controlling it. When we see the question from this perspective, the natural question is whether we could invent some way in which bargaining could operate effectively despite these transaction costs. One solution is a system of marketable permits which allows polluters to reallocate the costs of pollution control among themselves, so as to obtain a given level of environmental quality at the lowest total cost. There are a variety of practical problems with this approach, as well as concerns that it legitimates pollution by creating a legal right to pollute. On the other hand, it was only this approach which made it possible for Congress to pass legislation dealing with acid rain. Whether or not the approach to acid rain ultimately does minimize costs, this was by no means a negligible achievement.[59]

NOTES

1. Ronald H. Coase, *The Problem of Social Cost*, 3 J.L. & ECON. 1 (1960). For convenience, page citations to this article will be given parenthetically in the text rather than in footnotes.

2. 257 N.E.2d 870 (N.Y. 1970).

3. Edmund W. Kitch, *The Fire of Truth: A Remembrance of Law and Economics at Chicago, 1932–1970*, 26 J.L. & ECON. 163, 221 (1983).

4. *Id.*

5. *Id.* at 226 (quoting Posner).

6. RICHARD A. POSNER, OVERCOMING LAW 406 (1995).

7. Steward Schwab, *Coase Defends Coase: Why Lawyers Listen and Economists Do Not*, 87 MICH. L. REV. 1171, 1189 (1989).

8. *Id.* at 1189 n.51.

9. ROBERT C. ELLICKSON, ORDER WITHOUT LAW: HOW NEIGHBORS SETTLE DISPUTES 2 (1991).

10. Schwab, *supra* note 7, at 1190.

11. ELLICKSON, *supra* note 9, at 2.

12. For an overview of the origins and early history of the law and economics movement, including Coase's role, *see* NEIL DUXBURY, PATTERNS OF AMERICAN JURISPRUDENCE 364–394 (1995).

13. In some ways, Coase's personal views were quite different from those of his followers, but his work also contains many of the future themes of law and economics. *See* Daniel A. Farber, *Parody Lost/Paradigm Regained: The Ironic History of the Coase Theorem*, 83 VA. L. REV. 397 (1997).

14. J. M. Balkin & Sanford Levinson, *The Canons of Constitutional Law*, 111 HARV. L. REV. 963, 979 (1998).

15. 257 N.E.2d 870 (N.Y. 1970). Farber, *supra* note 13, contains a fuller treatment of the material discussed in this section.

16. Alternatively, the government could assess a tax of $2,000 (equal to the amount of pollution harm) against Atlantic, leaving Atlantic with the choice of ceasing its pollution or else paying the tax. Either way, making Atlantic "internalize" the harm to its neighbors will result in an economically efficient level of pollution.

17. This point was basically correct as far as it goes, although Coase does point out a complication regarding the correct method of calculating damages. *See* Pierre Schlag, *An Appreciative Comment on Coase's* The Problem of Social Cost: *A View from the Left*, 1986 WIS. L. REV. 919, 921 n.5 (1986).

18. The hypothetical is simpler than Coase's because he took into account not only the behavior of the polluter, but the possibility that the victims might be able to take steps to control the degree of damage.

19. Thus, it is a misunderstanding to think that Coase viewed the zero-transaction assumption as a plausible basis for policy. *See* Farber, *supra* note 13.

20. For example, as early as 1979, over 150 articles had been published dealing with the economic analysis of contract law. *See* Daniel A. Farber, *The "Law and Economics" Movement*, 4 RES. IN SOCIAL PROBS. & PUB. POL'Y 21, 23 (1987).

21. *See* Lawrence A. Cunningham, *Cardozo and Posner: A Study in Contracts*, 36 WM. & MARY L. REV. 1379 (1995) (documenting, with some misgivings, the remarkable influence of Posner's judicial decisions).

22. For an explanation, *see* A. MITCHELL POLINSKY, AN INTRODUCTION TO LAW AND ECONOMICS 37–44 (1983). The most problematic assumption is risk neutrality. *See id.* at 66–71.

23. MANCUR OLSON, THE LOGIC OF COLLECTIVE ACTION: PUBLIC GOODS AND THE THEORY OF GROUPS (1965).

24. *See* Jonathan Macey, *Promoting Public-Regarding Legislation Through Statutory Interpretation: An Interest Group Model*, 86 COLUM. L. REV. 223, 224, 229–36 (1986); Frank Easterbrook, *Foreword: The Court and the Economic System*, 98 HARV. L. REV. 4, 15–18, 51 (1984).

25. Daniel Rodriguez, *The Positive Political Dimensions of Regulatory Reform*, 72 WASH. U.L.Q. 1, 29 (1994).

26. Einer Elhauge, *Does Interest Group Theory Justify More Intrusive Judicial Review?*, 102 YALE L.J. 31, 35 (1991).

27. *Id.* at 44.

28. *Id.* at 45–46.

29. WILLIAM RIKER, LIBERALISM AGAINST POPULISM: A CONFRONTATION BETWEEN THE THEORY OF DEMOCRACY AND THE THEORY OF SOCIAL CHOICE (1982).

30. *Id.* at 192. *See also id.* at 167. A similar view is expressed in Frank Easterbrook, *Statutes' Domains*, 59 U. CHI. L. REV. 533, 547–48 (1983).

31. Jerry Mashaw, *The Economics of Politics and the Understanding of Public Law*, 65 CHI.-KENT L. REV. 123, 126–27 (1989).

32. *Id.*

33. For instance, the first full-scale law school textbook has only recently appeared. *See* MAXWELL STEARNS, PUBLIC CHOICE AND PUBLIC LAW: READINGS AND COMMENTARY (1997). A shorter earlier work was DAVID W. BARNES & LYNN A. STOUT, THE ECONOMICS OF CONSTITUTIONAL LAW AND PUBLIC CHOICE (1992).

34. DANIEL A. FARBER & PHILIP P. FRICKEY, LAW AND PUBLIC CHOICE: A CRITICAL INTRODUCTION (1991).

35. Elizabeth Hoffman & Matthew L. Spitzer, *Experimental Law and Economics: An Introduction*, 85 COLUM. L. REV. 991, 1012 (1985).

36. DONALD GREEN & IAN SHAPIRO, PATHOLOGIES OF RATIONAL CHOICE THEORY: A CRITIQUE OF APPLICATIONS IN POLITICAL SCIENCE 125–36 (1994). For a discussion of the Green and Shapiro book and the ensuing debate within political science, *see* Daniel Farber & Philip Frickey, *Public Choice Revisited*, 96 MICH. L. REV. 1715 (1998) (reviewing STEARNS, *supra* note 33).

37. Robert Ellickson, *Of Coase and Cattle: Dispute Resolution Among Neighbors in Shasta County*, 38 STAN. L. REV. 623 (1986).

38. John Donohue, *Diverting the Coasean River: Incentive Schemes to Reduce Unemployment Spells*, 99 YALE L.J. 549 (1989). Indeed, some individuals were so far from efficiency that they failed even to pick up checks for which they had already qualified.

39. Gary T. Schwartz, *Reality in the Economic Analysis of Tort Law: Does Tort Law Really Deter?*, 42 UCLA L. Rev. 377 (1994).

40. *Id.* at 444.

41. FARBER & FRICKEY, *supra* note 34, at 33.

42. *See* GREEN AND SHAPIRO, *supra* note 36.

43. Richard A. Posner, *The Ethical and Political Basis of the Efficiency Norm in Common Law Adjudication*, 8 HOFSTRA L. REV. 487, 492–93 (1980).

44. *Id.* at 498. As Posner's critics were quick to point out, his decision to imply actual individual consent rather than hypothetical consent leads to some conceptual difficulties.

45. *Id.* at 497.

46. For a good recent synthesis of the critiques, *see* ERIC RAKOWSKI, EQUAL JUSTICE 199–226 (1991). Posner responded to the critics in two essays, Richard A. Posner, *A Reply to Some Recent Criticisms of the Efficiency Theory of the Common Law*, 9 HOFSTRA L. REV. 775 (1981); Richard A. Posner, *The Value of Wealth: A Comment on Dworkin and Kronman*, 9 J. LEG. STUDIES 243 (1980). Posner's replies focus on criticisms unrelated to the conceptual difficulties of the ex ante argument and are not relevant to the present discussion.

47. Some of the other arguments against recognizing economic efficiency as a social value are discussed in DANIEL A. FARBER, ECO-PRAGMATISM: MAKING SENSIBLE ENVIRONMENTAL DECISIONS IN AN UNCERTAIN WORLD ch. 2 (1999).

48. Ronald Dworkin, *Is Wealth a Value?*, 9 J. LEG. STUDIES 191 (1980).

49. *Id.* at 220.

50. Dworkin made the same argument again in a later book. *See* RONALD DWORKIN, LAW'S EMPIRE 286–88 (1986). For a fuller discussion of the Dworkin/Posner debate, *see* Daniel A. Farber, *The Shift to the Ex Ante Perspective* (forthcoming).

51. RICHARD A. POSNER, THE PROBLEMS OF JURISPRUDENCE 379 (1990). *See also* Richard A. Posner, *The Ethics of Wealth Maximization: Reply to Malloy*, 36 KAN. L. REV. 262, 263–64 (1988).

52. *See* Thomas F. Cotter, *Legal Pragmatism and the Law and Economics Movement*, 84 GEO. L.J. 2071 (1996).

53 Jane B. Baron & Jeffrey L. Dunoff, *Against Market Rationality: Moral Critiques of Economic Analysis in Legal Theory*, 17 CARDOZO L. REV. 431, 433 (1996).

54. *Id.* at 495.

55. Ronald A. Cass, *Coping with Life, Law, and Markets: A Comment on Posner and the Law-and-Economics Debate*, 67 B.U. L. REV. 73, 76–77 (1987).

56. *Id.* at 89.

57. Of course, just as we need to be careful about the limitations and appropriate use of economics, we would also need to take the same degree of care in using narrative. *See* Daniel A. Farber & Suzanna Sherry, *Telling Stories Out of School: An Essay on Legal Narratives*, 45 STAN. L. REV. 807 (1993).

58. Cass, *supra* note 55, at 97.

59. For a summary of the marketable permit idea, and its application to acid rain, *see* ROGER FINDLEY & DANIEL FARBER, ENVIRONMENTAL LAW: CASES AND MATERIALS 355–63 (4th ed. 1994).

# Part III

# The Canon and Groups

# Chapter 8

# Race Relations Law in the Canon of Legal Academia

## *Randall Kennedy*

Should a course on race relations law be part of the curricular canon of a law school? If so, what should such a course offer? If such a course is offered, with what political and pedagogical attitude should it be taught? These are the primary questions addressed in this essay.

### I

Law schools should equip students with knowledge and techniques that the legal academy is well positioned to explore and impart and that will be of benefit to society. From this premise it follows that a law school should offer a course that investigates the ways in which race relations have affected and been affected by legal institutions, particularly the judiciary. After all, racial conflicts and efforts to regulate them have played a large and ongoing part in the development of American common law, statutory law, and constitutional law. On one level, this is an obvious point. Anyone with an appreciable knowledge of the United States knows that race matters and has long mattered to Americans. On another level, even well-educated people are often unaware of the pervasiveness of the influence of racial conflict upon Americans' preferences, habits, conduct, and institutions. Many are aware at some vague, abstract level that racial "slavery" and "segregation" and other forms of "oppression" have mocked the high-minded ideals voiced in the foundational documents of the United States. Relatively few, however, receive instruction in secondary schooling or college that enables them to have a vivid and detailed understanding of these evils and of their ramifications.

Law schools should also allocate substantial resources to the study of race relations law because of the peculiarly influential role of attorneys in the United States. Attorneys constitute a significant group even when they stay within a narrow professional niche; after all, one of the three branches of federal power, the judiciary, is virtually an exclusive preserve of attorneys. The influence of attorneys as a group, however, extends far beyond the judiciary insofar as many lawyers pursue careers in legislatures, administration, journalism, and business. Given the depth, complexity, and pervasiveness of racial controversies in the United States, an attorney who is ignorant of the American Dilemma is an attorney with a deficient education. Given the influence of lawyers, the prospect that an appreciable number of them might be undereducated about a matter that is so vital to American democracy is a cause for concern and an impetus to support the study of race relations law.

Wherever one turns in the legal universe, one encounters disputes that have often reached their most intense pitch in the crucible of struggles over "the race question." Americans have come to blows with one another over a variety of divisions—class conflict, gender distinctions, ideological splits, religious differences. But it was disagreement over the fate of racial slavery that erupted into civil war. The effort to recreate a shattered union in the aftermath of that war led to three amendments to the United States Constitution (the Thirteenth, Fourteenth, and Fifteenth Amendments) that changed fundamentally the relation of the individual to state and federal governments and the relation of the states to the central government. A very large portion of constitutional law today stems from this transformation. This includes not only judicial, legislative, and executive actions that are explicitly racial in nature. It also includes most of the actions taken by states that are alleged to violate the federally guaranteed rights of individuals. A course on race relations and the law should be a central curricular offering at every law school because every lawyer should know as part of his or her mastery of the key elements of American legal institutions that the struggle against racial injustice has been *the* great seedbed for advances in civil liberties and civil rights for all persons.

Responses to racial abuses of power have led to the creation of much of the law that protects due process and freedom of expression.[1] Such responses have also led to important achievements in other areas as well. Citizenship, for example, is a fundamental legal status. It distinguishes members of a polity from those who are nonmembers. It thus implicates what Michael Walzer describes as the most important questions in adjudicating matters of distributive justice: who constitutes the relevant community and how is that community constituted.[2] The Constitution of 1787 neglected to define national citizenship. But in the infamous case of *Dred Scott v. Sandford*, the Supreme Court decided that, whatever the full meaning of national citizenship, it meant at least the exclusion of African Americans. Blacks, the Court ruled, whether slave or free, could never become citizens of the United States. To change that radical act of rejection required a constitutional amendment. The Fourteenth Amendment stipulates that "all persons born . . . in the United States, and subject to the jurisdiction thereof, are citizens of the United States."[3] Birthright citizenship is a distinctive feature of American political culture. Without a knowledge of race relations and its effect on legal developments, one cannot understand satisfactorily the roots of this definition of American citizenship and the reason why proposals even to consider changing it generate high anxiety, if not outright condemnation.[4]

Being born in the United States is not the only way to become a citizen; one can also attain citizenship through naturalization. The history of naturalization is another story significantly shaped by racial conflict. From 1790 until 1952 federal law stipulated that, with certain exceptions, a person had to be "white" in order to be eligible for naturalization.[5] The enforcement of this law created a jurisprudence of racial classification that deemed people of certain nationalities or ethnicities to be "white"— and therefore eligible for citizenship, and people of other nationalities or ethnicities to be "nonwhite", and therefore doomed to permanent status as aliens.[6]

Many people take for granted the demographics of the United States, as if the character of the population was merely an accident of history. A properly constructed course on race relations law would teach students that, to a substantial extent, racial considerations have shaped immigration policies.[7] This is an important matter of contemporary relevance: absent the anti-Chinese animus that led to the Chinese Exclusion Act of 1882 and the anti-Japanese prejudice that led to the Japanese Exclusion Act of 1924, there would be a considerably larger presence of Asian Americans in the United States today.[8] Many people also take for granted the geography of the United States, as if that, too, simply emerged as a fact of nature. A good course on race relations law, however, would show that racial conflict significantly shaped the negotiations, transactions, and conquests pursuant to which the United States, dominated by "white" people, wrested a continent away from various peoples who were perceived as colored: the "red" Indians and the "brown" Mexicans.[9]

Many people take for granted their racial identity and that of their friends, kin, lovers, and neighbors. A comprehensive course on race relations law would show, however, that, in substantial numbers of cases, the question "Who is 'white'?" or "Who is 'colored'?" has generated sharp conflict, giving rise to some of the most poignant disputes in all of American law.[10] Consider, for example, *Green v. City of New Orleans*[11] which arose from the following heartrending facts: A white woman gave birth to a baby. Soon afterward, the woman died. The woman's sister took the baby to her home and planned to raise the child. As time went on, however, the baby's skin began to darken, which led to complaints from white neighbors. The baby's aunt soon capitulated, returning the child, a little girl, to city authorities. These authorities placed the child with black foster parents who, falling in love with her, sought to adopt the child. The authorities initially approved this effort but then resisted it when an examination of the child's birth certificate disclosed that she was registered as "white" by the state Bureau of Vital Statistics. A Louisiana law prohibited adoption across racial lines. The foster parents sought to change the racial designation on the child's birth certificate from "white" to "colored." But this effort, too, was thwarted. Considering that the mother was white, that the identity of the father was unknown, that experts in racial classification disagreed, that the child's racial character was ambiguous, and that initial official declarations of racial identity were entitled to a strong presumption of validity, the authorities refused to change the child's racial designation. The Louisiana Court of Appeals affirmed this ruling, stating that a change in racial designation should occur only when the relevant evidence "leaves no room for doubt," because the registration of a racial birthright "must be given as much sanctity in the law as the registration of a property right."[12] This ruling left the child in limbo. A white, she could not be adopted by the black foster parents who had grown to love her. A person of color, she stood no chance of being accepted socially by whites in segregationist Louisiana regardless of what was stated on her birth certificate. Few cases illustrate more vividly the cruel lunacy of American pigmentocracy.

Granted the significance of the race question in American legal culture, why explore it in a specialized course? Would not such a course be relegated to an academic ghetto by professors and students who perceived it as a sop to "political correctness"? Why not explore the subject throughout the law school curriculum?

Exploring the racial dimensions of a subject ought to be done wherever pursuing such a tack would be enlightening given the aims at hand. For example, if one seeks, in a course on contracts, to investigate the duty to speak, misrepresentation, caveat emptor, and related concepts, one might well do so in the context of cases in which men have sought to escape matrimonial obligations on the grounds that wives or fiancés had concealed or failed to disclose their racial ancestries.[13] A teacher of property concerned with exploring arguments for and against various modes of governmental regulation of housing markets should certainly consider using as heuristic vehicles the laws that prohibit racial discrimination in housing transactions.[14] A teacher of civil procedure can do no better than *Walker v. City of Birmingham*—a case arising from racial conflict on a grand scale—to introduce students to the collateral bar rule.[15] And a teacher of torts, interested in generating lively and instructive class discussion on the intentional infliction of emotional distress, should consider including for reading one or more of the many cases in which the word "nigger" has prompted a lawsuit.[16]

There are many other contexts as well in which, outside of a course specifically devoted to race relations, the race question can be usefully explored. If one seeks in a course on jurisprudence to probe the conditions under which people are obligated to obey the law or justified in taking up arms against the state, one should consider including in the syllabus cases, speeches, and other materials generated in the eighteenth and nineteenth centuries by Americans (e.g., Nat Turner, David Walker, John Brown, John C. Calhoun, William Lloyd Garrison, Jefferson Davis) who faced these questions in concrete form as combatants for or against Negro slavery. In teaching a course on professional responsibility, an instructor might want to ask whether an attorney's Jewishness ought to figure into her decision to accept or decline as a client a bank accused of hiding Nazi war loot, or whether an attorney's blackness ought to figure into his decision to accept or decline as a client a firm charged with illegal racial discrimination in hirings or promotions.[17]

Without any sort of overreaching, then, there exist plenty of opportunities for professors teaching basic subjects to highlight the racial aspects or consequences of a given problem or doctrine. Teachers should seize upon these occasions when doing so furthers the academic mission of the project at hand. It is unlikely, however, that professors teaching a course on contracts, torts, civil procedure, and so on will have time to assess comprehensively the distinctly *racial* aspect of their subject, for example the development of various racial ideologies within the American judiciary. After all, the primary aim of a course on contracts or torts or civil procedure is to develop a mastery of those subjects. Although studying racial conflict may shine a light on this or that sector of those areas, they encompass far more territory than even the large area of racial conflict. In order to study as a primary focus of inquiry the relationship between race relations and the law a school needs a stand-alone course, a course in which the race question itself can be at the center of attention.

## II

The canon of race relations law in the United States should consist of materials that convey an understanding of the ideas, events, movements, and personalities that are essential to know in order to appreciate the large influence of race relations upon American legal culture. This field is too massive to cover comprehensively in any one casebook, or monograph, or course. Hence the need in this field as in many others for difficult choices governing the allocation of time, energy, and attention. For teachers facing the difficult task of selecting what to include (and thus what to exclude), I offer the following suggestions.

The first stems from questions posed by J. M. Balkin and Sanford Levinson. In "The Canons of Constitutional Law," after describing Chief Justice Roger Taney's opinion in *Dred Scott v. Sanford* and Frederick Douglass's speech "The Constitution of the United States: Is It Pro-Slavery or Anti-Slavery?" they ask:

> Should either of these two texts, or both, or neither, appear in contemporary constitutional law casebooks? Which should American law students study and discuss, which should educated citizens know about, and which should inform the work of legal academics in the present era? Which of these writings, in short, should form part of the "canon" of American legal materials?[18]

I agree with their conclusion that Douglass's speech warrants inclusion. I use it and have found that it adds considerable vitality to class discussions regarding slavery, antislavery, and the secession crisis, and in my view teachers should import into their monographs, casebooks, syllabi, lectures, and classes anything that makes the subject in question more vivid, accessible, and meaningful to audiences. Frederick Douglass's biography and the vigor of his speech and writings make work by him an especially attractive prospect for study and discussion. Indeed, students are missing something very important if they do not have direct access to the voices and rhetorics of Douglass, Sojourner Truth, Solomon Northrup, William Wells Brown, Harriet F. Jacobs, and other black abolitionists who skillfully transmuted into a distinctive critique of the Slave Power their experience as former slaves, runaway slaves, or semifree antebellum Negroes. The same is true of the voices and rhetorics of Fannie Lou Hamer, Bayard Rustin, Malcolm X, Martin Luther King, Jr., and other champions of the Second Reconstruction. Even in a law school course focused rather narrowly on legal doctrine, something important is missing if students are unaware of the substance of King's "I Have a Dream" speech or his "Letter from a Birmingham Jail."

Levinson and Balkin, however, do not answer the question of priority. As between Taney's infamous opinion and Douglass's stirring speech, they do not say which text a teacher should choose to study *more* or choose to study at all in the event that scarcities of time, space, or attention preclude the possibility of studying both. A suitable answer depends upon the aims of the teacher. I can imagine a wonderful course on constitutional law that gave priority to Taney's opinion, and I can also imagine a wonderful course that gave priority to Douglass's speech. I would be likely to give priority to Taney's opinion on two grounds. The first has to do with the academic division of labor. My marginal intellectual advantage over colleagues in other parts of the university stems from my specialized training in the understanding and manipulation of judicial texts. I can probably best allocate the fruits of that advantage to law school students by focusing my energies primarily on such texts, using other materials as supplementary aids. The second reason has do with my impression of the relative social significance of the two documents. Horrible though it was, Taney's opinion has exercised more influence than Douglass's speech on the American constitutional regime and is thus, in my view, a more important document for law students to know about. Underlying this pedagogical judgment is my sense that of the various types of canonicity, the cultural literacy canon is the most appropriate for a teacher to embrace. According to Balkin and Levinson, the cultural literacy canon is constituted by "the materials that any educated person should know about in order to participate in and contribute to serious discussions about American law."[19] For purposes of a serious analysis of the secession crisis, Taney's opinion is even more crucial to know about than Douglass's great speech.

The fact is, however, that seldom if ever is a teacher faced with the stark choice of discussing one text to the total exclusion of another. Usually teachers are in a position to discuss several texts at once, though they give priority to some over others. To throw useful light on classic legal texts, teachers should consider assigning stories, poems, and novels. The two classic texts concerning the federal constitutional propriety of de jure racial segregation are *Plessy v. Ferguson*[20] and *Brown v. Board of Education*.[21] Both are essential texts in any good course on race relations law in the United States. Neither, however, reflects vividly what segregation actually meant as a matter of day-to-day lived experience. A useful supplement that performs this task admirably is Richard Wright's collection of short stories *Uncle Tom's Children*.[22] Another type of text that should be considered for inclusion is music. For example, one way of vividly illustrating the change in black consciousness reflected and nourished by the successful campaign of litigation against de jure segregation would be to play in a classroom Louis Armstrong's despairing 1930s rendition of "What Did I Do to Be So Black and Blue" and contrast it to James Brown's exuberant 1960s rendition of "Say It Loud, I'm Black and I'm Proud."

My second suggestion is that law school teachers focus more attention than they currently do on lawmaking institutions other than the courts.[23] One cannot, for example, obtain an adequate understanding of the Reconstruction constitutional amendments and civil rights legislation by viewing them solely through the lens of Supreme Court decisions. Teachers of race relations law (and other subjects as well) should revisit the debates held in Congress and state legislatures in order to grasp the political and social circumstances that gave rise to these enactments and affected their design. For example, in evaluating provisions enacted, it helps to know about proposals rejected. In considering the propriety of official racial distinctions in light of the Fourteenth Amendment, it helps to know that the thirty-ninth Congress rejected a proposed fourteenth amendment that would have expressly prohibited the making of racial distinctions.[24] Similarly, to understand adequately the Fifteenth Amendment, it helps to know that Congress rejected a version of that amendment that would have provided citizens with a right to vote and instead embraced a far more limited provision which merely provides a right to be free of racial exclusions from the franchise.[25]

Another source of lawmaking to which scholars of race relations law ought to devote more attention is the executive branch. Balkin and Levinson are right to decry the marginalization of Abraham Lincoln in the legal academic canon.[26] Regrettable, too, is the marginalization of Andrew Johnson, Lincoln's successor and a fierce opponent of the nation's first federal civil rights act, and, indeed, the Fourteenth Amendment. Johnson's veto message of the Civil Rights Act of 1866 is a document particularly worthy of inclusion in the canon of race relations law. Commenting upon the provision of the act which attempted to bestow citizenship upon all native-born Americans, regardless of race or previous condition of servitude, Johnson objected that such a policy "proposes a discrimination against large numbers of intelligent, worthy, and patriotic foreigners, and in favor of the negro."[27] Commenting upon the provision of the act which mandated that states permit all persons to contract, sue, own property, and give evidence on the same terms as whites, Johnson objected that it sought to "establish for the security of the colored race safeguards which go infinitely beyond any that the General Government has ever provided for the white race. In fact, the distinction of race and color is by the [act] made to operate in favor of the colored and against the white race."[28] These comments, so strikingly resonant of contemporary struggles over affirmative action, indicate that the current debate has a longer lineage than is often supposed. They also suggest the alacrity with which some representatives of the white majority have typically resorted to charges that measures seeking racial equality for long-oppressed racial minorities are instead illegitimate ventures into racial favoritism.

Third, I suggest that constructors of the canon of race relations law focus more attention than heretofore upon certain significant silences in the law. In addition to teaching (or at least alerting students to the presence of) the huge amount of constitutional, statutory, and administrative law that regulates race relations, a good course on the subject should also note and explore important lacunae. Silence can be as important as noise in law (as in life). The virtual absence of "noise"—ie., law—regarding the rape of enslaved black women, for example, speaks volumes about the brutal reality of slavery; it signals that, for the most part, legal regimes left slave women unprotected against sexual violence. Similarly, the absence of a federal anti-lynching law speaks volumes about the tenor of race relations between the 1890s and the 1920s, a period during which hundreds of blacks were lynched annually under the tolerant gaze of a largely indifferent public. These silences need to be recognized and explored.

Another type of silence that warrants more attention is that which stems from the apparent desire of decision makers to ignore the racial element of a controversy even when that element is, in fact, a major presence in the controversy. Two examples of this phenomenon are *Bailey v. Alabama*[29] and *Frank v. Mangum*.[30] *Bailey* brought into question the validity of a state law that criminalized breaching a labor contract while failing to repay an advance on wages. Racial sentiments played a key role in the enactment and administration of this statute; its purpose and effect were to intimidate black labor. In striking down the statute, however, the Court went out of its way to avoid mentioning the racial aspect of the case.[31] Similarly, racial sentiments played a key role in the miscarriage of justice that led to the rape conviction and, later, the lynching of Leo Frank, accused of sexually abusing and murdering a white Christian teenager in the pencil factory he managed.[32] Frank's Jewishness provoked a massive outpouring of anti-Semitic fear, resentment, and hatred that transformed his "trial" into a spectacle. The prosecution of Leo Frank marked a high point in the expression of anti-Jewish prejudice in America. Yet, in reading the Supreme Court decision that denied habeas corpus relief to Frank—a major landmark in the history of the great writ—one would never know that anti-Semitism had had anything to do with the defendant's predicament. Silence of this sort and the reasons for it warrant notice and greater study in investigations of race relations law.

A fourth suggestion is that teachers of race relations law revisit subjects that were once significant but that are now largely unknown. An example is the case law that arose from the enforcement of antimiscegenation statutes. Over the course of three hundred years, some forty-one colonies, territories, or states prohibited marriage across racial lines. This generated an extraordinary array of fascinating cases in which judges had to answer questions such as these: For purposes of deciding whether a couple was lawfully married, how should a judge determine whether a man or woman was "black" or "white"? In a jurisdiction prohibiting interracial marriage, should a judge enforce a will in which a white man bequeathed all of his property by deed of gift to his black mistress? What should happen if an interracial couple married in a state that permitted their union moved to a state that prohibited miscegenation?

The law created by these questions has largely disappeared from legal academic consciousness (though some of this law is being reconsidered because of its relevance to heated struggles today over same-sex marriage).[33] Virtually all that remains is the aptly titled case *Loving v. Virginia*,[34] in which the federal Supreme Court belatedly invalidated antimiscegenation laws.[35] It is possible that a scholar who is familiar with the case law generated by enforcement of the antimiscegenation laws would choose to forgo any investigation of this area insofar as it no longer gives rise to live legal disputes and insofar as there are other subjects that are, on balance, more worthwhile to study. It is also likely, however, that many scholars' inattentiveness to prohibitions on interracial marriage reflects not a conscious decision respecting pedagogical priorities but mere ignorance; many scholars, particularly those born during or after the civil rights revolution, are simply unaware of the human misery caused by antimiscegenation statutes. Those who become aware of this facet of race relations law may decide that, given scarcities of time and energy, they are better off focusing attention on other matters. But an informed decision cannot be made without knowledge of this "lost" subject. Moreover, after gaining familiarity with it, some scholars may find that the antimiscegenation case law is surprisingly relevant to contemporary concerns and therefore worthy of attention, even at the cost of spending less time on other matters.

Akin to the problem of the lost subject is the problem of the lost case. Even within well-known, deeply researched subjects, such as voting rights, there exist neglected cases which scholars ought to make more prominent. At the top of the list of such cases is *Giles v. Harris*,[36] a federal Supreme Court decision that should be essential reading in the canon of race relations law.[37] In *Giles*, in an opinion by Justice Oliver Wendell Holmes, Jr., the Court assumed that the state of Alabama had embarked on a racial policy to exclude blacks from the ballot box in violation of the Fifteenth Amendment. Nonetheless, the Court declined to grant equitable relief to the plaintiffs. According to Justice Holmes, the complaint in *Giles*

> imports that the great mass of the white population intends to keep the blacks from voting. To meet such an intent something more than ordering the plaintiff's name to be inscribed upon the [lists of eligible voters] will be needed. If the conspiracy and the intent exist, a name on a piece of paper will not defeat them. Unless we are prepared to supervise the voting in that state by officers of the court, it seems to us that all the plaintiff could get from equity would be an empty form. Apart from damages to the individual, relief from a great political wrong, if done, as alleged, by the people of

a state and the state itself, must be given by them or by the legislative and political department of the Government of the United States.[38]

Written at the beginning of the twentieth century, the *Giles* decision sounded themes that resonate loudly at the end of the twentieth century in ongoing struggles over judicial power to enforce the mandate of *Brown v. Board of Education.*

My fifth suggestion regarding the canon of race relations law scholarship stems from a basic question concerning the contours of the field: What should be the racial coverage of race relations law? As things currently stand, the black-white racial frontier continues overwhelmingly to dominate the field. This is so for a variety of reasons. White-black racial conflict has had more of an effect on broadly applicable law than any other racial conflict. White-red racial conflict has generated a tremendous amount of law, too, much of which has been gathered together and organized under the rubric of federal Indian law.[39] All three branches of the federal government, however, have long treated the Indian tribes as a sui generis group for whom unique laws are appropriate. This sharply limits the applicability of decisions in that area of the law and concomitantly limits interest in that area.

If the Fourteenth Amendment had been limited to the protection of blacks, it would be of far less concern to far fewer people than it is today. That federal Indian law has been effectively segregated doctrinally in courts and in law schools both reflects and explains, at least in part, the isolation of Indian affairs from major currents of intellectual life in legal academia, including courses and books on race relations law. The splitting off of federal Indian law from race relations law in general is a development and practice that ought to be reconsidered and undone. Considerable enlightenment about the (mis)treatment of Indians and other nonwhite peoples could be generated by systematically exploring the differences in treatment accorded to these various groups. To note briefly just one example: at the same time that federal and state governments imposed racial separation on blacks, they imposed racial assimilation on Indians. This is an important juxtaposition to which more attention should be called. It suggests the variety with which racial prejudice can express itself and suggests, too, the variety of racial ideologies that vulnerable racial minorities have had to confront. The same influential decision makers who believed that Indians could be "saved" through a process of assimilationist whitening saw blacks as irredeemably alien, incapable of assimilation, and thus fit only for a social existence safely distant from white society.

The bright and harsh light that Alexis de Tocqueville shed on race relations law in *Democracy in America* was enriched by his comparative focus on whites, blacks, and Indians, what he called "the three races of America."[40] Writing in the 1830s, Tocqueville demonstrated an admirable comprehensiveness in examining the interrelationship of those three races.[41] Subsequently, however, the United States has been peopled by many "races," including "yellow" people from China, Japan, and other Asian countries and "brown" people from Mexico, the Philippines, Hawaii, and other places that have been gripped by American imperialism.

States and the federal government in the United States have subjected peoples of color to all manner of racial abuses that have generated controversies that have spilled into legislatures and courts and given rise to a large body of law that ought to be part of the canon of race relations law. This is a relatively uncontroversial point; it is hard to imagine any course substantially concerned with race relations law that would fail to include for discussion *Yick Wo v. Hopkins*[42] or *Korematsu v. United States*.[43] At the same time, there is discernible in legal academia and beyond a growing impatience with analyses of race relations law that marginalize the history, participation, and concerns of colored peoples other than the white, black, and red.[44] This dissatisfaction is justified.[45] The United States is not simply a triracial society; it is a profoundly *multi*racial society. Attending to that fact poses yet more problems for teachers and writers who already face daunting dilemmas of selectivity. That fact also indicates, however, the extraordinary possibilities latent in the field of race relations law—possibilities that await realization in the years ahead.

My sixth suggestion is that scholars of race relations law (and scholars in general) canonize materials and techniques that clarify what happened on the ground as a consequence of a constitutional amendment, statutory provision, or judicial or administrative ruling. Too often, discussions of legal developments proceed on the assumption that realities mirror formal changes in rules. To some extent reality does change whenever a lawmaking body renders a decision. Even if onlookers ignore the decision, the ruling itself changes the contours of law and thus effectuates a reform, albeit limited, that is worthy of notice. To that extent, no decision is totally hollow and every decision is somewhat significant. Worthy of notice too, however, is the degree to which social practices change as a consequence of judicial, legislative, or executive lawmaking. Too little study is devoted to this inquiry. To be sure, some investigations of the actual social consequences of lawmaking have been undertaken.[46] Even when they exist, however, such studies receive too little attention in the legal academic canon.

## III

I turn now to the question: With what political and pedagogical attitude should a course on race relations law be taught? I approach this inquiry with some trepidation because recently my own attitude—or at least my perceived attitude—has been harshly criticized. In "The Strange Career of Randall Kennedy," Professor Derrick Bell expresses regret that I became his successor as the teacher of the basic course on race relations law at Harvard Law School.[47] He maintains that I started off my teaching and scholarly career on the right track, stating that my "first few articles were stunning models of racial advocacy,"[48] "hard-hitting writing filled with bite and passion."[49] They seemed to foretell that I "would become a powerful voice for a people whose expectations that the civil rights era would gain its racial justice goals were fading fast." But then, in his view, I took a wrong turn. I became "impartial" and all too ready to criticize publicly righteous positions embraced by champions of civil rights. According to Bell, I seemed to have forgotten whose side I was on and comported myself intellectually "in ways that—whether intended or not—serve to comfort many whites and distress blacks."[50] "Disgruntled students complained," Bell reports, "that Kennedy spent more time challenging and even denigrating civil rights positions than he did analyzing the continuing practices and policies of discrimination that made those policies, whatever their shortcomings, necessary."[51]

Bell's critique raises a variety of fundamental issues. First, by charging that I have abandoned the "advocacy orientation" of the course that he bequeathed to me, Bell implicitly asserts that a course on race relations law—and perhaps all courses—should be taught with an advocacy orientation. Unfortunately, Professor Bell neglects to define clearly what he means by advocacy orientation. I believe that what he means to refer to is an attitude of engagement in which the teacher is seeking to change the world (at least a bit) by shaping the perspectives of his or her students. An advocacy orientation is a commitment to challenge unjust aspects of the status quo and recommend needed reforms, no matter how radical. If this is what Professor Bell means by an "advocacy orientation"—and I think it is—then he and I agree on a fundamental point. For in my view, professors in every law school class are constantly, indeed unavoidably, taking a position, either implicitly or explicitly, with respect to the legitimacy or illegitimacy of the system of law they are attempting to analyze. Professor Bell wants his colleagues to be conscious of the political stances that they are taking in their books, articles, lectures, and other pedagogical tasks, including letters of recommendation and votes for tenure. I applaud his realistic appraisal of the unavoidably political elements of pedagogy and his insistence on a high degree of ideological self-awareness. Where, then, do we disagree in ways relevant to constructing a course on race relations law? Conflicts arise in a variety of areas, three of which are particularly important.

First, Bell is supremely confident that he knows what policy positions are *the* correct civil rights positions to adopt and thus the ones to urge his students to follow. Because Bell is so confident, he is impatient with others who lack his certitude, an impatience he displays by routinely portraying opponents as either racists or opportunists. I lack his certitude, believe that there is good reason to be open-minded about a variety of hotly contested debates regarding race relations policy, and therefore believe that a well-constructed course on race relations law should provide room for a patient, tolerant exploration of alternative resolutions to the dilemmas we face.

It is ironic, in the extreme, for me to be saying this in response to Professor Bell. After all, one of his signal contributions to the legal academic literature is "Serving Two Masters: Integration Ideals and Client Interests In School Desegregation Litigation,"[52] which sharply questioned the propriety of civil rights attorneys' pressing for one sort of remedy in school desegregation cases while their putative clients seemed to prefer a different sort of remedy. "The time has come," Professor Bell concluded, "for civil rights lawyers to end their single-minded commitment to racial balance, a goal which, standing alone, is increasingly inaccessible and all too often educationally impotent."[53] Bell's article was considered heretical in some circles.[54] Indeed, to some, unfortunately, it was cause for political and intellectual excommunication. Wherever one stands on the merits of the dispute, however, the important point here is Bell was a participant in a bona fide dispute between bona fide champions of African American advancement over the best strategy to pursue. Then as well as now, properly determining how best to proceed takes more than an emotional commitment to "doing the right thing." It requires as well an intellectual investment to figure out what constitutes doing the right thing, a task that is even more complicated today than it was in 1973 when Professor Bell published the first edition of *Race, Racism and American Law*, a wonderful compendium of source material for which all scholars owe him a large intellectual debt.

A properly constructed course on race relations law at the dawn of the twenty-first century should provide students with educational materials and psychological space so that they can determine for themselves appropriate responses to difficult questions: whether it is better to press for maximum racial integration in public schooling or for maximum educational quality regardless of the racial demographics of the students involved;[55] whether it is better to compel black workers to pursue racial grievances at the workplace through standard procedures obtained by collective bargaining or to allow black workers to engage in wildcat strikes for purposes of racial protest;[56] whether it is better to invest more in securing public safety in high-crime, majority-minority neighborhoods (even at the cost of encroaching upon personal privacy) or to insist that residents of such neighborhoods be accorded the same degree of privacy afforded to residents of safer, whiter, more affluent neighborhoods;[57] whether it is better to prefer to place black orphaned children in black adoptive families or to stipulate that such children will be placed with the first adoptive home available, regardless of race;[58] whether redistributive reforms primarily animated by a desire to help blacks are best packaged as race-specific or race-neutral.[59] A course on race relations law should make clear that enlightened, nonracist activists, jurists, and commentators can be found on several sides of these controversies. Contrary to Professor Bell's rhetoric, these issues are not, forgive the expression, black and white. They are multidimensional and should be portrayed and seen and dealt with as such.

A second broad area of pedagogical conflict between me and Professor Bell arises from differing premises concerning the normative aims of a course on race relations law. He seems to assume that its aim should be to advance the interests of black people. As I indicated above, what actually constitutes the best interests of black people is more contested and more difficult to discern than Bell's rhetoric suggests. But even if a broad consensus among African Americans was reached over what constituted the best interest of black people, major difficulties would still loom over an approach, like Bell's, which measures the political virtue of any given policy in terms of "Is it good for the blacks"? Blacks, after all, constitute only one portion of the American polity. What is good for that portion will likely often be good for the whole or good for social justice in general. But that need not always be the case. The interests of blacks might come into conflict with the interests of other groups whose claims in a given situation are more pressing or weighty than those of blacks. When that happens I see no reason to prefer the position of blacks, just as I see no reason to prefer *necessarily* the position of whites, Jews, Catholics, or any other particular social group.[60] A good course on race relations law in the United States would show that any group, like any person, is capable of perpetrating racial harms upon others. It would show how people of Chinese ancestry have attempted to deflect anti-Asian animus by scapegoating Indians and blacks,[61] how some Indians enslaved African Americans even as they themselves were being cruelly ousted from their lands by Euro-Americans;[62] how people of African ancestry have attempted to escape antiblack animus by scapegoating Indians,[63] how Jews have attempted to escape anti-Semitism by scapegoating Negroes;[64] how some African Americans have racially targeted Korean Americans;[65] and, how, of course, whites of various ethnicities have attempted systematically to subordinate blacks and other peoples of color.

Professor Bell is interested only in the last of these topics. For example, when one looks up the key term "racism" in the latest edition of *Race, Racism and American Law*, one finds the following entry: "Racism. See White racism." This elliptical comment stems from a theory that has, unfortunately, been gaining influence steadily over the past thirty years. Under that theory, blacks and other racially oppressed peoples cannot be "racist" because "racism" can be manifested only by groups with power. According to this theory, "racism" equals prejudice plus power. According to proponents of this theory, blacks can be prejudiced but blacks cannot be racists because they lack the power to effectuate the prejudices they may harbor. Materials that should be part of a good course on race relations law—sociological materials on the racial demographics of authority within the society—would enable a student to see the speciousness of this theory. They would enable a student to demystify the myth of black powerlessness. For the fact is that in an appreciable number of significant locales and institutions blacks do occupy positions of authority from which they could, if they so chose, effectuate prejudices. Scores of cities, police departments, military units, prisons, personnel offices, and social service agencies are directed by black officials who, like their white counterparts, make numerous low-visibility, discretionary choices that are routinely granted tremendous deference both within and without the bureaucracies in which they function. Furthermore, under certain circumstances, even weak individuals or groups can exercise power over others who, in the normal course of things, occupy a much higher social status. I think here of the lowly rapist or a group of historically victimized rapists. I think of what happened to a thirty-year-old woman who was told by her assailant before she was raped that before she died he would make sure that she knew what it felt like to "have a nigger cock."[66] Fortunately, she lived. The same cannot be said for Kristin Huggins, the victim of a rape-murder in 1992 at the hands of Ambrose A. Harris. Harris and an associate agreed to perpetrate a carjacking so that they would have an automobile with which to commit a robbery they were planning. Offering clarification as to what would be done with inconvenient prisoners, Harris reportedly said that he would "tie them up and leave them somewhere" if they were black but kill them if they were white. When Huggins unluckily drove her car near to Harris, he is said to have muttered, "I'm going to get that bitch."[67] Finally, I think of a tragedy that occurred in 1992, near Charleston, South Carolina. Four black men abducted a white woman, Melissa McLauchlin, raped her, and then killed her. Seeking to explain their actions, one of the perpetrators stated that it constituted retaliation for "four hundred years of oppression."[68]

Beyond the empirical fact that blacks can and do exercise appreciable amounts of power in America (even while they remain subjected to invidious racial subordination) is the further fact that circumstances sometimes change with breathtaking rapidity, empowering those who have been oppressed and lowering those who have been ascendant. It is important, then, to be attentive to the moral hygiene of the weak. For world history shows quite vividly that persons and groups who have been dealt with unjustly—I think, for example, of certain Serbs and Jews—are quite capable of donning cloaks of victimhood and visiting terrible injustices on others.

Given these considerations, teachers of courses on race relations law in the United States should definitely be self-conscious as they proceed to advocate favored policies; otherwise they will simply proceed to be un-self-conscious advocates. But in advocating one policy, or doctrine, or outcome over others, a teacher's conclusion should rest on a firmer foundation than that it advances the fortunes of the race with which the teacher happens to identify. Thus, knowing the racial demographics of who was helped or hurt by a given policy or who now supports or opposes a given reform is an insufficient basis for judging its propriety. An appropriate basis is whether the policy, doctrine, or outcome satisfies a conception of justice that is broader, grander, and more attractive than the simple preferences, racial identity, or naked subjectivity of the teacher in charge.

Professors should also keep in mind that even amongst those united in their desire to achieve "racial justice," the way toward that goal is not at all clear. People differ over what they mean by racial justice. Some mean preventing all forms of private or public racial discrimination. Some mean preventing all forms of invidious racial discrimination. Some mean preventing all forms of invidious racial discrimination *and* redressing the discernible vestiges of racial wrongs done in the past. On the other hand, some mean merely prohibiting governments from engaging in invidious racial discrimination, while expressly permitting private parties to do so. Furthermore, even people who embrace one of these competing visions of racial justice differ over strategies to pursue to reach their agreed ends. Against this backdrop of complexity, flux, and contestation, teachers ought to inculcate within students a willingness to experiment, an appreciation for empirical research that might shed light on the actual consequences of various policies, and a tolerance for listening closely to competing views.

### NOTES

1. *See* RANDALL KENNEDY, RACE, CRIME, AND THE LAW (1997); HARRY C. KALVEN, THE NEGRO AND THE FIRST AMENDMENT (1965); CLEMENT ETON, THE FREEDOM OF THOUGHT: STRUGGLE IN THE OLD SOUTH (revised and enlarged ed. 1964); ERIC FONER, THE STORY OF AMERICAN FREEDOM (1999); WILLIAM LEE MILLER, ARGUING ABOUT SLAVERY: THE GREAT BATTLE IN THE UNITED STATES CONGRESS (1996); MICHAEL KENT CURTIS, NO STATE SHALL ABRIDGE: THE FOURTEENTH AMENDMENT AND THE BILL OF RIGHTS (1986).

2. *See* MICHAEL WALZER, SPHERES OF JUSTICE (1983).

3. U.S. CONST., amend. XIV, § 1.

4. *See* PETER H. SCHUCK & ROGERS M. SMITH, CITIZENSHIP WITHOUT CONSENT (1985); Gerald L. Neuman, *Back to Dred Scott?*, 24 SAN DIEGO L. REV. 485 (1987).

5. In 1870, for example, Congress made persons born in Africa and outlanders of African descent eligible for naturalization. As anticipated, however, in

the nineteenth century relatively few people in these categories immigrated to the United States and became naturalized citizens. In the twentieth century, the numbers have grown but are still strikingly small in comparison with peoples from other areas of the world. *See* Bill Ong Hing, *Immigration Policies: Messages of Exclusion to African Americans*, 37 How. L.J. 237 (1994). *See also* Charles Gordon, *The Racial Barrier to American Citizenship*, 93 U. PA. L. REV. 237 (1945).

6. *See* IAN HANEY LÓPEZ, WHITE BY LAW: THE LEGAL CONSTRUCTION OF RACE (1996).

7. *See* Gabriel J. Chin, *The Civil Rights Revolution Comes to Immigration Law: A New Look at the Immigration and Nationality Act of 1965*, 75 N.C. L. REV. 273 (1996).

8. *See* BILL ONG HING, MAKING AND REMAKING ASIAN AMERICA THROUGH IMMIGRATION POLICY, 1850–1990 (1993).

9. *See* REGINALD HORSMAN, RACE AND MANIFEST DESTINY: THE ORIGINS OF AMERICAN RACIAL ANGLO-SAXONISM (1981).

10. *See, e.g.*, CHARLES S. MANGUM, JR., THE LEGAL STATUS OF THE NEGRO 1–18 (1940) ("Who is a Negro?"); GILBERT STEPHENSON, RACE DISTINCTIONS IN AMERICAN LAW 12–25 (1910) ("What Is a Negro?"); VIRGINIA R. DOMINGUEZ, WHITE BY DEFINITION: SOCIAL CLASSIFICATION IN CREOLE LOUISIANA (1986); JAMES F. DAVIS, WHO IS BLACK? ONE NATION'S DEFINITION (1991); Christopher A. Ford, *Administering Identity: The Determination of "Race" in Race Conscious Law*, 82 CALIF. L. REV. 1231 (1994); Ariela J. Gross, *Litigating Whiteness: Trials of Racial Determination in the Nineteenth Century South*, 108 YALE L.J. 109 (1998); *Note, Who Is a Negro*, 11 U. FLA. L. REV. 235 (1958); *Note, "Who Is a Negro" Revisited: Determining Individual Racial Status for Purposes of Affirmative Action*, 35 U. FLA. L. REV. 683 (1983); Peggy Pasco, *Miscegenation Law, Court Cases, and Ideologies of "Race" in Twentieth-Century America*, 83 J. AM. HIST. 44 (1996); Christine Hickman, *The Devil and the One Drop Rule: Racial Categories, African Americans, and the U.S. Census*, 95 MICH. L. REV. 1161 (1997).

11. 88 So.2d 76 (1956).

12. *Id.* at 80–81.

13. *See, e.g.*, Van Houten v. Morse, 162 Mass. 414 (1894); Theopanis v. Theopanis, 244 Ky. 689 (1932); Estate of Monks, 120 P. 2d 167 (1942).

14. For a first-year casebook on property law that spends a considerable amount of space exploring issues involving racial conflict, *see* JOSEPH WILLIAM SINGER, PROPERTY LAW: RULES, POLICIES, AND PRACTICES (2nd ed. 1997). *See also* CLEMENT VOSE, CAUCASIANS ONLY: THE SUPREME COURT, THE NAACP AND THE RESTRICTIVE COVENANT CASES (1959); John CHARLES BOGER & JUDITH WELCH WEGNER, RACE, POVERTY, AND AMERICAN CITIES (1996).

15. 388 U.S. 307 (1967). *See generally* ALAN F. WESTIN & BERRY MAHONEY, THE TRIAL OF MARTIN LUTHER KING (1974).

16. *See, e.g.*, Johnson v. Fambrough, 706 So.2d 739 (1997); Motley v. Flowers

& Versagi Court Reporters, 1997 Ohio App. Lexis 5542 (1997); Alcorn v. Anbro Engineering, 468 P.2d 216 (1970). *See also* Richard D. Bernstein, *Note, First Amendment Limits on Tort Liability for Words Intended to Inflict Severe Emotional Distress*, 85 COLUM. L. REV. 1749 (1985); Charles R. Lawrence, *If He Hollers Let Him Go: Regulating Racist Speech on Campus*, 1990 DUKE L.J. 431; Richard Delgado, *Words That Wound*, 17 HARV. C.R.-C.L. L. REV. 133 (1982); Marjorie Heins, *Banning Words: A Comment on "Words That Wound,"* 18 HARV. C.R.-C.L. L. REV. 585 (1983).

17. *See* David B. Wilkins, *Race, Ethnics and the First Amendment: Should a Black Lawyer Represent the Klu Klux Klan*, 63 GEO. WASH. L. REV. 1030 (1995); Sanford Levinson, *Identifying the Jewish Lawyer: Reflections on the Construction of Professional Identity*, 14 CARDOZO L. REV. 1577 (1993).

18. J. M. Balkin & Sanford Levinson, *The Canons of Constitutional Law*, 111 HARV. L. REV. 963, 967–68 (1998).

19. *Id.*, at 977.

20. 163 U.S. 537 (1896).

21. 347 U.S. 483 (1954).

22. RICHARD WRIGHT, UNCLE TOM'S CHILDREN (1938).

23. This, too, echoes a point made by Balkin and Levinson, *supra* note 18, at 1003–1004. A somewhat dated text that is attentive to the need to take into account, at the state and federal levels, all lawmaking agencies (including organs of propaganda and scholarship that regulate public opinion) is THE CIVIL RIGHTS RECORD: BLACK AMERICANS AND THE LAW, 1849–1970 (Richard Bardolph ed. 1970).

24. *See* ANDREW KULL, THE COLOR-BLIND CONSTITUTION (1992).

25. WILLIAM GILLETTE, THE RIGHT TO VOTE (1969).

26. Balkin & Levinson, *supra* note 18, at 1016.

27. *See* STATUTORY HISTORY OF THE UNITED STATES, CIVIL RIGHTS, Part I at 151 (Bernard Schwartz ed. 1970).

28. *Id.* at 154.

29. 219 U.S. 219 (1911).

30. 237 U.S. 309 (1915).

31. *See* ALEXANDER BICKEL & BENNO C. SCHMIDT, JR., HISTORY OF THE SUPREME COURT OF THE UNITED STATES: THE JUDICIARY AND RESPONSIBLE GOVERNMENT 820–908 (1984).

32. *See* LEONARD DINNERSTEIN, THE LEO FRANK CASE (1968).

33. *See, e.g.*, David Orgon Coolidge, *Playing the Loving Card: Same-Sex Marriage and the Politics of Analogy*, 12 B.Y.U. J. PUB. L. 201 (1998); Andrew Koppelman, *Same-Sex Marriage, Choice of Law, and Public Policy*, 76 TEX. L. REV. 921 (1998).

34. 388 U.S. 1 (1967).

35. Mention of *Loving* offers an opportunity to combat the tendency to focus

excessively on the federal Supreme Court in derogation of state supreme courts and other lawmaking bodies. The federal Supreme Court confronted antimiscegenation laws in 1967 near the end of the civil rights revolution and only after scores of state legislatures had repealed their prohibitions against interracial marriage. Nineteen years *before* Chief Justice Earl Warren's opinion for the federal Supreme Court in *Loving*, Judge Roger Traynor authored an opinion for the Supreme Court of California that invalidated on federal constitutional grounds that state's antimiscegenation law. *See* Perez v. Sharp, 198 P.2d 17 (1948).

36. 189 U.S. 475 (1903).

37. I am not claiming to have discovered or rediscovered *Giles*. For valuable discussions of the case *see* DERRICK BELL, RACE, RACISM AND AMERICAN LAW 94, 516 (1st ed. 1973); BICKEL & SCHMIDT, *supra* note 31, at 923–27. I am merely noting that the case lacks the salience that it should have and urging that arbiters of the race relations law canon redress this neglect. A contributing reason, perhaps, for *Giles*'s obscurity is that the federal Supreme Court has dropped it from its own historical memory. In *South Carolina v. Katzenbach*, 388 U.S. 301 (1966), the Court presents a short history of efforts to evade or nullify the Fifteenth Amendment on its way to justifying as policy and upholding as a matter of constitutional law challenged provisions of the Voting Rights Act of 1965. In the course of presenting this history, the Court relates its own history in the voting rights area. It bears noting, however, that the Court cites only those decisions in which it invalidates efforts aimed at excluding blacks from the franchise. It reduces to invisibility decisions such as *Giles* or *Grovey v. Townsend*, 295 U.S. 45 (1935) (insulating from constitutional attack a version of the white primary)(overruled by *Smith v. Allwright*, 321 U.S. 649 (1944)), rulings in which the Court itself became complicit in nullifying the Fifteenth Amendment. Perhaps the Court's presentation of its history was designed to further the struggle for racial justice by inventing a tradition of unbroken judicial solicitude for the rights of African Americans at the ballot box. But whatever the motivation or strategy, scholars need to be aware that they cannot depend upon the Court to describe thoroughly its own institutional history. This is an important matter since teachers frequently use cases as historical narratives. It may be. that one reason why *Giles v. Harris* has dropped from the legal academic canon is that it was dropped by the justices from the Supreme Court's canon.

38. 189 U.S. at 488.

39. The most significant scholarly engagement in this field remains FELIX S. COHEN'S HANDBOOK OF FEDERAL INDIAN LAW (1942), a text that is canonical along several dimensions.

40. ALEXIS DE TOCQUEVILLE, DEMOCRACY IN AMERICA (Phillips Bradley ed. 1945).

41. *See* Randall Kennedy, *Tocqueville and Racial Conflict in America: A Comment*, 11 HARV. BLACKLETTER J. 145 (1994).

42. 118 U.S. 356 (1886).

43. 323 U.S. 214 (1944).

44. *See, e.g.*, *Symposium: Race and Remedy in a Multicultural Society*, 47 STAN. L. REV. 819 (1995)(especially Deborah Ramirez, *Multicultural Empowerment: It's Not Just Black and White Anymore); Latcrit: Latinas/os and the Law: A Joint Symposium by California Law Review and La Raza Law Journal*, 10 LA RAZA L.J. 1 (1998), 85 CALIF. L. REV. 1087 (1998).

45. I have been insufficiently attentive to the full panoply of race matters in my own work. *See* Viet D. Dinh, *Race, Crime and the Law*, 111 HARV. L. REV. 1289 (1998) (reviewing Randall Kennedy, *Race, Crime, and the Law*). Others have been insufficiently attentive as well. In the first edition of Derrick Bell's wonderfully useful casebook, RACE, RACISM AND AMERICAN LAW, he sets apart a twenty-three-page chapter entitled "American Racism and Other 'Nonwhites.'" The remaining thousand pages are devoted to the race question along the black-white frontier. In the second edition of *Race, Racism and American Law*, no attention at all is given to the "Other Nonwhites."

46. *See, e.g.*, CLEAR AND CONVINCING EVIDENCE: MEASUREMENT OF DISCRIMINATION IN AMERICA (Michael Fix & Raymond J. Struyk eds. 1993); Jesse Choper, *Consequences of Supreme Court Decisions Upholding Individual Constitutional Rights (Part I)*, 83 MICH. L. REV. 1 (1984); *(Part II)*, 83 MICH. L. REV.; Michael J. Klarman, *Rethinking the Civil Rights and Civil Liberties Revolutions*, 82 VA. L. REV. 1 (1996); Michael J. Klarman, *Brown, Racial Change and the Civil Rights Movement*, 80 VA. L. REV. 7 (1994); Kenneth J. Melilli, *Batson in Practice: What We Have Learned about "Batson" and Peremptory Challenges*, 71 NOTRE DAME L. REV. 447 (1996); Michael J. Raphael & Edward J. Ungversky, *Excuses, Excuses: Neutral Explanations Under Batson v. Kentucky*, 27 U. MICH. J. L. REF. 229 (1993); John J. Donahue III & Peter Siegelman, *The Changing Nature of Employment Discrimination Litigation*, 43 STAN. L. REV. 983 (1991).

47. Derrick Bell, *The Strange Career of Randall Kennedy*, NEW POLITICS 55 (Summer 1998).

48. *Id.* at 56. The articles to which he refers are Randall Kennedy, *Race Relations Law and the Tradition of Celebration: The Case of Professor Schmidt*, 86 COLUM. L. REV. 1622 (1986); Randall Kennedy, *Persuasion and Distrust: A Comment on the Affirmative Action Debate*, 99 *Harv. L. Rev.* 1327 (1986); and Randall Kennedy, *McCleskey v. Kemp: Race, Capital Punishment, and the Supreme Court*, 101 HARV. L. REV. 1388 (1988).

49. *Id.* at 66.

50. *Id.* at 57. To preclude charges that I have quoted Professor Bell "out of context," I shall offer a full paragraph of his comments:

Kennedy, like Thurgood Marshall, is a contrarian. He loves to argue and play the devil's advocate. This is a useful talent in a classroom and is quite helpful in fine-tuning litigation strategies. Justice Marshall, though, never forgot whose side he was on, particularly in proclamations as opposed to private discourse. In public, he was the ultimate advocate for the black cause as reflected in his civil rights career and his judicial tenure. Kennedy, on the other hand, is quite willing to take his differences with black people public in ways that—whether intended or not—serve to comfort many whites and distress blacks. It is not that his criticisms are new. White conservatives have made similar arguments and worse. It is that he is relinquishing a much needed advocacy role and taking positions that render him an apologist [for aspects of a system] that are less overtly racist than in earlier times but no less ominous in the threat they pose for all blacks. *Id.* at 57.

51. *Id.* at 56.

52. Derrick Bell, *Serving Two Masters: Integration Ideals and Client Interests in School Desegregation Litigation*, 85 YALE L. J. 470 (1976).

53. *Id.* at 516.

54. *See* Nathaniel R. Jones, *Correspondence: School Desegregation*, 86 YALE L. J. 378 (1976).

55. For writings by champions of African American advancement who sharply question the integrationist-assimilationist approach to educational opportunities that prevailed during much of the civil rights era of the 1950s and 1960s, *see* Bell, *supra* note 52; Kevin Brown, *Has the Supreme Court Allowed the Cure for De Jure Segregation to Replicate the Disease?*, 78 CORNELL L. REV. 1 (1992); Alex M. Johnson, Jr., *Bid Whist, Tonk, and United States v. Fordice: Why Integrationism Fails African-Americans Again*, 81 CALIF. L. REV. 1401 (1993). Some of the sentiments that nourish this perspective have deep historical roots. *See* W. E. B. Du Bois, *Does the Negro Need Separate Schools?*, 4 J. NEGRO EDUCA. 328 (1935); Davison M. Douglas, *The Limits of Law in Accomplishing Racial Change: School Segregation in the Pre-Brown North*, 44 UCLA L. REV. 677 (1997). For the view of champions of African American advancement who steadfastly embrace integrationist approaches, *see* GARY ORFIELD, SUSAN E. EATON, & HARVARD PROJECT ON SCHOOL DESEGREGATION, DISMANTLING DESEGREGATION: THE QUIET REVERSAL OF BROWN V. BOARD OF EDUCATION (1996).

56. Consider the debate between those who maintain that labor law should empower black workers to engage in self-help protest that is independent of established unions and those who contend that black workers and workers in general will be better served by centralizing authority in the hands of unions obligated to represent workers fairly regardless of race. Voicing the former position, Judge Wyzanski maintained that "[i]n presenting non-white issues non-whites cannot, against their will, be relegated to white spokesmen, mimicking black men. The day of the minstrel show is over." *Western Addition Community Organization v. NCRB*, 485 F.2d 917 (D.C. Cir. 1973)(Wyzanski, J., dissenting). Ironically it was none other than Thurgood Marshall who wrote the Supreme Court deci-

sion which rejected Wyzanski's position. *Emporium Capwell Co. V. Western Addition Community Org.*, 420 U.S. 50 (1975). That Marshall, America's first black Supreme Court justice, wrote the opinion does not make it right or even in the best interest of blacks. It is safe to say, though, that Thurgood Marshall would not favor the perpetuation of a minstrel show.

57. Consider the debate between Tracey Meares and Dan Kahan, who argue in favor of enhancing police authority for the benefit of crime-ravaged and impoverished minority communities, and more traditional civil libertarians who see enhanced police power as a likely menace to racial minorities. *See* TRACEY L. MEARES & DAN M. KAHAN, URGENT TIMES: POLICING AND RIGHTS IN INNER-CITY COMMUNITIES (1999); David Cole, *Foreward: Discretion and Discrimination Reconsidered: A Response to the New Criminal Justice Scholarship*, 87 GEO. L.J. 1059 (1999); Dorothy E. Roberts, *Foreword: Race, Vagueness, and the Social Meaning of Order-Maintenance Policing*, 89 J. CRIM. L. & CRIMINOLOGY 775 (1999).

58. Some commentators fervently believe that it is in the best interest of orphaned black children for the state to attempt to place them for adoption with black adults. *See* Ruth-Arlene Howe, *Old Prejudices and Discrimination Float Under a New Halo*, 6 B.U. PUB. INTEREST L.J. 409 (1997); James S. Bowen, *Cultural Convergences and Divergences: The Nexus Between Putative Afro-American Family Values and the Best Interests of the Child*, 26 J. FAM. L. 487 (1987); Cynthia G. Hawkins-Leon, *The Indian Child Welfare Act and the African American Tribe: Facing the Adoption Crisis*, 36 J. FAM. L. 201 (1997). Other commentators fervently believe that it is a terrible disservice to black orphans for the state to attempt to place them for adoption with black adults, given the delays and other problems that such efforts cause. *See* ELIZABETH BARTHOLET, FAMILY BONDS: ADOPTION, INFERTILITY, AND THE NEW WORLD OF CHILD PRODUCTION, 86–100 (Beacon Press ed. 1999); NOBODY'S CHILDREN: ABUSE AND NEGLECT, FOSTER DRIFT, AND THE ADOPTION ALTERNATIVE, 113–40 (1999); Randall Kennedy, *Orphans of Separatism: The Painful Politics of Transracial Adoption*, 17 AMERICAN PROSPECT 38 (1994); Kim Forde-Mazrui, *Note, Black Identity and Child Placement: The Best Interests of Black and Biracial Children*, 92 MICH. L. REV. 925 (1994).

59. Among those on the leftward side of the political spectrum, support for race-specific reforms is broad and intense. *See, e.g.,* CHARLES R. LAWRENCE III & MARI J. MATSUDA, WE WON'T GO BACK: MAKING THE CASE FOR AFFIRMATIVE ACTION (1997); CHRISTOPHER EDLEY, JR., NOT ALL BLACK AND WHITE (1996); Duncan Kennedy, *A Cultural Pluralist Case for Affirmative Action in Legal Academia*, 1990 DUKE L.J. 705; Paul Butler, *Affirmative Action and the Criminal Law*, U. COLO. L. REV. 841 (1997); A. Leon Higginbotham, Jr., Gregory A. Clarick, & Marcella David, *Shaw v. Reno: A Mirage of Good Intentions with Devastating Racial Consequences*, 62 FORDHAM L. REV. 1593 (1994). There are progressives, however, who have expressed doubts about whether race-specific policies will broadly

advance the interests of most African Americans. *See, e.g.*, WILLIAM JULIUS WILSON, THE TRULY DISADVANTAGED: THE INNER CITY, THE UNDERCLASS, AND PUBLIC POLICY (1987); KENNEDY, *supra* note 1.

On the rightward end of the political spectrum there exists a substantial literature that argues that race-specific social policies, albeit well-intentioned, negatively affect their presumed beneficiaries. *See, e.g.*, SHELBY STEELE, THE CONTENT OF OUR CHARACTER (1990); Glen Loury, *Beyond Civil Rights*, NEW REPUBLIC, Oct. 7, 1985, at 22; Antonin Scalia, *The Disease as Cure*, 1979 WASH. U.L.Q. 147.

60. *See* Randall Kennedy, *My Race Problem—And Ours*, ATLANTIC MONTHLY, May 1997.

61. In *People v. Hall*, 4 Cal. 399 (1984), the California Supreme Court ruled that state law excluded Chinese, along with blacks and Indians, from testifying against whites. In the course of its decision the court described Chinese as "[a people] whose mendacity is proverbial; a race . . . nature has marked as inferior, and incapable of progress or intellectual development beyond a certain point." *Id.* at 402. A prominent Chinese merchant responded in the following terms: The whites "have come to the conclusion that we Chinese are the same as Indians and Negroes. . . . And yet these Indians know nothing about the relations of society; they know no mutual respect; they wear neither clothes nor shoes; they live in wild places and [in] caves." *Quoted in* Charles J. McClain, Jr., *The Chinese Struggle for Civil Rights in Nineteenth Century America: The First Phase, 1850–1870*, 72 CALIF. L. REV. 529, 550 (1984). The Chinese merchant argued, in other words, that it was understandable to exclude Indians and blacks from the witness stand but an injustice to do the same to people of Chinese ancestry.

62. See THEDA PURDUE, SLAVERY AND THE EVOLUTION OF CHEROKEE SOCIETY, 1540–1866 (1979); ANNIE HELOISE ABEL, THE AMERICAN INDIAN AS SLAVEHOLDER AND SECESSIONIST (Bison Book ed. 1992); C. Calvin Smith, *The Oppressed Oppressors: Negro Slavery Among the Choctaw Indians of Oklahoma*, 2 RED RIVER VALLEY HIST. REV. 240 (1975); Kathryn E. Braund, *The Creek Indians, Blacks, and Slavery*, 57 J. S. HIST. 602 (1991); William S. Willis, Jr., *Divide and Rule: Red, White and Black in the Southeast*, 48 J. NEGRO HIST. 157 (1963).

63. In 1914, a group of African Americans rightly objected to an Oklahoma statute that authorized railroads to provide first-class service only to whites. They prevailed in the United States Supreme Court which ruled that the statute in question violated the formal equality under which de jure segregation was justified. *See* McCabe v. Atchison, Topeka & Sante Fe Railway, 235 U.S. 151 (1914). Unfortunately, in the course of pleading their case, they participated in the unjustified vilification of other oppressed people. Complaining that Indians were protected from exclusion while blacks were not, the plaintiffs objected that Indians are "far more vicious as well as unclean and unhealthy." *Quoted in* BICKEL & SCHMIDT, *supra* note 31, at 778 n.146.

64. In an effort to defend Leo Frank against rape charges, *see supra* at 32, sup-

porters pointed to a black man who should have been a prime suspect. They attempted to foment anger against him by resorting to racist, antiblack stereotypes that depicted black men as rapacious sexual beasts. A sign of the extraordinary character of the animus against Frank is that the Negro-baiting tactics of his defenders failed. They "expressed outrage that a while employer was indicted, rather than a black worker with a criminal record, and shock that their appeals to white supremacy failed to rally the jury or the public." Nancy MacLean, *The Leo Frank Case Reconsidered: Gender and Sexual Politics in the Making of Reactionary Populism*, 78 J. AM. HIST. 917, 925 (1991). Many blacks reacted angrily to this attempt to supersede anti-Jewish prejudice with antiblack bigotry. See Eugene Levy, *"Is the Jew a White Man?": Press Reactions to the Leo Frank Case, 1913–1915*, 35 PHYLON 212 (1974).

65. *See* KOREANS IN THE HOOD: CONFLICT WITH AFRICAN AMERICANS (Kwang Chung Kim ed., 1999).

66. *See* Reynolds v. Commonwealth, 367 S.E2d 176, 178 (Ct. App. Va. 1988).

67. *See* State v. Harris, 716 A.2d 458, 465 (1998).

68. *See* Chris Sosnowski, *Death Penalty to Be Sought for Garner*, POST & COURIER, Apr. 14, 1995; Richard Green, Jr., *Trials Are Judge's Swan Song*, POST & COURIER, Mar. 2, 1998.

# Chapter 9

# Recognizing Race in the American Legal Canon

## *Fran Ansley*

### *Constitutional Memories*

Sometime during my second year in law school, around 1976, I had a powerful encounter with the Fourteenth Amendment. It started in a class called Con Law II, in which I understood that we were to study primarily the Bill of Rights. Coming into the course, I already had a vague idea about what some of those rights might be—certainly I felt favorably disposed toward them. But my overall grasp was, to put it charitably, weak. I did recall that we had discussed at length something called "due process" in our civil procedure class the year before, in the context of learning about the constitutional rights of certain corporations to resist defending themselves in unfavorable jurisdictions. From those discussions I had at least come away with a strong though unanchored sensation that due process was a big deal—widely influential, and guaranteed by the U.S. Constitution. Still, my knowledge was spotty.

That second year, in Con Law II, however, I learned with more clarity—I believe as a brief foundation for our taking up the incorporation doctrine—that due process was specifically a feature of the Fourteenth Amendment. As the semester wore on, I could see that this amendment was indeed a powerful thing, even beyond due process. It had sweepingly restructured the reach of the Bill of Rights, and it seemed to crop up repeatedly in an amazing range of constitutional controversies.

Particularly remarkable to me was the fact—briefly noted in passing in our casebook and in class discussion—that the amendment had been proposed and ratified just after the Civil War as part of the Reconstruction struggle over the status of freed slaves. I am a white Southerner whose childhood was spent under segregation, and whose earliest imprinting lessons about the fact and meaning of social injustice had to do with race. So it was moving to me, a proud and pleasurable surprise, to learn that the Fourteenth Amendment, apparently a central feature of our Constitution, an amendment whose clauses had turned out to be a fountainhead of rights for all kinds of people, had been born out of the black freedom movement.

Characterizing the Fourteenth Amendment in this way is maybe controversial. Not all would agree that the Fourteenth Amendment is "central" to the Constitution,[1] or that a "black freedom" amendment has yet succeeded in creating or enforcing meaningful equality for black people or any other racial minority,[2] or even that legal "rights" or strategies based upon them are of much use in any case.[3] Despite these important questions, I think my instincts at the time were right. I am no doubt more sophisticated about the law and legal history at this juncture than I was in my second year of law school, and nowadays I believe that the valence of constitutional rights as a force for good or ill is more deeply contingent and contextual than I suspected back then. Nevertheless, I am *still* thrilled at the story of the Fourteenth Amendment. I am still proud that it and its scarred and imperfect sister amendments (the Thirteenth which abolished slavery, and the Fifteenth which prohibited racial restriction of the right to vote) are embedded where they are, in the heart of our most canonical of American legal texts.

At the time I was first encountering the impact of Reconstruction on the Constitution, I found myself worrying about the students who did not take Con Law II. Would they somehow, through some other route, learn this inspiring and thought-provoking fact about the amendment's genesis? It seemed important to me that they should. And so one day, as I was talking with my friend and fellow student, whom I will here call Ruby—an African American woman a little older than I, who had grown up in the rural South—I asked her brightly and with feeling if she knew that the Fourteenth Amendment had been framed and adopted during Reconstruction. Did she know that it sprang from the fight for emancipation and for the eradication of the ravages of slavery?

Ruby sucked her teeth and cocked an amused and incredulous eye in my direction. "Of course I know that, child. Who do you think I am?"

Who *did* I think she was? It didn't occur to me that Ruby might be significantly better off than I in terms of her access to constitutional literacy.

In those days I had little information about the complex history of African American schools in the South before the *Brown* decision, or who had made those schools and how.[4] For these and other reasons I had few clues about what Ruby was likely or unlikely to know about the U.S. Constitution.

On that day, Ruby began to explain. She told me a little about her education in the segregated grade schools of south Georgia. She related how her black teacher there had insisted that every child in her elementary school class *memorize* the words of the Thirteenth, Fourteenth, and Fifteenth Amendments. That achievement, she said, took the children weeks. Ruby and her classmates learned these texts by heart, and then stood and recited them before each other while the teacher presided from the back of the room. Ruby remembered walking to school in the mornings and saying the amendments over with her sister in anticipation of the public performance she would soon be called upon to give. By my calculation, these events would have taken place sometime in the early 1950s: a time, in other words, when *Plessy v. Ferguson*[5] was still "good" law.

I cannot tell you what an effect this story had on me. I pondered the image of Ruby and her sister as little girls, walking down that hot south Georgia road, reciting the Fourteenth Amendment from memory upon the open air.

The story gave me more than an arresting image, however. It surprised me with a new sense of the Constitution and its history. Ruby's story suggests that African Americans have a particular historical claim upon the Constitution, and can take a particular kind of historical credit for some of the best aspects of its evolution. It manifests in a particularly vivid way that African Americans have sustained—through untold adversity, often from the bottom up, and at least in important part with the tools of a decentralized oral tradition—an insurgent interpretation of that document's meaning.

As someone who now teaches in law school classrooms, I am struck by the fact that this important learning moment happened "off the books." It was extracanonical, if you will, at least in the context of my formal schooling. But it forever changed my own view of one of the central texts of the tradition into which I was being inducted.

As for the quality of the educational experiences I could claim up to that point, the civic efficacy of the official canon to which I had been exposed, it is worth noting that I owed this knowledge to Ruby, a product of a scandalously underfunded Jim Crow Georgia school. Now she was here to tell her well-meaning but somewhat backward friend, with the bachelor's degree from Harvard and the year and a half in law school, a little something about the U.S. Constitution and one of its most important interpretive communities.

The story of Ruby and her teacher and their part in the intergenerational black stewardship of the post–Civil War amendments has continued to raise questions for me about race and the American legal canon as that canon is presently being taught and recreated in U.S. law schools.

This essay will argue that race is a central and generative feature of the American legal canon, but that its role and significance have too often been obscured or written out of the conventional wisdom transmitted through American legal education and scholarship.[6] It will urge that legal academics, in their roles as teachers, scholars, and public intellectuals, should challenge the grand racial narratives and "grand racial silences" of the official canon, that they should help to resurrect and construct counternarratives, in important part by attending to the experiences and words of those who can offer perspectives from the bottom and from the margins of the racial order as it is currently constituted. Such challenges will be crucial to the creation of a better canon: one that is more contentious and open-ended, perhaps, but truer to the nation's actual history and better suited to helping the peoples of the United States achieve a more just and peaceful future.

## Race and the American Legal Canon

Canonicity can mean many things. Certainly by any standard the legal canon would encompass the cases and materials that law professors assign to law students.[7] More embedded aspects of the taught canon are also an important part of the message conveyed. Such aspects include the pedagogical methods that law teachers use in their classrooms, who those teachers are, the general argument categories they encourage their students to learn how to make, the overall outline and sequence of the curriculum, and not least, the bar examination and the picture transmitted to students about the existing market for legal services and how they can or should fit themselves into it.[8] Beyond the preparation of students, legal scholars continually recreate and constitute another sort of legal canon through doctrinal and theoretical conversations carried on in a set of perhaps increasingly divergent academic and professional discourse communities. Further, beyond both the academy and the profession, there is a "popular canon" of American law. The Constitution, for instance, is an object of near-religious veneration for many members of the American public.[9]

In this essay, I will approach the legal canon in a way that cuts across various kinds of materials and audiences, focusing on its role as a source of cultural literacy, a collection of core narratives (or "stock stories")[10] that Americans tell themselves about the nation's history and its system of law. In doing so, I take as a given, and will not try to convince readers here, that the nation's history is strongly marked by racial oppression backed in many instances by the full authority of law, and that racist ideas, arrangements, and practices powerfully persist in the United States today. I believe it follows that stories about racially oppressive relations, about attempts to overcome them, and about ways that law has been involved in both, should not be muffled or repressed, but should be a prominent part of the canon transmitted in and through the law schools, addressed and debated in the scholarly community, and shared with the populace at large.[11] Subordinate narratives and perspectives about race should be sought from the bottom and from the margins, while presently dominant stories about race should be subjected to searching analysis, just as they have been in other disciplines.

## Challenging the Canon: Two Visions

### Adding

I have argued that legal educators should treat race as a canonical feature of the American legal tradition, should recognize the signs of race that mark our most important texts and defining moments, and should find ways of highlighting those signs for their students and their colleagues. However, the task may not be as simple as it sounds. As a first approach to better understanding where some of the difficulties lie, I will contrast two different visions of what a racially progressive change in the canon might entail. Both of these visions are at work in current writing and theorizing about "the Western canon" generally, and both are relevant for thinking about the American legal canon as well. The first I will call here the "additive vision" of canon transformation. It parallels some of the more primitive discussions in higher education about affirmative action in admissions or faculty hiring, and it focuses primarily on a need to be more "inclusive." In the context of race, the additive approach to canon change in liberal arts has often meant expanding course reading lists to include works by or explicitly about people of color, or expanding the list of course offerings to include courses explicitly about, for instance, "black" history, or the art and culture of non-European nations or ethnic groups.

Texts by and/or about people of color, so the argument runs, should be placed in the core, not only texts or courses by and/or about (dead? European? male?) white people. Similarly, "diversity" courses—that is, courses about "other" or "different" cultures, or courses focusing explicitly on people of color—should be included more generously in the elective curriculum, or perhaps more radically, should be required for completion of relevant academic degrees.[12]

The additive vision has a lot to recommend it. We do need inclusion and diversity.[13] In an earlier essay, I used the additive vision as a starting point for arguing that legal education might be able to make faster strides than other university disciplines in facing up to the centrality of race for our field and its traditions.[14] I hypothesized that legal education, though it had largely ignored the canon debates up until that point, might paradoxically be more advanced than the rest of the university in "desegregating" its canon. After all, I then argued, in legal education we didn't need to fight for the addition of a race-relevant text to our canon. Surely, at the pinnacle of American legal canonicity, as defined by anybody's standard and plain as day for all to see, sits the U.S. Constitution. And the Constitution is saturated with racial meaning and racial conflict—as even I had dimly seen in my second year of law school, and as Ruby had so strikingly illuminated for me in her reminiscences and gentle jibes.

Further, since Ruby's original tutorial, I had studied with other teachers as well, and had learned how to decode the places in the founders' Constitution where slavery had been accommodated while remaining unnamed. Those provisions included the three-fifths clause that allowed slave states to increase their political power by including enslaved persons (albeit fractionally) in their population counts for purposes of congressional representation; the slave trade clause that insulated the transatlantic slave trade from legislative prohibition by Congress for twenty years; and the fugitive slave clause that committed even free states to the recognition and enforcement of property rights in slaves who had escaped from bondage.

Given these marks left by slavery on the face of the Constitution, the centrality of race and racism to the American legal canon should be, at least relatively speaking, noncontroversial, and legal educators should face significantly lower barriers to teaching a racially integrated canon than scholars in many other disciplines.

Further experience, however, has cast doubt on my original thesis. In the first place, if race is in fact so self-evidently central to the Constitution, then why don't we teach it that way? Why is the Constitution of 1787 so seldom presented to our students in any depth?[15] Why do they so seldom read *Prigg v. Pennsylvania*?[16] How, even in my second year, could I have been left to wonder whether other students would be aware of the origins of the Fourteenth Amendment? Why, a few years ago, when I asked a third-year law student in my trusts and estates class where the Fourteenth Amendment came from, did he pause, think quizzically for a moment, and then venture hesitantly, "1964?"?

And the problem is not confined to our students. Most legal scholars would, of course, do better on dating and situating the Fourteenth Amendment than the unfortunate guy I called on that day. But no small number of my colleagues in law teaching have confessed to me that they were unacquainted with the slavery compromises in the founders' Constitution before I pointed them out.

Beyond constitutional law, a similar pattern of silence on matters of race characterizes other foundational areas of the law school's curriculum. American criminal law, property law, and legal ethics, for instance, are as marked by race as the Constitution. Yet they too are often taught with little or no overt or rigorous examination of the ways that racism and resistance to it have figured in their doctrinal development and social impact.[17]

In other words, experiential data from my own time in law school, both as a student and as a teacher, do not support my wishful hypothesis that we in legal education could reach an easy consensus on the centrality of race to our mission. Race, in many colors, may have been in our legal canon all along, but seeing and interpreting it will require a struggle.

## Beyond Adding

The limitations of the additive approach have been targeted repeatedly in the scholarship and the polemics of the larger canon debates. Scholars of color in anthropology, for instance, have refused to restrict their role to that of "native informant" or data gatherer about the lives or cultures of colored people. They have insisted as well upon critically examining the practices of white colonial and postcolonial anthropology. Race-conscious scholars of color in other parts of the academy too are likely to have turned their analytical gaze[18] on "whiteness" as well as "color," to have moved on to analyze closely the sacred texts and customary practices of the dominant racial group.[19] Toni Morrison has been pursuing this line in the context of literary criticism. One passage of Morrison's in particular has always struck me as powerfully suggestive for a full reading of the founders' Constitution, with that document's multiple accommodations to slavery, and yet its studied avoidance of any explicit invocation of the peculiar institution by name. Morrison calls for

> [an] examination and re-interpretation of the American canon, for the "unspeakable things unspoken"; for the ways in which the presence of Afro-Americans has shaped the choices, the language, the structure—the meaning of so much American literature. A search, in other words, for the ghost in the machine. . . .
>
> We can agree, I think, that invisible things are not necessarily "not there". . . . In addition, certain absences are so stressed, so ornate, so planned, they call attention to themselves; arrest us with intentionality and purpose, like neighborhoods that are defined by the population held away from them. Looking at the scope of American literature, I can't help thinking that the question should never have been, "Why am I, an Afro-American, absent from it?" It is not a particularly interesting query anyway. The spectacularly interesting question is, "What intellectual feats had to be performed by the author or his critic to erase me from a society seething with my presence, and what effect has that performance had on the work?"[20]

This sort of canon work moves beyond addition and opens for reexamination and reevaluation (by old-timers and newcomers alike) the entire received tradition.

## A Race-Conscious Canon for American Law

Thanks to decades of heightened effort to move beyond the kind of pale "de jure desegregation" that has characterized too many post-*Brown* law schools, there are now unprecedented numbers of teachers and scholars of color in the previously all-white legal academy. This achievement, as incomplete and as vulnerable as it is,[21] nonetheless has opened a new and exciting era of interpretive contestation on matters of race in the American legal canon.[22] It requires no essentialist illusions to see that new scholars of color in the legal academy have played a powerful role in unsettling old assumptions and infusing new themes into the canonical conversation.[23] Building on pioneering work by their scholarly and activist predecessors, and working across various sorts of racial and ethnic lines, they have introduced a wider legal audience to previously neglected racial texts and events that should clearly be part of the established canon; they have dramatized real and allegorical stories about race and law in America; they have helped white people in the legal academy to better understand the whiteness of so much of what we do; they have put forward new interpretive claims about the existing canon.[24]

This good work, coupled with that of others inside and outside the legal academy, puts us in a position to more fully and productively recognize and respond to race in the American legal canon. It allows us to identify racial problems that should be a recurring subject of study and racial narratives that should be among the stock stories of our culture. The work has also discovered and created materials with which we as legal academics can help construct and tell the "legal side" of those core stories about race.[25]

It is worth noting that some such narratives will be inspiring and others will be shameful. That is as it should be. *Dred Scott*, like *Lochner*, is a canonical case for American law, not because it is admirable, but because it is indispensable to understanding how we arrived at the present, because it stands as a (contested and variously interpreted) cautionary tale.

What follows are my own nominations for some grand problems of race and law in America that I believe should be part of the canon as taught in American law schools. I am not suggesting that all members of the legal community or of the nation will reach harmonious accord on the meaning or significance of these problems or of the racial stories that accompany them. But all of us should at least know that these problems exist, and all of us should be familiar with the major texts and events connected to them. We should be aware of the major contending interpretations of their meaning (including especially on questions of race the interpretations and perspectives of people and communities of color). This essay will not suggest a blueprint for how and where these themes can or should be fit into the curriculum or a course. Precisely the challenge I intend to pose is that we should be "teaching race across the curriculum," and all law teachers should be asking themselves how and where they can best do so. I choose the following problems involving race and law because each has had a strong imprint on American history, and each continues to be relevant for important decisions facing the nation today.

*1. Slavery.* One would think this nomination is so self-evident as to be unnecessary, but as I have complained above, experience suggests that is not the case. At the risk of belaboring the obvious, I note that the imprint of slavery on U.S. history is unmistakable: among other things, the institution helped to amass the nation's wealth, led to the costliest war in U.S. history, and was the source of revolutionary amendments to the Constitution. Further, slavery left behind a caste system that is even now only half dismantled, whose continued existence is still one of the most striking social facts about American society, and which today confronts policymakers and communities with some of the most difficult questions they face. Slavery's institutionalization, formal abolition, and informal afterlife are largely creatures of law, and the materials available for tracing and telling this story through a legal lens are abundant and ready to hand. Since I have written elsewhere about these materials and some of my pedagogical adventures in attempting to teach them, I will not repeat those stories here,[26] but will simply state that slavery is at the heart of American experience and is memorialized at the heart of our legal canon. It should be taught and debated accordingly.

When I first heard Ruby's story, I took from it that because of slavery and the nature of its overthrow, African Americans have a special claim upon the American legal tradition in general and upon the Constitution in particular. It seemed to me then and seems to me now that the rest of us owe our African American neighbors for much, including our reconstructed Constitution, and that we should study and acknowledge the nature of that debt.

In more recent years, as the economy of the nation and the world have undergone dramatic changes, as "globalization" has raised unprecedented questions about the meaning and future of national sovereignty, as millions of impoverished migrants have set forth to find work around the globe, and as disparities in wealth and life experience between those at the top and bottom of the world's economy widen to almost unimaginable proportions, I have begun to recognize other stories of race and law in America's past that I believe could also help the nation understand the challenges confronting us. The global economy forces us to think anew about the nature of territorial boundaries, for instance, and raises hard questions about the U.S. role in the new world order.

A more global perspective on the national racial canon also reminds us to revisit the story of American slavery itself in the context of its birth in the days of European empire and the Atlantic Triangle. The slave trade's involuntariness distinguishes it crucially from other sorts of immigration, but there are important common themes at work as well, such as the worldwide search for cheap labor, and the multiple ways that race and geography can be deployed in the construction of segmented labor markets.

Such a perspective on the U.S. place in the world also suggests the value of attending to some of our "other" racial minorities. Native American Indian tribes, Asians, and Latinos have stories that are particularly helpful in casting light on some of these pressing problems.[27] In this context, I want to propose two additional problems of race and law that should be treated as part of the American legal canon at century's end.

*2. Conquest.* If slavery is at the "heart" of the story of American law, what defines that law's outer perimeter? In more instances than not, the edge of our polity has moved through space by force of arms, in acts of conquest. The story of the European and then American conquest on this continent should be canonical in the study of American law.

The Constitution is strikingly silent about the extent of its own reach, never clearly addressing how the nation purported to exercise sovereignty over the lands of the original colonies, much less how the Constitution and the other laws of the union should or should not apply to territories and peoples not present at the founding in 1787.[28] This omission is as noticeable as the document's silence on slavery, since expansion was plainly an issue on the nation's agenda from the first. Since the acquisition of new territories and the admission of new states into the union continued apace well into the present century, the question could not continue to go unaddressed. Accordingly, we have the benefit today of various explanatory and declaratory sources that can help us understand the ways that the American legal system came to be imposed upon (or withheld from) various territories and populations.

The expansion of the United States, with the many incremental impositions of sequentially new boundaries upon newly acquired territory, was always importantly about race. Key American thinkers and leaders, including many with roles in the legal system, were gripped by the ideology of Manifest Destiny, the expansionist idea that the white race—or the United States as an instrument of the white race—had a calling and a responsibility to dominate (and thereby to save or uplift) the rest of the world. Accordingly, expansion of U.S. territory has in almost every instance been accompanied by racial narratives about the legitimacy of expansion, the likely benefits to be visited upon the darker people whose territory has been acquired, and the ways such people and their rights should or should not be recognized by American law.

For instance, the first Justice Marshall was once asked to resolve a dispute between two white property owners, one claiming title through purchase from an Indian tribe, and one claiming title through a grant from the federal government. He chose the path of candor, offering the following Genesis-like pronouncements about the nature of the European presence in America:

> On the discovery of this immense continent, the great nations of Europe were eager to appropriate to themselves so much of it as they could respectively acquire. Its vast extent offered an ample field to the ambition and enterprise of all; and the character and religion of its inhabitants afforded an apology for considering them as a people over whom the superior genius of Europe might claim an ascendency. The potentates of the old world found no difficulty in convincing themselves that they made ample compensation to the inhabitants of the new, by bestowing on them civilization and Christianity, in exchange for unlimited independence. But, as they were all in pursuit of nearly the same object, it was necessary, in order to avoid conflicting settlements, and consequent war with each other, to establish a principle, which all should acknowledge as the law by which the right of acquisition, which they all asserted, should be regulated as between themselves. . . .
>
> The British government, which was then our government, and whose rights have passed to the United States, asserted title to all the lands occupied by Indians, within the chartered limits of the British colonies. It asserted also a limited sovereignty over them, and the exclusive right of extinguishing the title which occupancy gave to them. These claims have been maintained and established as far west as the river Mississippi, by the sword. . . .[29]

Whatever undertones a reader may detect as to the justice's personal reservations about the proffered ideology, he did not shrink from enforcing it. In other instances, images of the racial inferiority of nonwhite peoples were used by American lawmakers in the context of conquest, not so much to justify taking over the land of such peoples as to avoid incorporating them into the larger body politic after their territory had been secured to the United States. In an 1848 speech against the Mexican-American War, Senator John Calhoun made the following argument:

> [W]e have never dreamt of incorporating into our Union any but the Caucasian race—the free white race. To incorporate Mexico, would be the very first instance of incorporating an Indian race; for more than half of all the Mexicans are Indians, the other is composed chiefly of mixed tribes. I protest against such a union as that! Ours, sir, is the Government of a white race. The greatest misfortunes of Spanish America are to be traced to the fatal error of placing these colored races on an equality with the white race. That error destroyed the social arrangement which formed the basis of society. . . . And yet it is professed and talked about to erect these Mexicans into a Territorial Government and place them on an equality with the people of the United States.[30]

Although Calhoun failed to dissuade the Congress from acquiring the land taken in the war, and although Calhoun's views were certainly more openly racist that those of the Congress generally, the fears he expressed were widespread. After the Mexican-American War was concluded by the Treaty of Guadalupe Hidalgo in 1848,[31] and the United States took over a vast territory that included present-day California, Arizona, Nevada, New Mexico, and parts of Colorado and Utah, New Mexican petitions for statehood were rejected for over sixty years, the longest wait imposed on a territory in U.S. history. In 1912 the white population of New Mexico for the first time became a majority, and New Mexico was at last admitted to the union.

Meanwhile, the conquered Mexican residents of areas acquired by the United States in the treaty were promised without racial reservation that their civil rights and property rights would be honored by the United States, but the promises were diluted from the beginning. For instance, dark-skinned ex-Mexicans often found themselves disenfranchised by racially exclusionary state voting laws that made no exceptions for treaty rights such as those the Mexicans were claiming.[32] Further, in the ensuing decades the vast majority of Mexican landholdings held by Mexicans at the time of the treaty were lost to Anglo hands through a confusing array of legal mechanisms and extralegal grabs, made all the more ironic as time wore on, and Mexican and Mexican American landless laborers formed the ill-paid backbone of so much of U.S. agriculture.[33]

After the Spanish-American war, a new conquest raised racial issues once more. At the close of hostilities in 1898, the United States signed a treaty with Spain through which it gained possession of the Philippines, Guam, Cuba, and Puerto Rico.[34] Although natives of Spain living in the territories retained the right to preserve their Spanish citizenship, the status of "the native inhabitants of the territories hereby ceded to the United States" was to be "determined by the Congress."[35] After the treaty, the Supreme Court was asked to rule on the legality of a tariff imposed on Puerto Rican oranges, in light of the fact that the island had become part of the United States. The Court ruled that the tariff was legal, but it felt constrained to address as well the question of the status of the inhabitants of the island:

> [T]he Constitution is applicable to territories acquired by purchase or conquest, only when and so far as Congress shall so direct. . . .
>
> We are also of opinion that the power to acquire territory by treaty implies, not only the power to govern such territory, but to prescribe upon what terms the United States will receive its inhabitants, and what their status shall be in what Chief Justice Marshall termed the "American empire." There seems to be no middle ground between this position and the doctrine that if their inhabitants do not become, immediately upon annexation, citizens of the United States, their children thereafter born, whether savages or civilized, are such, and entitled to all the rights, privileges and immunities of citizens. If such be their status, the consequences will be extremely serious. . . . In all its treaties hitherto . . . there is an implied denial of the right of the inhabitants to American citizenship until Congress by further action shall signify its assent thereto [quoting language from treaties related to the Louisiana Purchase, the acquisition of lands from Mexico, Alaska, and the instant case].
>
> Grave apprehensions of danger are felt by many eminent men,—a fear lest an unrestrained possession of power on the part of Congress may lead to unjust and oppressive legislation. . . . These fears, however, find no justification in the action of Congress in the past century. . . . There are certain principles of natural justice inherent in the Anglo-Saxon character, which need no expression in constitutions or statutes to give them effect or to secure dependencies against legislation manifestly hostile to their real interests. . . .
>
> It is obvious that in the annexation of outlying and distant possessions, grave questions will arise from differences of race, habits, laws, and customs of the people, and from differences of soil, climate, and production,

which may require action on the part of Congress that would be quite unnecessary in the annexation of contiguous territory inhabited only by people of the same race, or by scattered bodies of native Indians.

A false step at this time might be fatal to the development of what Chief Justice Marshall called the American empire.[36]

It is clear that policymakers in America have justified our expanding circumference by reference to race, and have also viewed that perimeter as having an important continuing racial function.

The Conquest deserves a place in a racially transformed canon because it had an important impact on the shape of U.S. history, coming close to fully accounting for our present national borders. Further, mythic tales of a sort of "citizen's conquest" along the advancing west-tending frontier, as white settlers displaced Indians and turned the land to productive use, come close to being synonymous with our official autobiography.

The themes and stories of conquest also have present-day significance. Numerous current issues could be better understood and resolved if informed by a better knowledge of the racial subtext to our nation's conquering past. Domestically, such issues include the stubborn persistence of an independence movement in Puerto Rico and the still-anomalous status of that island and its people within the larger structure of the U.S. polity;[37] the newly arisen and quite active sovereignty movement among native people in the state of Hawai'i;[38] the attitudes and demands of Mexican American communities whose diverse constituents include many residents descended from Mexican settlers who "came" to the United States only because the U.S. Army conquered the territory in which they were living and the earlier U.S.–Mexico border moved south;[39] not to mention the continuing struggle of Indian tribes to establish and defend a meaningful system of tribal sovereignty within the severe constraints imposed upon them by federal law and policy.[40]

Internationally, the history of conquest is also relevant for contemporary disputes. Since the time of the founding, the temper of the global geopolitical consensus has changed significantly. Today, ideologies of racial egalitarianism and of self-determination have, at least in a formal sense, prevailed, and human rights norms have taken frail but persistent root. A more thorough and thoughtful understanding of the law and practice of U.S. conquest might help us reconcile the continuing legacies of imperial past practice with the announced ethic of the postcolonial world in which we find ourselves today.

Finally, as the excerpts quoted above suggest, conquest implicates law. There is a body of legal texts and legal documents pertaining to conquest. These sources can help elucidate the ways law has accompanied conquest, has legitimated wars and structured their aftermath, has defined (or denied) the rights of the conquered, has constructed a series of second-class citizenships for those conquered persons (such as Indian tribes in the early republic, or New Mexico when it was still too brown, or Puerto Rico in the twentieth century) who have not been viewed as belonging to a white enough community to be fully integrated into the American body politic.

*3. Immigration.* Immigration is my third nominee for canonical status in the American racial story. It is often but not always related to the theme of conquest, and in any event has its own characteristic dilemmas and issues.

Disagreements over immigration policy often turn out to be disagreements about race. For much of its history U.S. immigration law has included explicitly racial criteria for admission to the territory of the United States, and then for the privilege of acquiring U.S. citizenship. For instance, following an upsurge of anti-Chinese agitation in California, Congress passed the Chinese Exclusion Act in 1882, suspending all immigration of "Chinese laborers" for the next ten years. This statute was followed by a stronger ban in 1888 which made it impossible for a departed laborer to return to the United States after a visit home, even if he had obtained a then officially sanctioned certificate for re entry before his departure.[41] The Supreme Court upheld Congress's power to set and change the rules in this way in 1889 in the *Chae Chan Ping* case, where Justice Field felt free to take judicial notice of the following:

> [The passage of this statute was occasioned by] a well-founded apprehension—from the experience of years—that a limitation of immigration of certain classes from China was essential to the peace of the community on the Pacific coast, and possibly to the preservation of our civilization there. A few words on this point may not be deemed inappropriate here, they being confined to matters of public notoriety, which have frequently been brought to the attention of congress.

> This discovery of gold in California in 1848, as is well known, was followed by a large immigration thither from all parts of the world. . . . The news . . . penetrated China, and laborers came from there in great numbers, a few with their own means, but by far the greater number under contract with employers, for whose benefit they worked. These laborers readily secured

employment, and, as domestic servants, and in various kinds of outdoor work, proved to be exceedingly useful.

For some years little opposition was made to them, except when they sought to work in the mines, but, as their numbers increased, they began to engage in various mechanical pursuits and trades, and thus came in competition with our artisans and mechanics, as well as our laborers in the field. The competition steadily increased as the laborers came in crowds on each steamer that arrived from China. . . . They were generally industrious and frugal. Not being accompanied by families, except in rare instances, their expenses were small; and they were content with the simplest fare, such as would not suffice for our laborers and artisans. The competition between them and our people was for this reason altogether in their favor, and the consequent irritation, proportionately deep and bitter, was followed, in many cases, by open conflicts, to the great disturbance of the public peace.

The differences of race added greatly to the difficulties of the situation. . . . [T]hey remained strangers in the land residing apart by themselves, and adhering to the customs and usages of their own country. It seemed impossible for them to assimilate with our people, or to make any change in their habits or modes of living.

As they grew in numbers each year the people of the coast saw, or believed they saw, in the facility of immigration, and in the crowded millions of China, where population presses upon the means of subsistence, great danger that at no distant day that portion of our country would be overrun by them, unless prompt action was taken to restrict their immigration. . . .

[Then the constitutional convention in California petitioned Congress] that their immigration was in numbers approaching the character of an Oriental invasion, and was a menace to our civilization; . . . that they retained the habits and customs of their own country, and in fact constituted a Chinese settlement within the state, without any interest in our country or its institutions. . . .

To preserve its independence, and give security against foreign aggression and encroachment, is the highest duty of every nation. . . . It matters not in what form such aggression and encroachment come, whether from the foreign nation acting in its national character, or from vast hordes of its people crowding in upon us. . . . If, therefore, the government . . . considers the presence of foreigners of a different race in this country, who will not assimilate with us, to be dangerous to its peace and security, their exclusion is not to be stayed because at the time there are no actual hostilities. . . .[42]

Following this case, which settled the unilateral congressional power to exclude aliens regardless of treaty provisions to the contrary, Congress passed the Geary Act which created a pass system applicable only to Chinese laborers, an internal identification regime based on race.[43] This statute was also upheld by the Supreme Court in *Fong Yue Ting v. United States,* another of the train of constitutional challenges mounted by Chinese activists to this and other anti-Chinese legislation.[44] Both *Chae Chan Ping* and *Fong Yue Ting* were important milestones in establishing Congress's plenary power over immigration and inaugurating what was to be a lasting attitude of deference by the Court toward federal immigration legislation.

Between 1921 and 1965 various national quota systems were adopted whereby immigration from each nation of the world was allowed only in accordance with quotas that were pegged by various formulas to past U.S. populations. These quotas operated in a specifically racial way. Their effect was to limit immigration from areas of Europe and of the world where disfavored racial and ethnic groups originated, and to preserve a "whiter" cast to immigration flows by tying them to the demographics of a whiter time. In addition, an "Asiatic Barred Zone" was in effect for a number of years. It prohibited all immigration from countries within specified latitudes and longitudes in Asia. Although the quotas were facially tied not to race but to nation, the intent of the legislation was evident from the context. Provisions such as the following reveal even more clearly Congress's underlying preoccupation with race:

> [An] immigrant born outside the Asia-Pacific triangle . . . who is attributable by as much as one-half of his ancestry to a people or peoples indigenous to not more than one separate quota area, situate wholly within the Asia-Pacific Triangle, shall be chargeable to the quota of that area.[45]

In addition to the immigration quota system for admission of persons desiring to become permanent residents or eventually naturalized citizens, the United States after World War II began a series of experiments with "guest worker" programs. When employers could show that there was a "shortage" of native-born or resident U.S. workers in a particular sector, they could import foreign workers—almost exclusively people of color from Mexico and the Caribbean—on a temporary basis to perform the specified job under supervision by the Department of Labor. The original "bracero" program with Mexico was ended in the 1960s, but today other guest worker programs are in existence, and the agricultural lobby is now pressing for an enlarged and liberalized regime.

Aside from the race-linked rules about immigration and temporary work authorizations, the law of citizenship was also racial in character during much of this time. For years, the chance to become a naturalized citizen was restricted to whites and people of African descent, a restriction that had an impact in its own right, but also could trigger other disabilities for those affected. (In California and a number of other states, for instance, no one ineligible for citizenship could own or lease agricultural land. Likewise the Immigration Act of 1924 excluded anyone from immigrating who was not eligible for naturalization, thereby in essence ending all legal immigration from Asia.) All of these measures were upheld in the face of court challenges.[46]

One by-product of the racial limits on naturalization was the creation of a forum for the repeated adjudication of whiteness, as people of various races and ethnicities attempted to establish that they were sufficiently "white" to be naturalized.[47] In one case, for instance, the Supreme Court was called upon to decide whether an Asian Indian man "of high-caste Hindu stock . . . and classified by certain scientific authorities as of the Caucasian or Aryan race" was eligible for naturalization as a "white person." Justice Sutherland, in holding that he was not, explained:

> What we now hold is that the words "free white persons" are words of common speech, to be interpreted in accordance with the understanding of the common man, synonymous with the word "Caucasian" only as that word is popularly understood. . . . [W]hatever may be the speculations of the ethnologist, it does not include the body of people to whom the appellee belongs. It is a matter of familiar observation and knowledge that the physical group characteristics of the Hindus render them readily distinguishable from the various groups of person in this country commonly recognized as white. The children of English, French, German, Italian, Scandinavian, and other European parentage, quickly merge into the mass of our population and lose the distinctive hallmarks of their European origin. On the other hand, it cannot be doubted that the children born in this country of Hindu parents would retain indefinitely the clear evidence of their ancestry. It is very far from our thought to suggest the slightest question of racial superiority or inferiority. What we suggest is merely racial difference, and it is of such character and extent that the great body of our people instinctively recognize it and reject the thought of assimilation.[48]

Not until 1965, the year after the passage of the Civil Rights Act of 1964, did Lyndon Johnson sign a bill abolishing the race-linked national origins quota.[49] Latinos and Asians of all nationalities are still branded with an "alienness" that is perceived as somehow "natural" by many Americans, but is in fact rooted in this long law-aided construction of highly stratified, racialized, and multinational labor markets.[50]

In legal education and in American communities, we should teach about the boundaries of American citizenship, should probe the meanings and the mechanisms behind this "nation of immigrants," and we should do so with the history of immigration law, the national quota system, and the long line of Mexican guest worker programs in plain view. Given the impact of immigration and immigration law on our society and economy, and given the difficult immigration questions confronting us today, this is an issue that should be prominently in the canon. Immigration even has its own national monument surrounded by controversy, surely a sign that it has canonical status in the American imagination.[51]

## Conclusion

We Americans inherit our national canon from its "original" authors, from their predecessors, and from intervening generations of official and unofficial readers, listeners, and responders, both winners and losers. We also create it continually anew, choosing which themes and values we will affirm, which national events we will remember and how, which past speakers, actors, and writers will command our attentive respect, which clauses and cases we will analyze, and which present-day problems we will treat as most pressing. Always and unavoidably, we carry out this canon-building and canon-destroying contestation in the light of contemporary concerns.

No contemporary concern is more important than that of race or has more resonance with our long national narrative. Structures and mandates of white supremacy, as well as diverse projects of resistance to it, have been central to the history of our country from before its founding to the present. Today, racial inequity and racial tension are epidemic in the national culture, and deep pessimism about the possibility of just or peaceful resolutions of racial differences and racial inequities is pervasive. Law has played a major role in both constructing and attempting to deconstruct the myriad institutions of white supremacy, and throughout our national history people of color, despite their racial subordination and their designation as unassimilable or inadmissible outsiders, have been active agents in making and changing that law. In the high and low texts of the American legal canon, signs of racial hierarchy and racial struggle are much in evidence, revealed both by what is included and expressed in those texts and by what is repressed and excluded from them.

Nevertheless, the teaching of these signs, the telling of these struggles, and the carrying on of vigorous and candid debate about their meaning within the context of the U.S. legal system are for the most part muted and peripheral within American legal education. The racial messages in the law school curriculum are ubiquitous but often inchoate, almost subliminal, and thus apparently invisible to many of us in the enterprise. We law teachers should find ways of speaking about these issues and breaking these silences, in our classrooms, in our writing and speaking, and in our work in the community. We should particularly seek out and generously use sources that examine three grand racial problems of American history that this essay has nominated for canonical status: slavery, conquest, and immigration.

A canon will always to some degree represent the victor's story, the version of national events and ideas most flattering to the powerful and most stabilizing for the status quo. But repressed narratives and "dangerous opposites" always remain in the canon as well, and they can provide alternative sources of inspiration and understanding. Since we are a society that claims a commitment to democracy, we should adopt a democratic canonical method, one that values and preserves bottom-up skepticism, a reiterative drive to revision, a restless and continuing search for the suppressed narratives of subordinated people, a suspicion of official wisdom, an acknowledgment that canons (and the challenges to them) are always in some sense provisional.

I will end this essay now as I began it, with a story about an African American child and the U.S. Constitution. Several years ago I delivered an earlier version of this essay to an audience of law professors. In that talk I told the story of Ruby and her Georgia teacher and told what I had learned from my friend about the transmission of the post war amendments to a new generation of black children in the Deep South in the early 1950s. I voiced my conviction that African Americans have particular claims on the Constitution and can take particular kinds of credit for some of its most admirable features. Not long after, I received a letter from an African American friend and colleague who had attended the talk. She told a constitutional story of her own, and I share it with you now:

My son was about five or six when he first learned about the enslavement of his ancestors in this country. He became very frightened that those days might return. I reassured him as best I could, but the only thing that seemed to provide him any comfort at all was to sit on the floor with him and read the words of the Thirteenth Amendment to the Constitution. I also explained to him several times how difficult it would be to amend the Constitution to allow the return of slavery. I read to him from one of those small pamphlet versions of the Constitution that law publishing houses put out. And do you know, that child wouldn't go to sleep without a copy of the Constitution under his bed that night, and for many months afterwards.[52]

### NOTES

To thank all those I owe on this topic would be impossible, but I want to mention a few people whose various contributions were indispensable: Derrick Bell, Bob Chang, Joe Cook, Juan Perea (who in an exemplary spirit of collegiality freely shared the results of his research with a novice), Jim Sessions, John Sobieski, Kathy Stillman, and Dick Wirtz. I am grateful as well for the support of the University of Tennessee Professional Development Awards Program and of the Faculty Development Fund of the University of Tennessee College of Law.

1. For instance, *compare* Christopher Eisgruber, *The Fourteenth Amendment's Constitution*, 69 S. Cal. L. Rev. 47, 48 (1995) ("[t]he Amendment . . . transformed the Constitution at its core, altering both the Constitution's political function and the principles that should govern its application") *with* Michael McConnell, *The Fourteenth Amendment: A Second American Revolution or the Logical Culmination of the Tradition?*, 25 Loy. L.A. L. Rev. 1159, 1160 (1992) (the amendment was simply "the logical culmination of the theory of the original Constitution").

2. *See* Donald Lively, *Equal Protection and Moral Circumstance: Accounting for Constitutional Basics*, 59 Fordham L. Rev. 485, 487–88 (1991) ("[T]he fourteenth amendment's meaning for minorities is primarily a function of evolving majority tolerance . . . [T]he history of Fourteenth amendment review reveals a pattern of judicial subservience to dominant social interests)." For people interested in full rights of citizenship for women of all colors, the Fourteenth and Fifteenth Amendments contained a bitter pill at their passage. Stringent efforts to win inclusion of women in their terms had gone down to failure. *See, e.g.,* Nora Basch, *Reconstitutions: History, Gender and the Fourteenth Amendment, in* The Constitutional Bases of Political and Social Change in the United States (Schlomo Slonim ed. 1990).

3. *See, e.g.,* Mark Tushnet, *The Critique of Rights*, 47 S.M.U. L. Rev. 23 (1993);

Alan Freeman, *Racism, Rights, and the Quest for Equality of Opportunity*, 23 HARV. C.R.-C.L. L. REV. 295 (1988); Patricia Williams, *Alchemical Notes: Reconstructing Ideals from Deconstructed Rights*, 22 HARV. C.R.-C.L. L. REV. 401 (1987); Mark Tushnet, *An Essay on Rights*, 62 TEX. L. REV. 1363 (1984).

4. *See generally* W. E. B. DuBOIS, BLACK RECONSTRUCTION IN AMERICA, 1860–1880; JACQUELINE JONES: SOLDIERS OF LIGHT AND LOVE: NORTHERN TEACHERS AND GEORGIA BLACKS, 1865–1873 (1980); Eric Bates, *Remembering the Good: Vanessa Siddle Walker Uncovers the Forgotten History of Segregated Black Schools*, SOUTHERN EXPOSURE, Summer 1994, p. 24.

5. 163 U.S. 537 (1896) (announcing that a Louisiana law mandating "separate but equal" public accommodations was not a violation of the equal protection clause).

6. Not all would agree with my characterization of legal education, of course. Richard Epstein, for instance, believes that "[t]he modern preoccupation with diversity has led to an excessive concern about matters of race and sex. Certainly within the legal community, the question of diversity has moved from being one consideration among many to a place of unquestioned dominance in university and law school life." Richard A. Epstein, *Legal Education and the Politics of Exclusion*, 45 STAN. L. REV. 1607, 1624 (1993). Whether universities in general and law schools in particular are primarily suppressing or primarily obsessing about matters of race (or engaging in some strange hybrid of both) is, of course, a matter of hot debate.

7. In their introduction to this volume, Balkin and Levinson mention cases and materials in relation to the "pedagogical canon." Cass Sunstein proposed this list of canonical elements in legal education: (1) authoritative texts, (2) the courses law professors teach, and (3) the choice of materials assigned in each. The occasion was a speech at the plenary gathering of the 1992 annual meeting of the Association of American Law Schools. Cass Sunstein, *In Defense of Liberal Education*, 43 J. LEGAL EDUC. 22 (1993).

8. On pedagogy, *see, e.g.*, Margaret Montoya, *Mascaras, Trenzas, y Greñas: Un/masking the Self While Un/braiding Latina Stories and Legal Discourse*, 17 HARV. WOMEN'S L. J. 185, 201–09 (1994), and in 15 CHICANO-LATINO L. REV. 1 (1994); Judy Scales-Trent, *Sameness and Difference in a Law School Classroom: Working at the Crossroads*, 4 YALE J. L. & FEMINISM 415 (1992); Charles R. Lawrence III, *The Word and the River: Pedagogy as Scholarship as Struggle*, 65 S. CAL. L. REV. 2231 (1992); Kimberle Crenshaw, *Foreword: Toward a Race-Conscious Pedagogy in Legal Education*, 11 NAT'L BLACK L.J. 1 (1989), *reprinted in* 4 S. CAL. REV. L. & WOMEN'S STUD. 33 (1994); Stephanie Wildman, *The Question of Silence: Techniques to Ensure Full Class Participation*, 38 J. LEGAL EDUC. 147 (1988).

On who teaches and why it might matter, *see, e.g.*, Deborah Jones Merritt, *Who Teaches Constitutional Law?*, 11 CONST. COMMENTARY 145 (1994); Jerome

Culp, *Autobiography and Legal Scholarship and Teaching: Finding the Me in the Legal Academy*, 77 VA. L. REV. 539 (1991); and Richard Chused, *The Hiring and Retention of Minorities and Women on American Law School Faculties*, 137 U. PA. L. REV. 537 (1988).

On the curriculum, *see* Duncan Kennedy, *The Political Significance of the Structure of the Law School Curriculum*, 14 SETON HALL L. REV. 1 (1983); *see also* Gerald Torres, *Teaching and Writing: Curricular Reform as an Exercise in Critical Education*, 10 NOVA L.J. 867 (1986).

On educational impacts of the job market, *see, e.g.*, Laurence Hellman, *Effects of Law Office Work on Value Formation*, 4 GEO. J. LEGAL ETHICS 537 (1991) (examining law firm clerkships, one channel through which the market can be seen to "leak into" legal education); ROBERT V. STOVER, MAKING IT AND BREAKING IT: THE FATE OF PUBLIC INTEREST COMMITMENT DURING LAW SCHOOL (1989).

9. For some provocative thoughts on Constitution worship, *see, e.g.*, Duncan Kennedy, *American Constitutionalism as Civic Religion: Notes of an Atheist*, 19 NOVA L. REV. 909 (1995); and Sanford Levinson, *Pledging Faith in the Civil Religion: or, Would You Sign the Constitution?* 29 WM. & MARY L. REV. 113 (1987).

10. J. M. Balkin and Sanford Levinson, *The Canons of Constitutional Law*, 111 HARV. L. REV. 963, 987 (1998).

11. Law professors can and should participate in making the popular legal canon. We have the freedom to function not only as teachers of law students, but also as public intellectuals or as community educators. We can help to develop more accessible materials and events. For an example of a text that aims to popularize a race-conscious version of the American legal canon, *see* NANCY SCHIFF, RACE, THE CONSTITUTION, AND THE SUPREME COURT: UNIT ONE OF A FOUR UNIT SERIES FOR TEENS ON LAW (The Center for Community Legal Education, University of San Francisco School of Law,1996). For an exemplary project by serious historians that aims to bring their findings to a wide audience, *see* ERIC FONER & OLIVIA MAHONEY, AMERICA'S RECONSTRUCTION: PEOPLE AND POLITICS AFTER THE CIVIL WAR (1995).

12. *Requiring* things is likely to lead to confrontations with the flip side of adding, that is, with subtracting. If the zero-sum view is often exaggerated or paranoid or a diversion, there are nevertheless realities of time, place, and credit hours that can and sometimes do force hard choices. Opting *not* to add or subtract anything is, of course, a choice.

13. For an article that includes a forcible argument for adding a particular case to the American legal desegregation canon, *see* Juan F. Perea, *The Black/White Binary Paradigm of Race: The "Normal Science" of American Racial Thought*, 10 LA RAZA L.J. 127 (1998), 85 CALIF. L. REV. 1213 (1997).

14. Frances Lee Ansley, *Race and the Core Curriculum in Legal Education*, 79 CALIF. L. REV. 1511 (1991).

15. Consider the views of the original Constitution presented in *Prigg v.*

*Pennsylvania,* 41 U.S. 536 (1842), which characterized the fugitive slave clause as foundational for the republic, in the context of a challenge to a Pennsylvania law that made the return of fugitive slaves to slaveholding states more difficult. Or *Dred Scott v. Sandford,* 60 U.S. 393 (1856), which justified the Court's mobility to exercise jurisdiction over an African American man's challenge to his enslaved status, on the ground that the founders had intended to exclude all persons of African descent from citizenship in the nation.

16. 41 U.S. 536 (1842).

17. I should note that this is less true than it was a decade ago. In property, for instance, there are now at least two casebooks that have begun to treat race as constitutive of property relations in the United States, not as an interesting after-thought on "policy." CURTIS BERGER & JOAN WILLIAMS, PROPERTY (1997); JOSEPH SINGER, PROPERTY (2d ed. 1997).

18. The metaphor of the "gaze" is a rich one, not my own. *See* Laura Mulvey, *Visual Pleasure and Narrative Cinema,* 16 SCREEN 6 (1975) (discussing the "male gaze" of many films and its power to construct the female as an object to be ob-served, a power that is all the greater for being implicit rather than overtly an-nounced or coerced). Said's observation in a related context is:

> [T]hese [colonial] accounts spirited away, occluded, and elided the real power of the observer, who for reasons guaranteed only by power and by its alliance with the spirit of World History, could pronounce on the reality of native peoples as from an invisible point of super-objective perspective, using the protocols and jargon of new sciences to displace "the natives'" point of view.

EDWARD SAID, CULTURE AND IMPERIALISM 168 (1994). In a similar vein, Toni Mor-rison once observed that whites in early American letters were able to write about people of color from a position where "there was never the danger of their 'writing back.'" Toni Morrison, *Unspeakable Things Unspoken: The Afro-American Presence in American Literature,* 28 MICH. Q. REV. 1, 13 (1989). For deployments of a related usage, *see* BILL ASHCROFT, GARETH GRIFFITHS, & HELEN TIFLIN, THE EMPIRE WRITES BACK: THEORY AND PRACTICE IN POST-COLONIAL LITERATURE (1989); and Henry Louis Gates, *The Empire Writes Back: Worlds Collide in Salman Rushdie's New Collection,* NEW YORKER, Jan 23, 1995, at 91.

19. The whiteness project is multidisciplinary and multiracial. For a few ex-amples beyond the legal academy, *see, e.g.,* DAVID R. ROEDIGER, TOWARDS THE ABOLITION OF WHITENESS (1994); THEODORE W. ALLEN, THE INVENTION OF THE WHITE RACE (1994); RUTH FRANKENBERG, WHITE WOMEN, RACE MATTERS (1993); TONY MORRISON, PLAYING IN THE DARK: WHITENESS AND THE LITERARY IMAGINATION (1993).

For examples of legal scholarship, *see, e.g.,* CRITICAL WHITE STUDIES (Richard Delgado & Jean Stefancic eds. 1997); IAN F. HANEY LOPEZ, WHITE BY LAW: THE

LEGAL CONSTRUCTION OF RACE (1996); Charles Lawrence, *The Id, the Ego, and Equal Protection: Reckoning with Unconscious Racism*, 39 Stan. L. Rev. 317 (1987).

20. Morrison, *supra* at 5 and 11–13.

21. *See* Hopwood v. Texas, 78 F.3d 932 (5th Cir. 1996), *cert. denied*, 116 S. Ct. 2582 (1996).

22. For an argument about the link between affirmative action in law school hiring and the improvement of legal scholarship, *see* Duncan Kennedy, *A Cultural Pluralist Case for Affirmative Action in legal Academia*, 1990 DUKE L.J. 801; *but see* Richard A. Posner, *Duncan Kennedy on Affirmative Action*, 1990 DUKE L.J. 1157.

23. Not everyone would agree about essentialist illusions or about the quality of the work. *See* Randall Kennedy, *Racial Critiques of Legal Academia*, 102 HARV. L. REV. 1745 (1989); *but see Colloquy: Response to Randall Kennedy*, 103 HARV. L. REV. 1855 (1990).

24. A full description of the growing literature is beyond the scope of this essay. For a start, *see* Richard Delgado & Jean Stefancic, *Critical Race Theory: An Annotated Bibliography*, 79 VA. L. REV. 461 (1993). There are also a number of helpful anthologies of critical race literature, e.g., CRITICAL RACE THEORY: THE KEY WRITINGS THAT FORMED THE MOVEMENT (Kimberle Crenshaw et al. eds. 1995); and CRITICAL RACE THEORY: THE CUTTING EDGE (RICHARD DELGADO, ed., 1995).

25. For reflections on how this new scholarship can support law school teaching, *see* Ansley, *supra* note 14.

26. For specifics, *see* Ansley, *supra* note 14, at 1539–54. Some particularly helpful sources out of many treasures are PEGGY COOPER DAVIS, NEGLECTED STORIES: THE CONSTITUTION AND FAMILY VALUES (1997); and Derrick Bell, *The Chronicle of the Constitutional Contradiction*, in AND WE ARE NOT SAVED, THE ELUSIVE QUEST FOR RACIAL JUSTICE (1987).

27. A forthcoming textbook will include materials on African Americans as well as "other" racial and ethnic minorities. I anticipate that it will make a canonical contribution, though still only a beginning. Richard Delgado, Angela Harris, Juan Perea, and Stephanie Wildman will soon publish RACE & RACES: CASES AND RESOURCES FOR A MULTIRACIAL AMERICA (2000).

28. Justice Bradley observed at a later date, in the context of discussing congressional power to govern territories, that "[t]he power of Congress over the territories of the United States is general and plenary, arising from and incidental to the right [*sic*] to acquire the territory itself. . . . The power to acquire territory . . . is derived from the treaty-making power and the power to declare and carry on war. The incidents of these powers are those of national sovereignty and belong to all independent governments." Church of Jesus Christ of Latter Day Saints v. United States, 136 U.S. 1, 34 (1890).

29. Johnson and Graham's Lessee v. M'Intosh, 21 U.S. 543, 572–73, 588 (1823).

30. CONG. GLOBE, 30th Cong., 1st Sess. 96–98 (Jan. 4, 1848).

31. 5 TREATIES AND OTHER INTERNATIONAL ACTS OF THE UNITED STATES OF AMERICA 213 (Hunter Miller ed. 1937).

32. California's "Gold Rush" Constitution of 1849, for instance, provided that "every white male citizen of the United States, and every white male citizen of Mexico, who shall have elected to become a citizen of the United States, under the treaty [of Guadalupe Hidalgo], shall be entitled to vote. . . ." CAL. CONST. art. II, § 1 (1849).

33. See, e.g., MALCOLM EBRIGHT, LAND GRANTS AND LAWSUITS IN NORTHERN NEW MEXICO (1994); and Guadalupe Luna, Agricultural Underdogs and International Agreements: The Legal Context of Agricultural Workers Within the Rural Economy, 26 N.M. L. REV. 9 (1996).

34. Treaty of Paris (1898), reprinted in CHARLES I. BEVANS, 11 TREATIES AND OTHER INTERNATIONAL AGREEMENTS OF THE UNITED STATES OF AMERICA 1776–1949, at 615–619 (1974).

35. Id.

36. Downes v. Bidwell, 182 U.S. 244, 279–280 (1901).

37. See Ediberto Roman, Empire Forgotten: The United States' Colonization of Puerto Rico, 42 VILL. L. REV. 1119 (1997).

38. See, e.g., Eric Yamamoto, Critical Race Praxis: Race Theory and Political Lawyering Practice in Post–Civil Rights America, 95 MICH. L. REV. 821 (1997); and Noelle M. Kahanu & Jon M. Van Dyke, Native Hawaiian Entitlement to Sovereignty: An Overview, 17 U. HAWAII L. REV. 427 (1995).

39. See, e.g., RODOLFO ACUÑA, OCCUPIED AMERICA: A HISTORY OF CHICANOS (1988) and DAVID J. WEBER, FOREIGNERS IN THEIR NATIVE LAND (1973).

40. See, e.g., SIDNEY L. HARRING, CROW DOG'S CASE: AMERICAN INDIAN SOVEREIGNTY, TRIBAL LAW, AND UNITED STATES LAW IN THE NINETEENTH CENTURY (1994); VINE DELORIA, JR. AND CLIFFORD M. LYTLE, AMERICAN INDIANS, AMERICAN JUSTICE (1983).

41. Chinese Exclusion Act, 22 Stat. 58 (1882); Scott Act, 25 Stat. 504 (1888).

42. Chae Chan Ping v. U.S., 130 U.S. 581 (1889).

43. Geary Act, 27 Stat. 25 (1892).

44. 149 U.S. 698 (1893). Interestingly, Justice Field issued a strong dissent in Fong Yue Ting, on the ground that once a friendly alien in time of peace had been legally admitted to the country, he could not be expelled for failing to have a pass without some guarantee of procedural fairness. For background on the efforts by the Chinese community to resist the tide of anti-Chinese legislation, see CHARLES J. MCCLAIN, IN SEARCH OF EQUALITY: THE CHINESE STRUGGLE AGAINST DISCRIMINATION IN NINETEENTH-CENTURY AMERICA (1994).

45. 66 Stat. 177 (1952). See also Hitai v. INS, 343 F.2d 466 (2d Cir. 1965)

where the court used this provision to deny permanent residency status to a Brazilian man born to Brazilian parents, despite the fact that immigration from Brazil was not then subject to a quota, on the ground that the applicant's parents, both Brazilian citizens, were born in Japan.

46. Restrictions on naturalization were upheld in *Ozawa v. United States*, 260 U.S. 178 (1922); alien land laws were upheld in *Terrace v. Thompson*, 263 U.S. 197 (1923).

47. *See* IAN HANEY-LOPEZ, WHITE BY LAW: THE LEGAL CONSTRUCTION OF RACE (1996).

48. United States v. Thind, 261 U.S. 204 (1922).

49. Accordingly, Professor Chin has suggested that the immigration act of that year should be seen as the third panel of a great civil rights triptych, together with the Civil Rights Act of 1964 and the Voting Rights Act of 1965.

50. Robert Chang, *Toward an Asian-American Legal Scholarship: Critical Race Theory, Post-Structuralism, and Narrative Space*, 1 ASIAN L. J. 1, 81 CALIF. L. REV. 1243 (1993).

51. *See* Juan Perea, "The Statue of Liberty: Notes from Behind the Gilded Door," *in* IMMIGRANTS OUT!: THE NEW NATIVISM AND THE ANTI-IMMIGRANT IMPULSE IN THE UNITED STATES (Juan Perea ed. 1997). *Compare* PETER BRIMELOW, ALIEN NATION: COMMON SENSE ABOUT AMERICA'S IMMIGRATION DISASTER (1995) at 15.

52. Letter to Fran Ansley from Judy Scales-Trent, Jan. 14, 1993, on file with author, used with permission of Professor Scales-Trent and of her son, Jason Ellis.

# Chapter 10

# Feminist Canon

## *Katharine T. Bartlett*

### A. Feminist Canon: A Contradiction in Terms?

Like any intellectual movement concerned with what comes to be understood as important, true, and just, feminists are concerned about canon. Feminist scholars in the field of law, like their counterparts in literature, science, history, philosophy, psychology, and virtually every other discipline,[1] have challenged the existing canons of their disciplines for defining what is important, what is true, and what is just, in terms that systematically omit, devalue, and subordinate women. They have found errors of fact, they have disproved assertions of objectivity, and they have questioned assumed values. Along the way, they have begun to develop a field of study with authorities—canon, if you will—of their own. This field, still lacking a single, agreed-upon label, is referred to as sex discrimination law, women and law, gender law, feminist legal theory, and feminist jurisprudence.[2]

There are a number of factors that make the emergence of a feminist academic canon unsurprising. First, a significant number of law professors wish to teach courses about sex discrimination and feminist jurisprudence—close to 250 are listed in the most recent AALS Directory of Law Teachers.[3] Their courses are in high demand, creating the need for a pedagogical canon.[4] Second, many of these professors wish to write on gender law subjects, and law journals wish to publish their articles. The last fifteen years have seen a proliferation of new law journals dedicated to feminist legal scholarship. Only a handful of such journals existed in 1978;[5] twenty years later, in 1998, there are at least eighteen.[6] Even the most established, prestigious law journals seek to publish feminist scholarship, and a number of the articles published in these traditional journals have begun to appear on various most-cited lists.[7] This publication explosion has both produced the raw materials for an academic theory canon,[8] and created the need for one to organize, prioritize, and evaluate these materials.

Finally, public interest beyond the academy in a number of subjects addressed in feminist theory is high. The Anita Hill/Clarence Thomas hearings, the trial of O. J. Simpson, and the Paula Jones case and its impeachment aftermath are among the public spectacles raising widely debated issues and public discussion about sex and law. Making sense of these public events and the issues they raise calls for what Balkin and Levinson refer to as a cultural literacy canon.[9]

While many of the preconditions of canon formation exist in the field of gender law, there are also factors that make a feminist canon seem improbable, or at least in need of an explanation. For one thing, the field defines itself in significant part by its opposition to the notion of accepted wisdom. Feminist theorists have not simply been critical of the contents of traditional legal canons. They have attacked the principles of objectivity and neutrality on which the notion of canon would appear to depend, arguing that such principles mask and perpetuate existing power inequities—specifically, the law's patriarchal underpinnings.[10] In the context of the feminist observation that the criteria by which authoritative texts are selected both reflect and help to perpetuate particular power arrangements, any set of authorities that feminist theorists might claim for their own use must be acknowledged to be also grounded in power, rather than in the higher, disinterested truth which canon claims to represent.

Just as a feminist canon appears to violate feminist substantive principles, it is also said to violate the standards for legitimacy by which canon is ordinarily judged. The fiercest critics of feminist scholarship attack its legitimacy on the grounds that it is political, subjective, trivial, and lacking in methodological rigor.[11] Many others who are not openly hostile to feminist scholarship accept the presence of gender law in the academy more as a concession to the interests of some students and faculty than out of recognition that there is a body of thought in this field with which the well-educated lawyer, or citizen, should be familiar. To these more silent critics, feminist teaching and scholarship by some faculty in the field of sex discrimination can be tolerated, but a feminist *canon* is a presumptuous overreaction to some correctable oversights in traditional legal canons.

Whether the notion of canon can accommodate feminist thought—indeed, whether feminism can accommodate the notion of canon—turns in part on whether there exists a workable line between feminism as a course of study and feminism as political action. Patrice McDermott characterizes the difference as one between a "way of seeing"—(i.e., "an analytical worldview presented through the prism of gendered relations of power which provides an interpretive framework for making meaning out of cultural experience")[12] and a "way of doing" (i.e., "a means of generating an array of individual and collective behaviors designed to improve the material, social, and intimate conditions of women's lives.")[13] Carol Sanger captures a similar distinction when she speaks of the difference between "feminists themselves and the teaching of feminism."[14] Feminist theory has demonstrated that academics and politics are inextricably intertwined.[15] Yet without some distinction between the two, it is difficult to see how a field of gender studies could exist, how a body of the relevant questions to be studied could be defined, how common reference points for study could be agreed upon, or even how arguments between those with different views in the field could proceed. These functions are served by canon, and to be performed require some separation—at least in theory—from the specific political programs that may claim support or validation therefrom. Such a separation does exist in the field of gender law, and it is the purpose of this essay to examine what it has produced.

## B. Feminist Legal Canon: The Case for Casebooks

This essay examines the feminist legal canon through a study of the leading academic casebooks used in teaching sex discrimination, women and law, gender law, and related courses.[16] These casebooks contain the material that is deemed worthy of teaching to law students, which overlaps considerably with the authorities and benchmarks that guide academic and public policy debates.[17] There are several possible explanations for this overlap. One is the more self-conscious attention placed in feminist thought on the relation between theory and practice. Many feminist academics began as practitioners. Their academic theory began as an effort to theorize and ground the litigation strategies they had used to open up the field of gender discrimination law. Barbara Allen Babcock, Ruth Bader Ginsburg, and Wendy Williams—all have been casebook authors, litigators, academics, and public spokespersons for women's rights.[18] Catharine MacKinnon and Lucinda Finley are two other examples of feminist teachers and scholars who have also been feminist legal advocates and public representatives of feminist perspectives.[19] The permeability of boundaries between teaching, scholarship, and public advocacy means that much of what might be said about the feminist legal canon on the basis of the pedagogical canon applies to the academic theory and cultural literacy canons as well.

The published casebooks do not tell the whole story, to be sure. First, an unusual number of courses have been taught in the field using unpublished collections of class materials that individuals and groups of professors have passed around between them and continually revised. While this caution should be made, it is fair to say that the published casebooks are a reasonable proxy for the larger whole. All of these casebooks began as unpublished teaching materials and developed over time as a result of collaboration. These casebooks are more widely used that the unpublished alternatives, and thus might reasonably be expected to have more influence in the field.[20] In any event, their accessibility gives them an irresistible advantage for an essay of this type.

Second, there are a number of edited anthologies of works in feminist legal theory that are used in law school teaching, especially in courses on feminist jurisprudence and feminist legal theory.[21] Insofar as these anthologies present fuller versions of some of the leading theoretical materials that "any serious legal academic . . . should know," they are arguably a truer source of the "academic theory canon."[22] A good many of the works reproduced in these anthologies, however, appear in briefer form in one or another of the casebooks, which may thus be fairly said to reflect the authority of the more theoretical work in the field itself.

Finally, it should be noted that the pedagogical canon is a more diverse and complex set of authorities than that which might be said to guide public policy debates. In such debates, feminist ideas tend to be presented as unified, uncompromising, and lacking all nuance. This is in part because of the way the media structures these debates as sound bites, or within confrontational formats in which much of what is understood about feminism comes from what its opponents, rather than its supporters, have to say about it. In any event, there is little doubt that a canon created by Camille Paglia, Anita Hill, Catharine MacKinnon, Susan Estrich, Naomi Wolf, and Katie Roiphe is a quite different canon from one which includes the works of such legal scholars as Kathryn Abrams, Angela Harris, Drucilla Cornell,

Reva Siegel, Dorothy Roberts, Mary Anne C. Case, and Robin West. This essay's focus on the pedagogical canon assumes that this canon is a fuller, more interesting body of work, although it may not always be a good reflection of the more public, cultural face of feminism.

The materials contained in the published casebooks I will examine, like the works found in more traditional legal canons, play different canonical roles. Some entries have primarily historical significance. Justice Bradley's concurring opinion in *Bradwell v. Illinois* is important in spelling out the separate spheres ideology used to justify the exclusion of women from certain "presumptively male" occupations and professions,[23] and has lasting effect as a "villain"[24] in the canon or as "negative precedent."[25] The Declaration of Sentiments, Sojourner Truth's "Ain't I a Woman?" speech, and Susan B. Anthony's comments made at her trial for violation of voting laws are also widely considered as important historical texts, even though these documents never had the status of law, because of their influence in the evolution of women's rights.[26]

Some works are canonical because of the legal propositions they established. *Reed v. Reed*[27] is without question a canonical text, for example, because it was the first modern case to overturn under the equal protection clause a state statute that discriminated on the basis of sex on grounds the classification did not bear a close enough relationship to the legitimate purpose of the statute. The case offered virtually no analysis and failed to justify why sex-based classifications should receive any closer scrutiny than classifications based on age, test scores, or other selection means. *Meritor Savings Bank v. Vinson*[28] is also in every casebook because it is the first U.S. Supreme Court pronouncement that hostile environment sexual harassment is a form of sex discrimination under Title VII. The case is more declarative than analytical and makes virtually no substantive contribution to a reader's understanding of what sexual harassment is, how it operates, or why the law should prohibit it.[29]

In contrast, other works find their way into the canon based on the power of the reasoning used, or because of its influence in how gender is understood in the law. *Wilson v. Southwest Airlines Co.*[30] is only a trial court case, and one of many cases addressing dress and appearance regulations under Title VII. All of the sex discrimination casebooks include the case, however, because of its categorical—for its day, gutsy—rejection of an airline's claim that hiring only attractive, female flight attendants was necessary to its business success.

Still other work is in the canon largely because it exhibits especially poor reasoning or results. An example is *Chambers v. Omaha Girls Club, Inc.*,[31] a case from the Eighth Circuit Court of Appeals that held that it was not a violation of Title VII for a private girls club to fire an unwed pregnant African American woman. This case has not been widely followed, but the court's acceptance of role model arguments in the context of unwed pregnancy and employment stands as an example of how the bona fide occupational qualification provision of Title VII can be interpreted to reinforce gender and race stereotypes rather than unveil them. Three of the five casebooks include it as a lead case,[32] and the other two refer to it at least once.[33] A 1974 case declining to find discrimination against pregnant women a form of discrimination based on sex[34] is another example of a case canonized—again, as a villain[35]—because it typifies a kind of faulty reasoning that is, in the mistake it makes, classic.

On some topics, scholarly writing forms the core of the canon, probably because no particular appellate case has the legal authority or the force of reasoning to have established itself as the authority in the field. Susan Estrich's accounts of stranger rape are an example.[36] Other works of feminist scholarship have been canonized, whether or not there are important appellate cases on the subject, because of the quality and originality of their analysis. Catharine MacKinnon's writing on pornography,[37] Wendy Williams's defense of equal treatment,[38] and Dorothy Roberts's work on punishing drug addicted pregnant women[39] are examples.

Drawing on all of these types of authorities, I trace in this essay the evolution of the feminist canon, from its first entry into the law schools in the late 1960s and early 1970s, to the most recent editions of gender law casebooks. This historical approach highlights characteristics of the feminist legal canon that both resemble and depart from more traditional legal canons. It brings to light both dependence on prior legal canons and resistance to the accumulated wisdom of the past. This approach also emphasizes relationships between how the field of gender law is organized in the leading casebooks and the substantive contents of those casebooks. My overall goal is to show both the instability of the feminist canon and its likely endurance.

## C. The First Generation Texts: The Canon of Progress

The subject of gender entered the law school curriculum through courses in "sex discrimination law" and "women and the law." The first such course appears to have been a student-generated course at New York University Law School in the fall of 1969.[40] Courses like it quickly spread to Yale, Georgetown, George Washington, Rutgers Law School (Newark), Harvard, Columbia, and the University of California at Berkeley (Boalt Hall).[41] These courses brought together and expanded material that seemed especially relevant to women, primarily from the existing fields of constitutional law, employment discrimination law, family law, and criminal law. Since the topics fit these already established courses, the question at the time was why a separate, synthetic course was necessary. The answer lay in the gap between the ideal and the real—that is, what could have been and what was. Issues of concern to women *could* have been covered in courses on employment law, family law, criminal law, and the like; but typically they were not. Women's marginalized status meant that questions of sex and gender were peripheral to standard courses, or missing altogether. In making sex discrimination a study of its own, these early courses tried to compensate for the exclusion of women from the law school curriculum and, along the way, to make more apparent the invisibility of women in the law itself. Two published texts became available during this early period. In 1974, Kenneth M. Davidson, Ruth Bader Ginsburg, and Herma Hill Kay published *Text, Cases and Materials on Sex-Based Discrimination*. This casebook was followed a year later by *Sex Discrimination and the Law: Causes and Remedies*, prepared by Barbara Babcock, Ann E. Freedman, Eleanor Holmes Norton, and Susan C. Ross. Both texts documented the traditional justifications for women's separate, inferior status, including women's divine and noble role as wife and mother, and then traced the gradual rejection of these justifications, through cases and statutes that invalidated laws and practices based on justifications. The progression of cases presented in these casebooks reflected the empirical, rational, and incremental theories and strategies of the time. The starting point was the 1971 case *Reed v. Reed*, which these early texts treated as the "turning point"[42] away from the tradition of women's subordination. From there, major Supreme Court cases and acts of Congress—many of them the result of litigation led by one or more of the authors of these early texts[43]—were presented as steady expansions in judicial and legislative understandings of the extent to which women are the same as men, and thus entitled to equal treatment.

Since the problem of women's exclusion was viewed in the 1970s principally as one of mistake, not vice or conspiracy, material that provided the bulk of the content of sex discrimination courses assumed that the problem could be addressed by relatively straightforward corrections of fact, under existing legal principles. Most feminists in the 1970s favored adoption of an equal rights amendment, but this measure was thought desirable largely because it would accelerate the corrective process rather than alter its course.[44] Reflecting this same sense of the correctability of existing law and institutions, the materials in these early books maintained the existing legal categories through separate chapters on constitutional law, employment discrimination law, family law, education law, and criminal law.[45] While the premise of these pioneer texts was that traditional courses in these areas gave inadequate attention to issues of gender,[46] the organization of the texts implied that the categories upon which the traditional courses were based provided ample expansion room to securing women's eventual equality.

## D. A Feminist Jurisprudence Develops

Two developments in the early and mid-1980s altered the way feminists conceptualized the field of sex discrimination law. The first was the emergence of the critical legal studies movement (CLS). Picking up where the legal realists had left off, members of CLS challenged the law's claim to objectivity and neutrality, emphasizing the extent to which law was partisan, morally impoverished, man-made rather than natural, self-legitimating rather than inherently legitimate. In the hands of feminists, some of whom had been in on CLS from the beginning, this critique observed that the dualities which gave the law its seemingly objective structure also tended to give advantage to men in relation to women. Clare Dalton, for example, showed how contract law distinctions—such distinctions as express and implied agreement, intent and form, consideration and gift—operated to systematically subordinate the interests of women who cohabited with men outside of marriage.[47] Feminists analyzed the division between the public sphere of business and commerce, in which the parties (mostly men) were protected by law, and the private sphere of the family in which the law did not intrude to protect those needing protection (mostly women).[48] The feminist critique of objectivity in law, refined in important respects by Catharine MacKinnon,[49] led to the identification of certain issues that had gone entirely unmentioned in the first-generation texts—namely, pornography, domestic violence, and marital rape.

The second development was a reassessment of the relationship between law and sexual difference. This reassessment began over the issue of how the law should treat pregnancy. To 1970s feminists, the answer seemed clear enough: pregnancy should be ignored, if possible.[50] Otherwise, it should be treated no worse, and no better, than any other job-related disability.[51] Reflecting the litigation strategies of the period, the sex discrimination texts of the mid-1970s uniformly presented pregnancy like other gender-based stereotypes: i.e., a factual blind spot. It had proved a particularly enduring one. While much sex-based discrimination in the 1970s had been identified and eliminated, courts saw pregnancy as unique to women, rather than a sex-based characteristic with respect to which sex-based discrimination could occur; on this basis, policies were upheld that allowed pregnant women to be excluded from jobs, or laid off, or otherwise disadvantaged.[52] Only with the hard-fought passage of the Pregnancy Discrimination Act of 1978 (PDA), when discrimination based on pregnancy was defined as discrimination based on sex,[53] did Title VII reach pregnancy discrimination.[54] The PDA was a clear victory on the part of feminists who had insisted on the similarity between pregnancy and other disabilities.

The consensus among feminists on the pregnancy issue did not last. At the point that discrimination against pregnant women became illegal in the workplace, a number of feminist scholars and advocates came to believe that the elimination of negative discrimination would not go far enough to equalize women's employment status with men's. The workplace, they argued, was designed specifically according to men's physical and social profiles, availabilities, and interests. Even if pregnant women were treated the same as other workers with disabilities, women's differences, including their disproportionate child-rearing responsibilities, would continue to handicap them in relation to men. Having used pregnancy's similarity to other disabilities to eliminate negative discrimination against pregnant women, these feminist scholars and advocates concluded that the prior premise of women's similarity to men was a barrier to addressing the different, and more burdensome, realities faced by working women. To get a better purchase on these realities, these feminists rediscovered the unique features of pregnancy and other disparate aspects of women's situations, and used these features to justify measures that would even up with the workplace advantages that men already enjoyed.[55]

The pregnancy debate came to a head in a 1987 California case challenging a state law requiring employers to provide up to four months' employment security for women disabled as a result of pregnancy.[56] The debate over *Calfed* pitted equal treatment theory, which had so successfully removed legal impediments to women's entry into the workplace and other public spaces by insisting on women's similarity to men, against a result-oriented substantive equality that insisted on women's entitlement to treatment that would equalize the material circumstances of men's and women's lives. Thus arose a split within the feminist legal community between those arguing that women's best hope for equality rested in a continued insistence on women's basic similarity with men, and those arguing that unless women's real differences from men were acknowledged and compensated for, a genuine, meaningful, real equality could never be achieved.[57]

From the CLS movement and the debate over pregnancy began to emerge something that came to be called feminist jurisprudence and, with this jurisprudence, changes in the way the subject of women and the law was defined. What emerged was not a single, uncontested alternative to the initial "liberal" consensus,[58] but rather a series of overlapping and competing possibilities. First, several versions of substantive (as contrasted with formal) equality were formulated, each designed to take account and equalize the effects of women's differences. Some favored accommodation only for sex-unique biological functions, such as childbearing and lactation.[59] Others pursued more comprehensive reform schemes that addressed social as well as biological difference.[60] All these different versions, however, had in common a shared commitment to evaluating the effects of various rules and practices on women, rather than their formal structure.

Another body of theory, influenced by psychology and moral theory, focused women's difference from men in a more affirmative way. "Different voice" theory emphasized women's tendency to think in terms of responsibility rather than rights, human connectedness rather than human individuality, and contextual experience rather than abstract and universal generalizations. In stressing these differences, this theory sought not to eliminate the disadvantages of women's differences, as if these differences were undesirable, but rather to celebrate these differences and model a better society based upon them. The point of this theory was not to facilitate women's adaptation to a male world; it was to change the world to adapt to women's superior instincts and values. Proposals emerged as wide-ranging as the imposition of a "duty to rescue" in tort law,[61] increased personal caretaking responsibilities on the part of corporate officers toward the victims of corporate mass torts,[62] work-place policies that better integrate worker responsibilities to their families and their employers,[63] and reforms in the tax[64] and bankruptcy law[65] to better reflect the ethical values of care, responsibility, connection, and sharing. Such proposals, in valorizing values traditionally associated with women, violated the tenet of equal rights feminism that women should be treated as individuals rather than as members of a group, but some feminist scholars saw in different voice theory the opportunity to forge a better society in a way that affirmed the value of women's differences rather than treating them as obstacles to be overcome.[66]

While debates about women's differences spawned various species of equality theory, Catharine MacKinnon broke loose from issues of women's sameness and difference with a still different framework of analysis she called "dominance theory." MacKinnon argued that it is the construction of women as sexual beings, rather than sex differences, that subordinates women to men. She observed, for example, that in the workplace sexually predatory conduct functions as the normal give-and-take between men and women, thus making men's control over women seem invisible or natural.[67] Likewise, in eroticizing the sexual use and abuse of women, pornography constructs women in ways that legitimate male coercion and female victimization. The law is complicit in these processes, MacKinnon contends, by providing regulatory systems that protect most of the objectionable behaviors, leaving the everyday con-struction of a sexually subordinated world untouched. Thus, the most ex-treme forms of sexually explicit material are criminalized through ob-scenity laws, while most pornography is protected and therefore legiti-mated by the First Amendment. The law assumes that whatever message is transmitted by pornography can be rebutted, like any other speech, through counterspeech. MacKinnon contends, however, that this oppor-tunity exists only at the level of theory, since once women are defined as objects-and-not-subjects, there is nothing they can say that anyone will think worth listening to.[68]

The influence of postmodern theory led feminists to still another set of approaches within feminist scholarship under which the fundamental premises of the liberal state were challenged. Among the challenged premises were that individuals have the capacity to have "intent," exercise "choice" or "consent," or act and think like "reasonable" people. Influ-enced by the "postmodern" view of the subject who is constituted from multiple institutional and ideological forces rather than as a "free" agent, feminist theorists have questioned what it means to "consent" to sexual intercourse,[69] to give up a child at birth,[70] to form a contract,[71] or to abuse drugs while pregnant.[72] At the same time, feminist theorists have observed that without a positive notion of individual agency, women are victims only and not agents. These kinds of observations pushed post-modern challenges to the law's premises of individual autonomy toward efforts to redeem a qualified concept of agency that takes into account both constraints on an individual's ability to choose and act reasonably and the individual's ability to resist and act.[73]

## E. The Second-Generation Texts: Reshaping the Field

The proliferation of theoretical perspectives on the relationship of gen-der to law destabilized both the organization of the field of sex discrimi-nation and the substantive contents of that field. With the exception of the second and third editions of the Kay casebook in 1981 and 1988, there was throughout the 1980s a reluctance to commit the materials used to teach these courses to formal publication. Dozens of law professors pre-pared and passed around their own materials, which tended to change every year in response to new developments in law and scholarship. A few efforts were made to establish "clearinghouses" for such materials, but the sheer volume and short shelf life made coordination extremely difficult.

The dams burst in the early 1990s, first with the posthumous publica-tion in 1992 of Mary Joe Frug's teaching materials, *Women and the Law*. These materials had been developed over years of Frug's teaching, until her violent murder in 1991. The materials were prepared for publication in 1992 by her spouse, Gerald Frug, and by Judi Greenberg and twenty-one other friends, mostly from northeastern law schools. The next year I published my own set of materials, also long in the works, as *Gender and Law: Theory, Doctrine, Commentary*. In 1994 followed a casebook by a group of Chicago-area law professors, Mary Becker, Cynthia Grant Bow-man, and Morrison Torrey, entitled *Feminist Jurisprudence: Taking Women Seriously*. The fourth edition of Herma Hill Kay's casebook was published in 1995, with the help of Martha West. The second edition of the Babcock book, with an enlarged cast of authors including Wendy Webster Williams, Rhonda Copelon, Deborah L. Rhode, and Nadine Taub, was published in 1996. In 1998, the second edition of my book was published, with the participation of Angela Harris. That same year, a second edition of the Frug book under the primary editorship of Judi Greenberg, Martha Minow, and Dorothy Roberts was published.

Several features of these second-generation texts deserve note. For example, the second-generation casebooks reflect less reliance on the traditional subject matter categories on which the earlier texts had relied. As noted above, organization of the first-generation texts according to the traditional categories of criminal law, employment law, constitutional law, and family law reflected the premise that the existing school canon was simply incomplete and, once filled in, could adequately address the unaddressed problems of women. Subsequent editions of these pioneer texts built upon, rather than revised, these initial orientations, and thus carried forward the same premise.

The second-generation texts appear uncomfortable with this orientation and, in varying degrees, have found ways of expressing this rejection. The first edition of the Frug book, for example, divided the field of women and the law into the three basic spheres of a woman's life—work, family, and body. Frug's spheres only minimally affect the clustering of materials around the traditional subject matter areas of employment law ("work"), family law ("family"), and the criminal law topics of domestic violence, prostitution, and rape ("body").[74] Still, her recharacterization of the field situates women's experience as the starting point, in an enterprise devoted first and foremost to discerning the law's impact on those experiences. Thus, along with the myriad nonlegal materials scattered throughout the volume, the book features women's lives as these lives interact with the law, rather than the law as it affects women. The second edition of the book self-consciously retains this orientation.[75]

The Becker book disrupts traditional subject matter boundaries by mixing, breaking up, and recombining conventional categories. Family law issues, for example, are explored in separate chapters entitled "Women and Reproduction," "Women and Marriage," and "Women and Children," rather than as a coherent, self-contained whole. Employment issues are divided into the headings of "Women and Wage Labor" and "Women and the Legal Profession." Theoretical material is extensive, and although the theory does not itself provide an organizing focus for the book, separate chapters on "Feminist Theory,"[76] and "The Construction of Female Sexuality,"[77] and a chapter entitled "Women and the State" at the end,[78] bookend a relentlessly coherent, critical perspective on the inadequacy of existing law and legal principles to correct the patriarchal bias of U.S. society.

Theory in my book is the primary organizing principle.[79] Following an introductory chapter which organizes the historical legacy into different theoretical foundations of gender subordination, the book devotes a chapter to each of the predominant theoretical perspectives for analyzing law and gender: formal equality, substantive equality, nonsubordination (or dominance theory), women's different voice(s), autonomy, and anti-essentialism.[80]

With the departure from the traditional subject matter categories into which the field of sex discrimination was at first divided, the field of gender law came increasingly to be understood as a field unto itself, with its own questions and perspectives, rather than a hodge-podge of topics owned by and lifted from more traditional subject matter areas.[81] Organized around its own perspectives and around themes that cross cut traditional subject matter fields, it has taken shape as an autonomous field, worthy of its own canon. Within this field, critiques and reform proposals relating to doctrines in fields previously considered unrelated to gender—contracts, torts, civil procedure, legal ethics, property law, welfare law, and bankruptcy[82]—accompany critiques and reform proposals relating to the most obvious subject matters relating to women, such as family and employment law.[83]

The different organizational schemes also produce a very different view of change and progress than the earlier casebooks portrayed. As noted above, the use of traditional subject matter categories in the two pioneering sex discrimination books suggests that change can and does occur within the traditional categories.[84] In addition, the historical sequencing of the materials reinforces the evolutionary quality of women's legal rights, emphasizing the law's success and downplaying its failures and the failures of feminist advocates. By way of contrast, the second-generation texts present a more mixed and ambiguous message about change. These casebooks include material that questions the theory or the success of the modern legal developments. Materials in these later texts give as much emphasis to the continued existence and resilience of sex discrimination as to the progress that has been made in addressing it. Thus, for example, while the first-generation casebooks show the development of sexual harassment law as a steady expansion of definitions and rights,[85] most of the second-generation texts include cases designed to show the limitations of contemporary doctrine.[86] Cases in the second-generation texts also emphasize the hidden traps in various legal reforms, in addition to the benefits these reforms may have accomplished. They reflect less confidence that the legal concepts for overcoming legal barriers to women's equality will emerge from within existing legal toolboxes. Two of the second-generation texts, for example, include portions of *Chambers v. Omaha Girls Club, Inc.*, the case holding that firing an unwed mother from a private, non-profit club for girls was justifiable as a bona fide occupation qualification.[87] The section headings in these second-generation texts help to reinforce the problematic nature of legal reform and an appreciation of the double binds produced from efforts to reform the law in an imperfect society with imperfect tools.[88]

Another consequence of the reworking of the field by the second-generation texts has been greater variety in the contexts in which common topics are understood. Abortion is one example. The Kay text classifies abortion as a subsection of family law, along with marriage contracts, divorce, and nonmarital families.[89] Classified in this way, its intimate or private aspects are foregrounded, as are questions about the interests of husbands and potential fathers that may compete with those of the pregnant woman. The Becker book treats abortion in a chapter on women and reproduction, in which the authors include material on state control of women's pregnancy, including control of drug addicts who have babies, midwifery, forced caesareans, and other topics not raised when abortion is viewed as a family law topic. In this context, abortion is less a private matter than part of a highly contested conflict between the woman's interest in her body and the state's interest in controlling irresponsible decisions she might make. My book addresses abortion primarily as an autonomy issue, along with rape, prostitution, drug abuse during pregnancy, and women's poverty. Viewed as part of the general problem of autonomy, abortion is less a contest of will between private individuals or between women and the state than it is one of many territories in women's lives in which choice and constraint coexist, and where a complex set of private and public pressures, including ideology, economic welfare, gender roles, and addiction, reinforce or help to combat one another. The Babcock book treats abortion as the major topic of a freestanding chapter on reproductive and sexual rights. This chapter considers separately (1) the evolution of reproductive rights; (2) the "contours and critiques of the abortion right," and (3) other reproductive modes and technologies, such as compelled cesareans, artificial insemination, and surrogate parenthood. Presented as a freestanding separate topic with its own history, law, and second-generation issues, abortion is more readily seen as an issue of independent and perhaps unique significance for women which has gradually evolved over time.

Domestic abuse is, similarly, framed in different ways by its placement in the overall scheme of each book. The topic, which is not treated in the early casebooks at all, appears as a criminal law issue in the most recent Kay text,[90] as a marriage or family law issue in Becker,[91] Frug,[92] and Babcock,[93] and as an issue of nonsubordination (along with sexual harassment) in my own book.[94] One approach constructs the problem as one of law enforcement, another as a problem of marriage, and still another as an issue of women's individual autonomy.

Still another example is child custody. In the Kay, Frug, and Babcock texts, child custody is viewed as a family law issue. My book treats the issue as an example of the different results that follow from the competing models of formal and substantive equality. The Becker book presents custody as one of a number of interconnected ways—along with maternity leave, child care, and child support—society deals with its children.

Discussion of economic issues also took on additional dimensions as the field was reworked organizationally. This discussion in the first-generation texts was limited to the economic consequences of divorce (in family law chapters), wage discrimination (in employment discrimination chapters), and constitutional issues connected to Social Security benefits and the like.[95] Once the field was organized into the different spheres of women's lives,[96] or into different perspectives including women's autonomy and self-sufficiency,[97] the need to consider deeper issues of poverty, welfare, and class became more obvious, and coverage—not just as add-ons to other topics, but as topics in their own right—was extended accordingly.

Differences also exist in the nature of materials included in the first-generation and the second-generation texts. The first-generation texts, like other pedagogical canons in the law, consisted primarily of appellate cases and statutes. Feminist theorists have observed, however, that a legal teaching canon that privileges appellate cases over other sources of information reinforces "the vision of law as an abstract and formal enterprise, derivable entirely within the closed universe of legal materials, and a notion that being a lawyer is merely being skilled at manipulating those materials."[98] To challenge the fundamental premises of this universe, the second-generation texts have tended to show greater interest in the underlying facts of a case, including how those facts are ascertained and presented. These are not mere gestures, for they can take many pages of valuable space. One of the longest single items in my own book is an ethics opinion from the California Supreme Court, presented to show how different approaches to legal reasoning might produce different decisions about relevance and thus different versions of the facts.[99] Ninety pages of the Babcock book are devoted to the confirmation hearings of Justice Clarence Thomas, much of it in the form of witness testimony relating to the sexual harassment charges made against him by Anita Hill.[100] Several of the texts have also made extensive use of legal briefs, to show the application, and limitations, of feminist theory to feminist practice.[101]

Finally, as with other critical perspectives, the feminist legal canon has been reaching beyond traditional legal materials to disciplines that might provide outside leverage for challenging existing legal authorities. From the beginning, the gender law canon has drawn more heavily than is the custom on speeches, letters, historical and social science materials, and writings from the popular press.[102] The most recent round of textbooks have an even more pronounced reliance on nontraditional sources. In addition to excerpts from articles in feminist legal theory, which abound, these books present portions of women's history,[103] literature, the popular press, gender bias studies, and medical or social science data. Narratives are also included.[104] Of the texts by Becker, Frug, and myself, no more than 50 percent of the principal items are appellate cases.[105] By way of comparison, over 90 percent of the items in two of the leading contracts casebooks are appellate cases, and the number of alternative sources is negligible.[106]

### F. Gender Law: Flash in the Pan or Enduring Canon?

Have I described a canon? Or a mere fad? Insofar as canonicity is derived from the authority yielded over time, only time will tell. A number of the observations I have made about the feminist canon, however, have a bearing on its staying power. In this final section, I pull together some of these observations. My purpose is to describe the characteristics of a feminist canon that make it likely, in my view, to endure. Here I emphasize the capacity to synthesize old and new understandings, and the capacity to accommodate multiple perspectives. My purpose is also to explain characteristics of a feminist canon that might change what is meant by canon. Feminist theorists are creating canon, in a conventional sense. But they also offer, by example, revised understandings of canon, and what it means to have authority. To this end, one of the most important characteristics of the feminist canon is the habit of self-critique. This habit has the capacity to alter how canon is understood and, ultimately, what canon means.

*1. The Capacity to Synthesize New and Old.* To qualify for the canon, an authority must be both distinct and understandable. To be distinctive requires new insight. To be understandable requires a connection to the familiar. Hence the double challenge for any candidate for the canon: to make better sense of social, political, economic, and other circumstances than what has come before, while using principles and concepts that are sufficiently recognizable and known for the insight to be understood and accepted.

There is a tendency to valorize one side of this equation at the expense of the other—that is, to put a premium on the freshness of the insight to the exclusion of its rootedness in existing understandings, or to value the longevity of an idea over its originality. This tendency finds its parallel in the way change and tradition are usually viewed as opposites—change representing a sharp break from tradition, and tradition representing the enemy of change. The change-tradition dichotomy makes it difficult to see two things: (1) that tradition is not static, but rather the accumulation of wisdom over time, requiring an endless series of syntheses of old and new understandings of the world; and (2) that change occurs less in opposition to tradition than as a consolidation of the best learnings of the past. Tradition cannot endure unless it adapts to change, and change cannot endure unless it takes account of the best learnings of the past.[107]

A canon represents nothing more than what has endured as a result of perpetual interactions between what is new and what is familiar. This is especially true about law, given the need of courts to follow legal precedent. Even with respect to authorities that do not have the force of law, however, what tends to endure in the canon is that which best synthesizes the new with the old, combining insights that challenge settled understandings with what is salvageable and worthy of saving from those understandings. The feminist concept of sexual harassment, for example, took conduct by men in the workplace that was previously taken for granted as the natural and accepted way men relate to women, and reconceptualized this conduct as offensive behavior that constructed women as sexual objects rather than as serious and capable employees.[108] This was a new understanding of the meaning and effect of a certain type of behavior, and thus qualified as insight. To take hold in people's minds as well as in the legal lexicon, however, required linking that theory to recognizable and accepted principles. Thus, the principle that the sexual harassment of women by men was a wrong against women took hold only when it was presented as an example of the familiar, if rearticulated, wrong of sex discrimination.[109]

Similarly, feminists have made understandable their critiques of doctrine in various subject matter fields by making it clear how these doctrines violated not only feminist precepts, but the principles of those fields themselves. Thus, for example, feminist critiques of the law of self-defense as applied to battered women are powerful not simply for pointing out that this law reflects male notions of a face-to-face "fair fight" between physical equals meeting in a one-time, time-bound confrontation and fails to take into account the realities of battered women who may kill their abusers in settings that do not have these characteristics. They are powerful because they show how the accepted objectives of criminal law are violated when the law does not recognize the special dangers women often face as a result of domestic violence.[110]

There is a corollary to the proposition that insights that are divorced from accepted wisdom are not likely to take root. This corollary is that principles that do not have the capacity to absorb new insights are not likely to endure. The staying power of principles such as equality, justice, and liberty rests in part on their ability to accommodate and reshape themselves to feminist insights. The endurability of the feminist canon, in turn, depends on how it responds to challenges to it. How the feminist canon has responded to challenges is explored further below.

*2. The Capacity to Accommodate Multiple Voices.* A canon cannot endure if it speaks with only one voice. Legal canons typically accept certain broad truths, and then provide alternate ways of viewing those truths. The constitutional law canon, for example, expresses its commitment to the rule of law and justice by offering multiple perspectives on how the Constitution should be interpreted—original intent theory, textualism, consequentialism, natural law theory, and critical race theory, to name a few.[111] The environmental law canon provides materials for looking at the problems it addresses through the lens of economic perspectives, environmental justice perspectives, conservationist perspectives, ecological perspectives, and others.[112]

Legal canons offer not only grand theories for thinking through legal issues, but more specific and detailed analytical frameworks to help resolve specific problems. Contract law assumes a basic principle that damages for breach of contract should put the promisee in the position it would have been in had the contract been performed. Yet how to measure these damages is not always a self-evident proposition. For example in some construction contract cases involving incomplete performance, damages might be measured by the cost of completing the project, or they might be measured by the diminution in value resulting from the incompleteness of the performance. The contract law canon includes the "classic" cases providing different ways of describing and resolving the choice between these two measures.[113]

In the 1970s, it was unclear that feminist thought offered much in the way of alternative analytical frameworks, large or small. Feminist analysis appeared as one framework, yielding one particular answer to every question having to do with gender and law: women are the same as men and thus should be treated the same—no better, no worse. So long as this remained the case, the possibility of a feminist party line seemed real enough, but the field hardly seemed rich enough to warrant an academic canon. As feminist thought has moved from speaking with one voice to many—the formal equality voice, the substantive equality voice (voices, actually), the "different voice" voice, the dominance theory voice, the postmodern feminism voice,[114] and the pragmatism voice[115]—the possibility of canon opened up. Today, the feminist canon contains authorities reflecting a range of views on many important topics. It offers, for example, one set of views favoring the treatment of pregnancy in the workplace as if it were no different from any other disability,[116] and another favoring solutions to work and family conflicts that assume pregnancy and child rearing require affirmative measures to insure that members of one sex are not systematically disfavored over the other in the workplace.[117] It includes opposing frameworks for analyzing such matters as whether pornography or "hate speech" should be regulated,[118] whether surrogate parent contracts should be enforceable,[119] and whether the law should prohibit all forms of female genital surgery performed for nonmedical reasons.[120]

The presence of alternative frameworks that may produce conflicting answers to specific problems makes feminist thought appear cacophonous, disputatious, and lacking in the kind of unified consensus that some would say is required to sustain a claim to "truth" (or relatedly, some feminists would point out, to support an effective political agenda). Ironically, however, it is the rich diversity of perspectives producing this chaos that gives feminist legal thought its claim to canon. A canon exists to encourage and organize the vigorous debates that go on in a field. Alternative analyses are a necessary part of this organization. Without them, authority in a field is more catechism than canon, which in the end makes for not only weak academics, but weak politics as well.

3. *The Capacity for Self-Critique.* An important part of feminist scholarship has consisted of turning critiques feminists have made of "male" law back against feminist thought itself. This process of self-critique has been self-conscious, deliberate, and pervasive. It has also been, by comparison to other fields, rather novel. Canon formation in more traditional fields is understood typically as a transparent process of choosing what is true, good, and important. The self is assumed to be absent from this process, for the point is to discover principles that transcend self-interest. Where no self is present, there is no meaningful role for self-critique. Where authority is understood more as a function of the perspectives of the persons or groups who assert it, the need for continual challenge, especially from the perspectives of those whose interests were not earlier factored in, is more evident.

Feminist self-critiques have substantial differences one from another, but there has been a tendency to refer to them all, somewhat confusingly, under the rubric "essentialism."[121] The first and perhaps most common of the "essentialist" critiques is that feminist theorists, in diagnosing and prescribing a society free from gender oppression, too often assume women who are white, middle class, heterosexual, able-bodied, and otherwise privileged.[122] This critique charges that just as traditional law masks male privilege with principles of objectivity and neutrality that presuppose male subjects and ignore women, so also feminists generalize about law and prescribe improvements that presuppose women of privilege and ignore women who are subject to other forms of oppression in addition to gender.[123]

A related "anti-essentialist" charge is that feminists rely too much upon gender oppression as the most fundamental or primary source of women's oppression, and thereby ignore other forms of oppression.[124] Those who raise this claim emphasize the extent to which oppression based on other factors, such as race, sexuality, class, ethnicity, or religion, is also significant, and not merely additive, and the danger that consideration of these different forms of oppression in isolation may mask the important interactive effects of a woman's multiple sources of identity.[125]

Extended more broadly, this "false universalism" critique sometimes comes in the form of a charge of gender "imperialism." For example, when some Western feminists criticize female genital surgeries practiced in other cultures often with the support, even leadership, of women, other scholars both inside and outside of those cultures insist that such criticisms inappropriately impose one culture's standards on another's, an imposition they claim is not unlike the imposition of male norms on women.[126]

Another anti-essentialist critique focuses on the assumption in some feminist analysis of the inherence of certain facts, especially facts about gender, when these facts are in reality "constructed" socially, man-made rather than preordained and inevitable.[127] Again, the critique represents an extension to feminist theory of observations feminists make about traditional law and legal theory. If male law is wrong for treating biological differences between men and women as necessitating different social and legal responses, so feminists are also wrong, it is claimed, for treating "woman" as a category that is self-explanatory, natural, or demanding certain inevitable responses. Some feminists are also critical of others for assuming that women had some "true identity" that could emerge once gender oppression was eliminated,[128] or indeed that any truths could be understood objectively, as opposed from the particular, limited perspectives of individual knowers. Some of the debate within this criticism of gender essentialism has focused on the relationship between "sex" and "gender," and on whether the male/female sex distinction is even valid.[129]

These various critiques within feminism occupy as important a role in the contemporary feminist canon as do the authorities to which they respond. Among the features these critiques share is a self-consciousness about feminist method and its relationship to law and authority. Each of them presupposes change and revision as expected components of authority, not signs of its absence. Each critique proves that it is possible to question authority even as it is being produced. Together they suggest that the foundations upon which any canon might be based are more tenuous and temporary than might have once been imagined, and that revision and rethinking are sources of a canon's endurance, not its enemies.

Feminist teachers and scholars have adopted canon as necessary and unavoidable. In living with the tension between having a canon and being ready to disown it, however, they bring some understandings to the notion of canon that are, if not unique, at least uniquely integrated with the substance of their own canon. In particular, these teachers and scholars bring a provisional stance toward authority which teachers and scholars in other legal fields might usefully borrow. The evolution of the feminist canon demonstrates how this provisional stance and a willingness to criticize authority, even one's own, do not weaken the authority of a field—*truth*, in some larger sense—but rather strengthen it. This lesson may be, in the end, a far more significant one than any single teaching about male patriarchy.

### NOTES

1. *See, e.g.*, FEMINISMS IN THE ACADEMY (Domna C. Stanton & Abigail J. Stewart eds. 1995); ELIZABETH KAMARCK MINNICH, TRANSFORMING KNOWLEDGE (1990); RECONSTRUCTING THE ACADEMY: WOMEN'S EDUCATION AND WOMEN'S STUDIES (Elizabeth Minnich, Jean O'Barr & Rachel Rosenfeld eds. 1988); SEX AND SCIENTIFIC INQUIRY (Sandra Harding & Jean F. O'Barr eds. 1987); MEN'S STUDIES MODIFIED: THE IMPACT OF FEMINISM ON THE ACADEMIC DISCIPLINES (Dale Spender ed. 1981).

2. On the questions of labels in this field and the possible significance of the different alternatives, *see* Clare Dalton, *Where We Stand: Observations on the Situation of Feminist Legal Thought*, 3 BERKELEY WOMEN'S L.J. 1 (1987–88).

3. *See* THE AALS DIRECTORY OF LAW TEACHERS 1997–98, at 1291–93. The number of professors teaching subjects in this field has grown substantially over the last decade, as shown by the fact that only 25 of those listed in this directory are shown as having taught in the field for over ten years, while 165 are listed as having taught between one and five years. A comparison with the listings of law teachers in more traditional fields is quite instructive. The number of law teachers having been in teaching between one and five years in the fields of contracts and property, for example, is about equal to the number having taught for over ten years. *Id.* at 1114–22, 1252–59. In torts, there are significantly more law professors in the more experienced age cohort than in the novice category. *Id.* at 1276–84.

4. I am using the typology offered by J. M. Balkin and Sanford Levinson, by which they divide legal canons into the pedagogical canon, the academic theory canon, and the cultural literacy canon. *See* Balkin & Levinson, *The Canons of Constitutional Law*, 111 HARV. L. REV. 963, 975–76 (1998). They define the pedagogical canon in constitutional law as the "key cases and materials [that] should be taught in constitutional law courses and reprinted in constitutional law casebooks"). *Id.* at 975.

5. *The Women's Rights Law Reporter* (Rutgers School of Law— Newark), first published in 1971, is the longest continuing women's law journal. *The Harvard Women's Law Journal* was begun in 1978, and continues today. Two other journals were begun in 1976. *The Women's Law Journal*, published by women from the major law schools in the southern California area, published only one or two issues. *The Women's Law Reporter*, published by Loyola University School of Law in Chicago, ran from 1976 to 1986.

6. These include, in alphabetical order with the starting date of publication in parentheses, *American University Journal of Gender and the Law* (1993), *Berkeley Women's Law Journal* (1985), *Cardozo Women's Law Journal* (1993), *CIRCLES: The Buffalo Women's Journal of Law and Social Policy* (1992), *Columbia Journal of Gender and Law* (1991), *Duke Journal of Gender Law and Policy* (1994), *Hastings Women's Law Journal* (1989), *Journal of Gender, Race and Justice* (University of Iowa College of Law) (1997), *Michigan Journal of Gender and Law* (1993), *Southern California Review of Law and Women's Studies* (1992), *Texas Journal of Women and the Law* (1993), *UCLA Women's Law Journal* (1991), *William & Mary Journal of Women and the Law* (1994), *Wisconsin Women's Law Journal* (1985), *Women's Law Journal* (Ohio Northern University College of Law) (1997), and *Yale Journal of Law and Feminism* (1989).

7. According to one set of such lists, four of the ten most-cited articles published in 1990 are works of feminist legal scholarship, as are three of the ten most-cited articles written in 1991. *See* Fred R. Shapiro, *The Most-Cited Law Review Articles Revisited*, 71 CHI-KENT L. REV. 751, 777 (1996). The 1990 articles include Angela P. Harris, *Race and Essentialism in Feminist Legal Theory*, 42 STAN. L. REV. 581 (1990); Katharine T. Bartlett, *Feminist Legal Methods*, 103 HARV. L. REV. 829 (1990); Vicki Schultz, *Telling Stories About Women and Work: Judicial Interpretations of Sex Segregation in the Workplace in Title VII Cases Raising the Lack of Interest Argument*, 103 HARV. L. REV. 1749 (1990); and Margaret Jane Radin, *The Pragmatist and the Feminist*, 63 SO. CAL. L. REV. 1699 (1990). The 1991 articles are Dorothy E. Roberts, *Punishing Drug Addicts Who Have Babies: Women of Color, Equality, and the Right of Privacy*, 104 HARV. L. REV. 1419 (1991); Catharine A. MacKinnon, *Reflections of Sex Equality Under Law*, 100 YALE L.J. 1281 (1991); Kathryn Abrams, *Hearing the Call of Stories*, 79 CALIF. L. REV. 971 (1991). It is noteworthy that all of these articles were published in prestigious, traditional law journals. Does this mean that student law review editors of prestigious journals are excellent judges of quality? Or that canon status is derived, at least in part, from the prestige of its publisher?

An analysis by William Landes and Richard Posner predicting the articles from Shapiro's most-cited list that will be most heavily cited in the lifetimes of these articles puts two articles of feminist scholarship in the top ten. *See* William M. Landes & Richard A. Posner, *Heavily Cited Articles in Law*, 71 CHI.-KENT L. REV. 825, 838–39 (1996). These articles are Angela P. Harris, *Race and*

*Essentialism in Feminist Legal Theory*, 42 STAN. L. REV. 581 (1990), and Martha Minow, *The Supreme Court, 1986–Foreword: Justice Engendered*, 101 HARV. L. REV. 10. Landes and Posner conclude that 20 percent of the publications in the top fourth of the lifetime publication list are works of feminist scholarship. *Id.* These are Katharine Bartlett, *supra* note 7; Robin West, *Jurisprudence and Gender*, 55 U. CHI. L. REV. 1 (1988); Frances E. Olsen, *The Family and the Market: A Study of Ideology and Legal Reform*, 96 HARV. L. REV. 1497 (1983); Catharine A. MacKinnon, *Feminism, Marxism, Methods, and the State: Toward Feminist Jurisprudence*, 8 SIGNS 635 (1983); Catharine A. MacKinnon, *Feminism, Marxism, Method, and the State: An Agenda for Theory*, 7 SIGNS 515 (1982); and Suzanna Sherry, *Civic Virtue and the Feminine Voice in Constitutional Adjudication*, 72 VA. L. REV. 543 (1986).

8. *See* Balkin & Levinson, supra note 4, at 976 (defining the academic theory canon in constitutional law as "the key cases and materials any serious legal academic . . . should know and any serious theory of constitutional law must take into account").

9. *See* Balkin & Levinson, supra note 4, at 976 (defining the "cultural literacy canon" as those "cases and materials any educated person should be aware of in order to participate in serious discussions about American constitutional development").

10. *See, e.g.,* MacKinnon, *Feminism, Marxism, Method, and the State, supra* note 7.

11. *See, e.g.,* Kenneth Lasson, *Feminism Awry: Excesses in the Pursuit of Rights and Trifles*, 42 J. LEGAL EDUC. 1 (1991); Arthur Austin, *Evaluating Storytelling as a Type of Nontraditional Scholarship*, 74 NEB. L. REV. 479 (1995); MICHAEL WEISS & CATHY YOUNG, FEMINIST JURISPRUDENCE: EQUAL RIGHTS OR NEO-PATERNALISM, at 47 (Cato Institute Policy Analysis Series No. 256, June 19, 1996). Some of these criticisms have come from disaffected feminists themselves. *See, e.g.,* DAPHNE PATAI & NORETTA KOERTGE, PROFESSING FEMINISM: CAUTIONARY TALES FROM THE STRANGE WORLD OF WOMEN'S STUDIES (1994); *see also* ELIZABETH FOX-GENOVESE, FEMINISM IS NOT THE STORY OF MY LIFE: HOW TODAY'S FEMINIST ELITE HAS LOST TOUCH WITH THE REAL CONCERNS OF WOMEN (1996).

12. Patrice McDermott, *The Meaning and Uses of Feminism in Introductory Women's Studies Textbooks*, 24 FEMINIST STUD. 403, 409 (1998).

13. *Id.* at 413–14. McDermott further distinguishes feminism as a "way of being," which she describes as "a critically conscious, open-ended feminist subject position which confers, not so much an identity, as a social location within feminist blueprints for social change." *Id.* at 409. Feminism as a way of being in the world "allows an individual to be critically conscious of, while simultaneously resisting and acting upon, existing structures of gender oppression." *Id.* at 417.

14. *See* Carol Sanger, *Feminism and Disciplinarity: The Curl of the Petals*, 27 LOY. L.A.L. REV. 225, 232 (1993).

15. See Bartlett, *supra* note 7, at 843–47, 862–63.

16. There are five such casebooks, all but one of which is in its second or later edition. The first, Kenneth M. Davidson, Ruth B. Ginsburg & Herma H. Kay, *Sex-Based Discrimination: Text, Cases and Materials*, was published by West Publishing Company in 1974 and has appeared in three subsequent editions. *See* Herma H. Kay, Sex-Based Discrimination: Text, Cases and Materials (2d ed. 1981); Herma Hill Kay, Sex-Based Discrimination: Text, Cases and Materials (3d ed. 1988); Herma Hill Kay & Martha A. West, Sex-Based Discrimination: Text, Cases and Materials (4th ed. 1996). For ease of reference, each of these editions will be referred to as "Kay," with the appropriate edition noted. The second, Barbara Allen Babcock, Ann E. Freedman, Eleanor Holmes Norton & Susan C. Ross, *Sex Discrimination and the Law; Causes and Remedies*, was published by Little, Brown & Company in 1975, and appeared in a second edition published by Aspen Law and Business in 1996 with a somewhat different set of authors. *See* Barbara Allen Babcock, Ann E. Freedman, Susan Deller Ross, Wendy Webster Williams, Rhonda Copelon, Deborah L. Rhode & Nadine Taub, Sex Discrimination and the Law: Causes and Remedies (2d ed. 1996). Both editions will be referred to in this essay as "Babcock" with the appropriate edition noted. The third casebook, Mary Joe Frug, *Women and the Law*, was published by Foundation Press in 1992. The second edition of this book was published in 1998, under the authorship of Martha Minow, Dorothy E. Roberts, and Judi Greenberg. This book will be referred to throughout this essay as "Frug." My own casebook, Katharine T. Bartlett, *Gender and Law: Theory, Doctrine, Commentary*, was published by Little, Brown & Company in 1993, and came out in a second edition with co-author Angela Harris in 1998, published by Aspen Law and Business. *See* Katharine T. Bartlett & Angela P. Harris, Gender and Law: Theory, Doctrine, Commentary (2d ed. 1998). Both editions will be referred to, again for ease of reference, as "Bartlett" (or as "my book") with the appropriate edition noted. The fifth casebook is Mary Becker, Cynthia Grant Bowman & Morrison Torrey, *Feminist Jurisprudence: Taking Women Seriously*, published by West Publishing in 1994. I refer to it here as "Becker."

Although my own book in this field is what led to the invitation to write this essay, there is a pretentiousness—unavoidable I think—in using this book as a principal reference point for a discussion of the feminist "canon." The awkwardness is enhanced by the fact that, at various points in this essay, I compare this book with books written by other scholars, many of whom are friends and for all of whom I have a great deal of professional respect. I have tried to be fair, but the reader will have to draw her own conclusions about whether I have succeeded.

I refer to all of these texts as "casebooks" because they were prepared for use in law school classrooms and contain excerpts of a significant portion of appellate cases. I should note, however, that these books depart, in varying degrees, from traditional casebook formats, especially in the sense that they contain a larger mix of noncase materials. *See supra* text at notes 98–106. For ease of reference and for want of any one term that accurately describes all of the course materials I discuss, I use interchangeably throughout the essay "casebook," "text," "book," and "materials."

17. Balkin & Levinson argue that the three types of canon—the pedagogical canon, the academic theory canon, and the cultural literacy canon—are more distinct in legal fields than in the liberal arts. *See* Balkin & Levinson, *supra* note 4, at 981–84.

Others have also noted differences between legal canons and those in other disciplines. Most especially, the important role of judges, juries, legislators, bar associations, and other professional groups in creating law distinguishes the legal canon from the canon in other disciplines, such as literature and philosophy, where the academy has a relatively free hand in setting the disciplinary standards for what is true, good, and important. *See* Cass R. Sunstein, *In Defense of Liberal Education*, 43 J. LEGAL EDUC. 22, 25 (1993) ("What literature departments do *creates* the canon; the same is less true, or at least it's differently true, of law schools, who have courts and employers to answer to"). *See also* Owen M. Fiss, *Objectivity and Interpretation*, 34 STAN. L. REV. 739, 757 (1982) (comparing the claim to authority of judges, which may be predicated "on virtue or power," with the authority of literary critics or moral philosophers, "who must rely on intellectual authority alone"); Richard A. Epstein, *Legal Education and the Politics of Exclusion*, 45 STAN. L. REV. 1607, 1610 ("as the courts go, so do the academics in their wake").

18. Ruth Bader Ginsburg (later an associate justice of the United States Supreme Court) was a litigator in some of the leading U.S. Supreme Court cases establishing the equal protection rights of women, a law professor at Columbia Law School, the author of several benchmark works of sex discrimination theory, and co-author of one of the first published casebooks in sex discrimination law published in the 1970s. Barbara Allen Babcock was assistant attorney general in charge of the Civil Division of the U.S. Department of Justice under President Jimmy Carter, a law professor at Stanford Law School, a well-known feminist academic, and the lead author of the other sex discrimination casebook that was published in the 1970s. Wendy Webster Williams was a founding partner of Equal Right Advocates, a San Francisco law firm dedicated to protecting the rights of women, a law professor at the Georgetown University Law Center, the author of some leading works of feminist legal theory, and co-author on the second edition of the Babcock book.

19. Lucinda Finley, a law professor at the State University of New York in Buffalo, has litigated important cases attempting to protect the safety of medical personnel and clients at abortion clinics, written some leading works of feminist scholarship, and spoken out in the national media. Catharine MacKinnon is perhaps the best and most prominent example of a feminist academic, legal advo-

cate, and public figure. MacKinnon is a law professor at the University of Michigan who helped to develop the theory of sexual harassment and has written legal briefs in specific sexual harassment cases, articulated a legal theory for regulating pornography and spearheaded campaigns to pass laws consistent with that theory, and written broadly and deeply on law and gender issues. She is also preparing her own casebook in the field.

20. To be sure, unpublished works can attain canonical status. Perhaps the best-known example is the set of legal process materials by Henry Hart and Albert Sacks that circulated originally in the mid-1950s in mimeographed form out of the Harvard Law School Dean's Office. These materials were designed as a "Tentative Edition" in 1958, and not formally published until 1994. *See* Henry H. Hart, Jr. & Albert M. Sacks, The Legal Process: Basic Problems in the Making and Application of Law vii (William N. Eskridge, Jr. & Philip P. Frickey eds. 1994). Some of the most-used materials in feminist jurisprudence courses in the 1980s were also unpublished and available only through informal networks. For example, I first saw the essay "The Sex of Law" by Frances Olsen in 1985, when it was already circulating widely among feminist law professors and included in course materials in feminist jurisprudence. It was not published, to my knowledge, until 1990. *See* Frances Olsen, *The Sex of Law, in* The Politics of Law: a Progressive Critique (David Kairys ed. 2d ed. 1990).

21. The anthologies with the broadest subject matter span include Feminist Legal Theory: Foundations (D. Kelly Weisberg ed. 1993); Applications of Feminist Legal Theory to Women's Lives: Sex, Violence, Work, and Reproduction (D. Kelly Weisberg ed. 1996); Feminist Legal Theory: Readings in Law and Gender (Katharine T. Bartlett & Rosanne Kennedy eds. 1991); Feminist Legal Theory Volume I: Foundations and Outlooks (Frances E. Olsen ed.1995); Feminist Legal Theory Volume II: Positioning Feminist Theory Within the Law (Frances E. Olsen ed. 1995) (selections of feminist legal theory organized in categories of traditional curriculum).

22. *See* Balkin & Levinson, *supra* note 4, at 975–76.

23. 83 U.S. (16 Wall.) 130, 139 (1872).

24. *See* Balkin & Levinson, supra note 4, at 1019.

25. *See* Deborah A. Widiss, *Re-viewing History: The Use of the Past as Negative Precedent in United States v. Virginia,* 108 Yale L.J. 237 (1998).

26. Babcock, Bartlett, Becker each include at least two of these three documents. *See* Bartlett, 2d ed., 55–57, 63–69; Becker, 3–6, 9–10; Babcock, 2d ed., 38–40, 76–78.

27. 404 U.S. 71 (1971).

28. 477 U.S. 57 (1986).

29. It is perhaps for this reason that neither of these cases (unlike, say, *Roe v. Wade*) is a household word outside of legal circles.

30. 517 F.Supp. 292 (N.D. Tex. 1981).

31. 834 F.2d 697 (8th Cir. 1987).

32. BARTLETT, 1059–66; FRUG, 241–46; BECKER, 732–36.

33. KAY, 4th ed., at 629, 766; BABCOCK, 2d ed., 521, 1290.

34. Geduldig v. Aiello, 417 U.S. 484 (1974).

35. See Balkin & Levinson, supra note 4, at 1019. Many "villain" cases, such as *Bradwell v. Illinois*, are out-of-date but kept around to remind us of how things used to be. Others, such as *Geduldig v. Aiello*, are still good law.

36. Excerpts from Susan Estrich's work on rape is set forth in FRUG, 763–77, BARTLETT, 2d. ed., 830–31; BECKER, 210–17, and KAY, 4th ed., 1166.

37. Selections from MacKinnon's various writings on pornography are included in BARTLETT, 2d ed., 630–33; BECKER, 325–334; and BABCOCK, 2d ed., 1434–43.

38. BABCOCK, 2d ed., 553–54; BARTLETT, 2d ed., at 326; KAY, 4th ed., at 769; *see also* BECKER at 65–66 (legal brief written by Williams).

39. BARTLETT, 2d ed., at 972–76; BECKER, 423–26.

40. According to the introduction to one of the first modern sex discrimination books, Susan Ross was one of the initiators of the student-run course at NYU. *See* BABCOCK, 1st ed., at v.

41. Ann Freedman helped bring the course to Yale, along with Barbara Babcock who had already taught the course at Georgetown. Susan Ross started the course at George Washington, and Eleanor Holmes Norton came to teach an early course at NYU. *Id.* Clare Dalton reports that Ruth Bader Ginsburg first taught a course in sex discrimination in 1970 at Rutgers Law School at Newark, at Harvard in 1971, and at Columbia starting in 1972. Dalton, *supra* note 2, at 4 n.5. Herma Hill Kay taught her first sex discrimination course in the spring of 1972 at the University of California at Berkeley School of Law (Boalt Hall). *Id.* In the spring of 1974, I took the first course she taught with her own published materials.

42. KAY, 1st ed., at 59.

43. Leading among them was Ruth Bader Ginsburg, who challenged sex-based classifications that discriminated against men as often as she did those that discriminated against women. *See, e.g.*, Kahn v. Shevin, 416 U.S. 351 (1974) (arguing, unsuccessfully, that widowers should have the same property tax exemption as widows); Weinberger v. Wiesenfeld, 420 U.S. 636 (1975) (arguing that widowers' Social Security benefits should be the same as widows'); Craig v. Boren, 429 U.S. 190 (1976) (on brief for amicus curiae ACLU, arguing that the drinking age for males should be the same as that for females); Frontiero v. Richardson, 411 U.S. 677 (1973) (on brief for amicus curiae, arguing that husbands should be entitled to dependency benefits under military benefits packages on the same basis as wives). Ginsburg was one of three authors on the original Kay text. Her commitment to formal equality, to be pursued by exposing inaccurate stereotypes and eliminating laws and practices based on those stereotypes, is

also apparent in her published scholarship. *See, e.g., Sex and Unequal Protection: Men and Women as Victims*, 11 J. FAM. L. 347 (1971); *Gender and the Constitution*, 44 U. CIN. L. REV. 1 (1975); *The Equal Rights Amendment Is the Way*, 1 HARV. WOMEN'S L.J. 19 (1978); *Sex Equality and the Constitution*, 52 TUL. L. REV. 451 (1978); *Sexual Equality Under the Fourteenth and Equal Rights Amendments*, 1979 WASH. U.L.Q. 151; *Ratification of the Equal Rights Amendment: A Question of Time*, 57 TEX. L. REV. 919 (1979).

44. *See* Ginsburg, Gender and the Constitution supra note 43 at 25 (ERA "should end legislative inertia that retards social change by keeping obsolete laws on the books.") Barbara A. Brown, Thomas I. Emerson, Gail Falk & Ann E. Freedman, *The Equal Rights Amendment: A Constitutional Basis for Equal Rights for Women*, 80 YALE L.J. 871 (1971). The first edition of the Babcock book devoted sixty pages to the Equal Rights Amendment. *See* BABCOCK, 1st ed., 129–89. Coverage was reduced in the second edition. See Babcock, 2d ed. at 178–191.

45. The books differ somewhat on how they organized family and education law. The Kay book grouped all covered family law topics, including abortion, in one chapter and had a separate chapter on educational opportunity. The Babcock book had a chapter on family law, and then a separate final chapter entitled "Women's Rights to Control Their Reproductive Capacities, Obtain Equal Education, and Gain Equal Access to Places of Public Accommodation."

46. Critiques along these lines include Nancy Erickson, *Final Report: "Sex Bias in the Teaching of Criminal Law*," 42 RUTGERS L. REV. 309 (1990); Mary Irene Coombs, *Crime in the Stacks, or a Tale of a Text: A Feminist Response to a Criminal Law Textbook*, 38 J. LEGAL EDUC. 117 (1988); Ann Shalleck, *Report of the Women and the Law Project: Gender Bias and the Law School Curriculum*, 38 J. LEGAL EDUC. 97 (1988); Elizabeth M. Schneider, *Task Force Reports on Women in the Courts: The Challenge for Legal Education*, 38 J. LEGAL EDUC. 87 (1988); Mary Joe Frug, *Re-reading Contracts: A Feminist Analysis of a Contracts Casebook*, 34 AM. U.L. REV. 1065 (1985). For a critique of the "informal" law school curriculum, *see* Marjorie Maguire Shultz, *The Gendered Curriculum: Of Contracts and Careers*, 77 IOWA L. REV. 55 (1991).

47. *See, e.g.*, Clare Dalton, *Deconstructing Contract Doctrine*, 94 YALE L.J. 997, 1095–1106 (1985). *See also* Olsen, *supra* note 7 (explaining how the dichotomy between the family and the market constructs legal relationships in ways that subordinate women). The history of the critical legal studies movement, from the point of view of the feminists who were either part of the movement or influenced by it, is told in Carrie Menkel-Meadow, *Feminist Legal Theory, Critical Legal Studies, and Legal Education or "The Fem-Crits Go to Law School,"* 38 J. LEGAL EDUC. 61 (1988).

48. *See, e.g.*, Olsen, supra note 7; Nadine Taub & Elizabeth M. Schneider, *Perspectives of Women's Subordination and the Role of Law, in* THE POLITICS OF LAW

117 (D. Kairys ed. 1st ed. 1982) (arguing that the public-private dichotomy operates in the law to subordinate women to men).

49. *See* MacKinnon's, *supra* note 7. MacKinnon did not self-identify, in print
at least, with the critical legal studies movement, but her critique of objectivity
was consistent with CLS views. Important differences existed, especially in regard
to MacKinnon's totalizing analysis of men as subjects and women as victims.
MacKinnon's dominance theory is described at infra note 67.

50. Cleveland Bd. of Educ. v. LaFleur, 414 U.S. 632 (1974).

51. This was the strategy in *Geduldig v. Aiello*, 417 U.S. 484 (1974). The U. S.
Supreme Court in *Aiello* held that discrimination against pregnancy did not constitute sex discrimination, since it distinguished between pregnant persons and
nonpregnant persons (which included both men and women). 417 U.S. at 497, n.
20. This reasoning has never been overruled as a matter of constitutional law, although legislation made it inapplicable in the employment context.

52. *See* KAY, 1st ed., at 484–510; BABCOCK, 1st ed. at 308–30.

53. 42 U.S.C. § 2000e(k) (1994).

54. The PDA extended the coverage of Title VII of the Civil Rights Act of
1964, but it did not alter *Geduldig v. Aiello* as a matter of constitutional law.

55. Linda J. Krieger & Patricia N. Cooney, *The Miller-Wohl Controversy: Equal
Treatment, Positive Action and the Meaning of Women's Equality*, 13 GOLDEN GATE
U.L. REV. 513 (1983).

56. California Federal Savings & Loan Ass'n v. Guerra, 479 U.S. 272 (1987).

57. Feminist individual groups joining an amici curiae brief written by Pro-
fessor Christine Littleton arguing on behalf of permitting pregnancy to be singled out for different, favorable treatment included the Coalition for Reproduc-
tive Equality in the Workplace; Betty Friedan; International Ladies' Garment
Worker's Union, AFL-CIO; 9 to 5, National Association of Working Women;
Planned Parenthood Federation of American, Inc. et al. (including seventeen
California labor, ethnic, and feminist organizations and sixteen individuals). *See*
Wendy W. Williams, *Notes from a First Generation*, 1989 U. CHI. LEG. FORUM 99,
101 n.6. On the other side of the issue in support of a brief written by Wendy
Williams and others were the National Organization for Women; NOW Legal
Defense and Education Fund; National Bar Ass'n, Women Lawyers' Division,
Washington Area Chapter; National Women's Law Center; Women's Law Project;
and Women's Legal Defense Fund in Support of Neither Party. *Id.*

58. The first full-blown comparison of feminisms of which I am aware that
identified "liberal feminism" and compared it with the alternatives is ALISON M.
JAGGAR, FEMINIST POLITICS AND HUMAN NATURE (1983). In feminist legal
thought, Catharine MacKinnon may have been the first to distinguish liberal
feminism from socialist feminism, and then radical feminism—which she
claimed was the one true feminism. *See* MacKinnon, *Feminism, Marxism,
Method, and the State: Toward Feminist Jurisprudence, supra* note 7; *see also*

Catharine A. MacKinnon, Feminism Unmodified: Discourses on Life and Law 16, 60, 118–20, 136–37 (1987) (criticizing liberal feminism).

59. *See, e.g.*, Sylvia A. Law, *Rethinking Sex and the Constitution*, 132 U. Pa. L. Rev. 955, 1007–13 (1984); Herma Hill Kay, *Equality and Difference: The Case of Pregnancy*, 1 Berkeley Women's L.J. 1 (1985); Ann Scales, *Towards a Feminist Jurisprudence*, 56 Ind. L.J. 375 (1980–81). Scales abandoned this position in favor of a broad-based nonsubordination approach in *The Emergence of Feminist Jurisprudence: An Essay*, 95 Yale L.J. 1177 (1990).

60. *See, e.g.*, Lucinda M. Finley, *Transcending Equality Theory: a Way Out of the Maternity and the Workplace Debate*, 86 Colum. L. Rev. 1118 (1986). Christine Littleton went even further, arguing that society has an obligation to eliminate the disadvantages of women's "socially female" activities, such as their disproportionate role in childrearing and their greater likelihood of crying in business meetings. Christine A. Littleton, *Reconstructing Sexual Equality*, 75 Calif. L. Rev. 1279, 1333 (1987).

61. *See* Leslie Bender, *A Lawyer's Primer on Feminist Theory and Tort*, 38 J. Legal Educ. 3 (1988).

62. *See* Leslie Bender, *Feminist (Re)torts: Thoughts on the Liability Crisis, Mass Torts, Power, and Responsibilities*, 1990 Duke L.J. 848.

63. *See* Finley, *supra* note 60.

64. *See* Majorie Kornhauser, *The Rhetoric of the Anti-Progressive Income Tax Movement: a Typical Male Reaction*, 86 Mich. L. Rev. 465 (1987).

65. *See* Karen Gross, *Re-Vision of the Bankruptcy System: New Images of Individual Debtors*, 88 Mich. L. Rev. 1506 (1990) (book review essay).

66. *See* Susan Wolf, *Comment, in* Multiculturalism and "The Politics of Recognition:" An Essay by Charles Taylor 75, 76–77 (Amy Gutmann ed. 1992). Feminists have tended to favor one side or another of this tension, rather than straddle the line. A remarkable conversation between feminists defining the battle lines is found in Ellen C. DuBois et al., *Feminist Discourse, Moral Values, and the Law*, 34 Buff. L. Rev. 11 (1985).

67. Catharine A. MacKinnon, Sexual Harassment: A Case of Sex Discrimination of Working Women (1979).

68. The dominance theory of Catharine MacKinnon assumes that women's pervasive construction as objects of male desire makes women's consent to sex sometimes, maybe usually, an unrealistic ideal. *See, e.g.*, MacKinnon, *supra* note 58. Opponents of MacKinnon's efforts to legally restrict pornography stress the value of the First Amendment to women. *See, e.g.*, Nadine Strossen, *A Feminist Critique of "The" Feminist Critique of Pornography*, 79 Va. L. Rev. 1099 (1993); Nan D. Hunter & Sylvia A. Law, *Brief Amici Curiae of Feminist Anti-Censorship Taskforce, et al., in American Booksellers Association v. Hudnut*, 21 U. Mich. J.L. Ref. 69 (Fall 1987–Winter 1988); Mary C. Dunlap, Sexual Speech and the State: Putting Pornography in Its Place, 17 Golden Gate U.L. Rev. 359 (1987).

69. *See, e.g.*, Jane Harris Aiken, *Intimate Violence and the Problem of Consent*, 48 S. C. L. Rev. 615 (1997); Martha Chamallas, *Consent, Equality, and the Legal Control of Sexual Conduct*, 61 Cal. L. Rev. 777 (1988); Frances Olsen, *Statutory Rape: A Feminist Critique of Rights Analysis*, 63 Tex. L. Rev. 387 (1984).

70. *See, e.g.*, Janet L. Dolgin, *The "Intent" of Reproduction: Reproductive Technologies and the Parent-Child Bond*, 26 Conn. L. Rev. 1261 (1994); Nancy Ehrenreich, *Surrogacy as Resistance: The Misplaced Focus on Choice in the Surrogacy and Abortion Funding Contexts*, 41 DePaul L. Rev. 1369 (1992) (review essay); Derek Morgan, *Making Motherhood Male: Surrogacy and the Moral Economy of Women*, 12 J.L. & Soc'y 219 (1985).

71. *See, e.g.*, Clare Dalton, *An Essay in the Deconstruction of Contract Theory*, 94 Yale L.J. 997 (1985).

72. *See, e.g.*, Michelle Oberman, *Sex, Drugs, Pregnancy, and the Law: Rethinking the Problems of Pregnant Women Who Use Drugs*, 43 Hastings L.J. 505 (1992).

73. *See, e.g.*, Kathryn Abrams, *Sex Wars Redux: Agency and Coercion in Feminist Legal Theory*, 95 Colum. L. Rev. 304 (1995).

74. Pornography was also covered in this chapter.

75. *See* Frug, 2d ed., at ix.

76. *See* Becker, at 50.

77. *See* Becker, at 155.

78. *See* Becker, at 868.

79. *See* Christine Littleton, *Whose Law Is This Anyway?*, 95 Mich. L. Rev. 1560, 1572 (1997).

80. The Becker book adds other frameworks, including hedonic feminism, pragmatism, and socialist feminism. *See* Becker, at 90–110. None of these frameworks, however, appears to play a role in how the materials are organized.

81. For the argument that these traditional subject matter divisions had hidden, gendered consequences, see Marjorie Shultz, *The Gendered Curriculum: Of Contracts and Careers*, 77 Iowa L. Rev. 55, 55–66 (1991) (traditional boundaries rigidify the division of the world into the public-market-male sphere of influence vs. the private-family-female sphere).

82. *See, e.g.*, Bartlett, 2d ed., at 778–86 (federal criminal sentencing), 728–37, 787–90 (tort law and civil remedies), 791–801 (legal ethics), 883–90 (health law).

83. New topics that did not exist when the first-generation books were written, such as sexual harassment and domestic violence, were added to the second-generation texts.

84. *See* text at notes 40–46.

85. *See* Kay, 4th ed., at 808–38.

86. *See, e.g.*, Bartlett, 2d ed., at 537–46 (excerpting two cases illustrating that courts have a tendency to recognize male-on-male sexual harassment more

easily than female-on-female harassment); Frug, 2d ed., at 286–99 (excerpting critical perspectives by Muriel Dimen and Rosemary Pringle that question the appropriate role of law in addressing workplace harassment issues).

87. 834 F.2d 697 (8th Cir. 1987). *See* Bartlett, 2d ed. at 1059–1066; Fry, 2d ed. at 250–255.

88. For example, the Becker book keeps questions about feminist strategies and goals at center stage with such subsection titles as "Theoretical Approaches to (In)equality," "Reproductive Technology: Boon or Bane for Women?" "Maternity Leave: Good or Bad for Women?" "'Choice' and Women's Traditional Roles," and "The Individual Rights of the Constitution: The Wrong Rights?" *See* Becker, at 67, 463, 574, 790, 869. The Bartlett book also uses subsection captions to emphasize questions and ambiguities rather than continuities and progress. Some examples include "Acquaintance Rape: Constructing Consent from Conflicting Truths," "Prostitution: Consent Under Conditions of Constraint," "The Pregnant Woman and Fetus as Adversaries," "The Primacy of Gender?" and "What Is a 'Woman,' Anyway?" *See* Bartlett, 2d ed., at 853, 865, 972, 1044, 1077.

89. *See* Kay, 2d ed., at 477–569.

90. Kay, 4th ed., at 1181–95.

91. Becker, at 524–61.

92. Frug, 2d ed., at 610–723. In the first edition of Frug, domestic violence was treated as an issue of women and their bodies (along with prostitution, pornography, and rape), rather than as a family issue. *See* Frug, 1st ed., at 554–624.

93. Babcock, 2d ed., at 1305–64.

94. Bartlett, 2d ed., at 617–629.

95. *See, e.g.,* Kay, 4th ed., at 290–319 (economic consequences of divorce), 917–972 (Equal Pay Act); Babcock, 2d ed., 211–226 (constitutionality of Social Security and other provisions designed to compensate women for past discrimination); 1193–96, 1227–58 (inequality in marriage and divorce).

96. *See* Frug, 2d ed., at 188–94 (comparable worth in the context of women's poverty); 491–98 (exploring cultural deficiency model of race and poverty), 567–74 (working women and child care), 765–81 (welfare reform and childbearing).

97. *See* Bartlett, 2d ed., at 972–87 (poor women's control of pregnancy), 987–1001 (welfare reform). Class is addressed throughout this text. *See, e.g., id.* at 49–95 (separate spheres ideology of the nineteenth century in the context of working-class women and professional women); *id.* at 1111–25, 1129 (class as an issue in an anti-essentialism law practice).

98. *See* Mary Irene Coombs, *Non-Sexist Teaching Techniques in Substantive Law Courses,* 14 S.Ill. U. L.J. 507, 514 (1990).

99. Bartlett, 2d ed., at 790–801.

100. Babcock, 2d ed., 617–707.

101. *See, e.g.*, Becker, at 409 (amicus brief of Feminist for Life in Bray v. Alexandria Women's Health Clinic); Bartlett at 581 & Frug at 697 (brief amici curiae of Feminist Anti-Censorship Taskforce, et al., in American Booksellers Association v. Hudnut).

102. For example, the original Kay and Babcock books both included the 1855 letter of protest by husband and wife Henry B. Blackwell and Lucy Stone, disavowing various legal incidents of marriage otherwise imposed on them by the state, as well as various speeches, position papers, and excerpts from the popular press and other nonlegal sources. *See* Kay, 1st ed., at 174; Babcock, 1st ed., at 647–48.

103. *E.g.*, the Frug, Bartlett, and Becker books all excerpt Linda Gordon's historical work on birth control, domestic violence, or both. Frug, 556–573, 2d. ed. at 611–625; Bartlett, 2d ed., 558–59; Becker at 354–58.

104. *See* Bartlett, 2d ed., 936–45 (setting forth Lucie White's narrative of handling "Mrs. G's" welfare case, as an example of practicing law in ways sensitive to the various critiques of essentialism).

105. About half of the entries in my book are cases, one-fourth are excerpts from traditional law reviews, and another quarter are readings from other disciplines or other non-traditional sources. The Frug book (1st ed.) contains about one-third of each. The Becker book has the highest number of nontraditional entries—close to 40 percent.

106. The two texts are John P. Dawson, William Burnett Harvey, & Stanley D. Henderson, Contracts: Cases and Comment (7th ed. 1998) (93 percent cases, 6 percent law review excerpts); E. Allan Farnsworth & William F. Young, Cases and Materials on Contracts (5th ed. 1995) (only 2 percent of entries are not cases). A notable exception among the contracts texts is Stewart Macaulay, John Kidwell, William Whitford & Marc Galanter, Contracts: Law in Action (1995), a book rich with commentary, empirical studies, descriptions of what happened to the real parties of a case, contract documents, and the like.

107. *See generally* Katharine T. Bartlett, *Tradition, Change, and the Idea of Progress*, 1995 Wis. L. Rev. 303.

108. One of the first to articulate this theory was Catharine MacKinnon. *See supra* note 67.

109. *Id.* The U.S. Supreme Court first recognized this theory in Meritor Savings Bank v. Vinson, 477 U.S. 57 (1986), and it has been developed and reinforced in its subsequent sexual harassment decisions. *See* Harris v. Forklift Systems, Inc., 510 U.S. 17 (1993); Oncale v. Sundowners Offshore Services, Inc., 523 U.S. 75 (1998); Faragher v. City of Boca Raton, 118 S. Ct. 2275 (1998); Burlington Industries, Inc. v. Ellerth, 118 S. Ct. 2257 (1998); Gebser v. Lago Vista Independent School District, 118 S. Ct. 1989 (1998).

110. *See* Bartlett, 2d ed., at 608.

111. For a presentation and analysis of these and other perspectives, *see* Michael J. Gerhardt & Thomas D. Rowe, Jr., Constitutional Theory: Arguments and Perspectives (1993).

112. *See* Robert V. Percival, Alan S. Miller, Christopher H. Schroeder & James P. Leape, Environmental Regulation: Law, Science, and Policy 15–31 (1996).

113. Most contract law casebooks compare *Groves v. John Wunder Co.*, 286 N.W. 235 (1939) (holding that cost of completion damages is appropriate) with *Peevyhouse v. Garland Bol & Mining Co.*, 382 P.2d 109 (Okla. 1962), cert. denied, 375 U.S. 906 (1963) (difference between market value of property as promised, and as left after the breach, is sufficient) or Jacob & Youngs v. Kent, 129 N.E. 889 (1921) (damages for failure to use correct pipe in constructing a house are limited to market value damages, unless parties manifested intent to the contrary). *See, e.g.*, John P. Dawson, William Burnett Harvey & Stanley D. Henderson, Contracts: Cases and Comment 11–22, 821–23 (7th ed. 1998) [hereinafter Dawson, Harvey].

114. The Bartlett book explicitly organizes its materials around these perspectives, but other books provide materials from these alternative perspectives as well.

115. *See* Becker, at 98–103.

116. *See* Wendy W. Williams, *The Equality Crisis: Some Reflections on Culture, Courts, and Feminism*, 7 Women's Rts. L. Rep. 175 (1982).

117. *See, e.g.*, Krieger & Cooney, *supra* note 55.

118. *Compare, e.g.*, Catharine A. MacKinnon, *Pornography as Defamation and Discrimination*, 71 B.U.L. Rev. 793 (1991) (favoring regulation of pornography), with American Booksellers Association, Inc. v. Hudnut, 771 F.2d 323 (1985), aff'd mem., 475 U.S. 1001, reh'g denied, 475 U.S. 1132 (1986) (overturning Indianapolis ordinance attempting to regulate pornography as a form of discrimination against women); Strossen, (opposing regulation of pornography); Carlin Meyer, *Sex, Sin, and Women's Liberation: Against Porn-Suppression*, 72 Tex. L. Rev. 1097 (1994) (arguing that pornography regulation does not satisfy its intended objectives and may do more harm than good).

119. *Compare, e.g.*, In re Baby M., 537 A.2d 1227 (N.J. 1988) (declining to enforce surrogate parent contract) with Marjorie Maguire Shultz, *Reproductive Technology and Intent-Based Parenthood: An Opportunity for Gender Neutrality*, 1990 Wis. L. Rev. 297 (defending surrogate parent contracts as a way of reinforcing the value of intent in the formation of parent-child bonds).

120. *Compare, e.g.*, Layli Miller Bashir, *Female Genital Mutilation in the United States: An Examination of Criminal and Asylum Law*, 4 Am. U.J. Gender & L. 415 (1996) (opposing female genital mutilation), with L. Amede Obiora, *Bridges and Barricades: Rethinking Polemics and Intransigence in the Campaign Against Female Circumcision*, 47 Case W. Res. L. Rev. 275 (1997) (justifying

genital scarification and reconstruction in terms of the cultural traditions which produced these practices).

121. Much of this section borrows heavily from the introduction to the chapter on anti-essentialism in Bartlett, ed., at 1007–1009.

122. *See, e.g.*, Harris, *supra* note 7.

123. Minow, *supra* note 7; ELIZABETH V. SPELMAN, INESSENTIAL WOMAN: PROBLEMS OF EXCLUSION IN FEMINIST THOUGHT (1988). A review of the Spelman book that is particularly attentive to the general problems of categorization and the twin difficulties of infinite fragmentation and overgeneralization is Jennifer Nedelsky, *The Challenges of Multiplicity*, 89 MICH. L. REV. 1591 (1991) (book review).

124. Bartlett, 2d ed., at 1008.

125. *See, e.g.*, Mari Matsuda, *When the First Quail Calls: Multiple Consciousness as Jurisprudential Method*, 11 WOMEN'S RTS. L. REP. 7 (1989); Kimberle Crenshaw, *Demarginalizing the Intersection of Race and Sex: a Black Feminist Critique of Antidiscrimination Doctrine, Feminist Theory and Antiracist Politics*, 1989 U. CHI. LEGAL F. 139; Judith A. Winston, *Mirror, Mirror on the Wall: Title VII, Section 1981, and the Intersection of Race and Gender in the Civil Rights Act of 1990*, 79 CALIF. L. REV. 775 (1991); Peggie R. Smith, *Separate Identities: Black Women, Work, and Title VII*, 14 HARV. WOMEN'S L.J. 21 (1991); Deborah King, Multiple Jeopardy, *Multiple Consciousness: The context of Black Feminist Ideology*, 14 SIGNS 42 (1988).

126. *See, e.g.*, Obiora, *supra* note 120; Isabelle R. Gunning, *Arrogant Perception, World-Travelling, and Multicultural Feminism: The Case of Female Genital Surgeries*, 23 COLUM. HUM. RTS. L. REV. 189 (1991–92); Karen Engle, *Female Subjects and Public International Law: Human Rights and the Exotic Other Female*, 26 N. ENG. L. REV. 1509 (1992).

127. *See, e.g.*, MARY JOE FRUG, POSTMODERN LEGAL FEMINISM (1992); Katherine M. Franke, *The Central Mistake of Sex Discrimination Law: The Disaggregation of Sex from Gender*, 144 U. PA. L. REV. 1 (1995).

128. *See, e.g.*, Katharine T. Bartlett, MacKinnon's Feminism: Power on Whose Terms?, 75 CAL. L. REV. 1559–1566 (1987) (Book Review).

129. *See* Mary Anne C. Case, *Disaggregating Gender from Sex and Sexual Orientation: The Effeminate Man in the Law and Feminist Jurisprudence*, 105 YALE L.J. 1 (1995); Franke, *supra* note 127; Francisco Valdes, *Queers, Sissies, Dykes, and Tomboys: Deconstructing the Conflation of "Sex," "Gender," and "Sexual Orientation" in Euro-American Law and Society*, 83 CALIF. L. REV. 1 (1995); Linda Nicholson, *Interpreting Gender*, 20 SIGNS 79 (1994); Anne Fausto-Sterling, *The Five Sexes: Why Male and Female Are Not Enough*, THE SCIENCES, Mar./Apr. 1993, at 10, 21.

# Chapter 11

# Homosexuals, Torts, and Dangerous Things

## Katherine M. Franke

Negligent, intentional, and strict liability torts. From a canonical standpoint, whatever else one might teach, it is not a first-year law school torts course if these three concepts are not covered. Torts has a canon, even a Restatement.[1] Yet a canon evolves only after some criterion of value has been established such that privileged texts can be identified according to an authoritative standard. Thus, a canon is the result of a process by which a rule of recognition identifies authoritative texts.

At what point can we say that torts became a legal field and an intact legal subject, the canon of which could be taught in law schools? Most often, casebooks reveal an existing canon, as is the case with most contemporary torts texts. However, during a period of field formation or reformation, casebooks can play a critical role in the evolution of a field, the creation of a disciplinary rule of recognition, and the concomitant development of a canon. In 1997, two casebooks, William Rubenstein's *Cases and Materials on Sexual Orientation and the Law*[2] and William Eskridge and Nan Hunter's *Sexuality, Gender, and the Law*,[3] entered legal education at a moment when they stand to have a profound effect upon the formation of a law school subject, a legal field, and a canon. What is, or should be considered, the canon of the field alternatively termed gay/lesbian, sexual orientation, sexuality, or queer law? What should we teach? If a canon is "a historical, political, and social product, something that is fashioned by men and women in the name of certain interests, partisan concerns, and social and political agenda,"[4] then these books reflect two competing social and political agendas.

## I. Canon Formation in Torts: The Persuasive Power of One Conceptual Scheme

In a well-established field such as torts, contemporary law school texts reveal to students an existing canon.[5] But a century ago, the struggle to define a coherent subject called torts was being waged within the academy and the larger legal community. Until the end of the nineteenth century, the American legal system approached the problem of personal injuries by resort to common law writs of trespass and case.[6] While eighteenth- and nineteenth-century lawyers knew there was a distinction between these two forms of action, few could have elaborated just what that distinction was:

> It was certain there was a distinction [between trespass and case] even if nobody knew what it was. . . . The law itself was seen as based, not upon elementary ideas, but upon the common law writs, as consisting in a range of remedies which had as it were come down from the skies. If a case fell within the scope of no writ, then in general there was no law. If it fell within the scope of one writ, then in general no other writ could be proper.[7]

In 1870, C. G. Addison published one of the first treatises on torts, in which he catalogued various common law forms of action but did not provide an overarching theory of torts.[8] In fact, Addison's timing was rather unfortunate, as he published the treatise at a time when the formal English writ system was losing favor in U.S. courts.[9] As a result, the book was not well received. An unsigned review, widely attributed to Oliver Wendell Holmes,[10] made a damning observation about Addison's book: "We are inclined to think that Torts is not a proper subject for a law book."[11] Between the lines of the review lay the judgment that the field of torts, such as it was in 1870 and such as it was captured in Addison's treatise, was merely an amalgam of procedural forms of action, rather than a coherent and unified system by which "to fix the dividing lines between those cases in which a man is liable for harm which he has done, and those in which he is not."[12]

Addison's treatise had been reviewed in no small measure because Harvard Law School had determined to teach torts as a separate law school subject in 1870 and it was regarded as the work best adapted for a textbook.[13] Sensing that the time might be right for a new field to emerge, but in a form that provided overriding philosophical and theoretical principles, the reviewer ended with the following entreaty: "We long for the day when we may see these subjects treated by a writer capable of dealing with them philosophically, and self-sacrificing enough to write a treatise as if it were an integral part of a commentary on the entire body of the law."[14]

That day was not long in coming. A second anonymous essay, again widely attributed to Holmes,[15] appeared in the *American Law Review* under the title "The Theory of Torts."[16] In this essay, the author outlined a tripartite conception of torts: liabilities in which culpability is in general an essential element (negligent torts); liabilities irrespective of culpability (strict liability torts); and liabilities arising from acts done intentionally (intentional torts).[17] Holmes would go on to develop more fully his metatheory of torts in *The Common Law* in 1881.[18] His project was "to discover whether there is any common ground at the bottom of all liability in tort, and if so, what that ground is."[19] He concluded that "[s]uch a theory is very hard to find. The law did not begin with a theory. It has never worked one out."[20] As such, the task fell to him to develop one. In so doing, Holmes located his conception of tort liability within a larger modernist discourse of human agency. Rather than relying upon arcane forms of action that organized wrongs by reference to the nature of the injury alleged, Holmes's theory was animated by a universal moral agent, the reasonable or prudent man: "The ideal average prudent man . . . is a constant, and his conduct under given circumstances is theoretically always the same."[21]

In 1874, convinced of the soundness of the case method recently introduced to Harvard Law School by Dean Christopher Columbus Langdell, Professor James Barr Ames published for his Harvard students the first torts casebook.[22] In this text, Ames did not heed the call to theory provided by Holmes, but rather offered his students eight hundred pages covering the common law forms of action for trespass, case, conversion, and defamation. Ames's book contained not one negligence case.[23] In 1893, however, the second edition of the book devoted "six chapters to negligence, including discussions of standards of care, the concept of duty, and contributory negligence."[24] From that time forward, Holmes's theoretical framework has defined the field by locating the reasonable person at the center of a tripartite system of civil liability. Within this structure, a canon of tort law has evolved, and contemporary torts casebooks invariably include canonical cases, such as *The T.J. Hooper*,[25] *United States v. Carroll Towing Co.*,[26] *Palsgraf v. Long Island Railroad Co.*,[27] and *Escola v. Coca Cola Bottling Co.*[28]

The process by which torts emerged as the field we know today mirrored a larger process taking place in American jurisprudence during the latter half of the nineteenth century: the maturation of a distinctly American legal system. The movement away from the English common law writ system, and toward a new conceptual scheme based on fault, individual responsibility, and the emergence of generalized standards of care, was provoked in significant part by the writings of Holmes. But it also reflected a response to changes in the U.S. economy, most notably the emergence of national railroads, large mills, and industrialized factories producing numerous accidents between strangers.[29] A new theory of civil liability was necessary to respond adequately to a newly industrialized United States. Thus the canonical cases of tort law came to enjoy a privileged status according to criteria of value that reflected particular historical, social, and political agendas.

In *Doing What Comes Naturally*, Stanley Fish observed that a powerful critic "can have a profound and direct effect on what gets taught in the schools, what appears in the curriculum, what gains entrance into the canon, what gets published, reviewed, anthologized, disseminated."[30] If ever this observation were true, it would be with respect to Holmes's theory of torts. With his general theory, Holmes created the field known as torts, shaped the curriculum of law school torts classes, and mapped out the contours of our contemporary torts canon. In the years since *The Common Law*, other torts theorists have tried to introduce new or alternative paradigms for conceptualizing the field of torts,[31] but with the exception of Guido Calabresi's introduction of law and economics,[32] the inertia of Holmes's model has been too powerful to resist.

## II. The Evolution of a New Field: Sexual Orientation/Sexuality and the Law

The Rubenstein and Eskridge/Hunter casebooks appeared at a critical point in the maturing of the gay rights movement and as a distinctly gay, some might say queer, American jurisprudence began to emerge. Gay men and lesbians have been found to have the right to marry under the Hawaii Constitution,[33] and the U.S. Supreme Court ruled that the Colorado Constitution cannot legitimately serve as the vehicle for the majority of Colorado citizens to express raw prejudice against gay people.[34]

When I was in law school in 1983, classes on sexual orientation and the law or sexuality and the law were not offered at my or any other law school. My fellow lesbian and gay law students and I, however, wanted to educate ourselves about gay rights law; some of us wanted to practice in this area, others were merely curious, and all of us felt the weight of our invisibility in the law school curriculum. This desire motivated us to put together our own self-taught course; certainly no one on the faculty had any greater expertise in the matter. We went to the library and found a few reported decisions that dealt with the rights of lesbians and gay men: a handful of employment cases,[35] a few lesbian custody cases,[36] cases concerning gay and lesbian student groups that had been denied official university recognition,[37] and a few sodomy cases.[38] We created an independent study course, and taught the material to ourselves. At that point no text revealed an overarching theory of sexual orientation or sexuality and the law.[39] As a result, not unlike C. G. Addison, we merely assembled existing reported decisions according to the type of harm alleged: employment discrimination, sodomy prosecutions, school recognition, and child custody, for instance. We shared with many gay rights advocates and scholars of the time a pre-*Hardwick* innocence grounded in the firmly held belief that soon the Supreme Court would dignify our lives by recognizing a right to privacy for consensual adult same-sex sexuality. Surely the judicial assault on our families, relationships, and public lives could not continue much longer.

Things have come a long way in the intervening years. While many commentators might have denied in 1983 that sexuality and the law was a legal field, few contemporary reviewers would maintain that "sexual orientation and the law" or "sexuality and the law" is not a proper subject for a casebook today. Unlike Ames's casebook on torts, the Eskridge/Hunter and Rubenstein casebooks have emerged not at the pedagogical moment when Harvard Law School determined to teach a course in sexual orientation and the law,[40] but after many American law schools have deemed this subject important enough to include it in their curricula. Indeed, as of 1995, one quarter of American law schools were offering courses devoted primarily to sexuality and/or sexual orientation,[41] and the percentage increases to one third if one counts courses that provide some significant or substantial coverage of these issues.[42] But what is being taught in these courses?[43] What is the proper subject of these courses and of these casebooks? What would a sophisticated and philosophic "commentary on the entire body of the law"[44] in this area look like? Would it promise "a 'critical' intellectual domain in American legal jurisprudence,"[45] or just a compilation of historic wrongs done to gay men and lesbians?

A survey of the syllabi used in the forty-eight law school courses devoted primarily to sexuality and/or sexual orientation and the law indicates highly idiosyncratic responses to the question of what to teach.[46] Some professors, in effect, ask the "gay question," just as many teachers of "Women and the Law" courses ask the "woman question"[47] and many teachers of "Race, Racism, and the Law" ask the "race question."[48] They seek to analyze the law's effect on gay men and lesbians as a class. Presupposing a fully constituted homosexual subject who is regulated by legal norms and rules, these courses examine the ways in which lesbians and gay men are treated or mistreated by the state through the enforcement of sodomy laws, denial of child custody, expulsion from the military, and limitations on the right to marry. Grounded in an acceptance of identity politics as the foundation of equality claims, this approach to the subject of sexual orientation and the law most often regards the aim of the struggle for gay rights as securing Fourteenth Amendment suspect-class status for gay men and lesbians, thus triggering "strict scrutiny" by courts and one would hope the invalidation of discriminatory laws.

In contrast, others approach this subject by considering the ways in which gay men and lesbians are not the object, but the effect of legal regulation. On this view, a course entitled "Sexual Orientation and the Law" is not about gay men and lesbians, but about the role that law plays in giving meaning to the notion of sexual orientation—whether it be heterosexuality, homosexuality, or bisexuality.[49] For instance, Jane Schacter has taught a course at the University of Wisconsin Law School that "examined "the relationship between sexual orientation and the law."[50] The course focused "on the interaction between the law and social, cultural and political attitudes about sexual orientation—that is, how social forces shape, and are shaped by, legal doctrine."[51] There are also those who approach this subject with their own particular intersectional interests. For instance, Mary Becker teaches a course at the University of Chicago entitled "Critical Race and Lesbian-Gay Legal Theory," while Twila Perry teaches "Race, Gender, and Torts" at Rutgers University-Newark.

Given that the question "What is the proper subject of sexual orientation and the law?" provokes as many different answers as there are courses so named, is this the proper topic for a casebook? Can we even begin to call such a diverse constellation of material a field? Just as

Holmes provided the philosophical framework within which to understand torts as a field, Eskridge/Hunter and Rubenstein provide frames to approach the subject of sexuality/sexual orientation. These two books, while providing very different views on the subject they purport to present, will have profound effects upon the evolution of sexual orientation, or queer theory, and the law. My hope, however, is that the effect these two casebooks will have on this field will differ significantly from the effect Holmes's metatheory had on the creation of the law of torts: No winner will emerge who, by virtue of winning, marginalizes the loser as naive, outdated, or irrelevant. Both of these books should receive equal respect in the academy, for they will keep alive an ongoing dynamic debate within the lesbian/gay/bisexual/transgender/queer communities with respect to the nature of sexuality, sexual identity, and the law.

## III. *Rubenstein's* Cases and Materials on Sexual Orientation and the Law

Rubenstein's *Cases and Materials on Sexual Orientation and the Law* provides one model by which to circumscribe the field of sexual orientation law. Essentially, he asks the "gay question." About this perspective he is quite up-front. He starts off by recounting the problems he had while a student at Harvard Law School searching for himself—a gay man—in the law school curriculum, in Harvard's well-stocked library, and in legal literature generally: "In the vast majestic expanse of Harvard Law School's library—where no subject was too obscure for its own shelf—the absence of legal materials about my life was itself awe-inspiring."[52]

This identity statement frames Rubenstein's approach: this is a field for and about gay men and lesbians. Should nongay people choose to take, or even teach, a class on the subject, they are welcome as fellow travelers. Yet the fundamental "aspects of gay and lesbian lives"[53] is what this book is about, a subject for which many students and teachers are looking. With the exception of sodomy and solicitation cases in criminal law and a few recent constitutional law cases, gay men and lesbians remain invisible in courses other than those that are explicitly dedicated to sexual orientation and the law. Until recently, traditional law school courses likewise ignored women's lives completely, yet to varying degrees women now appear in the cases and problems that are used in mainstream casebooks. If it were not for courses dedicated to sexual orientation, gay men and lesbians would still be wandering the halls of their law schools hopelessly looking for themselves in the curriculum, just as Rubenstein and I did during the early to mid-1980s.

The Rubenstein book begins with a chapter he titles "Basic Documents," which is divided into six subjects: Sexuality, Identity/History, Religion, Psychiatry, Philosophy, and Queer Theory. What makes these documents "Basic" is not entirely obvious; I wonder, basic to what? or to whom? Certainly Rubenstein is trying to set a cultural stage for the legal materials that follow. However, by calling them basic, Rubenstein leaves the impression that these documents—which include both fictional and nonfictional essays, amicus briefs, news articles, and academic studies—reflect a snapshot of background materials necessary to understand gay men, lesbians, and the law. It is unclear why these materials were determined significant enough to be considered basic, and why other materials were ruled out. They admittedly provide a nice, albeit brief, introduction to the history of the gay rights movement, including the coercive treatment of gay people by institutions such as the church and the psychiatric profession; but as a substitute for an introductory course in lesbian and gay studies and as a framing device, the first chapter provides an unnecessarily partial account of the fundamental aspects of lesbian and gay lives by focusing the reader on gay men. For instance, most of the material Rubenstein includes in the first section, entitled "Sexuality," describes gay male sexuality. Lesbians are the subject of less than a quarter of the material in this section, and what is included is dated—for instance, Alfred Kinsey's uniformly discredited observations that women exhibit same-sex sexual behavior much less frequently than men do,[54] and Marilyn Frye's essay "Lesbian 'Sex,'" which advances the dubious notion that lesbians prefer cuddling to penetration.[55] There is so much good pro-sex writing by lesbians available these days.[56] It is unfortunate that none of it was included in this section.

The "gay question" is further probed by Rubenstein by focusing on five substantive areas in which gay men and lesbians have experienced institutionalized discrimination: sodomy laws, identity (as expressed in schools, private associations, or coerced through outing), the workplace (private and public employment, including a new section on the equal protection clause), coupling (marriage and legal instruments that replicate marriage rights, such as guardianships and domestic partner benefits),[57] and parenting. Each of these chapters provides evidence of the law's coercive treatment of lesbians and gay men—sodomy law prosecutions, military discrimination against homosexuals, and the denial of custodial rights to lesbian and gay parents.

It is an unfortunate reality that the overwhelming majority of plaintiffs in gay rights cases are white men, and thus, asking the gay question by looking at legal opinions brings with it the responsibility to correct this demographic bias. Sensitive to this obligation, Rubenstein supplements the cases he uses with readings, both legal and nonlegal, written by or about the many types of people who make up the lesbian and gay communities. "Basic Documents" includes an interview with James Baldwin;[58] Audre Lorde's "Tar Beach"[59] and Paul Butler's "At Least Me and Rafael Tried"[60] appear in the "Coupling" chapter; and Lorde's "Man Child: A Black Lesbian Feminist's Response"[61] is included in "Parenting." To the extent that the lives of gay men and lesbians are generally hidden from and unknown to heterosexual people, the lives of gay men and lesbians of color are even more invisible—even within the gay community. Rubenstein's book reflects a sensitivity to this problem, although it could go further still. The section on marriage would benefit from the inclusion of writings such as Barbara Omolade's "The Unbroken Circle: A Historical and Contemporary Study of Black Single Mothers and Their Families,"[62] and the "Parenting" chapter would be enhanced by Regina Austin's "Sapphire Bound!"[63] or excerpts from Martha Fineman's *The Neutered Mother, the Sexual Family and Other Twentieth Century Tragedies.*[64]

In sum, Rubenstein's book seems to put to rest the first-order question: Is sexual orientation and the law a proper subject of a law book? To the more difficult second-order question—What is the proper object of sexual orientation and the law?—Rubenstein's answer is the lives of gay men and lesbians: "The organizing principle of the book remains the life experiences of lesbians, gay men, and bisexuals."[65] His book makes pedagogical space in the academy for gay men and lesbians; it "serves as a treatise or 'deskbook' on lesbian/gay law."[66] In a curious way, Rubenstein's approach to sexual orientation and the law relies upon a form of secular humanism similar to that employed by Holmes in *The Common Law.*[67] Just as the reasonable person is the animating subject of modern torts doctrine, the gay person centrally animates Rubenstein's approach to his subject. Rubenstein's casebook reflects a maturation of the legal discourse about gay men and lesbians, from object of legal regulation to moral subject who has certain vested natural, legal, political, and social rights.

The social and political agenda Rubenstein brings to this project thus creates a rule of recognition that identifies authoritative texts, which with time may make up the canon in this field. If your subject is the lives of lesbians and gay men, then the canonical cases are, to name a few, *Bowers v. Hardwick*,[68] *Hurley v. Irish-American Gay, Lesbian & Bisexual Group*,[69] *Romer v. Evans*,[70] *DeSantis v. Pacific Telephone & Telegraph Co.*,[71] *Watkins v. United States Army*,[72] *Baehr v. Lewin*,[73] and *Braschi v. Stahl Associates*.[74] These cases are privileged because they evidence the struggle between the gay or lesbian subject and legal institutions that seek to deny that subject full civil rights.

## IV. Eskridge and Hunter's Sexuality, Gender, and the Law

Eskridge and Hunter's book raises the specter of a competing conceptual scheme, one that will potentially assemble a different set of canonical cases than those selected by Rubenstein. Rather than examining the law's treatment of the fundamental aspects of lesbian and gay lives, *Sexuality, Gender, and the Law* is primarily concerned with readings that illustrate how there is "[a] mutually constitutive dynamic operat[ing] between sexuality and the state, just as one operates between the market and the state."[75] Rather than take the lives of lesbians and gay men as the object of legal analysis, the text consider[s] "sexuality" in its broadest sense. "Our enterprise ... is the deconstruction and analysis of sexual identity, and we do not limit that to gay, lesbian, and bisexual identities. We explore how the law constructs homosexuality and heterosexuality in diacritical relationship to each other. . . . [so as] to render visible the lives of lesbians and gay men, who are often invisible in the law, and at the same time to analyze the social meanings of heterosexuality, which is often unquestioned in the law."[76]

Recognizing the dynamic relationship that a casebook can have within the development of a field, Eskridge and Hunter openly confess their aspiration: "We hope that this book will help shape the field itself."[77] But what is their field? Is it the same field Rubenstein's book seeks to capture? Rather than focus upon the multiple ways in which the law interferes with or fails to take account of the lives of lesbians and gay men, Eskridge and Hunter seek to show how the law's regulation of sexuality permeates all facets of public and private life, and, indeed, produces a coherent boundary between the public and the private spheres. For these authors, law is a regulatory practice that has the power to create lesbian, gay, bisexual, transgendered, and heterosexual subjects.

As the title indicates, however, the book does not limit its focus to sexuality alone. The authors are committed to exploring the degree to which sexual norms and gender norms cannot be fully understood independent of one another: "[W]e view sexuality and gender in intellectual terms as so inextricably linked as to cast doubt on the ability to separate them completely and still attain a thorough understanding of either."[78] To this end, they include readings from natural law theorists such as John Finnis,[79] materialists such as Richard Posner,[80] feminist deconstructionists such as Judith Butler,[81] and queer theorists such as Eve Sedgwick.[82] One of the strengths of this text is the manner in which these difficult theoretical readings are paired with cases that ground abstract insights from cultural and gender studies in real life problems.[83]

Although Eskridge and Hunter do not start off with a chapter entitled "Basic Documents," it would have looked quite different from Rubenstein's had they done so. Their basic documents would touch on fundamentals of privacy doctrine; sex discrimination; scientific and cultural theories of sexual identity; First Amendment treatment of sexual speech, association, coming out, and the problem of conflicting norms about homosexuality under the religion clauses; and the law's construction of consent in an array of sexual contexts.

Instead, the Eskridge and Hunter text is organized within three clusters of four chapters each, covering a wide array of topics that all generally fall within the domain of sexuality. The first cluster provides constitutional, historical, and theoretical materials; it emphasizes theories of privacy and equality, the medicalization of sexuality, and competing philosophical visions of sexual identity.[84] Recall that Rubenstein includes the Kinsey study of lesbian sexuality in his "Basic Documents."[85] Eskridge and Hunter, however, discuss Kinsey in a chapter entitled "Medicalization of Sex, Gender, and Sexuality."[86] In so doing, they better situate Kinsey's *Sexual Behavior in the Human Female* within the evolving medicalization of sexuality that began with sexologists of the eighteenth century, continued through Freud in the nineteenth, and concludes with feminist critiques of Freud[87] and anticlinicians such as Foucault.[88] This first third of the book ends with a chapter entitled "U.S. Military Exclusions and the Construction of Manhood," in which the authors use the norm of masculinity in the military as a way of practically illustrating the intersection of race, sexuality, gender, and sexual orientation. In Rubenstein's section on the military, he first considers important regulations with regard to sodomy and homosexuality,[89] then excerpts two academic accounts of the subject,[90] and concludes with two significant legal challenges to the Pentagon's policies that exclude gay men and lesbians from military service.[91] In contrast, Eskridge and Hunter situate many of these same materials within a larger discussion of the military's history of racial segregation and exclusion[92] and the prohibition of women from combat positions.[93] In so doing, they render the subject in terms that implicate both gender- and race-based norms of masculinity, rather than framing the matter in merely gay/straight terms, as Rubenstein does. The latter approach reflects a kind of civil libertarian, equal access view of the problem, while Eskridge and Hunter are more concerned with exposing the powerful cultural work done by the military's policies in shaping modern notions of masculinity.

The second cluster of the Eskridge and Hunter text, beginning with a chapter entitled "Identity Speech in the Body Politic," examines the role of sexuality and gender in various aspects of public and political life. Here, the readings cover First Amendment rights to speak about sexual identity and about sex, hate speech, outing, and the relationship between sexuality and citizenship. With respect to this last topic, the materials suggest an interesting connection between domestic antigay referenda and asylum petitions made on behalf of women who seek to escape cultural practices such as female circumcision.[94] If we can understand *Romer v. Evans*[95] to stand for the proposition that a moral majority may not express its disdain for a minority's sexual practices by disenfranchising that minority, then does this precedent estop a majority of the Western world from expressing its disdain for African sexual practices by allowing asylum petitions from African women who object to those practices? In other words, does *Romer*'s mandate of a norm of tolerance between competing moral views on the domestic level require the same degree of cross-cultural tolerance when we encounter a conflict of values on the international level? The inclusion of these materials by Eskridge and Hunter illustrates the thoughtful and nuanced approach they bring to the intersection of sex, sexuality, and culture.

One of the book's shortcomings, expressly acknowledged by the authors, is its inattention to the relationship between sex, gender, and race. The disclaimer provided at the end of the introduction[96] reiterates, in a now familiar fashion, what has come to be the familiar footnote to Kim Crenshaw's "intersectionality" article[97] in almost every article written on feminist jurisprudence by a white woman. Yet the jurisprudence of equality and identity has moved beyond the point where all one needs to do is flag for separate discussion the complex implications of race. The un-marked terms "sexuality" and "sexual orientation" cannot now, and never could, legitimately denote an aspect of human identity that transcends or traverses racial locations.[98] We can, and must, do better. Mary Becker's course at the University of Chicago on "Critical Race and Lesbian-Gay Legal Theory" represents a laudable and serious effort to move beyond the phantasm of deracialized sexuality. In this course, she provides read-ings that address the intersectional identities of gay men and lesbians of color, the sexualization of African and gay Americans, and the limitations of gay marriage for dismantling sexism and racism, as well as readings that critique paradigms of formal equality that have been more successful for white gay men than for other lesbian and gay peoples.

While Rubenstein's book is predominately descriptive in nature—doc-umenting the legal treatment of lesbians and gay men—the Eskridge and Hunter book is more normative. Rather than assuming lesbian and gay subjects, the readings in the latter over and over again suggest the regula-tive and constitutive power of law to create sexed subjects. Its structure, case selection, and commentary reflect a theory of sexuality that is both problematizing and, for some, problematic in nature. Many people who teach in this area love Rubenstein's book precisely because gay men and lesbians are neither an afterthought—as is the case in some texts on women and the law or feminist jurisprudence—nor relegated to the sta-tus of exemplar of some larger theory. Yet others will regard the Eskridge and Hunter treatment as more successfully framing the central and cut-ting edge debates in contemporary queer theory with respect to the na-ture of sexual identity and the role of law and culture in the creation of subjects who possess a sexual orientation. These two books provide com-peting accounts of the proper object of gay and lesbian legal theory, ac-counts that mirror an ongoing debate in the field of women's studies. It is from this parallel debate that I want to draw some insights, which will help illuminate the canonical significance of the Rubenstein and Es-kridge/Hunter books.

## V. Canon Formation in Women's Studies: The Power of Two Ideas

The evolution of the torts canon provides a model of field production in which one powerful critic, scholar, and jurist was able to impose his view of the field and vanquish all others. I hope that something different takes place with respect to the evolution of the field of sexuality and the law. Rather than having one view prevail, my hope is that the academy, and the law more generally, can entertain competing canons within one field loosely termed sexuality and the law. The evolution of the discipline called women's studies provides an alternative model of field and canon creation.

Beginning with the work of Simone de Beauvoir,[99] and as interpreted by American feminist writers such as Betty Friedan,[100] Nancy Chodorow,[101] Susan Brownmiller,[102] and Catharine MacKinnon,[103] a field known as women's studies emerged in the late 1970s and early 1980s that understood its proper object of study to be the lives and experiences of women. These early second-wave feminists took on several important political and theoretical projects. They began by identifying and valorizing the ways in which women arguably are different from men.[104] They also sought to document the many forms of patriarchal power that subordinate women at home, at work, and on the street. Thus, much of the work of this time was devoted to voicing women's experiences of rape,[105] sexual harassment,[106] and domestic violence.[107]

The integrity of women's studies, as originally defined, came under attack in the mid- to late 1980s, when the thinking of postmodern continental philosophers became fashionable. The early writing of Joan Scott,[108] Seyla Benhabib,[109] and Gayatri Spivak[110] among others, provoked a theoretical rift within the field of women's studies that has yet to be resolved. These writers called into question the metaphysics of the subject as formulated by enlightenment feminists. It was during this period that "essentialist" became an epithet—to be charged with advancing essentialism was to have one's work attacked as naive, outmoded, and, to some, counterproductive.[111] Instead, these feminists questioned the normative function of a fixed female identity and were more concerned with the ways in which a constellation of social practices, some of which were patriarchal, produced male and female subjects. The category "woman" was not something that could merely be asserted and then valorized; it was, rather, a normative fiction. As such, sexual difference could not be disaggregated from culture.

> This rupture provoked an anguished, and often impatient, cry from some quarters: Why is it that just at the moment when so many of us who have been silenced begin to demand the right to name ourselves, to act as subjects rather than as objects of history that just then the concept of subjecthood becomes

problematic? Just when we are forming our own theories about the world, uncertainty emerges about whether the world can be theorized. Just when we are talking about the changes we want, ideas of progress and the possibility of systematically and rationally organizing human society become dubious and suspect. Why is it only now that critiques are made of the will to power inherent in the effort to create theory?[112]

Right around the same time, both essentialist and anti-essentialist feminists launched class and race critiques of women's studies, claiming that the object of study—woman—was in fact a white, middle-class woman who mirrored those individuals who had secured tenured appointments in women's studies departments. Anti-essentialists appropriated these arguments to undermine the legitimacy of cultural feminists who claimed to be vocalizing a universal woman's voice. At the same time, essentialists used these critiques to advance a more diverse identity politics that recognized and validated the experiences of women of color and low-income women. In the end, both sides—essentialists and anti-essentialists—called each other racist.[113]

The early 1990s saw the field(s) of women's studies struggle with a reconciliation between the defenders of identity politics and those who regarded it as bankrupt, or at best a naive or quaint notion. A new critique of the critique of essentialism evolved that recognized the counterproductivity of the binarism that the anti-essentialist critique had engendered, and sought to move the discussion to a new, less polarized discursive space. Several good books appeared that attempted to move the debate to new terrain,[114] and many writers took up a strategy Spivak termed "strategic essentialism":[115] "[Strategic essentialism entails] consciously choosing to essentialize a particular community for the purpose of a specific political goal. Strategic essentialism ideally should be undertaken by the affected community, which is best situated to undertake the process of selecting the appropriate circumstances in which to offer cultural information."[116] Interestingly enough, the feminists drawn to "strategic essentialism" are frequently, although not exclusively, women of color. Joan Williams offered a third way beyond the binarism:[117] Rather than providing a theory as to whether women are the same as or different from men, Williams suggested that "sameness and difference are not arguments about the essential nature of human beings. Instead, they are questions that stem from the fact that 'neutral' standards systematically disadvantage outsiders."[118] Our strategy should be to "describe differences between outsiders and the mainstream in ways that do not reinforce stereotypes, [while forging] working agreements on the most effective strategies to pursue in the face of the supposedly 'neutral' standards of a tradition that disinherits us."[119] As Williams acknowledged, her solution was "tidy in theory but difficult in practice."[120] But it did have the effect of dislodging the sameness/difference logjam.

Women's studies, as a field, is now experiencing a quite interesting framing moment. The various sides, if I can describe them so grossly, are speaking to one another in a new way. There are three, although not only three, possible outcomes of this intramural conversation. First, one side or the other could win the debate, just as Holmes's vision of a coherent theory of tort law vanquished once and forever the defenders of the old school, organized around forms of action, as well as other theorists who structured the field around types of injuries. This is unlikely, given the problematic nature of the notion of winning in this context, and the compelling and legitimate investment each side has in the integrity of its position. On the one hand, the power of the women's movement resides in identity-based assertions, and women's studies continues to have strong ties to the women's movement. At the same time, no serious scholar can any longer reject out of hand the insights of poststructuralist thinking that at a minimum have shifted questions of subjectivity from the realm of metaphysics to phenomenology, from the fact of being a woman to the process of becoming one. Given that resolution in the form of victory for one side is unlikely, the second and more likely alternative is that women's studies will rupture into two distinct fields: the study of culture in which women remain the proper objects of investigation, and gender studies, a discipline committed to the critique of cultural practices and norms that are understood as antecedent to the emergence of viable male and female subjects. Thus understood, "gender is not something we have, but something that has us."[121]

Equally possible, and I believe more desirable, is a third alternative whereby we keep talking to one another and maintain a creative tension between identity politics and the politics of identity. At present, it is unclear what kind of insights will emerge from a discourse that retains a dynamic investment in the uncertainty and provisionality of identity claims. But with the death of grand theory, women's studies, like all other fields, must develop new ways of doing theory itself. A synthesis of insights about the interrelationship between power and the subject holds out the promise of a new paradigm. In a faculty workshop in which I recently participated, a colleague offered that the theory of sex discrimination she prefers is one in which women always win. Even in this postmodern era, outcomes should still count—and count for a lot. The power of a theory still lies not only in critique, but in what it can do for the lives of subordinated people.

The field of women's studies stands at the threshold of a paradigm shift, in which the category of things that are considered proper objects of study is not characterized solely by the properties shared by all members—femaleness—but rather by a system of principles that give meaning to or make sense of what it means to be a woman.[122]

Against this backdrop, the Rubenstein and Eskridge/Hunter casebooks have appeared. Both attempt to define an emerging field. Both do so in very different ways. My hope is that the proper subject of this field will not be defined according to the winner of these two competing visions, but instead will be made up of a combination of the two. For some time to come, lesbian and gay law students will want to see themselves mirrored as intact subjects in law school curricula, and heterosexual students should be made aware that there are gay people in their midst. Furthermore, given the violence and discrimination that some gay people qua gay people experience every day, it remains important that explicitly gay legal organizations such as Lambda Legal Defense and the ACLU Lesbian and Gay Rights Project address the legal needs of a community defined in the terms of identity politics. This is well understood by Bill Rubenstein and Nan Hunter, both of whom headed the ACLU's Project prior to entering academia full-time.

At the same time, "gay politics" needs to be shaken from its roots in identity politics. The push for gay marriage, as framed by the plaintiffs in the Hawaii case,[123] represents to my mind a shortsighted example of "me too-ism," reflecting a kind of "institutional domestication [whereby] normalizing the queer would be, after all, its sad finish."[124] To demand entrance into an institution such as marriage without providing a critique of the meaning of marriage for both hetero- and homosexuals is not only naive, but dangerous as either a theoretical project or a political strategy. For this reason, the identity politics implicit in the Rubenstein text must be informed by the cultural critique that motivates the Eskridge and Hunter book; at the same time, the critique of identity underlying the Eskridge and Hunter approach cannot lose sight of the enduring political and personal need to make identity claims.

## VI. Conclusion

When the Supreme Court issued its decision in *Romer v. Evans*,[125] many members of the gay community jubilantly took to the streets proclaiming, "This is our *Brown!*" Particularly after *Bowers v. Hardwick*,[126] we needed a *Brown*-like judicial recognition of the equality rights of lesbians and gay men. But *Romer* is not that case to the extent that the Court refused to include gay people within a traditional civil rights discourse animated by suspect classes. Instead, *Romer* could very well signal the end of the equal protection jurisprudence grounded in identity politics, of which *Brown* is the paradigm example: Discrete and insular minorities deserve special protection under the Fourteenth Amendment, so the argument used to go.[127] Clearly this Court is not going to expand the members of the classes termed suspect; disabled[128] and gay people[129] have been denied such exalted constitutional status. Nonetheless, *Romer* opens the door to thinking about the equal protection clause in a whole new light, one that redirects the equality inquiry toward practices endorsed or enforced by the state that vilify their objects as legal strangers.[130] In this sense, *Romer* is entirely consistent with a theory of equality that at once prefers neither of the contested paradigms of identity and equality framed by Rubenstein and Eskridge/Hunter and draws from both. Hopefully, in this postidentity era, other victims of state-sanctioned bigotry, such as immigrants and single mothers, will one day rejoice: "This is our *Romer!*"

These books appear as part of the field-formation process, and will play a dynamic role in the creation of a subject within the law. But it is my hope that these casebooks will play a different role in the creation of a field, and of a canon, than did James Barr Ames's 1893 torts casebook.[131] Rather than answer the Holmes-like call for a philosophical approach that neatly and rationally unifies an "entire body of law,"[132] the best effect these texts can have is to frame an ongoing discussion, such as the one now taking place within women's studies, between those for whom the subject is the place to start and those for whom the subject is where you end up.

### NOTES

1. *See* RESTATEMENT (SECOND) OF TORTS (1965).
2. WILLIAM B. RUBENSTEIN, CASES AND MATERIALS ON SEXUAL ORIENTATION AND THE LAW (2d ed. 1997).

3. William N. Eskridge, Jr. & Nan Hunter, Sexuality, Gender, and the Law (1997).

4. *Canon Busting: The Basic Issues—An Interview with Stanley Fish*, Nat'l F.: Phi Kappa Phi J., Summer 1989, at 13, 13 (quoting Stanley Fish).

5. *See, e.g.*, Dan Dobbs, Torts and Compensation (2d ed. 1993); Richard A. Epstein, Cases and Materials on Torts (5th ed. 1990).

6. The writ of trespass provided relief for injuries, usually between strangers, that were the result of direct and immediate harm from the unauthorized use of physical force, whereas actions on the case were appropriate for harms inflicted between parties who had a relationship of either contract or status. *See* S. F. C. Milsom, Historical Foundations of the Common Law 393 (2d ed. 1981).

7. *Id.* at 309.

8. *See* C. G. Addison, The Law of Torts (Boston, Little, Brown, & Co. 1870).

9. The emergence of the Field Code in 1848 is one example of this trend. *See* Lawrence M. Friedman, A History of American Law 391–94, 403–06 (2d ed. 1985).

10. *See* G. Edward White, Tort Law in America: An Intellectual History 12 (1980).

11. *Book Notice*, 5 Am. L. Rev. 340, 341 (1871) (reviewing Addison, *supra* note 8).

12. O. W. Holmes, Jr., The Common Law 79 (Boston, Little, Brown, & Co. 1881).

13. *See Book Notice, supra* note 11, at 340.

14. *Id.* at 341.

15. *See, e.g.*, White, *supra* note 10, at 12.

16. *The Theory of Torts*, 7 Am. L. Rev. 652 (1873). Compare the implicit confidence displayed by Holmes's use of the word "the" in the article's title with the humility of the indefinite article used by John Rawls, certainly a no less important legal philosopher, in the title of his germinal work. *See* John Rawls, A Theory of Justice (1971).

17. *See The Theory of Torts, supra* note 16, at 653.

18. Holmes, *supra* note 12.

19. *Id.* at 77.

20. *Id.*

21. *Id.* at 111.

22. *See* James Barr Ames, Select Cases on Torts (Cambridge, Mass., n.pub. 1874).

23. *See* White, *supra* note 10, at 18.

24. *Id.* at 18–19. Ames's colleague Jeremiah Smith authored these six chapters as part of a supplement to the original work. See *Id.*

25. 60 F.2d 737 (2d Cir. 1932) (considering industry custom in establishing standards of care in negligence cases).

26. 159 F.2d 169 (2d Cir. 1947) (establishing risk-utility rule in negligence cases).

27. 162 N.E. 99 (N.Y. 1928) (establishing "risk rule" approach to limiting tort liability).

28. 150 P.2d 436 (Cal. 1944) (applying doctrine of res ipsa loquitur to injuries sustained from defective product).

29. *See* FRIEDMAN, *supra* note 9, at 468; MORTON J. HORWITZ, THE TRANS-FORMATION OF AMERICAN LAW, 1780–1860, at 95 (1977).

30. STANLEY FISH, DOING WHAT COMES NATURALLY 306 (1989).

31. *See, e.g.,* LEON GREEN, THE JUDICIAL PROCESS IN TORT CASES (1931). Dean Green suggested a conceptual scheme with which to approach tort law grounded in kinds of harms, rather than kinds of duties. As such, he organized the field into categories such as "Threats, Insults, Blows, Attacks, Wounds, Fights, Restraints," "Surgical Operations," "Keeping of Animals," and "Power, Telegraph, Water, and Gas Companies." *Id.* at ix. Green's casebook was never widely adopted.

32. *See* GUIDO CALABRESI, THE COSTS OF ACCIDENTS (1970).

33. *See* Baehr v. Miike, CIV No. 91-1394, 1996 WL 694235, at *22 (Haw. Cir. Ct. Dec. 3, 1996).

34. *See* Romer v. Evans, 116 S. Ct. 1620, 1629 (1996).

35. *See, e.g.,* Beller v. Middendorf, 632 F.2d 788 (9th Cir. 1980); Singer v. United States Civ. Serv. Comm'n, 530 F.2d 247 (9th Cir. 1976); Norton v. Macy, 417 F.2d 1161 (D.C. Cir. 1969); Gay Law Students Ass'n v. Pacific Tel. & Tel. Co., 595 P.2d 592 (Cal. 1979).

36. *See, e.g.,* S v. S, 608 S.W.2d 64 (Ky. Ct. App. 1980); Jacobson v. Jacobson, 314 N.W.2d 78 (N.D. 1981).

37. *See, e.g.,* Gay Lib v. University of Mo., 558 F.2d 848 (8th Cir. 1977).

38. *See, e.g.,* Doe v. Commonwealth's Att'y, 403 F. Supp. 1199 (E.D. Va. 1975); People v. Onofre, 415 N.E.2d 936 (N.Y. 1980).

39. In 1985, Roberta Achtenberg, then directing attorney at the National Center for Lesbian Rights, edited a treatise on sexual orientation and the law that employed the Addisonesque approach of cataloguing the material. *See* SEXUAL ORIENTATION AND THE LAW (Roberta Achtenberg ed. 1985). It was merely a more comprehensive compilation of cases than we were able to assemble as second-year law students.

40. Harvard Law School has included courses such as "Sexual Orientation and the Law" and "Law, Sex, and Identity" in its curriculum for several years now, all of which have been taught, however, by adjunct or visiting professors (including Bill Rubenstein).

41. *See* Francisco Valdes, *Tracking and Assessing the (Non)Inclusion of Courses on Sexuality and/or Sexual Orientation in the American Law School Curriculum: Reports from the Field After a Decade of Effort,* 1 NAT'L J. SEXUAL ORIENTATION L. 150, 151 (1995) <http://sunsite.unc.edu/gaylaw/files/ valdes2.pag>.

42. An example of the latter is "AIDS and the Law." *See id.* Of course, these numbers reveal that the majority of law schools do not offer courses on sexuality or sexual orientation law. This fact can be explained in several ways, the most generous of which is that these courses, like "Feminist Jurisprudence" and "Critical Race Theory," tend to be offered with greater frequency at the more elite schools that feel they have more freedom to offer non-black-letter, jurisprudential courses.

43. The first edition of Rubenstein's book, WILLIAM B. RUBENSTEIN, LESBIANS, GAY MEN, AND THE LAW (1993), was adopted for use in roughly 25 to 30 classes, including non-law school courses on the rights of gay men and lesbians.

44. *Book Notice, supra* note 11, at 341.

45. Victor F. Caldwell *Book Note*, 96 COLUM. L. REV. 1363, 1363 (1996) (reviewing CRITICAL RACE THEORY: THE KEY WRITINGS THAT FORMED THE MOVEMENT (Kimberle Williams Crenshaw et al. eds. 1995)).

46. *See* Valdes, *supra* note 41.

47. *See* Katharine T. Bartlett, *Feminist Legal Methods*, 103 HARV. L. REV. 829, 837 (1990) ("'[T]he woman question'... is designed to identify the gender implications of rules and practices which might otherwise appear to be neutral or objective") (footnote omitted); Patricia A. Cain, *Feminist Legal Scholarship*, 77 IOWA L. REV. 19, 20 (1991) ("Feminist legal scholarship seeks to analyze the law's effect on women as a class").

48. *See, e.g.*, PATRICIA WILLIAMS, THE ALCHEMY OF RACE AND RIGHTS (1991).

49. At a 1996 American Association of Law Schools' conference in Washington, D.C., on lesbians and gay men in law teaching, Nan Hunter suggested that the attendees consider teaching a course entitled "Heterosexuality and the Law" as a way of unmasking the powerful normative priority of heterosexuality.

50. Jane S. Schacter, Sexual Orientation and the Law 1 (Spring 1994) (syllabus, on file with author).

51. *Id.*

52. RUBENSTEIN, *supra* note 2, at v.

53. Jane S. Schacter, *Poised at the Threshold: Sexual Orientation, Law, and the Law School Curriculum in the Nineties*, 92 MICH. L. REV. 1910, 1915 (1994) (book review).

54. *See* RUBENSTEIN, *supra* note 2, at 14–19 (excerpting ALFRED KINSEY ET AL., SEXUAL BEHAVIOR IN THE HUMAN FEMALE 446–501 (1953)).

55. *See id.* at 28–33 (excerpting Marilyn Frye, *Lesbian "Sex", in* WILLFUL VIRGIN: ESSAYS ON FEMINISM, 1976–1992, at 109 (1992)).

56. *See, e.g.*, DOROTHY ALLISON, SKIN: TALKING ABOUT SEX, CLASS & LITERATURE (1994); AUDRE LORDE, ZAMI: A NEW SPELLING OF MY NAME (1982); THE PERSISTENT DESIRE: A FEMME-BUTCH READER (Joan Nestle ed. 1992); MINNIE BRUCE PRATT, REBELLION: ESSAYS 1980–1991 (1991); Amber Hollibaugh, *Desire for the Future: Radical Hope in Passion and Pleasure, in* PLEASURE AND DANGER: EXPLORING FEMALE SEXUALITY 401 (Carol S. Vance ed. 1984).

57. Curiously, the chapter entitled "Legal Recognition of Lesbian and Gay Relationships" in the first edition is renamed "Coupling" in the second. Notwithstanding the name change, the first and second editions cover the same material: gay marriage, domestic partnership, and other legal fictions through which lesbian and gay men in relationships can gain some of the financial and legal benefits afforded married heterosexuals. Given the thorough and complex critique of monogamy, marriage, and traditional family structures that the gay liberation movement has developed, it is unfortunate that Rubenstein chose to rename the chapter on gay and lesbian relationships "Coupling."

58. *See* RUBENSTEIN, *supra* note 2, at 71–78 (excerpting Richard Goldstein, *"Go the Way Your Blood Beats": An Interview with James Baldwin, in* JAMES BALDWIN: THE LEGACY 173 (Quincy Troupe ed. 1989)).

59. *See id.* at 688–98 (excerpting Audre Lorde, *Tar Beach, in* HOME GIRLS: A BLACK FEMINIST ANTHOLOGY 145 (Barbara Smith ed. 1983)).

60. *See id.* at 699–704 (excerpting Paul Butler, *At Least Me and Rafael Tried*, AURORA, Spring 1982, at 17).

61. *See id.* at 802–08 (excerpting Audre Lorde, *Man Child: A Black Lesbian Feminist's Response, in* SISTER OUTSIDER: ESSAYS AND SPEECHES 72 (1984).

62. Barbara Omolade, *The Unbroken Circle: A Historical and Contemporary Study of Black Single Mothers and Their Families*, 3 WIS. WOMEN'S L.J. 239 (1987).

63. Regina Austin, *Sapphire Bound!*, 1989 WIS. L. REV. 539.

64. MARTHA FINEMAN, THE NEUTERED MOTHER, THE SEXUAL FAMILY AND OTHER TWENTIETH CENTURY TRAGEDIES (1995).

65. RUBENSTEIN, *supra* note 2, at vi (emphasis omitted).

66. *Id.* at x.

67. HOLMES, *supra* note 12.

68. 478 U.S. 186 (1986) (upholding constitutionality of Georgia sodomy statute as applied to gay man).

69. 115 S. Ct. 2338 (1995) (finding that private association has First Amendment right to exclude gay organization from its St. Patrick's Day parade).

70. 116 S. Ct. 1620 (1996) (invalidating state constitutional amendment that prohibited state or localities from enacting laws forbidding sexual-orientation-based discrimination).

71. 608 F.2d 327 (9th Cir. 1979) (holding that Title VII does not prohibit sexual-orientation-based discrimination).

72. 875 F.2d 699 (9th Cir. 1989) (ordering reinstatement of gay member of U.S. Army on equitable estoppel grounds).

73. 852 P.2d 44 (Haw. 1993) (finding that prohibition of gay marriage is presumptively unconstitutional under Hawaiian constitutional provision barring sex-based discrimination).

74. 543 N.E.2d 49 (N.Y. 1989) (allowing surviving gay partner of leaseholder to inherit tenancy as family member).

75. Eskridge & Hunter, *supra* note 3, at v.

76. *Id.* at vii–viii.

77. *Id.* at v.

78. *Id.* at vii.

79. *See id.* at 230–32 (excerpting John M. Finnis, *Law, Morality, and "Sexual Orientation,"* 69 Notre Dame L. Rev. 1049, 1063–69 (1994)).

80. *See id.* at 241–44 (excerpting Richard A. Posner, Sex and Reason 146–47,157–59, 174–78 (1992)).

81. *See id.* at 280–82 (excerpting Judith Butler, Gender Trouble: Feminism and the Subversion of Identity 6–7, 22–23, 24–25 (1990)).

82. *See id.* at 289–300 (excerpting Eve Kosofsky Sedgwick, Epistemology of the Closet 67–68, 71–76, 78–90 (1990)).

83. These materials, particularly Butler and Sedgwick, are hard going for most law students. Indeed, after several attempts, I have given up trying to teach Butler.

84. *See id.* at vi.

85. *See supra* note 58 and accompanying text.

86. *See* Eskridge & Hunter, *supra* note 3, at 145–48.

87. *See, e.g.,* Nancy J. Chodorow, Feminism and Psychoanalytic Theory (1989).

88. *See* 1 Michel Foucault, The History of Sexuality (Robert Hurley trans. 1978).

89. *See* Rubenstein, *supra* note 2, at 585–95.

90. *See id.* at 595–607 (excerpting Judith Hicks Stiehm, *The Military Ban on Homosexuals and the Cyclops Effect, in* Gays and Lesbians in the Military 149 (Wilbur J. Scott & Sandra Carson Stanley eds. 1994); and Posner, *supra* note 80, at 314–23).

91. *See* Rubenstein, *supra* note 2, at 610–41, 650–63 (excerpting Watkins v. United States Army, 837 F.2d 1428 (9th Cir. 1988), and Thomasson v. Perry, 80 F.3d 915 (4th Cir. 1996) (en banc)).

92. *See* Eskridge & Hunter, *supra* note 3, at 321–41.

93. *See id.* at 342–65.

94. *See id.* at 755–61.

95. 116 S. Ct. 1620 (1996).

96. The authors write:

One shortcoming that we must acknowledge is the insufficient depth to which this book examines the interrelationship between sexuality and race. We have, we hope, demonstrated some of the ways that sexuality is racialized and race is sexualized in American law. We realize, however, that the issue goes much deeper, to the point where, at least in the United States, meanings of race and sexuality are often mutually dependent. Developing the materials necessary to fully explore this proposition was simply beyond the abilities of the authors to do in the time allotted to produce this book. We invite our readers to join the scholarly project of helping fill that gap. ESKRIDGE & HUNTER, *supra* note 3, at viii.

97. *See* Kimberle Crenshaw, *Demarginalizing the Intersection of Race and Sex: A Black Feminist Critique of Antidiscrimination Doctrine, Feminist Theory and Antiracist Politics,* 1989 U. CHI. LEGAL F. 139.

98. Thirteen years ago, Hortense Spillers demanded that feminists appreciate that black women's sexuality and experience of sexism are not identical to those of white women: "With the virtually sole exception of Calvin Hernton's Sex and Racism in America and less than a handful of very recent texts by black feminist and lesbian writers, black women are the beached whales of the sexual universe, unvoiced, misseen, not doing, awaiting their verb." Hortense J. Spillers, *Interstices: A Small Drama of Words, in* PLEASURE AND DANGER, *supra* note 56, at 73, 74 (citation omitted); see also *id.* at 79 ("Black American women in the public/critical discourse of feminist thought have no acknowledged sexuality because they enter the historical stage from quite another angle of entrance from that of Anglo-American women").

99. *See* SIMONE DE BEAUVOIR, THE SECOND SEX (H. M. Parshley trans. 1953).

100. *See* BETTY FRIEDAN, THE FEMININE MYSTIQUE (1963).

101. *See* NANCY CHODOROW, THE REPRODUCTION OF MOTHERING: PSYCHOANALYSIS AND THE SOCIOLOGY OF GENDER (1978).

102. *See* SUSAN BROWNMILLER, AGAINST OUR WILL: MEN, WOMEN AND RAPE (1975).

103. *See* CATHARINE A. MacKINNON, SEXUAL HARASSMENT OF WORKING WOMEN (1979).

104. *See e.g.,* Chodorow, *supra* note 101 (articulating the theory that woman's role as primary parent has a significant effect on the different cognitive development of male children and female children).

105. *See* BROWNMILLER, *supra* note 102.

106. *See* MacKINNON, *supra* note 102.

107. *See* SUSAN SCHECHTER, WOMEN AND MALE VIOLENCE (1982).

108. *See* JOAN WALLACH SCOTT, GENDER AND THE POLITICS OF HISTORY (1988).

109. *See* SEYLA BENHABIB, CRITIQUE, NORM, AND UTOPIA: A STUDY OF THE FOUNDATIONS OF CRITICAL THEORY (1986).

110. *See* GAYATRI CHAKRAVORTY SPIVAK, IN OTHER WORLDS: ESSAYS IN CULTURAL POLITICS (1987).

111. *See, e.g.,* Alison M. Jaggar, *Sexual Difference and Sexual Equality, in* THEORETICAL PERSPECTIVES ON SEXUAL DIFFERENCE 239, 245 (Deborah L. Rhode ed. 1990).

112. Nancy Hartsock, *Foucault on Power: A Theory for Women?, in* FEMINISM/POSTMODERNISM 157, 163–64 (Linda J. Nicholson ed. 1990)

113.  *See, e.g.,* Paula Giddings, When and Where I Enter: The Impact of Black Women on Race and Sex in America (1984) (arguing that the absence of African-American female intellectuals in the academy results in feminist theory that promotes the idea of the universal female subject that reflects the white middle-class identity of the theorists themselves); Angela P. Harris, *Race and Essentialism in Feminist Legal Theory,* 42 Stan. L. Rev. 581 (1990).

114.  *See, e.g.,* Conflicts in Feminism (Marianne Hirsch & Evelyn Fox Keller eds. 1990); Feminism Beside Itself (Diane Elam & Robyn Wiegman eds. 1995); Feminist Nightmares (Susan Ostrov Weisser & Jennifer Fleischner eds. 1994); Diana Fuss, Essentially Speaking (1989).

115.  *See* Gayatri Chakravorty Spivak, *Subaltern Studies: Deconstructing Historiography, in* Selected Subaltern Studies 3, 13–15 (Ranajit Guha & Gayatri Chakravorty Spivak eds. 1988).

116.  Leti Volpp, *(Mis)Identifying Culture: Asian Women and the "Cultural Defense,"* 17 Harv. Women's L.J. 57, 95–96 (1994); *see also* Kimberle Crenshaw, *Mapping the Margins: Intersectionality, Identity Politics, and Violence Against Women of Color,* 43 Stan. L. Rev. 1241, 1296–99 (1991); Trina Grillo, *Anti-Essentialism and Intersectionality: Tools to Dismantle the Master's House,* 10 Berkeley Women's L.J. 16, 21 (1995); Angela P. Harris, *Forward: The Unbearable Lightness of Identity,* 2 Afr.-Am. L. & Pol'y Rep. 207, 211 (1995).

117.  *See* Joan C. Williams, *Dissolving the Sameness/Difference Debate: A Post-Modern Path Beyond Essentialism in Feminist and Critical Race Theory,* 1991 Duke L.J. 296.

118.  *Id.* at 323.

119.  *Id.*

120.  *Id.*

121.  Katherine M. Franke, *What's Wrong with Sexual Harassment?,* 49 Stan. L. Rev. 501, 574 n.390 (1997).

122.  George Lakoff drew the distinction between a classical view of categorization in which categories are made up of sets defined by common properties shared by all objects within the category, and new theories of categorization in which "our bodily experience and the way we use imaginative mechanisms are central to how we construct categories to make sense of experience." George Lakoff, Women, Fire, and Dangerous Things: What Categories Reveal About the Human Mind, at xii (1987). Lakoff illustrates how the process by which humans categorize the world is not grounded in the perception of objective qualities that all members of the category share, but rather is based upon culturally contingent norms that produce similarities and differences. As an example, he cites the category "balan" in the Australian aboriginal language Dyirbal. Things that are balan include women, fire, and dangerous things. *See id.* at 92–96. This kind of categorizing seems incoherent to us, but makes perfect sense within the logic that underlies Dyirbal.

123.  *See* Baehr v. Lewin, 852 p.2d 44 (Haw. 1993); Baker v. State of Vermont, 1999 WL 1211709 (Vt. 1999); *see also* ANDREW SULLIVAN, VIRTUALLY NORMAL: AN ARGUMENT ABOUT HOMOSEXUALITY (1996); WILLIAM ESKRIDGE, JR., THE CASE FOR SAME-SEX MARRIAGE: FROM SEXUAL LIBERTY TO CIVILIZED COMMITMENT (1996).

124.  Judith Butler, *Against Proper Objects*, DIFFERENCES, Summer–Fall 1994, at 1, 21; MICHAEL WARNER: THE TROUBLE WITH NORMA: SEX, POLITICS AND THE ETHICS OF QUEER LIFE (1999).

125.  116 S. Ct. 1620 (1996).

126.  478 U.S. 186 (1986).

127.  *See* United States v.Carolene Products Co., 304 U.S. 144, 153 n.4 (1938).

128.  *See* City of Cleburne v. Cleburne Living Ctr., Inc., 473 U.S. 432 (1985).

129.  Romer declined to reach this question, *see* 116 S. Ct. at 1627, but virtually every federal appellate court that has decided it has eschewed heightened scrutiny, *see, e.g.*, Nabozny v. Podlesny, 92 F.3d 446, 454 (7th Cir. 1996); Thomasson v. Perry, 80 F.3d 915, 928 (4th Cir. 1996) (en banc); High Tech Gays v. Defense Indus. Sec. Clearance Office, 895 F.2d 563, 571 (9th Cir. 1990). *But see* Watkins v. United States Army, 847 F.2d 13429, 1349 (9th Cir. 1988), *vacated and aff'd on other grounds*, 875 F.2d 699 (9th Cir. 1989) (en banc).

130.  *See* Romer, 116 S. Ct. at 1629 ("A State cannot so deem a class of persons a stranger to its laws").

131.  *See* AMES, *supra* note 22.

132.  *Book Notice, supra* note 11, at 341.

# Part IV

# The Constitutional Canon

# Chapter 12

# The Constitutional Canon

## Philip Bobbitt

Texts may speak, but they do not decide. When we wish to resolve a dispute according to law, we must perforce interpret the Constitution because that is necessary in order to apply the provisions of the Constitution that underlie all American law. Thus *constitutional interpretation* is the means by which legal conclusions are ultimately drawn.

Although interpretation is unavoidable, however, this does not mean that just any method will do; quite to the contrary, there are well-defined rules that govern the uses of the Constitution in resolving disputes. These rules generate the legitimate forms of legal argument. Certain parts of the text of the Constitution, and other derivative texts, are "canonical" to this enterprise—that is, they are authoritative in our legal and political culture—owing to their role in defining, exemplifying, or explaining the legitimate methods of constitutional argument. Indeed it is hard to see how the normal operations of constitutional law in the United States could legitimately manage without such exemplars and directions.

The works of this canon describe the prosody of constitutional conflict—that is, the rules by which the formal structure of constitutional argument is maintained in order to resolve such conflicts. These means of resolution I consider the highest achievement of the American culture, and to map them is, for me, an exploring of the hauntingly familiar and yet excitingly ever new.[1] The rules described by these canonical works will be well-known to any lawyer or judge, even if he or she has never thought of them as rules as such, or knows these works only though the derivative texts of commentators. It is not in my power to revise or extend the canon; I can only hope to accurately describe it.[2] It is the result of the continuing struggle of our culture's attempt at what no society before ours has attempted, the making of justice through a constitution. I realize that it is unusual these days to assert the autonomy of constitutional argument, and to deny that law is either dependent upon, or reducible to, economics, political science or political philosophy, or morals. Yet I am certain that the legitimacy of constitutional argument derives not from any link it may or may not possess to the philosophical fashions of the hour, but rather from its traditional modalities of reasoning; and that it is legitimacy that gives constitutional law—indeed all law—its authority. A canon of texts that show us how to maintain this legitimacy is thus indispensable to law in the way that memory is indispensable to the preservation of the identity of the person. The canon shows us how to derive rules that enable us to go on, to know that we are acting appropriately even in new and only half-understood contexts. I have selected thirteen central, core works that compose this canon; and another nine that I believe to be likely to join that core.

The first six texts are drawn from the texts of the Declaration of Independence and the United States Constitution. It is significant for the subject of constitutional interpretation that these particular texts do not provide any substantive powers or rights but rather offer specific directions as to how to construe the substantive provisions of the Constitution.

## 1. The Declaration of Independence

> We hold these Truths to be self-evident: that all men are created equal, that they are endowed by their Creator with certain unalienable Rights . . . That to secure these rights Governments are instituted among men, deriving their just powers from the consent of the governed. . . ."[3]

This immortal passage provides the fundamental basis of the structure of the new American state: that this state will be a limited sovereign (there being no human agents that are sovereign over others because "all men are created equal"), that its powers can extend only to that authority that is duly authorized by the persons to be governed, and that basic human rights belong to the People—are not granted to them by a sovereign, as for example with Magna Carta. The U.S. Constitution is the legal mechanism by which the Declaration's statement that government will be put under law is given concrete form. Thus the fundamental institutional relationships that are ordained by the Constitution (e.g., federalism, the separation of the branches, the single national market) must operate in a way that is in accord with the foundation set forth in the Declaration. For example, a single state cannot tax a federal instrumentality because the state legislature draws its legitimacy not from the consent of the citizens of the entire union, who will ultimately pay the tax, but only from its own state citizens; government may not set out to place restrictions on political speech because without such speech—and the various cultural freedoms on which it depends—the "consent of the governed' cannot be manifested. The government may not abridge fundamental human rights because the purpose of government is to secure the rights of the people—even a properly passed law, evidencing consent, could not arrogate to the government power over rights that are unalienable and thus can't be waived or bartered away. The Declaration does not specify what specific institutions will be created by the Constitution; rather it provides the initial, fundamental model of an institutional structure—the union of states—and its relationship to the people. From this model all arguments from structure and relationship flow.

## 2. The Necessary and Proper Clause

At the end of the list of substantive powers in article 1, section 8, of the Constitution and in contrast to them is the provision enabling Congress to "make all Laws which shall be necessary and proper for carrying into Execution the foregoing Powers."[4] This clause provides Congress with the explicit authority to employ reasonable means to execute its enumerated powers. It is true, however, as Madison observed in Federalist 44[5] and as John Marshall wrote in *McCulloch v. Madison*,[6] that Congress would have had this power by implication owing simply to the practical necessity of providing it. In contrast to the claims of the Anti-Federalists at the time of ratification, the clause does not add to the list of enumerated powers, as if it were an open-ended grant of federal power,[7] but is rather an indispensable consequence of enumeration. Implicit or explicit, such a provision is indispensable to any system of limited powers. How else could we avoid the impossibility of listing all the implied powers—of means required to execute the limited number of authorized ends contained in the enumerated powers—while also avoiding the inference of unlimited power implied by the suggestion that the list can be supplemented at the will of Congress? For our present purposes, the main contribution of the clause is thus not its substantive content, which is negligible, but the interpretive direction it gives us. Because a means must be plainly related to an enumerated end (otherwise the whole point of enumeration would collapse, and its purpose of restraint would be circumvented), we are required in every case to assess this relation. The necessary and proper clause explicitly legitimates the use of practical inquiries to assess the constitutionality of any means chosen by the Congress. It directs that the assessment of the relationship between means and ends must be made on the basis of necessity and propriety—both prudential inquiries, dependent on the factual context and reasonableness of the means chosen.

### 3. The Ninth Amendment

The Ninth Amendment is yet another nonsubstantive provision whose function is to provide direction for constitutional interpretation. This often overlooked fact has bedeviled advocates and judges who feel forced either to ignore the amendment altogether because the text gives us no guidance as to the content of the substantive rules to be protected, or to supply that content by such imaginative pyrotechnics that these have been, thus far, widely unpersuasive and broadly criticized. The Ninth Amendment provides, "[t]he enumeration in the Constitution of certain rights shall not be construed to deny or disparage others retained by the people."[8] Its true import is to tell us how to determine what rights the people enjoy. These are, the text states, not only those of the first eight amendments, and various specific guarantees of the unattended text (such as those prohibitions against bills of attainder and ex post facto laws), but also the entire universe of rights not compromised in the original grant of powers to the federal government.[9]

The Ninth Amendment traces the constitutional ethos of the United States: that the government, because it takes its limited sovereignty from the people (Declaration), is therefore limited in its powers to those granted it (the Tenth Amendment), with all remaining powers and rights being retained by the people and the states. This ethos may be visualized in familiar mathematical terms as a closed set of specified powers within a universe of retained rights (with specific exceptions, or subsets within the general set of powers, that are the explicit, "enumerated" prohibitions). This gives us an interpretive rule to determine whether any right is retained by the people, namely: Is a particular exercise of governmental power a necessary and proper means to an enumerated end, or is it implicitly prohibited because such ends were withheld from the federal gov-

ernment, or explicitly prohibited by the enumerated rights? The jurisprudence of the Constitution could scarcely account for such rights as the
right to marry[10] without this understanding.[11]

## 4. The Tenth Amendment

The Tenth Amendment basically restates the underlying premise of the
Declaration of Independence and the Ninth Amendment, by providing
that "[t]he powers not delegated to the United States by the Constitution,
nor prohibited by it to the states, are reserved to the States respectively, or
to the people."[12] It is therefore, as Justice Stone remarked, a "truism" and
does not contain substantive import beyond that which it amends.[13] It is
not, however, trivial. Rather, the Tenth Amendment importantly directs
our interpretive efforts to the textual: unless there is an underlying power
explicitly provided for in the text—"delegated to the United States by the
Constitution"—the government is without legitimate authority to act. I
suppose it is obvious that a written constitution must give force to textual
provisions, but this is no more obvious than the fact that the people in
such a system as that described by the Declaration retain all the rights not
delegated to the government and not merely those expressly listed as
such, or that the Congress must have the authority to effectuate its delegated powers through various nonprohibited means. Also, however, the
fact that a written constitution relies upon its textual provisions was the
source of genuine concern with respect to the retained, and thus untextu-
alized, rights. Thus the pairing of the Ninth and Tenth, appended to the
substantive provisions of the preceding eight amendments. There was
sufficient anxiety among the framers, as evidenced in Federalist 84 (with
respect to rights)[14] and among the Anti-Federalists (with respect to powers),[15] that these obvious interpretive directions would be mislaid that
they sought to underscore their crucial role by adding them explicitly.

## 5. The Supremacy Clause

Unlike the Ninth and Tenth Amendments, and the necessary and proper
clause, the supremacy clause has both an interpretive and a substantive
aspect. Substantively, it provides that the laws and treaties of the United
States will take precedence over any contrary state action, and that the

states are bound by federal law. Its interpretive dimension, however, is equally important. The words of the supremacy clause that provide, "[t]his Constitution, and the Laws of the United States *which shall be made in pursuance thereof* . . . [bind the] Judges in every State . . . any Thing in the Constitution or Laws of any State to the Contrary notwithstanding,"[16] provide the explicit basis for judicial review, as well as for constitutional interpretation generally. Any judge[17] asked to settle a case according to law must first determine whether or not it is made in pursuance of the Constitution if it is a federal law, or if it is a state law, whether it conflicts with a federal statute that is made in pursuance of the Constitution or if that state law is itself "to the contrary" of the Constitution. This ought to be so obvious that it is beyond question, and indeed it was not questioned by the authors of *The Federalist Papers*[18] or the members of the First Congress[19] or the public that greeted the otherwise controversial case of *Marbury v. Madison*, but the wisdom of the framers in explicitly stating this rule has been vindicated by the absurd attacks on the constitutional basis of judicial review—the necessity for courts to review all governmental acts for their constitutionality—in our own century. When Marshall wrote in *Marbury* that "it is emphatically the province of the courts to say what the law is," he meant no more than that this is unavoidable in a system of limited sovereignty in which otherwise validly passed acts must be squared with the Constitution if they are to have the force of law. *Marbury* did not "establish," indeed could not have established, judicial review; it was rather the first notable, though not the first, instance of a negative result of that review applied to an act of Congress. Without that holding, we would still face the necessity of developing case law—doctrine—by which courts and other institutions determine whether the acts of government are in fact made "in pursuance" of the Constitution, in order to decide issues according to law.

## 6. The Preamble

Finally, the Preamble provides another part of the Constitution that is without substantive significance[20] but which directs us to an interpretive rule. As Joseph Story wrote, the role of the Preamble "is to expound the nature and extent and application of the powers actually conferred by the Constitution, and not substantively to create them."[21] The Preamble, written after the Convention had debated and voted on all the substantive provisions of the Constitution, sets forth the purposes for which the Constitution was written. It provides, "We the People of the United States, in Order to form a more perfect Union, establish Justice, insure domestic Tranquillity, provide for the common defence, promote the general Welfare, and secure the Blessings of Liberty to ourselves and our Posterity, do ordain and establish this Constitution for the United States of America." The reference to the "People of the United States" was denounced by some of the Anti-Federalists who urged that it should read, "We, the States. . . ."[22] but this would have been inconsistent with the Declaration of Independence which had declared that the Americans were "one people" and had named their union the "United States." The Preamble's continuity with this formulation is significant in that it asserts the judicial continuity with the people who dissolved by force of arms those political bonds that had united them with Great Britain and thus also—as by chain of title—with the sovereignty formerly held by Great Britain.

The list of purposes of the Constitution which the Preamble sets forth track the fundamental relationship of the people to the structure of government set forth by the Declaration of Independence: that the purpose of government is to secure the inalienable rights of the people to life, liberty, and the pursuit of happiness, or, in the words of the Preamble, to "secure the blessings of liberty" for the people, that is, the ratifiers then living and their successors. This statement of purpose directs us to the interpretive significance of purpose itself. It explicitly presents the purposes and intentions of the framers and ratifiers, which serve as a guiding rule in applying the text.

In summary, there are six interpretive texts originally proposed by delegates of the People of the United States, and each provides the basis for a particular form of constitutional interpretation: the Declaration of Independence, which sets forth the fundamental structural relationship of the United States, that of the limited government to the sovereign People; the Necessary and Proper Clause, which urges the use of prudential considerations in interpreting the text; the Ninth Amendment, which affirms the basic ethos of the Constitution, its division between retained rights and enumerated powers; the Tenth Amendment, which directs us to the text of the written Constitution; the Supremacy Clause, which provides a basis for the development of interpretive doctrine; and the Preamble, which calls to our attention the original purposes of the framers and ratifiers. These texts form the basic canon of the original, constitutive framework of interpretation. In addition to these, there are eight further works that have the authority of the canon: The Federalist Papers, the opinion in *McCulloch* v. *Maryland*, The Commentaries on the Constitution by Justice Story, Frederick Douglass's Speech at Glasgow, Washington's Farewell Address, Lincoln's Gettysburg Address, and Holmes's The Common Law and The Path of Law.

## 7. The Federalist Papers

In the crucial period between the signing of the Constitution and its ratification, Alexander Hamilton, James Madison, and John Jay wrote a series of eighty-five essays explaining the terse 4,543 words of the proposed Constitution. These were published in various newspapers around the country, and collected in a two-volume book called *The Federalist*. The object of this enterprise was to make clear to the voters, and the ratifying delegates chosen by them, what thinking lay behind the many choices made by the Constitutional Convention. Contemporaries of the authors observed that simpler and briefer expositions were likelier to persuade the public of the wisdom of ratification, but it is clear that the authors of *The Federalist* had more in mind than simply a series of advertising supplements. Rather, they regarded their work as an interpretive gloss to be considered by their successors. Jefferson observed that the Papers were "the best commentary on the principles of government which ever was written."[23] Nevertheless, it was the role of the Papers in ratification that gave them the canonical status they now enjoy as the principal interpretive document outside the constitutional text itself. That is because the "advertising" with which the ratifiers were presented as representing the purposes of the Constitution is the best guide we have, outside the Constitution, to the ratifiers' intentions in adopting that constitution. And it is the ratifiers' intentions, not the framers', that have legal consequence since they were the legal conduit of the people's sovereignty. To employ a homely metaphor: the Constitution is like a trust agreement, endowed by a testator. Its drafters, the framers, were only the lawyers who drew up the agreement. It is the ratifiers alone, like the testators, who were empowered to give the instrument legal significance. *The Federalist* tells us what the lawyers told their clients the latter were agreeing to, when they gave their consent to the document.[24] For this reason *The Federalist* has been, as Marshall wrote in *McCulloch*, "justly supposed to be entitled to great respect [by those] expounding the constitution."[25]

*The Federalist* makes clear that the new American constitution departs from the political philosophies of Montesquieu, Locke, and Hume and is grounded on an innovative view of sovereignty and the operations of government. With respect to government operations, for example, the framers rejected Montesquieu's view of the necessary separation of powers; the U.S Constitution provides a system of linked and sequenced powers whereby no one branch can give legal effect to its decisions without the concurrence of at least one other branch (e.g., the signing of a treaty by the president does not affect ratification until consent is had from the Senate.)[26] In contrast to Locke, the American framers rejected a sectarian basis for the new state,[27] and disclaimed any union between the Constitution and a particular religion, or indeed any religion at all. Equally important, the American Constitution takes an entirely novel view of sovereignty. In contrast to Hobbes and Hume, the American framers rejected the European concept of sovereignty, which derives from the body of the prince, i.e., its autonomy and identity, and introduced instead the idea of limited sovereignty. This notion radically departs from the limitations on the sovereign, such as Magna Carta, with which Europeans were familiar and holds instead that the government can never be truly sovereign because all power resides in the people and they, the endowing people, necessarily retain a residuum of power—"unalienable" power—that is nondelegable. Of course these two strands of innovation, philosophical and operational, are intertwined. For example, Hamilton's defense of judicial review in Federalist 78 depends upon the distinction between the paramount constitution as an expression of the people's will and the acts of government that is their delegee.[28]

Nor is *The Federalist* a comforting and easily assimilated document for contemporary attitudes today. Our current advocates of "civic virtue"[29] can scarcely be at ease with the framers' ideas of this term, as expressed in the latter's view that persons ought to be moved by "the love of fame, the ruling passion of the noblest minds" as the animating motive for undertaking "extensive and arduous enterprises for the public benefit."[30] Similarly, the frequent use of the term "justice" meant for the authors of *The Federalist* an "impartial protection of the right to exercise one's faculties . . . in the acquisition of property and in other [pursuits], not equal provision for the satisfaction of one's needs and desires."[31] Rather *The Federalist* takes its canonical authority from its influence on the ratifiers of the Constitution, and what we must presume to be their understanding of the way in which the text of the Constitution would be given meaning and effect.

Thus *The Federalist Papers* at once give us the legal warrant to resort to historical or originalist inquiries regarding the intent of the ratifiers (because they supply the legal theory that is the basis for the delegation of sovereignty to the government) and provide us with the raw materials that enable us to conduct that inquiry. They are of immeasurable significance to constitutional interpretation, though they at present await a fuller and more accessible edition that will make clear their relevance to a wide range of contemporary constitutional conflicts.

## 8. McCulloch v. Maryland

Ernest Hemingway is reported as having said that all American literature comes out of Huckleberry Finn.[32] Of *McCulloch v. Maryland*[33] it may be said that all American constitutional analysis comes from that case; it is the foundation case for the doctrinal analysis of constitutional questions, because there the United States Supreme Court announced a test for constitutionality that, with the appropriate variation for the particular doctrine to be employed, has served ever since as the template for constitutional review. In addition, it also provides the model for the structural analysis of constitutional issues. Of this case, William Draper Lewis wrote that it was "the most celebrated judicial utterance in the annals of the English speaking world."[34]

The facts are well known: The establishment of a federal central bank had been an important element in Hamilton's economic proposals to President Washington in 1791; whether Congress had the power to charter a bank—it is not among the enumerated powers—was hotly debated within Washington's cabinet. The president determined that Congress did have this power, and in due course a bank bill was submitted to Congress and the original Bank of the United States Act was approved. The statutory charter of this bank ran for twenty years. It was allowed to lapse during President Madison's term; the president was on record as having opposed the bank's constitutionality while a member of Congress. The government's need for borrowing at the time of the War of 1812 and the ensuing financial chaos of that period, however, changed many opinions, including Madison's. In 1816 he signed into law a bill chartering a second Bank of the United States with the support of many—including Clay and Calhoun—who believed the bank would provide the necessary credit to expand development in the West. In fact, the bank's shift to a restrictive monetary policy contributed to a depression, provoking a widespread re-action against it in the states. Two states prohibited the bank from oper-ating in their jurisdictions; six other states adopted taxes on the bank's operations in their states. In 1818, the Maryland Assembly imposed an annual tax of $15,000 on all banks or branches of banks within the state that were not chartered by the state legislature. The only bank that fit this description was the Bank of the United States, whose local cashier, J. W. McCulloch, refused to pay the tax. Maryland successfully sued McCul-loch in the Maryland courts; McCulloch appealed to the U.S. Supreme Court.

*McCulloch v. Maryland* addresses two questions: (1) Is the Bank of the United States constitutional (because if it is not, then its operations are null and void and it cannot be taxed but must be closed—the obvious ob-ject of the Maryland legislature); (2) If the bank is constitutional, can Maryland impose a tax on its operations?

The first question can be restated as "Does the Congress have the power to provide for the federal incorporation of a bank?" and thus can be broken into two issues:

1. How do we determine what is a legitimate federal power?
2. How do we know when a federal power is legitimately exercised?

The first issue can be restated as "Who determines whether the scope of federal power includes the incorporation of a bank and how is it deter-mined?" and as such can be broken into three parts:

1. Who created the union (because if it is the states, they must deter-mine the scope of federal power)?
2. If the states do not determine the scope of federal power, where does the Court get the authority to do so?
3. If the Court is obliged to determine the scope of federal power be-cause the Constitution mandates a system of enumerated powers, must a legitimate federal power therefore be an enumerated power?

The second issue can be re-stated as "If the exercise of federal power de-pends on powers implied by the enumerated powers (or "means"), when are these means actually implied?" and can be broken into three issues:

1. Must the means be indispensable to be actually implied?
2. Or are actually implied means those that are merely rationally re-lated to an enumerated power?

3. Does the necessary and proper clause decide the issue between (1) and (2)?

The ultimate result of this inquiry[35] was the conclusion that the enumerated powers provide only the ends, or goals, of government, and that the choice of means to achieve the goals must be left to Congress, subject only to the constraints that they must be rationally related to the enumerated goal (otherwise this is a path of evasion of enumeration) and must not be explicitly or implicitly prohibited. This conclusion yields the Great Test, which provides, "Let the end be legitimate, let it be within the scope of the Constitution, and all means which are appropriate, which are plainly adapted to that end, which are not prohibited, but consistent with the letter and spirit of the Constitution, are constitutional."[36]

This sequence of questions—power, means, prohibition—repeated in Shakespearean cadence with the doubling of each clause reinforcing its potency serves as the framework for American constitutional analysis. This analysis operates with different questions being asked at each stage, depending on whether the action in question is that of the state or federal governments (that is, whether the power relied upon is enumerated or plenary—whether the prohibition, for example, arises from the heavily doctrinalized inquiries of the First Amendment or the implicit restraints of federalism, and so on) and whether the fit between power and means need be only a plausible one or a compelling one. Thus the Great Test is the double helix of American constitutional interpretation, creating from its structure ever new answers by the juxtaposition of a limited number of questions requiring specific information.

Marshall uses the entire range of interpretive forms in the discussion of question 1. For example: the means by which Congress can act need not be enumerated because it would be impractical to provide a list of all the possible means appropriate to government power (such a constitution would be impossibly prolix and would require constant amendment as new means became available; because the actual practice of government (in requiring oaths of office, among other examples given) reflects the widespread assumption on which countless acts rely that means need not be enumerated; because the framers and ratifers clearly intended Congress to be able to choose those means it thought, after due deliberation, to be most efficacious; because the necessary and proper clause, interpreted according to its import in common language, does not require absolute or indispensable necessity ("necessary" means useful, needful, conducive to) but rather requires a range of means which can therefore be assessed for their propriety ("necessary *and* proper"); because a substantial body of case law and precedent, while not deciding the matter directly, has assumed the constitutionality of the bank in deciding cases arising from its operation;[37] because the spirit of a government of limited sovereignty implies that the enumerated powers given to the government by the people[38] are in fact enumerated responsibilities that Congress is to meet, implying that the selection of means related to those responsibilities is not a power per se but an incumbent duty of Congress; because a court has to decide the constitutionality of Congress's exercise of its power in order to render judgment in the case since if Congress's own decision as to its powers were assumed to be definitive the court could not act independently as prescribed by the structure of the constitutional system; and so on.

The second question in *McCulloch*—whether Maryland can validly tax a federal instrumentality—has also been productive for constitutional interpretation. For this question, however, he reserves one particular form, structural argument, which he deploys with such elegance and power that it has become the model for all structural analysis ever since. It must immediately be said that Marshall does not rely on the argument that the power to tax is the power to destroy, and that therefore Maryland's tax is incompatible with federal supremacy. This argument would require an inquiry by the Court into the actual effects of a $15,000 tax—whether it is, in fact, destructive of Congress's purpose. Rather, Marshall concludes that any tax, whether destructive or not, is implicitly forbidden to the states on purely structural grounds. First, a state tax on a federal operation—imagine for example a Maryland tax on the mails, the mint, even the federal judicial process—falls on all the taxpayers of the union, whereas the Maryland legislature is empowered only to tax its own citizens. Thus the tax is inconsistent with the relationship of representation that undergirds the constitutional structure and is enshrined in the Declaration of Independence. Second, if Maryland could tax federal operations it could manipulate the choices made by Congress by making some choices more or less expensive than others. This too is incompatible with the constitutional structure because it gives to the state a commanding role inconsistent with federal supremacy. With these arguments a prohibition on government acts can be inferred from the constitutional structure and its relationships.

From *McCulloch*, then, two forms of argument can be modeled: doctrinal and structural.

## 9. *Story's* Commentaries on the Constitution of the United States

Joseph Story, associate justice of the United States Supreme Court for thirty-four years, is perhaps most esteemed for his opinion in *Swift* v. *Tyson*,[39] which created the constitutional basis for a national body of commercial law, and his eloquent dissents in *Mayor of New York v. Miln*[40] and *Charles River Bridge Co. v. Warren*,[41] but his influence on constitutional interpretation is tied to his important *Commentaries*. For sixteen years, Story was concurrently a justice of the Supreme Court and a professor of law; his lectures in the latter role gave rise to a series of volumes of commentary, the second of which in 1833 was his *Commentaries on the Constitution*.[42] This was the most admired and widely influential treatise on constitutional law in the antebellum period, and was an important source for the constitutional ideas of both Webster and Lincoln, as well as a major if rarely acknowledged source of Tocqueville's *Democracy in America*.[43] For our purposes, the *Commentaries* are important because they provide a model for the use of prudential argument in constitutional interpretation.

Story sought to bring "practical science" to the interpretation of the U.S. Constitution, and attacked the theoretical underpinnings of historical argument which held that the original understanding of the social compact alone gave legitimacy to constitutional interpretation because that understanding provided the basis on which this compact had been endowed with legal authority by the sovereign people. By contrast, Story maintained that "no human government can ever be perfect; . . . it is impossible to foresee, or guard against all the exigencies which may, in different ages, require different adaptations and modifications of powers to suit the various necessities of the people."[44] Indeed the "only true test [of the meaning of the Constitution] must . . . be experience, which corrects at once the errors of theory. . . ."[45]

As the constitutional historian Jefferson Powell has written, "Even a cursory reading of [*The Commentaries*] reveals Story's constant and consistent use of the notion of [practical argument] in his interpretation of the Constitution. Repeatedly Story warned that the Constitution must not be read as the product of "metaphysical . . . subtleties' but instead as a 'practical instrument.' 'adapted to the business and exigencies of human society.'"[46] Story insisted that the framers had created a constitution which entrusted the government with "a very large mass of discretionary powers" capable of expansion or contraction according to circumstances.[47]

This mode of argument—prudential argument—is in sharp contrast to historical argument. In reaction to the Court's opinion in *Cohens v. Virginia*,[48] foreshadowed by Story's opinion in *Martin v. Hunters Lessee*,[49] Jefferson wrote in 1823,

> On every question of construction, [we should] carry ourselves back to the time when the Constitution was adopted, recollect the spirit manifested in the debates, and instead of trying what meaning can be squeezed out of the text or invented against it, conform to the probable one in which it was passed.[50]

The *Commentaries*, on the other hand, assert:

> [W]hatever may have been the private intentions of the framers of the constitution, which can rarely be established by the mere fact of their votes, it is certain that the true rule of interpretation is to ascertain the public and just intention from the language of the instrument itself, according to the common rules applied to all laws.[51]

> [A] far more exact and comprehensive knowledge is now necessary to preserve its adjustments and to carry on its daily operations, than was ... even dreamed of at its first institution. . . . And the important changes in the world during its existence have required very many developments of its powers and duties which could hardly have occurred, as practical truth, to its enlightened founders.[52]

Prudential argument itself, however, is not without its vulnerabilities. The *Commentaries* repeatedly assert that the Constitution's protection of human rights is relative and not absolute,[53] a concession that adversaries of this form of argument have attacked in our own period.[54]

What Story referred to as "science" we might today think of as "social science." As Perry Miller remarked, "the gospel of science was, in America, converted to stark utilitarianism."[55] Thus today the inheritors of Story's approach can be found in the law and economics movement, among others.

### 10. Frederick Douglass's Speech delivered at Glasgow, Scotland, March 26, 1860: "The Constitution of the United States: Is It Pro-Slavery or Anti-Slavery?"

Because constitutional interpretation legitimates more than one form of construction, and there is no hierarchy of constitutional arguments, partisans of different political positions can each claim the Constitution as their own. There is no more powerful or more moving example of this than the speech of Frederick Douglass, abolitionist leader and former slave, which attempts to reclaim the U.S. Constitution for the antislavery position.[56]

Although the text of the Constitution employs various euphemisms, and studiedly avoids the actual term slavery, there can be no doubt that there were several provisions that accommodated slaveholding. First, there was the three-fifths clause according to which slaves were to be counted for the congressional census.[57] Second, there was the grace period of twenty years during which the slave trade was to be permitted.[58] Third, there was the "slave insurrection" clause that provided that the states could call on the federal government for help in cases of slave revolts.[59] Fourth, there was the fugitive slave clause which provided that "[n]o person held to Service or Labour in one State . . . escaping to another shall . . . be discharged from such Service or Labour but shall be delivered up on Claim of the Party to whom such Service or Labour may be due."[60]

In a brilliant tour de force of constitutional argument, Douglass uses the disingenuous fact of euphemism in order to frame textual arguments that the Constitution permits an antislavery interpretation. Referring to the three-fifths clause as a "downright disability . . . which deprives [the slaveholding] States of 2/5 of their natural basis of representation," he concludes that the Constitution "encourages freedom by giving an increase of 2/5 of political power to free over slave States."[61]

Similarly, he treats the slave trade clause as "say[ing] to the slave States, the price you will have to pay for coming into the American Union is that the slave trade, which you would carry on indefinitely out of the Union, shall be put an end to in twenty years if you come into the Union."[62] Further, Douglass asserts that "[indeed] so far as the slave trade is concerned, this part of the Constitution became a dead letter more than 50 years ago and now binds no man's conscience for the continuation of any slave trade whatever."[63]

Douglass deals with the slave insurrection clause in much the same way. Suppose, he asks, that an antislavery person were president. "The right to put down an insurrection carries with it the right to determine the means by which it shall be put down. If it should turn out that slavery is a source of insurrection, that there is no security from insurrection while slavery lasts, why the Constitution would be best obeyed by putting an end to slavery."[64] No slaves, no slave insurrections.

With respect to the fugitive slave clause, Douglass adopts a more aggressive textual approach. He simply reads its terms, which on their face do not specify the true object of the provision, viz, to prevent slaves from escaping to free states, as applying to an entirely different class of laborers, the indentured servants. This clause "applies to a very large class of persons—namely redemptioners—persons who had come to America from Holland, from Ireland, and other quarters of the globe. . . . To such persons this applies, and only to such persons. The plain reading of this provision shows that it applies, and that it can only properly and legally apply, to persons 'bound to service . . .' [whereas] the legal conditions of the slave put him beyond the operation of this provision [because he] is a simple article of property. He does not owe and cannot owe service. He cannot even make a contract."[65] Therefore he cannot be the subject of a constitutional provision that speaks of a party "to whom Service . . . is *due.*"

Throughout, Douglass's interpretive approach is rigorously textual. The Constitution, he says, "is no vague, indefinite, floating, unsubstantial, ideal something, coloured according to any man's fancy, now a weasel, now a whale and now nothing. On the contrary it is a plainly written document, not in Hebrew or Greek but in English. . . . [T]he mere text, and only the text, and not any commentaries or creeds written by those who wished to give the text a meaning apart from its plain reading, was adopted as the Constitution of the United States."[66]

Story had written, "Let it be remembered that tests, which scarcely cover the breadth of a finger, have been since interpreted, explained , limited, and adjusted by judicial commentaries, which are now expanded into volumes."[67] Douglass asserted instead, "No court in America, no Congress, no President can add a single word [to the Constitution], or take a single world [from it]."[68] The importance of the fact that the text of the Constitution "is not in Hebrew or Greek" is that its meaning can be ascertained by every ordinary person, and it is their understanding of the text that gives it its ongoing legitimacy, and thus to which the interpreter must strive to give effect.

Similarly, Douglass rejects historical argument, the approach that relies on the original intentions of the framers and ratifiers. Of this form of argument he writes, "[The debates at the Convention] were purposely kept out of view, in order that the people should adopt, not the secret motives or unexpressed intentions of anybody, but the simple text of the paper itself. Those debates form no part of the original agreement. I repeat, the paper itself, and only the paper itself, with its own plainly written purposes, is the Constitution."[69]

Jefferson's unforgettable text—"all men are created equal"—may have been drafted with the idea in mind that this claim casts doubt on the sovereignty of a king, but it is a phrase capable of the understanding that Lincoln gave it, that all men are brothers. In the same way, Douglass takes the words of the Preamble and soars beyond their original intent because they are words that will allow this growth. The Preamble's "language is 'we the people,' not we the white people, not even the citizens, not we the privileged class, not we the high, not we the low, but we the people . . . we the human inhabitants; and if Negroes are people, they are included in the benefits for which the Constitution was ordained and established."[70]

Using the same textual approach, Douglass goes beyond the intentions expressed by the original generation of founders in construing other provisions of the Constitution when he observes simply, "The Constitution forbids the passing of a bill of attainder; that is, a law entailing upon the child the disabilities and hardships imposed upon the parent. Every slave law in America might be repealed on this very ground."[71]

These principles—that the text of the Constitution is the exclusive source of legitimate meaning, that no sources outside that text (either of practical affairs or recondite learning) can serve to enable interpretation because they do not convey the legitimacy of contemporary consent—are directions for constitutional interpretation and proceed, it should be noted, not from any particular provision of the Constitution, but from its being a written text per se.

## 11. Washington's Farewell Address

When Thomas Jefferson and James Madison were drawing up the primary reading list for the University of Virginia in 1825—the canon of its day—they described Washington's Farewell Address as one of the best guides to the distinctive principles of the American Government.[72] Although widely summed up in the misquoted warning against "entangling alliances,"[73] Washington's Farewell Address deals broadly with the most profound issues of statecraft and state formation. Its three subjects are the constitutional order at home—the union, the strategic independence of the United States abroad, and the relation between the two.

From the beginnings of the first modern states in Italy at the end of the fifteenth century, two inseparable principles have characterized statehood. The state must be able to coerce obedience within its jurisdiction, and it must be free of coercion beyond that jurisdiction. This is the relationship between law and strategy, that is, between the inner and the outer domains that are drawn by the territorial membrane of the state. If either of these two conditions is not met—if the state is unable to achieve a monopoly on legitimate violence within the state, or if it is unable to separate itself from the dictates of a foreign state—then it is not a viable state.

The sort of state founded by the Americans at the end of the eighteenth century may aptly be called a "state-nation." A not entirely dissimilar state was founded by Napoleon in France; the record of the Great Powers of the ninteenth century is an account of the spreading of this constitutional order to them and then by them throughout the globe. The legitimacy of this constitutional order is founded on the state acting as the apotheosis of the nation. (By contrast, the nation-state derives its legitimacy from the claim that it acts on behalf of the welfare of the nation.) Such states are witness to the high-water mark of patriotism, because the patriot is acting for the nation by acting on behalf of the state.[74]

Washington's Farewell Address is directed to the development of what he called the "national character" what we might call the national ethos— of the new American state. The address is not much attended to these days[75] because that ethos has substantially changed with the birth of the nation-state in the Civil War. Nevertheless, the address is of more than simply antiquarian interest. In the first place, it shows that the relationship between constitutional law and international security is a matter of the ethos of the state; in the second place, it describes what that ethos ought to be for the American state, and while that has to some extent changed with the change in the constitutional order from state-nation to nation-state, the methods of cultivating and giving expression to such an ethos are as necessary now, in the interpretation of the Constitution, as they ever were.

What were the elements of this ethos? Government by consent is one such element, although it must be distinguished, as we are inclined to overlook in the present period, from self-determination. Self-determination by national groups, so characteristic of the nation-state, was not one of Washington's "ethical" elements. On the contrary, Washington held that because the Constitution had been founded upon consent, it was "sacredly obligatory upon all" until it was changed by the consent *of the whole people.*[76] A second such element was the denial of party faction, and its submersion in the force of public opinion. This also exalts the interests of the state above those of its citizens when they form groups to reflect those interests. Union, by enlarging the scope of the state, and suppressing the jealous and petty spirits of subgroups, is the most important ethical element of the American state-nation. Third, the cultivation of those traits that best serve the republican state was recommended. "Promote, then, as an object of primary importance, institutions for the general diffusion of knowledge. In proportion as the structure of a government gives force to public opinion, it is essential that public opinion should be enlightened."[77] In contemporary constitutional terms, we might say that for Washington (and the state-nation) education is a fundamental interest, not a fundamental right—that is, it is to be protected because of its importance to the state, not its intrinsic importance to the individual. Fourth, of "all the dispositions and habits which lead to political prosperity, Religion and morality are indispensable supports. . . . [R]eason and experience both forbid us to expect that National morality can prevail in exclusion of religious principle."[78] There is something anachronistic in the current admiration of "civic virtue" if it ignores this religious element. Particular faiths—or faith itself—may be characteristic of the nation-state, but religion (not faith) is what cultivates the private virtues of self-sacrifice, self-discipline, modesty, attention to duty, and the like that are essential for the success of the state-nation. It is religion, not faith, that restrains the false patriotism of the demagogue. Fifth, Washington recommended that the United States avoid any "permanent Alliances with any portion of the foreign world."[79] He did this on the ground that such alliances tend to corrupt the domestic operation of politics (as indeed was the case with the Federalist/British, Franco-Republican split of the early nineteenth century. Washington did not recommend the abstention from foreign affairs sometimes attributed to him; he advised rather that the United States place itself in a position to defy external threats so as to be able to determine its own fate and maintain its own independence. Sixth, Washington emphasized his own role as "citizen" and addressed his fellow Americans as "citizens" rather than as "Americans." The address begins with Washington referring to himself as a "dutiful citizen" and concludes by speaking of "my fellow citizens."[80] Repeatedly he emphasized the importance of affection and friendship—qualities that are not associated with groups. He referred to this state paper as "these counsels of an old and affectionate friend"[81] and urged that the people be bound together by "affection."[82]

Washington's Farewell Address explicitly stresses the importance of the Constitution and the rule of law. For our purposes, the address is important as a guide to the construction of the Constitution; it traces the "national character" of the people, and therefore provides us with a guide in making ethical arguments in order to interpret the terms of the Constitution.

## 12. Lincoln's Gettysburg Address

Lincoln's Gettysburg Address[83] is as well-known to most Americans as Washington's Farewell Address is obscure.[84] Its description of the national ethos is radically different. The Gettysburg Address, as a state paper on constitutional interpretation, may be divided into two parts. First, Lincoln links up his vision of the new constitutional order with the classic forms of constitutional description. Second, he gives explicit directions on how future constitutional decisions are to be governed by providing us with a statement of the new constitutional ethos.

The introductory passage—"Four score and seven years ago, our forefathers brought forth upon this continent a new nation"—begins the address with a reference to the historical ground of legitimacy, dating the beginning of the constitutional order with the Declaration of Independence.[85] Notice that Lincoln attributes to the Declaration the creation of a nation (though this term is nowhere found in the Declaration itself). Moreover this is a new nation, an idea that would have struck the founding generation as unlikely because the term "nation" applied then, as throughout the eighteenth century, to ethnolinguistic groups. In this sentence Lincoln is attaching a historical argument to his assertion of the creation of a "new nation'—namely, he implies, that it was the intention of "our forefathers" to create a new nation. The next phrase—"conceived in liberty"—refers to the relationship between the constitutional structure of the United States and both foreign states (from whom it is free) and the people (who are free to create the new state).[86]

The next phrase—"dedicated to the proposition"—directs us to the ethos of the Declaration. It asserts simply that the Declaration, and the form of government based on it, are consecrated to an idea.[87] This is followed by a quotation from the text of the Declaration, "that all men are created equal."[88] There then follows a factual description of the context of the controversy ("Now we are engaged in a great civil war...). This is then followed by the declaration by the decision maker (in this case, the president) of the grounds of his decision (in this case, to oppose secession and to order armed forces to war, and consequently, to this battlefield and to their deaths): "those who have given their lives *that that nation might live.*" [89] Putting it this way enfolds the goals of both the abolition of slavery and the preservation of the union. The president, as commander-in-chief, has ordered men into battle in order that a particular constitutional form might be preserved. It follows that other presidents, in making a similar decision, might rely and actually quote this precedent for their decisions.

Finally, Lincoln reminds us of the practical import of the battle, that the triumphant Union forces have effectively decided a great constitutional conflict far more decisively than any political rhetoric could have done.[90] In Lincoln's words, the "brave men, living and dead, who struggled here, have consecrated it, far above our powers to add or to detract."[91] Notice the inclusion of the "living," which takes the proposition beyond the scope of a mere eulogy.

The second half of the address is devoted to a single form of constitutional argument. From start to finish it is a direction to Lincoln's contemporaries and posterity as to what sort of state is to issue from this great struggle. "It is for us ... to be dedicated ... to the great task remaining before us ... that we here highly resolve ... that the nation shall, under God, have a new birth of freedom, and that government of the people, by the people, for the people, shall not perish from the earth."[92] From this we learn that the "nation" is being refined, given a new being. Henceforth it will be a "nation" of many races, defined only by their shared "freedom." Second, we learn that the government of this nation shall not merely be a single union (as opposed to the constitution of the Articles of Confederation, or the constitution of the confederate states, which did not permit the central government to have a direct legal relation with the people, but only acted upon them through the states) or merely a single union constituted on the basis of consent (government by the people—the previous, state-nation ideology), but a single union constituted also on the basis of its service to the welfare of the people.

The hostile historian who wrote of this passage that in it Lincoln "reforged the old federal Republic into a nation 'dedicated to a proposition' which [has] meant, in practical terms, Wilsonian crusades to save and extend democracy, the New Deal with its labyrinth of welfare entitlements, and the civil rights revolution" was near the truth.[93] The ethos expressed in this passage from the Gettysburg Address is that of the nation-state,[94] not the state-nation. It is the progenitor of the American state of the twentieth century in both its achievements and its paradoxes.[95]

It is well to recall, if we are to understand this new constitutional ethos, that it was not the only candidate for such a role in the new nation-state. Listen to these words of Alexander Stephens, the vice-president of the Confederacy, contrasting his vision of the new constitutional ethos with that of the founders:

> The prevailing ideas entertained by [Jefferson] and most of the leading statesmen at the time of the formation of the old constitution, were that the enslavement of the African was in violation of the laws of nature; that it was wrong *in principle*, socially, morally, and politically. It was an evil they knew not well how to deal with, but the general opinion of the men of that day was that, somehow or other in the order of Providence, the institution would be evanescent and pass away. . . . Our new government is founded upon exactly the opposite idea; its foundations are laid, its cornerstone rests upon the great truth, that the negro is not equal to the white man; that slavery—subordination to the superior race—is his natural and normal condition. This, our new government, is the first in the history of the world, based upon this great physical, philosophical, and moral truth.[96]

This is the nation-state of Bismarck, a model that, at least initially, attracted far more adherents than that of Lincoln. It expresses a kind of protofascism, exalting a particular ethnic group and subordinating others whose misfortune was simply being proximate. These two models share the ethos of the constitutional order of the nation-state, the animating spirit of service on behalf of the welfare of the people, but they differ as to important elements of that constitutional ethos. For Lincoln, this ethos was characterized by the definition of the "nation" as a people united by citizenship—the element of that ethos to which Lincoln directed us in the Gettysburg Address[97]—rather than by ethnicity.

When we are called upon to make ethical arguments in construing the Constitution, the Gettysburg Address gives us guidance. When, for example, we want to determine the unenumerated rights of the people which are a principal inference of the ethos of limited government, Lincoln's text tells us, first, that they are the rights with which the Creator has equally endowed all human beings—the rights to determine one's own life, the uses to which one puts one's own liberty, and the ways in which one will pursue happiness (and even to discover what it is)—because Lincoln incorporates these ideas of the Declaration of Independence into the meaning of the Constitution. Second, because all persons have these rights equally, no person can determine for another how government shall advance these rights, except with that person's consent and within the rule of law. For Lincoln, as for Stephens, slavery was a defining issue in this element of the constitutional ethos: for Lincoln, those "who live under the law share equally in the making of the law they live under, and . . . those who make the law live equally under the law that they make."[98] The slave owner "governs the slave without his consent; but [moreover] he governs him by a set of rules altogether different from those which he prescribes for himself."[99]

Accordingly, in matters as contemporary as the abortion question, the right to die, lawful access to contraception, the right to marry a person of one's own choosing, to educate one's children as one prefers, we must first ask if the rights at issue have been equally allocated to all, and second, whether the location of the power to make such decisions does not lie in those unalienable rights reserved to the people, for the enhancement of which (not merely their security) the government of the nation-state is constituted.

There is a thriving scholarly debate over the influence of Pericles' Funeral Oration on the drafting of the Gettysburg Address.[100] For our purposes this similarity is to be noted: both men used the funeral oration as the occasion for a state paper, expressing the constitutional ethos of the state. When Pericles says, "We enjoy a form of government which . . . not being administered for the benefit of the few but of the many, . . . is called a democracy; but with regard to its laws, all enjoy equality . . . while with regard to public rank . . . each man . . . is preferred for public honors, not so much from consideration of party, as of merit; nor, again, on the ground of poverty, while he is able to do the state any good service, is he prevented by the obscurity of his position,"[101] he is directing his fellow citizens to act in a certain way, just as surely as he is describing their state.

## 13. *Oliver Wendell Holmes, Jr.,* The Common Law *and* The Path of the Law

The most important act, for the purposes of interpretation, of the new American political society occurred when that society determined to enshrine the Declaration of Independence, with its relationship of limited government and popular sovereignty, in a written constitution. From this one act derives the various forms of constitutional argument—textual, historical, prudential, structural, doctrinal, and ethical. These modalities of interpretation[102] are taken from the common law. There they are used as the ways of arguing over conflicts arising about property, promises, negligent and intentional harm. The new United States, by putting government itself under law, imported into the realm of constitutional law these forms of argument. Therefore it is not as surprising as it might otherwise seem that the immensely influential works about the development of the common law by Holmes have had a profound effect on constitutional interpretation.

The famous opening passage of *The Common Law* begins,

> The life of the law has not been logic: it has been experience. The felt necessities of the time, the prevalent moral and political theories, intuitions of public policy . . . even the prejudices which judges share with their fellow men, have had a good deal more to do than the syllogism in determining the rules by which men should be governed. . . .[103]

This observation, which must seem to us today a commonplace, struck at an acute vulnerability of the American constitutional system which, having just undergone such profound change owing to the Civil War, was therefore susceptible to charges that its legitimacy could not be axiomatically assured through long tradition. If Holmes was right, then constitutional interpretation was not a matter of following prescribed rules of legal analysis, but rather the result of the creative role of the judge in making choices that reflected the influence of external factors, like politics. Hitherto it was widely asserted that conscientious judges "found" the law to be applied in a particular case because the law's long existence preceded any case that came before them. It was merely a matter of locating the logically relevant precedents, or extrapolating logically from them. This deductive method Holmes characterized as the "*elegantia juris,* or logical integrity of the system as a system."[104] He sought to replace this picture of judging with a more realistic, inductive method wherein the judge tested a wide range of possible choices permitted by the precedents. In these tests the judge was partly influenced by unconscious preferences, and partly by the immediate social and intellectual demands of the day. This was true, Holmes believed, of all judges, whether they acknowledged it or not.

In 1897 Holmes published *The Path of the Law*.[105] This work was similar to *The Common Law* in its philosophical classification of legal subjects and quasi-historical methods of analysis, but it broke new ground with its assertion that law was merely "prophecies of what the courts will do in fact."[106] This too had profound implications for constitutional interpretation. When Charles Evans Hughes said, in 1907, "We are under a Constitution, but the Constitution is what the judges say it is . . . ,"[107] he uttered the fateful words linking Holmes's insights about the common law to the process of judicial review. Constitutional law was "what the judges say it is" because law itself was no more than a prophecy of what a judge would say were he confronted with a legal question; and "what he would say" was now widely thought to be influenced by extrajudicial considerations. With these two works, Holmes had become "the dominant influence on American jurisprudence in the first half of the century"[108] and touched off a crisis in constitutional interpretation that would dominate the second half of the century.

## 14. Nine Likely Additions

The nine works discussed in this section[109] have as assured a place in the canon as one can judge from so short a distance. All seek to respond to the crisis in constitutional interpretation wrought by the Holmesian revolution in attitudes toward common law reasoning. Interestingly, each one of them settles on a particular form of argument and renovates it in light of that revolution.

Justice Hugo Black, for example, developed textual argument, and a set of supporting doctrines, with a simplicity and power they had never had before. His innovation was to propose that the Constitution had a certain number of absolute prohibitions that, because of their phrasing without qualification in the constitutional text, barred any extension of governmental power into the prohibited areas. By the same rationale, legislatures are given considerable leeway to act when there are no explicitly textual prohibitions. Thus a judge need not decide whether such an extension of power is wise or prudent; he becomes instead a mere conduit for the language of the Constitution. He is not, as the Holmesian realists charged, enforcing his own views; indeed he may sometimes be, as Black noted of himself in a famous interview, in the exquisite position of affirming legislation he had opposed as a senator.[110] Most important, the judge in doing so acts on a basis readily apprehendable by the people, giving a common-language meaning to constitutional provisions. The most significant result of this view of interpretation was the verbatim incorporation of the texts of the first eight amendments[111] into the otherwise sparse text of the Fourteenth Amendment.

Hart's and Weschler's answer to the realist challenge was to reformulate doctrinal argument, changing the matrix from the application of precedential, substantive rules to the application of rules of precedential process. It's not what judges do, Hart and Wechsler tell us, it's how they do it. Conceding that substantive justice is a matter of political ideology, the reformed doctrinal approach holds that justice is a matter of fairness, and that fairness will result—regardless or even in spite of a judge's biases—if the methods of judging which all concede to be fair are scrupulously followed. These methods include adherence to traditional standards of dispassion and disinterest, the elaboration of convincing reasons for deciding one way or the other, the mutual opportunity for persuasion extended to both sides. The rule of decision that results from this process must be neutral with respect to the parties and general rather than specific with respect to the application of the rules to similar cases. Thus judicial acts are distinguished in their rule following and their rule creation from the ad hoc, unprincipled decisions of the legislature, which may act without giving reason, may legislate for one situation only, is not confined to a factual record, and may favor one interest over another.

Crosskey was adopting Holmes wholesale[111] when he renovated historical argument by asking "not what [the framers and ratifiers] meant, but what those words mean in the mouth of a normal speaker of English, using them in the circumstances in which they were used."[112] Avoiding the realist attack on historical methods as arbitrary, anachronistic, and subjective, Crosskey sought to rehabilitate those methods by relying on examples of word usage drawn from eighteenth-century newspapers, pamphlets, letters, diaries, articles, and other documents, in order to recreate an objective, factual record on the basis of which the Constitution could be interpreted. By expressing scorn at the idea of a "living constitution," he intended to remove the discretionary elements from constitutional interpretation and thereby restore its legitimacy.

Bickel too sought to embrace rather than deflect the Holmesian insight. If judges were inductive, fact-conscious deciders and not mere logicians, so much the better. "The accomplished fact, affairs and interests that have formed around [a precedent] and perhaps popular acceptance of it—these are elements . . . that may *properly* enter into a decision to abstain from rendering constitutional judgment or to allow room and time for accommodation to such a judgment; and they may also enter into the shaping of the judgment, the applicable principle itself."[113] The basis for the legitimacy of such judgments is, broadly speaking, consequentialist: and who can dispute that a "better" judgment is made more likely by an attention to the real world in which it will have an impact? A strong case can be made that the truly "canonical" work in this vein is either Mr. Justice Brandeis's concurrence in *Ashwander v. TVA*,[114] or his unpublished opinion in *Atherton Mills*.[115] These works introduced the modern form of prudential argument into the American constitutional jurisprudence, though sharply limiting it to the judiciary's protection of its own role. A similar case can be made for Justice Frankfurter's *A Note on Advisory Opinions*.[116] But because these earlier works, important as they are historically, are assimilated into Bickel's broader prudentialism, it seems reasonable to focus on the later work.

Charles Black attacked the reaction to the Holmesian turn rather than its insights. Accepting the realist revolution, he nevertheless rejected its principal contribution to constitutional law, the so-called Countermajoritarian Objection. This objection may be stated as follows:

> A Supreme Court decision that strikes down a statute on grounds of its unconstitutionality effectively casts a virtually unchallengeable veto against the acts of elected officials, despite the fact that the Court's members have not themselves been elected to do so nor have been authorized by the Constitution to do so. By thwarting the will of the prevailing majority it exercises an essentially anomalous role in a democracy.[117]

Black, by rehabilitating a role for structural argument it had not enjoyed since Marshall, endeavored to show not only that the explicit structural commitment of the Constitution endorsed judicial review, but that its complex system of legitimacy by consent (as reflected in majoritarian elections) actually infused the judicial branch (whose members were chosen with the consent of Congress and whose jurisdiction, save that provided by the constitutional text to the Supreme Court, was entirely within the hands of the Congress). It is not too strong to say that structural argument has made a post-Holmesian return to the very core of the legitimate forms on account of Black's work. Black was able to demonstrate that such inferences from the structure and relationships created by the Constitution were perfectly legitimate—some of our most important precedents, like *McCulloch v. Maryland*, depended upon them—but they did not depend on entirely determinate texts for this legitimacy.

Dworkin responded to the realist challenge by both denying its central premise of logical indeterminacy within legal logic and embracing its allegation of the judge's reliance on rules drawn from outside that logic. He maintained that there were demonstrable right answers to legal questions, and that their rightness could be assessed by comparing them with the results commanded by the best moral theory available. This meets the criterion for ethical argument asserted by some critics,[118] but denounced by others as going beyond the *constitutional* ethos in that it conflates moral and legal argument.[119] Dworkin also held that "some parts of any constitutional theory must be independent of the intentions or beliefs, indeed the acts [of the authorizing persons]. Some part must stand on its own political or moral theory; otherwise the theory would be wholly circular."[120] Accordingly, there was nothing suspect about the judge deciding cases on the basis of an "external" theory.

But one reason why legitimacy can't rest on an external philosophical basis, that is, one apart from actual practice, is that the people don't agree on what that philosophical basis might be. So the philosophers must take the position either that the system is illegitimate, or that legitimacy does not come from the people, or that things are legitimate on the basis of a popular commitment of which the people are unaware (i.e., once analyzed, the everyday concepts that people do sign on to turn out to be the favored ones of the philosophers). If one takes legitimacy to derive from practice, on the other hand, then various different justifications can be held by different persons all of whom share a commitment to the legitimacy of the system. "Circularity" is a fatal problem when we insist on a justification for our choices in order to legitimate them, but philosophical justification may not in fact be crucial or even relevant to their legitimacy.

President Johnson's speech to a joint session of Congress following police attacks on demonstrators in Selma, Alabama, must rank with the most enduring and formative characterizations of the American ethos.

Johnson was clearly aware of the historic genealogy of such moments: "At times history and fate meet at a single time in a single place to shape a turning point in man's unending search for freedom. So it was at Lexington and Concord. So it was a century ago at Appomattox. So it was last week at Selma, Alabama."[121] And he was also aware of the larger purpose of his message: to frame the constitutional ethos of the American state in such terms that his proposed voting rights act, and the constitutional reforms of which it was a part, would be implied by that ethos. Extending the mission of the nation-state beyond merely the advance of the welfare of its people, Johnson added, "Rarely are we met with a challenge, not to our growth or abundance, our welfare or our security, but rather to the values and the purposes and the meaning of our beloved Nation. The issue of equal rights for American Negroes is such an issue. And should we defeat every enemy, should we double our wealth and conquer the stars, and still be unequal to this issue, then we will have failed as a people and as a nation. For with a country as with a person, 'What is a man profited, if he shall gain the whole world and lose his own soul?'"[122]

Johnson, too, was responding to the Holmesian challenge. Like Lincoln, he tried to enhance the legitimacy of his position by linking it with the Declaration of Independence as a constitutional instrument, i.e., drawing attention to the legal significance of the commitments of the Declaration. "This was the first nation in the history of the world to be founded with a purpose. The great phrases of that purpose still sound, 'All men are created equal'—'government by consent of the governed.' ... Well, those are not just clever words, or those are not just empty theories. . . . These words are a promise to every citizen that he shall share in the dignity of man. [These words] say that he shall share in freedom; he shall choose his leaders, educate his children, and provide for his family according to his ability and his merits as a human being. To apply any other test . . . is not only to do injustice, it is to deny America. . . ."[123] In this phrase we see the distinction drawn in some of the constitutional commentary between moral argument and ethical argument: "to deny America," Johnson tells us, is to deny the specific constitutional promises of the American state, not simply the inferences from a moral theory about the state.

After listing the various farragoes ("[e]very device of which human ingenuity is capable has been used to deny this right") by which Negroes were tricked out of an otherwise valid registration to vote, Johnson concluded, "In such a case our duty must be clear to all of us. The Constitution says that no person shall be kept from voting because of his race or his color. We have all sworn an oath before God to support and to defend that Constitution. We must now act in obedience to that oath."[124] Johnson attempted to meet the realist challenge that the indeterminacy of constitutional interpretation cuts the ground out from under controversial constitutional decisions by claiming that a simple resort to the conscience—a conscience shaped of course by the constitutional culture of the United States—would yield the conclusion for which he was arguing. He was aware of the difficulty of knowing his assessment to be sure: "Beyond this great chamber, out yonder in the 50 states, are the people we serve. Who can tell what deep and unspoken hopes are in their hearts tonight as they sit there and listen."[125] But he asserted, even with some self-doubt, that his claim was so manifestly in the spirit of the country that it was finally undeniable. Thus he concluded the address by saying, "Above the pyramid on the Great Seal of the United States it says—in Latin—'God has favored our undertaking.' God will not favor everything that we do. It is rather our duty to divine His will. But I cannot help believing that He truly understands and that He really favors the undertaking that we begin here tonight."[126]

These twenty-one works compose the body of the canon that is crucial to the interpretation of the U.S. Constitution. There are today living authors (in addition to the remarkable Charles Black, who continues to publish fundamental work[127]) whose work may yet prove to have a similar centrality. Some of these authors fall within the categorical forms of argument, generalizing to what amounts to an ideology from the perspective of a single interpretive approach.[128] Some address the more fundamental question of how to decide the various forms of argument.[129] Of all of these, the one of whose ultimate centrality I am inclined to be most confident is Hans Linde.

Linde, a former judge of the Oregon Supreme Court, is perhaps best known for his work in bringing the potentialities of state constitutional adjudication to bear on constitutional cases.[130] This effort, which promises to have important effects on constitutional adjudication, does not depart from the basic forms of argument for constitutional interpretation at the federal level. With regard to such forms, Linde is widely admired as a constitutional textualist. But it is my guess that his most enduring insights have to do with the unavoidable decisional role of nonjudicial actors in constitutional interpretation.[131]

During the nullification crisis, John Quincy Adams wrote in his diary that Jefferson "more than any other man, contributed to introduce and make prevalent" what Adams called the "insatiate rage of debating the question of constitutional power upon everything. . . ."[132] Both theoretically and historically, nonjudicial constitutional interpretation has played a decisive role in American constitutional life. As a theoretical matter, every act by a state official must, in a limited sovereignty, be held in a kind of legal suspense until it has been determined to be constitutional. Because all officials take an oath to uphold the Constitution, because as a doctrinal matter there are many areas of constitutional conflict that have been held to be nonjusticiable, because as a practical matter only a tiny number of the constitutional acts of the state are ever in fact adjudicated, it is beyond dispute that all government officials must scrutinize their own acts for their constitutionality. A legislator who blindly waves off constitutional objections to his bill with the comment that "the courts will handle that" is hardly behaving in a conscientious way.[133] In the absence of decisive judicial review, this results in a "meaningless constitutionalism which asserts that anything is all right if it is permitted [and] nothing is all right if it is forbidden, by an Act of"[134] the legislature.

Perhaps, however, because the escalation to constitutional battle that bedeviled political discussion before the Civil War proved so disastrous to the country, it is a move that has been disfavored in our own era. Ironically, constitutional review by nonjudicial actors has been on the wane (at least until recently)[135] from about the same time that the Countermajoritarian Objection began to cast doubt on the legitimacy of judicial review,[136] that is, from the time at which the judiciary was made to bear more of the burden of constitutional interpretation than was supposed to be its natural share.

As a matter of constitutional interpretation, such review by presidents, congressmen, governors, and their colleagues does not differ from that by judges. The methods—the six basic forms of constitutional argument and explanation—are the same. Therefore the canons of interpretation (and the canon itself) are the same. There are, of course, notable instances of such review. Washington's refusal to turn over the notes of the Jay Treaty negotiations to the Senate debating its consent to that treaty, the Virginia and Kentucky Resolutions, Jackson's veto of the second bank, Lincoln's suspension of habeas corpus and his determination that secession was unlawful without the consent of the union, the rejection of the Versailles Treaty and the Court Packing Plan by the Senate: all these are notable instances of constitutional review outside the courts. One example will suffice.

*McCulloch v. Maryland* upheld the power of Congress to charter a federal bank in 1819. In 1832, the Congress extended the term of this charter by statute. Despite the holding in *McCulloch*, the bank statute was vetoed by President Andrew Jackson on constitutional grounds. He observed that "[m]ere precedent is a dangerous source of authority and should not be regarded as deciding questions of constitutional power except where the acquiescence of the People and the States can be considered as well settled."[137] Each branch of the federal government must "be guided by its own opinion of the Constitution" because every public official swears an oath to support the Constitution "as he understands it, and not as it is understood by others."[138] Moreover, Jackson concluded that the veto ought to be used to effect such a constitutional review by the president, and not for merely political reasons. Guided by these two principles, Jackson then considered the constitutional issue taken up in the first question in *McCulloch*, concluding to the contrary that a national bank was not an appropriate means to any power enumerated to Congress.

The texts that evidence such historic incidents—like Jackson's Veto Message of July 10, 1832—are not canonical to constitutional interpretation. These events are merely incidents of such interpretation. What is wanted is scholarship that will link up the basic methods of constitutional interpretation with "cases" of unadjudicated, constitutional conflicts that have been decided by nonjudicial actors. If it is true that constitutional interpretation owes its methods to the common law, it is also true that the customs of legal study associated since Langdell with the common law—the so-called case method—gravely distort constitutional decision making. The case method depends on edited cases, that is, written opinions that have been clipped from a federal or state reporter. These are of little help to the constitutional decider who is not a judge, or who may be acting in an area for which there are no available precedents. or in an area in which he may not consider himself bound by court precedent. The lack of available training at the level of the law school, where "casebooks" of edited opinions dominate constitutional law classes as if they were property or torts classes, or of available commentary showing how previous nonjudicial actors resolved the constitutional questions they faced without, or contrary to, judicial guidance, is appalling. How did Jefferson determine that the Louisiana Purchase was constitutional? How did Truman decide that a declaration of war was not necessary in order for him to commit troops to Korea? How did Governor Sam Houston determine that the secession of Texas was unconstitutional, or

Governor Orville Faubus decide that the mandate of the Supreme Court to integrate the Little Rock public schools was unconstitutional? One must hope that this lack of collected materials will soon be remedied.

Studying the works of this canon will not necessarily make one a better lawyer, or a better citizen, but it can teach us how to overhear ourselves,[139] how to guide and correct our thoughts, when we are struggling to resolve a constitutional conflict by legal means. The essential task in constituting a canon lies in exclusion as much as inclusion; in an age in which so many persons are captivated by political theories that attempt to justify our constitutional practices, identifying the canonical can be a salutary if bracing exercise. It is a useful reminder of the point expressed by Mr. Justice Holmes in his *Lochner* dissent that the Constitution does not enact Mr. Herbert Spencer's "Social Statics"; no one, I assume, can really maintain that "A Theory of Justice" or "Law's Empire" or "The Economics of the Law," no matter how worthy these works may be, are *canonical* with respect to constitutional interpretation.

There is a canon in constitutional interpretation. It is captured in the major casebooks, taught in the introductory courses in constitutional law, relied upon explicitly, but more often implicitly, by judges and presidents and members of Congress. Most profoundly, its precepts dwell in the half-memories of our restless and earnest people.

## NOTES

1. *See* J. HOLLANDER, RHYME'S REASON 3 (1981) (eloquently describing the joy he felt in mapping out poetry's rules of prosody).

2. Though any description of the canon must to some degree be cumulative because later works build on earlier ones. *See e.g.*, the discussion of the Gettysburg Address, which builds on the Declaration of Independence.

3. THE DECLARATION OF INDEPENDENCE para. 2 (U.S. 1776).

4. U.S. CONST. art. I § 8, cl. 18.

5. THE FEDERALIST No. 44 at 285 (J. Madison) (C. Rossiter ed. 1961) ("Had the Constitution been silent on its head, there can be no doubt that all the particular powers, requisite as means of executing the general powers, would have resulted to the government, by unavoidable implication. No axiom is more clearly established in law, or in reason, than that wherever the end is required, the means are authorized; wherever a general power to do a thing given, every particular power necessary for doing it, is included"). *See also* THE FEDERALIST, *supra*, No. 33 at 202 (A. Hamilton) (the clause declares "a truth, which would have resulted

by necessary and unavoidable implication from the very act of constituting a federal government and vesting it with certain specified powers").

6. 17 U.S. (4 Wheat.) 316, 406–07 (1819).

7. *See* Letters of Centinel V (Nov. 30, 1787), reprinted in 2 THE COMPLETE ANTI-FEDERALIST 168–169, (Herbert J. Storing ed. 1981) (under the necessary and proper clause "whatever law congress may deem necessary and proper for carrying into execution any of the powers vested in them, may be enacted"); Letters from the Federal Farmer IV (Oct. 12, 1787), reprinted in 2 THE COMPLETE ANTI-FEDERALIST, *supra*, at 247 (while people may hope Congress will act consistently with traditional limiting principles, under the necessary and proper clause, Congress "will not be bound by the Constitution to pay respect to those principles"); Essays of Brutus XI (Jan. 31, 1788), reprinted in 2 THE COMPLETE ANTI-FEDERALIST, *supra*, at 421 (the clause "leaves the legislature at liberty, to do every thing, which in their judgment is best").

8. U.S. CONST. amend. IX.

9. Thus the Ninth Amendment must be read in conjunction with the Tenth Amendment and the Declaration of Independence (the latter of which states what rights preexisted the Constitution and therefore are "retained," the former stating what powers have been delegated to the United States).

10. *But see* Zablocki v. Redhail, 434 U.S. 374, 384 (1978) (affirming the right to marry without regard to the Ninth Amendment).

11. It should be added that the privileges or immunities of United States citizenship (the rights of the people *vis-à-vis* the federal government) arise from this rights/powers description and, but for The Slaughterhouse Cases, 83 U.S. (16 Wall.) 36 (1872), are superimposed on the states by the provisions of the Fourteenth Amendment. Thus the interpretive rule for determining whether or not a particular *state* action transgresses the human rights guaranteed by the U.S. Constitution asks: Could the federal government, with respect to its enumerated powers, employ the means here used by the states in pursuit of its plenary, police powers? If not, then the state has trenched upon the rights retained by the people. *See* P. BOBBITT, CONSTITUTIONAL FATE 151–52 (1983). The privileges or immunities clause is thus a substantive and not an interpretive provision, although its work is usually done by the Fourteenth Amendment as a whole, *see* Adamson v. California, 332 U.S. 46, 68 (1947) (Black, J., dissenting) or by the due process clause, *see* Roe v. Wade, 410 U.S. 113, 164 (1973), or sometimes by the equal protection clause, see Skinner v. Oklahoma, 316 U.S. 535, 541 (1942) owing to various doctrinal developments that have sought to compensate for the *Slaughterhouse* debacle.

12. U.S. CONST. amend. X.

13. U.S. v. Darby, 312 U.S. 100, 124 (1941).

14. The Federalists were concerned with imperfect enumeration, fearing that an imperfect list of protected rights might be read as being exhaustive. *See* THE

FEDERALIST, *supra* note 5, No. 44 at 513 (J. Madison) ("[B]ills of Rights, in the sense and to the extent in which they are contended for, are not only unnecessary in the proposed Constitution but would even be dangerous. They would contain various exceptions to powers which are not granted; and, on this very account, would afford a colorable pretext to claim more than were granted"). See also 1 ANNALS OF CONG. 435 (remarks of J. Madison) (J. Gales & W. Seaton eds. 1789): "It has been objected also against a bill of rights, that, by enumerating particular exceptions to the grant of power, it would disparage those rights which were not placed in that enumeration; and it might follow by implication, that those rights which were not singled out were intended to be assigned into the hands of the General Government, and were consequently insecure. This is one of the most plausible arguments I have ever heard urged against the admission of a bill of rights into this system; but I conceive, that it may be guarded against. I have attempted it, as gentlemen may see by turning to the last clause of the fourth resolution." This clause later became the Ninth Amendment. *See also* 2 THE DEBATES IN THE SEVERAL STATE CONVENTIONS ON THE ADOPTION OF THE FEDERAL CONSTITUTION AS RECOMMENDED BY THE GENERAL CONVENTION AT PHILADELPHIA IN 1787, at 436–37 (J. Elliot 2d. ed. 1836) (Remarks of James Wilson in the Pennsylvania Convention, Oct. 28, 1787) [hereinafter ELLIOT's DEBATES]; 2 THE DOCUMENTARY HISTORY OF THE RATIFICATION OF THE CONSTITUTION 387–90 (M. Jensen ed. 1976) (Speech of James Wilson, Nov. 28, 1787) (arguing that a bill of rights was not necessary).

15. 3 ELLIOT's DEBATES, *supra* note 14, at 313, 317 (Patrick Henry, Virginia Ratifying Convention, June 12, 1788) (arguing that a bill of rights was needed because relying on construction of enumerated powers in the Constitution was insufficient: basic liberties "ought not to depend on constructive, logical reasoning").

16. U.S. CONST. art. VI, cl. 2.

17. I am inclined to think "the judges in every state" may be taken to include federal judges as well as state judges.

18. THE FEDERALIST, *supra* note 5, No. 78 at 467 (A. Hamilton) ("No legislative act . . . contrary to the constitution, can be valid").

19. Judiciary Act of 1789, 1 Stat. 73.

20. Jacobson v. Massachusetts, 197 U.S. 11, 22 (1905).

21. 1 J. STORY, COMMENTARIES ON THE CONSTITUTION OF THE UNITED STATES 445 (1833) [hereinafter referred to as COMMENTARIES, cited by volume number and page number only].

22. 3 ELLIOT's DEBATES, *supra* note 14, at 22 (P. Henry at the Virginia Ratifying Convention).

23. Letter to Madison (Nov. 18, 1788) in 5 THE WRITINGS OF THOMAS JEFFERSON 53 (A. Lipscomb ed. 1904).

24. For a slightly different use of this metaphor, *see* P. BOBBITT, CONSTITUTIONAL INTERPRETATION 4 (1991).

25. 17 U.S. (4 Wheat.) 316 (1819).

26. Similarly the framers' view of federalism rejects Montesquieu's view of a "society of societies" in favor of a single, supreme union; and rejects also Montesquieu's opinion that only small republics can effectuate popular rule. D. EPSTEIN, THE POLITICAL THEORY OF THE FEDERALIST 51 (1981); THE FEDERALIST, *supra* note 5, No. 9 at 73–76 (A. Hamilton).

27. This is not to deny the role of religion in developing the character of the American people, however; *see* Washington's Farewell Address, *infra*; *and see* text at note 78, describing the original purpose of the establishment clause to protect the established churches in the states.

28. "[Judicial review does not] suppose a superiority of the judicial to the legislative power. It supposes that the power of the people is superior to both, and that where the will of the legislature, declared in its statutes, stands in opposition to that of the people, declared in the Constitution, the judges ought to be governed by the latter rather than the former." THE FEDERALIST, *supra* note 5, No. 78 at 468–69 (A. Hamilton).

29. *See generally* NEW COMMUNITARIAN THINKING: PERSONS, VIRTUES, INSTITUTIONS, AND COMMUNITIES (A. Etzioni ed. 1995); COMMUNITARIANISM AND INDIVIDUALISM (S. Avineri & A. De-Shalit eds. 1992); M. Walzer, *Civility and Civic Virtue in Contemporary America, in* RADICAL PRINCIPLES: REFLECTIONS OF AN UNRECONSTRUCTED DEMOCRAT (1980).

30. THE FEDERALIST, *supra* note 5, No. 72 at 437 (A. Hamilton).

31. *See generally* EPSTEIN, *supra* note 26, at 72–81.

32. Echoing a remark by Dostoyevsky that all Russian short story writers emerged from Gogol's overcoat.

33. 17 U.S. (4 Wheat.) 316 (1819).

34. W. D. Lewis, *John Marshall*, in 2 GREAT AMERICAN LAWYERS (W. Lewis ed. 1907). Similarly Beveridge described it as "among the very first of the greatest judicial utterances of all time," while James Bradley Thayer thought "there is nothing so fine as the opinion in McCulloch v. Maryland." A. BEVERIDGE, 4 THE LIFE OF JOHN MARSHALL 289 (1919); J. B. THAYER, JOHN MARSHALL 85 (1901) (1974 republication).

35. To outline this part of the opinion schematically would look like this:
I. Is the Bank constitutional? [2–45]
   A. What is a legitimate federal power? [2–21]
      1. Who created the Union? [7–11]
      2. Why should a court decide? [12–15]
      3. Must a power be enumerated? [16–21]
   B. When is such a power legitimately exercised? [22–37]
      1. Must the means be indispensable? [23–28]
      2. Or must they be rationally related? [29–32]
      3. Does the necessary & proper clause restrain? [33–37]

Based on this rationale, Marshall derives the Great Test, given in [38], and applies it in [39–44].

36. McCulloch v. Maryland, 17 U.S. (4 Wheat) 316, 421 (1819).

37. In 1809 Marshall had avoided taking up the question of the first Bank's constitutionality when he found that a controversy arising from a state statute taxing branches of the Bank lacked the requisite diversity of parties necessary for jurisdiction. See United States v. Deveaux, 9 U.S. (5 Cranch) 61, 85 (1809).

38. It is seldom commented on that Abraham Lincoln drew his phrase "government of the people, by the people, and for the people" from Marshall's language in *McCulloch* that the federal government is "emphatically and truly, a government of the people. . . . Its powers are granted by them, are to be exercised directly on them, and for their benefit." Abraham Lincoln, Gettysburg Address (Nov. 19, 1863), reprinted in LINCOLN ON DEMOCRACY at 308 (M. Cuomo and H. Holzer eds. 1990); McCulloch v. Maryland, 17 U.S. (4 Wheat) 316, 404–05 (1809).

39. 41 U.S. (16 Pet.) 1 (1842).

40. 36 U.S. (11 Pet.) 102, 153o (1837) (Story, J., dissenting).

41. 36 U.S. 420, 583 (1837) (Story, J., dissenting).

42. 1–3 STORY, *supra* note 21.

43. *See* E. BAUER, COMMENTARIES ON THE CONSTITUTION 1790–1860 at 356–57 (1952).

44. 3 COMMENTARIES, at 686.

45. 2 COMMENTARIES, at 25; *see also* 1 COMMENTARIES, at 270–71, 316, 343, 358; 2 COMMENTARIES, at 407; 3 COMMENTARIES, at 757–58.

46. 1 COMMENTARIES, at 436–37; 3 COMMENTARIES, at 37; quoted in J. Powell, *Joseph Story's Commentaries on the Constitution: A Belated Review*, 94 YALE L.J. 1285, 1296 (1985).

47. 1 COMMENTARIES, at 409. This view was given most controversial expression in Story's doctrine of the dormant commerce clause. In *Mayor of New York v. Miln* and elsewhere, Story argued that the mere grant to Congress of the power to regulate interstate commerce displaced the states from making any regulation that Congress could have made. The argument is: when Congress is given the power to regulate a particular market, it puts into place that mixture of regulation and market self-regulation that it considers appropriate. This mixture will change according to circumstances. As a practical matter the congressional scheme—even if Congress chooses to have an entirely deregulated market—is frustrated whenever a state undertakes to apply its own regulations. Therefore, as a practical matter, the mere grant of the commerce power, whether actively engaged or "dormant," displaces the states. This, as Story predicted, is a position far more appealing to a society, such as ours today, that is in the throes of deregulation of national markets than to the agrarian society that envisioned Congress's actions in a more circumscribed context. "And so far is it from being true, that the na-

tional government has by its familiarity become more simple and facile in its machinery and operations that it may be affirmed, that a far more exact and comprehensive knowledge is now necessary to preserve its adjustments, and to carry on its daily operations, than was required, or even dreamed of, at its first institution. . . . And the important changes in the world during its existence have required very many developments of its powers and duties, which could hardly have occurred, as practical truth, to its enlightened founders."

48. 19 U.S. (6 Wheat.) 264 (1821).

49. 14 U.S. (1 Wheat.) 304 (1816).

50. Letter to William Johnson (June 12, 1823), *reprinted in* 9 WRITINGS OF THOMAS JEFFERSON *supra* note 23, at 439, 449.

51. 3 COMMENTARIES, at 143–46.

52. 2 COMMENTARIES, at 84–85.

53. *See* Powell, *supra* note 46, at 1311.

54. H. Black, *The Bill of Rights*, 35 N.Y.U. L. REV. 865, 867 (1960).

55. P. MILLER, THE LIFE OF THE MIND IN AMERICA 290 (1965).

56. F. Douglass, *The Constitution of the United States: Is It Pro-Slavery or Anti-Slavery?* Speech delivered at Glasgow (Mar. 26, 1860), reprinted in 2 THE LIFE AND WRITINGS OF FREDERICK DOUGLASS at 467 (P. Foner ed. 1950).

57. U. S. CONST. art. I, § 2, cl. 3.

58. U. S. CONST. art. I, § 9, cl. 1.

59. U. S. CONST. art. I, § 8, cl. 15.

60. U. S. CONST. art. IV. § 2, cl. 3.

61. DOUGLASS, *supra* note 56, at 472.

62. *Id.* at 473.

63. *Id.*

64. *Id.*

65. *Id.* at 475.

66. *Id.* at 468–69.

67. J. STORY, A DISCOURSE UPON THE LIFE, CHARACTER AND SERVICES OF THE HONORABLE JOHN MARSHALL 695 (1835).

68. DOUGLASS, *supra* note 56, at 468.

69. *Id.* at 469.

70. *Id.* at 477.

71. *Id.* at 478.

72. Matthew Spalding, *George Washington's Farewell Address*, 20 WILSON Q. 65 (1996).

73. This phrase is actually from Thomas Jefferson's First Inaugural Address. Thomas Jefferson, First Inaugural Address, in 1 MESSAGES AND PAPERS OF THE PRESIDENTS 323–24 (J. D. Richardson ed. 1908). It seems to be a feature of canonical works that a misleading, not-quite-correct "quotation" sums up the work in the popular mind, e.g., *McCulloch*'s "the power to tax is the power to destroy."

74. It is characteristic of the state-nation that one of its heroes should say, "I regret that I have but one life to give for my country" (Nathan Hale). Of the nation-state a more typical remark by one of its heroic patriots might be "The object of a soldier is not to die for his country, but to make some other poor bastard die for his" (attrib. to General George S. Patton).

75. A welcome exception is the work of Matthew Spaulding. *See* Spaulding, *supra* note 72. *See also* his recent book with PATRICK GARRITY, A SACRED UNION OF CITIZENS: GEORGE WASHINGTON'S FAREWELL ADDRESS AND THE AMERICAN CHARACTER (1996).

76. George Washington, Farewell Address, para. 16, reprinted in SPAULDING & GARRITY, *supra* note 75, at 175, 180.

77. *Id.* at 183, para. 28.

78. *Id.* at 183, para. 26.

79. *Id.* at 186, para. 39.

80. *Id.* at 175, 188, para. 50.

81. *Id.* at 187, para. 42.

82. *Id.* at 176, para. 6.

83. Lincoln, Gettysburg Address, *supra* note 38.

84. Similarly, parts of the Western canon of literature—Cicero and Tasso come to mind—are more cited than read. In any era, parts of the canon will have fallen into disuse or abandon. How then do we know these remain canonical works and not just the prescriptions of pedants? Because of the progeny of these works in other canonical texts in recent history. This is especially clear with Washington's Farewell Address, which continues to influence the growth and shape of our constitutional ethos and to provide a model for new state papers on that subject.

85. Lincoln, Gettysburg Address, *supra* note 38, at 307.

86. *Id.*

87. *Id.*

88. *Id.*

89. *Id.* at 308.

90. Or in Charles Black's memorable phrase, the question of secession and human rights was settled by "the constitutional experts on Missionary Ridge."

91. Lincoln, Gettysburg Address, supra note 38, at 308.

92. *Id.*

93. T. Fleming, *Abraham Lincoln: Speeches and Writings*, 41 NAT' REV. No. 23, at 38, 40 (1989) (book review).

94. *Cf.* Anthony Lake, *The Need for Engagement*, 5 U.S. DEPARTMENT OF STATE DISPATCH 804 (1994).

95. Because of these words, as Garry Wills has recently observed, "we live in a different America. . . . Up to the Civil War, 'the United States' was invariably a plural noun: 'The United States are a free government.' After Gettysburg, it be-

came a singular: 'The United States is a free government.' This was the result of the whole mode of thinking Lincoln expressed in his acts as well as his words, making union not a mystical hope but a constitutional reality." see G. WILLS, LINCOLN AT GETTYSBURG 145 (1992).

96. Cornerstone Speech at Savannah, Georgia (Mar. 21, 1861), *reprinted in* 4 ENCYCLOPEDIA OF THE CONFEDERACY 1783, 1785–1786 (R. Current ed. 1993).

97. Speaking of the Confederate Constitution, Lincoln wrote, "Our adversaries have adopted some declarations of independence, in which, unlike the good old one, penned by Thomas Jefferson, they omit the words 'all men are created equal.' Why? They have adopted a temporary national constitution, in the preamble of which they omit 'We the People,' and substitute 'We, the deputies of the sovereign and independent states.' Why? Why this deliberate pressing out of view the rights of men and the authority of the People?" A. Lincoln, Message to Congress in a Special Session (July 4, 1861), *in* LINCOLN ON DEMOCRACY, *supra* note 38, at 223.

98. Harry Jaffa, *Abraham Lincoln, in* 3 THE ENCYCLOPEDIA OF THE AMERICAN CONSTITUTION 1164 (L. Levy, K. Karst, D. Mahoney eds. 1986).

99. A. Lincoln, Speech on the Kansas-Nebraska Act (Oct. 16, 1854, Peoria, Ill.), *in* LINCOLN ON DEMOCRACY, *supra* note 38, at 71.

100. *See, e.g.,* the persuasive article by J. Stevenson, *Pericles's Influence on the Gettysburg Address,* 35 MIDWEST Q. No. 3, 338 (1994).

101. THUCYDIDES, HISTORY OF THE PELOPONNESIAN WAR 112 (trans. Henry Dale 1841) (1855 ed.).

102. *See* BOBBITT, *supra* note 24, at 11–22.

103. O. W. HOLMES, THE COMMON LAW 1 (1881).

104. O. W. Holmes, *Book Notice,* 14 AM. L. REV. 233, 233–34 (1880) (reviewing 1 C. C. Langdell, A Selection of Cases on the Law of Contracts (2d ed. 1879)).

105. O.W. Holmes, *The Path of the Law,* 10 HARV. L. REV. 457 (1887).

106. *Id.* at 461.

107. Charles Evans Hughes, Speech before the Elmira, N.Y., Chamber of Commerce (May 3, 1907) *reprinted in* ADDRESSES OF CHARLES EVANS HUGHES 179 ( J. Schurman ed. 1916).

108. Saul Touster, *Holmes's Common Law: A Centennial View,* 51 AM. SCHOLAR 521, 526 (1982).

109. Hugo Black, *The Bill of Rights,* 35 N.Y.U. L. REV. 865 (1960); CHARLES BLACK, STRUCTURE AND RELATIONSHIP IN CONSTITUTIONAL LAW (1969); W. W. CROSSKEY, POLITICS AND THE CONSTITUTION IN THE HISTORY OF THE UNITED STATES (1953); ALEXANDER BICKEL, THE LEAST DANGEROUS BRANCH (1962); Henry Hart, *The Supreme Court Foreword: The Time Chart of the Justices,* 73 HARV. L. REV. 84 (1959); Herbert Wechsler, *Toward Neutral Principles of Constitutional Law,* 73 HARV. L. REV. 1 (1959); RONALD DWORKIN, TAKING RIGHTS SERIOUSLY (1977); Lyndon B. Johnson, Special Message to the American People

(March 15, 1965); Hans Linde, *Judges, Critics, and the Realist Tradition*, 82 YALE L.J. 227 (1972).

110. *Justice Black and the Bill of Rights*, CBS interview with newsmen Martin Agronsky and Eric Sevareid and U.S. Supreme Court Justice Hugo Black (Broadcast Dec. 3, 1968) (sound recording on file at the University of Texas School of Law Media Center).

111. Compare Holmes's "objective" method, *see infra* note 112.

112. "We ask, not what this man meant, but what those words would mean in the mouth of a normal speaker of English, using them in the circumstances in which they were used." C. W. Holmes, *The Theory of Legal Interpretation*, 12 HARV L. REV 417–18 (1899). Crosskey sets this quote out as an epigraph on the title pages to both volumes of his POLITICS AND THE CONSTITUTION IN THE HISTORY OF THE UNITED STATES (2 vols.) (1953).

113. A. BICKEL, THE LEAST DANGEROUS BRANCH 116 (emphasis added) (1962).

114. 297 U.S. 288, 341 (1936).

115. *Atherton Mills v. Johnston*, unpublished opinion Jan. 26, 1920, reprinted in A. BICKEL, THE UNPUBLISHED OPINIONS OF MR. JUSTICE BRANDEIS 5 (1957).

116. J. Frankfurter, *A Note on Advisory Opinions*, 37 HARV. L. REV. 1002 (1924).

117. Bobbitt, *supra* note 24, at (paraphrasing BICKEL, *supra* note 113, at 17).

118. *See* RICHARD MARKOVITS, MATTERS OF PRINCIPLE: LEGITIMATE LEGAL ARGUMENT AND LEGITIMATE CONSTITUTIONAL INTERPRETATION IN THE AMERICAN LIBERAL, RIGHTS-BASED STATE (1999).

119. BOBBITT, *supra* note 24, at 21.

120. R. Dworkin, *The Forum of Principle*, 56 N.Y.U. L. REV. 469, 496 (1981).

121. Lyndon Baines Johnson, Special Message to the American People: The American Promise (Mar. 15, 1965), *in* 1 PUBLIC PAPERS OF THE PRESIDENTS OF THE UNITED STATES: LYNDON B. JOHNSON 1965, at 281 (1966).

122. *Id.* at 281–282.

123. *Id.* at 282.

124. *Id.* at 282–83.

125. *Id.* at 287.

126. *Id.* Of course, some may take issue with my assertion that such ethical claims are "undeniable." *See* W. Van Alstyne, *The Fate of Constitutional Ipse Dixits* (Book Review), 33 J. LEGAL EDUC. 712 (1983).

127. C. BLACK, A NEW BIRTH OF FREEDOM: HUMAN RIGHTS, NAMED AND UNNAMED (1997).

128. J. H. ELY, DEMOCRACY AND DISTRUST : A THEORY OF JUDICIAL REVIEW (1980); B. ACKERMAN, PRIVATE PROPERTY AND THE CONSTITUTION (1977).

129. M. TUSHNET, RED, WHITE AND BLUE (1988) ; J. POWELL, THE MORAL TRADITION OF AMERICAN CONSTITUTIONALISM: A THEOLOGICAL INTERPRETATION (1993); L. TRIBE, CONSTITUTIONAL CHOICES (1985).

130. H. Linde, *E. Pluribus: Constitutional Theory and State Courts*, 18 GA. L. REV. 165 (1984); *First Things First: Rediscovering State's Bills of Rights*, 9 U. BALT. L. REV. 379 (1980).

131. H. Linde, *Judges, Critics and the Realist Tradition*, 82 YALE L.J. 227, 251 (1972); H. Linde, *Due Process of Lawmaking*, 55 NEB. L. REV. 197 (1976).

132. 8 J. Q. ADAMS, MEMOIRS OF JOHN QUINCY ADAMS 308 (diary entry Feb. 1, 1831) (1876).

133. P. Brest, *The Conscientious Legislator's Guide to Constitutional Interpretation*, 27 STAN. L. REV. 585 (1985).

134. SIMON JENKINS, ACCOUNTABLE TO NONE: THE TORY NATIONALIZATION OF BRITAIN 9 (1995).

135. Note, *When May a President Refuse to Enforce the Law?*, 72 TEX. L. REV. 471 (1994) (examining constitutional review performed by the president).

136. J. B. THAYER, LEGAL ESSAYS (1908).

137. Andrew Jackson, Veto Message (July 10, 1832) in 3 A COMPILATION OF THE PAPERS OF THE PRESIDENTS 1789–1897, at 1139, 1144–1145 (J. D. Richardson ed. 1897).

138. *Id.*

139. *See* H. BLOOM, THE WESTERN CANON: THE BOOKS AND SCHOOL OF THE AGES (1994).

# Chapter 13

# The Canon in Constitutional Law

## *Suzanna Sherry*

Forced programming is not so much a way of getting a
message to the public (the public will probably tune
out), as it is a way of showing off power by hoisting flags
on other people's flagpoles.

—Charles Fried

[The canon is] an institutional configuration. It's societal. *Everybody's* in on it.

—Henry Louis Gates, Jr.

Vertigo: are we talking about can(n)ons with two *n*'s or three? A casual
peruser of the literature would be forgiven a momentary bewilderment.
The canons are everywhere under attack. Their detractors view them as
loaded weapons in the service of hierarchy, hegemony, and oppression.
Canons (and anticanons) are one of the weapons of choice in what has
been labeled "the culture wars": the struggle for control of the hearts and
minds of the educational system of the United States, and ultimately of
its legal and political apparatus. To write an essay prescribing "the canon
in constitutional law" is to take sides in the war, and it would be disingenuous to do so without justifying that choice. I cannot define my canon
until I defend its right to exist.

## I. Defending the Canon

In the next section, I will suggest a particular canon for constitutional
law. It is only a suggestion, and even as a suggestion it leaves individual

teachers with many choices. As Amy Gutmann has so aptly observed, disagreement over the *content* of a canon is neither surprising nor troubling: with so many works from which to choose, contemporary canon builders are bound to quibble over details.[1] But the attack on canons is more insidious than simply a claim that they canonize the wrong works. That kind of attack is always fair, and deserves a considered response of the sort I try to give in section 2. For example, I will try to argue that Sanford Levinson is right to call for a greater recognition of history, including more discussion of slavery cases, but wrong to abandon *Marbury v. Madison.*[2]

The attack on the canon is also more than simply a claim that the process by which works are selected for inclusion in the canon is biased by race and gender, although opponents of the canon do make such a claim. I don't agree that the selection process is biased. Indeed, I would argue that the canonization process is so unlike what we normally think of as a "selection process" that attributing bias—which suggests a deliberateness not present in the canonization process—is fundamentally mistaken.[3] It is, as Henry Louis Gates remarks in the quotation with which I began this essay, a societal project.[4] The claim of bias, however, is not my main concern in this essay, primarily because it is only a minor part of the argument against the canon.

The contemporary attack on the canon is, at base, one manifestation of the current infatuation with postmodernism, especially radical social constructionism.[5] Radical social constructionism contends that reality is socially constructed and that all judgments or choices are therefore wholly culturally contingent. There can be no objective standards of knowledge, or merit, or judgment, or morality. All such standards are necessarily the product of our current system of oppression, whereby the dominant class—usually described as straight white males—maintains its hegemony. Postmodernists "view common standards as masks for the will to political power of dominant, hegemonic groups."[6]

Lest the reader find this summary to be an implausible exaggeration, I offer a few examples from the legal academy. Deborah Rhode states unequivocally that "knowledge is socially constructed rather than objectively determined," and Catharine MacKinnon rejects standard scientific norms for testing hypotheses as "a specifically male approach to knowledge." Richard Delgado rejects the primacy of "linear, rationalistic thought," and Lucinda Finley condemns "[r]ationality, abstraction [and] a preference for statistical and empirical proofs" as inherently male. "Objectivity" itself is "by definition male." All "normative orderings . . . reflect the views of the powerful," and all "[s]tandards are nothing more than structured preferences" of the powerful. Judgments of merit are merely "white people's affirmative action." Nor is the rejection of objectivity confined to the radical left: Frederick Gedicks, defending the role of religion in political life, suggests that "the allocation of creationism to the marginalized world of subjectivity, and evolution to the privileged world of objectivity, is merely the exercise of social power rather than a natural, value-neutral distinction."[7]

If there can be no judgments apart from those dictated by the social status of the judge, if all knowledge is created by, and used to perpetuate, hierarchies of oppression, then it is a foregone conclusion that canons are weapons of war. To specify "an authoritative list of books" or "a sanctioned or accepted group or body of related works"—two of the multiple definitions of "canon" in my office dictionary—is perforce to dictate the content of knowledge and to mistake the subjective views of the powerful for objective and universal knowledge.[8] Thus postmodernist attacks on how we determine what counts as knowledge necessarily spill over into questions about the content of our canons. Most postmodernists do not explicitly challenge the constitutional law canon.[9] Nevertheless, their position that knowledge is socially constructed and can never be objective leads naturally to a conclusion that the canon is just another means by which the powerful perpetuate their power.

What would it mean to take seriously this charge that the canon is purely an exercise of political power? As many others have noted, the postmodernist claim both endangers the university as a unique haven for knowledge and ultimately deconstructs itself.[10] It endangers the university because it negates the university's very purpose of "fostering knowledge, understanding, intellectual dialogue, and the pursuit of reasoned argument in the many directions that it may lead."[11] The claim that the canon is about power rather than about knowledge, understanding, and judgment is a profoundly anti-intellectual stance, incompatible with the underpinnings of the modern university.[12] Indeed, why have universities at all, since politics can be practiced more easily and directly in other milieux? (The answer for the postmodernists, I think, is that their ideas will not win them power in the larger world, but only in the university, where academics focused on objectivity and knowledge can be taken unawares by the sudden onslaught of politically motivated postmodernists.) That universities are about fostering knowledge rather than about politics is a central constitutive rule of the system of universities, and changing that rule would change universities in the same way that counting any physical knocking down of the king as a checkmate would change the game of chess.[13]

Even if we were to accept the new vision of a university inherent in the postmodernist demands, there is another problem. The postmodernists do not simply attack the existing canon; they often suggest substitutes and alterations. But they cannot simultaneously claim that canons are power *and* that there are good reasons to include in the canon the particular materials they favor. If the old canons are merely the exercise of power, so is the postmodernist canon. It is an attempt, as the opening quotation from Charles Fried suggests,[14] to force others to salute the postmodernist flag. It precludes the kind of debate I try to engage in section 2, in which I ask why certain materials should or should not be included in the canon. For postmodernists, the answer to such questions can only be that particular canon choices are good politics: the choice to include or exclude affirms or discredits certain power relations. In these circumstances, discussion about what well-educated lawyers simply ought to know seems pointless.

The postmodernist attempt to change the canon is also self-defeating. By demanding inclusion as a matter of power rather than as a matter of intrinsic worth (which postmodernists deny can exist), they are making an argument that "ultimately ends in contempt for the very practice of justification, for the vocabulary of critical appreciation and for anything that could serve as a basis for authentic respect."[15] In destroying the legitimacy of the canon, the postmodernists necessarily defeat themselves, because their own canon will be held in equal contempt. And the postmodernists can, in any case, give no reasons for altering the canon, since reasons presuppose objective standards of knowledge and judgment. Thus their demands for inclusion are internally contradictory: "After all, if there is no such thing as [objective knowledge], then the present arrangement is no worse than any alternative; 'worse' presupposes a standard."[16]

There is a cruel irony in the postmodern reduction of knowledge and objectivity to politics. Postmodernism, by urging the oppressed to reject all current knowledge and standards as motivated by bias, may pose an even greater danger to the oppressed than to the powerful. Those who do not assimilate the accumulated knowledge of their society—whether it is the literary canon or the mores of behavior—will not be able to succeed in that society. Richard Bernstein eloquently describes the problem:

> What if the ideas coded in multiculturalism do not so much prepare people for real life as foster illusions about it, or, worse, provide a pretext for repudiating the values and behaviors that have traditionally led to success, such as objectivity and achievement, on the grounds that they are the values of the despised Eurocentric group?
>
> The rich and advantaged of our society will survive even if they are taught to believe something different. But to teach the poor and the disadvantaged that they can ignore the standards and modes of behavior that have always made for success in American life is more than mere silliness. It is a lie.[17]

The irony of all this is that it is often the advantaged imposing the new canon on the disadvantaged. As Richard Rodriguez puts it: "Now the American university is dismantling the American canon in my name. In the name of my father, in the name of Chinese grocers and fry-cooks and dentists, the American university disregards the Judeo-Christian foundation of the American narrative. The white university never asked my father whether or not his son should read Milton. . . ."[18]

In the end, the postmodernists cannot mean what they say. They act as if the canon is important—else why would they want to be included? They assume that some works merit inclusion in the canon, thus implicitly accepting that there are some valid standards for judgment. Their demands are motivated by a desire to gain respect for currently excluded works, and yet respect presupposes standards independent of power. They are, as Charles Fried describes proponents of speech codes who claim to be silenced by hate speech, "like annoying children who whine at their parents, 'you're not listening to me,' when what they mean is 'however much I go on, you don't think I'm right.'"[19] As I often tell my six-year-old daughter, whining will get you nowhere (except perhaps multiple publications and endowed chairs at prestigious universities).

The postmodernist critique fails to take into account what John Searle has called "institutional facts." Institutional facts are socially created but nevertheless objectively true: that a certain piece of paper is money does (or does not, depending on the particular piece of paper to which I refer) correspond to an external reality, but that reality is contingent rather than necessary. As Searle puts it, "Facts about money can be epistemically objective even if the existence of money is socially constructed, and, therefore, to that extent, ontologically subjective."[20] Searle makes several important points about institutional facts: institutional facts are collective and power-conferring, and they permeate our social lives. The workings and contours of the university and the canon are examples of institutional facts, and the postmodernist critique implicates several misconceptions about such facts. In arguing against canonicity, postmodernists mistakenly assume both that the canon is inherently epistemically subjective—which, as Searle's example of money shows, is not necessarily true—and that it is imposed as a matter of power and therefore subject to alteration by the exercise of power. Searle's intricate dissection of social facts reveals that while canonization *imparts* power (it gives a particular work more authority than it had before), canonization is not itself an exercise of power but rather a continuing collective acknowledgment of a status. That collective intentionality is a fundamental feature of human culture. It will not disappear, and it cannot be commanded.

This is not to suggest that canons can or should remain unchanging. The less radical critiques of canonicity focus on the need for continuing change and adaptation. Amy Gutmann, for example, quotes Emerson: "'Each age,' Emerson concludes, 'must write its own books.' Why? Because well-educated, open-minded people and liberal democratic citizens must think for themselves."[21] Taken as a moderate suggestion that canons cannot remain unchanged, this statement is unexceptionable. The very nature of a canon—the creation of accumulated societal judgments—mandates incremental change. Thus, in defending the canon from postmodernist charges that it merely reflects current hierarchies, I do not mean to immunize it from change. Nevertheless, the existing canon should always form the starting point, because it presumptively represents accumulated wisdom.

It seems particularly foolish for postmodernists to suggest that existing legal canons reflect only politics, and thus deserve little respect. As Balkin and Levinson note in their contribution to this volume, there are vast differences between law and literature.[22] However valid constant regeneration may be with regard to the literary canon, it is close to nonsensical in the context of the law. American law rests on a foundation several centuries deep, and we cannot begin to understand the modern architecture of law without examining that foundation. That foundation is, and must be, our canon. We may tinker with the canon at the margins, varying the modern frills, the illustrative cases, and the topical focus. But the postmodern critique of the canon as merely an exercise of power severs our connection with the past, and law then loses any possibility of being an autonomous discipline: law becomes solely politics by other means. The insights of the legal realists and their intellectual successors notwithstanding, law is not wholly political. The common law method, the doctrine of stare decisis, and the need to explain decisions in a way that integrates them with the past all provide law with the ability to rise above politics and, in Alexander Bickel's memorable words, "to appeal to men's better natures, to call forth their aspirations, which may have been forgotten in the moment's hue and cry."[23] Politics produced Ronald Reagan, one of the most conservative Republican presidents in this century, but law produced *Casey*, in which two Reagan appointees (as well as one Bush appointee) upheld abortion rights in the face of strong conservative opposition. Politics produced a federal law banning flag burning, enacted nearly unanimously by the House and Senate, but law struck it down. We cannot eliminate politics from law altogether, but a system of law that is purely political will quickly lose all legitimacy— as well it should.

There is another difference between literature and law that makes postmodernism particularly difficult to translate from the one to the other. An English major who reads Rigoberta Menchu[24] instead of Shakespeare—especially at the undergraduate level—may be poorly educated, but she will be able to function adequately as a holder of a degree in English. A lawyer who reads Roberto Unger instead of John Marshall, however, is unlikely to be able to function as a lawyer. Marshall, as lawyer, politician, and judge, instantiated the complex transformation from English common law to American constitutional law that has subsequently served as a foundation for our constitutional jurisprudence.[25] To probe Marshall's opinions is to explore the tensions, ambiguities, and contradictions inherent in a federal constitutional democracy. Indeed, I have often thought that it would be an interesting experiment to teach a basic introduction to constitutional law using only Marshall opinions. We can find in those opinions explorations of most, if not all, of the metaquestions that dominate constitutional law: about methods of constitutional interpretation, about the precarious balance between majoritarianism and tyranny, about the role of legislative intent and the ever-present fear of legislative bias.

To a great extent, the basic shape of our canon is mandated by what lawyers will need to know. A lawyer who does not understand how judges interpret wills or contracts will not be able to write either effectively, and one who cannot interpret and apply case law will be a poor advisor and a worse litigator. Even at the level of specifics, American lawyers need to have read certain cases. For example, some fringe groups like the Freemen have been establishing their own judicial system, apparently encouraged by a belief that in 1938 the Supreme Court subverted the original constitutional system by abolishing "common law courts."[26] Only a lawyer who has read and understood *Erie Railroad v. Tompkins*[27] can pierce the maze of misunderstandings underlying this belief. Any well-educated lawyer should be able to read or hear the claim about the abolition of "common law courts," with its telltale date, and be able to straighten out nonlegally trained clients, journalists, or others.

In law, then, a canon is not only defensible but necessary. It is unfortunate that we have to waste so much time—and kill so many trees—debating this basic point, for the much more interesting question is what belongs in that canon.

## II. Defining the Canon

There are two ways of approaching the question of the canon in constitutional law, one normative and one purely descriptive. A list of cases that appear prominently in the leading casebooks might be interesting, but it is of limited value.[28] A normative specification of the contents of the canon is likely to spark a much more interesting discussion, and that, therefore, is the approach I take.

To define the canon is to specify the basic and essential reading materials for students in constitutional law. But, as Balkin and Levinson point out in their contribution to this volume, we cannot do that without asking what it is that we mean our canon to convey. And this, in turn, requires us to explore our duties to our students. Who are these law students who have temporarily been placed in our charge? They are, first and most broadly, citizens of the United States (most of them, anyway). They will someday be practicing lawyers, and many of them will assume formal or informal positions of leadership. Our goal—indeed our duty— is to help them to become the best citizens, lawyers, and leaders they can be. These three related but independent roles each contribute to shaping our canon.

As Balkin and Levinson also note in their essay, sometimes these goals can conflict. These conflicts, as well as the need to specify a basic constitutional canon at all, arise largely because of time pressures. As Levinson has said elsewhere, "[T]here is neither time nor paper enough to include everything that one might legitimately want to cover. Choices, almost none of them easy, must inevitably be made."[29] In trying to describe the minimal material that in my view *must* be taught, I do not mean to exclude anything else a particular teacher might find relevant. The constitutional canon need not—and probably should not—fill the entire constitutional law course. The constitutional canon I describe in this essay begins with a core of key materials, but it also leaves room for many choices.

How, then, do we specify even the minimal key materials? As others have noted, the fact that we are training lawyers imposes some constraints on our canon.[30] Not only are there some things that lawyers simply must know, but lawyers' primary tools of the trade are certain kinds of materials: statutes, cases, and related texts. A lawyer who relies in her brief (or in her drafting of a contract or a public offering) solely on Shakespeare, or even on an article in the *Harvard Law Review*, is not likely to serve her client very well. With a limited amount of time and an externally imposed need to include cases in the canon, then, it makes sense to make them the centerpiece. The decisions of the Supreme Court, in particular, provide the most information in the fewest number of cases, since those decisions must be the starting point for all other cases in constitutional law. Finally, the set of potentially useful supplemental materials is so much vaster than the set of potentially useful Supreme Court cases that it makes little sense to try to specify canonical instances of the former. Thus, in the description that follows, I begin with canonical Supreme Court cases and—with one categorical exception—only sketch the possibility of further embellishment with other texts. Moreover, adhering to the conventional formulation of the subject matter of constitutional law courses, I eschew any discussion of the constitutional rights of criminal defendants or the niceties of federal jurisdiction.

As citizens, and particularly as well-educated citizens, our students should know something about the history of their country. They should understand its formative moments and its foundational struggles. No constitutionally literate citizen can ignore the great cases that established fundamental principles and engendered nation-threatening controversy: *Marbury, McCulloch, Dred Scott, Plessy, Abrams* (or *Whitney*), *Brown*, and *Roe*.[31] Indeed, all of constitutional law might be taught out of any one of these cases. Each has implications for methods of constitutional interpretation, for structuring a constitutional democracy, for protecting individual rights. Each also captures, with the misleading precision possible only in the judicial snapshot we call a case, the social and political undercurrents of its particular era. Taught without embellishment, the cases provide our students with at least a passing knowledge of basic American history. Supplemented with historical, political, social, or moral discussion, they can provide a framework for serious thought about our decidedly mixed heritage.

It is a type of knowledge that many of our students, unfortunately, do not acquire as undergraduates. In the fall of 1995, the University of Minnesota gave its entering students a short quiz on American history and civics. Large numbers of students did not know what Reconstruction was, could not define "Jim Crow," and could not name two Civil War battles. (In addition to the many who listed various Revolutionary War battles, two students included the Battle of the Bulge and two named Waterloo.) A significant minority could not name four American presidents who served before 1900. (And some listed those who never served, including Hamilton, Franklin, Irving, Hale, Pope, Samuel Adams, "Washington's son," and Adam Smith.) Twenty percent of the class thought the Constitution had been adopted in 1776; answers ranged from 1765 to 1889. The foundational cases, always significant for explaining our legal history and traditions, must now also become vehicles for conveying more basic knowledge.

Then there are the cases that, while not as crucial historically, set the framework for debates that continue today, and are therefore necessary for a full understanding of modern constitutional doctrine: the reach of the Constitution itself is explored in *Shelley* and *The Civil Rights Cases;* the abortion controversy is incomprehensible without *Lochner* and *Griswold;* and interbranch disputes are still governed, at base, by the *Steel Seizure Case* (all the rest is commentary).[32] Passing fads are illuminating too, to the extent that they illustrate the recurrent upheavals in even our most basic constitutional principles. The perorations in the slavery cases, the commerce clause and Tenth Amendment cases, the substantive due process cases, or the free speech cases can all serve as reminders that the road has been—and will continue to be—less than smooth, and that we are not always headed in the right direction.

Finally, as citizens, our students will be living in a diverse and heterogenous society. They will sorely need the virtues of tolerance, justice, and a concern for others that allow such a society to function. Here it is difficult to know how best to teach them the value of such virtues. Do we offer conspicuous failures? Teach *DeShaney, Buck, Abrams, Korematsu,* and *Bowers,* in addition to *Dred Scott* and *Plessy.*[33] Tell them about the conditions in the mines along with *Carter Coal*, read them the newspapers in *Near*, and don't let *Brown* rest on its sanitized footnote.[34] Do we instead give them the hard cases, where personal sympathies might be at war with broader principles of democratic constitutionalism, and make them struggle with the resulting dissonance? Give them *R.A.V.*, or any affirmative action case, or the abortion funding and parochial school funding cases (to catch both sides of the political spectrum).[35] Do we offer them examples worthy of emulation? My favorites include *Barnette, Loving, Plyler*, Brandeis's concurrence in *Whitney*, and Harlan's dissent in *Poe v. Ullman*, but there are, fortunately, a wealth of other choices.[36]

Our duty to our students as future lawyers is more specific, but in many ways less important. Few of them will actually practice constitutional law, and in any case the basic doctrines are less complex than in many other subjects. Three tiers, five classes, a few balancing tests, and a basic distinction between intended and unintended consequences, and voila! you're a relatively competent constitutional lawyer. (This is not to minimize the difficulty of conveying these concepts to the students, but compared with the rule against perpetuities or the vagaries of the *M'Naughton* rule these doctrines are relatively straightforward and intelligible.) How many of our students will really need to know that discrimination based on alienage is treated differently depending on whether it is enacted by the state or federal government and whether it implicates a vital state function? And, for those few who do, learning the basics of class-based tiers of scrutiny will enable them to master the alienage cases with little difficulty.

Constitutional law, like many other core courses, is important for training future lawyers primarily for the skills it imparts rather than the specific doctrines we teach. Here again the canon can be quite flexible. Give them opinions that are well argued and well written to hone their skills of expression. Give them opinions that are dense and difficult to understand to improve their ability to comprehend legal materials. Give them opinions that rest on fallacies and weak arguments, or that are internally contradictory, to strengthen their critical skills. Again, any number of cases can serve these purposes well (although those in the first category are in the shortest supply).[37]

Finally, there is a small category of nonjudicial constitutional works with which all American lawyers should have a passing familiarity. An eighteenth-century American lawyer who had not read Blackstone, or a nineteenth-century American lawyer unfamiliar with Story, or later Kent, or later still Cooley, would have been considered illiterate and unprepared to practice law, however technically skilled. The suggestion that such a category exists—or should exist—at the end of the twentieth century is, of course, the most vulnerable to the attacks on canonicity. For the works in this category are most like Shakespeare or Chaucer: my argument is that a lawyer unfamiliar with them is poorly educated, despite their lack of utility in day to day legal practice. Nonetheless, ask yourself whether you would be annoyed if a student law review editor asked for a detailed citation for a passing reference to one of these works, or if you would think less of a practicing lawyer who had no inkling of what you were talking about if you mentioned the work in casual conversation.

The list of extrajudicial canonical works in constitutional law is not long, in part because of how canons are formed. These are all works that have withstood the test of time, that are still central to modern discussions. They are, in Gates's words, "indispensable to an understanding of the shape, and shaping, of the [American legal] tradition."[38] I can think of only four that fit these rather stringent qualifications: James Madison, Alexander Hamilton, and John Jay, *The Federalist Papers*; Alexander Bickel, *The Least Dangerous Branch*; Alexander Meiklejohn, *Free Speech and Its Relation to Self-Government*; and Herbert Wechsler, "Toward Neutral Principles in Constitutional Law."[39] It is no coincidence that the latest of the four was first published more than thirty years ago, and that all of the authors are dead. (And it is not simply because by listing only works by these few authors, I avoid offending any friends I might leave out!) By rejecting the radical argument that canons are about power, I am necessarily committed to believing that they are formed by accretion and acclamation. That process takes time. It might be interesting to speculate about which more recent works will eventually enter the canon, but it cannot be more than speculation.[40]

And what about preparing our constitutional law students to be future leaders? Here we face an interesting dilemma: How are we to know what problems leaders will confront ten or twenty or more years into the future? Questions of constitutional law that are problematic now may be entirely uncontroversial twenty years from now. For example, the question of homosexual rights is currently a hot topic in constitutional law: despite the absence of a single Supreme Court case, one casebook allotted the topic 34 pages in its 212-page 1995 supplement, more than it allotted to affirmative action, voting rights, or congressional power under the commerce clause, each of which included a major Supreme Court case in the time period covered by the supplement.[41] Nevertheless, my guess is that within twenty years this will become a nonissue. Leaders of 2016, having diligently examined the question of homosexual rights in law school, will have no more use for their knowledge than they would have for knowledge of the law of slavery—not the history or the morality or the constitutionality of slavery, but the legal doctrines governing sale, manumission, and the like. Studying cases on homosexual rights may serve other purposes, including the general purpose of providing future leaders with the tools to grapple with difficult and controversial moral questions. *Bowers v. Hardwick* will always represent a moral failure in the same way that *Plessy v. Ferguson* does, and will therefore remain part of the canon. But the exact contours of the current doctrinal disputes— such as the Hawaii state decision on gay marriage, and cases on the military's "don't ask/don't tell" policy, both of which were included in the supplement—will not be relevant.

Since particular topics and cases, however irrelevant they may be doctrinally to future leadership, may be useful in other ways, there is no real harm in including them in the canon (as long as they do not displace more important cases). The more difficult task is to predict what issues, quiescent now, might be vital for leaders of the future to have mastered. Again, an example might illustrate my point. By the 1970s, the core principle of freedom of speech—specifically, the notion that the government may not prohibit speech simply because it is unpopular or offensive— had become so well settled that it was almost dull. In the Supreme Court, free speech cases were eclipsed by the exciting developments in substantive due process and equal protection law.[42] Even within the context of the First Amendment, jurists and law professors alike focused their attention on such difficult questions as government subsidies, special contexts, and other issues beyond the basic doctrine. One casebook, first published in 1975 and meant as a text for an introductory constitutional law course, left out any discussion of the First Amendment entirely.[43] Another, more comprehensive in scope, devoted 100 pages to the core concept, and 300 to less central but presumably more interesting free speech issues.[44] We are experiencing the fallout from that complacency two decades later, as legislators and law professors—*law professors!*—try to censor speech they don't like.

In the absence of a crystal ball, how should we best guard against such lapses? Here is where the whole idea of canonicity becomes especially useful. Because the canon grows and changes only incrementally, it is less susceptible to the personal interests of those who write (and teach) the casebooks. As anyone who has ever prepared a subsequent edition of a casebook knows, cases pass out of the canon only after they have long outlived their usefulness. The idea of a canon produces a natural disinclination toward sudden change, which provides a safeguard against the transient whims of any single generation of lawyers and law teachers. If we approach the canon with presumptive respect but not uncritical acceptance, we can avoid both the chaos that comes from too much change for its own sake and the stagnation that accompanies an overly tenacious adherence to tradition. A canon, with its built-in responsiveness to incremental change, is a good place to start.

## III. The Content of Our Canons

Astute readers will notice that every work in my canon is authored by a white male. Women and people of color appear only as passive subjects. This is not deliberate, but it cannot go unremarked. Much of the criticism of the legal canon—especially the call to change rather than to abandon the canon—comes from those who object to its white male character.[45] Indeed, radical feminists and critical race theorists are at the forefront of the postmodern movement in law generally: they are, for example, leading the charge against concepts such as "merit" and "reason." According to these postmodernists, the standards that lead to canonization—as well as to more mundane decisions on hiring, tenure, reading recommendations, and the like—are "white people's affirmative action. . . . A way of keeping their own deficiencies neatly hidden while assuring only people like them get in."[46] My all-white, all-male canon is just another example of the hidden conspiracy that masquerades as standards of judgment.

The simplest response is to return to my earlier descriptions of how works get into the constitutional canon. The primary source of the canon is opinions by the Supreme Court of the United States, which was all-white for 178 and all-male for 192 of its 207 years. Only four of its 107 justices have not been white males—and two of those might be the two least influential justices on the current Court.[47] It should thus come as no surprise that a limited selection of twenty-four cases includes none authored by those four.[48] The probability of a white male canon increases when we recognize that older cases are more likely to be foundational, thus weighting the canon more heavily toward the period during which there were no female justices or justices of color. Similarly, nonjudicial works enter the canon only over time, and the presence of significant numbers of women and people of color in positions to write about law is a relatively recent phenomenon. Immediate representation of diverse groups in the canon can be achieved only by fiat; as I explained earlier, canonization by command deprives the canon of any legitimacy, thus defeating the very purpose for including a work in the canon.

Of course, the postmodernists often disagree that Supreme Court cases should form the centerpiece of the constitutional canon, or that works by legal academics should provide the primary supplemental material. This quarrel ultimately derives from the basic social constructionist argument that our reliance on certain categories of works—such as those by Supreme Court justices and legal academics—is merely an exercise of social power. Again, social constructionism is at the heart of the critique of the canon.

The response that opinions of the Supreme Court, at least, derive their significance—and thus their place in the canon—from their socially created power is not very helpful. First, of course, to the extent that we are educating lawyers, we are necessarily a part of the same reality (socially constructed or not) that gives the Supreme Court its authority. Unless the social constructionists are suggesting that we ought not to educate lawyers—those who will work within, study, and perhaps modify *our* legal system—but instead ought to produce revolutionaries who will topple that legal system, it seems to me irrelevant whether or not the Supreme Court's power is socially constructed. Second, to say that the Supreme Court's authority is socially constructed has little explanatory power: *everything*, except what Searle calls "brute facts" (such as the existence, height, and weather conditions of Mt. Everest), is socially constructed in the sense that it depends for its existence on human perceptions and beliefs. That does not make the fact that the Supreme Court *does* have power any less objectively true, nor does it detract from the significance of their opinions. Thus the same sort of weaknesses that beset the postmodernist critique of canonicity also undermine any argument based on the Supreme Court as a socially constructed institution.

That our students ought to begin with Supreme Court opinions does not, of course, tell us what else they should read. The Supreme Court, as Justice Jackson once pointed out, is infallible only because it is final;[49] since the Court is not inherently infallible, we should equip our students with the tools they need to criticize—and perhaps ultimately to change—wrongheaded decisions. But there is no need for, and indeed potentially great danger from, a canonical set of materials from which to launch challenges. Thoughtful use of any materials that develop our students' critical skills, including those otherwise in the canon and additional assignments of each individual teacher's choosing, will enable them to approach Supreme Court decisions with appropriate skepticism. Unlike (at least some) Supreme Court opinions, which are significant regardless of their persuasiveness or morality, attacks on the Court vary in importance. The relative weight to assign to works of critical race theory, or law and economics, or even classic critiques such as those of Frederick Douglass, William Lloyd Garrison, or John Calhoun, is a matter of personal choice, not canonicity. Specifying a canon for criticizing the Court risks turning what should be an exercise of critical faculties into a prescription of orthodoxy.

There is, finally, one last response to the complaint that the canon is insufficiently diverse. I noted earlier that it is primarily—although not exclusively—radical feminists and critical race theorists who have launched the postmodern attack on the legal canon. Does this observation tell us anything useful? Christopher Wonnell has speculated that it does. He suggests that these two groups of scholars have gravitated toward postmodernism for a particular reason: affirmative action, by applying different sets of standards to different populations, creates a sort of cognitive dissonance that can be resolved only by criticizing the very idea of standards.[50] To be hired to provide "diversity," and then to be judged instead by whether one produces traditional scholarship, is profoundly disturbing. Social constructionism, with its insistence that the standards of judgment are arbitrary, is inevitably psychologically comforting.

If this explanation is accurate, what should we make of the postmodernist disputes over the canon? It might, perhaps, make us more sympathetic toward the psychological discomfort of the postmodernists, but it should make us less willing to accept their claims on the merits. Like a patient parent with a whining and obviously unhappy child, perhaps we can find a way to assuage the underlying concerns without giving credence to the whining itself. Maybe we should start talking seriously about the costs and benefits of affirmative action, instead of parroting catchwords like "diversity" and "reverse discrimination."[51] Maybe we should continue to talk about the purposes of legal scholarship—trying to avoid recriminations, dogmatism, and irresponsible charges of racism or sexism. But we should stop blaming the canon for injuries and explosions it has little or nothing to do with.

## NOTES

I thank Jack Balkin, Jim Chen, Paul Edelman, Dan Farber, Sandy Levinson, and Mike Paulsen for their helpful suggestions. Kaitlin Hallett, Minnesota J.D. 1998, provided excellent research assistance.

1. Amy Gutmann, *Introduction, in* MULTICULTURALISM: EXAMINING THE POLITICS OF RECOGNITION 3, 21 (Charles Taylor et al. eds. 1994).

2. On slavery, *see* Sanford Levinson, *Slavery in the Canon of Constitutional Law*, 68 CHI.-KENT L. REV. 1087 (1993). On *Marbury, see* J. M. Balkin & Sanford Levinson, *Constitutional Canons and Constitutional Thought*, in this volume, note 36.

3. My argument here is analogous to Robert Post's suggestion that "self-determination . . . is something that happens within public discourse; there is no external Archimedean point from which it can be compelled or its outcome anticipated." Robert Post, *Meiklejohn's Mistake: Individual Autonomy and the Reform of Public Discourse*, 64 U. COLO. L. REV. 1109, 1119 (1993). Similarly, "canonization" occurs on an ongoing basis, and no set list of canonical works is likely to be successfully imposed. Any list of such works is more in the nature of a recognition than a specification of canonical status.

4. HENRY LOUIS GATES, JR., LOOSE CANONS: NOTES ON THE CULTURE WARS 6 (1992).

5. *See* Francis J. Mootz III, *Legal Classics: After Deconstructing the Legal Canon*, 72 N.C.L. REV. 977, 981 (1994).

6. Gutmann, *supra* note 4, at 18.

7. The quotations in this paragraph are taken from the following articles: Deborah L. Rhode, *Missing Questions: Feminist Perspectives on Legal Education*, 45 STAN. L. REV. 1547, 1555 (1993); CATHARINE A. MACKINNON, FEMINISM UNMODIFIED: DISCOURSES ON LIFE AND LAW 54 (1987); Richard Delgado, *Rodrigo's Tenth Chronicle: Merit and Affirmative Action*, 83 GEO. L.J. 1711, 1721 (1995); Lucinda M. Finley, *Breaking Women's Silence in Law: The Dilemma of the Gendered Nature of Legal Reasoning*, 64 NOTRE DAME L. REV. 886, 893 (1989); A. W. Phinney, *Feminism, Epistemology and the Rhetoric of Law: Reading Bowen v. Gilliard*, 12 HARV. WOMEN'S L.J. 151, 177 (1989); Richard Delgado, *Norms and Normal Science: Toward a Critique of Normativity in Legal Thought*, 139 U. PA. L. REV. 933, 951 (1991); PATRICIA J. WILLIAMS, THE ALCHEMY OF RACE AND RIGHTS 103 (1991); Richard Delgado, *Rodrigo's Chronicle*, 101 YALE L.J. 1357, 1364 (1992); Frederick M. Gedicks, *Public Life and Hostility to Religion*, 78 VA. L. REV. 671, 686 (1992). For a survey of the literature, including other examples, *see* Suzanna Sherry, *The Sleep of Reason*, 84 GEO. L.J. 453, 457–64 (1996); Daniel A. Farber &

Suzanna Sherry, *Is the Radical Critique of Merit Anti-Semitic?* 83 Calif. L. Rev. 853 (1995).

Catharine MacKinnon is a slightly different breed of postmodernist (indeed, she denies being a postmodernist at all). She believes in the possibility of objective knowledge—and even claims to *have* objective knowledge—but argues that everything we *think* we know is in fact the product of male dominance. For purposes of attacks on the canon, however, her argument is analogous to the argument that knowledge is simply raw power translated into silkier language.

8. The dictionary I keep in my office happens to be *Merriam Webster's Collegiate Dictionary*, Tenth Edition (1993), and one of the other definitions it lists further illuminates the problems that radical social constructionists have with canons: "a criterion or standard of judgment."

9. *But see* Mary Becker, *Obscuring the Struggle: Sex Discrimination, Social Security, and Stone, Seidman, Sunstein & Tushnet's Constitutional Law*, 89 Colum. L. Rev. 264 (1989). Some postmodernists do seem to have a disdain for constitutional doctrine. *See, e.g.*, Robert A. Williams, Jr., *Vampires Anonymous and Critical Race Practice*, 95 Mich. L. Rev. 741 (1997); Richard Delgado, *Rodrigo's Thirteenth Chronicle: Legal Formalism and Law's Discontents*, 95 Mich. L. Rev. 1105 (1997).

10. Many of the arguments I make in this paragraph have been previously made. *See* Charles Taylor, *The Politics of Recognition, in* Taylor, *supra* note 1; Gutmann, *supra* note 1, at 18–21. Charles Fried, *The New First Amendment Jurisprudence: A Threat to Liberty*, 59 U. Chi. L. Rev. 225 (1992).

11. Gutmann, *supra* note 1, at 20.

12. For reviews of those underpinnings, *see, e.g.*, Neil W. Hamilton, Zealotry and Academic Freedom: A Legal and Historical Perspective (1995); J. Peter Byrne, *Academic Freedom: "A Special Concern of the First Amendment,"* 99 Yale L.J. 251, 269–72 (1989). For a similar sentiment, *see* Larry Laudan, Science and Relativism (1990) ("The displacement of the idea that facts and evidence matter by the idea that everything boils down to subjective interests and perspectives is—second only to American political campaigns—the most prominent and pernicious manifestation of anti-intellectualism in our time").

13. *See* John R. Searle, Speech Acts: An Essay in the Philosophy of Language 33–35 (1969).

14. Fried, *supra* note 10, at 253.

15. Susan Wolf, *Comment, in* Taylor, *supra* note 1, at 75, 78. *See also* Taylor, *supra* note 10, at 69–70 (describing inclusion on postmodernist terms as "unsufferable patronizing" and "breathtaking condescension").

16. Alan R. Madry, *Analytic Deconstructionism? The Intellectual Voyeurism of Anthony D'Amato*, 63 Fordham L. Rev. 1033, 1036 (1995).

17. Richard Bernstein, Dictatorship of Virtue: Multiculturalism and the Battle for America's Future 10–11 (1994).

18. RICHARD RODRIGUEZ, DAYS OF OBLIGATION: AN ARGUMENT WITH MY MEXICAN FATHER 171 (1992).

19. Fried, *supra* note 10, at 252.

20. JOHN R. SEARLE, THE CONSTRUCTION OF SOCIAL REALITY 190 (1995). The ideas in the rest of this paragraph are also taken directly from Searle's excellent book.

21. Gutmann, *supra* note 1, at 17 (footnote omitted) (quoting Ralph Waldo Emerson, *The American Scholar, in* SELECTED ESSAYS, Larzer Ziff ed., at 87 (1982)).

22. Balkin & Levinson, *Constitutional Canons and Constitutional Thought*, at 11–14.

23. ALEXANDER M. BICKEL, THE LEAST DANGEROUS BRANCH: THE SUPREME COURT AT THE BAR OF POLITICS 26 (1962).

24. One of the trendiest books on undergraduate reading lists these days is RIGOBERTA MENCHU, I RIGOBERTA MENCHU: AN INDIAN WOMAN IN GUATEMALA (1984).

25. *See generally* G. EDWARD WHITE, THE MARSHALL COURT AND CULTURAL CHANGE, 1815–35 (1988).

26. *See* David Howley, *'Common-Law' Court Sits at Capitol*, ST. PAUL PIONEER PRESS, Apr. 17, 1996, at 1A.

27. 304 U.S. 64 (1938). *Erie* held that federal courts exercising jurisdiction over suits solely on the basis of diversity jurisdiction—that is, because the suit is between citizens of different states—must apply state law, rather than federal common law. It thus reversed a century-old practice of federal courts creating and applying federal common law in diversity cases.

28. Nevertheless, a survey of the principal cases found in all of seven leading law school casebooks in constitutional law produces a surprisingly short list: Marbury v. Madison, 5 U.S. (1 Cranch) 137 (1803); McCulloch v. Maryland, 17 U.S. (4 Wheat.) 316 (1819); Gibbons v. Ogden, 22 U.S. (9 Wheat.) 1 (1824); The Civil Rights Cases, 109 U.S. 3 (1883); Lochner v. New York, 198 U.S. 45 (1905); Shelley v. Kraemer, 334 U.S. 1 (1948); Youngstown Sheet & Tube Co. v. Sawyer (The Steel Seizure Case), 343 U.S. 579 (1952); Brown v. Board of Education, 347 U.S. 483 (1954); Griswold v. Connecticut, 381 U.S. 479 (1965); Board of Regents v. Roth, 408 U.S. 564 (1972); Roe v. Wade, 410 U.S. 113 (1973); San Antonio Independent School Dist. v. Rodriguez, 411 U.S. 1 (1973); Frontiero v. Richardson, 411 U.S. 677 (1973); Plyler v. Doe, 457 U.S. 202 (1982); INS v. Chadha, 462 U.S. 919 (1983); Garcia v. San Antonio Metropolitan Transit Authority, 469 U.S. 528 (1985); Bowers v. Hardwick, 478 U.S. 186 (1986); Morrison v. Olson, 487 U.S. 654 (1988); City of Richmond v. J.A. Croson Co., 488 U.S. 469 (1989); Rust v. Sullivan, 500 U.S. 173 (1991); New York v. U.S., 505 U.S. 144 (1992); R.A.V. v. City of St. Paul, 505 U.S. 377 (1992); Planned Parenthood of Southeastern Pennsylvania v. Casey, 505 U.S. 833 (1992). For one of the seven, I could not locate supple-

ments beyond 1994, but the other six all contained three additional cases: Romer v. Evans, 517 U.S. 620 (1996); United States v. Lopez, 514 U.S. 549 (1995); Adarand Constructors, Inc. v. Pena, 575 U.S. 200 (1995). Five of the six also contained U.S. v. Virginia, 518 U.S. 515 (1996).

I counted only principal cases, excluding any that were discussed only in notes. The seven casebooks are the ones I happened to have on my shelf (I knew there was a reason that publishers send out all those free copies!): PAUL BREST & SANFORD LEVINSON, PROCESSES OF CONSTITUTIONAL DECISIONMAKING: CASES & MATERIALS (3d ed., Little, Brown, 1992 & 1994 Supplement); WILLIAM COHEN & JONATHAN D. VARAT, CONSTITUTIONAL LAW: CASES & MATERIALS (10th ed., Foundation, 1997); DANIEL A. FARBER, WILLIAM N. ESKRIDGE, JR., & PHILIP P. FRICKEY, CASES AND MATERIALS ON CONSTITUTIONAL LAW: THEMES FOR THE CONSTITUTION'S THIRD CENTURY (West, 1993 & 1996 Supplement); GERALD GUNTHER, CONSTITUTIONAL LAW (12th ed., Foundation, 1991 & 1996 Supplement); WILLIAM B. LOCKHART, YALE KAMISAR, JESSE H. CHOPER, STEVEN SHIFFRIN & RICHARD H. FALLON, JR., CONSTITUTIONAL LAW: CASES, COMMENTS, QUESTIONS (8th ed., West 1996, & 1996 Supplement); RONALD D. ROTUNDA, MODERN CONSTITUTIONAL LAW: CASES & NOTES (5th ed., West, 1997); GEOFFREY R. STONE, LOUIS M. SEIDMAN, CASS R. SUNSTEIN & MARK V. TUSHNET, CONSTITUTIONAL LAW (3d ed., Little, Brown, 1996 & 1996 Supplement). Cases decided after 1996 were not included in this survey which was done in early 1997. I would be surprised though if current (i.e. 2000) casebooks did not include (at least) United States v. Printz, 521 U.S. 98 (1997) and City of Boerne v. Flores, 521 U.S. 507 (1997), of the spate of recent cases limiting the power of Congress and the national government (and concomitantly, enhancing the role of the Court).

It is interesting to compare this list with a similar list compiled in 1993. *See* Jerry Goldman, *Is There a Canon of Constitutional Law?*, AM. POL. SCI. ASS'N NEWSL. (Law and Courts Section), Spring 1993, at 2–4, *cited in* Balkin & Levinson, *Constitutional Canons and Constitutional Thought*, in this volume, note 67. One case from the earlier list has disappeared: *New York Times v. United States* (Pentagon Papers Case), 403 U.S. 713 (1971), is not in the Farber, Eskridge & Frickey casebook, which was not included in the earlier survey.

Intriguingly, over half the pre–1992 cases on my list do not appear on Goldman's: The Civil Rights Cases (1883); Shelley v. Kraemer (1948); Board of Regents v. Roth (1972); San Antonio Independent School Dist. v. Rodriguez (1973); Frontiero v. Richardson (1973); Plyler v. Doe (1982); INS v. Chadha (1983); Bowers v. Hardwick (1986); Morrison v. Olson (1988); City of Richmond v. J.A. Croson Co. (1989); Rust v. Sullivan (1991). (Cases decided after 1991, of course, also do not appear on the earlier survey, which was published in 1993 and likely written before the 1992–93 term appeared in the casebooks.) Goldman deliberately surveyed books used primarily by undergraduates in political science courses, and in fact only four casebooks were considered by both surveys: Brest & Levinson; Gunther; Lockhart,

Kamisar, Choper & Shiffrin; and Stone, Seidman, Sunstein & Tushnet. This suggests that perhaps the additional cases on my list are part of the constitutional law canon only for future lawyers, and not for general students of American law and government. Or it may simply reflect a tendency for undergraduate courses to cover fewer cases, perhaps in more depth, than do law school courses.

29. Sanford Levinson, *Slavery in the Canon of Constitutional Law*, 68 CHI.-KENT L. REV. 1087, 1091 (1993).

30. *See, e.g.*, Cass R. Sunstein, *In Defense of Liberal Education*, 43 J. LEGAL. EDUC. 22, 25 (1993).

31. For nonlawyers (or constitutionally illiterate lawyers): In *Marbury v. Madison*, 5 U.S. (1 Cranch) 137 (1803), Chief Justice John Marshall firmly established the practice of judicial review, solidifying the power of the Supreme Court to interpret the Constitution and invalidate laws inconsistent with it. *McCulloch v. Maryland*, 17 U.S. (4 Wheat.) 316 (1819), also authored by Chief Justice Marshall, set out the framework for both testing the powers of Congress and mediating disputes between Congress and the states, determining once and for all that federal power is supreme where it exists. *Dred Scott v. Sandford*, 60 U.S. (19 How.) 393 (1857) is perhaps the most infamous Supreme Court case, invalidating the Missouri Compromise, denying that blacks could be citizens, and most likely precipitating—or at least hurrying the onset of—the Civil War. *Plessy v. Ferguson*, 163 U.S. 537 (1896), is another blot on our constitutional landscape, for it upheld state-mandated segregation of railway cars under the theory that separate but equal violated no part of the Constitution. *Abrams v. United States*, 250 U.S. 616 (1919), and *Whitney v. California*, 274 U.S. 357 (1927), both upheld legislation that censored politically unpopular speech, and in each the majority opinion is ultimately overshadowed by that of a single justice: Holmes's dissent in *Abrams*, and Brandeis's concurrence in *Whitney*, are the classic explication of core principles of free speech. (Here the canon is somewhat flexible: *Cohen v. California*, 403 U.S. 15 (1971), in which the Court overturned Mr. Cohen's conviction for wearing a jacket that said "Fuck the Draft," might make a nice substitute, although it is not as stirringly written.) *Brown v. Board of Education*, 347 U.S. 483 (1954), struck down both the doctrine of "separate-but-equal" and segregated education, effectively—although not explicitly—overruling *Plessy*. *Roe v. Wade*, 410 U.S. 113 (1973), held that the Constitution protects a woman's right to abort her pregnancy, invalidating almost all of the contemporary state anti-abortion laws and triggering a political and cultural battle that still rages.

32. To continue the lesson: In *The Civil Rights Cases*, 109 U.S. 3 (1883), the Supreme Court held that the Fourteenth Amendment did not confer on Congress the power to outlaw private discrimination. *Shelley v. Kraemer*, 334 U.S. 1 (1948), by contrast, broadens the reach of the Fourteenth Amendment itself, invalidating racially restrictive real estate covenants; the case represents the farthest the Court has gone in allowing the Constitution to reach private actors. *Lochner*

*v. New York*, 198 U.S. 45 (1905), used substantive due process to strike down maximum hours legislation. Discredited in the late 1930s, substantive due process returned in a different guise to invalidate anti-abortion laws. The stage was set for that return in *Griswold v. Connecticut*, 381 U.S. 479 (1965), when the Court invalidated Connecticut's ban on the use of contraceptives. There was some dispute among the justices as to whether they were engaging in what has come to be called Lochnerizing. Justice Jackson's concurring opinion in *Youngstown Sheet & Tube Co. v. Sawyer* (The Steel Seizure Case), 343 U.S. 579 (1952), used a flexible approach to defining presidential power in the face of congressional action or inaction, and—with a brief formalist interlude in the mid-1980s—that approach has governed separation of powers doctrine ever since.

33. As Sanford Levinson has suggested, it is possible that "life under the American Constitution may be a tragedy." SANFORD LEVINSON, CONSTITUTIONAL FAITH 59 (1988). Again, for the uninitiated and the illiterate: In *DeShaney v. Winnebago County Social Services Dept.*, 489 U.S. 189 (1989), social workers failed to take action on recurrent reports of parental abuse, and four-year-old Joshua DeShaney's father ultimately beat him so severely that he suffered profound and permanent brain damage and was confined to an institution for the rest of his life. The Court held that neither the social workers nor the county which employed and supervised them was liable for his injuries. *Buck v. Bell*, 274 U.S. 200 (1927), upheld a state law mandating sterilization for certain people thought to be hereditarily mentally defective. Justice Holmes's opinion for the Court declared memorably that "three generations of imbeciles are enough," *id.* at 207, but Carrie Buck, whose sterilization was ultimately authorized by the nation's highest court, turned out to be of normal intelligence. *See* Stephen Jay Gould, *Carrie Buck's Daughter*, 2 CONST. COMMENTARY 331 (1985). In *Korematsu v. United States*, 323 U.S. 214 (1944), Justice Black, that great civil libertarian, wrote an opinion for the Court upholding relocation orders for Japanese Americans during World War II. *Bowers v. Hardwick*, 478 U.S. 186 (1986), upheld criminal penalties for engaging in homosexual acts. The other three cases are described in note 28, *supra*.

34. *Carter v. Carter Coal Co.*, 298 U.S. 238 (1936), decided at the height of the Great Depression, invalidated various federal laws—including minimum wage and maximum hour limitations—designed to alleviate the misery of the nation's coal miners. The case's primary relevance lies in its interpretation of Congress's power under the commerce clause, but it can be supplemented to teach about the plight of workers during the Depression and the federal efforts to erect a safety net. *Near v. Minnesota*, 283 U.S. 697 (1931), is the key case holding that prior restraints on the press are nearly impossible to justify; the state of Minnesota had tried to suppress a nasty anti-Semitic article, and the Supreme Court invalidated the restraint. Many students are entirely unaware of the depth and viciousness of anti-Semitism in those halcyon days. In *Brown v. Board of Education*, 347 U.S. 483

(1954), the Court bolstered its conclusion that segregated education harmed black schoolchildren with a bland footnote citing various sociological and psychological studies. As with *Near* and anti-Semitism, amplification of this footnote can expose the horrors of Jim Crow.

35. In *R.A.V. v. City of St. Paul*, 112 S. Ct. 2538 (1992), the Supreme Court invalidated St. Paul's hate speech regulation, under which R.A.V. had been charged for burning a cross on the lawn of a black family. The case raises conflicts between principles of freedom of speech and principles of equality. The affirmative action cases, including *Regents v. Bakke*, 438 U.S. 265 (1978), *City of Richmond v. J.A. Croson Co.*, 488 U.S. 469 (1989), and *Adarand Constructors, Inc. v. Pena*, raise difficult questions about the meaning of equality, many of which are well rehearsed in the multiplicitous opinions. *Maher v. Roe*, 432 U.S. 464 (1977), and *Harris v. McRae*, 448 U.S. 297 (1980), held that the government need not fund abortions even if it funds childbirth; the many—and conflicting—cases defining the permissible boundaries of government funding of religious education include *Everson v. Board of Education*, 330 U.S. 1 (1947) (upholding state subsidization of bus transportation for parochial students); *Board of Education v. Allen*, 392 U.S. 236 (1968) (upholding state loan of books to parochial school students); *Wolman v. Walter*, 433 U.S. 229 (1977) (invalidating state loan of maps and other instructional materials—excluding books—to parochial school students); *Lemon v. Kurtzman*, 403 U.S. 602 (1971) (invalidating a salary supplement for parochial school teachers who taught courses offered by the public schools using the public school textbooks); *Aguilar v. Felton*, 473 U.S. 402 (1985) (invalidating the use of publicly paid remedial teachers in parochial schools). This series of cases raises questions about the worth of a right in the absence of a government obligation to fund the right. *See* Michael W. McConnell, *The Selective Funding Problem: Abortions and Religious Schools*, 104 HARV. L. REV. 989 (1991).

36. Board of Education v. Barnette, 319 U.S. 624 (1943), struck down mandatory flag salute laws in the public schools, and Justice Jackson's majority opinion contains these memorable words:

> [F]reedom to differ is not limited to things that do not matter much. That would be a mere shadow of freedom. The test of its substance is the right to differ as to things that touch the heart of the existing order. If there is any fixed star in our constitutional constellation, it is that no official, high or petty, can prescribe what shall be orthodox in politics, nationalism, religion, or other matters of opinion. . . .

*Id.* at 642. Chief Justice Warren, writing for the Court in *Loving v. Virginia*, 388 U.S. 1 (1967), invalidated Virginia's antimiscegenation laws on the grounds that "[t]he clear and central purpose of the Fourteenth Amendment was to eliminate all official state sources of invidious racial discrimination in the States," and there can be no "'valid legislative purpose . . . which makes the color of a person's skin the test of whether his conduct is a criminal offense.'" *Id.* at

10, 11 (quoting McLaughlin v. Florida, 379 U.S. 184, 198 (1964) (Stewart, J., concurring).

In *Plyler v. Doe*, 457 U.S. 202 (1982), the Court invalidated a mean-spirited attempt to deny a public education to the innocent children of illegal aliens. Justice Brennan wrote for the Court:

[The challenged statute] imposes a lifetime hardship on a discrete class of children not accountable for their disabling status. The stigma of illiteracy will mark them for the rest of their lives. By denying these children a basic education, we deny them the ability to live within the structure of our civic institutions, and foreclose any realistic possibility that they will contribute in even the smallest way to the progress of our nation. In determining the rationality of [the statute], we may appropriately take into account its costs to the Nation and to the innocent children who are its victims.

*Id.* at 223–24.

Justice Brandeis's concurrence in *Whitney v. California*, 274 U.S. 357, 372 (1927), eloquently defended the principles of free speech embodied in the First Amendment:

Those who won our independence . . . believed that freedom to think as you will and to speak as you think are means indispensable to the discovery and spread of political truth; . . . that the greatest menace to freedom is an inert people; that public discussion is a political duty. . . . [T]hey knew that . . . it is hazardous to discourage thought, hope and imagination; that fear breeds repression; that repression breads hate; that hate menaces stable government; that the path of safety lies in the opportunity to discuss freely supposed grievances and proposed remedies; and that the fitting remedy for evil counsels is good ones.

*Id.* at 375.

In *Poe v. Ullman*, 367 U.S. 497 (1961), the Court dismissed, on a procedural technicality, a challenge to Connecticut's law banning the use of contraceptives. Justice Harlan dissented, reaching the merits and concluding that the law was invalid. His opinion stands as a monument to sensitive and faithful constitutional interpretation:

Due process has not been reduced to any formula; its content cannot be determined by reference to any code. The best that can be said is that through the course of this Court's decisions it has represented the balance which our Nation, built upon postulates of respect for the liberty of the individual, has struck between that liberty and the demands of organized society. . . . The balance of which I speak is the balance struck by this country, having regard to what history teaches are the traditions from which it developed as well as the traditions from which it broke. That tradition is a living thing. A decision of this Court which radically departs from it could not long survive, while a

decision which builds on what has survived is likely to be sound. No formula could serve as a substitute, in this area, for judgment and restraint.
*Id.* at 542.

Congratulations! If you have read all the footnotes thus far, you are now constitutionally literate.

37. A colleague, who shall remain nameless, suggests that the first category includes anything by Brennan, the second includes anything by O'Connor, and the third includes anything by Scalia.

38. Gates, *supra* note 4, at 32.

39. ALEXANDER HAMILTON, JAMES MADISON & JOHN JAY, THE FEDERALIST PAPERS (1787) (reprinted in various editions); Bickel, *supra* note 23; ALEXANDER MEIKLEJOHN, FREE SPEECH AND ITS RELATION TO SELF-GOVERNMENT (1948); Herbert Wechsler, *Toward Neutral Principles of Constitutional Law*, 73 HARV. L. REV. 9 (1959).

40. You didn't really think I would actually list my own candidates, did you? I would wager, however, that most readers would nominate at least JOHN ELY, DEMOCRACY AND DISTRUST: A THEORY OF JUDICIAL REVIEW (1980).

41. DANIEL A. FARBER, WILLIAM N. ESKRIDGE, JR. & PHILIP P. FRICKEY, CASES AND MATERIALS ON CONSTITUTIONAL LAW: THEMES FOR THE CONSTITUTION'S THIRD CENTURY (1995 Supp., West, 1995). This supplement was published before the decision in *Romer v. Evans*, 116 S. Ct. 1620 (1996), and thus does not include it. The 1996 Supplement also devotes 34 pages to the topic, substituting the United States Supreme Court's decision in *Romer* for the earlier decision by the Colorado Supreme Court.

The Supreme Court cases to which I refer in the text are *Adarand Constructors, Inc. v. Pena*, 115 S. Ct. 2097 (1995) (striking down federal affirmative action set-aside programs and changing the level of scrutiny accorded federal affirmative action); *Shaw v. Reno*, 113 S. Ct. 2816 (1993) (striking down a state redistricting plan containing a majority-minority district and intimating that such districts would be disfavored in the future); *United States v. Lopez*, 115 S. Ct. 1624 (1995) (striking down an exercise of Congress's power under the commerce clause for the first time in almost sixty years).

42. The first abortion case, *Roe v. Wade*, 410 U.S. 113 (1973), was decided in 1973, and the Court continued to develop the law throughout the decade. Around the same time, the Court first began to notice that sex discrimination might be unconstitutional, struggling between 1973 and 1976 to define the level of scrutiny it should be accorded. *See* Frontiero v. Richardson, 411 U.S. 677 (1973); Craig v. Boren, 429 U.S. 190 (1976).

43. PAUL BREST, PROCESSES OF CONSTITUTIONAL DECISIONMAKING: CASES AND MATERIALS (1st ed., Little, Brown & Co., 1975).

44. GERALD GUNTHER, CONSTITUTIONAL LAW: CASES AND MATERIALS (9th ed., Foundation Press, 1975).

45. *See, e.g.*, Derrick Bell, *Multiple Cultures and the Law: Do We Have a Legal Canon?*, 43 J. LEGAL. EDUC. 1 (1993); Jerome McCristal Culp, Jr., *Firing Legal Canons and Shooting Blanks: Finding a Neutral Way in the Law*, 10 ST. LOUIS U. PUB. L. REV. 185 (1991); Frances Lee Ansley, *Race and the Core Curriculum in Legal Education*, 79 CALIF. L. REV. 1511 (1991); Judith Resnik, *Constructing the Canon*, 2 YALE J.L. & HUM. 221 (1990).

46. Delgado, *Rodrigo's Chronicle, supra* note 7, at 1364. *See also* MACKINNON, *supra* note 7, at 36 (describing standards of merit as an "affirmative action plan" for men).

47. *See* Paul Edelman & Jim Chen, *The Most Dangerous Justice: The Supreme Court at the Bar of Mathematics*, 70 S. CAL. L. REV. 219 (1996).

48. A quick calculation confirms that if one assumes that all justices authored exactly the same number of opinions and the opinions were chosen entirely randomly, there is a 40 percent probability that all the cases chosen would have been written by white males. There is a 76 percent probability that at least 23 of the cases would have been. The 24 cases are those actually listed by name in the text; I did not count cases cited only in notes. If the cases cited in note 28 are included, then of 34 total cases, 32 were written by white males. Making the same assumptions as before, the probability that at least 32 of 34 randomly chosen cases would have been written by white males is 87 percent. For an explanation of these calculations, *see* EMANUEL PARZEN, MODERN PROBABILITY THEORY AND ITS APPLICATIONS 52–54 (1960).

49. Brown v. Allen, 344 U.S. 443, 540 (1953) (Jackson, J., concurring).

50. Christopher T. Wonnell, *Circumventing Racism: Confronting the Problem of the Affirmative Action Ideology*, 1989 B.Y.U. L. REV. 95, 119–41. Two sociologists have suggested that the radical form of postmodernism (which they label DECONSTRUCTION, to distinguish it from the everyday practice of deconstruction) arises when a discipline lacks "social solidarity, organizational cohesion, and professional communication," and when the members of that discipline "have little confidence in the robustness and accuracy of their intellectual projects." Stephan Fuchs & Steven Ward, *The Sociology and Paradoxes of Deconstruction: A Reply to Agger*, 59 AM. SOC. REV. 506, 506 (1994); Stephan Fuchs & Steven Ward, *What Is Deconstruction, and Where and When Does It Take Place?: Making Facts in Science, Building Cases in Law*, 59 AM. SOC. REV. 481, 484 (1994).

51. Daniel Farber has made a similar suggestion about further conversation. *See* Daniel A. Farber, *The Outmoded Debate over Affirmative Action*, 82 CALIF. L. REV. 893, 893–94 (1994).

# Chapter 14

# Constitutional Canons and
# Constitutional Thought

## J. M. Balkin and Sanford Levinson

### I. Introduction

In March of 1860, Frederick Douglass addressed an audience in Glasgow, Scotland.[1] Douglass, the son of a white man and a part-Indian slave, had escaped to freedom, had taught himself to read and write, and by 1860 had become one of the most prominent abolitionists in the United States.[2] His subject that day in Glasgow was how to interpret the Constitution of the United States. In particular, Douglass asked whether the Constitution protected the institution of slavery or whether, on the contrary, the correct reading of the Constitution made it an antislavery document.[3]

Douglass spoke three years after the Supreme Court's infamous decision in *Dred Scott v. Sandford*,[4] in which Chief Justice Roger Taney held that American blacks, even free blacks, were not and could not be citizens of the United States.[5] Purporting to rely on the original understandings of the persons who framed and ratified the 1787 Constitution, Taney argued that by 1787 a century-long consensus held that blacks "had no rights which the white man was bound to respect and that the negro might justly and lawfully be reduced to slavery for his benefit."[6] Moreover, Taney insisted, Congress lacked the power to bar slavery in the territories of the United States.[7] In Taney's view, the Constitution written by the framers was clearly pro-slavery.[8]

Douglass disagreed. He did not dispute Taney's reading of American history but insisted that the original intentions of the framers and ratifiers of the Constitution were irrelevant. The founders were long dead, "but the Constitution is for ages."[9] The meaning of the Constitution was to be found in its text, because "only the text, and not any commentaries or creeds written by those who wished to give the text a meaning apart from its plain reading, was adopted as the Constitution of the United States."[10] The Constitution, Douglass argued, "is no vague, indefinite, floating, unsubstantial, ideal something, coloured according to any man's fancy, now a weasel, now a whale, and now nothing."[11] Rather, it is "a plainly written document," "full and complete in itself."[12]

Nowhere in the text, Douglass pointed out, did the words "slave" or "slavery" explicitly appear.[13] Hence, the Constitution could hardly be interpreted as pro-slavery. Indeed, it was antislavery. "In all matters where laws are taught to be made the means of oppression, cruelty, and wickedness," Douglass thundered, "I am for strict construction."[14] Where its text was unclear or open-ended, the Constitution should always be interpreted strictly in favor of maximizing justice and expanding human rights.[15] Thus, nothing prevented the Congress or the states from eliminating slavery through legislation.[16]

Moreover, Douglass claimed that there were strong textual reasons to think that slavery was itself unconstitutional. "The Constitution," Douglass noted, "forbids the passing of a bill of attainder: that is, a law entailing upon the child the disabilities and hardships imposed upon the parent."[17] Hence, "[e]very slave law in America might be repealed on this very ground."[18]

We do not mention Douglass's Glasgow Address merely to promote its particular constitutional arguments, or even to endorse its general approach to constitutional interpretation.[19] The question we are concerned with is this: Given that Roger Taney's famous remarks in 1857 about the meaning of the Constitution appear and have appeared for decades in American constitutional law casebooks, should Douglass's 1860 Glasgow Address also appear, perhaps in juxtaposition? Is his speech as valuable or as important a presence in constitutional law casebooks as *Dred Scott* or a dozen other U.S. Supreme Court cases that regularly appear in introductory courses on constitutional law?

Taney's opinion was written by the Chief Justice of the United States, the highest judicial officer in the land. By contrast, Douglass's address was offered by a former slave who—as a result of *Dred Scott* itself—was not even a citizen of the United States, much less a professionally trained lawyer or a government official. Moreover, Taney's opinion, although immediately denounced and vilified by opponents of slavery, was nevertheless the supreme law of the land for a time; it required not one but two constitutional amendments to overrule.[20] In contrast, Douglass's Glasgow Address was a political speech that never had any binding legal effect. Indeed, what makes Douglass's speech so interesting is precisely the fact that it was out of step with the consensus of legal opinion of his time. Although many abolitionists surely agreed with Douglass's view that the Constitution prohibited slavery,[21] probably most well-trained lawyers in 1860, and certainly all those who might have been politically viable candidates for appointment to the federal judiciary, regarded his arguments as specious or "off-the-wall" interpretations of the Constitution. Indeed, even many abolitionists would have agreed that Douglass's arguments were specious. William Lloyd Garrison, for example, agreed with Taney that the Constitution protected slavery, and therefore denounced it as "a covenant with death, and an agreement with hell,"[22] and insisted that the northern states had a moral and political duty to secede from the Union.[23]

But how, precisely, are these facts relevant, if at all? Should either of these two texts, or both, or neither, appear in contemporary constitutional law casebooks?[24] Which should American law students study and discuss, which should educated citizens know about, and which should inform the work of legal academics in the present era? Which of these writings, in short, should form part of the "canon" of American legal materials?

In our introduction to this volume we pointed out that what is regarded as canonical in law depends very much on the audience for whom and the purposes for which the canon is constructed. For example, legal materials can be canonical because they are important for educating law students (the pedagogical canon), because they ensure a necessary cultural literacy for citizens in a democracy (the cultural literacy canon), or because they serve as benchmarks for testing academic theories about the law (the academic theory canon). And we pointed out that some of the most important forms of canonicity have less to do with the choice of materials than with the tools of understanding that people use to think about the law—the background structures of "law-talk" that shape conversations within and concerning the law.[25] These elements of "deep canonicity" include characteristic forms of legal argument, characteristic approaches to problems, underlying narrative structures, unconscious forms of categorization, and the choice of canonical examples.

Arguments about the canon in literature assume for the most part that there is some connection between the materials that constitute a canon and how individuals think. The materials that students and educators most frequently encounter set the agenda for problems—they establish what is normal and what is deviant, what is expected and what is out of the ordinary, and what are good and bad examples of practice. However, as we have noted, in a deeper sense what are most canonical are habits of thought. These habits of thought lead to the selection and retention of those materials that are called canonical. Exposure to those materials, in turn, helps reproduce and reinforce the habits of mind that shape what materials are deemed canonical. Thus, it is false to say that canonical materials by themselves shape thought, for they may simply reflect the kind of thought that leads to their continued selection. Because canonical materials are both causes and effects of thought, the causal story of how canons influence us is inevitably a complicated one.

When we speak of a canon, we are really speaking of a process of reproduction—a reproduction of the tools of understanding, the "cultural software" that people use to formulate problems, to understand the world, and to understand their own actions.[26] From this perspective, what makes canons canonical is precisely that they do reproduce themselves in successive generations of human minds. The establishment of a canon leads to an accentuated focus on some materials as opposed to others. Because space and attention in human minds are limited, frequent transmission of canonical works helps draw greater attention to them and thus helps ensure their perpetuation and proliferation. Indeed, the effect is even more profound. By capturing more and more of the limited space in human minds and imaginations, canonical materials begin to define the very nature of what is worth talking or thinking about. They have a bootstrapping effect that helps ensure their continued centrality as well as their future reproductive success.[27] Thus, things do not become canonical simply because they are important; often they become important because they are canonical.

In this essay, we explain how canonical features of constitutional pedagogy and academic theory shape, for good and for ill, both how students learn the law and how academics study and theorize about the law. In particular, we contend that the pedagogical canon in constitutional law is much too centered on the opinions of the Supreme Court of the United States. This focus on Supreme Court opinions and the increasing subdivision of the constitutional law curriculum have subtly affected the content of constitutional theory. We also think that, as in the liberal arts, there may be some advantages to expanding the range of materials included in the study of law, but we think the reasons for expanding or changing the canon may be different with respect to law and the liberal arts. Because legal canons rely heavily on pronouncements of courts and legislatures, liberal arts scholars have more control over their canon than do legal scholars. Nevertheless, legal scholars do have some agency in forming their canon, and the canon of constitutional law needs serious revision. The current study of constitutional law makes a fetish of the opinions of the Supreme Court and lacks comparative and historical perspective. The narrowness of current canonical materials has had unfortunate effects for constitutional theory and legal education: it encourages too much specialization and focuses attention away from basic questions about the justice of the legal system. We think that a revitalized constitutional canon should pay attention to structural questions that do not often come before courts, and it should include nonjudicial interpreters of the Constitution, particularly representatives of political and social movements whose interpretations often shape and influence the direction of constitutional interpretation.

## II. Comparativism and Court-Centeredness

In our introductory essay we identified the pedagogical or teaching canon in constitutional law as those cases and materials (historical examples, legislative history, speeches by legislators and presidents, etc.) that are regularly taught and read in constitutional law courses, or that should be regularly taught and read in those courses. Any inquiry into the pedagogical canon must be concerned not only with content, but also with form. It must be concerned not only with the issues that are taught but also with the kinds of materials that are used to teach them, whether they be cases, statutes, academic arguments, or factual studies. This latter question of form is likely to be overlooked. The question is not what Supreme Court cases should be taught, but rather whether what should be taught are Supreme Court cases rather than Lincoln's first inaugural address or James Madison's speech about the constitutionality of the Bank of the United States.

Here sociological questions merge with prescriptive ones. One reason why the constitutional canon is almost exclusively constructed in terms of U.S. Supreme Court cases is the general court-centeredness of legal education. Indeed, it is more than court-centeredness—it is U.S. Supreme Court–centeredness. Although much important constitutional law is decided in circuit and district courts,[28] constitutional law casebooks tend to emphasize only the Supreme Court's decisions.

Juxtaposing Supreme Court opinions with the interpretations of such distinguished statesmen as James Madison, Wendell Phillips, Frederick Douglass, and Abraham Lincoln casts a very different light on the Supreme Court's purported role as the sole authoritative interpreter of the meaning of the Constitution. The U.S. Supreme Court–centeredness of the pedagogical canon in constitutional law has important ideological effects. It tends to reinforce the Supreme Court's finality in matters of constitutional interpretation. Conversely, it tends to downplay the possibility (and desirability) of "protestant" interpretations of the Constitution, which view each citizen as having the duty to interpret the Constitution for herself.

Moreover, the Supreme Court–centeredness of the constitutional canon means that law students quite literally never consider, in any systematic way, those aspects of the Constitution that never become the subject of litigation, such as fixed periods between elections, bicameralism, the two-term limit for presidents, or the remarkable hurdles facing anyone who wishes to engage in formal constitutional amendment under Article V. These structural features of the Constitution are at least as important as the dormant commerce clause or the First Amendment protections accorded to commercial speech, but they almost never become part of the law student's consciousness.

That might not be such a problem if legal pedagogy were concerned only with preparing students for legal practice. Almost no practicing lawyer will ever be called upon to address, in a litigated case, whether it is really defensible that Vermont has the same number of senators as Texas. (Of course, most law students will also rarely litigate cases involving the dormant commerce clause or the First Amendment.) However, many law professors believe that it is their function to train lawyer-citizens as well as legal practitioners, especially because the United States continues to draw an excessive number of its leaders from the ranks of professionally trained lawyers. We must recognize that, by neglecting these important structural features of the Constitution, we are inflicting on the nation graduates whose ignorance of fundamental structural issues leaves them ill equipped to discuss many vital issues of governance. Trained in law schools to have entirely too much faith in the Constitution and never having considered some of its manifest imperfections—indeed, outright stupidities[29]—our students will have few tools with which to think about the adequacy of the institutions bequeathed to us by our long-dead founders.

Just as the pedagogical canon is innocent of these important issues, it also seems completely uninterested in comparisons with the constitutions of other lands and times. Extraordinarily few casebooks in any subject include material from foreign legal systems. This absence is particularly glaring in constitutional law courses. Of course, if one wants comparativism, one need hardly go past our own shores. The first comparisons might be made to other domestic constitutions, including the discarded Articles of Confederation, the fifty state constitutions that complement the United States Constitution,[30] and even the Constitution of the Confederate States of America, which bears many interesting differences from the antebellum Constitution. But beyond our borders, one might also look to the written constitutions of well over one hundred other countries,[31] the United Nations Charter, and the Treaty of Rome.[32] And this list, of course, does not even include judicial opinions by constitutional courts in other countries. Through these opinions we might compare not only the treatment of particular structural or human rights issues, but also the modes of interpretation that these courts employ. Just as there is more than one way to design a democracy, there is surely more than one way to interpret a constitutional provision.[33]

Both historical and what is generally called "comparative" study (i.e., the study of other legal cultures) are really special cases of comparativism. Comparativism operates either temporally or spatially—it takes us either back in time or outward to other places. In both cases, the purpose is the same. It is to make the object of our study—in this case the United States Constitution—"strange" to us. (Literary critics are well aware of the similar technique of "defamiliarization.") We hope to see how a problem dealt with in one way might be dealt with in another way, or how a particular feature of our political life looks when it is separated from concomitant features that we unthinkingly blend together.

The American legal academy's general failure to consider other constitutions and other constitutional opinions in constitutional pedagogy has two significant ideological effects. First, it tends to reinforce the idea that the U.S. Constitution is the standard case of a written constitution; hence other constitutions will be judged with respect to their similarity to or their difference from this norm. Second, it tends to make the U.S. Constitution not only a descriptive but a prescriptive norm for constitutional design. This tendency is revealed whenever American constitutional lawyers eagerly offer advice to emergent political systems struggling with the task of constitution writing. Like all too many of their professors, students rarely grapple with the possibility that there are other ways of structuring governments or dealing with the problems of democratic institutions—for example, the choice between proportional representation and "winner take all" elections, or between parliamentary models and models that feature separation of powers.[34] Students who read these and other confident pronouncements are rarely informed just how dubious are many judicial descriptions of the world outside the courtroom. Perhaps one should not expect judges trained in law schools to be skilled in sound empirical and social analysis, but if so, this raises rather important questions about the judicial role.

### III. Practice Concerns and "Timeless Problems"

"Legal practice" concerns exert a somewhat different influence on the pedagogical canon. Casebook authors often think it important to map the way legal doctrine is "actually" practiced. To the extent that casebooks shape the way that certain problems are thought about, this may be a self-fulfilling prophecy. Nevertheless, it is by no means clear that casebooks match existing legal practice. Rather, they tend only to reflect practice as imagined by academics. Most academics have little sense of how many cases are litigated in different areas, or how much of the bar's attention is devoted to some questions rather than others. Nevertheless, legal academics create a sense—possibly too often derived from the opinions of the Supreme Court—of what issues are "hot" and therefore worthy of imposing on their students.

This need to map practice as the academic imagines it leads to an emphasis on "current problems." Here again court-centeredness—and particularly Supreme Court–centeredness—plays an important role. Hence, one sees a large amount of material devoted to areas in which legal doctrine changes virtually every Supreme Court term. In the field of equal protection, for example, school desegregation cases have been followed by affirmative action cases, and now considerable attention seems to be focused on voting rights. One can trace the changing imaginations of academics by noting when certain issues begin to get a significant degree of space in constitutional law casebooks. One might look at the number of pages devoted to racist speech before and after *R.A.V. v. City of St. Paul*,[35] for example. Moreover, the rise of particular forms of legal scholarship (for example, feminist legal scholarship) can change the content of casebooks, even if the Supreme Court no longer hears a large number of gender discrimination cases. The pedagogical canon surely responds to driving forces in the academy and in legal culture generally as well as in the courts.

Even so, the notion of canonicity is usually posed *against* the issues of the moment and toward issues that are considered "timeless." This leads to an inevitable conflict between covering the "leading cases" and covering problems that, in the view of the academic, are the truly important problems that lawyers and judges face (or should be facing).

The desire for timelessness is often related to the desire for "good teaching cases." Often this means cases and materials that raise what the teaching community considers to be important (and "timeless") issues of constitutional law. Nevertheless, the timelessness of the canon may be partially illusory; it may reflect the anxieties of the moment dressed up as timeless concerns. After all, the question of what is "important" and "timeless" is constructed by the legal culture, and changes over time. If the historical study of the canon teaches us anything, it is that timelessness isn't what it used to be.

The concept of timelessness, however, does lead us to the notion of imparting a tradition, which brings us to a different conception of canonicity. The cultural literacy canon consists of those cases and materials best designed to acculturate the student into the "tradition" of American constitutional discourse, and to introduce her to that which a member of a particular interpretive community should know. What is this interpretive community? It is an interpretive community as imagined by another interpretive community consisting of legal academics. Academics imagine a community of intelligent, educated, everyday lawyers, judges, and scholars. (We might compare this community with the imagined community of educated men and women that liberal arts education is supposed to produce.)

Everything that we have said about form versus content (what kinds of materials versus what kinds of issues) also applies to this tradition. Court-centeredness, and in particular, U.S. Supreme Court–centeredness, is surely central to the current definitions of cultural literacy. Judging from existing constitutional law casebooks, apparently everyone needs to know *Marbury v. Madison*,[36] but not Andrew Jackson's Bank Veto,[37] the European Charter on Human Rights, or the German Basic Law.

This tradition, like so many others, is an "invented tradition." It comes into being at a particular point in history, and then regards itself as always having been there. We can uncover the inventedness of this tradition by investigating when certain materials enter and leave the canon of things every lawyer, judge, law student, or constitutional scholar should know, and connecting these changes to political and social issues of the time. Here are just a few examples of the questions one might ask about the canon of cultural literacy in constitutional law:

1. What is the relationship between the rise of legal casebooks and the court-centeredness of the cultural tradition? In the nineteenth and early twentieth centuries, constitutional theory was more the province of political scientists than law professors.[38]

2. When do law review articles become essential parts of the academic theory canon? We suspect the answer is only recently. When do treatises become important to the canon, and when do they begin to lose their importance? Joseph Story's and Thomas Cooley's treatises were surely influential during the nineteenth century, as were treatises by Williston, Corbin, and Wigmore in later years. However, student-edited law reviews have gradually replaced treatises as the major venue for scholarly commentary in our own time.[39] Interestingly, constitutional law provides the one major exception: Laurence Tribe's *American Constitutional Law*.[40]

3. When does *Marbury* become a central case in the cultural literacy and pedagogical canons? One guess is that *Marbury* gains particular importance in the twentieth century. It would be interesting to note the treatment of *Marbury* during the period leading up to the constitutional controversies over the New Deal when judicial supremacy was a major concern. Surely *McCulloch* and *Gibbons v. Ogden*[41] must have assumed new importance during a time of expanding federal legislative power.

4. Along the same lines, we might ask when *Calder v. Bull*[42]—which contains one of the earliest discussions of natural law—becomes central to the constitutional canon. Was it always seen as central or did its importance rise around the time of *Griswold v. Connecticut*[43] or *Roe v. Wade*?[44] Similarly, we suspect contemporary concerns are giving new prominence and importance to Justice Harlan's dissent in *Lochner v. New York*.[45] The most famous dissent in *Lochner* has always been Justice Holmes's,[46] peppered as it is with memorable aphorisms and quotable slogans. Yet while Holmes's canonical dissent offers little more than relentless majoritarianism, Harlan's careful consideration of the actual purposes and likely effects of legislation probably resonates more deeply with contemporary liberal constitutionalists searching for nuanced approaches to judicial scrutiny. In an earlier age trying to free itself from the excesses of *Lochner*,

Holmes's aphoristic embrace of majority will sounded positively heroic and well worth canonizing. But in an age where unconstitutional conditions, positive liberties, affirmative action, and gay rights are on the scholarly agenda, Harlan's more judicious approach may seem increasingly relevant and attractive.

These questions presuppose a more general point: some cases and materials may languish in relative obscurity for decades or even centuries—except perhaps to a few cognoscenti—and then suddenly become central to the pedagogical, theoretical, or cultural literacy canons. This change in fortunes is usually not accidental, but is related to the constitutional problems of the present moment. Cases and opinions become timeless, in other words, when the time is right.

Indeed, several early casebooks did not begin with what many now consider the crown jewel in the constitutional canon, *Marbury v. Madison*; rather, they began with the amendment processes listed in Article V.[47] This may reflect the interests of political scientists, who still dominated the field in the early part of the century. It may also reflect a more continental way of thinking about constitutional law: the student should begin with structural features and the rule of recognition, asking first how we know something is part of the Constitution and how one adds things to the Constitution. In many of these early casebooks, individual rights issues are considered secondary,[48] whereas they are considered central to American constitutional law today.

## IV. Pedagogy and Academic Theory

Although the pedagogical and cultural literacy canons are conceptually distinct from the canons of academic theory, they surely affect the structure of normative constitutional theory. The selection of cases and materials in casebooks and other teaching materials both reflects and perpetuates particular (some would say outmoded) understandings of legal issues. Through organizational decisions, the pedagogical canon can direct our attention toward certain problems and issues and away from others, or cause us to see certain situations as paradigmatic and others as secondary or inconsequential.

The treatment of the First Amendment is a good example. For many years, the paradigm of seditious libel by a political dissenter has been taken as the canonical example for free speech theory; this conception gains its apotheosis in *Brandenburg v. Ohio*,[49] in which the Supreme Court laid down doctrines about seditious advocacy that strongly protect dissenting speech.[50] Few teachers who concentrate on the classic canon of free speech cases seem to acknowledge that extremely few dissenters today face the prospect of criminal punishment for what they say. This may be the result of liberal legal doctrines themselves or it may be the result of deeper changes in our culture. In any event, the truly central First Amendment controversies of our era—campaign finance, government speech, broadcast regulation, and unconstitutional conditions—do not fit easily into the paradigmatic example of a lone dissenter spewing out unpopular opinions. As a result, casebooks have found no completely adequate way of dealing with them.[51] A particularly pronounced example of this phenomenon occurs in Gerald Gunther's popular casebook, which for many years divided the world of free speech into subversive advocacy, time, place, and manner regulation, symbolic expression, and "Additional Problems."[52] When almost all of the key free speech issues of our time have become "additional problems," one senses that the central theoretical approaches to the First Amendment desperately need rethinking.

A second kind of effect on theoretical imagination stems from the increasing specialization of constitutional law resulting from the explosion of constitutional law cases and claims of constitutional rights that must be protected by judicial review. We might think of this as the victory of the exceptional cases described in footnote 4 of *United States v. Carolene Products Co.*[53] over the normal case of judicial review described in the text of that opinion.[54] The more opportunities that exist for judicial review of individual rights, the more specialization occurs.

For example, especially after the 1960s, constitutional law casebooks started to carve off the criminal procedure materials for reasons of space. At present only the casebook edited by William Lockhart, Yale Kamisar, Jesse Choper, Steven Shiffrin, and Richard Fallon retains a substantial amount of these materials, largely, we suspect, because Professor Kamisar, a noted expert on criminal procedure, is one of the editors.[55] Criminal procedure, in short, has unfortunately become a specialty that is no longer taught by most ostensible "experts" on constitutional law (including ourselves). This has two unfortunate effects.

First, constitutional theorists may tend to neglect the many instances of constitutional interpretation that occur in criminal procedure cases, and that may affect or help predict judges' and justices' views in other types of cases. For example, the dispute between Justices Black and

Frankfurter over incorporation was largely waged in the area of criminal procedure.[56] In our own day, Justice Scalia's interpretations of the confrontation clause seem linked to his formalist interpretations of other parts of the Constitution.[57]

Second, if constitutional theorists do not pay attention to criminal procedure issues, these issues will tend to be thought of as administration of justice issues rather than questions of constitutional interpretation. The criminal procedure amendments will, in short, be written out of the legal imagination of an entire generation of constitutional scholars.[58]

We have witnessed in our own time the "shrinking" of the Bill of Rights so that in the imagination of constitutional law professors it encompasses only the First Amendment, the takings clause, and the due process clause. This way of thinking destroys the sense that the component parts of the Bill of Rights are interrelated.[59] For example, one of us (Levinson) believes that a mindless textualism has led professors who teach "the First Amendment" to include subversive advocacy and federal aid to parochial schools in the same course—because both the free speech clause and the religion clauses appear in the text of that amendment—while ignoring the implications of the Second Amendment. These implications should be important for anyone who emphasizes the "checking value" that underlies the free speech and press provisions of the First Amendment, for many members of the founding generation viewed popular possession of arms as the ultimate "check" on corrupt governments.[60]

Today, only specialists in criminal procedure follow and critically comment on the Supreme Court's interpretation of large parts of the Bill of Rights. Hence, there is a loss of a common culture of discussion among legal scholars about the Supreme Court's work in interpreting the different parts of the Constitution. A related problem may now be appearing on the horizon as free speech courses are increasingly taught separately from equal protection and due process courses.

Indeed, even within the remaining areas of the constitutional law casebook, certain parts of the Constitution are treated as peripheral and are often left out of courses (for example, interstate taxation and intergovernmental immunity) or are taught only in specialized courses (for example, voting rights).[61] The marginalization or exclusion of certain features of the Constitution may well affect which paradigms dominate discussions of constitutional theory and which shape the imaginations of constitutional scholars.

In other words, as specialization increases apace, scholars who do constitutional "grand theory" may view only a narrower and narrower part of constitutional law as their job to explain. If so, their theoretical views may become increasingly parochial, or increasingly subject to the blinders and limitations that arise whenever a theory is tested against only a limited set of situations.

Often the choice of cases and materials in a constitutional law casebook reflects a narrative about the development of the Constitution and constitutional law. For example, the casebook author can present materials as the historical evolution of doctrine toward a particular goal, the "present situation." This present situation can be portrayed as either a good thing or a bad thing, but the point of the narrative is to envision constitutional law as working toward a certain state of affairs. The evolution of constitutional law can be a story of progress or one of gradual decline from an earlier, golden era, whether it be the era of the founders, Reconstruction, the New Deal, or the halcyon days of the Warren Court.[62] One can arrange cases and materials as an ongoing dialectic of principle and counterprinciple, struggling with each other in the materials of the law.[63] Finally, if one wants to take a strongly genealogical approach, one can simply present the cases as reflecting the political and cultural anxieties of their times, showing how the law has been different before and no doubt will be different again. Every casebook tells a story, if we will only listen to it; indeed, it is almost impossible to organize a casebook that tells no story at all.

## V. Expanding the Canon

In the debates over canon formation in the humanities, the contestants have disagreed less about whether canonical writers like Shakespeare or Homer should be retained, and more about whether the canon should be expanded to include new materials written by women, minorities, or non–Western European writers. The analogous question in law is whether students should be exposed to "marginalized voices" in their study of law. The expression is placed in quotation marks because its meaning is essentially contested. To be sure, examples of marginalized voices in contemporary constitutional discourse might include women, homosexuals, and racial and ethnic minorities. But marginalized groups might also include laypersons of whatever race, gender, or sexual orientation, for their lack of professional status means that they have almost always been excluded from serious constitutional debates. The student of the canon should ask to what degree this exclusion is parochial or unfair.

Marginalization is a normative as well as a descriptive matter. *Many* people have been forgotten or marginalized in present-day legal discussions. Any reviser of subject matter canons must choose among them and must also be prepared to offer convincing reasons for her choice. To the narratives of slaves and suffragettes one might consider adding the following marginalized voices: the Mormon settlers of Utah, who were forced to abandon important tenets of their religion (including polygamy) so that the Utah Territory might enter the Union;[64] contemporary religious fundamentalists,[65] who are often despised or treated with condescension by secular America; members of the contemporary "militia" movement, who have developed distinctive views about the interpretation of constitutional and common law;[66] William Lloyd Garrison, who argued that the North should secede from the South because the Constitution was "a covenant with death and an agreement with hell";[67] and John C. Calhoun, who was not only a staunch supporter of slavery, but also a constitutional theorist of great imagination whose doctrine of concurrent majorities is strikingly relevant to today's debates over voting rights and the constitutionality of race-conscious redistricting.[68] Several of these examples may suggest that marginality is sometimes well deserved; yet one can hardly deny that decisions about which of these marginalized groups should be recognized and which consigned to oblivion are heavily politicized.

"Marginalization" includes issues of form as well as content. To the law professor's court-centered mind, the most obvious examples of "new" materials that might be added to the legal canon are older, neglected U.S. Supreme Court cases; thus, people might debate whether slavery cases like *Prigg v. Pennsylvania*[69] or *The Antelope*[70] should enter the pedagogical canon, and, conversely, whether anything is really lost by dropping taxation of interstate commerce cases or even regulation of pornography cases from the first-year course to make room. Yet an equally important question concerns whether court decisions should be replaced or supplemented by nonjudicial materials. We coedit a casebook[71] that has consciously chosen to eliminate quite a few of the standard cases[72] while including speeches by James Madison and Frederick Douglass, Andrew Jackson's veto of the bill renewing the charter of the (Second) Bank of the United States, an opinion of the United States attorney general concerning the delivery of abolitionist mail in Mississippi, and excerpts from the Lincoln-Douglas debates about the proper respect due the Court's decision in *Dred Scott*.[73] Because we no longer devote full coverage to the First Amendment, omitted materials include such classics as *New York Times Co. v. Sullivan*[74] and the entire corpus of cases involving pornography and election finance. However, the omission of the First Amendment has other repercussions as well. Both of us feel that election finance is one of the most important issues in contemporary constitutional law, and thus the omission of First Amendment challenges to campaign finance legislation is a clear example of where pedagogical interests in introducing students to the study of constitutional law and constitutional interpretation must trump the concerns of academic theory and the interests of practicing lawyers.

One reason to include the Lincoln-Douglas debates is that they are important to cultural literacy. But they also raise fundamental issues about constitutional theory and the role of canonical materials in undergirding one or another approach to the Constitution. We believe that it is vitally important to emphasize the crucial role that nonjudicial officials (and, indeed, the citizenry at large) play in constitutional interpretation. Few Supreme Court justices have had as much theoretical and practical influence on our constitutional order as Abraham Lincoln. Yet because most contemporary casebooks and courses are so unrelentingly U.S. Supreme Court-centered, they offer a highly distorted understanding of the American constitutional system to the hapless students exposed to them. These students will almost inevitably end up believing that constitutional interpretation is the exclusive province of the judiciary—and particularly the Supreme Court—as both a theoretical and an empirical proposition. As a theoretical proposition, this is pernicious. As an empirical proposition, it is preposterous. This willful ignorance of nonjudicial interpreters is a form of marginalization quite different from those we are accustomed to, but it is no less serious.[75]

Almost equally neglected in most casebooks is the phenomenon that, after all, explains the events of 1861 to 1865: the presence within the United States of a legally sanctioned system of chattel slavery. We think there are many reasons to include materials on slavery in the canon of constitutional pedagogy.[76] One purpose, though, is simply to point out that the American constitutional tradition—and, beyond that, the notion of the rule of law itself—has often been intertwined with and used to promote the enforcement of evils like slavery. In the antebellum period—

a formative period of American constitutional thought—competent lawyers were quite able (and indeed were expected) to offer any number of legal arguments concerning slavery, just as they offered arguments about the constitutional status of navigation, the immigration of paupers, or the regulation of interstate commerce. Focusing on slavery shows that the record of the Constitution and of constitutional lawyers is considerably more mixed regarding the issue of slavery than many admirers of the Constitution might wish to concede. More generally, students must recognize, despite their natural admiration for the Constitution, that the constitutional tradition is full of racism and sexism fully responsive to what Holmes unforgettably labeled "the felt necessities of the time."[77] When these "felt necessities" included the ruthless suppression of what we in our own era consider "basic human rights," the "authoritative interpreters" and elite lawyers ensconced in Washington and elsewhere had no difficulty whatsoever in accommodating their interpretations of the Constitution to those necessities.

This justification for the inclusion of materials on slavery is historicist. The intention is to show the student that at different points in history constitutional arguments have been evaluated and constructed very differently and that the Supreme Court has often changed its mind about what counts as sound constitutional analysis. Moreover, the approach is also critical, for it seeks to remind students that, while purporting to speak in the name of the Constitution, the Supreme Court has often done very wicked things whose effects are still with us today. If we recognize the Constitution's checkered past, we can better understand that the constitutional interpretations of our own time may also be complicit in evils many of us would rather not confront.[78]

At first glance, this critical or historicist approach appears to have much in common with feminist and minority critiques of the literary canon; these critiques also seek to expose social injustice through expansion of the canon. Yet their approaches differ in several important respects. In literature, constructors of the canon are much less likely to dredge up forgotten racist novels of the nineteenth century for inclusion in the canon than to focus on demonstrating the inherent racism of currently accepted parts of the received literary canon and to suggest the inclusion of African American writers unjustly neglected. In like fashion, feminist literary theorists might be interested in sexist or male supremacist elements common in the popular literature of the past, but they would probably not argue for the permanent inclusion of sexist literature in the canon in order to encourage people to read and be challenged by it. Thus, the purposes of expansion are quite different in law and in literature. Both a constitutional historicist and a feminist literary critic would attempt to reveal the history of sexism or racism in their respective fields. However, the result in the case of law would be to enshrine these examples in the canon so that students would have to confront them and learn about the historicity of constitutional views of what is just and right. By contrast, a feminist literary critic might discard these texts after revealing them as examples of the injustices of the past (and as continued in the ideology of the present). Like the inclusion of slavery in the constitutional canon, the feminist attack on the literary canon is designed to reveal ideology. But it is done for different reasons and with different consequences for the educational process.

## VI. The Symbiosis of Theories and Canons

The academic theory canon does not include all of the cases and materials that lawyers and courts regularly use in defending constitutional arguments. These materials tend to be comparatively recent and driven by specific doctrinal considerations. Rather, the academic theory canon consists of cases and materials that are sufficiently important to the arbiters of this canon (legal academics) that any theory of constitutional law must account for them. Here the canon is like a set of doctrinal dots that any theory of constitutional law must connect. Thus, we might also call it the "theory construction" canon. It is the canon used to construct and test relevant theories of constitutional law and constitutional adjudication. The classic example of a "must explain" case, of course, is *Brown v. Board of Education*.[79]

The construction of an academic theory canon is accompanied by the formation of an "anticanon" of cases that any theory worth its salt must show are wrongly decided. Examples are *Lochner v. New York*,[80] *Plessy v. Ferguson*,[81] and *Korematsu v. United States*.[82] Our notions of what is canonical tell us that we have to justify *Brown* (a good case) and explode *Lochner* (a bad case). In contrast, no one thinks it *as* important to explain why *Bunting v. Oregon*[83] or *Hebe Co. v. Shaw*[84] is rightly or wrongly decided.[85] Indeed, these twin notions of normative canonicity and anti-canonicity are also central to the pedagogical and cultural literacy canons. Cases become important to teach and remember because they serve as the icons (and demons) of an invented constitutional tradition.

The "canonical" problems of justifying *Brown* or decrying *Lochner* are presented repeatedly as we are educated in constitutional law. Doctrinal heroes and villains appear to us already identified and waiting for us to confront them. Indeed, the standard constitutional law course might well be understood as organized around the ritual justification and demonization of specific canonical cases. (How many constitutional law courses have taken as their central theme "The Ghost of *Lochner*"?) One sometimes feels that all of modern constitutional theory is driven by a desire to justify (or condemn) five cases (and we all know which ones they are).

One of the most interesting features of the academic theory canon is precisely its tendency to force us to recognize certain cases as "heroes" or "villains"—so that a libertarian can safely be considered "out of the mainstream" if she, like Richard Epstein, actually approves of a case like *Lochner*. This is a point of no small importance. It reveals the canon and canonicity as vehicles for the normalization of beliefs and interpretive assumptions, and hence as instruments of social control for the relevant interpretive community. A constitutional theorist has to explain why *Dred Scott* or *Plessy v. Ferguson* is bad constitutional law (and not just morally appalling) or she is out of the game.[86] Thus, central to any struggle over the constitutional canon is the demarcation of the icons and the demons of constitutional law, and inherent in this demarcation is the normalization of positions that can then be used to normalize discourse (and thought) about constitutional law.

Indeed, the most remarkable evidence of this normalization concerns the constitutional text itself. Not only are non–Supreme Court materials relentlessly excluded from the teaching canon and the cultural literacy canon, but it is by no means clear that the entire text of the Constitution itself is necessarily part of these canons. There are significant parts of the constitutional text that no one in the legal academy thinks it very important to explain; within this interpretive community these portions have for all intents and purposes been read out of the Constitution. Candidates might include the Second Amendment, the republican form of government clause, and the privileges or immunities clause of the Fourteenth Amendment.[87]

One challenges the academic theory canon by offering a counter-canon—a different set of cases and materials. One offers a countercanon (pedagogical or cultural literacy) to rediscover cases and materials and parts of the constitutional text that have been neglected, that point in opposite directions, or that are embarrassing to currently fashionable academic theories created to explain the existing canon.

Thus, one important purpose for expanding the pedagogical canon or the cultural literacy canon is to critique existing normative theories of constitutional law. That is because constitutional theories tend to be adapted to solve certain canonical problems: for example, legal process theories were adapted to address concerns of federalism and separation of powers. Yet there is often an awkward fit between these theories and different sorts of problems. So it can be an amusing as well as an instructive exercise to apply a well-known theory—for example, the principle of institutional competence, the notion of law as integrity, or *Carolene Products*-style theories of process protection—to a "different" area of constitutional adjudication, for example, slavery. When one starts talking about making slave law the best it can be, preserving democratic deliberation about the regulation of slavery, or the relative importance of state versus federal competence in the regulation of slaves, one begins to see the limitations and narrowness of contemporary constitutional theories.

In particular, these thought experiments help us see how constitutional theories actually tend to avoid putting the basic justice of the legal system into question by offering intricate and intellectually demanding forms of legal analysis as a substitute for and a diversion from potentially de-legitimating inquiries about our constitutional system. When these theories are applied to universally condemnable practices, we more clearly understand how they encourage a flight from substance.

Thus, it should not surprise us that leading constitutional theories exist in a symbiotic relationship with the pedagogical and cultural literacy canons whose materials they describe and justify: normative constitutional theories help construct what parts of the constitutional tradition to explore and emphasize (because these theories work best with respect to these areas). At the same time, the pedagogical and cultural literacy canons tend to give these constitutional theories greater purchase and plausibility than they might otherwise have. The construction of the pedagogical and cultural literacy canons allows contemporary constitutional theories to escape certain embarrassing moments and proceed with their project of legitimation.

## VII. Conclusion

We began this chapter by asking whether Frederick Douglass's Glasgow Address should become part of the pedagogical canon, perhaps in juxtaposition with Roger Taney's infamous *Dred Scott* opinion. We think that it should; indeed, we think that it is a particularly good example of how the constitutional canon might be expanded.

In saying this, we fully recognize that we cannot create or enforce a constitutional canon by ourselves. That task belongs to no single person or set of persons. Rather, canons are made by all of us, just as our ways of thinking are shaped by them in turn. Even so, we are participants in building the canon that we will bestow upon the next generation, and so we have as much right as duty to offer our own views, in the hope that they will influence others. Thus, we gladly affirm that Douglass's Glasgow Address deserves a place in the canons of constitutional pedagogy; indeed, we think it is something that every educated lawyer and every constitutional theorist should know. We believe this for three reasons.

First, Douglass's speech is important because it is made by a person who is not a member of any governmental body or even a professionally trained lawyer. In this sense, it reveals to the student that all Americans, even those who have heretofore been excluded from the People, have the right, and the duty, to interpret the Constitution and to decide for themselves what that document means.

Second, Douglass's speech is important because it is made by a prominent figure in a social movement, the antislavery movement. We think American constitutional development is too often taught as the history of decisions by judges who, even if they are to some degree influenced by the events around them, nonetheless move either in response to autonomous legal norms or in ways that are ultimately idiosyncratic and mysterious. Alternatively, the history of constitutional law is taught as the history of great jurists who show the rest of us the way through their wisdom or their folly. Imagining constitutional development in this way neglects the fact that constitutional changes—including changes in constitutional interpretation—are often the result of mass political action, which is later recognized and sanctified by various legal and judicial elites.[88]

The members of the International Workers of the World (IWW) had far greater prescience about the meaning of the First Amendment than did Oliver Wendell Holmes or even Louis Brandeis.[89] Conversely, the standard narrative that emphasizes the Supreme Court's "leadership" in *Brown v. Board of Education* usually overlooks the limited impact of that opinion in the decade following it.[90] It also ignores the significance of President Truman's willingness to defy American military leaders in 1947 and to order the desegregation of the armed forces. The 1948 election, among other things, confirmed that the general electorate—even if not that in the Deep South—was willing to reward a president who committed himself to civil rights. And, of course, Truman's willingness to make such decisions itself reflected changes in American political demographics and the rise of an increasingly activist black constituency.

Legal academics who look to the Supreme Court to "lead" public opinion must explain, among other things, why the president would nominate, and the Senate confirm, persons significantly out of step with the conventional wisdom at the time of their selection. We strongly suspect that public opinion much more often leads the Supreme Court—even if in suitably complex ways—than the other way around.[91] If we paid more attention to the empirical realities of American politics—an attention that is rare in any constitutional law casebook—we might have a very different view of the so-called "Countermajoritarian difficulty" as *the* central theoretical issue of constitutional law.[92] Legal academics often ask themselves whether the courts should defer to conventional practices or wait for the creation of new rights by legislation or amendment. What they should ask themselves instead is whether judicial decisions do not already reflect the political and ideological struggles playing out in the larger culture, translated into the professional discourse of the law.

Today, homosexual rights are on the agenda of the federal courts not because judges locked up in their ivory towers have decided that it is time to start talking about them, but because of a revolution in the social meanings of heterosexuality and homosexuality precipitated by the growth of a movement for homosexual rights following the Stonewall riots. Nor is it irrelevant that an increasing number of political officials, both elected and appointed, are willing to acknowledge being gay or lesbian. Social movements play a key role in influencing the development of culture, and hence in changing social meanings so that judges can later "discover" new rights in the Constitution, often making arguments first offered by dissidents outside the bounds of professional discourse. Douglass's speech reminds us that the interpretation of the Constitution, while provisionally in the hands of professionally trained elites, ultimately rests in the hands of the larger political culture of the United States, or to put it in more storied terms, it rests in the hands of the people.

Third, Douglass's speech deserves a place in the constitutional canon—along with *Dred Scott* and *Prigg v. Pennsylvania*—because it brings home to the student, to the practicing lawyer, to the citizen, and to the legal academic a central question of constitutional law, a question that creates enormous dissonance in our souls, a question that we and generations before us have tried in countless ways to avoid asking or confronting: How can a person be faithful to a constitution in a country with deeply unjust conditions that claims that those conditions are justified or permitted by that very text? What shall we do if we discover that the Constitution itself might be an evil document that keeps evil in place, if we suspect that it might even be "a covenant with death and an agreement with hell?"

Should we, like William Lloyd Garrison, declare the Constitution to be such an agreement and refuse to enforce it? Should we, like Roger Taney, the author of *Dred Scott*, embrace current conditions, and the Constitution that permits them, because we are upholding the rule of law and the intentions of the framers? Should we, like Joseph Story, the author of *Prigg v. Pennsylvania*, return the escaped slave to her master, enforce a constitutional bargain with slave states that we believe to be deeply unjust, precisely because it is a bargain and because it is necessary to avoid some even greater calamity—namely, civil war? Or should we, like Frederick Douglass, refuse to acknowledge evils in the Constitution while denouncing the evils done in its name? Should we construe the Constitution to permit evil, knowing that it may be evil, or perhaps convincing ourselves that it is not so evil after all? Or should we construe the Constitution "strictly" in favor of our vision of human rights and justice, regardless of the original understandings, or even the current consensus about its meaning, in the hope that the Constitution, and the country, may someday become what they presently promise to be?

Our reasons for including figures like Douglass and Garrison—as well as Taney and Story—in our own courses on constitutional law reveal our sense of what is most important about the task of legal pedagogy. We are teachers of law, not of justice, and yet the question of justice—and law's persistent failure to attain it—can never remain out of our minds for long. When we teach our students law, we introduce them to a world.[93] It is a world that they will inhabit for many years to come, one that we hope will enable them, not only as lawyers, but as citizens, to lead better, more worthwhile lives. But our very entry into such a world is simultaneously the successful inculcation of a canon, a rule of practice and a discipline of thought that shapes our imaginations, colonizes our consciousness, and helps make us, for better and for worse, the kind of people that we are. To imagine that one can escape this canonicity is a fantasy. To imagine that we can exercise a greater degree of self-consciousness about the canons that constitute our professional lives is not. It is time that we did so.

NOTES

We are grateful to Akhil Amar, Bruce Ackerman, John Langbein, Carol Rose, and Reva Siegel for their helpful comments on an earlier draft of this essay.

1. Frederick Douglass, *The Constitution of the United States: Is It Pro-Slavery or Anti-Slavery?*, Address at Glasgow: (Mar. 26, 1860), *in* 2 THE LIFE AND WRITINGS OF FREDERICK DOUGLASS 467–80 (Philip S. Foner ed. 1950).

2. *See* FREDERICK DOUGLASS, *Life and Times of Frederick Douglass, in* FREDERICK DOUGLASS: AUTOBIOGRAPHIES 453, 526–28, 532, 642–46, 661–64 (Henry Louis Gates, Jr. ed., First Library of Am. College Edition 1996) (1994); FREDERICK DOUGLASS, MY BONDAGE AND MY FREEDOM 44–45, 113–15, 248–58 (Johnson Publ'g Co. 1970) (1855); FREDERICK DOUGLASS, NARRATIVE OF THE LIFE OF FREDERICK DOUGLASS 16, 40, 57–58, 60 (David W. Blight ed. 1993) (1845); 1 THE LIFE AND WRITINGS OF FREDERICK DOUGLASS, *supra* note 1, at 11, 16–18; *see also* WILLIAM MCFEELY, FREDERICK DOUGLASS 8 (1991) (discussing Douglass's racial identity).

3. *See* DOUGLASS, *Life and Times of Frederick Douglass, supra* note 2, at 467.

4. 60 U.S. (19 How.) 393 (1857).

5. *See id.* at 432.

6. *Id.* at 407.

7. *See id.* at 451–52. Thus, Taney's opinion in effect ruled unconstitutional the platform of the new Republican Party. *See* DON E. FEHRENBACHER, THE DRED SCOTT CASE: ITS SIGNIFICANCE IN AMERICAN LAW AND POLITICS 202 (1978) (indicating that the Republican Party's 1856 platform affirmed the "sovereign powers" of Congress over U.S. territories and declared that Congress should exercise those powers to prohibit slavery in the territories).

8. Buried in the above paragraph is a wonderful anecdote about canons and canonicity in law.

When we published the original version of this essay, the *Harvard Law Review* informed us that its settled practice was always to refer to justices of the United States Supreme Court by their ceremonial titles. *See* A UNIFORM SYSTEM OF CITATION 52 (16th ed. 1996). Thus, we committed a law review faux pas by referring to "Taney" rather than "Chief Justice Taney" in the above paragraph. Of course, one of our major themes is that constitutional interpretation is much too centered on the worship of the Supreme Court and its pronouncements. The *Harvard Law Review*'s style manual is a wonderful symbol of how pervasive this idolatry has become. One might think that the use of ceremonial titles for justices was part of a more general practice of respect, but in fact the courtesy seems to be focused particularly on members of the judiciary. Thus, for example, while Roger Taney must always be described as "Chief Justice Taney" in articles appearing in the *Harvard Law Review*, apparently Abraham Lincoln may be mentioned without adding his ceremonial title of president. We are grateful to the *Review* for allowing us to depart from its custom in our essay, and thereby allowing us to suggest, if only symbolically, that Frederick Douglass is on at least the same level of interpretive authority as Roger B. Taney.

9. Douglass, *supra* note 1, at 469.

10. *Id.* Nevertheless, Douglass suggested that there was no serious conflict between text and original understandings, and he emphasized that "the intentions of the framers of the Constitution were good, not bad," with respect to the future of slavery in America. *Id.* at 473.

11. *Id.* at 468. Douglass's reference is to Hamlet's mocking of Polonius concerning the appearance of a cloud. *See* WILLIAM SHAKESPEARE, HAMLET act 3, sc. 2, ll. 358–68 (G.R. Hibbard ed., Oxford Univ. Press, 1987).

12. Douglass, *supra* note 1, at 468.

13. *See id.* at 471.

14. *Id.* at 475–76.

15. *See id.*

16. *See id.* at 478.

17. *Id.*

18. *Id.*

19. We note, however, that Douglass's central interpretive rule—that, "[w]here a law is susceptible of two meanings, the one making it accomplish an innocent purpose, and the other making it accomplish a wicked purpose, we must in all cases adopt that which makes it accomplish an innocent purpose," *id.* at 476—has interesting parallels to the theories of contemporary scholars like Ronald Dworkin. *See* RONALD DWORKIN, LAW'S EMPIRE 313–14 (1986) (promoting the idea that legal interpretation should make the law "the best it can be").

20. The Thirteenth Amendment abolished slavery but did not settle the question of citizenship. *See* U.S. CONST. amend. XIII. The Fourteenth Amendment guaranteed that all persons born or naturalized in the United States were citizens of the United States and of the state in which they resided. *See id.* amend. XIV, § 1.

21. *See* WILLIAM M. WIECEK, THE SOURCES OF ANTISLAVERY CONSTITUTIONALISM IN AMERICA, 1760–1848, at 269 (1977). The most notable antislavery constitutionalist was Lysander Spooner, who almost certainly influenced some of Douglass's arguments. For a discussion of Spooner's work, *see* Randy E. Barnett, *Was Slavery Unconstitutional Before the Thirteenth Amendment?: Lysander Spooner's Theory of Interpretation*, 28 PAC. L.J. 977 (1997).

22. WALTER M. MERRILL, AGAINST WIND AND TIDE: A BIOGRAPHY OF WM. LLOYD GARRISON 205 (1963).

23. Douglass began as a Garrisonian, but broke away; his Glasgow address is a clear rejection both of Garrison's separatist beliefs and of Garrison's pessimism about the practical political meaning of the Constitution. *See* Douglass, *supra* note 1, at 478–80; 2 THE LIFE AND WRITINGS OF FREDERICK DOUGLASS, *supra* note 2, at 48–66. For an exchange about the legal and political significance of Douglass's Glasgow Address, *see* J. M. Balkin, *Agreements with Hell and Other Objects of Our Faith*, 65 FORDHAM L. REV. 1703, 1709–10 (1997), and Dorothy E. Roberts, *The Meaning of Blacks' Fidelity to the Constitution*, 65 FORDHAM L. REV. 1761, 1766–69 (1997).

24. In the interest of full disclosure, we report that Douglass's Glasgow Address *is* currently reprinted in one (and only one) of the standard constitutional law casebooks, a casebook that, not at all coincidentally, we co-edit. *See* PAUL BREST, SANFORD LEVINSON, J. M. BALKIN AND AKMIL REED AMAR, PROCESSES OF CONSTITUTIONAL DECISIONMAKING: CASES AND MATERIALS 173–181 (4th ed. 2000).

25. For a discussion of the concept of "law-talk," see J. M. Balkin & Sanford Levinson, *Constitutional Grammar*, 72 TEX. L. REV. 1771, 1774–78 (1994).

26. J. M. BALKIN, CULTURAL SOFTWARE: A THEORY OF IDEOLOGY (1998).

27. We have made a similar claim about citations to legal scholarship, which also tend to create a set of canonical materials. *See* J. M. Balkin & Sanford Levinson, *How to Win Cites and Influence People*, 71 CHI.-KENT L. REV. 843, 845 (1996).

28. *See, e.g.*, Action for Children's Television v. FCC, 58 F.3d 654, 659–70 (D.C. Cir. 1995) (en banc) (upholding the constitutionality of a statute prohibiting indecent broadcast programming between 6 A.M. and 10 P.M.); Mozert v. Hawkins County Bd. of Educ., 827 F.2d 1058, 1063–70 (6th Cir. 1987) (rejecting a free exercise clause claim by fundamentalist Christian parents who sought to avoid exposing their children to secular materials).

29. *See* William Eskridge and Sandford Levinson, eds., CONSTITUTIONAL STUPIDITIES/CONSTITUTIONAL TRAGEDIES (1998).

30. State court judges have sometimes interpreted state constitutional provisions to reach results quite different from U.S. Supreme Court decisions. For example, after the Court refused to recognize the existence of a right to equal educational resources in *San Antonio Independent School District v. Rodriguez*, 411 U.S. 1, 54–55 (1973), a number of state courts found such a right in their state constitutions, including Texas, the state in which *Rodriguez* was originally brought, *see* Edgewood Indep. Sch. Dist. v. Kirby, 777 S.W.2d 391, 397 (Tex. 1989) (interpreting the Texas state constitution to include a right to "substantially equal opportunity to have access to educational funds").

31. *See, e.g.,* CONSTITUTIONS OF THE COUNTRIES OF THE WORLD (Albert P. Blaustein & Gisbert H. Flanz eds. 1997).

32. See, for example, J. H. H. Weiler, *The Transformation of Europe,* 100 YALE L.J. 2403 (1991), a fascinating article that compares developments under the Treaty of Rome to early developments in the history of the U.S. Constitution.

33. We note, alas, that the contemporary Supreme Court seems determined to aid and abet the ignorant disregard of the constitutions of other countries. Justice Breyer's recent suggestion in *Printz v. United States* that the Court consider the experience of the European Union was roughly dismissed by Justice Scalia's majority opinion: "We think such comparative analysis inappropriate to the task of interpreting a constitution, though it was of course quite relevant to writing one." Printz v. United States, 117 S. Ct. 2365, 2377 n.11 (1997). Yet if the framers themselves engaged in comparativism, one would think that a devotee of original understanding should have a similar interest, at least as an aid to divining their larger purposes. Nevertheless, Scalia insists, in a fit of nationalistic fervor, that such inquiries are completely unnecessary, for "our federalism is not Europe's." *Id.* at 2378 n.11. It is "the unique contribution of the Framers to political science and political theory." *Id.* (quoting United States v. Lopez, 514 U.S. 549, 575 (1995) (Kennedy, J., concurring) (citing Henry J. Friendly, *Federalism: A Foreword,* 86 YALE L.J. 1019 (1977))) (internal quotation marks omitted). That claim may or may not be true, but it seems quite irrelevant to the point of comparativism, which is to understand ourselves better through comparison with others. By contrast, what Scalia offers us is the kind of self-satisfied strutting that gives chauvinism a bad name.

34. Indeed, one of the elements most sorely missing from the current constitutional canon is a concern with facts. Rarely do constitutional law casebooks present the kinds of empirical data that would let students judge the accuracy of the Supreme Court's sometimes astonishingly cavalier pronouncements about the outside world.

Consider, for example, the "chilling effect" that liberal legal scholars fear will arise from regulation of the press. Do we have any reason to believe that the fear of libel judgments has a greater effect on press behavior than, say, the fear of retribution from a paper's leading advertiser? *See* Frederick Schauer, *Liars, Novelists, and the Law of Defamation,* 51 BROOK. L. REV. 233, 246–47 (1985); Frederick Schauer, *Uncoupling Free Speech,* 92 COLUM. L. REV. 1321, 1329–30 (1992).

Next consider conservative paeans to the virtues of federalism. Striking down a federal scheme regulating radioactive waste, Justice O'Connor proclaimed: "State sovereignty is not just an end in itself: 'Rather, federalism secures to citizens the liberties that derive from the diffusion of sovereign power.'" New York v. United States, 505 U.S. 144, 181 (1991) (quoting Coleman v. Thompson, 501 U.S. 722, 759 (1991) (Blackmun, J., dissenting)). Yet as Larry Kramer points out, few scholars, let alone members of the Supreme Court, have done enough work to justify any such confident pronouncements about the relationship between fed-eralism and liberty. *See* Larry Kramer, *Understanding Federalism*, 47 Vand. L. Rev. 1485, 1490, 1561 (1994). There are many different forms of federalism, and many different liberties that might be protected in greater or lesser degrees by these various forms. Moreover, if decentralization is the key to promoting liberty, it is by no means clear that power should be concentrated at the level of states rather than at the level of counties or municipalities.

35. 505 U.S. 377 (1992).

36. 5 U.S. (1 Cranch) 137 (1803). In fact, one of us (Levinson) confesses to having stopped teaching *Marbury* altogether, because it costs far too much class-room time to teach it well relative to the gains that teaching it would produce. This confession is simply another way of articulating the quasi-Darwinian point made earlier that all canons must be understood in "competitive" or "economic" terms. Canons are composed of materials that are engaged in a never-ending competition for space in the scarce resources of scholarly consciousness and for time in the limited hours that can be devoted to any given course. If we had infi-nite time and infinite memory there might be no need for canons; we could read and absorb *everything*. In fact we live in conditions of ever more imposing cogni-tive and temporal scarcity, where the very notions of "keeping up" with one's field and giving one's students a "comprehensive" overview of that field seem in-creasingly ludicrous. A teacher must decide what is worth teaching in a course that usually lasts no more than 42 hours. A casebook editor inevitably faces page limits that require, at best, vigorous editing of texts and, at worst, the ruthless ex-clusion of otherwise meritorious materials.

37. *See* Brest and Levinson et al, *supra* note 24, at 51.

38. This situation began to change with James Bradley Thayer, a law professor whose work on judicial review became highly influential. *See* Jay Hook, *A Brief Life of James Bradley Thayer*, 88 Nw. U.L. Rev. 1, 5–6 (1993).

39. This change occurs as the audience for contemporary legal scholarship increasingly becomes fellow academics rather than judges and members of the practicing bar. The latter two groups now form the primary audience for legal treatises.

Mary Ann Glendon, in her critique of the contemporary legal academy, picks out "the declining prestige of the legal treatise" for special censure. Mary Ann Glendon, A Nation Under Lawyers: How the Crisis in the Legal Profes-sion Is Transforming American Society 204 (1994). "Up to the mid-1970s," Glendon writes, "treatises like [Louis] Loss on securities regulation, [Phillip] Areeda on antitrust, [Charles Alan] Wright and [Arthur] Miller on civil proce-dure, and [John H.] Wigmore on evidence were widely regarded as the highest form of legal scholarship. Their authors were the superstars of the legal acad-emy." *Id.* In Glendon's view, this happy state of affairs was disturbed in the late 1970s, when the legal academy was joined by "a new generation of professors" who "began to avoid purely 'doctrinal' scholarship" and turned away from older traditions of treatise writing. *Id.* As a result, Glendon asserts, "[t]he ratio of 'practical' to 'theoretical' essays published in leading law journals dropped from 4.5:1 in 1960 to 1:1 in 1985." *Id.* She contrasts her affection for the treatise tradition with the "harsh judgment" of Yale professor George Priest, who claimed in 1983 that treatise writing "has been cast off to practitioners" and that "[t]he treatise is no longer even a credit to those competing on the leading edge of legal thought." *Id.* at 204–05 (quoting George L. Priest, *Social Science Theory and Legal Education: The Law School and the University*, 33 J. LEGAL EDUC. 437, 441 (1983)) (internal quotation marks omitted).

40. LAURENCE H. TRIBE, AMERICAN CONSTITUTIONAL LAW (2d ed. 1988).

41. 22 U.S. (9 Wheat.) 1 (1824).

42. 3 U.S. (3 Dall.) 386 (1798).

43. 381 U.S. 479 (1965).

44. 410 U.S. 113 (1973).

45. 198 U.S. 45, 76 (1905).

46. Id. at 74.

47. *See, e.g.*, NOEL T. DOWLING, CASES ON AMERICAN CONSTITUTIONAL LAW 1–20 (1937) (beginning with "The Constitution; and The Amending Process"); OLIVER PETER FIELD, A SELECTION OF CASES AND AUTHORITIES ON CONSTITUTIONAL LAW 1–18 (1930) (beginning with "The Formulation and Modification of the Constitution of the United States"); JAMES PARKER HALL, ILLUSTRATIVE CASES ON CONSTITUTIONAL LAW 1–17 (2d ed. revised and enlarged 1927) (beginning with a section on the "Establishment and Amendment of Constitutions"). One should compare these casebooks with the "Harvard" casebook published during the heyday of the legal process era, *see* 1 PAUL A. FREUND, ARTHUR E. SUTHERLAND, MARK DEWOLFE HOWE & ERNEST J. BROWN, CONSTITUTIONAL LAW: CASES AND OTHER PROBLEMS 3–39 (1954). This casebook begins, as most contemporary casebooks do, with the historic basis of judicial review. By his fourth edition in 1950, Dowling had dropped the introductory remarks on amendment and replaced them with the "Origin of [the] Doctrine of Judicial Review." NOEL T. DOWLING, CASES ON CONSTITUTIONAL LAW 1–69 (4th ed. 1950). Interestingly, and symbolically, this material appears even before the text of the Constitution itself. For the successor to Dowling's casebook, *see* NOEL T. DOWLING & GERALD GUNTHER, CASES AND MATERIALS ON CONSTITUTIONAL LAW (7th ed. 1965), which appears in its latest incarnation as GERALD GUNTHER & KATHLEEN M. SULLIVAN, CONSTITUTIONAL LAW (13th ed. 1997). The discussion of constitutional amendments and Article V has by now been relegated to a single, lengthy footnote on "Other Congressional Powers." *Id.* at 250 n.1.

48. *See, e.g.*, HALL, *supra* note 41, at xiii–xiv (table of contents devoting primary coverage to structural issues); HENRY ROTHTSCHAEFER, CASES ON CONSTITUTIONAL LAW vii–viii (1932) (same).

49. 395 U.S. 444 (1969) (per curiam).

50. *See id.* at 447.

51. In contrast, the problems of racist speech and pornography have been assimilated with much less difficulty into the organization of the pedagogical canon. They fit easily into the standard paradigm of the lone individual (or group of individuals) saying things that others do not like. After all, one of the earliest racist speech cases was *Beauharnais v. Illinois*, 343 U.S. 250 (1952), and even *Brandenburg* itself might be viewed as a racist speech case. Indeed, the most prominent racist speech case of our era, *R.A.V. v. City of St. Paul*, 505 U.S. 377 (1992), is an old-fashioned criminal prosecution. In like fashion, casebook authors can (and do) simply insert discussions of feminism and pornography after the traditional materials on obscenity. *See, e.g.*, GUNTHER & SULLIVAN, *supra* note 44, at 1126–55. We do not doubt that it might be better to treat these materials in a different way—for example, as part of the study of the equal protection clause. Our point is rather that casebooks have had much less trouble working them into a traditional schema, even if that schema is ultimately mistaken.

52. GERALD GUNTHER, CASES AND MATERIALS ON CONSTITUTIONAL LAW 1105–1545 (10th ed. 1980). These "additional" First Amendment problems included defamation, obscenity, prior restraint, commercial speech, labor picketing, freedom of association, and campaign finance. *See id.* at lxviii–lxxiv. However, Gunther shrewdly placed *Red Lion Broadcasting Co. v. FCC*, 395 U.S. 367 (1969), and *Miami Herald Publishing Co. v. Tornillo*, 418 U.S. 241 (1974), with the public forum cases. *See* GUNTHER, *supra*, at 1302–05.

53. 304 U.S. 144, 152 n.4 (1938).

54. This is the argument of J. M. Balkin, *The Footnote*, 83 Nw. U. L. REV. 275, 301 (1989).

55. The Lockhart casebook is also unique in continuing to include substantial material on capital punishment. *See* WILLIAM B. LOCKHART, YALE KAMISAR, JESSE H. CHOPER, STEVEN H. SHIFFRIN & RICHARD H. FALLON, JR., CONSTITUTIONAL LAW 555–81 (8th ed. 1996). Indeed, among the other standard casebooks, only BREST & LEVINSON includes as a major case *McCleskey v. Kemp*, 481 U.S. 279 (1987), which rejected a challenge to death penalty procedures on the ground of racial discrimination. *See id.* at 290–91; BREST ET AL, *supra* note 24, at 884–882 (edited version of *McCleskey*). It says much about the current canon that the index entry under "death" in the Gunther & Sullivan casebook directs the reader to "Right to die." GUNTHER & SULLIVAN, *supra* note 44, at I-2. This is, no doubt, because the right to die fits easily under the categories of substantive due process that are still central parts of the pedagogical canon, while the right to be *free* from death is conceptualized under the Eighth Amendment's cruel and unusual punishments clause and hence is relegated to courses on criminal procedure.

56. *See, e.g.*, Rochin v. California, 342 U.S. 165 (1952); Adamson v. California, 332 U.S. 46 (1947).

57. *See* George Kannar, *The Constitutional Catechism of Antonin Scalia*, 99 YALE L.J. 1297, 1330–34, 1355 (1990).

58. *But see* AKHIL REED AMAR, THE CONSTITUTION AND CRIMINAL PROCEDURE (1997) (approaching the criminal procedure provisions of the Bill of Rights through the lenses of textual and structural constitutional interpretation).

59. Akhil Amar's work on the Bill of Rights is one of the few recent attempts to read the amendments together as part of a single Constitution. *See* AKHIL REED AMAR, THE BILL OF RIGHTS: CREATION AND RECONSTRUCTION (1998).

60. *See* Sanford Levinson, *The Embarrassing Second Amendment*, 99 YALE L.J. 637, 648–50 (1989); *see also* L. A. Powe, Jr., *Guns, Words, and Constitutional Interpretation*, 38 WM. & MARY L. REV. 1311 (1997) (elaborating possible connections between First and Second Amendment doctrines).

61. These new courses, in turn, give rise to new and more specialized casebooks. *See, e.g.*, SAMUEL ISSACHAROFF, PAMELA S. KARLAN & RICHARD H. PILDES, THE LAW OF DEMOCRACY: LEGAL STRUCTURE OF THE POLITICAL PROCESS (1998).

62. *See* Robert W. Gordon, *The Struggle over the Past*, 44 CLEV. ST. L. REV. 123, 127–31 (1996).

63. An excellent example is FRIEDRICH KESSLER & GRANT GILMORE, CONTRACTS: CASES AND MATERIALS (2d ed. 1970), which appears in its most recent incarnation as FRIEDRICH KESSLER, GRANT GILMORE & ANTHONY T. KRONMAN, CONTRACTS: CASES AND MATERIALS (3d ed. 1986).

64. *See* Davis v. Beason, 133 U.S. 333, 348 (1890); Murphy v. Ramsey, 114 U.S. 15, 42–47 (1885); Reynolds v. United States, 98 U.S. 145, 166–67 (1878); THOMAS G. ALEXANDER, MORMONISM IN TRANSITION: A HISTORY OF THE LATTER-DAY SAINTS 1890–1930, at 3–15, 60–73 (1996) (detailing the persecution of Mormons); LEONARD J. ARRINGTON & DAVIS BITTON, THE MORMON EXPERIENCE: A HISTORY OF THE LATTER-DAY SAINTS 185–205 (2d ed. 1992) (same).

65. *See, e.g.*, Mozert v. Hawkins County Bd. of Educ., 827 F.2d 1058 (6th Cir. 1987).

66. *See, e.g.*, Susan P. Koniak, *When Law Risks Madness*, 8 CARDOZO STUD. L. & LITERATURE 65, 67–68 (1996); David C. Williams, *The Militia Movement and the Second Amendment Revolution: Conjuring with the People*, 81 CORNELL L. REV. 879 (1996).

67. *See* MERRILL, *supra* note 22, at 205.

68. *See, e.g.*, 4 THE WORKS OF JOHN C. CALHOUN 338–47 (R. Crallé ed. 1851).

69. 41 U.S. (16 Pet) 536 (1842).

70. 25 U.S. (12 Wheat.) 546 (1827).

71. PAUL BREST, SANFORD LEVINSON, J. M. BALKIN, AND AKHIL REED AMAR, PROCESSES OF CONSTITUTIONAL DECISIONMAKING (4th ed. 2000).

72. Jerry Goldman's recent survey notes that BREST & LEVINSON has by far the fewest cases (98) of any of the major law school casebooks. The Gunther casebook has the most (129), and the Stone casebook is not far behind with 122. *See*

Jerry Goldman, *Is There a Canon of Constitutional Law?*, AM. POL. SCI. ASS'N NEWSL. (Law and Courts Section), Spring 1993, at 4.

73. These choices reflect the view that these materials are far more canon-worthy than, say, *Carter v. Carter Coal Co.*, 298 U.S. 238 (1936), a hoary relic of the Bad Old *Lochner*-era Court and one of the cases omitted in the third edition of BREST & LEVINSON.

74. 376 U.S. 254 (1964).

75. Indeed, no casebook, including BREST & LEVINSON, has paid sufficient attention to the problem of amendments (whether legal or illegal) outside of article 5. This question, central to Bruce Ackerman's important recent work, *see* 1 BRUCE ACKERMAN, WE THE PEOPLE: FOUNDATIONS 53–54 (1991); 2 BRUCE ACKERMAN, WE THE PEOPLE: TRANSFORMATIONS (1998), has yet to be assimilated adequately into the constitutional canon. Although all casebooks spend countless pages on varying interpretations of the Fourteenth Amendment, none devotes more than scant attention to the problematic status of the Fourteenth Amendment's ratification. In order to guarantee a two-thirds majority in favor of the amendment, the Reconstruction Congress refused to seat southern senators and representatives. *See id.* at 99–119. Moreover, Congress refused to reseat those southern congressional delegations or to recognize the legitimacy of southern state governments—including governments thought necessary for ratification of the Thirteenth Amendment—until those governments ratified the Fourteenth Amendment. *See id.* Ackerman, in contrast, argues that the deepest single question of American constitutional theory is how to develop a truly satisfying account of the legitimacy of this necessary yet problematic amendment. *See id.* We think that confronting Ackerman's questions seriously would require disruptions in all of the canons of constitutional law—pedagogical, cultural literacy, and theoretical.

76. *See generally* Sanford Levinson, *Slavery in the Canon of Constitutional Law*, 68 CHI.-KENT L. REV. 1087, 1094–95 (1993) (discussing justifications for including materials on slavery in law school constitutional law classes).

77. O. W. HOLMES, JR., THE COMMON LAW 5 (Mark DeWolfe Howe ed., Harvard Univ. Press 1963) (1881).

78. *See* J. M. Balkin, *Agreements with Hell and Other Objects of Our Faith*, 65 FORDHAM L. REV. 1703, 1720 (1997).

79. 347 U.S. 483 (1954).

80. 198 U.S. 45 (1905).

81. 163 U.S. 537 (1896).

82. 323 U.S. 214 (1944).

83. 243 U.S. 426 (1917).

84. 248 U.S. 297 (1919).

85. *Bunting v. Oregon* upheld a cap on working hours and required time-and-a-half pay for overtime. *See Bunting*, 243 U.S. at 438–39. *Hebe Co. v. Shaw* upheld

a regulation of adulterated foodstuffs. *See Hebe,* 248 U.S. at 302–03. Both cases are interesting because they were decided during the *Lochner* era, when the Supreme Court was generally thought to be hostile to such legislation.

86. Michael Klarman has offered an extremely provocative critique of such "normativism" in constitutional scholarship. *See* Michael J. Klarman, *Rethinking the Civil Rights and Civil Liberties Revolutions,* 82 VA. L. REV. 1, 25–31 (1996). Mark Graber has recently noted that "[c]ontemporary constitutional theory rests on three premises[:] *Brown v. Board of Education* was correct, *Lochner v. New York* was wrong, and *Dred Scott v. Sandford* was also wrong." Mark A. Graber, *Desperately Ducking Slavery:* Dred Scott *and Contemporary Constitutional Theory,* 14 CONST. COMMENTARY 271, 271 (1997).

87. Among the words not discussed in most constitutional law courses are those of the Preamble, which, among other things, demand that the Constitution be employed to promote "the general Welfare" and "to establish Justice." U.S. CONST. preamble. It is possible that the reason why the Preamble has not figured more prominently in constitutional interpretation is that it does not appear to be self-executing. However, this begs the question why it could not be so interpreted. Even if the Preamble does not contain any new rights or powers, it might, like the Ninth and Tenth Amendments, be considered a rule of interpretation that applies to the entire document. Perhaps the best analogy is to the Second Amendment, which contains a clause about the necessity of well-ordered militias that presumably explains why the right to bear arms is guaranteed. In like fashion, one might argue that the provisions of the Constitution are to be liberally interpreted to promote the goals set forth in the Preamble.

88. For a discussion of the central role of social movements in shaping elite discourse about the Constitution, *see* J. M. Balkin, *The Constitution of Status,* 106 YALE L.J. 2313, 2338–42 (1997).

89. *See* DAVID M. RABBAN, FREE SPEECH IN ITS FORGOTTEN YEARS 77–128 (1997). Rabban states:

> Commentary generated by the IWW free speech fights refutes the conventional understanding that Americans before World War I did not pay much attention to the meaning of free speech. . . . This commentary overwhelmingly took place outside the judicial system. Most of it was more sophisticated analytically, and more sensitive to free speech concerns, than typical judicial decisions of the period. . . .

*Id.* at 128.

90. *See, e.g.,* GERALD N. ROSENBERG, THE HOLLOW HOPE 39–41 (1991).

91. As Mr. Dooley once put it, "no matter whether th' Constitution follows th' flag or not, th' Supreme Coort follows th' iliction returns." FINLEY PETER DUNNE, MR. DOOLEY AT HIS BEST 77 (Elmer Ellis ed. 1938).

92. *Cf.* Mark A. Graber, *The Nonmajoritarian Difficulty: Legislative Deference to the Judiciary,* 7 STUD. AM. POL. DEV. 35, 37 (1993) (internal quotation marks

omitted) (noting that the Court often is willing to resolve issues delegated to it by a grateful Congress unwilling to pay the political costs of resolution).

93. Or, as Robert Cover would have said, we make them part of a *nomos*. *See* Robert M. Cover, *The Supreme Court, 1982 Term—Foreword:* Nomos *and Narrative*, 97 HARV. L. REV. 4, 4 (1983).

# Contributors

*Fran Ansley* is Professor of Law at the University of Tennessee College of Law in Knoxville. She has written about the past and present of race and other identity categories in law and in legal education. Some of her more recent work looks at the ways that law is shaping and being shaped by the globalization of low-wage labor markets in the United States and abroad.

*Ian Ayres* is the William K. Townsend Professor at Yale Law School. He is author of more than seventy articles applying law and economics to a variety of issues including contracts and civil rights.

*J. M. Balkin* is Knight Professor of Constitutional Law and the First Amendment at Yale Law School and author of *Cultural Software: A Theory of Ideology*.

*Katharine T. Bartlett* is the Dean and A. Kenneth Pye Professor of Law at Duke University School of Law, where she teaches family law, gender and law, and contracts. She has written extensively in the area of gender and law and on family law issues.

*Philip Bobbitt* holds the Walker Centennial Chair in constitutional law at the University of Texas where he has taught since 1976, with intervals in the U.K. and Washington, D.C. His latest book is *The Shield of Achilles: How Military Invention and Constitutional Transformation Change the World*.

*Paul D. Carrington* is Chadwick Professor of Law at Duke University. He has taught Civil Procedure since 1958, at fifteen American law schools. He conducted a study of federal appeals courts for the American Bar Foundation and served as Reporter to the Advisory Committee of the Judicial Conference.

*Martha Chamallas* is Professor of Law at the University of Pittsburgh where she teaches torts, employment discrimination, feminist legal theory, and constitutional law. Her scholarship in torts and civil rights has focused on race and gender discrimination, covering such topics as sexual harassment, occupational segregation, and hidden biases in the computation of damages for accident victims. She is the author most recently of *Introduction to Feminist Legal Theory*.

*Daniel A. Farber* is Henry J. Fletcher Professor and Associate Dean for Research at the University of Minnesota School of Law. His scholarship encompasses constitutional law, environmental law, and law and economics. His most recent book is *Eco-Pragmatism: Making Sensible Environmental Decisions in an Uncertain World*.

*Katherine M. Franke* is Professor of Law at Columbia Law School. She has written extensively on issues related to sexual harassment, racial and gender-based identity, sexuality, and American racial history. She is also Co-Chair of the Board of Directors of the International Gay and Lesbian Human Rights Commission.

*Randall Kennedy* is Professor at Harvard Law School and author most recently of *Race, Crime, and the Law*.

*Sanford Levinson* is W. St. John Garwood and W. St. John Garwood, Jr., Regents Chair in Law and Professor of Government at the University of Texas, Austin. He is the author, most recently, of *Written in Stone: Public Monuments in Changing Society*.

*Carol M. Rose* is the Gordon Bradford Tweedy Professor of Law and Organization at Yale Law School. She is the author of *Property and Persuasion* and co-author of *Perspectives on Property Law* (with Robert Ellickson and Bruce Ackerman), and has written numerous articles on environmental law, land regulation, water law, and the history and theory of property.

*Suzanna Sherry* is the Cal Turner Professor of Law and Leadership at Vanderbilt University Law School. Her essay was written while she was the Earl R. Larson Professor of Civil Rights and Civil Liberties Law at the University of Minnesota. She is the author of several books and numerous articles in constitutional law, federal jurisdiction, and related subjects.

*Robert Weisberg* is Edwin E. Huddleson, Jr., Professor of Law at Stanford University. He has written in the areas of criminal law and criminal procedure, as well as cultural studies of law. He is co-author of *Literary Criticisms of Law*.

# Permissions

The editors gratefully acknowledge permission to reprint the following articles.

J. M. Balkin and Sanford Levinson, "The Canons of Constitutional Law." This article first appeared in 111 Harv. L. Rev. 964 (1998). Copyright 1998 by the Harvard Law Review Association. Reprinted by permission of the Harvard Law Review.

Ian Ayres, "Empire or Residue: Competing Visions of the Contractual Canon." This article first appeared in 26 Florida State Law Review 897 (1999). Copyright 1999 Florida State University Law Review. Reprinted by permission of the Florida State University Law Review.

Carol M. Rose, "Canons of Property Talk, or Blackstone's Anxiety," reprinted by permission of the Yale Law Journal Company and Fred B. Rothman & Company from The Yale Law Journal, Vol. 108, pages 601–632.

Paul Carrington, "Teaching Civil Procedure: A Retrospective View." This article first appeared in 49 J. Leg. Educ. 311 (1999). Reprinted by permission of The Journal of Legal Education.

Katherine M. Franke, "Homosexuals, Torts, and Dangerous Things," reprinted by permission of the Yale Law Journal Company and Fred B. Rothman & Company from The Yale Law Journal, Vol. 106, pages 2661–2683.

# Index